CALIFORNIA WAGON TRAIN LISTS

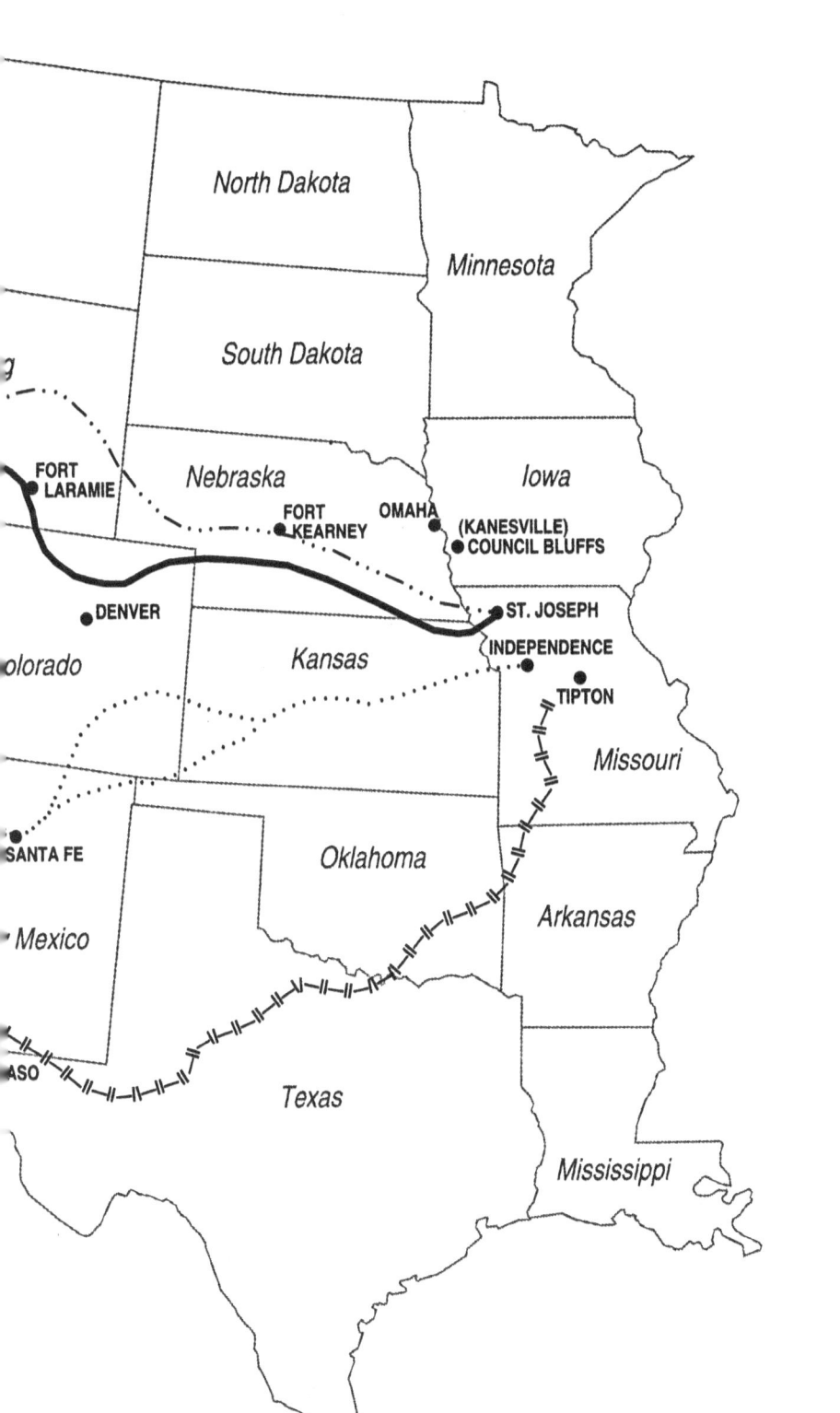

CALIFORNIA WAGON TRAIN LISTS

VOLUME I
April 5, 1849 to October 20, 1852

By

LOUIS J. RASMUSSEN

JANAWAY PUBLISHING
Santa Maria, California

Copyright © 1994, Louis J. Rasmussen

ALL RIGHTS RESERVED.
No part of this publication may be reproduced, stored in a retrieval system, or transmitted in any form or by any means whatsoever, whether electronic, mechanical, magnetic recording, or photocopying, without the prior written approval of the Copyright holder or Publisher, excepting brief quotations for inclusion in book reviews.

Originally published
Colma, California
1994

Reprinted and Published by:

Janaway Publishing, Inc.
732 Kelsey Ct.
Santa Maria, California 93454
(805) 925-1038
www.janawaygenealogy.com
2015

Publisher's Note:
No Volume II of *California Wagon Train Lists* was published. Louis J. Rasmussen, the author, died shortly after this book was completed.

Library of Congress Catalog Card Number: 94-67422

ISBN: 978-1-59641-347-4 (Paperback)

ISBN: 978-1-59641-346-7 (Hardbound)

Made in the United States of America

To

Dad

ACKNOWLEDGEMENTS

On behalf of Louis J. Rasmussen and myself, I would like to thank those that made this book possible:

First, my father, Otto W. Balser, who encouraged Louis to continue his research and supported us with his love and faith. Harry Rutledge, whose correspondence and sharing of resources with Louis became part of the foundation of the work. Harold Schindler who provided the motivation for completing the project. The Rev. Kathy Ray for her instrumental role in giving me the tools to work with. Beverly Buhs, Beverly Weber, Lianne Buhs, Barbara Bruxvoort, Diane Myers and Randy Myers for their unflagging support, willingness to work with us, and friendship.

Many libraries opened their collections to Louis in his research, and he would especially like to thank the Bancroft Library at the University of California at Berkeley.

Also, I'd like to thank our friends and family who provided enthusiastic interest and optimism that sustained us through the hard work.

Barbara K. Rasmussen
Secretary and Editor

CONTENTS

Acknowledgements iv
Contents Page v
Key to Abbreviations and Symbols vi
California Wagon Train Lists 1
Notes 181
Geographical Notes 205
Surname Index 207
Geographical Index 304
Subject Index 316

KEY TO ABBREVIATIONS AND SYMBOLS

Certain abbreviations, symbols and figures are used in footnotes, indexes, endnotes and text. The below key defines their corresponding meanings

(x)   - An "x" following a page number in the Index indicates more than one entry for cited surname, town, state or country will be found on the page; e.g., 165(x).

(-)   - A dash (-) between page numbers in the index denotes that the citation is repeated on each intervening page; e.g., 150-154.

(?)   - A surname or given name followed with a question mark, in brackets, indicates that the passenger name (or residence) may have been listed incorrectly in the original source. For example, William Speai (William Spear?). In all cases the first listed spelling represents the name as it appeared in the original source. The secondary spelling, in brackets, denotes the original listing was obviously incorrect, or translation impossible. The bracketed name is the author's translation.

____   - Denotes surname or given name not listed in original source. For example, ___Smith. Where one or more letters of a name were missing this is reflected by a corresponding space. As an example, "John J_nes." This could be interpreted as "John Jones."

*   - Indicates additional data on subject or individual will be found in a footnote.

sic   - Exactly as written, even though incorrect (quoted).

Arch. - Archibald	Dr. - Doctor	Maj. - Major
bro. - brother	Esq. - Esquire	Rev. - Reverend
Capt. - Captain	fam. - family	Sec. - Secretary
chldrn - children	Gen. - General	Sen. - Senator
Col. - Colonel	Gov. - Governor	Sgt. - Sergeant
Co. - Company	Hon. - Honorable	svt. - servant
dau. - daughter	Lt. - Lieutenant	svts. - servants

CALIFORNIA WAGON TRAIN LISTS

INDEPENDENCE, MISSOURI (April 5, 1849)

On the morning of April 5, 1849, a number of small companies were encamped on the Santa Fe roadside, awaiting a sufficiency of grass to enable them to start to California. For several days the weather had been very disagreeable. Several of the emigrants, from the exposure they had to undergo, were sick and considerable fear was manifested by many in consequence of reports of deaths from cholera in the vicinity. One emigrant, supposed to be from North Carolina, named Robert Umberfield, died on the evening of April 4, 1849 at the campsite. He was alone, and intended emigrating with the first emigrant group listed below.

The first wagon train group listed as being in this area on April 5, 1849 was one from Lower Sandusky, Ohio. It was composed of John M. Smith, J.A. Johnson, L.E. Boren, H.H. Caldwell, Isaac Sharp, J.W. Stevenson, John Stuben, George Taylor, Grosvenor Gallagher, and Henry Loveland. Their train consisted of three wagons, sixteen mules, two tents capable of accommodating fourteen persons, goods for nine months, and all necessary arms. Some of the foregoing group planned to locate in the California gold field region, while others, when they obtained a sufficiency of the "dust," would return to Sandusky.

Near the above train was a company from Cincinnati, composed of Joseph Louge (or Lange), Abram Sanborn, William Crawford, and James Wood. This company had one wagon, six mules, a tent, and provisions for six months.

The next company found in quarters was from Knox County, Kentucky, and was composed of A.E. Pogue, J.G. Pogue, E.F. Arthur, John P. Thatcher, T.J. Woodson, John Woodson, H. Woodson, R. Hale, with attached wagon train members consisting of Dr. P. Fulkerson, John Mills and James R. Fitts, of Lea County, Virginia.

In the vicinity were camped two small companies, one from White County, Indiana, composed of William Orr, L.M. Burns, Dr. H.B. Russell and P.S. Russell; and one from Henry County, Indiana, which was composed of J.B. Harris, J. Font, L. Laughlin, and R. Hutchinson. Each company had a tent, wagon and oxen.

The Bellevue Mining Company, from Sandusky County, Ohio, was also in the locality. This wagon train had formed themselves into a joint stock company with any gold discovery to be equally divided, share and share alike, at the expiration of two years. They had provided themselves with four light wagons, to be drawn by mules and oxen, two large tents and provisions for nine months. Members of this train were:

N.S. Cook	C. Close	S.H. Cook

P.T. Sharp	A.G. Yottey	R. Burleson
S. Dean	J. Findley	R.B. Burleson
C. Smith	A. Raymond	Isaac Banta
H. Holm	H. Conklin	C. Durham
B. Fox	William Sharp	Peter G. Sharp
J. Scroford		

Camped near the foregoing train was a small company consisting of J. Hamman, of Sandusky County, Ohio, and P.Y. Hough and S.N Turvill, of Erie County, Ohio. This small group intended to join with a larger train for safety.

A two wagon train from Anderson County, Kentucky was also in camp. This group was comprised of Charles N. Ford, John M. McBrayer, James B. Miller, A.J. Miller, F.M. Miller and H. Taylor.

The next group in the vicinity traveled in a single wagon and it was composed of:

James Quinton (of Nashville, Tenn.)	William Beatty (of Nashville, Tenn.)	Thomas J. Stum and two sons (of Nashville, Tenn.)
M. Smith (of Rutherford County, Tenn.)	W.M. Clark (of Rutherford County, Tenn.)	John Harris (of Rutherford County, Tenn.)

Preparing to move out of the camp area was a three wagon train composed of the below Virginia residents. Pulling their wagons were eighteen mules.

R.W. Crenshaw (of Lynchburgh, Va.)	R.A. Webber (of Lynchburgh, Va.)	W. McClanaham (of Lynchburgh, Va.)
D.C. Ward (of Pittsylvania Cty)	C.A. Hunt (of Pittsylvania Cty)	W.W. Pestross (or Peatross) (of Pittsylvania Cty)
Dr. Thomas Gillard (of Pittsylvania Cty)	Thomas J. Brown (of Campbell County)	Capt. J. Clements (of Franklin Cty)
J. Kean (of Franklin County)	Mr. ____ Scott (of Franklin County)	A.B. Clements (of Franklin Cty)
E. Kean (of Franklin County)	Dr. J. Haynes (of Franklin County)	John T. Cole (of Henry County)

Two small companies from Illinois were also camped on the Sante Fe roadside. The first consisted of J. Tackaborry, G. Young, John Rees, William Easley and James Dow, from Tazewell County; the second company, composed of Elisha Bassett, Julius Benedict and Lorenzo Kendall, from Bureau County.

The last train camping in this area on April 5, 1859 was made up of New York residents as follows:*

C.C. Lagrange	J.W. Smith	E.H. DeGracie
M.A. Richard		

INDEPENDENCE, MISSOURI (April 6, 1849)

In a camp, about two miles west of Independence, was a wagon train of residents of Cincinnati, Ohio. The group was organized into messes of five, were provided with ten wagons, twenty tents and five marquee, and calculated to commence their trip to the West with eleven mules to the wagon. Two of the wagon bodies were made of sheet iron, and were capable of being used as boats; as such they had been tested, and found capable of

(*) All members of this train were from Albany, New York and they intended to make the journey as a mess in a larger company, under the guidance of Colonel W.H. Russell.

bearing twenty men, or 2,500 lbs of freight, at the same time drawing only four inches of water. This group was organized under a military regulation concept, for their better protection in making the trip to California. Two hundred weight of bread and twenty-eight pounds of bacon were the individual allowances authorized for the journey, and provisions for twelve months, after their arrival in California, had been shipped by way of Cape Horn. The foregoing wagon train was made up of the below individuals:*

J.H. Levering (President)	Mr. L.M. Rogers	Mr. C. Mohr
W.B. Norman (Vice President)	Mr. J. Johnson	Mr. E.A. Stokes
	Mr. S. Whitehead	Mr. C. Long
David Kinsey (Treasurer)	Mr. T.W. Kinsey	Mr. J.P. Harley
S.T. Jones (Secretary)	Mr. A.G. Kinsey	Mr. P.K. Urner
A.H. Colter	Mr. M. West	Mr. W. Kerr
John Bell	Mr. G.J. Gullford	Mr. R.W. Cook
Mr. J. Bird	Mr. R.L. McGowan	Mr. F. Moreland
Mr. H. Ruffner	Mr. S. Withington	Mr. F. Hamlin
Mr. A.T. Perry	Mr. J.W. Anderson	Mr. J. Graham
Mr. A.J. Vorhees	Mr. T.A. Bishop	Mr. J.D. Benedict
Mr. A.F. Gove	Christopher Bell	Mr. Charles Eberle
Mr. A.B. Nixon	Mr. J. Pearson	Mr. W. Wilson
Mr. J. King	Mr. H. Helm	Mr. H. Urner
Mr. N. Graves	Mr. G.W. Fosdick	Mr. J. Eistner
Mr. A. Johnson	David Scott	Mr. W.B. Diver
Mr. J. Talbert	Mr. H. Probasco	George Martin
Mr. G.W. Litter		

On April 6, 1849, on the Santa Fe road, about four miles from Independence, a company of fifteen men from Summit County, Ohio were making ready to move out behind the Cincinnati wagon train. The Summit train was organized as a joint stock company and it consisted of three mule drawn wagons. Members of the company were:

John Decker	H.S. Long	Jonathan R. Gilbert
A. Kellog /sic/	L.P. Buckley	R. Abbey
J.O. Garrett	Ira Rose	P. Fisher
L. Wistendorf	C. Gressard	J.L. Gilbert
George Ayliffe	G. Carr	E. Steinbacker (or Steinbecker)

In the same vicinity a company of thirty-five men from Wayne County, Indiana, were in camp and preparing to move out. This train was composed of seven wagons, six tents, nine months of provisions, and mules and cattle sufficient to make the trip. They were organized and governed by a constitution and by-laws. All gold found in California was to be mutually shared and in case of the death of any member of the company, then his widow or other lawful heir was to receive the share he would have received. They were composed as follows:

William V. Davis (President)	A.B. Knode (Recording Secretary)	Thomas Williams (Treasurer)
Robert Houston		Henry Miller

(*) See notes p. 181 for further information on this group.

W. Williams
(Corresponding
Secretary)
William Buck
Charles Trisa
J.M. Fritch
B. Manifold
William S. Porter
Jacob Weaver
Enoch Myers
H.J. Sahumbrie
George Neese (of
Champaign County,
Ohio)

A. Cunningham
Willets Starr
J.N. Puntney /sic/
(Putney?)
James Puntney /sic/
(Putney?)
N. Baldridge
William F. Koch
George W. Beeler
A. McDowell
H.A. Echelbarger
Samuel Neese (of
Champaign County,
Ohio)

Adam Gates
Peter Boothe
J. Echtenock
R. Cochran
William McAfee
A. Saunders
Samuel McMurray
Samuel Pifer
C. Rathfun /sic/
(Rathbun?)
L. Don Meek

Camped at the same site as the above train were three young men from New Carlisle, Ohio, who proposed to go to California with a Dr.____ Woodworth, of St. Joseph, Missouri. This group was organized as a separate mess and it consisted of Mr. F.P. Ward, Dwight Herbert and Jacob Stetzel. *

INDEPENDENCE, MISSOURI (April 7, 1849)

On the above date, several officers of various companies put ashore at Independence. They had booked passage on the steamer "Mary Blane," from St. Louis, Missouri. These officers were preparing to take their companies to California from Independence.

James McElrath
W.C. Hayes
S.K. Dundass
W.L. Morris
George Crewes
Jonathan Hagen

Oliver C. Gray
O.P. Stodger(?)
A.A. Ackley
S.E. Barr
James Taylor

J.L. Algeo
John M. Algeo
John Rainey
Timothy Montgomery
Thomas McKay

At a campsite on the Santa Fe road, about ten miles from Independence, the following members of a wagon train were found on April 7, 1849:

Lieut. G.W. Paul (of St.
Louis, Mo.)
William Zabriskie (of
New Jersey)
William Paul (of
Pennsylvania)
Mr. ____ Crosby (of
Pennsylvania)

Mr. H. Martin (of Boston,
Mass.)
W. Wells (of New
Hampshire)
George Lukens (of
Pennsylvania)

James Sharp (of
Independence, Mo.)
Robert Jackson (of
Pennsylvania)
John Taylor (of
Pennsylvania)

Encamped in company with the above was a command of William Pye, of Palmyra, Missouri, consisting of Edward R. Pye and son, and Mr. F.D. Gilbert of New York; C.D. Smith, E.L. Nichols, C.B. Wheeler and C. Youngs, of Connecticut; James Stewart, John S. Webb, Shorty Ray, and J.W. Harper, of Independence, Missouri.

Three companies from the State of Michigan were also camped on the Santa Fe road, just out of Independence, on April 7, 1849. The first company, a joint stock group, were

(*)See notes pp. 181-182 regarding this group.

to be bound together for two years, and all were residents of Monroe City, Michigan. They were to travel in three horse-drawn wagons and carried provisions for six months. The company consisted of:

George Kirland /sic/	George Wethington	A.J. Mason
Horace Besby	William Wilson	H. Bulkley
J.B.Swzo___ (Swzort?)	M. Sweeny	D.B. Scott
	D.R. Ashley	

The second company was from Adrian County, Michigan, with two horse-drawn wagons loaded with one large tent and provisions for six months. It was composed of:

E.F. Gleeson	L.A. Hammond	D.A. Woodbury
S.G. Crittenden	G.Chafey	F.A. Parke

The third company was from Cass County, Michigan and consisted of Aaron Brown, E.J. Bonine, and William H. Brice and his wife. The group was to travel in one wagon and was planning to join a large train for safety.

The wagon train known as the "Iron City Rangers" was also at a campsite out of Independence, Missouri on April 7, 1849. This group was organized into messes of five, were provided with eight light mule-drawn wagons, and each man, in addition, had a mule to ride and one pack mule. In the company was an experienced chemist. Members of this wagon train were:

A.W. Brockaway	A. Rudolph	James B. Mitchell
T.B. Kennedy	S. Grubb	William Laury
H.W. Myers	G. Kinzenbach	F. Rockenbaugh
J.C. Rieber	Robert Wightman	(Rookenbaugh?)
Lorain Robbins	A.J. Tingle	S.D. Brown
Joseph C. Kennedy	Thomas S. Hart /sic/	R.S. Wingham
J.C. McKibben	W.B. Sharp	Robert S. Mart /sic/
(McKibbon?)		

(all the above were from Pittsburgh)

D.M. Whitehill (of Wooster, Ohio)	Walter Taylor (of Mansfield, Ohio)	Eli Smith (of Mansfield, Ohio)
Isaac Brecker (of Mansfield, Ohio)	George Miller (of Mansfield, Ohio)	Joseph Smith (of Mansfield, Ohio)

A second company from Pennsylvania was camping on the Santa Fe road out of Independence on the same date as the forementioned. This group, though smaller, was well provided with two wagons, ox teams, one tent and 400 lbs of provisions for each man. It hailed from Centre County, Pennsylvania and was composed of:

John Miller	Samuel Sankey	George M. Wasson
Edward Montillius	William Frederick	G. Miller
Jonathan Moore	Mathias Piaff	William Bartlett

A third Pennsylvania group, one from Pittsburgh, was also camped on the Santa Fe road on April 7, 1849. It operated under the name of "Diamond K. Company" and was composed of six men. This company proposed to move from its site in approximately five days, joining up with the Lieutenant G.W. Paul wagon train, but acting as an independent organization. This party traveled by two mule-drawn wagons and carried provisions for two hundred days, allowing three pounds a day to each man. The company was organized as follows:

Crawford Washingon (Captain)	C. Kincaid	W.G. Johnston
Joseph L. Moody	W.O.H. Scully	W.B. McBride

A single wagon party from Schuylkill county, Pennsylvania was camped in close proximity to the foregoing wagon train, ten miles out of Independence, on April 7, 1849. The party was organized as a joint stock company and was composed of:

C.S. Cockill (Cockrill?)	Thomas Small	Robert John
	H.L. Bird	____ Jenkins

There were two additional single wagon companies camped on the Santa Fe road on April 7, 1849. The first, an independent joint stock company, from Tioga County, Pennsylvania consisted of:

J.B. Hill	J.G. Scutter	N.B. Allworth
Samuel R. Smith	Philemon Doud /sic/	

The second single wagon company intended travelling as an "independent" company, and under no contract or stipulation to each other. It was composed as follows:

Robert Faulkner (of Erie County, Penn.)	P.H. Moody (of Erie County, Penn.)	J.L. Keefer (of Steuben County, Kentucky)

One train, consisting of four wagons from Middleburgh, Ohio, was preparing to leave the Independence, Missouri area on April 7, 1849. This group was organized as a joint stock company and would disband one year after arrival in California, unless sooner called for by a two-thirds vote. Train members were:

S. Newton	I. Sumner	William A Ostrom
T.B. Hickcox	F.A. Nash	N. Palmer
J.W. Evans	S. Britton	N. Wait
A.S. Cleveland	G.W. Rhodes	F.W. Wait

Also camped on the Santa Fe road, out of Independence, on April 7, 1849 was a train of Grant County, Indiana residents. They were organized into messes of five, each mess being provided with a wagon, tent and other necessary equipment. Members of this train consisted of:

William Harlan	Levi Hummer	Edmund Brown
Thomas St. John	John Hummer	Josiah Draper
John St. John	Jesse Swift	M. Cleveland
Royal Webster	Peter Stout	Thomas Pratt
David Hite	Anthony Inman	L. McCormick
Andrew Patterson	Joshua Hersey /sic/	H. Hendricks
Jonathan Dubois	C. Morehead	William Hendricks
Barney Luger	J.W. Hurlburt	Benjamin Stout

ST. JOSEPH, MISSOURI (April, 1849)

On April 7, 1849 a wagon train known as the "Washington California Mining and Trading Association" arrived at St. Joseph, Missouri. The group encamped on the side of a hill on the north side of town before beginning its trip to California. Members of this train were from Washingon County, New York and the group consisted of : *

Samuel McDoual /sic/	A.F. Bliss	D.T. Harshaw
J.H. Tilford	D.M. Hall	William Owen
H.S. Crandall	J. Robertson	William Harrison
J. Cowan	R. Gourlay	James Hill
James H. Newton	A. McNaughton	Andrew Telford

(*) This train still at St. Joseph on April 14, 1849. See notes section p. 182 and page 24.

The Schaghticoke California Mining Company emigrants landed at St. Joseph, Missouri on April 7, 1849. The group had booked passage on the steamer "Mustang" and after debarking they encamped a quarter mile north of town. After purchasing horses and oxen in St. Joseph, they left for California via Fort Kearny (Nebraska). * The majority of the company was from Schaghitocke (or Schagtiocoke) New York. The group was still encamped at St. Joseph on April 14th, and by that time had acquired 3 wagons, 10 yoke oxen, one large tent and 6 months provisions. *The following were members of this company:

Almon Boomer (Captain)	Alexander Button	John T. Bowers
Dr. Thomas B. Small	*John Henley	Morgan Dyer
Thomas Cain	William Good	

(*) The Schaghticoke group also purchased mules and departed St Joseph on April 20, 1849.
(all above residents of Schaghticoke, N.Y.)

*Edward McClellan (of Cambridge, N.Y.)	George Greatrake (of Allegheny, Pa.)	Albert G. Eldridge (of White Plains, New York)
*Francis Brezel (of Schoharie, N.Y)	Harbut Bowers	
	Benjamin D. Bowers	

(*) One source lists John Henley as "J. Hurley," Francis Brezel as "Frances Burzell" and Edward McClellan as "E. McClelland."

The "Buffalo Exploring and Mining Company" left St. Joseph, Missouri, on April 12, 1849 for California. This New York wagon train was organized as a joint stock company and it consisted of 5 wagons pulled by 16 yoke oxen. Provisions transported were to last for six months. Two tents were also carried by the group which consisted of:

M.W. Burnett(Captain)	*William A. Albro	John McIntosh
James DeBois (Secty)	*William D. Witwer	M. McIntosh
O.A. Post (Treasurer)	*Charles Paxson	H.S. Dodge
Wiliam Isaac Williams	Henry H. Buchanan	Tristran Winn
* George B. Efner	B.F. Smith	**Hiram A. Crerran

(*) One source lists these names as H.A,. Curran, W.D. Witmer, William H. Albre, C. Patton, George B. Einer.

On April 14, 1849 a wagon train known as the Mackinac Mining Company was in a camp outside of St. Joseph, Missouri ready to move to California as soon as nature provided sufficient grass upon the plains for the sustenance of their stock. This group had provided themselves with three wagons, twelve yoke oxen, one tent and ample provisions for one year. All the members of the company were from Mackinac County, Michigan, with the exception of P.M. Dorsey, who was from Buchanan, Michigan. The following composed the company:

P.M. Dorsey	John S. Dunn	Philip Burns
William Crawford	John B. Carter	Joseph Gardner
E.P. Hill		

INDEPENDENCE, MISSOURI (April 9, 1849)

Large numbers of emigrants began pouring into Independence by April 9, 1849. Many of the companies came completely outfitted, and others only partially. Some of the emigrants were in town, boarding not fully equipped for the trip to California. The companies and wagon trains below were encamped within the vicinity of Independence on April 9, 1849.

The "Pontotoc and California Exploring Company" was organized into messes of six men each, bound together as a joint stock company until August 1, 1850. This train had ten wagons, seven tents and forty yoke of oxen. For better security in traveling, they operated as a military organization. Members of this train were:

T.H. Vaughn (President)	H.N. Calloway /sic/	S.G. Turner
H.N. Calloway (Vice President) /sic/	L. Morrow	J.A. Denton
	A. Morrow	M. Hardin
John Thomasson (Vice President)	J.H. Edmondson	H.A. Walter
	William M. Cunningham	Reuben Soo (?) (Son?,
J.A. Formevaul (Secretary)	J.G. Cunningham	Soo___?)
	* J.E. Wetherall	J.T. Cunningham
J.P. Carr (Treasurer)	L.B. Goodrich	William McEwen
J.H. Payne (Surgeon)	* S.W. Wetherall	D.B. Bramlett
J.W. Prude	A.J. Hanna	R. Lilies
Mark Hardin	F.A. Lamb	W.T. Osborne
William N. Nesbit	J.A. Parks	C.R. Harris
A.R. Calloway	J.H. Hall	William H. Findley
S.G. Calloway	W.C. Wright	W. Dickson
		C.M. Leland

(above members from Pontotoc, Mississippi)

P.A. Towne	F.W. Carr	W.A. Rayburn
C. Turner	R. Williams and two servants	

(above members from Coffeville, Mississippi)

A single wagon company which intended to travel to California in company with some large party is indicated below. The wagon was pulled by three yoke of oxen and the group carried one tent. The composition is as follows:

J.S. Groom (of Wilkerson Cty, Miss.)	R. Groom (of Wilkerson Cty, Miss.)	V.C. Groom (of Wilkerson Cty, Miss.)
A. Reynolds (of Hamilton Cty, Penn.)	Robert Harper (of Pennsylvania)	

(*) Consider the alternatives of J.E. Wetherell and S.W. Wetherell.

The next train camped outside of Independence, Missouri on April 9, 1849 consisted of a group organized into messes of four each, provided with four wagons, three tents and other necessaries for the trip. It was composed of:

George Martin	John Perry	O. Jennings
Alexander Nunn	James Alexander and family	William Quigley

(all above from Wisconsin)

Dr. J.H. Dixon	T.J. Parker	J.H. Moore

(all above from Beaver County, Penn.)

William Dennison	George W. Bard	Jacob Wells
L.M. Dennison		

(all above from Pittsburgh, Penn.)

James Kiernan (of Somerset County, Penn.)   John Fleck (of Somerset County, Penn.)

The below group was ready to move out of Independence on April 9, 1849 in a train consisting of four wagons, twenty mules, four ponies, three tents, and provisions for six months:

C.J. Willis, of Virginia	W.P. Jackson, of Floyd County, Ga.	Johns, Fla.
A.C. Harrison, of Virginia	E.F. Garrison, of Floyd County, Ga.	D.F. Sanger, of Floyd County, Ga.
S. Jones, of Paulding Cty, Ga.	C.C. Winn, of Cobb County, Ga.	A.T. Harper, of Floyd County, Ga.
A. Jones, of Paulding Cty, Ga.	John G. Phillips, of St. Johns, Fla.	Thomas Berry, of Chattanooga Cty, Ga.
J.G Papy, of St. Johns, Fla.	R.S. Hernandez, of St.	W.C. Boyle, of Chattanooga Cty, Ga.
M.J. Kirk, of South Carolina		

A small company camped outside of Independence on April 9, 1849 was preparing to move out with the "Pontotoc and California Exploring Company." Accompanying the larger group was a safety factor. The small group which traveled in a single wagon pulled by an ox team consisted of:

Green Wallack, of Butler County, Ala.	Edward J. Cook, of Lowndes Cty, Ala.	H.M. Hurburt, of Lowndes Cty, Ala.
J.L. Lunnice, of Rankin County, Miss.		

A company from Fort Wayne, Indiana was preparing to move out of Independence on April 9,. 1849. It was intending to move with the company of Colonel ____ Russell.*
No wagon complement was listed for the below group:

Samuel Ballow	Charles Lamb	Joseph Whitaker
Charles F. Colerick	George E. Smith	E.D. Bartlett
G.A. Sherland	A.S. Hall	Thomas T. King

(*) See footnote on Page 2 relative to Col. W.H. Russell

A three-man group encamped outside of Independence on April 9, 1849 was intending to leave for California with the "Pontotoc and Califonia Exploring Company." All of the men were from Hyde county, North Carolina, completely outfitted, but with no wagon complement indicated. The group was composed of:

Robert S. Jennett	Dr. William Sparrow	A.B. Gardener

* The eleven wagons of the "Newark Overland Company" were camped in a field outside of Independence, Missouri on April 9, 1849. This train was under the command of General John S. Darcy and it carried sufficient provisions for six months. The wagons were believed to have been pulled by mules. The company was also provided with eleven tents, necessary maps, a field glass, compass and telescope, and each man was armed with a revolving pistol, double-barrelled gun and a rifle. The group carried sufficient clothing for three years. Each man was to work on his own after arrival in California. The train members were:

John S. Darcy and servants	Thomas Young	A. Jobes
Andrew J. Grey	Col. J.R. Crockett	L.B. Baldwin
Charles Hicks	William D. Kinney	S.H. Meeker
A. Jerohnen	Robert Bond	J.A. Pennington and servant
B. Easterline	Moses Camfield	G.W. Martin
C.B. Gillespie	John C. Richards	Joseph Denman
J.W. Shaff	William F. Lewis	Thomas Fowler
Wallace Cook	James Lewis	Cyrus Currier
George Sayre	S. DeHart	A. Gibbons
S. Freeman	B. Carey	D.S. Bardsall
T. Woodruff	H. Johnson	

(above were from Newark, New Jersey)

William Emery, of Elizabethtown, N.J.	Joseph T. Doty, of Elizabethtown, N.J.	I. Overton, of Elizabethtown, N.J.
David Emery, of Elizabethtown, N.J.	C.D. Bogleston, of Elizabethtown, N.J.	B.F. Woolsey, of Jersey City, N.J.
T.W. Seeley, of New York City, N.Y.	Alexander J. Cartright Jr. /sic/ of New York City, N.Y.	Charles Grey, of New York City, N.Y.

On April 9, 1849 a Kentucky train was camped in a field close to Independence, Missouri. This party, under the command of Captain Edward Bryant, intended to depart for California on April 20, 1849. Bryant, the author of "What I Saw in California," had ensured that his company was one of the best prepared for the journey that lay ahead. The unit numbered forty-eight men and the trip was to be made upon mules, packing their provisions. They were provided with eleven tents, one wagon, an India rubber boat capable of receiving and bearing the weight of the wagon body, a medicine chest, hospital stores and other goods. Each man had three mules for his own use, with three extra mules to every mess group of four. All personnel were armed with a rifle, a pair of holster pistols and a pair of belt pistols. Provisions for one hundred and twenty days were on hand. The majority of the group was from Louisville, Kentucky and residence listings for the remainder are

(*) See "Notes" pp. 182-183 for variations on this company.

indicated as follows:

*Captian Edward Bryant	John Todd	C. Benham
John Kaye	R.W. Moore	George Rees (?) (Ress?)
W. McFarland	J. Burdsall	R.A. Wingate
T. Bland	H. Conroy	Samuel Carey
F.A. Kaye Jr.	W.G. Stewart	Wallace Pope
E. Gogerty	W.P. Richardson	M.Griffin
Robert Pope	Z.D. Parker	E. Neblitt (?) (Noblitt?)
L.W. Ludwig	J. Swayer (?) (Sawyer?)	James J. Stewart
E.F. Dulsey	E. Crawford	Andrew Musselman
John T. Moore	O.T. Murray	F. Brison
G.G. Moore	L.K. Thomas	

(above from Louisville, Kentucky)

Dr. H.P. Slaughter, of Henderson, Ky.	F. Tilford, of Lexington, Ky.	Sandy Brown, of Lexington, Ky.
C.C. Morgan, of Lexington, Ky.	M. McCracken, of Lexington, Ky.	H. Marshall, of Lexington, Ky.
M.A. Chinn, of Shelbyville, Ky.	F.M. Weams, of Franklin, Tenn.	J.H. Marshall, of Lexington, Ky.
H.D. Martin, of Paris, Ky.	Joseph McCleary, of Owensborough, Ky.	W.B. Wakeman, of Wheeling, W. Va.
D.D. Martin, of Paris, Ky.	F.W. Sheaffer, of New Madrid, Mo.	Thomas L. Sturgeon, St. Louis, Mo.
___Faulds of St. Louis, Mo.		

One wagon, drawn by ponies, was encamped near Independence on April 9, 1849. This unit, which was enroute to California, consisted of:

Mersay Oliver, of Madison Cty, Ky.	William Riddle, of Anderson Cty, Ky.	John Kearns, of Ohio

A two-wagon train, pulled by oxen, was in the field outside of Independence on April 9, 1849. Personnel in this group were from Richmond County, Ohio and the train was composed of:

James C. Lee	James J. Knox	James M. Marshall
Thomas Dansbee	William Heston (?) (Huston?)	William Broner
Alexander Fulton		

Another two-wagon group from Ohio was encamped in the same area as the foregoing train on April 9, 1849. This unit was from Woodford County, Ohio and it had provisions for six months. The wagons were drawn by eleven mules. Members were:

Henry Merryman	Joseph Booth	Benjamin Moseley
James E. Davis	S. Johnson	E. Wilbright
Samuel Davis	L. Smith	George Grey

Still another group from Ohio was camped in the same area as the above train. With wagons pulled by mules, it was very military--so completely organized even its members dressed uniformly. From Hamilton County, it had two wagons, sixteen mules, a horse and tents. The train, which intended to depart for California in company with Colonel Russell and his group, was composed of the following Hamilton County, Ohio residents:*

John Friend	A. Price	J. McKune
C.W. Friend	H. Wyckoff	J. Dumont
P. Campbell	A.J. Riddle	J. Langeman
William Elliot /sic/	L.N. Dunn	

A fourth group from Ohio camped on the outskirts of Independence on April 9, 1849 was a group from Morgan County. This company had one wagon, two tents, mules and other goods necessary for the trip to California. Members encamped were:

P. Burgess (?) (Burgeon?)	G.B. Wright	R.T. Sprague
Major J.S. Lone /sic/	W.C. Palmer	A. Hawkins
		J.A. McConnell

Another company from Ohio, camped at Independence on April 9, 1849, was from Huron County. This train was made up of three wagons with provisions for two hundred days. They also carried three tents and intended to utilize mules on the wagons. The unit was formed as a joint stock company and was the first to leave Ohio for the State of California. They procured their mules and outfit in St. Louis in February, 1849 and had been camped out of Independence for four weeks. Personnel in the company consisted of:

Stephen Dunton	Elisha Guthrie	John Jonson
____Beech	____Talbert	L.H. McGeorge
S.G. Whipple	T.B. Gardiner	D. Jefferson
W.C. Pettibone	Solomon Bardshar	M.M. Young
H.M. Jennings	H.B. Barney	

The final Ohio company camped out of Independence, Missouri on April 9, 1849 was at a point six miles out of town, where the eye of a traveler seldom penetrated, and so located for good reason. This small group of individuals was from Richland County and had selected a remote campsite to isolate one of its members, a solitary female— the only one in all the wagon trains parked around Independence that day. The company had one wagon, an ox team, one large tent, and was organized as a joint stock venture. It carried ample provisions for six months. Members of this group consisted of:

Simon Hackett	Jonas Brantney	W. Van Scoyse
Susan Hackett (an orphaned sister of Simon Hackett)	John Welkel	

A single wagon company from Knox County, Tennessee was also encamped near Independence on the same day as the above listed company. Bound to California to dig gold, this company was moving by ox team and it was composed of:

John L. Osborne	D.F. Wood	A.W. Rogers, of Knox County, Tenn.
A.P. Osborne	Samuel Hunter, of Knox County, Tenn.	
C. Harvey, of Knox County, Tenn.		

(*) See footnote on Colonel W.H. Russell, page 2.

The final company that was located out of Independence on April 9. 1849 was a small unit from Wisconsin. Their goods were aboard two wagons and the group consisted of:

L. McCummings, of Racine County	Perry McCummings, of Racine County	Andrew Stanton, of Racine County
C.F. Jenks, of Rock County	William Pixley, of Rock County	

ST. JOSEPH. MISSOURI (April 10. 1849) A number of wagon train units were in the vicinity of St. Joseph, Missouri on April 10. 1849. Most of them were getting ready to move out within two or three days. Great fears were anticipated that large wagon trains, moving together, would reduce the grass on the plains faster than nature could replenish it for the traveling stock. To obviate this, companies were departing in parties barely large enough for their own protection, and starting at intermediate times. The following trains were at St. Joseph on April 10, 1849 and preparing to move:

The "South Bend Joint Stock California Mining and Operating Company" had six tents, twelve wagons, thirty-six yoke of oxen, and provisons for six months. The company had purchased most of their goods in St. Louis, Missouri. It was bound together for a year after their arrival by by-laws, and organized into messes of five for traveling. Each man was armed with a rifle, bowie knife and a pair of pistols. They anticipated leaving St. Joseph within a few days, moving to a camp ground in the Indian territory, there awaiting a sufficiency of grass to justify proceeding on to California. Members of the train were:

C.M. Tutt (President)	Abin Allen	A.G. Robinson
G.W. Haines (Secretary)	E.C. Johnson	D.E. Gish
C.S. Fassett (Treasurer)	Charles Traver	C.W. Lewis
T. Lindsey	P.N. Johnson	W.S. McCullogh
William Norton	John Day	J.E. Woodward
W.G. Whitman (?) (W.O. Whitman?, WB. Whitman?)	P.W. Kinsey	J.A. Miller
	Samuel Harris	Francis Donohoe
	C. Caldwell	E.G. Carpenter
	J. Armstrong	L. Bressett
	A.G. Ford	

(above from South Bend)

M.A. Kidwell, of Plymouth, Ind.	G.S. DeGraff, of Michigan City, Ind.	J. Trainer, of LaPorte, Ind.
Enoch Belangee, of Plymouth, Ind.	William W. Stewart, Captain of the Company of New Buffalo, Michigan	J.S. Sillsbridge, Physician, of Chicago, Illinois

A company on the field and ready to move on this date was a group from LaPorte, Indiana. They were organized as a joint stock company and they possessed one large tent, two wagons, ten mules, and carried provisions for six months. Members were:

Samuel J. Gist, Captian	J.B. Lemon, Secty and Treasurer	James Lemon
M.M. McCoy	Benjamin Rusk	Stephen Oakes

The previously mentioned LaPorte, Indiana company and the below three LaPorte, Indiana companies intended traveling as a wagon train together to California. They were camped out of St. Joseph and were preparing to move:

The first company consisted of the following personnel who shared one wagon and a tent:

John Cutler, of LaPorte, Indiana	Henry Cutler, of LaPorte, Indiana	E.R. Alexander, of Richland, Ohio

The second company was provided with a wagon, six mules, a tent and six months of provisions. Members were:

T. Price	N. Van Tasser (?) (Van Tasson?)	S. Van Tasser (?) (Van Tasson?)
Andrew Hume		

The third LaPorte, Indiana Company was organized as a joint stock company for the period of two years. It shared three wagons, nine yoke of oxen, two tents and provisions for six months. Company consisted of:

M.T. Wickham	C. Barney	S. Walbridge (?) (G. Walbridge?)
G.W. Brandon	J.H. Dunham	
L. Findley	F.B. Everts	A.F. Lane
C.R. Patterson	Gideon Pratt	Francis Rose

A threesome consisting of Samuel Wayburn and A.D. Callander, of Milford, Indiana, and William Case of Middlebury, Indiana were camped in the vicinity of St. Joseph, Missouri on April 10, 1849. Organized as a joint stock company, this small group intended to journey to California in one wagon, a tent and other necessaries. They intended to join a large train for protection.

A number of trains from Michigan were in the field out of St. Joseph on April 10. 1849. The first Michigan train was organized as a joint stock company and it was bound together for two years by a set of by-laws instituted at the time of organization. This train was provided with five wagons, twenty yoke of oxen, four tents and provisions for six months. Members of the train were:

B.F. Brown, Captain	L.W. Tubbs, Commissary	D. Gee
George Engle, Lieutenant	D.K. Benedict	E.S. Gilkerson
Samuel Jennings, Secretary	J. Coles	C.P. Ludwick
George Stone, Treasurer	D.H. Austin	John Fisk
A.B. Montrass	Leander Strong	Robert Pollock /sic/
G.W. Pocock /sic/	J. Macomber	W.H. Vaughn
John Abbott	J.C. Duree and son	H.A. Hecox /sic/

The next wagon train from the Michigan area was divided into fourteen messes, each mess being provided with a wagon, four yoke of oxen, and a tent, and carrying 2,500 pounds of freight, chiefly in provisions. This train was preparing to depart within a week. Members of the wagon train were:*

Robert W. Wilson	Isaac Babcock	C. Martin
William H. Compton	B. Guard	Henry Myers
Asa Dow	George S. Freese	J.C. Smith

(above from Cass County, Michigan)

(*) One contemporary source varies composition of this company (see notes pp. 183-185).

R. Maranville   H. Rudd   G.W. Jones
Ezra Guard   J. Rudd   Leonard Crane
Eli Eck   J.P. Thompson   James Wiley
H. Schenefelt   George Eancs (?)
                           (Evans?)

(above from Cass County, Michigan)

J. Cronkhite   David Nobby   C.Towner
S. Saulpan   H. Kingsley   E. McDougall
H. Smith   George Fay   Thomas Brady
James Tooly /sic/   J.O. Nickel   James Hull (?) (Hall?)

(above from St. Joseph, Michigan)

Samuel Hastings   E. Ford   William B. Howard
Lyman Hastings Jr.   F. Barker   L. Kimble
Lyman Hastings and son I. Steinbaugh   F. Van Horn
G. Pike   J. Hartsall   A. Smith

(above from Berrien, Michigan)

William Hood, of   John Hale, of LaPorte N. Hudson, of Elkhart
  Wisconsin   Indiana   County, Indiana
____Bleauster, of   Benjamin Veszey, of   Eli Paxon, of Elkhart
  Wisconsin   Elkhart County, Indiana   County, Indiana
John Winchester, of   F.W. Earl, of Jackson John Heisz (?) (Heinz ?),
  Elkhart County, Indiana   County, Iowa   of Winnebago County,
Charles Kane, of   Illinois
  Winnebago County,
  Illinois

The third wagon train, camped out of St. Joseph, Missouri on April 10, 1849, was organized under the name "Pawpaw Mining Company of Michigan." It traveled with five wagons, fifteen yoke of oxen, two tents and was loaded with provisions for six months. The train members had organized themselves as a joint stock company and were bound together for the period of two years. Train members were:

Dr. B. Hard, President   F.S. Stanton   A. Bryant, Treasurer
Z.P. Davis   W.G. Barrett, Secretary   R. Hinkley
John Mead   G.H. Brown   G.H. Emory
J.T. Hart, Captain   T. Boyd, Commissary   A.S. Jones
A. Bangs   A. Taylor   G.S. Anderson
A.M. Herron   E. Taylor   S. Demarest

(above from Paw Paw, Michigan)

A three-wagon train from Virginia was also camped in the same general area as the above train on April 10, 1849. The wagons were pulled by mule teams and the group was organized as a joint stock company for the period of two years. Train members were:

C. Dunkum (?)   James Davidson, of   John H. Douglass, of
  (Dunkam?), of   Rockbridge, Va.   Rockbridge, Va.
  Powhatan County,   Samuel Davidson, of   David Orbison, of
  Virginia*   Rockbridge, Va.   Rockbridge, Va.

(*) carried in one source as Pocohantas County, Va.

William B. Dorman, of Rockbridge, Va.
John Ward, of Rockbridge, Va.
William B. Whitlock, of Augusta, Va. /sic/
Joseph Bodkin, of Bath, Va.
C.R. McDonald, of Bath Va.
John McDonald, of Bath, Va.

A second unit from Virginia was a small group that travelled in two wagons pulled by mule teams. It was also organized as a joint stock company. Members were provided with two tents to shelter the group while enroute to California. On April 10, 1849 the wagon unit consisted of:

Robert Stephens
Luke Stephens
John E. Herbst
Robert Paxton

(above from Roanoke County, Virginia)

Dr. N.E. Cargill
William H. Gwaltney
Willaim F. Harrison
Rufus K. Harrison
E.T. Chappel

(above from Sussex County, Virginia)

A four-wagon group from Ashtabula County, Ohio was camped out of St. Joseph, Missouri on April 10, 1849. This train was bound together as a joint stock company for two years. They had provided themselves with two tents, four wagons, twelve yoke of oxen and carried provisions for nine months. Members of the train were: *

H.B. Stone, Captain
A.W. Webster, Secretary
C. Tinker /sic/
H. Tinker
H.M. Way
Charles Tinker, Lieutenant /sic/
A.N. Kenk
John Packer
G. Perkins
L. Beckwith, Treasurer
Lyman Luce
G. Kendall
G. Hayner

A second small train from Ohio was encamped in the vicinity of St. Joseph on April 10. 1849. Formed as a joint stock company, this group was provided with two wagons, two tents, ox teams and provisions for six months. Members of the company were from Oxford, Butler County, Ohio and the train consisted of:

John Martindale
Hamilton Cluff
Hermann Bond
Jesse Ogle
John Lyttle
O. Greer
Manning Corey
P. Redenor

The five wagons of a train from LaPorte, Indiana parked out of St. Joseph on April 10, 1849. Members were bound as a joint stock company and they carried with them sufficient capital to engage in other business if the gold digging in California was not lucrative. Train personnel consisted of:

J.B. Travey, Captian
William Everhart
Charles Wees
J.R. Hall
John Holland
G.N. Turner
J.D. McDonald, Treasurer & Secty
Samuel Miller
William Miller
Henry Miller
J.C. Degraff
B.C. Harris (?) (R.C. Harris?)
A. Rodgers
H. Cramb

ST. JOSEPH. MISSOURI (April 13, 1849 For two weeks rain and cold weather had been adding to the hardships of camp life of the emigrants parked out of St. Joseph. Some, rather than undergo the further exposure and hardships which awaited them on

(*) See notes p. 185 regarding this train

the trails to California, had forsaken the wagon trains and decided to settle in Missouri.

Encamped out of St. Joseph on the forementioned date was the "Pittsburgh and California Enterprise Company." This train was divided into fifty-two messes, each mess was provided with a tent, wagon, six mules, and every other necessary for comfort. The train was to move out of St. Joseph in a week. Members were: *

M. Kane Jr., /sic/ President	T. Dunn (?) (Dune?)	P. Kane
Charles Coleman, Vice-President	James M. Aitkin	J.B. Chamberlain
	W.R. Guy	A.M. Litman
Charles T. Officer, Secretary	G.A. Walker	J.S. Willock
	R. Silcox	J. McCandless
William J. Ankrim, Captian	W.H. Taylor	A.L. Sample
	Dr. ____ Orendorf	L. Crepps
William Rankins, Lieutenant	J. Knowland	James Witty
	William Cooper	W. Blakely
James M. Braden, Lieutenant	B.C. Quigley	J.A. McGee /sic/
	J. Dorrington	L.G. Berger
J.S. Tallanalle	J. Connor	J. Nesmitte
A.W. Gug	B. Messersmith	J. McGraw
E.C. Gug	W.C. Beck	James McCarter
P. Ward	John Davison	R.P. Glass
A. McMurray	James Melville	A. McClory
Thomas Suce	J.R. Riddle	J. Leckey
W. McClory	M. Kane Jr. /sic/	James McKee /sic/
Thomas Barker	J. Huyett	J. McClaskey (?)
W. Mehan	S. Trisbie (?) (Trisbin?)	(McCloskey?)
R. McKee /sic/	J. McCowan	R. Phillips
J. Aiken	Samuel Ward	S. Gayne
W.F. Marthens	N. McIlwine	J. McDonald
C.O. Flynn	T. Jones	A. Spear
C. Lent	J. Amberson /sic/	H.S. Wynne
J. Joyce	F. Anderson /sic/	J.B. Fulton
J.M. Meredith	J.S. Wilson	Jacob Cupps
William C. Meredith	R. Wilson	J.C. Anderson
A. Ingram	D.W. Wilson and two sons	J. Hughes
W.J. Ingram	W. Shaffer	R.K. Pelrouski (?)
A.J. McNulty	J. Merabin	(Polrouski?)
W.P. Skelly	C. Rabun	J. Ludwick
George E. McCrady	W. Patterson	J. Hunker (?) (Hunter?)
W.M. Murray	T. Maxwell	J. Oliver
J. McGreggor	J. Morrison	L.L. Whiting
H. Wallace	J. Moore	E. Alsip
A.F. Blythe	J. Morgan	E. Holifant
H. Dixon	D. Blair	B.T. Latshaw
W.H. Call	James Kane	C.C. Blair
R. Spencer		

(above from Pittsburgh, Penn)

(*) See notes section p. 185-188.

William Cadda (?) (Cadde?)   W. Estep /sic/   Samuel Deal /sic/
W. Angenbraigh   F.J. Beal /sic/   J.L.F. Johnson
M. Miller   A. Beal /sic/   T. Galbraith
J. Martin   W.G. Bender   T. Daft /sic/
J. Dixon   S.H. Sarler   Thomas Daft /sic/
E.D. Harding   Isaac N. White   W. Bishop
James A. Irwin   John Heiss (?) (Heise?)   John Flood
W. Minis   G. Sythe   J. Glenn
W. McIlbeny   J.G. Gallagher   H. Wilson
J. Fulton   A. Wilson   W.D. Graham
J.P. Harbach   D. Darragh   J.D. Robinson
J. Matthews   J. Darragh   F.P. Robinson
J. Walls   J.K. Vankirk /sic/   M. Boreland
J. Means   J. Templeton   J. Warren
M. Goodfellow   C. Templeton   J.P. Boyd
J. Jack   L. Eckhoff   J. Goodwin
B. Brown   A.J. Jack   M. Hayden
J.P. Irwin   J.B. Henderson   J.G. Woods
J. Day   J.O. Nilson   H.J. Brunot
J. Estepp /sic/

(above from Pittsburgh, Pennsylvania)

A.D. Patterson   W. Hughes   C.G. Smith
J. Groves   J.W. Eggleston   S.B.F. Clark? (S. Clark and B.F. Clark?)

(above from Rochester, New York)

Thomas B. Dunn, of Jefferson County, Virginia   S. Sugder   F.A. McMillan
   J.N. Sinclair, of Mercer County, Pa.   R.G. Robinson
T. Reynolds   G. Winebiddle
J. Caldwell   J. Cook   A. Harris
W.C. Reed   J. Reynolds   J. Kearnes
D. Davis   D. Hughey   Thomas Perkins
Thomas Thornburgh   R. Jacobs   M. Fisher
H. Gotsman (?) (Gotzman?)   John Thornburgh   R.B. Butler
   B. Fiffer /sic/   A.S. Goodwin

(above from Alleghany County, Pa.)

W.J. Beatty   M. Meckling   J.W. McCandless
W.J. Stewart   E. Yetter

(above from Butler, Pennsylvania)

John Morgan   W. Wychoff (?) (Wyckoff?)   M. Courtright
G.W. Curtis   James Jones

(above from Short Creek, Virginia)

G. Steiner   J.A. Markle   J. Shotts
E. Taylor   J. Ellcessor   J.A. Foster
J.R. Johnson   W. Johnson   J. Smith
J. Latshaw Jr.   M. Holzman

(above from Westmoreland County, Pa.)

T.W. Rodgers   S.H. Squire   J. Kerr
E. Marquis   D. Estep /sic/   F. Ball

(above from New Brighton, Pa.)

J.S. Steel	W.M.O. Shelton	F.C. McClure
Thomas Gregg	R. Crosby	

(above from Birmingham, Pa.)

J.R. Dinnin	R. Wilson	George C. Taylor
G. Mitchell	S.M. Stowe	

(above from Jamestown, N.Y.)

F.C. Negley	G. Lemon	A. Young
J. Barrachman	J. Kiser	R.C. Gilchrist
Thomas McNair	R. McNair	D. McBride
J. Boreland	F. Phipper /sic/	B. Grape
J. Coppersmith	R. Staley	P. Smoker
P. Bergen		

(above from Butler County, Pa.)

J.B. Hartley	R. Wilson	C. Truesdale
H. Sheppard	C.T. Kirkland	D. McGill
D. Houck	O. McConnell	William F. Alderman /sic/
J.F. McGaughey		

(above from Mohoning County, Ohio)

H. Halderman /sic/	George Horne	C. Peters
P. Halderman /sic/	Guy Haines	

(above from Lancaster County, Pa.)

* The "Illinois Sucker Company" was encamped on the Indian Territory, opposite St. Joseph, on April 13, 1849. Several parties intending to join this wagon train had not yet arrived on the scene. This group had forty wagons, ox and mule teams and each of its organized messes had a tent and a riding pony. David Adams, of St. Louis, Missouri was to act as wagon train guide as far as Sutter's Fort. Members of this train hailed from St. Clair, Morgan and Macoupin Counties, Illinois and St. Louis, Missouri. Train members as of April 13, 1849 were:

H. Buffum	A. Ferguson	J. Godfrey
A. Stevens and family	B. Hutton	M. Louis
David Booz /sic/	William Bowers	J.G. Beeler
___ Taylor	J. Gifford	Samuel Truitt
Thomas Lock	C. Record	William Mitchell
George McBride	Robert S. Green	F.H. Curtis
Rollin Post	George M. Boxer (?)	J.W. Buffum
G.W. Carr	(Bozer?)	J.N. Dow
Samuel McPhaill /sic/	C. Vaugh	W. Boothsinger
John Bills (?))Bells?)	E. Pomeroy	Ellis Elwell
J. Vedder	F. West (?) (Went?)	John Rislin and son
Thomas T. Rainey	___ Vanntee	John Godwin /sic/
A. Schenitoski	___ Wardzinuski	___ Brooks /sic/
___ Joblauski	M.T. Smith	John Brooks /sic/
H.A. Latham	R.F. Grisihline	M. Bratagan
R.W. Camfield	W.R. Latham	W.V. Moody
N.M. Dorsey	John Hughes	D.W. Aldrich and family
A. Starr	F. Starr	J. Flanagan
John Sales	John Post	

(*) One contemporary source varies composition of this company (see "notes" pp. 189-191).

E. Randall	J. Patrick	T. Woods
T. Oakes	____ Purseley	A. Curree /sic/
H. Rice	R. Kirkwood	J. Spruance
Peter Lottim	E. Case and family	L. Post
G. Sittibruive	Charles Sinclair	C.A. Walker
C.J. Palmer	____ Keller	D. Settlemyer
J.D. Powers	John Douglass	J. Layman
Charles Chaney	B. Luken	William Benson
J.F. Burton	William White	J. Longwell
____ Guild	____ Croghan (?)	C. Mitchell
H. Martin	(Crogham?)	John Hogus
Mr. ____ Anderson and family	A. Groetfield	J. Haltzwert
	C. Mizendorfer	G.S. Hanly /sic/
J. Johnson	C. Johnson and brother	J. Rowe
R. Whyers		

On April 13, 1849 the "St. Clair Mining Company" wagon train was encamped in a grove about seven miles from St. Joseph, Missouri, on the opposite side of the river. The train consisted of twelve light wagons, four mules to each, ten tents, and the unit carried provisions for six months. Each man, excepting the drivers, was mounted on a pony. Members of the train were:

Vital Jarrot, Captain	B.C. Renois	Robert McCracken
Thomas Short	N. Boismenue /sic/	H. Frotier
John Boles	Robert Carnes	Joseph Frotier
Louis Amel	J.J. Statis	N. Sexton
____ Everson	B. Delorine	____ King
M. Morrison	John Chandler	G.W. Hook
John Christy	M. De Rousue (?) (De Rousse?)	B.Delude
A. Robinson		L. Thatcher
William Ogden	N.C. Cornoier	A. Gamlin
M. Lecompte	J.O. Adams	Jeremiah Hotus
John Greer	N. Turcot	L.D. Stewart
P. Peron	John Boismenne /sic/	Dr. A.X. Illinski
John H. Butler	J.O. Butler	P. De Noville

A wagon train from Shelby County, Illinois was encamped a short distance from St. Joseph, Missouri on April 13, 1849. The train was ready to move out to California in its eleven wagons pulled by ox teams. Two light carriages were also a part of the train and they were drawn by four mules to each carriage. Six months provisions were on hand for the journey. This train was composed of:

Benjamin F. Hunter and family	William H. Rankin	R. Madison
	L. Hunter and family	J.W. Madison
William Bevins	John Scruggins	Joseph Stewart
David L. Wright	David Evey	R.L. Williams
John Turr	John Evey	William Harsman
John Sullers	Dr. ____ Reeves and family	Joseph Evey
James Perryman		Mathias Rice

A small company of Germans hailing from Chicago, Illinois was also camped a short distance from St. Joseph, Missouri on April 13, 1849. They were enroute to California in two wagons drawn by ox teams and carried six months of provisions. The unit was organized as a joint stock company and consisted of:

Eli Knower (?) (Elk Knower?)	C. Van Gardiner	A. Fraunborger (?) (Fraunberger?)
F. Werner	C. Zeager	
	G. Zeager	

Camped in the same general area as the foregoing train was an eight wagon train from Will County, Illinois. This train was made up into three messes sheltered by three tents. Oxen were used to pull the wagons. Train members were:

Joseph Zumalt and family of nine children	Peter Bayley and family	James S. Waite and family
_____ Connor	D. Whitemore	S. Whitemore

ST. JOSEPH, MISSOURI (APRIL 14, 1849) The weather continued to be cold and disagreeable at St. Joseph. There was a heavy frost on the night of April 13th and the following morning ice, three quarters of an inch thick, was found on still ponds of water. Camp fires were blazing in every direction around St. Joseph. Wherever emigrant wagons were parked there was a shivering mass, wrapped in their blankets and robes, huddling together, cheering each other on the golden prospect before them.

Many members of trains "bolted" the campsite areas out of St. Joseph and took to hotels in the town, having become convinced that there would be time enough on the trail for a man to do camp duty when he had no other accommodation. Some four hundred emigrants were boarding in town on April 14th. Insubordination had manifested itself in several of the trains. Most of the following trains were ready to move out as soon as nature had provided sufficient grass upon the plains for the sustenance of their stock.

There follows a list of the wagon train companies camped near St. Joseph on April 14, 1849 were:

A company from Wisconsin which was organized into messes and provided with wagons drawn by ox teams. This group was awaiting the arrival of additional persons from Wisconsin before departing. Members of the train as of April 14, 1849 were:

Abel Minard and family	J.A. Short	Anson Oland
M. Connover /sic/	C. Ingersoll	Dr. E.B. West
Randalll Fuller	G.C. Cone	John Doliver (?)
John Howell	E. Lyman	(Dolliver?, Dollver?)
J. Goodrich	William H. Elder	J. Fishelor
Henry Root	Leander Hill	George Woodward
T.C. Ward	William West	
	Dr. E.R. Hoyt and family	

(above from Waukesha County, Wisconsin)

John Edwards	George Villinger and family	Dr. _____ Slye and family
A. Ostrander		

(above from Milwaukee, Wisconsin)

James Cline   Fred. Weshe   ____Weshe
A. Lewis

(above from Milwaukee, Wisconsin)

A one wagon group from Ionia County, Michigan was encamped out of St. Joseph on April 14, 1849. The wagon was pulled by three yoke of oxen and the group had also provided themselves with a tent. Members of this unit were:

G.S. Isham   Susan Isham   W.W. Fitch

The "Pokehagan California Company" was also in camp. It was a joint stock company from Cass County, Michigan and the train moved in five wagons pulled by fifteen yoke of oxen. It was ready to leave for California and its members were:

Henry Hass	Z.W. Ashley	William Welsh
Esquire Hass	Henry Kimmer	George Benton
Charles Shatlock	Henry Shatlock	Ezekiel Benton
J.S. Bradley		Leonard Benton

*A company from Adrian, Michigan was in camp and ready to move. It traveled by one wagon and four yoke of oxen. Providing additional shelter was a tent. Members of the company were:

Ephraim Lapham	Edward Lapham	John Densmore /sic/
H. French	H. Crandall	

Another small company from Michigan was camped out of St. Joseph on April 14, 1849. From Kalamazoo Michigan, this unit moved by wagon and had temporarily stopped at St. Joseph. Members of the company:

R. Barber   S. Hagan   E. Tobin

The above four groups, although independent of themselves, were preparing to travel with larger trains for protection. The same circumstance applied to the below unit from New Haven, Connecticut, consisting of:

Dr. J.R. Wakefield and wife   Lieut. Asa A. Stoddard

A wagon train from New Albany, Indiana was in camp and ready to move out for California. Four young men in the group were not identified as were three men hired as drivers. Unit composed as follows:

John Keller, wife and 5 children	Dr. L. Hoover, wife and 5 children	John Abbot /sic/, wife and child
G. Abbot /sic/, wife and 3 children	Ira Gilchrese, wife and 3 children	Mr. ____Schaffer and four young men
Three hired men (as drivers)		

Eight companies from Ohio were camped out of St. Joseph on April 14, 1849. The first, from Columbiana County, consisted of:*

A.V. Kinnear	F. Esholtz	H. Jordan
Z. Downer	A. McMillan	A.J. Hagan

*See "notes" p. 192 for additional data on this company.

S.M Holland	J.S. Smith	E.O.F. Hastings
J.W. Evans	J. Lindsay	A. Schindler
N.B. Wean	A. Anderson	Hugh Lee
George Grice	Daniel Williard	

The second Ohio wagon train was from Medina County and it was composed of:

George Case	J. Sawyer	D. Fullman
J.G. Briggs	B.B. Briggs	K. Chandler
H. Chandler	P. Chandler	

The third Ohio wagon train was from Lorain County and it was composed of:

E.W. Brooks	A. Forbes	L.I. Burril
J.W. Hall	H. Garfield	P. Garwick

(above from Lorain County)

S. Bethel of Morgan, Ohio

The fourth wagon train from Ohio was from Allen County and its members were:

James A. Hoover	Joshua B. Hoover	M. Mahan
J.A. Armstrong	W.H.C. Mitchell	Stephen Clingaman

The fifth Ohio train, known as "The Cincinnati and California Joint Stock Company", consisted of:

J.W. Wilson	Charles Robinson	H.J. Richards
William C. Conway	W.P. Harrington	William Huntington
E. Burr	Samuel Ayres	P. Chambers
T. Morrow	W. Endicott	John B. Louck /sic/
_____Frisbee	J. Loach (?) (Leach?)	D.S. Ross

(above from Cincinnati, Ohio)

Dr. J.F. Ankney of Kenton, Ohio   Dr. J.F. Robinson, of Beaver, Penn.

A sixth train from Ohio was known as the "Experiment Club" and its members were:

H. Winslow	Samuel Wright	M. Williams
Silas Smith	William Poor	

(above from Cincinnati, Ohio)

G.K. Fitzgerald	A.P. Rarison	Peter Myers

(above from Philadelphia - no State listed)

The seventh unit was from Cleveland, Ohio and it was composed of:

G.J. Chapman	F. Hooper	A. Curfes
A. Allardt	H. Fuhrup	

The final company from Ohio was composed of George Parry and John Evans of Cincinnati; and Isaac Parry of Richmond, Indiana.

A number of wagon trains from New York were also encamped on the outskirts of St. Joseph, Missouri on April 14, 1849. The first train was composed of individuals from Washington County and operated as a joint stock company. The train was made up of three wagons pulled by twelve yoke of oxen. Members were:*

Samuel McDoul /sic/	A.F. Bliss	A. McNorton
W. Harrison	John Robertson	B.F. Harshaw
D.M. Hall	John H. Tilford	John Cowan
James Hill	James H. Newton	H.S. Crandall
William Owen	A. Tilford	Robert Gourley

A second New York unit was from Cattaraugus County and it was preparing to move out to California in one wagon. This group consisted of:

J.T. Clark	Mr. ___Johnson	Mr. ___Sargeant

Another New York train was known as the "Albany Overland Association". It was from Albany, New York and its members were camped near the above group. This train was composed of:

James Roach	D.R. Haswell	B.F. Post
J.A. Becker	Henry Steele	Dr. E. Taker
N. Gasaway	Charles S. Perry	A.S. Brayton

In the same vicinity as the above was a two-man company from Rhode Island, consisting of P.R. Arnold and S.J. Vickory. Camped near the Rhode Island unit was a company consisting of J.G. Westfall of New Jersey, Philip Burne, of New Hampshire and William Smith, of New York.

Several trains from St. Louis were in camp a short ways out of St. Joseph, Missouri on April 14, 1849. The first St. Louis unit had provided themselves with one wagon, six mules, one large tent and provisions for nine months. It was bound together as a joint stock company for one year after arrival in California. Members were:

M.P. O'Connor	Thomas Murphy	John Drum /sic/
Andrew Murphy	Mathew Murphy /sic/	James Garvin
Thomas Flinn /sic/		

The second St. Louis, Missouri group called itself the "St. Louis Proc Company"(sic) and it was organized as a joint stock company. This unit intended to go by way of Fort Kearny and was set to move out of St. Joseph in a few days. Its members would travel in one wagon which was pulled by four yoke of oxen. A tent would be used to provide additional shelter. Members were:

T.S. Wright	John Fisher	A.S. Currie /sic/
J.A. Budd	A.N. Peters	John Atwood

The third St. Louis company was composed of Patrick McLaughlin, J. Sage and Redmond Sage, all of St. Louis, Missouri, and James McCann, of Randolph County, Illinois. This unit, a joint stock company, traveled by one wagon and four yoke of oxen.

The fourth group from St. Louis encamped out of St. Joseph, Missouri on April 14,

(*) This train had been at St. Joseph for one week.

1849 was bound together as a joint stock company for the period of one year. This group called itself the "Mound City Association of St. Louis". J.C. Davis, one of the members of this train, was well informed as to the route to the California gold fields, having once made the trip in company with Colonel John Fremont. This association had provided themselves with three wagons, two light spring carriages, four mules to each, two tents and all the necessary provisions. Several other trains were planning to go in company with this train, under the guidance of Mr. Davis. Members of the association were:

J.C. Davis	John Suydam	J.C. Smith
Charles Cutter	James E. Gallaway	James R. Dewitt/sic/
C.B. Suydam	W. Buckholder	

The final St. Louis company camped out of St. Joseph on April 14, 1849 was under the direction of S. Thorpe, of St. Louis, Missouri. It traveled with two wagons and the group consisted of:

S. Thorpe	William Miller	William States
Job Newton	William Cooper	Mr. ___Williams

Two companies from Virginia were encamped in the Indian Territory out of St. Joseph on April 14, 1849. Both of the companies were ready to move out for California. The first train, known as the "Sacramento Union Company of Wheeling" was planning to move out in five wagons, six mules to each wagon. They carried six tents and provisions for six months. Additionial provisions had been forwarded ahead by sea routing for use after their arrival. This train was organized as a joint stock company and consisted of:

W. McK. Lambdin	R.B. Woods	J.A. Agnew
J.E. Wade	R.T. Morrison	C.J. Chapman
George Rigby	Moses Ray	Dr. J.R. Brotherton
George Hobbs(?)	E.E. Hamilton	R.S. Hopkins
(Hobbe?)	John Burgy	V. Brown
R.P. Buckley	J. McCulloch	G.D. Curtis
G. Arthur	G. Currey/sic/	A.B Olney
William Drennon	B.A. Goode and servant	

The second group from Virginia was a joint stock company which was planning to move out in two wagons pulled by ox teams. Members of this train were from West Wheeling and the group was composed of:

Charles Thompson	John Curley	Joseph Tuttle
Charles Hall	E. Thomas	P. Thomas
Amos Curley	F. Thomas	

Encamped in the vicinity of the above party was a company of fifteen Germans. Members of this train would not reveal their identity for fear of taxation. The unit was under the supervision of a Mr. ___Pettit.

A company consisiting of J.B. Forye, W.H. Chever, John Lewis, of Davenport, Iowa; and J.A. Beddison, of Rock Island, Illinois was also encamped out of St. Joseph, Missouri on April 14, 1849.

Another small train encamped on the same date was composed of William McDowell, of Dayton, Ohio; J.H. Boyd, N.C. Cannon and Charles Cannon of Peru, Illinois. It was preparing to move out of St. Joseph, Missouri as soon as possible.

Also ready to move out of its St. Joseph campsite on April 14, 1849 was a train consisting of four wagons. Each wagon in this train was pulled by six mules. Members of this unit were:

Dr. J.S. Ormsby, of Peru, Illinois	Major William Ormsby, of Kentucky	A. McLain, of Westmoreland, Penn.
L.P. Ormsby, of Peru, Illinois	J.K. Trumbull, of Kentucky	J. Moats, of Westmoreland, Penn.
J. Shutt, of Westmoreland, Penn.	M.L. Detter of Westmoreland, Penn.	J. McManus, of Westmoreland, Penn.
Samuel Stoufer, of Westmoreland, Penn.		

Two wagon trains from Wisconsin were camped out of St. Joseph, Missouri on April 14, 1849. The first train was made up of the below Racine County residents: *

J.B. Howe	L. Dutton	E. Gordon
E. Stebbins	A.H. Blake	W. Dodge
E. Lowry	W. Spofford	E. Pearce
___Simonds	H. Blake	___Kimball
___(name unlisted)	___(name unlisted)	

The second group from Wisconsin was composed of Jonathan Mavey, wife and six children, of Rock County.

Three groups from Indiana were encamped out of St. Joseph, Missouri on April 14, 1849. The first unit consisted of:

John H. Manlove, of Tippecanoe County	John N. Manlove, of Tippecanoe County	M.D. Manlove, of Tippecanoe County
W.P. Mc___, of Tippecanoe County		

The second group from Indiana consisted of John Bartlett, James Hammin, J. Ridgeway, A. Staunton, W. Woodfon /sic/(Woodson?), and A. Leeds.

The third Indiana group was composed of B. Kamp /sic/(Camp?), wife and eight children, David Anderson, wife and two children, of New Albany; and in company, Andrew Jackson, of Ireland, and Thomas Kyle, of Kentucky.

A number of individuals from Tennessee were in camp, ready to move to California, on April 14, 1849. They were:

Albert Moss, of Montgomery County	James Brown, of Montgomery County	Thomas Hart, of Campbell County

(*) See "Notes" p. 193 for another listing on this train composition.

William Hart, of Campbell County
J. O'Callahan, of Nashville
J.O. Gordon, of Nashville
Thomas Coffin, of Nashville
William Wayman and son, of Summit County
Patrick Kinney, of Nashville
F. Kinney, of Nashville
B. Finnin and lady, of Nashville
Allen Thorpe, of Summit County
F.A. Goole, of Nashville
D. Miller, of Nashville
William A. Boggs, of Nashville

The following Pennsylvania residents were in camp out of St. Joseph, Missouri on April 14, 1849:

William Bancroft, of Erie County
R. Carter, of Philadelphia
J.D. Thomas, of Chester County
William Nash, of Erie County
M. Nash, of Erie County
George W. Jacobs, of Chester County
A. De Foe, of Erie County
D. Evans, of Philadelphia
Charles Jacobs, of Chester County

The below individuals were suitably equipped and organized into a company. They were camped out of St. Joseph on the forementioned date and were preparing to move out to California. The company consisted of:

J.R. Wheeler, of Harrison County, Ohio
J.M. Brumbarry, of Nacogdoches, Texas
John Heager, of Holland
Samuel Sneade, of Lynchburg, Va.
James Ladew, of Galena, Illinois
James Casey, of Ireland
Charles Casey, of Ireland
*From Columbia County, Ohio:
James R. Wiley
M.W. Wiley
C. Boorsman
John Daye and lady

A family from Hampden County, Massachusetts was in camp on April 14, 1849 and ready to move out to California. The family consisted of Hector Campbell, William B. Campbell, Samuel L. Campbell, Hector B. Campbell, Charles A. Campbell and six unidentified females.

The following residents from Illinois were in camp out of St. Joseph, Missouri on April 14, 1849, ready to move out to California:

James Robinson, of Coles County
Arthur Carr, of Shelby County
Calvin Rowley, of Will County
George A. Sanford, of Kane County
Amos Church, of LaSalle County
Henry White, of Grundy County
Peter Hoffman, of Coles County
E. Gilford, of Shelby County
James H. Taylor, of Will County
A.F. Hagan, of La Salle County
George Perry, of Grundy County
Samuel Ayres, of Grundy County
John Gordon and son, of Shelby County
John Johnson, of Shelby County
William Patterson, of Will County
William Lawrence, of LaSalle County
Mr. ___Pierce, of Grundy County
Henry Brown, of Grundy County

(*) County listed as found in source. Residence should be "Columbiana County, Ohio."

S.K. Turner, of Grundy
County

Dr. ___Antecs(?)
(Antees?), of Grundy
County

INDEPENDENCE, MISSOURI (April 19, 1849) California emigrants continued to congregate in the vicinity of Independence, Missouri. Handmaiden to influx was dissension. Cases of "accidental shooting" occurred almost daily in the wagon train campsites. Carelessness in the handling of firearms was generally the cited cause of the "accidents" and many of the shooting encounters were never reported on the pretext that the wounded parties were "in a fair way to recover".

Disagreements over procedural matters, route decisions, purchasing of provisions and selection of cattle were complaints that resulted in some instances in the complete dissolution of companies of wagon trains. One of the dissolutions, or winding up of affairs, came near proving fatal to an innocent party. In an encounter between two members of the company, Thomas S. Sawyer and a Mr. ___Walters, of Illinois, respecting a balance claimed by Sawyer as due him, shots were exchanged, and a Mr. Alexander H. Baldwin, of Elmyra, New York, who chanced to be passing the belligerents at the time, received the contents of a gun, fired by Sawyer, into his loins. Baldwin is said to have recovered. Sawyer was arrested; pleaded guilty to an assault, and was fined the sum of $1.00 and costs.

Very few of the large number of emigrants congregating in Independence took time to consider that they might be disappointed in their quest for gold in California. "Gold is plenty in California" was the motto. Few anticipated failure. One of the rare groups that displayed foresight was "The Western Mining Company of Cincinnati". This train was from Hamilton County, Ohio and it was mostly composed of mechanics, who carried with them their tools, and complete running gear for a saw mill. Very few emigrants took similar precautions, nearly all relied for subsistence upon their success at finding gold. This unit had wisely considered that if they were unsuccessful in their search for gold, their all was not lost. Even if necessary tools were available in California, most of the emigrants found it impossible to pay the exorbitant prices.

Thus, in spite of the fact that the men of the "Western Mining Company of Cincinnati" could not average two dollars each in their pockets, they were better off than most of the emigrants in camp on that day in April, 1849. The unit had been formed as a joint stock company and they carried ample provisions for nine months. They had provided themselves with seven tents, seven wagons, 26 yoke of oxen, and a mule for each man to ride. Members of the company were:

Alexander W. McCoy	John Ellison	A.J. Liggett
D. Aber	P.W. VanWinkle	C. Beard
W.P. Jeffreys /sic/	John Marbley	W.W,. Knapp
N.M. Harris	G.D. Sheppard	W.B. Otway
F. Cassim	S.T. Curtis	M. Terman
R. Barrett	Edward Owens	N. Terman

Dr. J. Thompson	C. Allesworth (?)	A. Rogers
M. Thompson	(Allenworth?)	Edward Hurd (?)
R. Thompson	J. Vansant /sic/	(Hard?)
M.J. Martin	J.B. Sargeant	B. McCormick
C.A. Anderson	T. Silmon	___Barnhart

Six other wagon trains were camped out of Independence, Missouri on April 19, 1949. The second Ohio train was from the city of Cincinnati and it operated under the name of the "Mutual Mining Association of Cincinnati". It was organized as a joint stock company and it moved in four wagons pulled by fourteen yoke of oxen. The unit carried provisions for six months plus three tents. All of the members of this train were from Hamilton County, Ohio with the exception of John W. Gray, of Madison County, Missouri. Train members were:

William Moore, Captain	Jacob Bennett	John W. Gray (of Madison
John B. Hart	William Millan /sic/	County, Mo.)
D.A. Powell	John Atkinson	J. Powell
N. Butterfield	D.C. Morris	John Johnson
L. Dewey	N. Clary	W.L. Isgnigg(?) (Isnigg?)
John Tuttle	W. Beach	John W. Walton
D. Van Trace	John H. Boyd	P.F. Shaw
		P. Boldman

The third Ohio wagon train was from Harrison County and it was composed of mechanics and professional men who were enroute to California with the intention of engaging in such business as their capacity and means would allow. This train consisted of two wagons, six mules to each, with two extra mules to ride. Members were:

Henry Johnson	Asbury Johnson	Lewis Lester
William Cady	___Vanborn	William Phillips
John Conwell	G.H. Jones	

The fourth train from Ohio which was camped out of Independence on April 19, 1849 consisted of a group organized as a joint stock company. The mode of transportaiton employed by this group is not known. Members of the train were:

Joseph Munn(?) (Mann?), of Marion County, Ohio)	George W. Larabee (?) (Larebee?), of Marion County, Ohio	Henry Larabee (?) (Larebee?), of Marion County, Ohio
Thomas Picketts, of Marion County, Ohio	George Rice, of Morrow County, Ohio	George A,. Weber, of Morrow County, Ohio
George Beckley, of Crawford County, Ohio		

The fifth Ohio wagon train was from Steubenville, Ohio. It was divided into eleven messes and was organized along the lines of a military unit. Its civil affairs were conducted by the officers and a board of trustees, consisting of one representative from each mess. The unit was formed as a joint stock company and it was provided with eleven tents, eighteen wagons, fifty-four yoke of oxen and provisions were on hand for nine months. This train was composed of:

J. McElrath, Captain	Thomas Trotter	H. Stokes
O.C. Gray, Secretary	J. Baltzell(?) (Baltgell?)	J. Morrison
George Hance, Treasurer	William Taggart	O.A. Worthington
H. McConnelly	William Briskell	S.R. Barr
Charles Sweeney	John Hoge	John Rainey
William C. Hayes	Edward Callendine	Dr. John Marshall
William H. Stokes	C.W. Haines	H.H. Maxfield
G. Jackson	S.V. Treadway	James Kell /sic/
Charles W. Richards	S.A. Ream	D.P. Keller /sic/
W. Solomon	William Fisher	S.D. Dundall(?) (Dandell,
M.S. Ruddy	O.T. Norton	Dandall?)
James Spencer	D. Burgett	J. Fugitt
James Shively	J.R. Collins	James Irwin
D. Connor	J. Parrott	George Todd
T.G. Morehead	A. McDonald	E. Brown
A. Morehead Jr.	John Matlock	B.F. Stokes
John Pacey	Daniel McGee	Thomas Loff (?) (Luff?)
William Daniels	E. Whittington	H.C. Scott
D.L. Forsinger	William Sherman	D. Anderson

The sixth unit was from Gallia County, Ohio and it consisted of S.D. Wood, Daniel H. Rose(?)(Prose?), Jacob H. Prose(?)(Rose?), Daniel Prose (?)(Rose?) and Lewis Childers. They traveled in one wagon pulled by three yoke of oxen. Necessary provisions were carried and a tent was taken for shelter.

The final Ohio group camped out of Independence, Missouri on April 19, 1849 was from Sandusky City. The unit was formed as a joint stock company and it was provided with two wagons, eight yoke of oxen, a yoke of cows, a span of ponies and other necessaries for the trip. Members of this group were:

W.E. Parish /sic/, Captain	John Ramsell /sic/	J. Hitching
A. Starr	D.A. Crowell	Edward Johnson
C.P. Cook	J.W. Beatty	

Two wagon trains from Illinois were in camp out of Independence on April 14, 1849. The first train consisted of three wagons, six mules to each, carrying provisions for one year. This train was composed of the following Peoria residents:

J.E. Carter	J. Fash	William E. Gunett /sic/
Robert Taylor	A.H. Fash	George Scott
J. Clegg	D..A. McConnell	___Peck

The second Illinois train moved in three wagons pulled by twelve yoke of cattle. The group carried provisions for seven months. Members of this train, all from Will County, were as follows:

A.F. Kercheval	J.W. Newton	William Parks

S. Runyan	A.N. Runyan	O.R. Runyan
A. Runyan	John Mahoney	David Mahoney
H. Rutherford(?)		
(R. Rutherford?)		

Two wagon trains from Kentucky were camped out of Independence on April 19, 1849. The first train, actually no more than one wagon, pulled by six mules, had been fitted out by a Mr. R. Mullons (?) (Mullens?) upon the conditions that he received, as compensation, a certain portion of the gold findings for a specified period. He had also, apparently, provided the provisions for the trip to California. Members of this train consisted of:

E.W. Hayes, of Kenton County	C.K. Snyder, of Pendleton County	J. Fritzland, of Woodford County
B.B. Mullons (?) (Mullens?), of Pendleton County	James Croslin (?) (Croalin?), of Campbell County	D.W. Thorpe, of Grant County
G. Young, of Jackson County	W. H. Childers, of Pendleton County	

The second Kentucky wagon train was kown as the "Green River Mining Company of Kentuck" (sic). It was organized as a joint stock company and was provided with nine tents, eleven wagons, forty-four yoke of cattle and provisions for five months. Members of this train were:

W.F. Summers	D.J. Campbell	W.H. Skiles
F.A. Jones	S.M. Crosthwait(?)	William Ellis
H.C. Gantt /sic/	(Croathwait?)	George Ellis
D. Torian	J.H. Paris	J. Hatcher
L.W. Landrow	L. Stern	R.C. McKainey
G.W. Feland	A.B. Anderson	James McCowan
H. Coleman	P.P. Johnson	J.K. Sale
J.P. Freeman	G.M. Earle	J.W. Cole
Capt. E.H. Herd	T.R., Darniell /sic/	James Shepard
C.W. Poindexter	D. France	George Carter
___France	M.D. Hare	G.W.D. Luck
William Bayley	W.W. Gray	M. Sherrill
J.F. Davis	J.H. Ingram	L.J. Sherrill
J. Hoy	R. Lavidge	L.W. Roberts
L.L. Sloss	B.F. Edmonds	J.R. Crail /sic/
J.O. Hill	B.Y. Samuels	John St. John and two servants

A company of Germans were encamped near Independence on April 19, 1849. They had provided themselves with a wagon and a team, and were ready for the move to California. Members of the company were:

C. Billings, of Ohio	J. Mann, of Ohio	L. Mischart, of Ohio
P. Straub, of Ohio	C. Criblin, of St. Louis, Mo.	___Swind, of St. Louis, Mo.

Mississippi had two wagon trains camped out of Independence on April 19, 1849. The first train was organized as a joint stock company and was made up of four wagons. Members of this train were:

A. Upchurch	William Worrell	D.C. White
H. Brown	R. Runnels	A. McMillan
O.R. Saddler	E. Sofley	C. Farmer
W.C. Thompson	J.T.J. Cain	C.W. Findley
R.M. Williamson	E. Hodges	J.L. Findley
H.M. Hart	S. Currell	

(above from Madison County)

The second Mississippi unit ready to move to California was from Lafayette County. Mode of travel employed was not revealed in research source. Members of this group were:

John Morris	F.J. Malone	A.M. Graham
James A. Weaver	J.M. Robertson	J.M. Humphreys
J.S. Lambert	H.S. Mitchell	William H. Owens

Indiana had three wagon groups in a camp out of Independence on April 19, 1849. The first unit was from Wayne County and it was organized as a joint stock company. This train had three wagons, three tents and carried nine months provisions. Mule teams were used to move the wagons. Members of this group were:

Samuel Sinex	Isaac Evans	A. Vaunxen
F. Fulghmer	J. Stiddins	C. Maule
James Talbert (?)	P. Stiddins	William Runnels
(Tolbert?, Telbert?)	L.D. Parsons	William Thatcher
Henry King		

The second Indiana unit was from Lafayette County and its members moved in a single wagon. This unit was composed of:

Samuel Hill	George M. Maxwell, Esq.	B. Cowdrey
William P. Henderson		

The third Indiana group also planned to make their journey to California in a single wagon, this one pulled by three yoke of oxen. Members of this company were:

Dr. Z.B. Gentry, of Clinton County, Illinois	R.M. Waters, of Clinton County, Illinois	D. Fudge, of Clinton County, Illinois
T.G. Titloo, of Kane County, Illinois		

Two small companies from Tennessee were in the field out of Independence on April 19, 1849. The first was from DeKalb County and it was composed of David Roger, James Davis, R. Dellmarch, James Walker and Thomas Elrod. The second company was made up of H.H. Means, and Alfred Means and two servants.

Two small companies from New York were also preparing to move to California. The first was composed of H. Webster, A. Kelsey, D.S. Sells and S. Kent of Monroe County; the second was composed of G.P. Webster and S.T. Johnson, of Oswego, New York and T.J. Marlett, of Aurora, Illinois.

A company consisting of E.B. Ute, Wayne County, Ohio; P. Finlock, of Campbell County, Virginia; and A. Coleman, of Washington County, Missouri, were in a camp out of Independence, Missouri on April 19, 1849. This company was suitably equipped and preparing to move out to California.

The final unit located at Independence on April 19, 1849 was a threesome from Adrian, Michigan. This small group was composed of B.M. Hance, E.A. Spooner and S.L. Ramsdall. They were ready to commence their journey to California and had provided themselves with sufficient provisions.

ST. JOSEPH, MISSOURI (April 20, 1849) A number of wagon trains were still encamped near St. Joseph on April 20, 1849. Many of the units had been in the area for two to three weeks waiting for sufficient grass on the plains to support their stock. The following groups were camped at sites around St. Joseph on April 20, 1849:

A wagon train from Milan, Ohio composed of the following California emigrants:

E.B. Atherton	Samuel Wickham	John Norton
Robert Smith	H. Allen	Snow Edison
M. Smith	Harry Paige	G.C. Choate
Charles Goodrich	J. Gregory	William Jennings

The "Mechanicsville and California Mining Company", from Evansville, Indiana, landed from the steamboat "Meteor" at St. Joseph, Missouri on April 10, 1849. The landing was actually made about 11 miles below St. Joseph owing to the rise of the Missouri River. This company was encamped about 4 miles below St. Joseph on April 20, 1849. The train was made up of wagons pulled by ox teams and they carried provisions for one year. Members of the train were:

Joshua W. Stephens, President	Christopher Hampton	S.J. McClure
	H.P. Vaughn, Secretary	David Darr
Thomas Conoway /sic/	Robert Parke /sic/	Rich S. Browning /sic/
Samuel R. Fickas	John Fairchilds	John W. Stephens
Clark Cody	John L. Fickas	Jesse McCallister

*The "Painsville Mining Company" from Lake County, Ohio arrived at St. Joseph, Missouri on April 18, 1849 and were still encamped at the site on April 20, 1849. This group, enroute to California, consisted of:

L. Thatcher, President	H.K. Fobes /sic/	M. Fox
S. Mathews /sic/, Director	A. Trowbridge	J.W. Amy /sic/
H.C. Ely	E. Bligh /sic/	George Reynolds
Major Downing /sic/	H.P. Cady	E. Manley
C. Turner, Director	B.F. Adams, Director	

(*) See "notes' p. 193 for reference to "Painesville Mining Company"

M. J. Turney   J. Green

On April 20, 1849 the Elk Horn California Company was still encamped out of St. Joseph, Missouri. This unit had come from Walworth County, Wisconsin and had spent approximately a week in St. Joseph. Members of the company were:

Zophar Chittenden   Edward Pentland   George M. Allen
Lewis Lewis /sic/

INDEPENDENCE, MISSOURI (April 20, 1849) Emigrants continued to arrive at Independence on their westward journey to California. Most of the emigrants arrived completely outfitted, except in stock. As stock was the principal and indispensable ingredient for the journey the selection was one of importance. Many of the emigrants, in purchasing their stock, were compelled to accommodate themselves to their purses. As a consequence of following this avenue there were a number of tragedies. Sales of oxen were made as low as $22 the yoke, and mules at $30 per head. However, these were not the general market rates. Stock sold for such prices would last just enough to carry their owners to a point where it would be impossible to replenish.

The supply of oxen and mules in Independence exceeded the demand. Ordinary to good mules were $40 to $60, and choice mules were selling for $70 to $100 per head. The supply of oxen was large and prices ranged from $45 to $55.

To the onlooker it was apparent that there would be immense suffering on the Plains due to poor selection of stock. Why hundreds of emigrants purchased inexpensive teams to undertake a journey of two thousand miles was a mystery. Many of the pioneers with large, heavy wagons were allowing but four mules, or two and three yoke of oxen; the empty wagon itself was a sufficient load to pull. In most cases the question of a duplicate team was never considered.

How to outfit-whether to start with mules or oxen-occasioned much discussion among many of the companies. Many companies, fully equipped, excepting in stock, came to the very point of dividing over the selection. Advocates for both actively engaged in setting forth the advantages of one type of team over the other.

Most of the experienced mountain men in Independence were fitting themselves out with light wagons, carrying light loads, and utilizing six to eight mules as a team to each wagon.

A wagon train from New York, known as the "German California Mining Company" was camped out of Independence on April 20, 1849. It was organized as a joint stock company and the group intended making the trip with mules and ox teams. Four tents were to be used as shelters. Members of this company were:

M. Carl   Seler Franz   A. Balm
G. Scimmers   K. Aulich   G. Schneider
W. Bachananer (?)   B. Aulich   P. Elergoff
   Buchananer (?)   A. Hill   H. Steinburg
C. Wisehoff   ___Diebrich   F. Thomas

F.S. Scheid	___Dutrich	N. Lange
F. Brantlach	F. Preness	___Klump
G. Deuz (?) (Douz?, Denz?)	L. Nussbarner	C. Knouer
	F. Schlagider	G. Schaibrock(?) (Scheibrock?)
B. Scharman	G. Roth	F. Kramer
H. Tupper	L. Roth	___Schrafft
A. Neihmert	C. Richter	F. Kaller (?) (Keller?)
F. Gross	A. Wichrowsky	V. Kopf
___Mattesheimer	T. Schmidt	W. Rusche
*Dr. F. Wallace	P. Hartman	D. Schneider (?) (Schnaeider?)
___Berling Sr.	A. Ferber	___Schneider (?) (Schnaeider?)
___Berling Jr.	T. Asgolm	
C. Anderform /sic/ (Anderson?)	T. Schaub	
F. Diefel	F. Weber	___Hubermann (?) (Habermann?)
George Topf	C. Haber (?) (Huber?)	___Ahrent (?) (Abrent?)
G. Pflagratu (?) (Pflagruter?)	F. Moore	
	J. Kelly	
	T. Scharman	

Another train encamped out of Independence on April 20, 1849 was made up of the below individuals. This company was made up of four wagons pulled by fourteen yoke of oxen and it was ready to move to California immediately. Members of the train were:

J.W. Turner, of Adrian, Michigan	Three hired men, all unidentified, of Pennsylvania	Pennsylvania
B. Sherman and family, of Pennsylvania	___Coney, of Wisconsin	Thomas Nelee, of Wisconsin
A. Conway, of Wisconsin	G.J. Smith and family, of	___Williamson, of Wisconsin
Allen Hubbard, of Adrian, Michigan		

A three wagon train which was organized into three messes was also encamped out of Independence on April 20, 1849. This unit was fully outfitted and ready to move, the wagons being pulled by twelve yoke of oxen. Members of this company were:

Joseph Knight	D.T. Eldridge	T.D. Warren
D.W. Paddock	William Freeman	T.L. Cutler

(above from Racine County, Wisconsin

P.E. Holcombe, of Bond
   County, Penn.

ST. JOSEPH, MISSOURI (April 25, 1849) The roads in every direction around St. Joseph were lined with wagon trains of emigrating parties enroute to California. Several trains had already departed St. Joseph and were now about one hundred miles from the frontier; they intended to remain in camp for some days at Grand Island, Nebraska, which was about two hundred and eighty miles from St. Joseph. From that point the roads from Independence, St. Joseph, Fort Kearny and Council Bluffs connected.

Many of the emigrants camped out of St. Joseph made it a point to eat one or two of their last meals away from their campsites. This practice of last meals "out" was also followed by emigrants at Independence, Missouri. The business merchants of St. Joseph

(*) While several members of the "German California Mining Company" were engaged in a shooting match, a gun in the hands of Dr. F. Wallace prematurely discharged and killed a young man named Werner Hill.

and Independence able to meet any demands for supplying emigrants with wagons, stock and trail supplies, but the landlords of hotels and houses were often guilty of gross and unpardonable remissness in not providing comfort and sustenance.

On April 24, 1849 one of the meals served at the "Edgar House" was tabulated by a disgruntled dinner guest. The landlord of this St. Joseph establishment served a "bill of fare" to forty hungry emigrants as follows: boiled ham, two dishes; fat pork, six dishes; fried ham, six dishes; potatoes, ten dishes; and about a dozen dishes of corn and wheat bread; desert, peach pie.

In reviewing the foregoing meal one gratification was apparent, that none of the emigrants were likely to be troubled with gout previous to moving out to the plains. Sustenance was not the only shortcoming in St. Joseph hotels and houses. The appearance of the rooms and sheeting to the beds indicated great scarcity of water, or gross negligence. The river being contiguous, and the town plentifully supplied with wells, lead the pioneer to suppose the latter was the case. This attitude of "they are only California emigrants" existed in most of the frontier towns through which the trail pioneers traveled.

A number of wagon trains camped out of St. Joseph on April 25, 1849 were from Ohio. The first train was from Cincinnati, Ohio and consisted of four wagons, twenty-three mules and three horses. The unit members intended to pull out of St. Joseph in approximately one week. This train was composed of:

S.G. Israel, President	Samuel Barret /sic/,	William Mullowy
J.C. Crane, Secretary	Treasurer	B. Fitzpatrick
S.B. Weller	J.A. Drake, Captain	William Glover
	J.A.Z. Jones	James O. Burns

*A second company from Cincinnati, Ohio who intended moving with the above train was a small joint stock company. This group had one wagon, seven mules and two tents. Members were:

J.G. Hubbell	W.J. Sperry	J.H. Moore
Barry Jones	G.W. Harrington	A.W. Griffin

Another single wagon unit from Cincinnati traveled as a joint stock company. Equipped with a tent and six mules the below company members were preparing to leave for California:

J.M. Kerr	George Krausz /sic/	D. Kloppenburgh
J.W. Way		

The fourth company from Cincinnati was provided with a tent, wagon, three yoke of oxen, and seven mules for packing. The members of this company were:

C.S. Coover /sic/	E. Stockton	C. Hiddon
George Mower	J.R. Johnson	J.B. Smart
L.H. Braley		

(*)See "notes" p. 194 for additional data

The fifth company from Cincinnati, Ohio consisted of a man named Jacob Son (___Jacobson?) and eight unidentified Germans. This group had one tent, eleven mules and two wagons.

A sixth company from Cincinnati, Ohio was made up of David Schaeffer and three unidentified Germans. They were preparing to move to California in a wagon pulled by two horses.

The seventh company from Cincinnati was provided with two tents, a wagon and eight mules. Members of this company were:

Isaac Stokes	Arch. De Butts	William Sloan
James H. Haslett	H. McConnelly	A.J. Atherton

Travelling with the above listed company was another group from Cincinnati, Ohio. This unit had two tents, one wagon, and eight mules. Members were:

Joseph Vance	John Shiner	Robert Gillmore/sic/
J.C. Arnold	J.C. Wingate	A.C. Baldwin

A ninth company from Cincinnati had a tent, wagon and six mules. This California-bound group was composed of:

John Millikin	Silas Prenell	C.H. Bell
John Delany	William D. Lawrence	L.D. Sunderly

A tenth company from Cincinnati, Ohio consisted of Samuel N. Goman, Theodore Ogle, M. Ogle, and Thomas Burnett. This company had a tent, wagon and six mules.

The eleventh company from Cincinnati was composed of J.V. Vredenburgh, J.S. Vredenburgh and Matthew Ruckle. They had provided themselves with a wagon and six mules.

The twelfth, and last company from Cincinnati, Ohio, was equipped with a wagon and seven mules. Members of this company were:

Joseph Howard	Joseph Gill	Joseph Dinney
Asbury Malay	J.W. Shaw	A. Culverson

A company from Trumbull County, Ohio was camped out of St. Joseph, Missouri on April 25, 1849. This group, a joint stock company, was equipped with a wagon and eight mules. Company members were:

C.W. Bidwell	W.W. Hyde	George S. Case
William H. Robbins		

Another Ohio unit in the camp was from New Carlisle. It was organized as a joint stock company and was provided with a wagon and five mules. Members were:

D. Hubbard	F.P. Ward	Jacob Stitzel

A company travelling in a wagon with eleven mules was from Columbus, Ohio. Like the foregoing Ohio wagon trains this group was bivouaced out of St. Joseph, Missouri

(*) See "notes" p. 194 relative to page 4 entry.

on April 25, 1849. Members of this unit were:

H.L. Morgan	B. Carpenter	L.E. Green
S.Y. Hoyt	B. John	J.W. Cowan
H.C. Rareden		

A company from Monroeville, Ohio was preparing to journey to California in one wagon pulled by six mules. Members of this group were:

W.C. Cook	William P. Thompson	C.P. Ross
Timothy Baker	George Goodhue	

A wagon train from Miamisburg, Ohio was also encamped out of St. Joseph on April 25, 1849. This train consisted of four wagons and sixteen yoke of oxen,. Members were:

William Anderson	William Reller	Robert Stewart
Charles Kurtz	D. Botts	Samuel Loree /sic/
John Gepheart	Joseph Howard	C. Watson
M.D. Whitbridge	Peter Backenbaugh	

A small wagon train known as the "Pittsburgh Independent California Company" was encamped out of St. Joseph on the foregoing date. The group was preparing to move out in two wagons pulled by eight mules. Train composition consisted of:

John D. King	W.T.A.H. Gross /sic/	George Stewart
William Gay	D. Boudelear	C. Robons /sic/
Alexander Moore	D.C. Ellis	(Robbins?)

A company from McDonough County, Illinois was also in camp. This train was made up of ten wagons, forty yoke of oxen, and two yoke of cows. Members of the train were:

T. Chandler	James Lupton	___Harris
L.G. Farwell	G. Chitham	L.H. Robinson
J.L. Anderson	D. Hamilton	John Willcox /sic/
J.H. Updegraff	John Wiley	J.W. Dellam
Mike Martin	Charles Fox	J. Naylor
R.H. Broadus	Dr. Thomas Luster	E. Bean
George Boughman	John Hunt	George W. Head
Joseph Neitesky	George W. Ayre	Elijah Step
Michael Yost	Edward Ayre	Frank Pierson
James Morrow	P. Cormany	

A small unit from Hancock County, Illinois intended travelling to California in two wagons pulled by eight yoke of oxen. This group consisted of:

D.C. Miller	Thomas B. Motts	Joseph Garrett
J.M. Cozad		James Garrett

A company provided with three wagons, eight yoke of oxen, seven mules and three horses was also in camp out of St. Joseph, Missouri on April 25, 1849. Members of this train were:

A. Pettibone, of Galena, Ill.	R.A. Drummond, of Galena, Ill.	David Wade, of Galena, Ill.

W. Galord /sic/, of Schuyler County, Illinois	S. Galord /sic/, of Schuyler County, Illinois	Joseph Galord /sic/, of Schuyler County, Illinois
Dr. J.E. Oatman, of Chicago, Ill.	Dr. Asa Clark, of Chicago, Ill.	Mr. ___Mecham /sic/, of Chicago, Ill.

A company from St. Louis, Missouri was encamped out of St. Joseph, Missouri on April 25, 1849. This group, provided with one wagon, four mules and a pony, consisted of:

J.M. Seward	James McFarland	Mr. ___Hilt

Also camped out of St. Joseph was a company from Adrian, Michigan. It was provided with a tent, one wagon and four yoke of oxen. This group consisted of:

S. Richmond	C. King	James Skinner
H. Crandall		

A company from Steuben County, New York was a bivouac out of St. Joseph. The group, preparing to travel to California in a wagon pulled by four yoke of oxen, consisted of:

B.F. Dudley	Eli Bidwell Jr.	H. M. Miller
Joseph Mellburn		

The next to last group camped out of St. Joseph, Missouri on April 25, 1849 was J.D. Van Allen and his son (unidentified). They were from Buffalo, New York and planned to move to California in a wagon pulled by five mules.

The final wagon train in camp on the foregoing date was one consisting of ten wagons, twenty-seven yoke of oxen, four mules and two horses. Camp site protection was in the form of four tents and all the wagon train members were from Rushville, Indiana. The company was under the direction of Captain N. Hayden. This group was composed of:

Capt. N. Hayden	George B. Findley	James Hillman
M. Sexton	W. Piercy	S. Bratton
A.J. Crawfrod	George Stone	R. Beall /sic/
J. Aldridge	Samuel Diffendaffer (Diffendoffer?)	H.E. Carr
M.W. Cox		O. Posey
William B. Maddox	J.J. Nichols	J.H. Carr
J. Murphy	Joshua Wolf	___Buchanan
James Wildridge /sic/	Charles Points	John W. Malone
William McMath	Smith Scott	

FORT KEARNEY (Nebraska) (April 25, 1849) On April 25, 1849 the steamboat "Dahcota" was wrecked at a point about eighteen miles below Fort Kearney, Nichtenabotna township (Nebraska).* On board the steamboat were a number of California emigrants.* Following the wreck, a group of the emigrants wrote to a Kanesville, Iowa newspaper seeking assistance. They requested that teams be sent to the narrows of the Nichtenabotna and Missouri River, then down the Missouri four miles until coming in contact with a Mr. Thomas Hughes. Members of the emigrant party aboard the "Dahcota" were identified as follows:

(*) For additional emigrants on board see page 58.

Colonel C.M. Johnson
Henry Boley
Elizabeth Johnson
Mrs. Mary Ann Gooch and child
John Fothingham and family
Mrs. Elizabeth P. Crombie (widow)
Edward Reeves and family

John Murry /sic/ and family (Murray?)
Sarah Worsley, wife of John Worsley, and six children
Thomas Binnel
Emeline Mangum (widow) and child
Robert Miller

G.P. Dykes
Peter ___cock (Babcock?, Hicock?)
Charles Nowlan /sic/ and family
Jared Graham
Joshua Gray and family
William Bean and family

ST. LOUIS, MISSOURI (April 28, 1849) On April 28, 1849 the steamer "Princeton" arrived in St. Louis from the Illinois river bringing California emigrants. Nine of the emigrants (all un-identified) were organized into a company called the "Westfield Mining Company". Also on board were the members of the "Granite State and California Mining and Trading Company" who were listed as:

Mr. G.W. Houston, President
J.B. Gage, Vice-President
Edward Moore, Secretary
Gilvin S. Tifield, Treasurer
James W. Stuart
Charles W. Childs
Austin Pinney
J.P. Lewis

Dr. ___Bachelder
Grovinor Allen
J. Lyon
Lafayette Allen
Thomas J. True
C.C. Barclay
Erastus Woodbury
Alden B. Nutting
Jonathan Haynes
Robert Thom /sic/
J.P. Hoyt

C. Hodgden
Dr. A. Haynes
S.W. Gage
J.D. Gage
Alfred Williams
Kimball Webster
James Butler
Benjamin Ellenwood (Ellanwood?)
Jacob Morris
G. Carlton

ST. JOSEPH, MISSOURI (April 27, 1849) On the morning of April 27, 1849, Captain Miles M. Goodyear with a party of gentlemen left St. Joseph, Missouri for California. Captain Goodyear indicated the group would travel with pack mules and they were determined to make the best time ever made across the plains. Goodyear, an old mountaineer, left St. Joseph with the following individuals in his party:

David Harkness, of Michigan
W. R. Marvin, of Michigan
Evan Lewis, of Wales
John Davis, of Maine
J.S. Vernon (?), of Michigan

N. Grant, of St. Joseph, Missouri
John Hughes, of Great Britain
Two un-identified California Indians
Dr. ___Burris, of Alabama
Charles Maddin, of Arkansas
Andrew Goodyear, of Maine
Capt. Miles M. Goodyear, of Maine

The "Dixon Company", from Dixon Lee County, Illinois, had left St. Joseph, Missouri by April 27, 1849, having crossed the river on April 24th. Members of this wagon train are listed as follows:

Leslie H. McKenney, Captain	J.B. Nash	D. Vroman
E. B. Baker, Lieutenant	R. Catherwood	P. McKenney
F. Pickle	S. Hatch	J. Porter
S. W. Franklin	E. Pinkham	D.C. McKenney
B.R. Stephens	V. Mason	M. Flatt
E. Sterling	A. Johnson	W. Seaman
F. Shobert /sic/	R. Johnson	W. Davis
J. Ramsey	H. McKenney	___Marsh
S. Hough	R. McKenney	T.C. Hicks
Long John /sic/	C. Taylor	H. Loveland
W. Ross	J. Miles	W.D. Dunn
J. Bligh	R. Moor /sic/ (Moore?)	___King
J. Earl	F.H. Burroughs	___Dresser

    *A wagon train consisting of some seventy-five members left St. Joseph, Missouri for California on April 24, 1849. A large number of this company were from Michigan, but only the names of the persons residing in Racine, Wisconsin are known at this writing. Before departing from St. Joseph, the Wisconsin segment acquired grain to insure that their cattle and mules had sufficient feed along the route. Racine residents in this train were as follows:

James B. How /sic/	Elisha Lowery	Ebenezer Pierce
Silas Simonds	Sheridan Kimball	A.K. Blake
D.L. Dulton /sic/	W.E. Dodge	A.C. Stebbins
Alex Connell	James Coughran	E.E. Gordon
George Taylor	W.P. Spaford /sic/	

    The Brookville California Company left St. Joseph for the gold mines during the last week of April, 1849. The approximate departure date was April 24, 1849. Members of this company joined with a large wagon train from Southern Illinois before it left St. Joseph. The Brookville California Company consisted of:

Benjamin Chafer	S.F. Rodman	H. Berry Jr.
John Hudson	John F. McCarty	Thomas V. Kimble
Elisha Skinner	Moses Forcum	L. Woods
Francis M. Kerme /sic/	Moses Renny	M.C. Winchester
Joseph D. Forcum	John Conrad	Andrew Berry

    Three residents from Columbia County, Pennsylvania were in St. Joseph, Missouri on April 27,. 1849. The trio, Thomas Smith, John Petrican and Samuel S. Wilson, were engaged in outfitting themselves for the trip to California.

    The Charleston, Virginia Mining Company had pitched their tents on a hillside north of St. Joseph before commencing their trip to California. Members of this company called their hillside retreat "Camp Bryarly". The encampment lasted several days and on April 27, 1849, the roster of the group was as follows:

B. F. Washington, of Jefferson, Virginia, President	Robert H. Kelland, of Richmond, Virginia, 1st Commander	Smith Crany, of Jefferson City, Virginia, 2nd Commander

(*) A secondary source varies spelling, see p. 26 and "notes" p. 194 relative to page 26.

J.E.N. Lewis of Jefferson Cty, Virginia, 3rd Commander	H. Conway	J.H. Murphy
	Wake Bryarly, Surgeon	E.M. Aisquith, Treasurer
	Nathaniel Seevers, Quartermaster	J. Harrison Kelly, Secretary
Daniel Cockrell		
T.C. Brapley	James H. Moore	Joseph Engle
F.A. Riely /sic/	James McCurdy	J.T. Humphreys
John Moore Jr.	W.J. Burwell	George W. Comegys /sic/
J.W. Gallaher /sic/	H.C. Harrison	Jacob Bender
C.F. Slagle	J.T. Boley	Morgan Miller
J.C. Walpert	J.H. Engle	Benjamin Hoffman
H.H. Moore	Andrew Wagner	John Purcell
Samuel Davidson	E. Rohter /sic/	J.A. Strider
P.B. Showman	F.W. Duke	M. Ferrill
J.T. Poland	N. Tavener	J.H. Garnhart
Asa Dlevinger /sic/	James Davidson	J.S. Showers
C.A. Hayden	T.C. Moore	I.K. Strider
V.E. Geiger	J.C. Davis	A.R. Miller
D. Fagan	A.J. Marmaduke	Charles Cunningham
Enos Daughtery	E. Lock	George Cunningham
John Allen	C.C. Thomas	James Cunningham
G.C., Stonebraker	T. Milton	B.F. Steevers /sic/
J.W. Bowers	J.C. Young	W.H. Mackaran
E. Hooper	R.H. Keeling	R.M. Blakemore
J.M. Lupton	F.R. Simpson	P.M. Ripler

*A company from Dayton, Ohio, who called themselves the "California Mining and Trading Company", arrived at St. Joseph, Missouri on April 19, 1849, on the steamboat "Embassy". The group encamped one mile north of St. Joseph to prepare themselves for the trip to California. On April 27, 1849 the unit was still in place and members of the company consisted of:

J.J. Hopkins, President /sic/	James Horton, Vice President	C.D. Flinn
		F.B. Creighton
O.D. Finch, 1st Lieutenant	A. Ferree /sic/	William Reed
D.P. Brown, 2nd Lieutenant	H. Marat	Charles Boden
	B.F. Kinsely /sic/	William Palmer
John M. Wentze, 1st Sergeant of this company	John Edmonson	John Smith
	William Roper	James Odell
	John S. Lewis	J.D. Possenoe
P. Wagner	W. Hoffman	S. Broadwell
W. Ewing	D.D. Gilman	I. Stouder
J. Haage /sic/	J. Hager /sic/	D. Kemp
S. Hoke	D. Fundiburgh	J. McClure
Dr. John Longenecker /sic/	R. Shadrick	Ira Tingley
	H. Winters	James Crow
W.H. Smith	William M. Smith	E.A. King
S.M. Keifer /sic/	W.H. Bickford	J.W. McCorkle
Thomas Clegg Sr.	J. Hisey	J.H.T. Morris
Thomas Clegg Jr.	D. Stibbins /sic/	James Pease
P. Baer, President /sic/	J.P. Clough Jr.	W. Coles

(*) See "notes" pp. 194-196 for further details.

J. Kreiner   D. Engles   J.C. Foster
Webster Clegg

*The "Cincinnati Mercantile Association", a group from Ohio, was camped across the river from St. Joseph, Missouri on April 27, 1849. This group had all the necessary provisions on hand for the trip to California and was intending to depart in six days. The following were members of the company:

Dr. John McKenzy /sic/	Dr. W. F. Ames	S. Merrill
William M. Stoder	R.S. Drummond	Joseph H. Merrill
John Bukham /sic/	David Horton	W. Name
Timothy Worthington	John R. Patten /sic/	John Henderson

A wagon train known as "The Independent Company", from Illinois, was in St. Joseph, Missouri on April 27, 1849 and was intending to leave for the plains in two days. This unit consisted of three wagons and eighteen mules. Members composing the company were:

William Rea /sic/, of Macon County	Jacob Hummell, of Macon County	Henry Prather, of Macon County
R.G. Oglesby, of Macon County	George Matsler, of Piatt County	Henry Sadorus, of Champaigne County
T.L. Loomis, of Macoupin County	Richard Piatt /sic/, of Piatt County	N.W. Pendicord, of Dewitt County

Four men from LaPorte, Indiana were in St. Joseph, Missouri on April 27, 1849. This foursome, who called themselves the "New Durham Temperance Mess", attached themselves to Rev. Isaac Owens' wagon train. The Owens' train was encamped on the opposite side of the river, six miles south of St. Joseph. The train, numbering about one hundred and seven persons, planned to leave their encampment for the plains in one week. Members of the "New Durham Temperance Mess" were:

Lemuel Robinson	John Griffith	Abraham Miller
L. Crumpacker		

The "Madison Company", from Jefferson County, Indiana, left St. Joseph, Missouri on April 27, 1849 for California. Members of this train were:

Dr. G. W. Cross	John Mulby	W.D. Vail
C. C. Elliott	S. D. Cowden	Samuel Keath
W. G. Taylor	W. Leffler	J. B. Woodburn
William Stewart	Jackson Ury	E. Dreher /sic/
Truvius Wilson		

The "Chautaugee Mining Company", from New York, left St. Joseph on April 23, 1849 for California. This company was composed of:

John Clarke	Alonzo Winsor /sic/	Lyman Rexford
A. J. Blackman	James Briggs	David Sabine

A small company from Pike and Ralls Counties, in Missouri, left St. Joseph, Missouri on April 26, 1849 for California. Members of this company, known as the "Spencer Creek

(*) See "notes" pp. 197-198 for additional details on this association.

Company", were as follows:

John H. Davis	R.S. Davis	R. Odell
D. Parker	M. Parker	One Negro (name not listed)

On April 27, 1849 the following individuals from Cleveland, Ohio were in St. Joseph, Missouri making preparations to leave for California:

M. Dyer	B.A. Peterson	B. Douglass /sic/
James E. Eddy		

A small company from Shelby County, Ohio was also in St. Joseph on the forementioned date. Members of this company were:

R.K. Cummins	A.C. Gerard	S. Whittlerey
H. Deaver	J. Shanely	

KANESVILLE, IOWA (May 2, 1849) The following individuals had arrived in Kanesville, Iowa and were destined to leave for the California "gold" regions within a short time. Names reflected were in Kanesville on May 2, 1849.

Edwin Hillyer, of Dodge County, Wisc.	Oscar Finley, of Calhoun County, Mich.	Francis McClasky, of Jefferson County, Wisc.
Andrew Shannon, of St. Louis, Mo.	Mr. ___Reynolds and brother, of Wisconsin	Robert Davidson, of Ann Arbor, Mich.
Philenus Howe, of Polk County, Iowa	Dr. ___Landsdale, of Polk County, Iowa	Mr. ___Traitkill (?) of Polk County, Iowa
A.W. Blair, of Polk County, Iowa	Hiram Beales /sic/, of Linn County, Iowa	William Abbey, of Linn County, Iowa
James Lytle /sic/, of Linn County, Iowa	Samuel W. Tolman, of Linn County, Iowa	Amos Fuller, of Cass County, Mich.
James Reed, of Linn County, Iowa	Charles Mulford, of Linn County, Iowa	John Van Vaulkenburgh /sic/ of Cass County, Mich.
John Gough, of Cass County, Mich.	R.S. Blackburn, of Schuyler County, Ill.	Michael Carr, of Wisconsin
L. Sparks, of Schuyler County, Ill.	J.D. Moore, of Schuyler County, Ill.	J.S. Downer, of Michigan
P. Sparks, of Schuyler County, Ill.	Lemuel Johnson, of Iowa	John Roberts and family, of Wisconsin
Marshall McNeal, of Illinois	Peter Wyrick, of Wisconsin	George Mitchell, of Bonaparte, Iowa
Mr. ___Bailey, of Wisconsin	D.C. Downer, of Michigan	R. Widener, of Bonaparte, Iowa
K. Davidson, of Michigan	Philip Johnson, of Wisconsin	A. Widener, of Bonaparte, Iowa
C.F. Walker, of Lee County, Iowa	Giles Wells, of Lee County, Iowa	John Mickelwait, of Van Buren County, Iowa
J.P. Walker, of Lee County, Iowa	Asa Fordice (?) (Fornier?), of Lee County, Iowa	
Whitcomb Mickelwait, of Van Buren County, Iowa	John Taylor, of Henry County, Iowa	

James Mickelwait, of Van Buren County, Iowa
Willerby Mickelwait, of Van Buren County, Iowa
Dr. S.L. Giles, of Van Buren County, Iowa
Buton Dodson, of Van Buren County, Iowa
G.B. Day of Sturgis Prairie, St. Joseph County, Michigan
Volney Palchen, of Sturgis Prairie, St. Joseph County, Michigan
Hiram Jacobs, of same town as above
John Major, of same town as above
Benjamin Ogden, of same town as above
W.H. Angevine, of same town as above
Robert Etderton(?), of same town as above
Michael Laird, of same town as above
Conrad Rainking /sic/ (Rankin?), of Fort DesMoines, Iowa
Edward Keller, of Fort DesMoines, Iowa
Mr. ___Smith, of same town as above
John Frederick, of same town as above
Michael Swingley, of Ogle County, Illinois
Robert French, of Calhoun County, Mich.
V.S. Newcomer /sic/, of same town as above
V. Blodgett, of same town as above
Valentine Haney, of Niles, Michigan
Joseph Coveney, of Berrien County, Mich.
Thomas Scott, of Henry County, Iowa
Andrew Frame, of Van Buren County, Iowa
Joseph Dodson, of Van Buren County, Iowa
William Hineman, of Van Buren County, Iowa
Edward Allander, of Van Buren County, Iowa
William Allander, of Van Buren County, Iowa
Jacob French, of Augusta, Lee County, Iowa
Augustus Fairbanks, of Augusta, Lee County, Iowa
Francis Richardson, of Wisconsin
Philip Johnson, of Watertown, Wisc.
Hezekiah G. Cable, of Fort DesMoines, Iowa
John Williams, of Fort DesMoines, Iowa
Isaac Cooper, of Fort DesMoines, Iowa
O. Welker, of same town as above
Mr. ___McHenry, of same town as above
Daniel Searles, of Racine County, Wisconsin
Dr. ___Scoffield /sic/ of same town as above
James Hartwell, of Mishawaka, Indiana
John Ruple (?), of Cleveland, Elkhart County, Indiana
Silas T. Mattax /sic/, Elkhart County, Indiana
Alexander Marshall, of Louisa County, Iowa
Alexander Hamilton, of Louisa County, Iowa
William Seaman, of Van Buren County, Iowa
Ell. Parr, of Van Buren County, Iowa
Joseph Crawford, of Van Buren County, Iowa
Joe Smith, of Augusta, Lee County, Iowa
Simon Brown, of Augusta, Lee County, Iowa
John Parley (?) (Porley?), of Augusta, Lee County, Iowa
Samuel Wallard (?) (Willard?), of Augusta, Lee County, Iowa
Ezekiel Rose, of Fort DesMoines, Iowa
Charles Goodnough /sic/, of Fort DesMoines, Iowa
John Brewer, of same town as above
Mr. ___Hinson, of same town as above
Jesse Searles, of Racine County, Wisconsin
George W. Light, of same town as above
Egbert Taylor, of Miles, Michigan
S.H. Griffin, of Niles, Michigan
H.W. Rood (?), of Niles, Michigan
Erastus Kimball, of Edwardsburg, Mich.

On May 2, 1849 a group of individuals known as the "Dowdle Family: had banded together in Kanesville, Iowa. It is believed this group was preparing to leave for California. Members of the "family" were as follows:

Dr. J. Hendricks, of South Bend, Ind.	A.P. Pinney, of St. Joseph, Berrien County, Michigan	W. Miller, of South Bend, Indiana
E.S. Reynolds, of South Bend, Indiana	A.M. Church, of same town as above	C. Johnson, of same town as above
M.B Miller, of same town as above	L.C. Wittermyer, of same town as above	W. Snavely, of same town as above
G. Pierson, of same town as above	J.M. Morton, of same town as above	W. Woodward, of same town as above
Dr. D.W.C. Willoughby, of same town as above	S. Huff, of same town as above	W. Maslin, of same town as above
L.B. Huff, of St. Joseph, Berrien County, Iowa	Robert Lee, of Chicago, Illinois	John Sales, of Chicago, Illinois
Edward Hicken, of Chicago, Illinois		George Hicken, of Chicago, Illinois

ST. JOSEPH, MISSOURI (May 4, 1849) On May 4, 1849 a group of men known as the "St. Joseph Company" announced their intentions of departing from St. Joseph, Missouri on May 11, 1849 for California. The company was made up of St. Joseph residents and they intended to make the trip in seventy days with pack mules. Company members were:

Sam Johnson	John Somerfield /sic/	B.D. Ellett /sic/
James Andrews	James Somerfield /sic/	Edward Bunall /sic/
J.W. Jones	Michael Camron /sic/	Samuel Willson /sic/
Thomas Fausett /sic/	John F. McDowell	T.F. Warner
Francis Brubaker	M.F. Moss	James Cirkwood /sic/
D.H. Moss	John Lewis	(Kirkwood?)
Joel Ryan		

*On April 29, 1849 the below individuals departed from St. Joseph for the California gold regions:

D.I. Wilmans and brother (un-identified)	A.D. McDonald	Mr. ___Lansdale
	John Warfield	

On May 2, 1849 a wagon train of from thirty to thirty-five wagons departed from St. Joseph for California. About one hundred and twenty men and four women were in this train,. Most of the company were from Cass County, Illinois with the remainder of the train consisting of two teams from Morgan County, Illinois, two from Hancock County, Illinois, two from Fulton County, Illinois, one form Madison County, Illinois, four from Joe Daviess County, Illinois and seven teams from other parts of the state. There were approximately fifty members of the train from Cass County. Only a portion of the train members are known at this writing and the names are as follows:

J.W. Overall	G.P. Allin /sic/	Jesse Cross
Henry Bomler	John Brown	Charles M'Crea

*See "notes" p. 198 relative to this group and also indexed names.

Henry S. Fitch	Henry Harfaclift /sic/	W. Rosenberger
George C. Fitch	James Jackson	Mr. ___Barnet /sic/
Frederick Krohe (?)	Chambers McLean	(Baranett ?)
(Krobe ?)	George Edgar	Conrad File
Mr. ___Bradford		Mr. ___Croft

(all above from Beardstown, Illinois)

Mr.___Robertson	George Edgar	John B. Thompson
C. Beady	W. Rosenberger	Thomans Deals

(above from Virginia)

Mr. ___Robinson, of Cass County, Illinois	Mr. ___Beard, of Cass County, Illinois	Thomas Smith, of Cass County, Illinois

On May 1 1849 a company from Troy, Lincoln County, Missouri, arrived in St. Joseph, Missouri. This group called themselves the "Troy Mining Company" and they were still in St. Joseph on May 4, 1849. Members of this California-bound company were as follows:

Colonel David Bailey	Henry A. Bailey	Shapburgh R. Woolfolk
Major Francis C. Clark	Lindley H. Ruland	William C. Shelton
Capt. F. M. Wright	James H. Manning	Charles L. Forbush
Henry Hall	Richard Hearld	George W. Wright
John H. Hilton		

On May 3, 1849 a company composed of six men, two wagons, twelve mules, two tents, and provisions for six months, left St. Joseph enroute to California. The following are the names of the company membes:

J.N. Johnson of Keokuk, Iowa	C.C. Graham, of Keokuk, Iowa	O. Dunks of Keokuk, Iowa
R.B. Smith, of Keokuk, Iowa	W.Y. Head, of Keokuk, Iowa	Thomas P. Grier, of Mecklenburg County (no state listed)

Members of a small company from Hollidays Cove, Virginia, were in St. Joseph on May 4, 1849. The group called themselves the "California Company" and it consisted of:

William Brown, Captain	William F. Knox, Treasurer	David Hindman
William Farnsworth	John Swearagen	John Pyatt
		Elijah Robinson

A wagon train known as the "Washington City and California Mining Association" was in St. Joseph, Missouri on May 4, 1849. This train consisted of:

J. Goldsborough Bruff, President	C.C. McLeod, Quartermaster and Adjutant	Augustus S. Capron
Gideon Brooks, Vice President	John M. Farrar, Asst. Commissary	Alexander Garrett, Ensign
Benjamin B. Edmonson, Treasurer	George Byington	James Foy, Blacksmith
A. H. Parish /sic/, Secretary	John Bates	C.G. Alexander
Henry Austin, Surgeon	*Charles Bishop	William N. Barker
John Cameron, Commissary	John T. Coumbe /sic/	James H. Barker
	Stephen J. Cassin	B.G. Burshe (?)
		Richard Culverwell
		Stephen Culverwell
		William H. Deitz

(*) Died of cholera on the Platte.

John Y. Donn /sic/ (Dunn?)	H.C. Dorsey	John V. Ennis
William Franklin	David Foible	Gregory Ennis
Thomas J. Griffiths	Charles Fenderich	James A. Ennis
W. Hillery	Josiah B. Hills	L.A. Iardella
S.D. Lewis	W. Jewell Jr.	T.P. Kinesbury
John M. Marden	W.W. Lloyd	F.M. Magruder
Isaac E. Owen	Joseph Murphy	C.G. Moseley
O.B. Queen	William Pope	Thadeus Provest /sic/
J.H. Queen	Charles Reed	Henry Wright
Edwin D. Slye /sic/	Joseph C. Reily /sic/	Thomas B. Scott
Robert Slight /sic/	W.J. Stoops	Joseph Thaw
M.M. Teprell	William H. Truman	Thomas Williams
F.R. Windsor	Henry Vermillion	D.R. Wall
James Wardell	Richard Washington	George A. Young
	J.C. Willis	

The Olentangy Mining Company, a wagon train from Delaware County, Ohio, was encamped near the bluff, seven miles west of St. Joseph, Missouri, on May 4, 1849. This California bound group had arrived in St. Joseph with horse teams, intending to go through with them, but abandoned the idea, and exchanged their horses for oxen. The company consisted of:

Dr. H.C. Mann, President	N.N. Lykes, Commissary	S. Forman /sic/
Joseph Barker, Treasurer	M. Armstrong	Isaac Dutton
William Said	William Patterson	S. Westbrook
S. Selandek	John Taylor	William A. Jones
P.A. Banehast	Jacob Taylor	H.H., Robinson
A. Carson	Henry Taylor	S. Robinson
Margon Savage /sic/ (Morgan Savage ?)	John D. Jacobs	M. Gillett
Dr. E. Field, Vice President	W.A. Loring, Secretary	A.S. Renyon

On May 2, 1849 the "Barry Union Pioneer Company", from Pike County, Illinois, crossed the river at St. Joseph, Missouri, enroute to California. They were joined by the "Mackinac Mining Company", and the "Buffalo Mining Company", under the command of Dr. G.W. Southwick. (See pages 7-8 for two wagon trains known as the "Buffalo Exploring and Mining Company" and the "Mackinac Mining Company." As noted on page 7, the Buffalo train is listed as leaving St. Joseph on April 12, 1849.)

Members of the "Barry Union Pioneer Company" consisted of:

Dr. G.W. Southwick	Daniel D. Grey	H.A. Parker
Rev. W. Mitchell	Nelson Grey	G.M. Mays
L.A. Walker	C.A. Adams	William Aldrich
G.K. Watson	Charles E. Mason	John Myers

A wagon train from Coles, Edgar and Clark Counties, Illinois, crossed the river out of St. Joseph, Missouri on April 30, 1849. This group expected to organize a train of twenty to thirty wagons and were determined to go through to California. Members were as below:

W. Titsner	C. Grove	G. Owsley /sic/

S. Lundrey	T.E. Stoddert /sic/	S. Mitchell
W. Evinger	J.R. Beverly	E. Parker
A. Evinger	J. Kennedy	J. Parker
J.C. Miller	R. Wiley	J.A. Mitchell
G. Yocmm /sic/ (G. Yocum ?)	J. Wilkinson	J. Skidmore
	T. Kelly	J.W. Roberts
		N. Norfolk

(*)On May 4, 1849 the members of a wagon train from Canton, Ohio announced that they would leave St. Joseph, Missouri for California on May 7th or 8th. They intended to cross the plains in ninety or a hundred days with their wagons and mule teams. The following persons were members of this train:

George B. Platt, President	James Anderson, Secretary	Alison Dunbar, Treasurer
William Haas		George S. Dunbar
John W. Wagner	Amos Peirrong /sic/	Darwin Estep
	Daniel Raffensperger	

The "Illinois and California Mutual Insurance Company, No. 1" arrived at St. Joseph, Missouri on April 27, 1849. The members of this wagon train were still in St. Joseph on May 4th and at that time the group consisted of:

William B. Broadwell	B.A. Watson	W.P. Smith
Jacob Uhler	William Odenheimer	E. Fuller
Henry Dorar /sic/	E.T. Cabinis	T. Billson
Lewis Johnson	B.D. Reeves	John Rodham
Richard Hodge	Benjamin Taylor	B.R. Biddle
J.B. Weber	J.B. Watson	F.S. Dean
Albert Saterty /sic/	Thomas Whiteburst	

A portion of the "Central Michigan California Emigrant Company" was encamped in the north part of St. Joseph, Missouri on May 4, 1849. They were awaiting the arrival of the residue of their company and expected to leave St. Joseph for California on either May 5th or May 7th. The advance party of this company consisted of:

H.C. Hodge, Captain	Mr. ___Dalamatter	William P. Pantlan /sic/
Mr. ___Hodgkins	J. Thorn	R.M. Fuller
Mr. ___Cranmore	E. Spencer	William Morris
H. Morris		

and fifteen unidentified members

(*)A wagon train from Wheelersburg, Sciota County, Ohio, was encamped in St. Joseph, Missouri on May 4, 1849. This train was to leave for California on the following day and it was composed of:

Dr. T.S. Moxly /sic/	William Crichton	William Raddock
Robert McConnell	William McKinney	W. Enslow
Uri Nurse	John Miller	T.S. Enslow
Morrison Nurse	W.J. Finton	A.F. Kendall
G.F. Dupe	T.J. Burke	

A wagon train from Beloit, Wisconsin was encamped in St. Joseph, Missouri on May 4, 1849. This group had adopted the motto "Excelsior" and they intended to leave for

(*)See "notes" pp. 198-200 for additional data.

California on May 7, 1849. Members of this wagon train were:

Mess No. 1
(all from Beloit, Wisconsin)

John Dyer	___Armstrong	Charles Marsh
Hubbard Moore	George C. Watson	J.C. Leonardson
Archibald Coe	C. T. Curtiss /sic/	

Mess No. 2
(all from Beloit, Wisconsin)

Andrew Whalen	C.C. Tuttle	J.S. Willson /sic/
James Ingersol		

Mess No. 3
(all from Beloit, Wisconsin)

Capt. William Thomas	Dr. Jesse Moore	J. Klein /sic/
A. Boengesser		

*Mess No. 4
(all from Beloit, Wisconsin)

Dr. G.W. Hicknell (?)	W. D. Hilyer /sic/	F.H. Hackett
(Bicknell ?)		

*Mess No. 5
(all from Beloit, Wisconsin)

D.C. Pinkham	George W. Haskell	E.W. Hackett

Mess No. 6

Mr. ___Brown, of Iowa	Samuel H. Culver, of	E.W. Barker, of Janesville,
William F. Kimball, of	Janesville, Wisc.	Wisc.
Janesville, Wisc.		

The members of the Springfield, Illinois Company, No. 3 were in St. Joseph, Missouri on May 1, 1849 and left that town on May 2nd for California. This small company consisted of J.T. Walters, James Walters and William Walters.

Three residents of Platteville, Wisconsin were in St. Joseph, Missouri on May 4, 1849. This threesome, James S. Gillis, William Palmer and E. O'Hana, were enroute to California.

INDEPENDENCE, MISSOURI (May 9, 1849) The first wagon train of the "Pioneer Line", comprising twenty passenger carriages, eighteen wagons for baggage and supplies, with one hundred and twenty-five passengers, left Independence for Upper California on May 9, 1849. Turner, Allen & Company were the proprietors of this line, and they had previous experience in the management of transportation trains through the Spanish country. The list of passengers, teamsters, muleteers and herders connected with the May 9 departure are as follows:

Capt. N.C. Cunningham,	P.D. Tiffany, of Belfast,	W.H. Gray, of Belfast,
of St. Louis, Mo.	Me.	Me.

(*)There is a possibility that some of the members of Messes 4 and 5 were from Jefferson, Wisconsin.

G. Cochran, of Belfast, Me.
J. James, of Belfast, Me.
S. Heath and son, of Belfast, Me.
A.V. Parker, of Waldo, Me.
J.J. Eastman, of Pittsfield, N.H.
E.S. Gross, of Boston, Mass
W.T. Watters /sic/ (Walters ?), of New York City, N.Y.
Stewart Morse, of New York City, N.Y.
J.J. O'Brian /sic/(O'Brien ?), of Philadelphia, Pa.
J.G. McKarsher, of Philadelphia, Pa.
J.A. Brewster, of Philadelphia, Pa.
Horace Guth, of Northampton, Pa.
J.M. Davidson, of Maryland
H.T. M. Spears, of Chesterfield, Va.
E.D. Bouz (?)(Booz ?), of Appomattock County, Virginia
E.D. Winslow, of Charleston, S.C.
A.C. Gale, of Courtland, Ala.
C.M. Kelsey, of New Orleans, La
G.W. Kelsey, of New Orleans, La.
C.C. Cranson, of Ann Arbor, Mich.
J.L. Peters, of Columbus, Ohio
J. Foster, of Massillon, Ohio
C.H. Wesson, of Chillicothe, Ohio
D. McDonald, of Indiana
A.C. Bonnell, of Indianapolis, Indiana
S.J. Upton, of Belfast, Me.
R. Usher, of Belfast, Me.
H.E. Pierce, of Waldo, Me.
S. Kingsbury, of Waldo, Me.
L.C. Fisk /sic/, of Sturbridge, Mass.
E.B. Chase, of Derby Line, Vermont
Dr. A.H. Steel /sic/ of Oswego, N.Y.
Arza Crane, of Oswego, N.Y.
R.S. Stoyell of Moravia, N.Y.
R. Whitman, of Pittsburgh, Pa.
S. McClure, of Shipensburgh, Pa.
B.J. Reid, of Clarion, Pa.
J.D. Roger, of Montgomery County, Pa
S. Purcy, of Greenbrier County, Virginia
G.W. Porter, of Powhattan, Va.
W.T. Brewer, of Elberton, Georgia
J.E.S. Jones, of Elberton, Georgia
B.E. Henry, of Elberton, Georgia
S. Camdee, of Munroe County, Michigan
D.F. McCullum, of Ann Arbor, Michigan
L.B. Ward, of Potosi, Wisconsin
J.H. Millenchop, of Potosi, Wisconsin
J. Ellison, of Ripley, Ohio
W.P. Jeffreys, of Ripley, Ohio
L.P.H. Virden, of Indiana
A. Duhring, of Belfast, Me.
S. Hupp, of Belfast, Maine
C. Treadwell, of Waldo, Me.
E.H. Jones, of Newcastle, Me.
J.B. Patterson, of Newcastle, Me.
L.A. Wooley, of Derby Line, Vermont
C.B. Dodson, of Geneva, N.Y.
C.W. Mulford, of Albany County, N.Y.
W. Ware, of Salem, New Jersey
J. Cooper, of Washington County, Pa.
E. Dye, of Washington County, Pa.
R. Lane, of Washington County, Pa.
P. Wolfe, of Washington County, Pa.
J.W. Kuntz, of Washington County, Pa.
W. Gilkinson, of Wheeling, W. Va.
G. Hutcherson /sic/ (Hutchinson ?), of Wheeling, W. Va.
D.C.H. Swift, of Turnball, Ala.
T.C. Marian, of New Orleans, La
Dr. F. Pitts, of New Orleans, La.
C.M. Sinclair, of Ann Arbor, Mich.
J. Wesson, of Iowa
W. Hauschute, of Fort Madison, Iowa
R. Hauschute, of Fort Madison, Iowa
R. Hauschute, of Fort Madison, Iowa
A. Flynn, of Zanesville, Ohio
P. Flynn, of Zanesville, Ohio
M. Virden, of Indiana

W. Millen (?) (Mitlen ?), of Lafayette, Ind.
J. King, of Lafayette, Ind.
W.B. Brunson, of Lafayette, Ind.
W. H. Slade, of Carlyle, Ill.
H. Wilcox, of Carlyle, Ill.
R.J. Updike, of Fremont, Ill.
W. Rogers, of Danville, Ill.
Dr. ___McDonald, of Prairie Du Rocher, Illinois
L. Sloss, of Louisville, Ky.
R. Morrie, of Louisville, Ky.
A.B. Floyd, of Lexington, Mo.
Dr. A.B. Hoy, of Lexington, Mo.
*R.W. Brogdin, of Canada West
Samuel Todd, Wagon Train Clerk
C.D. Faulkner, Train Commissary
H. Seawgoos /sic/, of Montgomery County, Indiana
C. Kinsey, of Edwington, Ill.
J. Elliott, of Lewistown, Ill.
S.D. Reynolds, of Lewistown, Ill.
S.F. Alsen /sic/ of Lewistown, Ill.
M.O. Andrew, of Lewiston, Ill.
C.C. Hutton, of Chicago, Ill.
J.C. Pierce, of Chicago, Ill.
H. Dunning, of Collinsville, Ill.
R. Smith, of Lebanon, Ky.
Ely McJilton, of Osage County, Mo.
A. Ferguson, of Montreal, Canada
*Fred Pearks, of Canada West
*Tousaint Chabot, of Canada West
W.J. Burns, Officer of Guard for Train
Robert C. Green, of Baltimore, Mo., Ass't Train Wagon Master
A.O. Garrett, of Peoria, Ill.
Dr. ___Pearons, of Peoria, Ill.
D. Hurff, of Peoria, Ill. (Dr. ___Hurff ?)
J.C. Hunt, of Peoria, Illinois
H. J. Reed, of Ottawa, Illinois
J.D. Olmstead, of Ottawa, Ill.
J.M. Bacon, of Ottawa, Ill.
B. Elden (?) (or R. Elden ?), of Ottawa, Ill.
E. Morse, of Ottawa, Ill.
W. H. Rumsey, of Madisonville, Ky.
J. Keith, of Lewis County, Missouri
*G.W. Cottrell, of Canada West
*J.C.P. Cottrell, of Canada West
O. Trowbridge, of London, Canada West
Moses Mallerson, of St. Charles, Mo., Train Wagon Master

<u>Teamsters</u>

J. Sacket, of St. Louis, Mo.
P. T. Lewis, of St. Louis, Mo.
D. Lionberger, of Payson, Adams County, Illinois
C. D. Gilman, of Scottsburgh, N.Y.
C. Coleman, of Bluffton, Ind.
J.H. Cunningham, of Bellaire, Ohio
B.D. Chapman, of Tiffin, Ohio
J.C. Dessieux, of Osage County, Mo.
S. Smith, of Van Buren County, Mo.
R. Dunlap, of Belleville, Ill.
G.F. Feiffer, of Belleville, Ill.
___Cody, of Boston, Mass.
A. French, of Fayette County, Pa.
J.G. Stafford, of Bellefontaine, Ohio
Five un-identified teamsters
W.B. Cox of Andrew County, Mo.
S.R. Turner, of Cedar County, Mo.
N. Greenwood, of Lake County, Ill.
Luke Colburn, of Oak Grove, Wisc.
R.M. Beadles, of Orange County, Va.
W. Maxwell, of Madison County, Alabama
M. Flanagan, of Roscommon County, Ireland

(*) It is possible that Tousaint Chabot referred to a town in Canada West and that G. W. Cottrell, J.C.P. Cottrell, Fred Pearks and R.W. Brogdin were from Tousaint Chabot, Canada West.

Muleteers and Herders

Francisco Guiteria	Mayo Domo	Philip Auchust (?)
(Guiteris ?, Guiterio ?)	John Vigiel	(Auschust ?)
Frank Romino	Manuel Pino (?) (Pico ?)	H. Marie Churbello

(all above from New Mexico)

INDEPENDENCE, MISSOURI (May 13, 1849) Word reached Independence on May 13, 1849 that a number of deaths had occurred in the wagon trains that had left for California, some deaths taking place as far out as eighty miles on the plains. Word of the following deaths had reached Independence, but the time and place of death were not revealed:

W.W. Knapp, of Massillon, Ohio	Mr. ___Cook, of Louisiana	Dr. ___Cotton, of Hinds County, Louisiana
Mr. ___Davies, of Van Buren County, Missouri	William McCaddin, of Zanesville, Ohio	___McConnell, son of Judge ___McConnell, of Ohio

On May 11, 1849 a difficulty occurred between William H. Freeman, of Randolph County, Missouri and ___Howard, of Cincinnati, Ohio, in which Freeman was shot in the abdomen, and died on May 12, 1849. The cause of the difficulty originated by each endeavoring to charge the other with counterfeiting and general villainy. Howard's wife was said to have killed her husband's mistress some weeks earlier in Cincinnati.

ST. JOSEPH, MISSOURI (May 11, 1849) The "Illinois Union Band" wagon train left its encampment near St. Joseph on May 11, 1849, bound for California. The place of rendezvous had been Wolf Creek, 18 miles from St. Joseph. Nine additional wagons, principally from the Illinois counties of Brown and Menard, were to unite with the train at Wolf Creek. Names of the occupants of the nine wagons are unkown at this writing but there follows a list of persons who were with the "Illinois Union Band" at Wolf Creek on May 11, 1849.

Dr. J.C. Gray	Thomas Hobbs	John C. Summers
C. Baker	J. Poling	E.L. Ward
		William Ward

(above from Jefferson County, Ill.)

Philip Clark	Enos Campbell	Samuel Secket
Rev. Moses Clampet	J.N. Campbell	E.F. McElwain
J.J.F. Clampet	Lewis Campbell	Jason Miller
Thomas Rucker	A. Clarke	H. Sims
J. Cow		

(above from Sangamon County, Ill.)

Joel Rice	W.H. Sorgenfry	W.H. Stewart
Abel H. Rice	W.M. St. Clair	W. Shoemaker
M. Gill	W.C. Myers	

(above from White County, Ill.)

J.M. Loring	Hiram Ogden	William Green
Philip Loring	J.R. Rutherford	J.R. Ellison
D.C. Robinson	B.R. Robinson	F. Paterson (Patterson ?)
W. Revfro /sic/		

(above from Morgan County, Ill.)

Ausby Fike	Henry Amos	William M. Howel /sic/
Moses P. Fike	James H. Richardson	(Howell ?)
A.Y. Fike	R. Hough	
	*(of St. Clair County, Ill.)	
W. M. Moore	J.C. Davis	T.B. Nichols
James Johnson	Joseph Gillespie	John Tolen (?) (Tolan ?)
Alfred Murray		
	*(of Bond County, Ill.)	
Robert Doing	Mills Wood	W.H. Wood
	(of Clark County, Ill.)	
W.H. Bingham	James Kimbell (?)	Patrick Smith
	(Kimball ?)	
	*(of Kendall County, Ill.)	
A. Peake	Luke Peake	B.R. Holiday /sic/
William Gum	W.M. Hawk	Z.F. Riggs
T.A. Kirkpatrick	Wiley Brazil	Ormsby Grooms
J.H. Howel /sic/ (Howell)	Thomas Jones	M.R. Barber
J.N. Bennett	Charles Weever /sic/	F. McMurray
	(above from Scott County, Ill.)	

The following are the names of a wagon train of emigrants from Galena, Illinois. This train was encamped at St. Joseph, Missouri on May 11, 1849 and was preparing to move across the plains to California. The names of approximately twenty-five others are missing from this roll.

Isaac Evans	Thomas Fehan /sic/	Archibald Drummond
Watson Evans	A.A. Stroud	Stephen Burip
George Rause	William Mackey	James McCleary
James Rause	E. Johns	A.E. Schwalka /sic/
William Rause	D. Gardner	S. Dail /sic/
Mr. ___Reeder	W.B. Whiteseas and lady	A. Shubar
R. McGowen /sic/	H. Bailey	William Reed
P.J. Donnevan /sic/	T.A. Livermore, wife and family	John Reed
J.D. Winters, wife and two daughters		Mr. ___McLaughlin
	Mr. ___Sanders	Joseph Harris
Theodore Winters and lady	Mr. ___Hammond	Mr. ___Meloney
Mr. ___Waterhouse	Asa Rowson	Mr. ___Brown
John Hughs /sic/	William Strawbridge	D.H.T. Moss and family
Mr. ___Barton	Mr. ___McKee	Mr. ___Couts /sic/
J. Dodge	Louis Quench	Lieut. ___Sampson
William Rice	William McGinnis	William Whitham /sic/
George Rice	Mr. ___Matticks /sic/	Mr. ___Cisson
Mr. ___Kilboin	John Drum	Robert Lightfoot
J. Townsend	Mr. ___Bruce	Andrew Murphy
J. Herrold and lady	Joseph Sutton	Joseph Lee and lady
James Fiddick	James Sutton	Mr. ___Barley
Thomas Enoor	William Gray	George Epperly
Mr. ___Bailey		

(*) Residence listings refer to name entries appearing above the citation line.

Another wagon train from Illinois was encamped at St. Joseph, Missouri. The train was well supplied with good wagons, oxen and mules, and it left St. Joseph on May 7, 1849 for the California gold regions. This company was from Rock Island, Illinois and they referred to their train as the "Rock Island Pioneers". Members of the group were:

Capt. ___Frizzle	Dr. J.W. Brackett	J.W. Barnet /sic/
P. Gallup	C.A. Spring	D. Dean
R. Calbough	W.H. Conway	O. Dimmick
J.T. Bean	J. Cook	C. Brook
Mr. ___Bumhiser	G. Cook	G. Campbell
E. Turner	L. McCoy	Mr. ___Ross
A.F. Cutter	W. Dean	J. Brun /sic/
R. Fairville	W. Tinny /sic/	J. Bruner
E. Fairville	P. Can /sic/	Mr. ___McPherson
A. Shuar /sic/	I. Littick	J. Miser
Mr. ___Wolf	Mr. ___Liddy	T. Chandler
Dr. ___Harckness /sic/	J. Anderson	H. Updergruff (?)
(Harkness?)	M. Martin	(Updergraff ?)
T. Luster	G. Head	J. Naylor
R. Broaders	L.H. Roberson /sic/	Mr. ___Harris
G. Ayres	J. Lupton	J. Wiley
G. Flox	Mr. ___Adams	

The "Buckeye Rovers" wagon train from Athens, Ohio, left St. Joseph, Missouri on May 10, 1849. This wagon train was bound for California and members of the train were:

Joseph Dickson, President and Commander	Dennis Drake	R.B. Barnes
	Hugh Dickson	Ara Conde /sic/
H.J. Graham, Treasurer	Seth Paine	Cyrus Giles
William L. Wilson, Secretary	James Rathburn /sic/	Charles Giles
	G.D. Stephens	Joshua Gardner
E.P. Smith	William Logan	Elijah Ferrall /sic/
James Shepherd	L. Townsend	Elijah Armstrong
William L. Stedman	G.W. Reeves	

On May 8, 1849 a small group from Edwardsville, Illinois crossed the ferry at St. Joseph. This unit was composed of A.C. Alexander, A.D. Treadway, Ed Norton, G.W. Prichett and one unidentified servant. They were bound for California and traveled with two small wagons and three pack mules. Their equipment included clothing, tools, tent, and provisions with a total weight of 1700 pounds.

A company consisting of D. Evans, of Pennsylvania, S.B.F. Clark, of Vermont, A. Dubois, of Michigan, and B. Irvine, of New York, left the Iowa Mission on May 9, 1849 for California.

A company from Dodgesville, Wisconsin, left St. Joseph, Missouri for California on May 10, 1849. Traveling with mules, the group consisted of Henry Robinson and lady, David Prothers, James Lillars, and J.B. Davis.

The "Buchanan Agricultural and Mining Company" wagon train left St. Joseph, Missouri on May 8, 1849, for California, by way of Santa Fe. The following were members of this train:

W.J. Everett	F. Williams	William T. Crockett
William M. Mainey	William H. Minster	Milton Everett
David M. Tobin	William Fitzhue /sic/	William Everett
Joseph Elliott	(Fitzhugh ?)	B.R. Everett
John Elliott	Robert McWilliams	Moses Swain
Woodford Shomaker /sic/ (Shoemaker ?)	Mr. ___Lancaster	Walker Bivins

On May 11, 1849 a wagon train calling itself the "Fulton Star Company" left St. Joseph to cross the plains. The train was composed of:

Eldridge Keeling	J.H. Davis	S.M. Roe
C. Cummins	E.P. Ingersoll	A.J. Loomis
G.W. Mull	G.W. Anderson	E. Walding
H. Meriner /sic/	E. Raywalt	A.G. Walding
E. Boden	C. Wallie /sic/	Jesse Collins
A.P. Malony /sic/	J.N. Perine	C.C. Davis
W.J. Foutch		

On May 5, 1849 a party of four men crossed the river near St. Joseph, Missouri on their way to California. They traveled with two ox teams and rode mules. The foursome consisted of Allin McLane, Dr. M. Caldwell, and J.M. Kay, all of Missouri, and A.S. Jones, of Michigan.

A train consisting of three wagons was camped near St. Joseph, Missouri on May 11, 1849. With thirteen yoke of cattle, this train expected to depart from St. Joseph within a few days and cross the Sierra Nevada by October 1, 1849. Members of the train were:

Dr. William Todd, of Farmington, Iowa	John Killen	Reson Ray /sic/
	R. Flinn	Hiram Bolter
Ebenezer Brown	M.A. Browning	

A small company from Fayette County, Pennsylvania was in St. Joseph, Missouri on May 11, 1849. They intended to leave within a few days for California. Members of the company were:

Richard Irwin, Captain	Joseph Troth, Treasurer	B.G. Krepps, Secretary
Samuel Minehart	Hamilton Booth	

The following were members of a company which was encamped in St. Joseph, Missouri on May 11, 1849 and were preparing to leave for California in a short time:

T.J. Northrup, of New York	A. Willongby /sic/ (Willowghby ?), (no residence listed)	Dr. J.E. Charles, of Ohio
J.F. Bean, of Ohio		Hugh Campbell (no residence listed)
Simeon Wheeler, of New York		

KANESVILLE, IOWA (May 16, 1849) The following individuals had arrived in Kanesville, Iowa and were destined to leave for California:

William A. Warney, of Albion, Michigan
N.D. Fitzgerald, of Waterloo, Wisc.
Amos Thompson and two sons, of same town as above
Randall Fuller, of Waukashaw County, Wisc.*
John Howell, of same town as above
Michael Thompson, of same town as above
Nelson Whitney, of Watertown, Wisc.
Charles C. Banks, of Rochester, Wisc.
L.C. Wittenmyer, of St. Louis, Mich.
Robert Jamison, of Washington County, Iowa
William Baker, of same town as above
Morrison Francis, of Henry County, Ill.
John More Jr. /sic/, of Henry County, Ill. (Moore?)
Dan Moore /sic/, of Henry County, Ill.
E.S. Congdon, of Ogle County, Ill.
W.M.C. Easton, of Keokuk, Iowa
R.S. Bates, of Fulton County, Ill.
S. Wilson, of Adams County, Ill.
John Nicholson, of Adams County, Ill.
Willis Stith and company /sic/ (Smith ?). of Chicago, Ill.
D.H. Holcomb, of Chicago, Ill.
David Corsaut (?) (Corsaul ?) of Ogle City, Illinois
John Richardson, of Keokuk, Iowa
O. Hamton /sic/, of same town as above
John Deutsch, of same town as above
Henry Swinerton, of Grant County, Wisc. (page 64)
W. Banks, of same town as above
Ira Dolliver, of Waukashaw County, Wisc.
Tunis Vanvecthen /sic/ of same town as above
B.F. King of St. Louis, Mich.
Henry S. Compton, of Niles, Mich.
Peter Mills, of Washington County, Iowa
Henry W. Chase, of Waterloo, Wisc.
Francis Graham, of Jo Daviess County, Illinois
Philip Hull, of same county as above
W.S. Jacks, (a smelter of Rock Island, Ill)
Charles P. Hamlins /sic/ (Hamlin ?), of Knoxville, Ill.
John Coakley, of Rock River, Ogle County, Illinois
W. Smith of Chicago, Illinois
Oscar M. Holton, of Chicago, Ill.
Dr. ___Shanks, of Shullsburgh, Wisc.
M.H. Tuttle, of Calhoun County, Mich.
E.R. Tyler, of Ogle County, Ill.
R. H. Martin, of Keokuk, Iowa
George Montaque, of Portland, Iowa
W. Ackers, of same town as above
Austin Ackers, of same town as above
George Gowley /sic/ of Grant County, Wisc.
O.A. Crane, Gross Point, Ill.
E.G. Hill, of Gross Point, Ill.
E. Gaffield /sic/, of same town as above
Henry Pratt, of same town as above
P. Graff, of Chicago, Illinois
Jonathan Brown, of Niles, Mich.
Harrison Brown, of Platteville, Wisc.
George W. Williams, of same town as above
P. Stone, of same town as above
William Rigg, /sic/, of Rock Island, Ill.
G.L. Shewer, of Ottawa, Illinois
Joseph Pagitt, of Nauvoo, Illinois
Augustus Teruter, of Fulton County, Ill.
Joseph Orr, of Adams County, Ill.
S. Orr, of same county as above
William Orr, of same county as above
J.N. Reilly, of Chicago, Illinois
H. Barnes, of Chicago, Illinois

(*) Listed as found in source. Consider entry as Waukesha County, Wisc.

Ashbel Burhitt, of Ogle County, Ill.
Galusha Bridge, of same county as above
Philander Osborn, of same county as above
T. Swartwout /sic/, of Woodstock, Ill.
Franklin Eels /sic/, of Ottawa, Ill.
A.J. Eels /sic/ of Ottawa, Ill.
Seymore Knight, of Buchanan, Mich.
N. Knight, of same town as above
W. Copur /sic/, of same town as above
G.W. Foote, of St. Joseph County, Mich.
J. Brooks, of same place as above

Thomas W. Small, of Henry County, Iowa
Frank Riggs /sic/, of Lafayette County, Wisc.
R. Reynolds, of Racine County, Wisc.
W. Reynolds, of same county as above
William Fink, of same county as above
Miss Elizabeth Jones, of same county as above
A. Freeman, of Little Fort, Lake County, Illinois
David Shupe, of same town as above
G.P. Russell, of Greenfield, N.H.
Elizabeth Rogers, of same town as above
J.A. Smith, of St. Joseph County, Mich.

Dr. R.E. Harrison, of Berrien County, Mich.
John Burrows, of Iowa County, Wisc.
Richard Williams, of Linn County, Iowa
Benjamin Lawson, of same county as above
Jeremiah Eaton, of Little Fort, Lake County, Ill.
C.F. Swartwout /sic/, of same town as above
Alden Putnam, of same town as above
J. Marsh, of same as town above
B. Crabtree, of same town as above
L.A. Crabtree, of Chicago, Illinois
E. Shallowhouse, of St. Joseph County, Mich.

The "Albion Company" from Michigan was in Kanesville, Iowa on May 16, 1849. This group had lost a great part of the equipment by the sinking of the steamer "Dahcota" on April 25, 1849 (see page 39 for details). The following were members of the "Albion Company":

Francis Clay
Uriel Young
George West
A. West
David Handy
Philip Goodrich
H. Goodrich
W.A. Warner
Oscar Finley

A.H. Colby
Oscar McGee
C.F. Finch
Robert Finch
Ezra Bradner
N. Flemming
Jesse Flemming
William Flemming
A. Blodgett

Thomas W. Grant
M. Tuttle
Lorin Markham
Adin Congleton /sic/
Austin Church
J.F. Gilliland
Alex. Moore
William M. Pearl

On May 16, 1849 the "Fayette Rovers" wagon train group had been in Kanesville, Iowa almost a week. This unit was from Jonesville, Michigan and it consisted of the following persons:

Henry Baxter, Captain
G.W. Holsted /sic/, Lieutenant
Ira Latham
Gustavus C. Cooley

A.S. Welch
Ambrose M. Dibble
A.J. Baker
Andrew Hartman

John S. Lewis
Calvin R. Ralph
Hirman Platte
Dr. Jonathan T. Onderdonk

Members of the "Daniel Boone" wagon train company were in Kanesville, Iowa on May 16, 1849. This group was from Chicago, Illinois and Niles, Michigan. Members of this group were as follows:

J.W. Noyes	L. Dana	W. Polk
J.B. Witt	H. Dana	E. Kelsey
A.C. Cross	J.H. Cross	

The "California Company" of Rochester, Wisconsin was in Kanesville, Iowa on May 16, 1849. Members of this company were:

C.W. Brown, Captain	Y.J. Kendall	John A. Bloomer
David Williams	William Jackson	Charles Linsley
Mr. ___Farr	J.W. Ames	G.W. Gamble
C.H. Patterson	O.N.J. Ames	Hiram Kellogg
	W. Hoyt	

A small group of men from Monroe, Wisconsin were in Kanesville, Iowa on May 16, 1849. This group consisted of:

William Brown	S.P. Condee /sic/	W.F. Jones
A. Goodard	P. Norton	A. Vansant
Dr. ___Woodford	A. Woodford	E. Witter

A company from Dubuque, Iowa, who were said to have experience in mining operations passed through Kanesville, Iowa on or about May 16, 1849. The unit was on its way to the California gold regions, and the following persons made up the company:

E.M. Whitesides	J.A. Langton	V. Glenat
J.B. Seere /sic/	T. DeSene	James Fanning
J. Crevier	A.R. Whitesides	Thomas Crane
Conrad Garner	J. Garner	P. Shervin /sic/

The "Red Rock Mining Company" was in Kanesville, Iowa on May 16, 1849. This group was from Marion County, Iowa and consisted of:

Simon Drouillard	James A. Chesnut /sic/	William Cayton
Thomas P. Cowman	(Chestnut ?)	Alex. B. Daniel
William Cotterell	James Chesnut /sic/	Leonard D. Fowler
Alex S. Cayton	(Chestnut ?)	Samuel Richardson
Ezekiel Clark	J.M. Clark	E.F. Clark
R.M. Billups	S.F. Donnell	A. Vertress /sic/
C.M. Gilkey	Simpson B. Matthews	G.D. Compton
Alonzo Reynolds	O. Matthews	William Beckwith
Mosby Childers	George E. Jewett	Lucian B. Reynolds
Elias Williams	Samuel Lucas	Austin S. Howard
Jonas Belknap	Silas Belknap	James Howard
James White	Joseph White	O. Bales
Charles Bales	H.W. McMillan	

The following persons from Kalamazoo, Michigan arrived in Kanesville, Iowa on or about May 16, 1849. They were enroute to California and this group consisted of:

Peter P. Acker	S.W. Bryan	C.L. Cobb
Henry Gregory	G.H. Gale	M.D. Smith
J.A. Rhodes	Obadiah Rood	George Hogle
Charles Johnson	J.C. Gibbs	Ambrose Dunn
Reuben Gates	Henry Greenwood	Sherman Hawley

A number of individuals from Stephenson County, Illinois had congregated in Kanesville, Iowa on May 16, 1849. They were enroute to the California gold fields and these Illinois residents consisted of:

E.H. Higgins	I.M. Luther	F.E. Young
William Patterson	R.N. Baker	William Jones
O.E. Kellogg	I. Benner	F.J. Lamm /sic/

A group known as the "Spartan Band" arrived in Kanesville, Iowa safely from McHenry County, Illinois. They intended to cross the Missouri River on May 16, 1849. The full roster of this group is not available, but among the various persons composing the band were:

James H. Vansickle	Lucian Wright	H. Lyon
Jedediah Rogers and son	Capt. ___Smith	Mr. ___Edwards
Thomas Durning (?) (Darning ?)	Ziba Dodd	Bradford Burbank
	John Quick	John Sewin (?) (Sawin ?)

The "Michigan Company" from Wayne County, Michigan arrived in Kanesville, Iowa on May 8, 1849. The members of this company sold their wagons in Kanesville and intended to pack from Kanesville to California. Names of the company members follow:

Dr. B.L. King	William Quirk	Nathan Travers
William Beals /sic/	Joseph Pardy	J.B. Reed
Lewis LaFountain	Oaks Bigelow /sic/	

(ST. JOSEPH, MISSOURI) On May 14, 1849 a group known as "H.C. Hodge and Company" left St. Joseph, Missouri for California. This party was from central Michigan.

On May 9, 1849 a company of California emigrants arrived in St. Joseph, Missouri by steamer, believed to be the "Timour". Their names are as follows:

Colonel J.W. Bicknell, of Knox County, Tenn.	T.D. Heiskell, of Monroe County, Tenn.	J. Brown, of Monroe County, Tenn.
H.B. Heiskell, of Knox County, Tenn.	Dr. O.P. White of Monroe County, Tenn.	A.A. Humphreys, of Monroe County, Tenn.
R. L. White, of Monroe County, Tenn.	C. Howard, of Monroe County, Tenn.	R. Campbell, of Hormer, Alabama
J.C. McIntosh, of Memphis, Tenn.	J.W. Campbell, of Knoxville, Tenn.	L.D. Thustin, of Hormer, Alabama
H.D. Smith, of Florence, Alabama	J.C.F. Wilson, of Florence, Alabama	J. Jackson, of Florence, Alabama
Mr. Boggs Russell, of Louisville, Kentucky	Mr. T.A. Lansforerd (Lansford ?), of Gravilly Spring, Alabama	D. Campbell and three servants, of Florence, Alabama
W.D. Bassett, no residence	A. Campbell, no residence	S.J. Johnston, no residence
J. Campbell, no residence	H. Guffith /sic/, no residence	*J. Johnston, no residence
Mr. ___Alvirus, no residence		Mr. ___Taplin, no residence

(*) Two entry listings for this name. No residence was listed for each entry.

D. Campbell, of Florence, Alabama, and three servants, departed from St. Joseph, Missouri for California on May 18, 1849. His arrival in St. Joseph is noted on page 60. W.D. Bassett, J. Campbell, A. Campbell. S.J. Johnston, J. Johnston (two entry listings), Mr. ___Alvirus, H. Guffith and Mr. ___Taplin, left St. Joseph, Missouri for California on May 17, 1849. Their arrival in St. Joseph is noted on page 60.

On May 25, 1849 word reached St. Joseph, Missouri that a wagon train which had left the city some weeks previously was now some 200 miles on their way to California. Members of this train were:

W. Coons	Isam Winer	J.R. Smith
J.F. Hawkins	O. Snider	Mr. ___Siman /sic/
*D.I. Wilmans	O.H. Harrison	*A.D. McDonald
*C. Wilmans	J.T. Ashby	G. Wise
W.B. Long	J.P. Raybum /sic/	B. Wise
J. Long	William Bird	H. Snider
J.H. Hawkins	W. Leer	J.W. Winstock
H. Howell	J. Lastley	C. Carter
W. Briggs	B.M. Hawkins	J.B. Haislep /sic/
John McFarland	C. Price	(Haslep?, Haslip ?)
J.E. Marrill /sic/ (Merrill?)	C. Ingram	T. Wilson
	J.P. Raybum /sic/	George Wise

(Note: Entry for J.P. Raybum appears twice. Listed as found in source.)

A company from Ogle County, Illinois crossed the river near St. Joseph, Missouri on May 5, 1849, and were on their way to California on May 7, 1849. This company consisted of the following:

John Hancock	J.V. Gale	F. Morrill
G.M. Shipman	C. Gray	G. Swingly /sic/
C. Newcomer	S.W. Chaney	A. Mulkins
D. Franklin	E. Kling	W. Brooke
J. Banden (?) (Bauden?, Bahden ?)	D. Kling	

A small wagon train from Southport, Wisconsin, left St. Joseph, Missouri on May 11, 1849 for California. They crossed the river with three wagons and three yoke of cattle to each wagon. Names of the company members were:

J.I. Bevens	J. Lock	J. Gates
S.C. Chase	B. Newell	Mr. ___Fitzhugh

On May 18, 1849 a small company from Elgin, Kane County, Illinois left St. Joseph, Missouri for California. Members of this group were:

Dr. H. Rosenkrans	E. Mansfield	H.C. McClare
Thomas Ellensworth	Benjamin Eleensworth	James Allen

On May 25, 1849 news reached St. Joseph, Missouri that a number of cases of cholera had been reported among the emigrant trains enroute to California. One reported death on the trail was a young man by the name of Samuel Wilson, formerly a resident of St. Joseph. The exact place and time of death were not revealed in the research source. Wilsons's

(*) See Indexed names for further data.

cause of death was cholera. In St. Joseph itself, there were cholera fatalities among the emigrants preparing to depart for California. Two emigrant brothers, Thomas and Daniel Pepper, from Green County, Kentucky, died of cholera, one on May 20, 1849 and the other on May 21, 1849.

Cholera was also raging along the river courses. Boats were disabled by it and were compelled to tie up. Several little towns along the Missouri River were nearly desolated. There was said to be sixty deaths on board the ill-fated "Mary" on her passage from St. Louis to Kanesville, Iowa. The deaths were mostly emigrants from England and Wales under the charge of a Captain Dan Jones.

KANESVILLE, IOWA (May 30, 1849) By May 30, 1849 the below named individuals had departed from Kanesville, Iowa and were on the plains on their way to the California gold regions. Some of these persons had attached themselves to wagon train companies, but the identity of the companies is not known.

C.H. Eastman, of Ogle County, Illinois
Capt. ___ Bell, of Canada West
John Van Allen, of Canada West
David Young, of Adams, Seneca County, Ohio

Samuel Swasey, of same town as above
John Coburn, of Linden, Whitesides County, Ill.
Horace Cochran, of Adams, Seneca County, Ohio
Bartlett Brown, of same town as above

Joseph A. Ferrington (Farrington ?), of Linden, Whitesides County, Ill.
A. Stewart, of Walworth County, Wisconsin
Mannassah Grover, of Adams, Seneca County, Ohio

A group of men traveling in what was termed the "Odd-Fellow Wagon" passed through Kanesville, Iowa on their way to California. The passage of this wagon through Kanesville took place shortly before May 30, 1849, possibly a week or two before that date. This unit had come from Chicago, Illinois and consisted of the following:

H.P. Woodworth, of Sterling, Illinois
William M. Hobbie, of same town as above
L.H. Woodworth, of same town as above
Thomas Gordon, of Mercer County, Ill.

Walter Hay, of Wabash, Indiana
Silas P. Chatfield, of McHenry County, Illinois
Henry Vanderhoof /sic/ of Berrien County, Michigan
Joseph Duncan, of same county as above

Coleman Wilks /sic/ (Wilkes ?), of Adams County, Illinois
C.S. Woodworth, of Peru, Illinois
O.M. Whitlock, of Platteville, Grant County, Wisc.
N. Nichols, of Berrien County, Michigan

The "Iowa Company No. 1, of California Emigrants" wagon train passed through Kanesville, Iowa on or about May 16, 1849. This train had sixty-four wagons, and its complement consisted of 192 men, all well armed; 10 women and 10 children. Members of the train had organized and elected Josiah M. Knight as its Captain, E. Bostwick as Lieutenant, H.M. McMillan as Secretary and Thomas Hanan (sic) as the wagon train guide. The Minutes of Organization and the Constitution of the company will be found in the "Frontier Guardian," (Kanesville, Iowa) of May 30, 1849. The following persons were members of this wagon train:

Thomas Hanan
James Hanan
Simon Parshall /sic/ (Marshall ?)
T.A. Russell
William G. Russell
S.B. Matthews
O. Matthews
G.E. Jewett
S.H. Stanfield
D.T. Durham
T. Durham
C.H. Durham
William Langdon
G. Cain
George McFarlane
Isaac Foster
J.G. Foster
Vincent Foster
J. Blote (?)
William C. Easton
E. Plumey (?)
D.S. Cowan
J.D. McLane
J. Shaffer
A. Donahoe
A. Tainter
E. Gaff
B. Benson
E. Bostwick
G.C. Smith
John Cole
Charles Bell
C. McDaniel
D. Ballantine
H. Julian
William Cunningham
C. Hurley
J. McNutt
H. Webster
J. Tansey
H.W. McMillen /sic/
Josiah M. Knight
John Carter
O. Bayles
C. Bayles
J. Rhodes
T.C. Smalley

John N. Taylor
Nathaniel N. Hasald /sic/
John D. Hanan
John J. Martin
M.B. Childers
E. Williams
G.D. Compton
L. B. Reynolds
N.P. Cocks
A. Trussell
J.F. Wolf /sic/
William Farnsworth
M.S. Farnsworth
John Longmire
S. Bristol
J. Crawford
S. Lewis
William Casson
H. Bremmer
G.B. Montgomery
D. Wise
John Wise
George Rogers
A.W. Hanvet /sic/
Thomas Hewett
R.S. Bates
W.S. Niles
E. Funck
P. Stone
C.H. Payne
B.M. Coats
Henry Webster
D.T. McCartney
C. Ball
J. Dubb
A.J. Carpenter
C.B. Gaston
E.D. Hurley
Levi Chase
Joseph Dutton
James White
Joseph White
Henry Britton (?) (Britten ?)
Jacob Beninger /sic/
Lewis Beninger /sic/
J. Merick /sic/
William Spencer

Philip Cline
Enoch Cobesty /sic/
John Barnes
J. Black
A. Reynolds
O. Reynolds
S. Lucas
William Beckwith
M. Kern (?)
J. Paggett
J. Head
M. Lewis
William Baker
J. Laidsy /sic/
G. Cline
S.F. Merick /sic/
L. Mason
H. Fick
P. Fick
J.P. Roberts
William Hardinbook
M.G. Smith
William McClelland
John McClelland
R. Dran /sic/
W.E. Smith
G. Sheldon
J. Girard
J.H. Street
C.P. Hamlin
R.B.F. Scott
J.D. Scott
W. Scott
A.C. Williams
A.N. Breeze
L. Slater (?) (Slator ?)
L.R. Paynter /sic/
H.H. Lewis
J. Thorn /sic/
D. Neal
J.H. Howard
J. McChesney
J. Belknap
D. Allen
Charles Mace
Willis Stith

J.P. Hill	James Robinson	P.T. Day
William Vaughn	William Bussell /sic/	John Loring
J. Swinerton	(Russell ?)	Willis Banks
Henry Swinerton (see p. 57)	George Gowdy	William Snodgrass
R.G. Rineney /sic/	J. Rider	A.S. McNeal
J. Badger	A.J. Heustis (?)	D.P. McNeal
Thomas Shin /sic/	S. Chapin	J. Blue
William Mosford	William D. Crawford	Peter Mills
William Barker	Robert Jameson	J. Boyd
C. Neal	A. Brazdon /sic/	William Crawford
J. Spears	J.Orr	John Nicholson
William Cooper	S. Orr	T. Westrope
S. Wilson	William Orr	J.B. Evans
S. Belknap	E. Bussell /sic/ (Russell ?)	William B. Westrope
J. Fowler	Norman Homer	Annie M. Huestis (?)
A.S. Howard	John E. Mory /sic/	(Annis M. Huestis ?)
Polly Belknap	Eleanor Bales	Wibor F. Huestis
Clarinda Belknap	Jasper Bales	Sarah M. Huestis
Rachel Howard	Margaret Bininger /sic/	Dorothy Gandemon /sic/
Clarinda Howard	Elizabeth Bininger /sic/	A. Bininger /sic/
Homer Howard	Caroline Josephine	Charles H. Bininger /sic/
Nancy Howard	Beninger /sic/	E. Manuel Bininger /sic/

A group of emigrants banded together during the latter part of May, 1849 and drew up the constitution and by-laws of the "Knox County, Illinois Company". This meeting took place in Kanesville, Iowa, and it is believed that this wagon train company had departed from Kanesville on or about May 30, 1849. Members of this train were composed of separate groups which had been congregating in Kanesville for a period of time (see "Notes" Section p. 200 for details). At a meeting of some of the company on May 12, 1849, a constitution and code of by-laws were adopted and the following persons were elected under it, viz: Asa Haynes, Captain; Cephas Arms, Lieutenant; Thomas Shannon, First Sergeant; Edward Doty, E.N. Taylor and Charles B. Mecum, second, third and fourth sergeants; R.C. Price, Clerk; Committee of Inspection, J.L. West, F.S. Kellogg, and J.R. Parker. Members of the "Knox County, Illinois Company" were:*

From Knox County, Illinois

J.L. Woolsey	Nath. Hurlbut /sic/	J. Grosscup
Ubin P. Davison /sic/	Oren Clark	H.B. Frans /sic/
C.B. Mecum	J.B. Colton	M.P. Edgerton
N.D. Morse	J.E. Hale	A.C. Clay
John Cole	J.W. Semple	Alex Ewing
R.C. Price	E.N. Taylor	L.D. Montgomery
Cephas Arms	John H. Ewing	Edward McGowan
Asa Haynes	J.W. Plummer	George Allen
Thomas McGrew	John L. West	Edward Doty
Bruen Byram /sic/	W.B. Rude	Aaron Larkin
Alex. Palmer	Thomas Shannon	Robert Kimble /sic/

From Warren, Illinois

H.J. Ward	John D. Thompson	J. Mackey

(*) Departure date of this train from Kanesville is uncertain, believed late May, 1849.

F.S. Kellogg
William Kellogg

From Peoria, Illinois

L. Bartholomew
E.F. Bartholomew

Edw. Kellogg

From Fulton, Illinois

J.R. Parker
S. Wise
John Lawrence
R. Cunningham
William Whaley
Otho Berkshire

Jacob Grimm /sic/
Theodore Ingersol /sic/
F.B. Shannon
Orville Jones
J.B.V. Wallace

J.B. Anderson
John Chatterton
H.D. Walker
James Dunn
John Short

From Adams, Illinois

H. Surmeier
J.B. Surmeier
John Spees /sic/

John Lake
John A. Roth

F. Muer
Fred Ketzler (?) (Katzler ?)

From Washington County, Iowa

J.D. Campbell
J.H. Cooper

D.L. Fidler
Alex Sandilan (?)
  (Saudilan?)

Peter Buck
George W. Buck

From Rock Island, Illinois

J. Hasbrook
William Petre /sic/

S. Shelhammer

John Herald

From Mercer County, Illinois

C.W. Miller
Thomas Gordon

John Evans
James Merrifield

L.F. Langford

S. P. Edgerton, of
  Galesburgh, Ill.
James H. Ellis, no
  residence listed

D.C. Norton, of Knox
  County, Ill.
A. Barton, no residence
  listed

R. Baldwin, of Erie
  County, Penn.

From Jonesville, Michigan

Henry Baxter, Captain of
  the Faette (Fayette ?)
  Rovers
G.C. Cooley
A.M. Dibble

G.W. Halsted, Lieutenant
H.W. Platt, Secretary
A.J. Baker
Andrew Hartman
J.S. Lewis, Treasurer

C.R. Ralph
A.S. Welch
Ira Latham
J.F. Underdouk (?)
  (Underdonk), M.D.

P.P. Acker, of Kalamazoo,
  Mich.
Henry Gregory, of
  Kalamazoo, Mich.
Luke Wells, of Rock
  Island County, Illinois

G.A. Gale, of Kalamazoo,
  Mich.
Robert Taylor, of Knox
  County, Ill.
Alex Wells, of Rock
  Island County, Ill.

C.L. Cobb, of Kalamazoo,
  Mich.
Ira Wells (Surgeon of the
  Company), of Rock
  Island County, Ill.

On May 19, 1849 a group of California-bound emigrants banded together to form a wagon train known as the "California Express Company". At this meeting J.B. Witt, E. H. Phetterplace, John M. Worcester, B.L. King and John Morrison were appointed to a committee to draft a constitution and by-laws for the wagon train rule and government. The initial meeting was held in Kanesville, Iowa, and on May 21, 1849 a second Kanesville meeting took place in which the wagon train members adopted the constitution, united themselves into a body under the name of the "Express Company" (known at times as the "California Express Company"), and elected their officers as follows: J.B. Witt, Captain; Lewis Lafountain, First Lieutenant; E.H. Phetterplace, 2nd Lieutenant; J.W. Worcester, 1st Corporal; N.N. Reiley, 2nd Corporal; Executive Committee members-J.W. Howard, O.M. Holcomb and B.L. King.

The members of the "California Express Company" wagon train consisted of:

J.B. Witt, of Chicago, Ill.
J.W. Noyes (?) (Neyes ?), of same as above
E.H. Phetterplace, of Chicago, Ill.
J.N. Riley, of Chicago, Ill.
William Beal, of Dearborn, Mich.
Nathan Travers, of Dearborn, Mich.
A. Smith, of Rock Island, Ill.
A.H. Guffy, of Moline, Ill.
J.M. Worcester, of Tichera (?), Marquette County, Wisconsin
G. W. Worcester, of same as above
T. McMichael, of Dodgeville, Iowa
James Leavitt, no state
Joseph Robson, of Macomb County, Mich.
Hiram Crippen, of Washington, Iowa
Daniel Fulmer, of Sharon, Ohio
Bartley Reeves, of Wabash County, Ind.
Oscar N. Holcomb, of Chicago, Ill. /sic/
D.H. Holcomb, of Chicago, Ill.

Hamilton Barnes, of Chicago, Ill.
B.L. King, of Dearborn, Mich.
William Quick, of same as above
Joseph Pandegan (?), of same as above
Erastus Kelsey, of Cook County, Ill.
William Bell, of Rock Island, Ill.
Loren Dana, of Chemung, Ill.
A.M. Orvis, of Lake Maria, Marquette County, Wisconsin
William Powers, of Burlington, Iowa
Daniel Klanbery (?) (Klaubery ?), of Burlington, Iowa
A. Green, of Macomb County, Mich.
Jonas Reed, of Washington, Iowa
E.D. Berge, of Wabash County, Ind.
Edward T. Williams, of Detroit, Mich.
Hiram Burlingame, of Chicago, Ill.

Jacob Burlingame, of Chicago, Ill.
Lewis Lafountain, of Wayne County, Mich.
John B. Reed, of same as above
O.O. Bigelow, of same as above
Wesley Polk, of Cook County, Ill.
Richard Ness, of Ann Arbor, Mich.
J.W. Howard, of Rock Island, Ill.
F. Selick, of Utica, Michigan
Robert Palmer, of Livonia, Mich.
N. P. Swan, of Oakland, Mich.
Ranson Ecleston, of Neville, Ohio
S.C. Tyler, of Macomb County, Mich.
David Moufort (?) (Monfort ?), of Macomb County, Mich.
Layfayette Hard (?) (Herd ?), of Wadsworth, Ohio
Schuyler Milliman, of Detroit, Mich.

The "Wisconsin and Iowa Union Company" was a group of emigrants that organized at their winter quarters near Council Bluffs, Iowa on May 23, 1849. It is believed they may have passed thru Kanesville, Iowa on their way to California during the latter part of May, 1849. This company adopted a constitution and set of by-laws, and it was commanded by an elected Colonel and two elected subordinate officers with the titles of Lieutenant Colonel and Adjutant. J.S. Kirkpatrick was chosen as the Colonel and W.W. Ferguson and A.M. Blackman were respectively elected as Lieutenant Colonel and Adjutant. The following persons were members of the "Wisconsin and Iowa Union Company":

Henry Utt	William Benwell	William R. Riggs
T.B. Cameron	S.W. McMaster	James P. Stillwell
Thomas Headly /sic/	R.W. Long	William Edwards
David D. Utt	M. Nicholson	Daniel Rosse /sic/
James DuPui	F.H. Chrismon /sic/	Thomas C. Underwood
W.W. Morran /sic/	William McIntire /sic/	Robert Tucker
Israel Inman /sic/	R.C. Brown	Robert Turner /sic/
H.H. Inman /sic/	John Burris	J.B. Horton
Henry Opt	Thomas T. Hawley	George W. Burr
W.H. Andrew	Andre J. Beney /sic/	Stephen Owen
Robert Turner /sic/	David Morell /sic/	John Owen
G.H. Lee	Isaac Franks	D.L. Pepper
David Stuart	John Franks	Martin Dreibelbis
D. Osterbury	William Bywater /sic/	Thomas Stuart
J. Vincent	John Ryan	P.H. Inmann /sic/
Samuel Love	D. Riggs	(Inman ?)
S. Watson	Robert Stewart	Charles deRo
Henry Robertson	Stephen Pierce	John Stuart
William Nesbit /sic/	George Peirce	Andrew J. Binney /sic/
G.B. King	John Waterworth	John Mickolson /sic/
John J. Robertson	William Morgan	G.D. Utt
Henry J.R. Robertson	Daniel J.C. Davies	Daniel Bennet /sic/
John McGrath	John Osborne /sic/	J. Southerland
Isaac Dicholson /sic/	James Mitchell	Roderick Southerland
Edward McGinny	Absolam Myers	___Chamberland
Sylvanus Peabody	P.M. Scott	John Glym /sic
Thomas C. Parry	George Scott	John McIntrye /sic/
B.N. Bonham	James H. Gillham /sic/	James McLaughin /sic/
	John McCamron /sic/	(McLaughlin ?)

On May 29, 1849 a group of California emigrants left Kanesville, Iowa, to begin the long journey across the plains. This wagon train was known as the "Badger Company" and members of the train were:

William Abbott	Amond Ohlson	Harmon Corwin
Dosson Baldwin /sic/	Jarvis Whitman	Lyman Arnwell
William Phillips	William Godwin /sic/	Stephen Betts
Francis Bedford	(Goodwin ?)	John C. Murphy
Joseph Ney	Wesley Hannan	Joseph B. Coffeen /sic/
T.A. Killer	James Hannan	(Coffey ?)
G.W. Williams	N.B. Hand	J.P. Lyon
S.S. Williams	E. Hand	Elias Call
J. Giess (?) (Giese ?)	O. Hand	S. Northrop
Lewis Parkhurst	E.O. Hand	J. Code /sic/
S. Phillips	A.B. Erman (Ermon ?)	O.C. Wilder
A.C. St. John	Richard Fuller	John Spring
Costellow D. Buck	Clark A. Hough	Samuel Gray
William Jones	F. Parker	F.J. Parker
John Coad /sic/	Isahel Bennett /sic/	

William Persell	E. Bennett	George H. Buck
A. Benson	S. Moony /sic/ (Mooney ?)	Richard Shatswell /sic/
Andrew J. Sluman (?)	William Roberts	(Shotswell ?)
(Shuman ?)	John Roberts	Moses Hale
Anton Keller	Robert Roberts	Hiram Nordyke
Charles McKile	M. Skinner	Jacob Nordyke
R. Moody	William N. Keys /sic/	William Daggett
Julius Beach /sic/	S. Dunham	William Souther
John S. Julian	D.J. Dillay /sic/	G.W. Harrington
Julius C. Beach /sic/	G. Worden	Walter Hay
D.R. Funk	Coleman Wicks	L. Clark, of Fort
C.D. Lackey	F.W. Merritt, of Fort	Washington, Wisc.
John L. Clark, of Fort	Washington, Wisconsin	J.R. Atwater, of same as
Washington, Wisconsin	___Wheeler	above
J.S. Cochran, of same as	Thomas Murray	
above		

It is possible that some additional individuals may have been attached to the foregoing "Badger Company". The added personnel were members of the "Johnston County Company", the "Jackson County Company" and the "Clinton County Company" units. Members of the three foregoing companies were:

C. Swan	D. McCormick	___McDonald
C.C. Catlett	G.W. Hess	J.B. Craig
Colonel S. Carpenter	New Pesen /sic/	Levy Bond
W.R. Pearsall	F.J. Parker	J. Adams

ST. JOSEPH, MISSOURI On May 31, 1849 the following men crossed the river at St. Joseph, Missouri with twenty mules and horses, and were on their way to California:

Dr. J.R. Riggs	William DeCamp	E.E. Willis
Charles Stanburough /sic/	Robert Henderson, driver,	Samuel E. Cross
J.Q.A. Cunningham	of New Jersey	Douglass Perkins
John Huntington	J. Stevens, of Marietta, Ohio	Zebedee Cheeseman

On May 28, 1849 a small wagon train from Waukesha, Wisconsin left St. Joseph, Missouri for California. The train carried provisions for six months and the following composed the train:

G.W. Woodworth	William H. Elliott	R. Dillon
D. Grant	William A. Olin	G.C. Cone
Monroe Conorer /sic/	G.C. Cornell	___Damon
(Connor ?)	H. Lyman	Connell Williams

KANESVILLE, IOWA On June 13, 1849 it was announced in Kanesville, Iowa that the following indviduals would be attached to a Mormon wagon train to go by the way of Salt Lake (Utah) to the California gold regions:

Noah Norton, of Adrian, Mich.	Abraham Mills, of Adrian, Mich.	Dr. ___Graham, of Adrian, Mich.
Mr. ___White, of same as above		

ST. JOSEPH, MISSOURI (June 24, 1849) On June 24, 1849 a small company of emigrants left St. Joseph for the California "gold region". The company consisted of the following:

Sashel Bynam, of Howard County, Missouri
E.R. Wilson, of Randolph County Missouri
W. Adams, of Chariton County, Missouri

Ruben Ba_gett (Badgett ?), of Howard County, Missouri
N. Terrill, of Randolph County, Missouri

Mr. ___Harris, of Howard County, Missouri
Dr. ___Adams, of Chariton County, Missouri

ST. JOSEPH, MISSOURI (June 19, 1849) The members of the Rollin Enterprise California Company wagon train arrived in St. Joseph, Missouri on June 19, 1849. This company consisted of:*

H. McGee
Adam Lull
John Adams
Charles H. Erickson

Thomas Kealy (?) (Kenly?)
H.M. Pell (?) (Pall, Bell, Ball ?)

William Smith
Francis Brooks
O.F. Fester

ST. JOSEPH, MISSOURI (July 11, 1849) Word reached St. Joseph on July 11, 1849 that numerous deaths were taking place in the wagon trains bound for California. Some of the fatalities were reported in a letter written by a Mr. H. Egan, a member of one of the westbound wagon trains.

Egan reported that his own wagon train passed a company which had five cases of cholera. One of the party, a Mr. George Thompson, of Atchison County, Missouri, had died on May 22, 1849. The point of encounter took place about two miles west of Salt Creek. Salt Creek is about sixty some miles from the Missouri River. Most of the members of the cholera stricken wagon train were from Gentry County, Missouri.

On the evening of May 23, 1849, Egan's wagon train came upon the Nodaway Company wagon train, the Captain, Robert Patten, of Nodaway County, Missouri, was very sick with cholera, and a young man by the name of Thomas O'Flowel (O'Flewel ?), of the same county, had died the previous night with cholera.

Egan's letter indicated that on the night of May 28, 1849 one Alfred Campbell, of the Nodaway Company, late of Gentry County, Missouri, and formerly of Indiana, died with the measles, forty-five miles east of Fort Kearney at Grand Island.

On May 29, 1849, Captain Robert Patten of the Nodaway Company died at a point 80 miles east of Fort Kearney.

FORT CHILDS (May 18, 1849) On May 18, 1849 the members of the "Missouri and Georgia California Mining Companies" published an indorsement in which they extolled the navigational attributes of Nathaniel Boman, of Oregon. The two companies had united for their mutual protection in traveling to California, and they hired Boman to serve as their guide. On reaching Fort Childs the two groups published an announcement in which they noted that Bowman had great familiarity of the western route, the location of different camping grounds and that he was untiring in his exertions to advance their interests. Members of the two companies signing this announcement were as follows:

(*) This is but a partial list of the Rollin Company. The company consisted of 72 persons and was under the direction of Judge Thomas H. Owen.

James H. Owens	G.W. Armstead	W.H. Ansett
G. Wasbely (?) (Wimbley?)	Thomas Allen	H.W. Brooks
	E.B. Brudlon	V. Brooks
E.B. Benrongles	H.S. Cumberford	B. Brooks
T.J. Daniels	H. Doyle	R. Duncan
T.D. Edwards	S. Garr	William Gibson
Charles D. Hammond	C. Harrington	William Hide /sic/
L.C. Jack	H. James	E.J.C. Milner
A. Jack	N.B. Mulville	John T. Milner
M. McCarty	William Morse	James F. Nichols
B.D. Nickson	James Mye	Samuel Oldham
J. Owens /sic/	J.C. Oldham	E.H. Parks
Thomas E. Owan /sic/ (Owens ?)	J.P. Pennell	John H. Royston
	J.W. Stean /sic/	John Rader
N. Owens	James Sims	F.H. Sanford
M.A. Owens	W.H. Travis	J. Whitworth
A.H. Mingfield	W.C. Winter	J.M. Ward
E.F. Park	F. Wilhinus	

FORT KEARNEY, NEBRASKA TERRITORY (May 31, 1849) On July 27, 1849 a letter was received in St. Joseph, Missouri from Mr. E.P. Howell, a member of a west-bound wagon train. Howell's letter was dated Platte River, 13 miles below Fort Kearney, Thursday, May 31, 1849. It had been sent by way of Council Bluffs, Iowa. Howell indicated that he was traveling in a company of 17 wagons, 51 men and 2 ladies, principally from Ray County, Missouri. Three of the wagons were from Carroll County, Missouri and three from Gentry County, Missouri.

Howell related in his letter that his group had crossed the Missouri River at old Fort Kearney, two weeks previously. On the evening of May 30th while hunting antelope, Howell fell in with some emigrants on the Independence and St. Joseph road, who informed him that there had been much sickness on their road-measles and cholera. Howell was told that the Randolph Company wagon train had buried one person on the morning of May 30th, being the second they had lost from cholera.

In his letter Howell related that there had been several deaths on their road from cholera. George Thompson (brother of General J.B. Thompson) had died as well as Alfred Campbell, of Gentry County, Missouri, and a young man by the surname of O'Howell.

In closing his letter Howell furnished the names of the emigrants traveling in his wagon train as follows:

Daniel Parker, Captain	John Smith	George Hughes
John Clarke	George Smith	William Dawson
Edward Woodroe	John Vanscoit	Samuel Bullock
John Temple	James Vanscoit	J.M. Carter
J.H. Cole	J.W. Handy	S.W. Sparks
J.J. Howell	J.B. Handy	R.K. M'Gee
William H. Williams	Amos Wright	Anthony Lutman
E.P. Howell	John H. Morehead /sic/	

R.J. Squires	G.W. Hubbard	Daniel Duncan
Milton Cundiff /sic/	Thomas Esry /sic/	B.D. Lucas
John Squires	Robert Lee	John Shackelford
Ephr. January Sen.	Wilson M'Kinney	James Shackelford
Ephraim P. January	William Colly	Thomas Alsop
Leonard Ballew	James H. Colley	William Gilpin
H.W. Wallace	E.W. Squires	Henry M'Clary and wife
Andrew Thompson	Daniel Duncan	Benjamin Sheilds /sic/
William Thompson	William Duncan	(Shields?)
John Hill		

FORT LARAMIE, WYOMING TERRITORY (June 19, 1849) On June 19, 1849, a California bound emigrant bearing the name of Mr. ___Brubanks wrote a letter from Fort Laramie in which he reported his arrival in that locality. The letter was received in St. Joseph, Missouri on August 3, 1849. Brubanks, formerly a citizen of Naples, Illinois, related that his group has reached the Fort after thirty days of hard travel and much sickness. Brubanks' train was originally from a Bloomington, Indiana company which had broken up into many small divisions, the final breaking up was on June 6, 1849.

Brubank and others (unidentified) formed a small company of thirteen wagons, of which he was in command. Brubank's letter noted that a Rev. Isaac Owen and family and Rev. James Corwine (sic) were in his wagon train.

On the same day that Brubank's letter arrived in St. Joseph, Missouri a second letter from Fort Laramie was received. The second communication was written by Dr. William F. Edgar, Assistant Surgeon in the United States Army. Edgar had been on a march which was more or less connected with the emigration movement. Dr. Edgar had left Fort Kearney (Nebraska) on May 10, 1849 and arrived thirty days later at Fort Laramie. The doctor had marched with two companies of Mounted Riflemen, officers, six ladies-male and female servants-and sixty odd teamsters. At Fort Kearney, Edgar's group was joined by Company "G" of the Regular Mounted Rifles.

When reaching a point known as Chimney Rock, Edgar related that the Army group was overtaken by a pack mule company. The pack mule company camped overnight with the Army and exchanged experiences. Edgar's letter indicated that the California bound pack mule company consisted of Messrs. Andrews, Johnson, Lewis, Love, Ryan, Summerfield and Moss. The given names of the men were not listed in the letter. One man in the pack mule company, a Mr. Wilson, died of cholera.

Edgar's letter also reported that a Mr. ___Roe, of Wisconsin, had been killed by Indians, supposed to be Sioux, on the north side of the Platte River, about 300 miles below Fort Laramie. This information being supplied to Dr. Edgar by an emigrant encountered during the course of the march.

ST. JOSEPH, MISSOURI (AUGUST 17, 1849) Word reached St. Joseph, Missouri on August 17, 1849 that the remains of a man, an emigrant, were found on August 4, 1849 by Mr. J.F. Foreman at the half way grove between St. Joseph and the great Nemaha Sub Agency, which had been dug up by wolves. Near the grave lay a board on which was written, "Samuel Campbell, from Mobile, Alabama, died of Cholera May 29, 1849".

Other graves had been dug into by the animals without success, one being that of a Nathaniel Clark, from Jefferson City (or County) Missouri, who died of cholera, in ten hours. No date of death was noted on the grave of Clark.

ST. JOSEPH, MISSOURI (August 31, 1849) On the foregoing date, word reached St. Joseph, Missouri that several cases of cholera had occurred in wagon trains which had reached points beyond Fort Laramie (Wyoming). News also arrived in St. Joseph that a Mr. J. McDowell, formerly a citizen of St. Joseph, had been killed by an Indian near Fort Laramie, a short time previous to August 31, 1849.

KANESVILLE, IOWA (September 19, 1849) On August 21, 1849, George A. Smith and Ezra T. Benson, two west-bound emigrants, wrote a letter from their camp at Spring Creek, 345 miles from Kanesville, Iowa. Smith and Benson sent their letter to Kanesville via a Mr. ___Babbitt, who came into their camp on his way back from the Salt Lake area.

Included in the letter was an account of how Smith and Benson had come upon the grave of a California bound gold digger. On August 9, 1849, Smith and Benson passed the grave and from a writing found upon the same they learned that it was the grave of Edward Haggard, of Askaloosa, Iowa, (of the Hawkeye Company) who died in June, 1849. Copy of the writing found upon the tomb follows:

> "To anyone who may read-June 7th, 1849.
> "May known the cause
> "The Hawkeye Company on their journey to California, to inform anyone who may read this letter, that mankind whilst journeying through this world are subject to troubles, crosses, and losses, of which we the Hawkeye Company have to say that we mourn the loss of one of our company, to wit, Edward Haggard, of Askaloosa, Iowa, who departed this life June 7th 1849—was taken ill at Loup Fork, (Loop Fork?) with diarrhea, of which was the cause of ending his existence, we mourn the loss of a friend, and particularly to be left in a decent land. We add nothing more.
>
> James McMurray
> J. Shrade
> W.W. Sampske
> W.G. Lee"

In another letter, which Smith and Benson sent to Kanesville, Iowa, they mentioned other graves found along the trail. This second letter had been sent from a camp near Fort Childs, 208 miles from Kanesville, and dated August 5, 1849. In it they made note of passing the grave of A. Kellogg, at Praire Creek, one hundred and fifty-seven miles from

Kanesville. Kellogg's grave indicated that he had died of cholera on June 23, 1849. The grave of Samuel Gully was found at a point one hundred and eight-fives miles from Kanesville, in the open prairie. His grave, neatly turfed over, stated that he had died of cholera on July 5, 1849, aged thirty-nine years.

Along side of Gully's grave was that of Henry Vanderhoof. Both Vanderhoof and Kellogg were members of a California bound group that was headed by O. Spencer. Vanderhoof died of cholera, according to his grave mark, on July 4, 1849.

ST. JOSEPH, MISSOURI (November 2, 1849) In November, 1849, a St. Joseph, Missouri newspaper ran an article concerning letters received from California by members of the St. Joseph pack mule company. The first letter was from D. H. Moss who datelined his letter, Sacramento City, California, August 7, 1849. Moss stated that he had left the Missouri River on May 12, 1849, arriving in Sacramento on August 5th. They had been detained on the route for seventeen days on account of sickness.

Moss noted that they had lost two of the company of seventeen, one of them Samuel Wilson, of St. Joseph, Missouri, was a victim of cholera and he died about 75 miles from the Missouri River. The other victim being Hugh Riddle, late of Baltimore, Maryland, who was accidentally shot by another member of the group, a Mr. ___ Kirkwood. Riddle was shot on the night of June 17, 1849 and died on the morning of June 19th.

Moss's letter related facts relative to conditions in California insofar as mining and business was concerned. Two other letters were printed, one from Joel Ryan, datelined Sacramento City, August 9, 1849, and the other from N. Grant, bearing the dateline of Sacramento City, August 11, 1849. Ryan and Grant were also members of the pack mule company and in substance contained about the same information as noted above.

ST. JOSEPH, MISSOURI (November 16, 1849) On November 16, 1849, word reached St. Joseph, Missouri that a wagon train known as the "Banner Company", composed of men from Wisconsin and Illinois, under the command of J.A. Gooding, and guided by Colonel J.H. Cutting, had reached California. The trip had been made with wagons drawn by mules from St. Joseph, on the Missouri River, to the gold mines of California in 79 days, of which twelve days were layby time. Of 3,000 teams that started before them, they passed all but about twenty.

ST. JOSEPH, MISSOURI (December 14, 1849) John and Andrew Scott, two California emigrants from St. Joseph, Missouri, wrote their father, John Scott, of St. Joseph, three letters dealing with their arrival and activities after reaching California. The first, datelined September 1, 1849, Sacramento City, California, announced their safe arrival. In this letter they noted that on the Big Platte they had connected themselves with the wagon train of Captain ___ Owen's company, and joined teams with B. Nickson, with whom they traveled to Carson River, where Nickson's cattle gave out.

The Scott's then joined teams with a man by the name of Sims, with whom they traveled through to California. The second letter from the Scott's was dated from

September 18, 1849 and it mentioned they were working on the American Fork, about half a mile below Sutter's mill. The third letter, written on September 23rd, stated that "the St. Joseph boys had all got through safely and were doing well".

ST. JOSEPH, MISSOURI (December 21, 1849) In the latter part of December, 1849, an extract of a letter written by W.T. Jackson was printed in a St. Joseph newspaper. Jackson's letter was datelined from Yuba River Diggins, September 2, 1849 and addressed to his mother, in Ralls County, Missouri. Jackson had crossed at St. Joseph early in the Spring of 1849 and made the trip without much difficulty. His letter stated that Henry Hawkins and Thomas Hildreth had started the previous day for a location to mine.

ST. JOSEPH, MISSOURI (December 28, 1849) Mr. J. Bennett, of Jackson County, Missouri, and Mr.____Baine, of Platte City, Missouri, were in St. Joseph on December 28, 1849. Bennett and Baine had just arrived from California. They had left Missouri for California by way of the plains on April 16, 1849, and arrived in California on July 27, 1849. Both men indicated they intended to return to the California mines in the spring.

WEAVER TOWN DRY DIGGINS, CALIFORNIA (November 1, 1849) On the foregoing date, Frederick Rohrer, formerly a resident of Andrew County, Missouri, addressed a letter to Judge C. F. Holly of Savannah, Missouri. Rohrer's letter was received and reported in a St. Joseph, Missouri newspaper on January 11, 1850.*

In his letter Rohrer noted they had left Salt Lake City (Utah) on August 13, 1849 with seven mules and five ponies, and after a tedious journey of 44 days-800 miles-they arrived in California on September 25, 1849.

Rohrer's correspondence did not reflect the names of his fellow travelers but did deal to some length with his impressions of the gold region and the route his group took to California. He placed Weaver Town Dry Diggins (Diggings) as 50 miles east of Sacramento, California, 2 miles north of Weavertown, and 1 1/2 miles southeast of Hangtown, California.

Rohrer's route lay up the valley of the Salt Lake 80 miles to the crossing of Bear River-thence to the Fort Hall road, a southwest course, through the mountains 100 miles. They reached the head of Mary's River on August 30, 1849, and followed the stream to its "sink"-300 miles. From the "sink" to Carson's River was a distance of 40 miles of desert-which they made in one day. On September 21st they crossed the summit of the Sierra Nevada. They left behind in Salt Lake some 2,000 emigrants that would cross the Sierra Nevada, at the head of Feather, Truckee and Carson Rivers-three different routes.

WEAVERS CREEK, CALIFORNIA (September 21 and 23, 1849) On the foregoing two dates Samuel Hawkins Jr. wrote letters from California to Mr. F. M. Colburn, of St. Louis Missouri. Hawkins, a recent arrival in California, spoke of his trip across the plains as a "pleasure excursion" rendered more pleasant by the opportunity it

(*) See notes pp. 200-201 on spelling of Frederick Rohrer name.

afforded for hunting. The route persued by Harkness led him by the Great Salt Lake. After leaving the lake, he found the roads bad to the Fort Hall road. Harkness and his party (absence of names in letter) left their wagons on the Atlantic side of the Sierra Nevada range and packed their outfit.

The Harkness letter placed Weavers Creek as 45 miles north of Sacramento, California.

SACRAMENTO, CALIFORNIA (November 19, 1849) Leo. Smith, Jr., formerly a resident of St. Joseph, Missouri, wrote a letter from Sacramento, California, to Jesse Holladay, of St. Joseph. Smith's letter, dated November 19, 1849, related the fact that he had been an invalid since his arrival in the Sacramento Valley. Smith had tried mining for two weeks, with no success.

In speaking of other California emigrants Smith noted that Samuel C. Steele and George Conner had done well. He mentioned that Mason F. Moss was selling goods at Coloma, California, and that ___Glazebrook was making money mining. Samuel Love and D. Wilmans were reported as selling goods at Hangtown, 60 miles from Sacramento, in the Dry Diggings. Smith's letter was received in St. Joseph on Feb. 1, 1850.

ALONG THE FEATHER RIVER, CALIFORNIA (September 29, 1849) While engaged in mining for gold along the Feather River, about 600 miles from Sacramento, California, Charles and Robert Springer took time to write a letter to Mr. S.W. Springer, of St. Joseph, Missouri. Their letter was received in St. Joseph on February 1, 1849.

Charles and Robert Springer had left St. Joseph in the spring of 1849 and reached the gold region about three weeks previous to the date of their letter (September 29, 1849). They reported that one of their company, David Compton, had died during the journey. Other members of the company were not listed in the letter.

ST. JOSEPH, MISSOURI (February 1, 1850) W.Y. Hitt, a citizen of Boone County, Missouri, returned to that county after overland trip to California which he commenced in the Spring of 1849. Hitt returned to St. Joseph on approximately February 1, 1850, after leaving his two sons engaged in mining at Dry Diggings, California. The given names of Hitt's sons were not listed in the basic research source.

KELSO DIGGINGS, CALIFORNIA (November 5, 1849) On the forementioned date, Sam Johnson, a member of the "St. Joseph Company" listed on page 46, wrote a letter from Kelso Diggings, California. Johnson's letter was received in St. Joseph, Missouri approximately February 22, 1850.

Johnson's letter stated that John and James Somerfield, Frank (Francis) Brubaker and the two Tracy's (one being John M. Tracy), Mr. ___Decker and Eli Skagg were all close together.* It would appear that Johnson meant they were close to Kelso Diggings. The letter continued with the statement that Mr. ___Ray and John were about two miles off. The two Moss's, Mason F. and David H., were listed as being

(*) Consider "Eli Skaggs" as alternative name.

about 15 miles from Kelso Diggings. Sam Johnson had seen Mason F. Moss two weeks previously and was told that David Moss had made $1,800.

On approximately the same date that the Sam Johnson letter arrived in St. Joseph, Missouri, the residents of St. Joseph were told that a letter from John M. Tracy was received. Tracy's letter was dated November 4, 1849 but the research source did not disclose the exact California location. In view of the reference to John M. Tracy in the forementioned Sam Johnson letter, it would appear that Tracy was near Kelso Diggings, California.

In his letter Tracy mentioned that Mr. ___Decker was suffering from diarrhea. He continued "that, Thomas Willis was probably dead with the same disease, the last time I heard from him he was speechless."

Tracy's letter then referred to the death of a "Mr. ___Stratton" by stating that Stratton and a companion had gone to the mountains to look for gold. While on the way Stratton's gun accidentally went off, and shot him in the foot; and while his comrade went for a horse, the Indians took Stratton prisoner, and burnt him.

Some details concerning a Jerry Lancaster were related in the Tracy letter. While crossing the plains Lancaster fell in love "with Jinkins' (sic) wife". Lancaster hired a man by the name of ___Bascom and Jinkin's nephew (unidentified) to shoot him. The wound did not prove fatal and Lancaster fled and had not been heard of up to the time the letter was written.

<u>GOLD MINING AREAS IN CALIFORNIA (November-December, 1849)</u> During the period of November-December, 1849 a number of St. Joseph, Missouri residents who had gone to California wrote letters to friends in St. Joseph. These letters were all received in St. Joseph by March 1, 1850. The research source did not indicate the California locale of the emigrants and in all instances the time period is not very specific. Extracts from the letters are as follows.

Mr. John Metcalf wrote to his daughter and stated he was doing well. The identity of the daughter is not revealed. Metcalf noted that he and his son (unidentified) had accumulated somewhere between $5,000 to $6,000 in gold mining efforts. Jacob Dehaven and the son of one A. Wells were reported as "doing well, making $25 a day at their trade".

A letter from a V. Thompson (in California) written to his father in St. Joseph revealed that his mining efforts were not successful. Thompson's letter was written in November, 1849 and he advised persons who were making twenty-five cents a day in Missouri to stay where they were, not to come to California.

<u>HANGTOWN, CALIFORNIA (December 14, 1849)</u> On December 14, 1849, Joel Ryan, formerly a citizen of St. Joseph, Missouri, wrote a letter to Sinclair K. Miller, of St. Joseph. Ryan, a member of the "St. Joseph Company" which had gone to California by pack mule train, wrote his letter from Hangtown, California. His letter was received in St. Joseph on approximately March 29, 1850. Ryan had departed from

St. Joseph on May 11, 1849 for California.

Ryan's letter related his experiences in mining and the cost factors for living in California. In referring to those who went to California with him he remarked they "have done tolerable well, many scattered about the gold regions." Ryan noted that Samuel E. Love and A.D. McDonald were with him in Hangtown. McDonald and Love were scheduled to leave for Sacramento, California in a few days.

David Moss, according to Ryan, was making good money by merchandising in a mill ten miles from Hangtown.

SAN FRANCISCO, CALIFORNIA (December 24 and 31, 1849) General John Wilson and his wife, who were supposedly lost in the mountains trying to reach California, managed to reach San Francisco, and there wrote friends of their safe arrival. Their letters were addressed to friends in Glasgow, Missouri and bore dates of December 24 and 31, 1849. References to these letters appeared in a St. Joseph, Missouri newspaper in March, 1850.

The two Wilson letters related the hardships they endured. Three days before reaching the California settlements, the Indians stole most of their mules, and the rest died thus forcing them to complete the trip on foot, having left and lost everything but their clothing and a blanket apiece.

The letter source did not reveal the names of any fellow emigrants.

SAN FRANCISCO, CALIFORNIA (December 26, 1849) Mr. N. McClure, a resident of Wisconsin, wrote to his friends in that State on December 26, 1849. While announcing his safe arrival in San Francisco he cautioned on the necessity of money to a man in California. "I can assure you," he wrote, "a man here without money had better be in hell." McClure noted that coffee was fifty cents a cup and "bleeding" costs twenty-five dollars. No mention was made of the whereabouts of any fellow emigrants. McClure's letter appeared in a St. Joseph, Missouri newspaper during March 1850.

AUGUSTA, MAINE (January 5, 1849) On the foregoing date a newspaper in Augusta printed an item which it had extracted from a Little Rock, Arkansas newspaper. The item noted that K. Thorndike, E.C. Spaulding and E.S. Graves, of South Thomaston, Maine and William T. Sayward, of Lime Rock (sic) (Limerick?, Limestone?) had recently departed for California. The four men were to go in company with Captain Otis M. Cutler of Lowell, Massachusetts, who was to be the Commander. This group planned to go by way of Corpus Christi (Texas); Matamoras, Mexico; Saltillo, Mexico; Monterey, Mexico and then to California.

BOSTON, MASSACHUSETTS (January, 1849) On the foregoing date a newspaper in Augusta, Maine stated that a group of New England pioneers left Boston, Massachusetts by railroad for California, by way of Vera Cruz, Mexico and Mexico City, Mexico. The group was commanded by Capt. Edward A. Paul of Boston, Lt.

Charles F. Read, of Lowell, Mass., Quartermaster Jonathan Gavett, of Boston; Charles Liscom, George A. Baker and C. Willard Gleason of Boston; T. Henry Hoskins of Gardiner, Maine; Charles Austin of Charleston, Maine; John L. Read of Brattleboro, Vermont; Edward L. Kittredge of Nelson, New Hampshire; James H. Fickett and Thomas M. Gridley, of Roxbury, Maine. A short time after this article was printed an additional item noted that the company was at Philadelphia, Pennsylvania and had left for Baltimore, Maryland from which they would sail in a few days to Tampico, Mexico.

AUGUSTA, MAINE (February 15, 1849) An Augusta, Maine newspaper printed a story on the foregoing date that James and Henry Thompson from Portland, Maine left St. Louis, Missouri on January 22, 1849 to go to California via Independence, Missouri. They were sending their goods by sea and expected to beat their merchandise to California by two months.

BELFAST, MAINE (April 12, 1849) On the foregoing date a Belfast newspaper carried a report that Cyrus Rowe, late senior partner of the "Republican Journal", would go to California by the overland route, via Independence, Missouri. The article also indicated that others taking the overland route to California were Charles Treadwell of the firm of Treadwell & Mansfield; Annis Campbell, Hiram E. Pierce and A.V. Parker, of Waldo, Maine. Solyman Heath (Soliman, Solomon?), an attorney at law, and his son were also scheduled to leave.

AUGUSTA, MAINE (May 31, 1849) The "Kennebec Journal" of Augusta printed an article on the forementioned date that Isaac B. Gore, part owner of the steamer "Edward Bates", was killed recently on the plains beyond Hannibal, Missouri, by Arthur Shearer, late Postmaster of that place. It appeared that Shearer, with his wife and five to six children, were on their way to California, when he discovered an improper intimacy between his wife and Gore, and rushing into the tent shot him dead.

AUGUSTA, MAINE (July 26, 1849) The "Kennebec Journal" of Augusta prints letters received from a Mr. ___Dudley and Mr. ___Webster, of Roxbury, Maine, who belonged to the "Congress and California Mutual Protection Association" which left Boston, Massachusetts in the Spring of 1849 for the overland route. At the time the lettes were written, Dudley and Webster were in the neighborhood of Fort Kearney (Nebraska).

INDEPENDENCE, MISSOURI (May 8, 1849) A group of individuals from Oxford, Ohio departed from Independence, Missouri on May 8, 1849 for California. Individuals in this company were:

Hiram Ogle	David Miller	John Blake
Franklin Ogle	Alexander Miller	McGonigle Peyton
Dr. John Garver	Samuel Blake Sr.	John Hadleigh
A.C. Stearns	Thomas VanNess	Isaac Smith
Jackson Van Scoyoc	Jonathan Van Scoyoc	A.C. Rynnearson

Ezra Bourne　　　　　　John Samuels

MOBILE, ALABAMA (April 6, 1849) *On the foregoing date Captain Blanton McAlpin's "Mobile Company" left Mobile, Alabama for Vera Cruz, Mexico with intentions of going to California. The group departed from Mobile aboard a British Mail Steamer and a reference to their departure was printed in the New York Daily Tribune of April 18, 1849. Members of this company were:

Capt. Blanton McAlpin, of Mobile, Alabama	C.R. Bostwick, of Mobile, Alabama	Robert T. Saunders and servant, of Mobile, Ala.
Dr. E.D. Bryne, of Mobile, Alabama	O. Bostwick, of Mobile, Alabama	William S. Cooke and servant, of Demopolis, Alabama
Daniel Crawley /sic/ of Alabama	Reuben T. Thorn and family, of Virginia	John R. Cooke and servant, of Demopolis, Alabama
F.H. Clements, of Georgia	Philip Gamble, of South Carolina	
William H. Dougherty, of St. Louis, Mo.	John D. Skinner, of Hartford, Conn.	Franklin Cunning, of Hartford, Conn.
Elisha Mather, of Hartford, Conn.	Justin Hodge, of Hartford, Conn.	V. Gassner, no residence listed
C. Moniche, no residence listed	George Patrin, no residence listed	

MILLEDGEVILLE, GEORGIA The New York Herald (N.Y.) of April 18, 1849 printed a number of departure notices of California-bound emigrants. These appeared as follows:

From Milledgeville, Georgia: (Departing about April 1, 1849)

Mr. ___Ellsworth	F. Park	Balling Breedlove
T.W. White	F.H. Sandford /sic/	Starke Park
E. King	F.D. Edwards	

The above group would unite with other emigrants at Atlanta, Georgia and then go to St. Louis, Missouri.

From Washington, D.C.:

Sixty-four men composing the "California Mining Company" left Washington, D.C. for St. Joseph. The date of departure did not appear in the Herald article.

From Juniata, Pennsylvania:

Following were listed as members of the "Juniata, Pennsylvania California Company": (departure date not listed)

James K. Kelly	Dr. E.D. Hammond	D.C. Salsbury
Dr. William A. Kelly	Robert Beck	James M. Duncan
Harrison Levy	E. J. Smith	William Scott
J. McMorrow	Abraham Vandling	Louis Franciscus
John F. Hayes	H.M. Campbell	J.G. Smith

From Dayton, Ohio: (departure date not listed)

H.T. Kyle	J.C. Frankelerger /sic/	S.C. Emily
J.L. McCain	J.M. Clegg	Daniel Boone

From South Carolina: (departure date not listed)

J. Smith	E. Cuthbert	J. Hazard
M.H. Stopp	E.J. McDonald	

From Greenville, Alabama: (departure date not listed)

A. Deming	D.W.C. Benshaw	J.L. Davenport

(*)See notes pp. 201-203 regarding these dates.

*Rufus Calwell /sic/
Jno. Deming
Jno. C. Otis
H. Cook
J.H. Chace /sic/
A.J. Spofford, of
  Perrysburg, Ohio

A.J. Richardson
I.G. House
*S. Colwell /sic/
William Rhodes
G.S. McKnight, of
  Belvedere, Ill.
Jno. P. Cook

Milton Cook
P.J. Rymer
Fed Bone /sic/ (Fred
  Bone?)
G.W. Clark, of
  Perrysburg, Ohio

From Port Lavaca, Texas:

The Herald article stated that four companies of California emigrants had left Port Lavaca on March 16, 1849 and they consisted of the "Defiance Company" from Defiance, Ohio; the "Clarksville Company" from Clarksville, Tennessee; a company from Natchez, Tennessee consisting of thirty men and a company from E. Mississippi consisting of fourteen men. The Herald also noted that a Dr. ___Brandes and a Mr. ___Wuestenfeld intended to go by way of Texas.

From Ft. Smith, Arkansas: (departing on March 12, 1849)

The following departed from Fort Smith for California, March 12:

Capt. M.M. Heath, of
  Illinois
S.F. Stanley, of Arkansas
J.H. Sellers, of Arkansas
M.J. Flynn, of Ireland
W.H. Hutchinson, of St.
  Louis, Mo.
W. Brokaw (no residence
  listed)

J.V. Wadsworth, of New
  York
Jesse Owen, of Arkansas
A. Scarborough, of
  Arkansas
H. Harris, of Germany
D.D. Bowman of St.
  Louis, Mo.
F.W. Lanweister, of
  Germany

T. Gerold /sic/ (no
  residence listed)
M. Marshall, of New York
G. Ballard, of Arkansas
John W. Waddie, of
  Pennsylvania
N. Rom /sic/, of Germany
S. Mullrey, of Germany
___Funnells, of Maine

From Louisville, Kentucky:

The following emigrants comprised the "Hule's California Company" and they intended to travel via the Independence, Missouri route:

J.B. Hule
Dr. ___Hule and lady
S. McMillen /sic/
C.P. Bardin
J.S. Coach
M.B. Johnston
Jacob Fox
Jacob B. Fox
Abraham Graf

Lt. ___Thompson, of U.S.
  Navy
J.S. Prather
A. Rankin
Justus Dunn
B. Stout
Matthew Harris
Ferdinand Graf
E. Buck

Dr. ___Martin
J.H. Baxter
M. Brown
D.C. Stone
I.D. Thompson
S.P. Reader
R.H. Redd
Henry Byers
S. Raphael

(all above of Louisville, Kentucky)

Dr. B. Miller

J.H.B. Miller and two
  unidentified
  accompanists

W. Percival
Henry Fox
Bernard Sheddel

(all above of Lexington, Kentucky)

J.T. Smith, of Hancock,
  Hancock County, Ky

W.D. Mayhall, of
  Hancock County, Ky

H. Haynes, of Breckinridge
  County, Ky

(*) Consider Rufus Colwell and S. Calwell as alternatives.

B. McDuffy, of
Breckenridge County,
Kentucky

From St. Louis, Missouri:
The following members of an overland company bound for California departed from St. Louis, Missouri on March 16, 1849:

Stephen O. Coleman	James Stewart	Thomas K. Wannell
Edward E. Hunter	O. Stewart	John J. Holiday
John Vorhees	F. Campbell	W. Paul
Samuel Hawkins Jr.	Solomon Wood	Carles Parks
Richard B. Dallam Jr.	William Brausheed	A. Hoffman
James Webster	John B. Smith	H. L. Brolaski
U.P. Coleman	William Vose	A.S. Vanpelt
William Brown	Ellis N. Leeds	A. Patterson
William Cleaver	Taylor Jones	C.W. Lightner
F.A. McDonald	Heath Jones	A. Burnett
A. Thompson	John Jones	William Gibson
A. Moody	Jackson Jones	R. Ludd
Charles Pickering	Stephen Jones	Samuel N. Holiday
George Massey	William Cruickshank	Peter Guisler
John Mullen	J.W. Alexander	Jonah Hunter
Lewis Legg	Gilbert Deacons	Henry C. Lynch
John S. Wells	George Mattoon /sic/	Casper Graulech
Charles L. Smith	John S. Wells /sic/	G. Yoster
C. Hoffman	B. Twomley /sic/	Thomas Cleaver
J. Getzendiner	Thomas Copperwaithe	Henry Cleaver
William P. Stebbins	J.W. Selser	Samuel Young
Granville O. Eads	William Selser	James Clark
A. Selser		

FORT SMITH, ARKANSAS (March 21, 1849) The Fort Smith Herald of the forementioned date published an announcement of a meeting held by the "Fort Smith California Emigrating Company". During the meeting a set of rules and regulations was drawn up and the following names appeared in the news article:

John F. Wheeler	Captain J.J. Dillard	Dr. ___Betner
___Van Buren	T.M.S. Gookin	J.W. Seaman

The same newspaper contained an article referring to the arrival of the steamboat "Celia No. 2" from Helena, Arkansas and on board were the following passengers who intended to unite with the "Fort Smith Company" (also known as the "Fort Smith California Emigrating Company"):

R. Biven	Hugh Martin	W.C. Stephenson
J.T. Moore	Dr. B .G. King	A.J. Heslip
J. Lock	R.H. Price	F. Bukes
J.C. Shell	J.B. Hurd	C. Russell

A third reference to individuals attaching themselves to the "Fort Smith California Emigrating Company" also appeared in the Herald issue of March 21, 1849 when the newspaper noted that the following emigrants from Philadelphia, Pennsylvania intended to join the California bound company:

T.B. Russum	C. E. Pleasants /sic/	J.P. Coolidge

D. Lake   J. Lake   R.A. Heazlitt
R.D. Smith   R.L. Allen   T.S. Allen

The <u>Fort Smith Herald</u> of June 6, 1849 printed a number of letters which it had received from members of wagon trains which were on the plains. The letters were from T.M.S. Gookin and J.W. Seaman, both of the "Fort Smith California Emigrating Company" and from John B. Hackett. A fourth letter was from H.J. Share, of Little Rock, Arkansas. One of the letters contained a reference to the death of J.G. Roberts, a member of the "Little Rock Company".

<u>FORT SMITH, ARKANSAS (March 21, 1849)</u> A list of the members of the "Knickerbocker Exploring Company", of New York, was printed in the <u>Fort Smith Herald</u> on the forementioned date. Company members intending to go to California were identified as follows:

Capt. John A.N. Ebbetts
1st Lt. George H. Blake
2nd Lt. Abram A. Van Gelder
Peter Lodewick, Treasurer
James P. Burr, Secretary
Cornelius Cornwell
John M. Hendricks
William Moore
Edgar Seabury
James Brown
Oliver B. Oakley
John Jones Jr.
Samuel Griffiths
Ira M. Allen
Samuel Kelly
Joel G. Candee
Josiah H. Bruen /sic/
William McCleland /sic/ (McClelland?)
James M. Hutchings
Samuel Y. Lum
E.O. Crane
Gerard Rancker
William F. Ford

Alexander H. Reed
George Derrick
Andrew Smith
William S. Ross
William W. Wyckoff
Hiram Green
Phineas U. Bl__
James E. Baker
James Helms
James H. Cooley
Patrick Garvey
James Lockheart /sic/ (Lockhart?)
John H. Bogert /sic/
Robert W. Nevins
John P. Hoyt
Schuyler Hoes
John Price
T.C. Sturges /sic/ (Sturgess?)
John A. Hunter
Melvin S. Gardner
William Larison /sic/
P.C. Wilson /sic/

Stephen Hyde
John Flynn
James Spencer
Jessee Brush /sic/
William Can_eld (Canfeld?)
Barnabas Pike
P.C. Wilson /sic/
George Churchill
Charles Churchill
Joseph Van Doren (Van Duren?)
James Broadmeadow
John Murphy
H.M. Sturges /sic/ (Sturgess?)
James L. Byers
J. Alfred Kanouse
John Jackson
James MacNally
John Hempreed (?)
William R. Goulding
E.L. Hughson
J.F. Hough

The <u>New York Daily Tribune</u> of July 4, 1849 stated that Captain Ebbett's "Knickerbocker Exploring Company" /sic/ had left Fort Smith, Arkansas on March 20, 1849 and reached Sante Fe on May 27, 1849. The company name seems to be used interchangeably in many contemporary sources appearing at times as the "Knickerbocker Emigrating Company".

On July 20, 1849 the <u>Tribune</u> printed a letter from George W. Churchill, of New York. Churchill, a member of the Knickerbocker Company appears in the foregoing list as "George Churchill". Churchill's letter, written to his father in New York, was datelined Sante Fe, May 29, 1849, and it furnished some account of the adventures the company was experiencing.

The New York Daily Tribune of November 13, 1849 printed another letter dealing with the "Knickerbocker Exploring Company", this one from Andrew Smith. Smith, a company member, indicated that the group broke up on the Sante Fe trail, and that he had reached the California mines safely. The letter also mentioned two other company members, John P. Hoyt and George Derrick.

FORT SMITH, ARKANSAS (April 4, 1849) The Fort Smith Herald of April 4, 1849 published a notice that the following company from Logansport, Louisiana was enroute to California:

S. Lasselle, Captain	J.S. Armstrong	T.A. Merrick
D.C. Buchanan	U.M. Nahan	J.M. Jones
Joseph Muse (Jos Muse?)	O. Hamilton	T. Sutherland
P. Kelley /sic/	A. Richardson	L. Sutherland
T.J. Bristo	G.W. Turner	A.J. Reams
William Tibbatts /sic/ (Tibbetts?)	Robert Metcalf, of Natchez, Tenn.	A. Jacobs, of Natchez, Tenn.
__ Liddell, of Natchez, Tenn.	C. Remington, of Louisiana	H.L. Lamford, of Louisiana
H.W. Pullam, of Louisiana	__ Vebler, of Louisiana	C.P. Colton, of Louisiana
Joseph Dale	Alex Learight	
James Dale	William Learight	

FORT SMITH, ARKANSAS (March 4, 1849) The "Western Rovers" company was formed at Fort Smith according to the Herald of the forementioned date. The membership list of this California-bound company appeared as follows:

Capt. John L. Bass	R.J. Featherstone, of Alabama	Sgt. Henry Hart, of Virginia
1st Lt. E.A. Cole	B. Lack, of Mississippi	Sgt. Elam Morrison, of North Carolina
2nd Lt. E.C. Bollinger (All above from Mississippi)	C.L. Martin, of Mississippi	Sgt. L.H. Humphreys, of Mississippi
3rd Lt. William K. Newman, of Tennessee	Cpl. I.J. Allen (?) (L.J. Allen?)	Sgt. William Skinner, of Alabama
John Lark, Surgeon, of South Carolina	Cpl. John S. Anderson	H.B. Bowden
C. Bendett (?) (C. Bennett?, G. Bennett?)	V.B. Burton	William D. Biffle
	A. Bullock	J.H. Boardman
Pike Clough	J. Chase	C. Claudet (?) (Claudot?)
James P. Clough	D. Carson	James Crouch
O. Crossman	Samuel T. Cochran	P. Clapp
John G. Day	James Cole	Henry Downs
J.A. Edwards	Benjamin Davis	J.H. Edson
John Ewing	William C. Davis	John Freeman
S. Fant	J. Eaton	W. Figgin
William B. Fant	P.W. Fulligan	Robert Gorman
A. Gore	Joseph Goodson	__ Hague
W.A. Hopkins	L.B. Gill (?) (I.B. Gill?)	L.H. Hill
S.W. Hurst	S. Hurst	Joseph Hurst

Thomas C. Hurvey (?) (Harvey?) /sic/	David Hays /sic/	J.F. Jones
James Harvey /sic/	R.F. Jennings	William W. Joyce
J. Killingsworth (?) (Kinningsworth?)	F. Jones	R.G. Kyle
	R. Lanier	J.J. Leahe
O. Margan (?) (Morgan?)	J.J. Mitchell	I. Magaw
J.R. Maltbey	J.W. Mitchell	J.H. Millner /sic/
J.R. Paxton	W.W.P. McCall	W.H. McClain
J. Riley	W.C. Neeley	Thomas Newman
Samuel E. Stentell	B. Phillips	J.H. Quisenberry
F. Stith	T.K. Rowe	J.R. Rendale
William G. Williams	__ Stephens	J.M. Stewart
W. Whatley	C.G. Stanley	Z.D. Steel /sic/
H. Whatley	Theodore O. Wheeler	T. Wallace
	W.W. Young	William Young

FORT SMITH, ARKANSAS (April 18, 1849) The Fort Smith Herald of April 18, 1849 printed a list of the members of the "New Orleans Mining and Trading Association" who were planning on going overland to California. The organizational membership was listed as follows:

Captain James Wright	Thomas Armitage,	Winslow Hubbard
A. Skarzynski	Treasurer and Secretary	David Morgan
W.T. Mallory	F.H. Hoffman	Charles Boudray
J. Olliod /sic/	Harman Baruh /sic/	Josh. S. Marsh
W.D. Rowand /sic/		

It is possible that there were more members of the "New Orleans Mining and Trading Association" for the New York Daily Tribune of May 15, 1849 printed a letter which had been written by Thomas Armitage, one of the association's officers. Armitage's letter spoke of the death of two of the members, Dr. __ Alford, the group's doctor, and the association President. The association President was not identified.

FORT SMITH, ARKANSAS (April 25, 1849) The Fort Smith Herald issue of April 25, 1849 printed the names of members of two groups planning to go to California in search of gold.

The first company, known as the "Maine & New York Company", consisted of the below individuals:

William H. Barnes	Gilbert Fowler	Benjamin Ross
Moses C. Jennett	James Wilber /sic/	Robert Dyer
	(all above from Maine)	
Samuel Jackson, of Virginia	William Golden, of New York	Abraham Wagner, of Bath, Maine
John M. Ellis, of Bath, Maine	Samuel Chesholm, of Bath, Maine	Peen Yan, of Bath, Maine
		Robert Morgan, of New York

The second group, the "Havilah Mining Association", was made up primarily of New York City residents. The residence sites of C.S. Schenck, of New York City, and William M. Bennett, of Fort Smith, Arkansas, were specifically listed as stated in the research source. The Havilah group was made up of the following emigrants:

John Conger	J.W. Thompson	Henry C. Langley
W. Teller	J.D. Drake	W.B. Grant
H. Vandever /sic/	C.H. Cole	William Fawcitt /sic/
E.F. Lasak	J. Brinkrhoff Jr./sic/	(Fawcett?)
W.D. Coleman	(Brinkerhoff?)	J.P. Hynard /sic/
J.J. Lott	Thomas Parsons	(Haynard?)
C.H. Van Wyck	C.B. Tappen /sic/	Isaac Johnson
G.F. Sniffin	F.A. Hoyt	G.K. Patterson
B.L. Noe	J.H. Macdonald /sic/	E.W. Ehrenstroen
J.G. Billing	John Brown	Edward Norton
E.E. Miles	S. Hickerson	F.W. Corsegner
F.G. Bents	J.F. Randolph	G.H. Andrews
C.S. Schenck, of New York City, N.Y.	William M. Bennett, of Fort Smith, Arkansas	

FORT SMITH, ARKANSAS (May 23,1849) On the forementioned date the Fort Smith Herald announced that the "Waterford Mutual Mining Association" would leave shortly for California. Members of the mining group had arrived some ten days previously on the vessel "Cotton Plant". Emigrants in the association were identified as:

C.F. Vandecar /sic/	Alexander Stewart	L.D. Aldrich
Roberts Vandercook /sic/	James V.S. Stewart	Alexander McDonald
William Vandecar /sic/	N.N. Scheuten	Joseph Dutcher
John W. Stewart	Robert Blake Jr.	

The same issue of the Herald also indicated that members of the "Osborne Company" (Osborn Company?) would unite with the "Waterford Association". In printing the list of members of the Osborne Company, the Herald did not include an "e" in the surname "Osborne" as noted below:

A.H. Osborn /sic/ (Osborne?)	J.A. Whaley William Woods	David Dick O.T. Beard
J.W. Osborn /sic/ (Osborne?)	James Johnson	Charles Johnson
	(above from Brooklyn, N.Y.)	
Joseph Boyle, of Martinville, N.J.	William H. Burgess, of Jackson, Mississippi	Fowler Fenn, of Hillsorough, Mississippi
C.E. Osborn /sic/ (Osborne?),of Jackson, Mississippi		

DEPARTURES FROM SCATTERED POINTS- (April-May,1849) The New York Daily Tribune of May 3,1849 printed a series of announcements which furnished the names of individuals and companies departing from various points for California. The list appeared as follows:

Buffalo, New York: A company left Buffalo, for the overland route through St. Louis, Missouri, under the command of Colonel C.H. Gratiot. Company members were:

A.S. Webster, of Buffalo, N.Y.	D.W. Heywood, of Buffalo, N.Y.	Dr. J.P. Dudley, of Buffalo, N.Y.

A.S. Bailey, of Utica, N.Y.
D.C. Bennett, of Cheektowaga, N.Y.

D.J. Baker, of Clarence, N.Y.

H.S. Conklin, of Clarence, N.Y.

*Boston, Massachusetts: The "Boston and Newton Joint Stock Association" departed from Boston on April 16, 1849 overland by way of St. Louis and Independence, Missouri. Several members of this company were machinist and one was reported to be a teacher. Complete membership list was not printed but the officers were identified as:

Bracket Lord, President
Jesse Winslow, Treasurer
A.C. Sweetser, Director
Thomas H. McGrath, Director

Walton C. Felch, V. President
D.J. Staples, Director
H.W. Dickinson, Director

S.D. Osborne, Secretary
A.J. Hough, Director
Ben. C. Evans, Director

Jackson, Tennessee: Albert Searsey and a Dr. __ Hancock departed for California from Jackson, Tennessee following an undisclosed route. Date of departure believed to be the middle of April, 1849.

Carroll County, Tennessee: Major V. Sevier, of Carroll County, departed for the California mines accompanied by his brother Joseph Sevier. Route not listed.

Sumner County, Tennessee: The following company departed from Sumner County for California, via Independence, Missouri:

Major R.B. Alexander
Timothy Johnson
Alexander Scrivener
J. Nicholson
William Lawson
James Crenshaw
Epaminondas Johnston
Lafayette H. Debow

J.H. Sarver
Lt. W.C. Bradley
James H. Martin
Simpson Bennett
A. Ellis
Thomas Duffy
Isaac Byrns /sic/ (Byrnes?)
T.P. Trott
William Akin

William Anthony
Jonathan White
Lewis Riddle
William Brevard
Francis Duffy Jr.
Henry Cox
J.S. Copeland
J. Burgess
Dr. Alex Anthony

Missouri: The "Wellington Mining Company", of Missouri, which was commanded by Captain O.S. Burnham, of St. Louis, Missouri, announced their intention to engage exclusively in mining for gold in California. The route the company was to follow was not indicated. Membership not listed.

Dubuque, Iowa: The following individuals had crossed the river and were ready to start for California:

L.M. Alverson
W.W. Corriell

R. Cox
S. Cox

W.S. Gillman /sic/

Madison, Wisconsin: The following emigrants had departed from Madison, Wisconsin for the California mines:

(*)For complete list of "Boston & Newton Joint Stock Association" see "Notes" section pp. 203-204.

T.W. Sunderland
William Raedall /sic/
E.R. George

A. Harazthy (?)
S. Powers
Luther Fairchild

William Cleghorn
O.B.W. Wilson

Ottawa, Illinois: Below California-bound emigrants departed from Ottawa, Illinois:

M.E. Maynard
Lemuel Wade /sic/
Haven Hines (?)
Gustavus Pierson
Sheldon Young
Hiram White
Jonas Larroway
Andrew Sterling
Thomas Wheeler
Francis L. Fellows
__ Wolf
Peter Bayley and family
Patrick Rowan
Hugh Rowan
Patrick Bannon
Mr. Tally A. McIntosh,
    late Editor & Prop. of
    True Democrat

T.P. Duncan
Jeremiah Lets (Letts?)
Jeremiah Lets Jr. (Letts?)
Stephen Ponner
Dr. D. Whitmore
Samuel Whitmore
William Fennesy /sic/
F. Gritzner
Henry Eddy and family
James Dunn
J.S. Waite and family of 5
    children
James Gallagher
A. Stillman, former Editor
    & Prop. of Joliet Signal
Thomas Clement

P.A. Haven
Carlos Haven
James Owen
Nelson Smith
William McGennes /sic/
    (McGinnis?)
James Connor
Col. George S. Fake
David Fake
J. Zunwalt /sic/ and family
    of 8 chldrn with 3 teams
Harry Wade and family
    /sic/
Peter McIntosh
Lyman Doolittle

Chicago, Illinois: The following company departed for California from Chicago in the early part of April, 1849:

E. Kimberly, a son of
    Dr.__ Kimberly
J.W. Norris, the author of
    the Chicago Directory
Mr. __ Wilson
Mr. __ Coleman

Charles Getzler, a son of
    A. Getzler
*Mr. __ Cowles, son of
    Alfred Cowles
Mr. __ Cartner
Mr. __ Lieser

Mr. __ Smith
R. Hamilton, a son of
    Col.__ Hamilton
Mr. __ Elmer
Mr. Henry Cook
Oliver Clark

Centerville, Indiana: On March 26, 1849 the following emigrants departed from Centerville for California:

Dr. John Pritchard
John Bloomfield
John Frazier
William Young

Isaac Suffrins, of
    Richmond, Indiana
Daniel T. Woods
Henry R. Hannah
Nathan Gibson

__ Simmers
David B. Woods, one of
    the editors of the Whig
John M. Williams, of
    Economy, Indiana

Rushville, Indiana: On April 2, 1849 the below individuals left Rushville for California:

G.R. Tingley
William R. Maddux
J.H. Carr
George Stone

N. Havden (?) (Hayden?)
J.J. Nicholas
Richard Beale
N.W. Cox

Houston Carr
A.J. Crawford
__ Aldridge

(*) Alfred Cowles was further identified as being the Register of the Land Office.

Franklin, Ohio: The "California Mining Company" from Franklin, Ohio, left that city on May 1, 1849 for an eighteen months stay in the California gold region. This group was equipped with ten wagons and forty mules. Members of the company were:

Joseph Hunter, Captain	S.J. Price	H. Moores /sic/
F.A. McCormack, Treasurer	G. Walton	C. Breyfogle
	D. Bryden	E. Barcus Jr.
C.E. Boyle, Physician	E.E. Canfield	G. Chadwick
W. Cain	A.B. Crist	C. Dewitt /sic/
J.S. Demgan	T. Davis	L.A. Denig
C.M. Fisk	J. Krumm	J.C. Lunn
P. McCommon	H. Ranney /sic/	T. Rugg
J.P. Stone	W. C. Stiles	D. Rugg
C.D. Wood	L.H. Sherman	
John Coulter, Lieutenant	J.M. Marple, Secretary	

Cambridge, Ohio: The "Cambridge, Ohio California Company" departed by way of Independence, Missouri for California in the early part of April, 1849. Members of the company were listed as:

Zaccheus Beatty, Captain	William Lofland	Samuel Johnson
James Allison	Dr. J.G. Moore, Secretary	Henry Shively
John M. Clark	John W. Davis	Benjamin Plummer
Jacob Ferguson	Jacob Gray	Adam Conrad
John McKelvy	Samuel M. Roberts	John Hutchison
James V. Davis	Abaslom Suusfrank /sic/	N.L. Wolverton
Campbell D. Bots /sic/ (Botts?)	Aaron Patterson	David S. Suydon
	John A. Scott	Alfred Cook
Thomas Beaham /sic/	James Kirkpatrick	Joseph Ax /sic/
John Boyd	Andrew Hanna	Seth J. Dickinson
William M. Blake	John Beall	

DEPARTURES FROM SCATTERED POINTS On May 16, 1849 the New York Daily Tribune printed another list of emigrant departures for California. In format, the departure lists were similar to the issue of May 3, 1849, furnishing the names of individuals and companies departing from different geographical sites but not always noting the exact departure dates.

The Victoria Company: The Tribune reference of May 16, 1849 indicated this company, under the command of Charles M. Creaner, an old citizen of Texas, had been formed at Victoria, Texas. On April 14, 1849 the New York Herald printed an item referring to the departure of the "Victoria California Company" /sic/ from Victoria on March 18, 1849 for the Sulpher Springs where it would unite with members from other parts going to California. The Herald item listed the company commander as Charles M. Creamer /sic/.

Mississippi & Alabama Emigrating Company: Only a minor reference to this company appeared in the Tribune. The company was listed as being composed of ninety men who would go to California via Fort Smith, Arkansas.

Batesville, Arkansas: Following individuals were identified as Batesville, Arkansas residents going to California with un-determined departure dates:

Thomas Hughes	Capt. Septius Williams	Peter Cheny
William B. Searcy	Harrison Dwinal /sic/	Dr. James E. Pelham
James R. Searcy	John Stone	Lloyd Magruder
Sandy Waugh	William Hughes	J.G. Malcomb /sic/
		Eli Ward and son

The May 16, 1849 issue of the New York Daily Tribune also mentioned that the "Baltimore and Frederick Mining and Trading Company" was enroute to California, and that George M. Harker, late Commercial Editor of the St. Louis Union, was enroute to St. Joseph, Missouri from St. Louis. The same newspaper also announced the arrival in St. Louis, Missouri of the "Berkshire Company" and "Capt. Dixon's Sacramento Company", both units enroute to St. Joseph, Missouri.

DEPARTURES FROM SCATTERED POINTS The New York Daily Tribune of May 1, 1849 printed a list of emigrant departures from various geographical points. The departure dates were not always reflected and routes seldom identified. There follows a compilation of the forementioned article:

Kalida, Putnam County, Ohio: The below emigrants departed for California from Kalida with departure route and date in 1849 not listed:

Lucius E. Hawley	H.G. Lee	Andrew J. Taylor
G.J. Wichterman	J.M. Lee	G.A. Holibaugh
Joseph Wichterman	Thomas Shehan /sic/	Josephus Goble
Jacob L. Beam	John Nicholis /sic/	

Trumbull County, Ohio: Following individuals departed from Trumbull County, Ohio for California during the early part of 1849:

Daniel Jagger	R. Quigly /sic/	Josiah Soule Sr.
John Reeves	__ Atwood	__ Baldwin
__ Wood	__ Hake	__ Packard
__ Baldwin		

Marion, Ohio: Following emigrants departed from Marion, Ohio for California during the early part of 1849:

| John Dumble | H. Van Houten | *G.W. Bowers |
| *J. Brady | John Smith | __ Cooper |

Oak Springs, Missouri: On April 14, 1849 the "Louisville, Kentucky Emigrating Company" met at Oak Springs, near Independence, Missouri, and elected Reuben F. Maury as Captain of the company. Members of this group were listed as follows:

Capt. Reuben F. Maury	George Phillips	George F. Gillis
John Seabaugh	L.S. Gilpin	E.W. Conner /sic/
B.F. Stewart	N. Peabody	__ Poor
B. Holochar	W. Schotin	John Smith
H. Eenboom (?)	John Edwards	John F. Edwards

(*) Preceded the company to purchase supplies.

J.T. Stewart
J.Q.A. Stewart
G. Holesberg
C.T. Darling
C.C. Adkins, of Tennessee
J.A. Bowlin
A.P. Tidball

H. Hickel
M.J. Warren
Jacob L. Seibert
R.W. Seibert
Nathaniel Benton
W. Robinson
A. Miller

John Trier
Alexander Bruner
J.B. Cording
A.S. Caldwell
A.P. Ruger
R.D. Kent

Burlington, Iowa: Following individuals departed from Burlington, Iowa for California during the early part of 1849:

P.F.W. Brooks (?) (F.W. Brooks?)
Peter Jackson
John S. Matthis
Lemon Fouts
Presley Dunlap
James Taylor
William Hendrin
D. Purcell
Jacob Arrick
Campbell Suttle
C. Denmark
Milton Blair
Lucius Austin
Jonathan Donald
J. Miner
William Chichester
__ Bond
Z. Kinsell
S.F. Sgevens /sic/ (Segvens?)
David Wheatley
A.W. Gordon
Joshua Holland
Peter Ke?hler
Daniel Rorer /sic/

Lafayette Brooks
J.S. McClure
Jer Freel /sic/ (Jerome Freel?)
L.P. Reed
M. McCaslin
Charles H. Jordan
Luther Mead
Jos. Myres /sic/ (Myers?)
Thomas Hutchinson
David Russell
Robert Anderson
J.C. Brant
D. Redding
__ Rankin
L.B. Austin
__ Fair
Harvey Blair
John Burkholder
Thomas Sater
Joseph Moffett
James Caudel
N.M. Ives
Jer Buford /sic/ (Jerome Buford?)

Reuben Worrel
George Worrell
Mr. __ Sidell and wife
Moses Jordan
Ephraim Moore
George Pearson
Josiah Suttle
John Farmer
William W. Scott
Arthur Sullivan
*Alonzo Sargent /sic/
Charleston Hughes
William Valentine
*Nahum Sargeant /sic/
C.F. Matthews
N.W. Wile
H. Wile Jr.
James Cochran
Samuel Eikenbury
Hiram Fairbanks
Charles Miller
Albert G. Walong
F.O. Becket /sic/
Jacob Elliott
Levi Moffett

(above emigrants traveling by wagons)

J.S. David
James Buttles
Andrew Sturgis

Oliver Cottle
William Ritchey
Jacob Leffler

Shannon Knox
F. Daniels

(above emigrants with mule teams)

Watertown, Wisconsin: Following emigrants, from Watertown, Wisconsin, departed for California during the early part of 1849.

Stephen Stimpson
Nelson Whitney
Luke Colburn

Henry Waldron
Louis Meyer
Ole Hanson

Amos Steck
James Stevens

Platteville, Wisconsin: Below individuals departed from Platteville, Wisconsin during early part of 1849 for California:

William B. Vineyard
J.H. Barton

E.T. Locke
__ Costs

Major __ Rountrees and Company

(*) Consider alternative listings of "Alonzo Sargeant" and "Nahum Sargent".

__ McKee   T.L. Hammonds   H. Tyler
Dr. W.B. Dows   William Myers

Quincy, Illinois: The following individuals left for California from Quincy, Illinois in the early part of 1849:

James Demares	S.K. Lawrence	Edward Felt
John S. Demares	M. Leach	Job Herring
William Ralph	__ Dobbins	__ Meredith
__ Wilton	Mark Foote	James Headley
J. Switzer	James T. Day and wife	Noah Ball
Stephen Kennard	Ether Page /sic/	__ Woods
O.F. Miller	Robert McGinnis	Oliver Kimball
William H. Benneson /sic/	George Case	H.B. Gibbs
John A. Flack	Dr. William H. Taylor	John L. Cochran
John Rogers	William Hurrell	Ethan Allan
James A. Parker	__ Arrowsmith	William Vaughn
George Adams	Benjamin Mikesell	Joe Pope
B. Minton	Dr. M. Walker	M. Kennard
James Griffith	__ Ireland	__ Ward and son
John Justire	Joseph Isham	Richard Ball
Jasper H. Lawrence	P. Lane	__ Houghton

Millcreek, Illinois: Following individuals residing in the neighborhood of Millcreek, Illinois departed for California during the early part of 1849:

J.O. Robinson	Jesse Thomas	James Connelly
Wesley Tibbs	Elisha Seehorn (?)	Daniel Innman /sic/
Robert Ware	(Seeborn?)	Peter Journey
Jackson Ammon	Eli Seehorn (?) (Seeborn?)	Mr. __ Brown
Abel Harrel /sic/	Alpha Seehorn Jr.(?)	__ Golder
Stephen Thomas	(Seeborn?)	William Blackwell
__ Fields	Royal Crandall	Matthew Wyatt (?)
John Lions /sic/	John Hayes	(Mathew Wyatt?)
William Burkslow	Andrew Innman /sic/	
Royal Herrel /sic/	John Innman /sic	

Winchester, Illinois: The below individuals departed from Winchester, Illinois for California in the early part of 1849:

Hezekiah Evans	Jacob Hamilton	John S. McConnell
James Evans	Edward Saers (?)	Charles Constable
James H. Evans (?)	William York	Samuel Wilson
(James E. Evans?)	James Staunton	John Wilson
Daniel Evans	Dennison Haggard	David Kilpatrick
Edward Evans	Alfred Pond	William Orr
J.S. Deleep /sic/	James Coons	Andrew Hammond
Thomas Tucker	Mr. __ Hardy	Mr. __ Trace
George Tucker	George W. Pettit	

Jacksonville, Illinois: Following Jacksonville, Illinois residents departed for California in the early part of 1849:

J.P. Lancaster   G.W.S. Callen /sic/   J.W. McFarland

William Babb	*__ McElwait	Mr. __ Scott
Henry Babb	John Caldwell	D.W. Nicholson
James Jordan	C.A. Moore	Henry Keener
Augustus Patterson	Isaac Handler	Joseph Swain
C. Patterson	W. Watson	S. Crum
William Wright	William Rockwell	L. Lindsay
E. Foster	Thomas Burker	George Meggison
		*__ McElwait

Additional Illinois Emigrants: In addition to the forementioned Illinois emigrants, the New York Daily Tribune of May 1, 1849 noted that the following Illinois residents departed from respective resident sites for California during the early part of 1849:

William Hanna Jr.	D. Boyd Findley	Hy Paine
John Hanna	Robert Glass	John Glass and family
Sam Hanna Jr.	George C. Smith	James Glass
Green Hanna		

(above from Center Grove, Ill.)

Gottlieb Kaemies (?), of Oquawka, Ill.	A.M. Richards, of Knoxville, Ill.	Daniel Lim (?) (Linn?), of Oquawka, Ill.
		Robert Rice, of Knoxville, Ill.

East Tennessee & California Gold Mining Company: The New York Daily Tribune of May 1, 1849 reported that this company had been rendezvousing for some time at Knoxville, Tennessee. The paper reported the commander of the company as George Alexander Anderson, but the names of the members of the unit were not printed in the cited issue.

SUPPLEMENTARY REPORTS OF EMIGRANT ACCIDENTS AND FATALITIES

The New York Daily Tribune periodically reported accidents and fatalities taking place in wagon train groups going to California. Extracts of these reports are noted below. The issue of the Tribune appears to the left of the incident report.

Newspaper Edition Date	Incident Report
June 6, 1849	Report of death of A.J. Neely, of Mississippi on May 9, 1849 and a Mr. __ Burrows, of New York, dies of cholera on same date. Based upon a letter from Independence, Missouri under date of May 11, 1849
June 18, 1849	Report of a man named __ Harris killed by __ Shields for making improper advances to Shield's wife. Foregoing based upon a letter from Fort Kearney dated May 21, 1849. The Tribune article also noted that General __ Anderson was leading a company from Knoxville, Tennessee. On July 30, 1849 the Tribune stated that Harris had been tried a year earlier for a rape upon a German girl.
July 30, 1849	Peter Kessler returns from a projected trip to California.

(*) Two individuals bearing surname of "McElwait".

Kessler had been shot through the lungs by a John Starkey who with a William Patton tried to deprive him of his property. Kessler succeeded in wounding Starkey and the two culprits were expelled from the overland company. Kessler returned to civilization in a Mormon wagon. He was going to California as member of Eickenberry's Company which left Fort Laramie on May 26, 1849.

August 7, 1849   Report of murder of Joseph King, of Missouri, by Robert Stanfield. This article is based on a letter from Santa Fe, dated July 7, 1849. Item also states that seven out of nine men enroute to California under Green Marshal (Marshall?) were killed on March 20, 1849 when two-hundred Apaches attacked them on the Gila River. Marshall and a Robert Ward were cut to pieces. Another item in this paper, which was based on a report from Fort Kearney, Nebraska, dated June 23, 1849, mentioned George McKinly (McKinley?), of Holton, Maine and John Newry, of Blainsville, Pennsylvania, being wounded by premature discharge of a gun.

August 10, 1849   Mention of graves on the plains of J.A. Park, of Pontotoc, Mississippi, aged 34 years; J.J. Hardy, of Winchester, Illinois, aged 24 years and __ Abbott, aged 79 years.

August 30, 1849   Mention of California emigrants fighting with Indians, which is based upon a letter from James Harris dated June 15, 1849, from Independence, Missouri. A company, enroute to California under a Captain __ Cunningham, was attacked and John Ransom, Joseph Spars and Joseph Nevland (Newland?) were killed. Wounded in the attack was Captain C. Todd, __ Dunlap, __ King and two men bearing surname of Gray.

September 11, 1849   Letter written ninety miles west of Fort Laramie on the Platte River, dated July 3, 1849, and signed "William". This letter announced the deaths of Dr. __ McBeth, H.O. Hays (Hayes?), Colonel __ Fay and the writer's brother, Albert. All deaths were due to cholera.

Another article in the <u>Tribune</u> of September 11, 1849 announced the death of a man named __ McDowell. McDowell had been shot by Indians who had lost family by cholera and blamed the whites for bringing the disease to the country. McDowell's death report was based upon a letter from Fort Laramie dated August 1, 1849.

A third letter in the Tribune furnished a list of graves which had been found between St. Joseph, Missouri and Fort Laramie. The list is reproduced below.

Samuel Campbell, d.May 27,1849, of Mobile, Ala.

William Chapman, d.May 28,1849, of Cincinnati, Ohio

Dr. __ Ryan, d.May 27,1849, no residence

Nicholas Bolemene, no death date, of Illinois

Joseph Sharpe, d.May 21,1849, no residence

John Deguire, aged 54 years, no residence

John Cannon, d.May 8,1849

Levi Smith, d.May 25,1849, of Wilmington, Ind.

E. Wilson, d.May 28,1849, age 17, of Washington Co.,Ark.

J. Land, no other data

H.T. Johnson, d.May 20,1849, of Florence, Alabama

John D. Bradshaw, d.June 20,1849, of Johnson County, Mo.

J.J. Hardy, d.June 9,1849, age 33, of Winchester, Ill.

B.F. Rogers, d.June 5,1849, of Paducah, Kentucky

Joseph Blake, d.June 19,.1849

E.F. Spencer, d.May 30,1849, of Michigan

S.T. Walbert, d.May 30,1849, of Hancock County, Ill.

James McAllister, d.May 21,1849, no residence

B.F. Adams, d.May 10,1849, no residence

Sloan McMillan, d.May 11,1849, no residence

John Albert, d.May 23,1849, aged 76 of New Albany, Ind.

George Winslow, age 25, of Newton, Mass.

James H. Groot, d.May 22,1849, age 25, of Essex, Virginia

John Eathey, d.May 28,1849, no residence

A.B. Donel /sic/ (Alex B. Daniel?) d.May 27,1849, of Red Rock, Iowa

Joseph Hunter, d.June 10,1849, age 56, of Columbus, Ohio

G.H. Corwell, d.June 10,1849, age 20, of Waukesha, Wisc.

William Wells, d.June 28,1849, of Cooper County, Ohio

John Ocland, d.June 22,1849, of Ohio

Levi Smith,
    d.June 19,1849, age 58,
    of Lawrence County,
    Mo.
J.W. Resley,
    d.June 14,1849
Lemuel Lee,
    d.June 3,1849, age 64,
    of Vandalia, Ill.
Capt. Pleasant Gray,
    d.June 9,1849, age 43,
    of Huntsville, Texas
__ Keenan, of Pleasant
    Hill, Mo.
John Hoover,
    d.June 18,1849, age 12
E. Morse, age 60, of
    Poland, Ohio (Masonic
    Symbol on marker)
John Campbell, age 18, of
    Fayette, Missouri, killed
    by accidental discharge
    of gun.
R.S. Croghin,
    d.June 13,1849, age 25,
    of Midway, Kentucky
W.S. Ferguson,
    d.June 21,1849, age 30
    years
F. Bunn, at Scott's Bluff
    (Nebraska)
Joseph Blakely, at Scott's
    Bluff (Nebraska)
Ellis Russell,
    d. June 14,1849, age 53
M. Conover,
    d.June 14,1849, age 27,
    of Waukesha Co.,Wisc.
Charles S. Gilman, from
    vicinity of Rochester,
    New York
L. Fredenberg, of Buffalo,
    New York, shot by
    accident July 5,1849
S.W. Moore,
    d.June 11,1849
Rachel E. Pattison,
    d.June 19,1849. age 19
Mrs. Matilda Taylor,
    d.June 9,1849, of
    Illinois
N.T. Phillips,
    d.June 17,1849, age 32
J.P. Wright,
    d.June 19,1849, age 16,
    of Pleasant Hill, Mo.
Preston Muir,
    d.June 21,1849, age 25,
    of Greene County,
    Kentucky
W.K. Colly,
    d.June 18,1849, age 46,
    of Ray County, Mo.
G.Griffin, grave at base of
    Chimney Rock
James Roby,
    d.June 21,1849, age 20,
    in Mounted Rifles,
    formerly of Ohio
Charles Bishop,
    d.July 8,1849, age 25, of
    Washington City
T.T. Lease, of Mt. Pleasant
    (rest defaced)

Edition Date
September 21,1849   Letter printed relative to the Ithica Pack Train and written from Green Horn Village, at base of Rocky Mountains. Mentions mule train under command of J. Heselp/sic/ and Dr. __ Roberts, of Menard County, Illinois, being captain of ox-team train. Letter notes that a Mr. __ Pixby, of Detroit, Michigan, almost being injured by a buffalo bull and a man from a nearby wagon train, Joshua Burton, of Boone County, Missouri, shot himself.

October 26, 1849   Letter from the Colorado River under date of July 24,1849 from a Mr.__ Anderson to his brother as published in

Edition Date	
	the Lexington, Missouri Express. Letter indicates they had left Fort Kearney on May 9, 1849 and that they were sixty-nine men in the company. There was fear that the company would be attacked by two hundred deserters of the Oregon Battalion who had been threatening them. The letter reported the death of Levi Slagle from the neighborhood of Lexington, Missouri.
November 5, 1849	List of graves west of Fort Laramie as contained in a letter dated August 19, 1849 and sent from Green River:

Dr. __ McDermett /sic/ d.July 21,1849, of Fairfield, Iowa, age 28 yrs.

John Woodside, buried at Warm Spring, d.June 10, 1849

T. George, died June 18, 1849

Jesse Clark Jr, of Breeden, New Jersey, d.June 28, 1849

David Hipes, of Madison County, Ill. d.June 20, 1849, aged 25

N. Glenat, of Dubuque, Iowa, aged 45, d.July 7, 1849

Herr Saltzer, of Indiana, age 22 yrs, d.June 10, 1849

John McDowell, of St. Joseph, Missouri

Mrs. __ Bryan, d.July 25, 1845 (old grave?)

*W. Rector, d.July 28, 1849

George C. Pitcher, late of Henry County, Illinois and formerly of New York, d.July 20, 1849 at Pacific Spring

J.M. Hay (no other data listed)

Mrs. Mildred Moss, late of Galena, wife of D.H.T. Moss, d.July 7, 1849 aged 25 years

John B. Mastin, of Pontatoc, Mississippi, d.July 5, 1849, age 15

Thomas M. Rankin, aged 28 years, d.June 25, 1849, of Missouri

W. Drennon, drowned May 20, 1849 at Platte Crossing, aged 35 yrs. late of Ohio

Nancy Tremble, d.June 25, 1849, at Willows Spring, age 24

William Moore, of Oswego, Indiana, age 56

Joseph Bartlett, d.August 26, 1844 (old grave?)

James Estell, of Lawrence County, Mo., d.June 20, 1849

J.R. Nelson, of Adams County, Illinois, d.June 26, 1849, at Big Sandy

ST. JOSEPH, MISSOURI (March 22, 1850) For the past week several companies had arrived at St. Joseph enroute to California. The following company from Mesheehakee, Indiana was encamped at St. Joseph on March 22, 1850:

William H. Moore and wife	N. Tuller	T. Garrett
C.L. Kemp	R. Cook	

(*) W. Rector also died at Pacific Sandy.

G. Cook	Mr. __ Brook, of	J.B. Kemp, of Centreville,
Mr. __ Leech, of Cass	Centreville, Mich.	Mich.
County, Mich.	Mr. __ Marshall, of Cass	Mr. __ Jones and
	County, Mich.	company, of Cass
		County, Mich.

ST. JOSEPH, MISSOURI (March 19,1850) The below company of emigrants arrived at St.Joseph on March 19,1850 enroute to California. All members were from Chicago, Illinois and they proposed to make the journey with horse teams.

S.P. Burgess	C. Holden	D.S. Moore
Henry S. Burgess	M. Deffenbach	W.S. Moore

Three emigrants from Michigan also arrived at St. Joseph, Missouri on March 19,1850. This company consisted of a Mrs. __ Shun, niece and nephew (both unidentified) and a Mr. __ Jerome. It is believed that several other emigrants accompanied this group but their names were not listed in the primary research source.

ST. JOSEPH, MISSOURI (March 17,1850) The "Penfield Company", from Kendall County, Illinois, arrived at St. Joseph on March 17,1850. This group was under the command of Captain D. Burroughs and they pitched their tents on the west side of the Missouri River where they remained until their departure for California. The group had twenty horses and intended to purchase more before leaving. All were in good health with the exception of William J. Umstad, who had broken a little finger while training his ponies. The company consisted of:

Capt. D. Burroughs	John Lent	Lewis Waterman
Asa G. Burroughs	Norman Eldridge	Freeman Giffard
Benjamin Darnell	James Peckett	Elihue Furgeson
William Ryon /sic/ (Ryan?)	Dennis Sailberry	Isaac Aldridge
Owen W. Jacobs	A. Brown	
John Timerman		
William J. Umstad		

MERCER, PENNSYLVANIA The New York Daily Tribune of April 1,1849 reported that the following party left from Mercer, Pennsylvania to go by the overland route to California:

Thomas P. Stewart	George W. Porter	William B. Woods
Daniel Stewart	John Findley Jr.	Lewis Woods
George Keener	James W. Smith	John M. Magoffin
James O'Neil	Henry Kerr	William Tanner
James Morrison	William Denniston, of	Nicholas Welch, of
James Livermore, of	Findley Township	Delaware
Springfield, Penn.	Henry Barnhart Jr. of	Henry Butterfield, of
Joseph Walker, of West	Pymatuning /sic/	North Liberty, Penn.
Greenville, Penn.	E.H. Downer, of Crawford	
	County, Penn.	

The same issue of the Tribune stated that the following persons departed for California from North Liberty, Pennsylvania at approximately the same time:

Jonathan McMillen	Francis Wadsworth	John Gyer
James Riddle Jr.	Cornelius Gill	Cowden Gyer
David Himrod	Joseph Woodworth	J.F. Satterfield

The <u>New York Daily Tribune</u> of April 1, 1849 also indicated that additional emigrants going to California, via St. Louis, Missouri, included the below group which departed from Brooklyn, Ohio:

E. Corbin, of firm of Corbin & Shaw	D. Sawtell	J. Newell
	Joel Chapman	A. Booth
L. Crittenden	Lewis Felton	Charles Brainard
		F. Ingham

KANESVILLE, IOWA (April 3, 1850) The following emigrants, enroute to California were reported to have arrived in Kanesville by the <u>Frontier Guardian</u> of the forementioned date:

From Illinois:

Dr. James Cameron	C.N. Netware	Dr. John Crim
Samuel Ewing	Reuben E. Lemoin	M.W. Robinson
James H. Breese	George W. Hodgins	G.W. Gale
Charles P. McNamara	S.B. Shumway	E.H. King
J.W.G. Ferris	Samuel Swift	Benjamin Despain
W. Allingham	D.D. Colton	Benjamin Despain Jr.
W.B. Skinner	Sebastin Adams	G.W. Bell
Thomas G. Richmond	John L. Smith	Harrison Presson

From Deseret:	From Indiana:	From Ohio:
Robert Pierce	Valentine Bennett	H.J.B. Seymour
From Iowa:	Samuel M. Weed	From Wisconsin:
James Blake	From Pennsylvania:	Paine Stillwell /sic/
Augustus Jones Jr.	Dr. William W.	
H.C. Ross	Stillwagon /sic/	
S.P. Woodman		

DEPARTURES FROM SCATTERED POINTS The issue of the <u>New York Daily Tribune</u> of April 4, 1850 reported the departure of the following California emigrants:

From Baldwinsville, New York: (via St. Louis, Missouri)

David Tappen	J.H. McClenthen	Henry Culver
John Taggart	___ Curtis	Collin Rouse
S.D. Pickens	Almer North	Alvah Hooker
James Williams	Calvin Randall	
Francis A. Smith	John Dwyer /sic/	

From Akron, Ohio:

A. Hart	D. Hanscom	N. White
I.Y. Young	J. McKibben	R. Carton (Carlton?)
J. Holmes	L. Washburn	H. Boyd
M.A. Wheeler	J. Sherwood	J. Patterson
O. Neal	William Shaw	E. Dugal
J.O. Neal	E. Cummins	C. Scriber
J. Hohner	R.C. Kimble	

William Smagg
S. Gibson
S. Chandler
James Chandler
William Bradley
William Ives
M. Michler
Lewis Kilbourne
James Root
___ Reynolds
W. Gunder
D. Kirby
B. Kirby
J. Gardiner
J.O. Garrett and wife
Emily Garrett
J.O. Garrett Jr.
Hiram Garrett
Sarah Garrett
Henry Garrett
Miss Lorinda Washburn
Miss Maria Dickerman

From Cuyahuga Falls, Ohio:
E. Morton
A. Coke (?) (Cooke?)
Samuel Rattle
George Lillie
Z. Jones
William Rattle
F. Rumrill

From Magadore (no state listed):
G.E. Kent
J.J. Myers
A. Kent
N. Gear
N. May
J.H. Leavitt

No Departure Points on Following Emigrants:
H. Willard
Mrs. ___ Willard
Theo. Willard
H.O. Willard
A. Packard Jr.
H.S. Williams
G. Bales
William B. Judd
John D. Miner
___ Fenn

P. Grifferman
G. Sumner
M. Hennesey /sic/
  (Hennessey?)
A. Kimble
John Cook
J. Wohmen
John Kidder
Joseph Kidder
L.L. Kidder
F. Sumner
J. Remington
J. McKelvey
Jones John /sic/ (John
  Jones?)
Mayer Weil (Meyer
  Weil?)
William White
Charles Carner
King Smith
E. Hull
John Steinbucher

J. Redick
D. Santon
H. Taylor
W. Taylor
Robert Cochran
Y.E. Clark
A. Vaughan

William Jones
N. Miller
C. Smith
J.D. Greene
A. Dehaven
M. Jewett

John Hill
J. Spicer
Eph. Bellows
S. Sparrowhawn
J.D. Whitney
D. Wright /sic/
D. Wright /sic/
O. Wright
M. Porter
A. Fenn
  (above from Aurora, Ohio)

O.H.P. Ayres
William Mease
Levi Krider
W.B. McCune
J. Wido /sic/
John Good
C. Holfemany
Dr. ___ Marshall
A. McDaniel
Lewis Asner
John Hermon /sic/
M.R. Paine
J. Morgan
C.J. Heys /sic/
Andrew Martin
F. Master
John Ticer
Henry Bake (?)(Henry
  Blake?)
George Richey
B.F. Dickerman and wife

S.D. McNeal
C. Ayliff
A. Wood
C. Gillett
E. Randall

B.B. Greene
A.B. Bradley
C. Hall
H. Kynion

William Lewis
Levi Allen
Edwin Allen
J.F. King
R.P. Smith
B. Stanton
P. Hickock
___ Davis
John Devin (Devine?)

William B. Stone	M. Bishop	Charles Kimble
John Allen	Theo. Fenn	John Baddle
James Newing	E. Beach	C. Haskins
L. Bradley	E. Hays /sic/	E. Cook
William H. Garrett	M. Asper	Daniel Powles
Calvin Holt	Joseph Spiker	P. Beale
William Lamb	Joseph M. Yocum	S. S. Peck
A. Chapman	Richard Fassett	C. C. Dewey
L. M. Comstock	S. Snow	J. B. Gibbons
W. D. McClure	John Dulin	Henry Jewett
James R. Jewett	Samuel Dulin	H. Baldwin

(all above from Aurora, Ohio)

F. Stees	John Kryter	T. Smith
G. W. Smith	J. Christy	

(above from Springfield, Ohio)

Georger Yorck	H. Lye	J. Rhinie

(above from Stark County, Ohio)

Seth Hamlin	E. Fry	Dr. L. Northrop
J. Felts	N. Baldwin	

(above from Lima, Ohio)

J. Gates	H. Hetsler	

(above from Suffield, Ohio)

G. Wells	D. Simson(?) (Simpson?)	W. Nelson
G. Andrews	D. Richmond	John Hamlin
J. Falm	M. Breem	J. Allen
		Hiram Stott(?) (Scott?)

(above from Randolph, Ohio)

William Parker	W. D. Myers	George Best
D. Everett	George McKey /sic/	

(above from Richfield, Ohio)

B. Lockwood	L. Davis	William Finch
John Stine	Milton Briggs	

(above from Copley, Ohio)

G. O. Lacey, of Bainbridge, Ohio	H. C. Lacey, of Bainbridge, Ohio	J. Pendleton, of Stow, Ohio
L. Frost, of Stow, Ohio		

ST. JOSEPH, MISSOURI (April 5, 1850) The Saint Joseph Gazette of April 5, 1850 reported that the following company of emigrants from Palestine, Illinois had arrived and were preparing to depart for California:

John Hendron	Enoch Newlin	Kelly Newlin
John Lackey	William McCoy	John McCoy
____Drake	Calvin Newlin	Jonathan Newlin
Frederick Newlin	John Johnson	Isaac Green
Perry Bogard	Nicholas Kellyhan	Bazle Green
Henry Varner	Levi Whitemore	Nicholas Green
George Miller		

In addition to the previously mentioned Illinois company the St. Joseph Gazette issue of April 5, 1850 indicated that the below California emigrant companies had arrived:

From Butler County, Pennsylvania:

C. E. Purviance	J. D. P. Taylor	John Young
A. M. Evans	James Grassman	Limon Young /sic/
J. Bredin	Robert Grassman	D. Barrow
Jacob Shugert	George Bleightner	Conrad Rityet(?)
N. Henchback	John Vageby	A. Kisner
Jacob Kearner	E. Vageby	

From Cynthiana, Kentucky: (arrived April 1, 1850)

M. W. Boyd	A. J. West	W. Russell
R. G. R. Moore	Philip Murphy	

ST. JOSEPH, MISSOURI (April 12, 1850) The St. Joseph Gazette of April 12, 1850 contained several articles dealing with the departure of emigrant companies to California from that city. One of the articles dealt with the departure on April 11, 1850 of a company who decided to make the trip to the mines by foot, without mules, oxen or horses. This group took provisions for forty days and its members consisted of:

Tacitus P. Zander of Milwaukee, Wisc.	Samuel Kelly, of Waterford, Wisc.	Joseph Galbreath, of Schuyler County, Illinois
John Buckingham, of Iowa County, Wisc.	Joseph Alstad, of Waterford, Wisc.	James Barnes, Jo Davis County, Ill.
George D. Hicks, of Shallburgh, Wisc.	Buroughs Thomas /sic/ of Risdon, Seneca County, Ohio	Robert M. White, Belmont County, Ohio
S. D. Pickens, of Baldwinsville, N. Y.	N. C. Kimberly, of Ohio City, Ohio	Ulysis S. Dewey, /sic/ of Elbridge, New York
H. A. Culver, same city as above	John H. Taggart, of Baldwinsville, N. Y.	John E. Duyer, /sic/ of Baldwinsville, N. Y.
A. C. Culver, same city as above	Stephen H. Karney, of same city as above	Almer North, of same city as above
James S. Williams, same city as above	David Tappin /sic/ same city as above	Edward Wright, of Hampshire Township, Hane County, Ill.
Alino F. Smith, same city as above	John M. Hancock, of Megadoar, Summit County, Ohio	
Solomon Watkins, of South Bend, Indiana		

The second departing company of California emigrants was from Rock Island, Illinois. This unit left St. Joseph on April 10, 1849, traveling by horse teams, taking two extra horses to each wagon. The members of this company were:

L. D. Dick /sic/	Delivan Dimick /sic/	Robert Middleham
L. R. Dimick /sic/	Joseph Farmbarge	George Reed
William Francis	Oliver Kincaide /sic/	
Amesworth Wood	N. Nazro Reynolds	

A third group of emigrants at St. Joseph was identified as being from Schoolcraft, Michigan. This wagon train consisted of:

Isaiah W. Pursel /sic/	D. T. Gilbert	Roan McClure

Oliver Eldred	Smith Dychman/sic/	William Finlay/sic/
William Irwin	James Kearney	James B. Finlay/sic/
Thomas Finlay/sic/

The final article regarding California emigrants appearing in the St.Joseph Gazette of April 12,1850 concerned a group that would be departing in a few days. Members of this unit were listed as:

Joseph P. Turner, of LaSalle County, Ill.	James Turner, of LaSalle County, Ill.	E.R. McLaughlin, of LaSalle County, Ill.
Robert B. Patcliff, of Milwaukee, Wisc.

KANESVILLE, IOWA (April 17,1850) On April 17, 1850 the FrontierGuardian printed a list of California emigrants who had arrived in Kanesville. The list appeared as follows:

From Michigan:
Lauren F. Fox	O.J. Day	R. Doan
Benjamin Cooly/sic/	Ira J. Saunders

From Indiana:
Wilkinson De Frees	Thomas Butler	Miller Shenabarger

From Illinois:
John A. King	A.A. Dexter	Cyrus E. Brown/sic/
John W. Shaffer	Nelson Martin	Dr. L.H. Cutler
George J. Niver	Ira Guiltner	William T. Smith
George M. Waters	J.C. Blandin	J.C. Brooks
Andrew Davis	John C. Chapman	Edwin Brooks
Judson Lamphere	Dr. I.S. Thompson	Joseph R. Forward
Alfred H. Rockwell	Theodore A. Cunningham	Cyrus E. Brown/sic/
Wesley D. Plummer	Moses Robinson	John W. Blackman
Edward Lally	G.R. Minchell/sic/	H.B. Miller
Mr. M.R. Patterson	(Winchell ?, Mitchell ?)	John E. Guild
William M. Glover	James B. Rockwell	Horace F. Babbitt
Jacob Wright	Edmund S. Cutler	H.W. Erskine
F.M. Justice	Isaac Hill	J. Nobles
Lewis Andrews	Silas Roe	Leicester King Jr.
Joseph Barlow	James Martin	Laertes S. Smith
E.H.M. Patterson	Zacchus Parker	James Hultz
Edwin Monroe	John H. Wynkop	Reuben Brownson
S.B. Hulse	J.C. Merryfield	John P. Yates
T.C. Orsborne/sic/	J.M. Harold	W.S. Cothrin
(Osborne?)	John Butler	S.C. Plummer, M.D.
Martin L. Shook	William T Hubbard	James Plumbner/sic/
Henry Shaffer	Andrew Fletcher	(Plummer ?)
A.W. Campbell	J.A. Brock	Peter Crayton
		L. Blanchard

From Iowa:
J. McMullin	Moses Dillon/sic/	William Jones Jr.
John A. McKinney	Jackson Schenck	James Jones
George G.G. deLorimier	Damas Robert/sic/	Thompson Jones
George Foster	Nelson Faucher	Isaac C. Hall
M.B. Mead	Morris Rodgers	Joseph C. Patterson
A. Stewart Jr.	M.J. Burton	O.A. Jenks

From Iowa (cont'd):
E. Creole (?) (Creele ?)   C.H. Steffey   J.M. Blanchard
Benjamin Higgins/sic/   Joseph P. Stauts   A.E. Harger (Hanger ?)
Joseph F. Guyer   Alex McDowell   Gary Conger
David Barnes   Joseph P. Heart   Horace Conger
Daniel Dillion/sic/   Reuben Barker/sic/   Russell S. Reynolds
Matthew J. Jinkin/sic/   John Barker/sic/   Robert T. Eaton
Thomas R. Brasher   Samuel J. Parker/sic/   D.C. Cleary
Robert Brasher   William Risk   O.W. Pence (Peace ?)

From Wisconsin:
Garner Aldrich   W.F. Prosser   Simeon B. Sarles
Fohann Frederick   L.L. Cole   Martin P. Owen
   Theuring   Byron N. Lowe   Levison Woodhouse
R.J. Lacey   Josiah Rice   Edgar Bennett
Lyman Gilmore   Marcellus Teetahorn   William E. Jones
Amos Blacknum   E.S. Redington   J.M. Stewart
Zenos Mann   O.H. Conger   Benjamin T.D.L. Harton
Francis Dodge   O.F. Wood(?) (Weed ?)   (Horton ?)
Richard Williams   Stephen Post

From New York: From Vermont: From Texas:
E. W. King   Dr. ____ Vaughan   J.W. Richards and Family
Orson Burlingame   Marvin Kimball

From Maine: From Ohio:
James A. Tibbetts   Harrison Wackman   Sherman Bills

From Fairfield, Iowa: (Members of the Union Company):

George M. Wilkinson   Alfred Colvin   C.S. Shaffenr/sic/
David P. Ramsay   James M. Rea (Res ?,   (Shaffner ?)
James M. Slagle   Ree ?, Ren ?)

ST. JOSEPH, MISSOURI On April 19, 1850 the St.Joseph Gazette published an article which reported California emigrant arrivals in St. Joseph. The following data appeared in the issue:

Arrived overland on March 26, 1850:-From Michigan:

Rev. G.B. Day   Brush Sutherland   A.B. True
Erastus Thurber   Marshall Hermane/sic/

Arrived by water on March 26, 1850:

James Wilson   Mr. ____ McKee   David Sturgis
Mr. ____ Hamilton   Mr. ____ Barnard

Arrived overland on April 13, 1850:-Now encamped at Savannah, Mo.

John Morrison   George W. Buck   Mr. ____ Gillum/sic/
Mr. ____ Smith

ST. JOSEPH, MISSOURI On April 26, 1850 the St. Joseph Gazette published several articles dealing with the arrival of emigrant groups in St. Joseph. The first emigrant unit was organized into a company which consisted of the following individuals:

John Davis, Captain   Samuel Ernis   L.W. Patchin
W.F. Davis, Secretary   J.N. Talley   T. Wyatt
Benjamin W. Shepard   F.B. Patchin   Edward D. Hicks
G.W. Kelly

William Wyatt	James Wyatt	Mathew Bigge/sic/
John Collins	Erastus Bow	M.F. Hamitt
William Hays	S.J. Leek	C.G. Goodrich
J. Hays	James A. Pique	W.F. Davis
F. Wyatt	S. Strong	

The second company of emigrants reported in the Gazette was a pack company from Washington County, Missouri which had arrived in St. Joseph on April 24, 1850 and intended to leave for California on May 1, 1850. This company consisted of:

James B. Spinger/sic/ (Springer ?)	S.W. Spinger/sic/ (Springer ?)	Thomas P. Shore/sic/ Warren H. Patton
John Tuffi (?) (Tufli ?)	Thomas Shore/sic/	John Q. Patton
One black boy named "Henry"	James Shore	

A third emigrant unit in St. Joseph Missouri on April 26, 1850 was a company from Butler County, Pennsylvania which had arrived in the city on April 7, 1850. Members of this company consisted of:

R.G. Jordan	A. Martin	S. Riddle
J.L. Jordan	D. Martin	J. Riddle

The following California emigrants were reported by the Gazette to have arrived in St. Joseph, Missouri on the indicated dates:

Arrived on April 9, 1850:

James Harris	Charles Coventry	Peter Uber
James Simpson	Hugh Lee	W. Williamson
F. Wadsworth	William Basset/sic/	T.J. McCoy
John Guger	Thomas McMillen	Daniel Blakeley
Cornelius Gill	William Rose	Oliver Piser
John Wootly/sic/	James Whittock	William Walling
J.W. Brown	John Kennedy	Samuel Dickey
	Alex. Mortland	John Thompson

Arrived on April 21, 1850:

George Smith	A. Eisler	A. Nicol
Gottich Wiseman	____ Keyser	____ Coppersmith

The final emigrant company reported by the Gazette of April 26, 1850 was a company from Jamestown, Grant County, Wisconsin, which was encamped seven miles out of St. Joseph, Missouri, on the west side of the river. This unit was intending to depart for California on April 29, 1850. The company was composed of:

W.B. Spencer	J.B. Penn	Dr. William Prentiss
Noah Vanvolkenburgh	William H. Whitesides	J. Lothrop/sic/
Josiah Rithey/sic/ (Ritchey ?)	Samuel Whitesides	Abraham Carnes
	James Virden/sic/	R. Killborne/sic/ and
C. J. Cumings (Cummings ?) and Company	Aaron Wels (Wells ?) and Company	company

ARKANSAS (April, 1850): The Daily Picayune of New Orleans, Louisiana printed an article on April 30, 1850 stating that Judge R.C.S. Brown would lead a company to

California and the group intended to depart on May 10, 1850. The Picayune based their article on an item which appeared in the Van Buren Intelligencer (Arkansas).

KANESVILLE, IOWA (May 1, 1850) On May 1, 1850 the Frontier Guardian of Kanesville, Iowa published a list of emigrant arrivals in that town. The below list reflects emigrants enroute to California:

From Iowa:
A.J. Henderson
V. de Lorimier
J.H. Jennings
Thomas Bandy (?)
  (Baudy?)
S. Chamberlain
Jackson McElroy
Jerome W. Coffin
Andrew Huffin
Nathan Bass (?) (Buss?,
  Bunn?)
Morris Eggleston
Milton B. Gordon
John Sloan
Charles L. Moss
William J. Saunders
H.C. Terrill
Noah J. Snow
Alfred B. Mecham
H.J. Mecham

William C. Rees
John P. Quigley
Caleb Bucknam
Robert Logan
William Hutton
W.J. Bucknam
Thomas Francis
David Jones
Augustus Jones
B. Ford
G.B. Hamilton
Jefferson Garner
J.M. Baker
F.B. Kleecker
Isaac Bullock
Edmund Shepherd
Eber L. Mansfield
Charles Crippen
Eli Pannell (?) (Pennell?)

H.B. Horn and Company
Dr. H.A. Silsby
Charles D. Davis
John Q. Myers
Charles W. Bryan
Thomas Cowan
George Hellis
Joel Bailey
G.W. Davis
T.S. Cannon
R. Stephenson
Morris Martin
J.B. Massick
E.M. Downs
John Bandy (?) (Baudy?)
J.N. Saunders
John B. Scott
James Triggs
William A. Hawthorn/sic/
A. Vaughn

From Wisconsin:
Edward L. Johnson
Ames Blackburn/sic/
O.N. Higley
Jerry Parsons
John Clegg
George Criger
Nelly Gray
Henry P. Starks
George Lemon
P.D. Lewis
Henry Smith
William D. Tourtclett
Paul Lindstram (?)
  (Lindstrom?)
Harrison P. Willard
Sylvanus de Lafayette Fox
John Carpenter
C.N. Norton
Clouden Stoughton
Thomas Eelbeck
Johnson A. McEwan

Levi Welden
Egbert A. Wiley
David McCommens
L.K. Greenleaf
John Woodhouse
Reuben Ellsworth
William Crites
Lucy P. Crites
James James Jr./sic/
James H. Scofield
L. Tannenwould/sic/
  (Tannenwood?)
James B. Boeknell (?)
  (Bucknell?, Bocknell?)
Levi Reynolds
Henry Himebauch/sic/
James Toay
W. Henry
Robert A. Wrisley
C.M. Putney
C.A. Forsyth

R.Y. Rendel (?) (Rundel?)
Lewis L. Cole
John W. Winders
Zenos Mann
Egbert R. Hurlbut
Leander Keyes
John Gorman
William Vincent
William G. Barrett
William Turner
Reuben Clark
Thomas M. Clark
N.W. Richardson
David Drerer/sic/
  (Drever?, Dreyer?)
Lorenzo Palmer
George A. Palmer
Ellis Seed
Dr. H. Van Vleck
Nelson V.A. Cron

From Wisconsin (con't):

J.J. Gilson
George Vincent
Dow Vincent

Edward Sumner
Loren A. Noyes
James Noyes
Henry Yaw

W.E. Sumner
George Colt
Charles Leonard Jr.

From Illinois:

Joel S. Barns/sic/ (Barnes?)
Elijah Camp
John Griffin
Rufus Moore
Bartlett Shaw
Morris S. Herrick
L. King Jr.
David Mumms
Norman Buck
Samuel Buck
Seth Gates
Erastas N. Ormsby
Sylvester Tiffany
Samuel Punches
James C. McBridge
Henry Johnson
J.P. Thompson
J.B. Thompson
James M. Humphrey/sic/
Marshal B. Burr/sic/
M.R. Patterson
John Knight
James F. Knight
S.B. Farwell
John Patterson
A. Bradbury
R.E. Lemoine
William Jones
James M. Humprhey/sic/
John Stephenson
Almon Ticknor
Cornelius Knapp
William Horton
George W. Brimhall
Almonson Metcalf

Luther Woodward
T.W. Lackore
Edward Fay and son
Joseph Lamb
Abner Gale/sic/
Harlow E. Bundy
Horace F. Babbitt
Jerome Holsted/sic/ (Halsted?)
Jacob Adams
John H. Paddock/sic/
William S. Sargent
Charles Beard
Wallis S. Buell
Phillip Lepper
Calvin Tiffany
William Terwilliger
Ziba Dimmick
John H. Paddock/sic/
James F. Rice
A.H. Dawson
Leonard Thomas
Daniel Louderback
Joseph Keith
Minor Hammond
Miles Sheppard
W.E. Parker
A.T. Thatcher
P.H. Postlethwaite
Stillman Slocumb
Levi Wheeler
Phelix M. Harris/sic/
J.D. Charles Crocker (Charles Crocker?)
Columbus Hesley (?) (Hosley?)

George H. Hall
Horace Dwelly
N.B. Bullock
Abner Gale/sic/
George D. Fowler
Stanton Prentiss
Almon Fowler
Henry A. Goodyear
Samuel B. King
William Clark Jr.
Samuel R. Taylor
Lorenzo P. Terwilliger
Lester F. Dana
William W. Thomson/sic/
George Longworth
Henry S. Bloom
John Butler
George Tyrie/sic/ (Tyler?)
Edwin W. Allen
A.A. Doxsee/sic/ (Dorsey?)
Joseph L. Blansett
Henry Cornagle
S.S. Bullock
Edward B. Bates
George Ibertson
Samuel Hall
George W. Lamfear
Jonathan Heywood
Leavitt Balloon
William F. Davis
Peter Shelton
Robert J. Kirk
A.D. Bishop

From Indiana:

A. Freeman
Daniel Pickrel/sic/ (Pickrell?)
James M. Rodgers
John Murphy and son
Christian Muffit/sic/
Robert Curl
Charles Noble

William Dougall
Joshua Harlan
Joseph Plum
John C. Peebles
Lewis F. Parker
William J. Denny
Jacob Haynes

Warren Dunning
James Branen/sic/ (Brannen?)
Joseph Ramsdell
Peter Keith
Elisha Keith
Robinson Ramsbey

From Tennessee:
Thomas Lawson
From Pennsylvania:
Frederick Schrader
From Vermont:
Marvin Kimball
From New York:
Darius Smith
From Michigan:
David Cronemiller
William Engle
James Campbell
Franklin L. Barnes
John G. Peak
B.S. Estlow
Casper Reed

From Missouri:
Thomas S. Dorey
From Virginia:
George M. Asbury/sic/
   (Ashbury,Asburry?)
From Isle of Man:
Willliam Christian

Adam Henderson
Enos Dutton
S. Scribner
Charles A. Lawrence
John A. Daniels
William Rose
Enos Himebouch (?)
   (Himebauch?)

From Ohio:
Jacob Kelley
Isaac Asburry/sic/
   (Ashbury,Asbury?)
James Hardestry/sic/
   (Hardesty?)
James Temple

John Hate/sic/
J.M. Wells
George Anderson
Thomas W. Glass
William L. Lawrence
Thomas Johnson

The Frontier Guardian of May 1,1850 also published a list of emigrants that were organized into companies as follows:

"Coldwater Company" (from Michigan)
Green Arnold   Harris Weaver   Amos Fox
"Extract Comapany" (from Waukegan, Illinois)
George Ferguson   Daniel Adams   Moses Chatburn
Alexander B. Ferguson Henry Hiers/sic/ (Hyers ?) Henry Porter
Hawley Dickinson   P. Cary
Mrs. ___Southwick   John Sherwood

"Desmoine Company, No.1"
The "Desmoine Company No.1" (sic)was organized on April 18,1850 and the following individuals were elected as officers: William Risk, Captain; Daniel L. Bowen,Lieutenant; Dr.J. Beirce, Sergeant of the Guard; Levi Eckley, Wagon Master; Rev. ___Presson, Chaplain. Risk, the Captain, had crossed the Plains in 1847, and returned in 1848. The company was to leave Kanesville, Iowa on May 2,1850 with twenty bushels of corn per team, being the first ox train to leave the Bluffs during the 1850 period. Members of the company were:

Hugh M. Leffler   Dr. A. J. Henderson   Dr. J. Peirce
Richard Leffler   William W. Hart   Moses Parker
Hans Garsey   James E. Goodrich   Harrison Presson
Samuel Roods/sic/   James Huff   Reuben Presson
   (Rhodes?)   M. Colt   Butler Presson
M.G. Standeford/sic/   Elias Loshmet   E. Hymer
   (Standford?)   A. Loshmet   J.B. Hymer
S. Robinson   Benjamin Colt   Miner Brown/sic/
Joseph Miller   Robert Morrison   J.H. Baxter
H. Hustin/sic/   Levi Eckley   Robert Harrell
J.M. Cooper   Dow Eckley   J.M. Miner/sic/
Onestis Anderson   John Eckley   N. Scott
Aaron Lemmons/sic/   William W. Anderson   J.L. Anderson
George Dismy(?)   James Smith   D.L. Bowen
Charles Benton   James Duncan/sic/   H.L. Wholly/sic/

Thomas Hays/sic/   James Friggs   Caleb Sales
William Dustan   J.T. Guinn   William Risk
J.G. Dustan   L. Roods /sic/ (Rhodes?)   Moses Dillon
Daniel Dillon   William Disnoph (?)
Samuel Russell   L. Hall

"Excelsior Company, No. 1"

This company was organized on April 22, 1850 and they departed the Kanesville, Iowa area on April 24, 1850 for California. Members of the unit who were elected officers were: G.J. Shaffer, Captain; J. Bonnet, Lieutenant; J.B. DeWolf, Sergeant; J.H. Moore, Wagon Master and Samuel C. Plummer, M.D., Engineer. Company members consisted of:

H. Shaffer	William T. Reed	John Herron
A. Shaffer	H. Griffin	William Brady (?)
Andrew Kyles	John Shellhammer	S. Macklin (?) (Mecklin?)
Peter Eby	Aaron Shellhammer	Alonzo Joy (?) (Jay?)
Daniel Cramer	T.A. Hitchcock	Eli Durben (?) (Durbin?)
Hiram Hilton	Joshua Wilder	W.W. Aldridge
James Blake	S.S. Sewell	J. Holstead(?) (Halstead?)
Jacob Frazier	H. Bartlett	L. Inman
C.D. Davis	D.D. LeFollett	George Prull
James Duncan/sic/	Orson Cord(?) (Card?)	P. Bly
H. Bundy (?) (Bandy?)	H. Goodyear	James Plummer
H. Norris	B. McDole (?) (McDale?)	W. Cothrin
Thaddeus Morrell	C. _____	C.B. Jarvis
E.M. Palmer	M.S. Herrick	N. Crooks
L. King Jr.	_____ Merryfield	William Proctor
Joshua M. H_____	George Wright	M. Shineberger (?)
P. Chesshire/sic/	G.L. Douglass	(Shimberger?)
(Cheshire?)	S. Lewis	John Mitchell
Thomas Butler	Russell Davis	
John Roberts	Lewis Quear (?) (Queer,	
W. Manning	Queen?)	

An additional eighteen men were members of this company. Due to the inability of the author to decipher entries in the research source, the eighteen names are missing from the above company list.

"Northern Illinois Union Company"

This company of California emigrants left Kanesville, Iowa on April 25, 1850. This unit was under the command of G.W. Bell with S. Shaw as First Lieutenant and William Patten holding the position of Second Lieutenant. The research source list contained the below names as members of this organization:

Stephen Post	Hugh McNeil	Henry Shafer
Robert Cook	Nelson Fuller	Thomas Garratt/sic/
J.W. Martling	George F. Vedder	*Capt. James Robertson
William Anderson	John Wesley Webley	Byron N. Lowe

Additional Members**
Alex Blair **   James Walker **   James McGrath **

(*) One source lists James Robertson as Captain in place of G.W. Bell.
(**) One source lists these as the only members of this company.

Joseph H. McGrath	G.H. Boynton	Thomas H. Loehr
Thos. C. Thompson/sic/ (Thomson?)	Robert J. Walker	Jacob Hotspiller
	A.H. White and Company	Andrew Campbell
James P. Thomson/sic/ (Thompson?)	Clark W. Childs	Charles Doss (Dess?)
	Frederick Sibeck	Aldrich M. Rowley/sic/
Augustus Huffman/sic/	George Marvin	Warren Morse
A.W. Hazard	James Horrison/sic/ (Morrison?)	
Andrew Jackson Drake		

In continuing its list of emigrants organized into companies, the <u>Frontier Guardian</u> of May 1, 1850 indicated that the "Pioneer Company of California Emigrants" had departed from Kanesville, Iowa on April 22, 1850. The California-bound unit was commanded by Captain R.B. Clark. F.C. Patterson was the company First Lieutenant and James M. Rae and David Ferris were designated as Second Lieutenants. Members of the unit were:*

D. Mumms	George Barnes	George Hay/sic/
E.W. Mandell	James Bertholf	John Taylor
Philip Wing	Peter Bertholf	James Paquin
Dr. D.H. Brewer	Leva Pratt (Levi Pratt?)	D. Kane
O. Cooley	J.C. Williams	L. Ferris
S. Dunn	G. Criger/sic/	F. Lewis
L. Hall	George Leland	H.J. Lewis/sic/
Hill Whitmore	F.C. Patterson	E.S. Risington (?)
L.W. Sanborn	Ira Hall	C.N. Widner

The following individuals, members of the "Union Company, of Fairfield, Iowa" were reported to be encamped in the vicinity of Kanesville, Iowa during the latter part of April 1850:*

Alfred Colvin	John Clark	Faucher Stimson/sic/
David P. Ramsay	Richard Williams	Daniel O. Rayner
O.F. Weed	Benjamin Jackson	L. Keyes
Harrisin Griswold	O.N. Congar	J.W. Winders
Theodore Kendall	John Fish	S.V. Thompson
L. Greenleaf	Alfred Hickox/sic/	George F. Hatch
George Coryell/sic/	Mark Hickox/sic/	Henry B. Hatch
O.R. Phelps	R.D. Hickox/sic/	Ezra Hatch
Mathew Moralew (?) (Morslew?)	Edward Heard	Griffin Frazier
	L.L. Cole	W.F. Prosser
William Daykon/sic/ (Dayton?)	Frederick Kessler	Mason Clark
	Rufus B. Clark	Levi Knowlton/sic/
S. Haysey/sic/ (Hasey?)	M.G. St. John	J.M. Stewart
A. Hasey/sic/ (Haysey?)	____ Latimer	S.P. Stoughton
A. Rickcord/sic/	C.B. Polkhamus/sic/ (Polhemus?)	William Weed
J. Davis		J. Burgess
Benjamin Schillinger	Sylvester Hall	Zacharias Squires
Oscar Matteson/sic/	Morris Willey/sic/	Ogden Squires
Charles Harris	Henry Harper	Reed Ferriss/sic/
Peter Cook	David Ferris/sic/	Henry Telver
George Wilkinson	James M. Rea/sic/ (James M. Rae?)	
Chris S. Shaffer		

(*) Because of listings of officers names, the "Pioneer Company of California Emigrants" and the "Union Company of Fairfield, Iowa" may have been inter-connected.

Rufus Stebbins
Samuel Pierce
Ezek Pierce/sic/
Augustus Jones
James Bertholf/sic/
Peter Bertholf/sic/
J. Hall
F.B. Lewis

Edward Smith
Charles Aviril (?) (Avirl?, Averill?)
Thomas Dow
W.H. Lamb
H.J. Lewis/sic/

Peter Johnson
Joel Bailey
J. W. Collin(?) (Coffin?)
J.S. Juce
H. Juce
Luther Juce

The <u>Frontier Guardian</u> of May 1, 1850 reported that the "Waukegan Banner Company of Californians" had been organized at Kanesville, Iowa during April, 1850. According to the source the members of this company "exclude the habits of gambling and profane language, all grossly immoral practices and they did not intend to travel on the sabbath day". The company departed Kanesville on April 20th, just after the election of Levi L. Lathrop, the new train's Company Captain, and A.B. Andrews, the unit's Secretary. Members of the company were reported to be:

Benjamin F. Porter
J.B. Porter
Henry Gadden
John Duell/sic/
C.B. Rose
Peter Lincbeck (?) (Lindbeck?)
William J.W. Johnson
Warren Hough
Patrick Deubar (?) (Denbar?, Dunbar?)
John Caltender
Daniel Woodford
H. Rose
John Woodhouse
Levison Woodhouse
Mark Hadley
George Evans
William Scott

H. Wallace
Alex Blumy/sic/
James Ferry
Samuel Reynolds
C. Clingman
John Gudley (?) (Gunley?)
George Gudley (?) (Gunley?)
James Cassidy
L.D. Dany
S.F. Dany
Henry Snessby
George Vandimack
Thomas C. Foreman
John Conig (?) (Cosig?, Cunig?)
____ Jeptha (?) (Jepths?)
C.P. Thompson

William B. Lathrop
A.F. Parker
Horace A. Kent
Theron Parsons
James Keiffer
Charles Burish
Chauncey Huffman
Patrick Coyle
Peter Duffy
David M. Rollins
Charles Leonard
James Byrge/sic/
A.K. Nichols
J. Hartnett (?) (Hartnell?)
____ Hall
Charles R. Woods
James B. Alger
Abner Alger

The "West Point Company" and the "Persifer Company" departed Kanesville, Iowa for California during the latter part of April, 1850. The departure date was either April 20 or April 29, 1850. These two companies were under the command of Major E. Creel, with Captain R.W. Miles in charge of the "Persifer Division" (at times listed as the "Persifer Company") and Captian C.H. Steffey in charge of the West Point Division (also listed as the "West Point Company"). The acting Surgeon of the two groups was L.S. Thomson. The following is a list of the individuals comprising the two units:

<u>Persifer Division:</u>
Andrew Fletcher
David White
Robertson White

Charles Hearn
Anthony W. Caldwell
A.J. Caldwell

Charles R. Lindsay
Lewis McAllister
William McAllister

William Bradford	R.N. Alexander	L.B. Hall
John Hearn /sic/	William Lindsay	George W. Fanning
Elias Thompson	William H. Thompson	Harvey Herrin /sic/
Clark Pierce	Smith Tutil /sic/ (Tuttle?)	
Edward Thorp /sic/	George McPherrin	

West Point Division

G.K. Minshall	John A. McKenney	Joseph P. Stotts
Alexander Stewart	William P. Casey	Joseph F. Guyer
Joseph P. Hart	Reuben Barker	David Barnes
Isaac Hatfield	John Barker	Andrew Harger
Ellis Seed	Bart Shaw	J.M. Strahan
H.B. Miller	J. Spears	John W. Blackman
L. Sims Thomson	Joseph C. Patterson	S.P. Woodman
Jackson Schenck	William Jones Jr.	Isaac Hill
T.B. Hall	James Jones	Wesley D. Plummer
E. Thompson (Ellus Thompson?)	Thompson Jones	S.F. Dodge
	A.S. Ireland	C.S. Stall
William Hastings	J.W. Moore	Lewis Andrews
Lorin Auger	David Grant	

According to the Frontier Guardian of May 1,1850 the "Grand Mustang Company, No.1" left Kanesville, Iowa for California on April 30,1850. This unit was from Ogle County, Illinois and it was under the command of Captain Alfred Mory. Rufus Moore had been selected as the company Lieutenant and Henry Benn, the Surgeon. Members of this organization were listed as:

Tilghman Slifer /sic/	J.H. Hunaden (?)	T.A. Cunningham
G.H. Landon	(Hunsden?)	Hiram Herrick
Henry Moore	Andrew Coakly /sic/	William Slaughter
John Moore	(Coakley?)	C.P. Bridge
William Welk	Patrick Dully /sic/	
John Wilson		

ST. JOSEPH, MISSOURI (May, 1850) The St. Joseph Gazette of May 3,1850 contains a list of members of the "McPike & Strother" wagon train. The issue also contains the constitution and by-laws of this organization and they note that R.B. Ellis was chosen as the train Captain; J.L. Taylor, as Secretary; J. Priest (also listed as John W. Priest) as train Lieutenant: and R.L. Ward as train Commissary. One section of the by-laws notes that the time of rising each day, while on the trail to California, would be by sound of a bugle at 4:00AM.

Members of the "McPike & Strother" train were identified as:

Dr.R.B. Ellis of St. Louis, Mo.	William H. Walker, of Scott County, Ky.	Dr. John L. Taylor, of Palmyra, Mo.
J.H. Netherland, of Scott County, Iowa	Dr. E.M. Bartlett, of Louisiana, Mo.	R.S. Lindsay, of Scott County, Ky.
James Stone, of Louisiana, Mo.	Samuel S. Kennedy, of Louisiana, Mo.	Marion W. Gorden /sic/ (Gordon?), of Louisiana, Mo.
James A. Henderson, of Clarksville, Mo.	Alfred Demming, of Marion County, Mo.	James W. Jeffries, of Marion County, Mo.
Elisha J. Carson, of Marion County, Mo.	John W. Childs, of N. Albany, Iowa	

Thomas J McClure, of N. Carlisle, Ohio
Jeremiah Penix, of Louisiana, Mo.
Benjamin Rose, of Louisiana, Mo.
John G. Penix, of Pike County, Mo.
William A. Mackey, of Clarksville, Mo.
James R. Bartmess /sic/ of Clark County, Mo.
John W. Priest, of Marion County, Mo.
E. L. Smoot, of Marion County, Mo.
James B. Wells, of Pike County, Mo.
John W. Martin, of Bonaparte, Van Buren County, Iowa
W. S. Roy Sr., of Marion County, Mo.
W. S. Roy Jr., of Marion County, Mo.
Samuel Sampson, of Lancaster County, Penn.
W. J. Williams, of Pike County, Mo.
John Kimderlin, of same as above
Harry Wilbarger, of same as above
James M. Hudson, of same as above
R. L. Ward, of Marion County, Mo.
Thomas Brothers, of Louisiana, Missouri
Henry Brothers, of same as above
Samuel Bryant, of Clark County, Mo.
W. H. Menefer, of Marion County, Mo.
M. Q. Townsend, of Westport, Ky.
B. L. Ulsie, of St. Louis, Mo.
F. W. Smith, of Washington, Iowa
R. W. Burnel, of Washington, Iowa
John R. Allison, of Pike County, Mo.
Samuel E. Hendricks, of Pike County, Mo.
B. F. Peck, of Clarksville, Mo.
William H. Roberts, of Scott County, Mo.
George Greene, of Scott County, Mo.
John White, of Lee County, Iowa
Edward Covington, of Edgar County, Ill.
Simeon H. Johnson, of Marion County, Mo.
William C. Barby, of Pike County, Mo.
C. H. Cull, of Adams County, Illinois
William Hay, of Pike County, Mo.
Thomas J. Newland, of Pike County, Mo.
John Kels, of Pike County, Mo.
Isaac J. King, of Pike County, Mo.
James Willis, of same as above
J. McCoy, of same as above
Richard H. Cornelius, of Marion County, Mo.
J. A. Haugh, of same as above
Thomas Majors, of same as above
A. W. Bailey, of same as above
Rev. Thomas Morrow, of Indianapolis, Iowa /sic/ (Indianola, Iowa?, Indianapolis, Ind.?)
John P. Lennen, of Pike County, Mo.
H. Seymour, of Grand Rapids, Mich.
A. M. Hannah, of Indiana
R. W. Ellis, of St. Louis, Mo.
C. E. Willis, of Pike County, Mo.
William Lynch, of Germantown, Tenn.
B. C. Strother, of Germantown, Tenn.
William C. Moore, of Germantown, Tenn.
John F. Kerr, of Ashley P. C., Missouri
D. L. Averell, of Frankfort P. C., Missouri
R. S Pendry, of Quincy, Ill.
William H. Bartlett, of Louisiana, Missouri
William L. Brown, of Louisiana, Missouri
John Richmond, of Hannibal, Mo.
B. Young, of Marion County, Mo.
George E. Sisson, of Pike County, Mo.
Ed. Sisson, of same as above
E. Hughes, of same as above
R. S. McOuat /sic/ (McQuat?), of Marion County, Mo.
Robert Trotter, of Ireland
James W. Marshall, of Missouri
J. E. Shaw, of Pike County, Ill.
John Parks, of same as above
____Bradley, of St. Louis, Missouri
John Foulkes Jr., of Louisiana, Mo.

Ferman Long, of Pike County, Mo.
Timothy Hoice, of same place as above
P. B. Sillheimer, of Wisconsin
Henderson Curty, of Wisconsin
Mrs. ____ Pollard, of St. Louis, Mo.

James McPike, of Pike County, Mo.
John McPike, of same as above
R. B. McDonald, of Illinois
A.J. Smith, of Wisconsin
Mrs. ____ Russell, of St. Louis, Mo.

J. W. Orr, of Pike County, Mo.
Alfred Pike /sic/, of sof Pike County, Mo.
John Spears, of Wisconsin
John Warmbaker, of St. Louis, Mo.
E. J. Strother, of Pike County, Mo.

The St. Joseph Gazette of May 3, 1850 also reported that a company of California emigrants from Beloit, Wisconsin, who called themselves the "Badger Gold Hunters", had arrived in St. Joseph, Missouri on April 25, 1850. The company was encamped about two miles from the town and the train consisted of ten wagons and sixty-two animals. Members of this unit were identified as follows;

Capt. W. D. Hilyer
J. M. Daniels
J. Bartlett
B. Harley
E. Stocking
E. J. Dole
W. Dole
N. Brown
L. Sawyer
E. Goddard

F. Allis(?) (P. Allis?)
Dr. O. T. Maxson
L. S. Perkins
H. A. Benson
S. G. Colley
S. Moore
H. E. Howard
H. Sanborn
E. Chesebrough /sic/
R. Ramsey

Dr. George Carey
J. Gordon
J. M. Tower
H. L. Warner
J. B. Colley
H. Hill
T. Griffiths
J. M. Cole
J. Roberts

The foregoing issue of the Gazette carried a report on a small group from Gundy County, Illinois that had arrived in St. Joseph, Missouri on April 25, 1850. This unit was scheduled to leave St. Joseph on April 27th and join the "Tailor McLean Company" (sic-Taylor McLean?), at old Fort Kearney. Individuals in this company were listed as:

Dr. B. E. Dodson and lady   Albert Knapp and lady   N. B. Dodson

In addition to the above companies, the St. Joseph Gazette of May 3, 1850 also reported that a company from Sidney, Shelby County, Ohio, had arrived in St. Joseph on April 15, 1850. This unit was to leave for California during the second week in May, 1850. The company was reported to consist of:

H. Mars (?) (Mara?)
J. D. Barkdell

J. W. ____
Christopher Mann

A. G. Miller

Another company from Shelby County, Ohio was reflected in the same issue of the newspaper. The company's arrival time and departure date was not listed. Members of this company were identified as:

M. S. Bush
G. E. Abbot

J. Caldwell
E. A. Eusey (?)

John Henley

ST. JOSEPH, MISSOURI (May, 1850) The St. Joseph Gazette of May 10, 1850 mentions a number of emigrant companies departing for California from St. Joseph, Missouri. The

Gazette reported that the following company from Fayette County, Ohio, left their camp in Nodaway County, Missouri on May 9, 1850 for old Fort Kearney:

No. 1-
Alfred M. Ogle	Francis A. Patrick	Thomas Brannon /sic/
Alfred Smith	James Smith	

No. 2-
John H. Robinson	Franklin L. Nitterhouse	William Blue
Andrew J. Jeffries		

No. 3-
Frederick Sprecher	David Headington	Baldwin Millihan
Benjamin F. Wiley		

No. 4-
James Lyly /sic/	James Cockerell	James Rowe
Morris Rowe		

No. 5-
Thomas Davis	Daniel B. Clark	John Robinson
James W. Bridwell /sic/		

No. 6-
John White	Thomas Wood	Daniel Leib
Thomas Prizer		

No. 7-
John Murray	John Glenn	Robert Duncan
Henry Morse		

The same issue of the Gazette reported the makeup of "D. McLean's Company". This California bound group was made up of the below segments:

No. 1-
William H. Beggs	George Sites /sic/	James M. Black
John Wood	Horris Sites /sic/	

No. 2-
William Hidy /sic/	William Pool	Thomas R. Grubb
David Pucket	W. K. Mahan	

H. Dale's Mess-
Henry Dale	James Aigen	James L. Williams
Adams W. Lemon /sic/	Adam S. Nigh	

Hendrickson's Mess-
Robert M. Hendrickson	Ferguson Malcom	George Michael
Daniel Fraggins	Presley Fraggins	

Dixon's Mess-
Ellis Dixon	Kelly Dixon	Jacob Sperry
Henry Hopps	Nelson Clouser	

Compton's Mess-
Thomas Compton	Harrison Bryant	Jackson Bryant
Eli Yeoman		

Dewitt's Mess-
Mr._____Dewitt /sic/	Jeremiah Allen	Francis Shannon
John Stokesberry	Thomas Rankin	Samuel Wilson

Wright's Mess-
Thomas Wright	David Wright	James H. Evans
Robert Stewart	Philip Lewis	

Smith's Mess-
Isaac Smith   Archibald McGahem /sic/   James J. Stewart
David Loofbourrow /sic/

Wendel's Mess-
Ham Wendel   Henry Burnett   Charles C. Latham
Samuel Millihan

The St. Joseph Gazette of May 10, 1850 also carried an item that a emigrant company from Meigs County, Ohio, bound for California, was encamped near the river, opposite St. Joseph. This group intended to leave for the plains within a few days. The company, travelling with eight wagons, consisted of the following:

E. Cotterel	R. Stivers Sr.	Dr. ____Byers
W. Cotterel	G. Stivers	____Tubbs
____Gardiner	A. Stivers	A. Carr /sic/
____Chase	C. G. Stivers	____Parker
____Mehany	R. Stivers Jr.	____Gilbert
____Hassetton /sic/	____Page	____Allen
(Haselton?)	____Cummins /sic/	____Probst
____Young	J. Stivers	____Thomson
____Beatty	J. Karr /sic/	____Hubbell
____Price	____Simson /sic/	J. Wilson
____Percy	Dr. ____Westfall	D. Wilson
____Sylvester	____Marsh	J. Riggs
____Anderson	____Brown	P. Riggs
J. Smith	____Whitemore	

A company known as the "Janesville Gold Hunters No. 1", from Janesville, Wisconsin, left St. Joseph, Missouri on May 6, 1850. The departure of the company was reported in the foregoing issue of the Gazette. Company members were listed as follows;

Colonel O. Guernsey	A. W. Hurlburt	W. B. Shipman
D. Cross	William F. Barker	James H. Campbell
William H. McGlovern	Jacob Walsath	
Frank Storm	L. F. Bennett	

The final emigrant company reported in the Gazette of May 10, 1850, was under the direction of Captain J. D. Barkdull. Mr. J. L. Hughes acted as Barkdull's Lieutenant. The company name could not be ascertained in the primary research source and a number of the names of the members were not distinguishable. The wagon train was apparently made up of the following sections:

No. 1-
Andrew Coffenberry   Christian Shanly /sic/ of   Stephen Wilkin Jr.
George Kizer   Shelby County, Ohio
William Edgar

No. 2-
William Sneveley   Ezra Pretzman   John McCullough
T. G. Meeker

No. 3-
John Hurley   M. S. Bush   E. A. Ensey
George E. Abbott   John Calwell /sic

No. 4-
Anthony Fleming /sic/   Jacob Allenbach   Daniel Harshbarger
Nicholas Frantz   George Rice
  No. 5-
J. D. Barkdull   C. B. Mann   Henry Marrs /sic/
J. W. Dingman   A. G. Miller
  No. 6-
John Irwin   Owen Kaho (?) (Kahe?)   S. J. Gamble
William G. Gamble
  No. 7-
John S. Stephenson   M. Honnell /sic/   Harvey Guthrie
George W. Neal   Eli B. Honnell /sic/
  No. 8-
A. Mayes   Jacob Sing   John S. Hodge
John Gish   Joseph Hill
  No. 9-
Samuel Perry   John Wise   Alfred Davis
Michael Gleich
  No. 10-
William Rodgers   Robert Notcrost (?)   Nicholas Trapp
Henry Martin   (Norcrost?)
  No. 11-
J. L. Hughes   E. G. Hamilton   Enos E. Barkdull (?)
R. T. Hughes   Jack Newbrach, of Allen   (Harkdull?)
  No. 12-   County, Ohio
John M. Ainsworth   ____Hartzel   D. J. Porter
R. M. Al____, of
  Covington, Ohio
  No. 13-
Francis McTarnahan   ____Carson   W. A. Hollaway
____ McTarnahan   Mrs. R. McTarnahan   Isaac McTarnahan
Miss M. C. McTarnahan,
  of Miami County, Ohio

KANESVILLE, IOWA (May, 1850) The *Frontier Guardian* of May 15, 1850 contained a number of articles dealing with the arrival and departure of California-bound emigrants.

The following individuals were reported to have arrived in Kanesville and were preparing to depart for California:

From Iowa:-
Truman B. Tripp   G. E. Cole   A. J. Loomis
Green Yarnell   J. D. Walworth   J. C. Smith
B. R. Skinner   Morgan Hart   A. Henderson
John Fern   Chandler W. Ellsworth   Moses Greene
Alfred C. Leveridge   James Crippen   William Gillman (?)
William W. Hollenbec   Benjamin Coffee (?)   (Gillmon? Gillmen?)
  /sic/   (Coffin?)   M. C. Terrell
Abraham Agnew   H. G. Creery (?) (Creary?) H. E. Terrell
John Newton   Washington Williams   L. D. Dutton
Anderson Pike   Jerome Dutton
William P. Wells   Leander V. Loomis

From Iowa (Cont'd):-
William H. Rockafellar
  (Rockefeller?)

From Illinois:-
James Hillman
Columbus S. Marshall
J. T. Nelson
Edwin Ray
Daniel Pike
Nathan R. Resseter
Amhal Hays Jr.
Jeremiah Moble (?)
  (Mabie?)
Hollis Newton Jr.
William A. J. Pierce
Hugh B. Taylor
Joseph R. Strickler
Evan Rea /sic/
Benjamin W. Reynolds
Morrison Gaston (?)
  (Garton?)
Phineas Sheurman (?)
  (Shearman?)
Theodore Jones
J. C. Chapman
Edwin Harvey Lord
Hezakiah Bruce
S. H. Herryford /sic/
  (Merryford?)
Isom Atkison /sic/
  (Atkinson?)
Charles Jewitt
James A. King
Joseph B. Tuttle
Walter Johnson and
  Company

From Indiana:-
W. Magury /sic/
Asa Haynes
A. P. Tibbetts
Amos Mendenhall

From Wisconsin:-
Dow C. Barry
Samuel Howard
George Jones
W. D. Truax
Edwin D. Robbins
George Biglow /sic/

John Gilliland
James Widener

Hiram Blackman
T. M. Underwood
A. S. Whitaker
John M. Messroll (?)
  (Messrell?)
Homer Lewis
William C. Barnes
William L. Abbitt /sic/
  (Abbott?)
John Murphy
Simon Emmet (?)
  (Bennet?)
John Rose
Joseph Gannon (?)
  (Ganson?)
William Callahan
Samuel Gillam (?)
  (Gilham?)
John Phalen /sic/
Howard Houghton
J. Kingsbury
William Kingsbury
Samuel McMullen
G. W. Hutchison /sic/
  (Hutchinson?)
Ezekiel Spicer
John B. Baker
James Matson
J. J. Whitney
S. Pinkham
Jedidiah Hubbard
Ames Lyon

James Irwin
A. D. Follett
Newton Nye (?) (Nys?)
John Oliver

William Bloxham
William F. Davis
B. C. Baker
Dr. John Lease (?)
  (Louse?, Leese?)
Frank Luck

117

Samuel McWilliams
Francis Moxley

John Rahu (?) (Rahn?)
W. P. Teats, M. D. (?)
  (Tents?, Teste?)
Theodore Taley (?)
  (Tuley, Teley, Toley?)
Joseph Stitles
William L. Stewart
B. Greenwood
Thomas Gregory
D. G. Shettenkirk (?)
  (Shottenkirk?)
Daniel Brown
Francis Trull (?) (Trall?)
Jacob Trenell (?)
George W. Yager /sic/
S. Sackeider
Columbus Henley(?)
  (Hesley?)
E. D. Butler
E. A. Shirley
Henry Purvis (?)
Albert Thomas
William Day
Isaac H. Mason
Theodore Graham
Charles Graham
Nathan Ellis
S. W. Boynton
J. W. Lakue and
  Company
Bryon W. McKinstry
John Hart

F. Flanders
David C. Lewis
Hiram Mendenhall

Isaac Allcock
Dr. S. L. Grew (?) (Grow?)
C. M. Washburn
Charles T. Ross
William O. Moore

From Wisconsin (Cont'd.):-

Jacob J. Brower /sic/ (Brewer?)	James Ashworth	Nathan B. Ellis
David Miller	Jeremiah Sanborn	William Howe
P. McDonnell	William McPherson	John Hay /sic/
L. Streeter	J. Hollenbeck /sic/	Charles Orvis (?) (Orvin?)
Augustus B_____ net (Bennet?, Barnet?)	Joseph Stone	G. D. Jenks
William Chreviston /sic/	Charles L. Durban	L. O. Whitman
Henry Saunders	L. M. Thompson	B. M. Soule
	Joseph M. Simmons	Oscar S. Higbee
	James L. Reynolds	

From Michigan:-

Hiram Hamilton	A. Radenbough (?) (Rodenbough?)	James P. Hanna
J. J. Hardy	J. M. Wells	Caleb P. Wray
Jonathan Engle	John Barker	Isaac D. Giddings
William Engle	William H. Millard	Ira Goodrich
George Hessler (?) (Hossler?)	S. W. Denion /sic/ (Deuion?, Deulon?, Denlon?)	Moray T. Speer
W. K. Conger		William A. Gibbs
J. C. Morley		Frederick Plummer
Orlando Freeland		L. C. Taylor

From Ohio:-

Cyrus Delano	Robert McGarren (?) (McGarron?, McGavren?, McGavron?)	James Vance
Abraham Agnew		Samuel Kirtland /sic/

From Virginia:- / From Massachusetts:- / From Maryland:-

From Virginia:-	From Massachusetts:-	From Maryland:-
John Stephenson	Marshall Curtis	Stephan Mahony /sic/

From New York:-

Alonzo L. Niblack (?) (Niblock?)	L. F. Thompson	M. D. Abbott

From the Chicago Excelsior Company:-

H. Emmons	J. C. Frisbie	J. Parker
P. Reinhart	P. H. Newton	

The <u>Frontier Guardian</u> of May 15, 1850 published lists of companies departing for California from Kanesville, Iowa noted below:

Birmingham Emigrating Company

This company departed from Kanesville on May 6, 1850 under the command of Captain C. L. Mers (Mors?). Other officers of the company were listed as Hiram Barns (Barnes?), 1st Lieutenant; Clement Wood, 2nd Lieutenant; Andrew Loomis, 3rd Lieutenant; E. D. Skinner, Secretary; David Lowry, Chaplain; and Joseph C. Spees, as Wagon Master. The company membership was reported as follows:

Hiram Barns /sic/ (Barnes?)	E. D. Skinner	Charles D. Skinner
	Seaton L. Harness	Jacob Griffith

William L. Plaskett (?)   J.S. Culbertson   Barnet Barnes /sic/
  (Pluckett?,   Jonas Speelman (?)   (Barns?)
  Pluskett?,Plackett?)   (Speekman?)   Abner Loomis
D. H. Lowry /sic/   Abel Butt   Frederick Peckham
Amelia Lowry /sic/   Clement Wood   Reason Barns /sic/
Samueel Perrine   Joseph C. Spees   (Barnes ?)
Jefferson Baird   Joseph Huey   Zenes Carter
Joseph W. Gale   Catharine Huey   J. J. Caldwell
B. F. Sandford (?)   Samuel Martin   Jonathan Sage
  (R. F. Sandford?)   William Bennett   E. B. Winner
J. Bickford   Rosetta Culbertson

Extract Company

This company was from Waukegan, Illinois and it operated under the command of Captain George Ferguson. The unit left Kanesville, Iowa for California on May 6, 1850. Memberships in the company were as follows:

Pennell Munson,   W. R. Defrase (?)   Henry F. Porter
  Secretary   J. W. Ellis   Pat Cary /sic/
M. J. Southwick   Moses Chatbourn /sic/   O. F. Noble
Daniel Adams   Henry Nellis   Edward Gorman
William McLean   William Shuhan   L. G. Farnham
R. Willard   Deland Campbell   Alex B. Ferguson
B. H. Dickinson   V. S. Andrews   H. P. Hires
John W. Herwood

Mutual Protection Company, No.1

This company was under the command of E.M. Downs and it departed St. Joseph, Missouri on May 6, 1850. The following is a list of its members:

E.M. Downs, Captain   Joseph Prentiss, Secretary   F.B. Kleecher
Robert T. Lawton   John Hull   William Kaser (?)
R. Hancock   R. Ostrander   (Keser?, Knear?)
John Grindell   John Sloan   R. West
Stephen Graham   John M. Knott   Abraham Ratan (?)
James E. Sheffield   Samuel Sloan   (____Abraham and
C.M. Bevard   William Wickham   ____ Ratan?)
William H. Shattuck   G.G. Blanchard   Thomas Calderwood

Union Packing Company

This company was made up of members from Michigan and Iowa. It crossed the Missouri River, near St. Joseph, Missouri, on May 8, 1850. The below individuals were members of the company:

*Leroy Garther, Captain   George Allen, Lieutenant   W. H. Spencer
  (Gurther?)   David Kendall   Company Clerk
I. Bradford   P. S. Derbyshire   Otis C. Thompson
C. M. Johnson   M. S. Sperry   Leonard Thompson
J. J. Hummer   A. Matoon   A. Rodenbough (?)
Eric Potter   F. H. Hughs /sic/   (Radenbough?,
*Faulkner Gurthrie   (Hughes?)   Redenbough?)
  (Guthrie?)

(*) Surnames listed as found in source. Consider alternatives of "Leroy Guthrie/Gurthrie" and "Faulkner Garther/Gurther".

Quincy Company

This company was organized at Kanesville, Iowa on May 13, 1850, under the supervision of Joel Emery (?) (Emory?), as Chairman. William Masters was elected as Captain; James G. Orr, 1st Lieutenant; James Evans, 2nd Lieutenant. They intended to leave Kanesville for California shortly after their organizational meeting. Members of the company were:

William Billings	William Masters	T. W. Goodwyn Jr. /sic/
F. S. P. Catherwood	Joel Emery (?) (Emory?)	J. B. Hicks
Nelson Strickland	James A. King	J. J. Whitney
James Evans	Thomas Cross	Joseph Watty
Chancy Hesler /sic/	F. G. Johnston	Job Valentine
George Knight	V. Blakeslee (?) (Blakelee?)	James G. Orr
Walter Emery (?) (Emory?)	T. W. Goodwyn /sic/	Henry Miller
T. S. Emery(?) (Emory?)		

California Banner Company

This company departed from Kanesville, Iowa to cross the Missouri River on May 9, 1850, for California. It was made up of the following individuals:

Joseph L. Durbin Captain, of Louisa County, Iowa	W. H. R. Thomas, Lieutenant, of Louisa County, Iowa	Robert Nixon
William Colton, Secretary, of Louisa County, Iowa	Eli Fite /sic/	Marvel Wheelock /sic/ (Wheellock?), Inspector of teams and wagons, of Louisa County, Iowa
John Ferris (?) (Farris?)	Leonard Cobinson /sic/ (Robinson?)	H. C. Marvel /sic/
John Donahoe	John Schelling (?) (Schilling?)	James B. Milligan
William Egan	P. M. Bird	Mark Carson
James Ray (?) (Roy?)		David Gregory
		Samuel Stephens

(Some sixteen additional men were members of this company but the author is unable to decipher the entries as they appeared in the Frontier Guardian of May 15, 1850. A portion of these names seem to be represented as follows)

Henry May	James Warnstaff	Henry Haight (?) (Height ?)
John Hunt	J. Homer	A. D. Hurley
Michael Wien	Francis Gulling (?) (Galling?)	Stephen Barr (?) (Burr)
Albert Penchal		John Stoddard
Gustavus Jones		

Social Band of Liberty

This wagon train company was primarily made up of individuals from Lewis and Clark Counties, Missouri. They departed from Kanesville, Iowa, for California, on or about May 14, 1850. Members of the train were:

Lewis Dufriend	Patrick McDermott, Wagon Master	John McCann
Nathan Cellars		Virgil Quiry /sic/

John Devillion (?)   Andrew Devillion (?)   Carles Hobbs /sic/
   (Devilbian?), Wagon   (Devilbian?), Secretary   (Charles Hobbs?)
   Captain   M. Barton   Robert Bennett /sic/
Samuel Cellars   J. W. Maddox   Herman Little (?)
James P. Jones   Richard Quinn (?)   ____ McCan /sic/
Thonmas K. White   (Richard Gaines?)   (____McCann?)
Edward Rocke (?)   Patrick Duffy   J. H. Williams
   (Rocks?)   Henry Bennet /sic/   William Findley
George Browning   W. A. McPherson   W. Easley (?) (Ensley?)
E. A. Johnson

The Cutler Company

On May 15, 1850, the <u>Frontier Guardian</u> published a letter it had received from the Secretary of the "Cutler Company." The article indicated that the company had crossed the Missouri River on April 22, 1850. The letter furnished names of the company members and reported the fact they had traveled about twenty-five miles the first day. Captain R. C. Petty was acting as the guide. Members of the group were listed as follows:

L. K. Cutler, Captain   Edwin Grieve   Lieutenant
John W. Shapper,   M. L. Sheek (?)   William Jolly
   Secretary   F. H. Dodge   Timothy Milarhy /sic/
Ira Glitner   Miles B. Dodge   David Jolly
Jacob Rose (?) (Ruse?)   William Johnston   Charles Leeland /sic/
George H. Hall   Miles Tyrel /sic/   (Leland?)
B. Dodge   John Baker   Albert Pickering
Richard Barrey (?)   William H. Baker   George J. Niver
   (Barney?)   Richard Robinson   Samuel T. Baker
Henry Keiner (?)   Samuel Parker   *Lemuel Huston /sic/
   (Kefner?, Ketner?)   L. C. Dow   William Scovill (?) /sic/
Dr. Samuel Houston /sic/   William Camp   William Cha(ddock?)
   (Huston?)   Oliver Camp   Owen Ruble
John Giler   Elijah Camp   Nathaniel ____
James J. Fairbanks   Mason Sutherland   William White
Orin Gray   Joseph P. Webster   A. Dewel /sic/
Harrison Brown   Charles D. W____   Martin Millet
John Metts   M.____D____   Christopher Bennett
William Scovill /sic/   James P. Webster   Sidney Sutherland
Phillip Carrson /sic/   Charles D. Hickox   Silas Sutherland
   (Carson?)   William Chaddock
D. Smith, First Lieutenant   E. Chapman, Second

<u>NEW ORLEANS, LOUISIANA (May 20, 1850)</u> On the foregoing date the <u>Daily Picayune</u> published a story stating that a company of one hundred individuals left from the vicinity of El Paso (Texas) on February 28, 1850 for California. The company included Gov. Henry Smith, James W. Robinson, W. W. Thompson, John R. Wooldridge, W. P. Huff, of San Felipe, Z. P. Glasscock, William S. Anderson and a Dr. ____Hoxie (a nephew of Dr. ____Hoxie, of Independence, Missouri).

(*)Note entry for Dr. Samuel Houston. Consider alternative of Lemuel Houston.

NEW ORLEANS, LOUISIANA (May 28, 1850) On the foregoing date the Daily Picayune prints a letter written by Dr. S. McAdow, of Weston, Illinois. McAdow writes that C.H. Moor, of Milford, Illinois, had died of cholera while enroute to California. On the following day the Picayune reported that Major Jacob Judy, of Edwardsville, Illinois, had died of inflammatory sore throat while enroute to the California mines. Judy was accompanying his brother (unidentified) to California.

ST JOSEPH, MISSOURI The Frontier Guardian of May 29, 1850 contained a number of articles dealing with the arrival and departure of California-bound emigrants.

The following individuals were reported to have arrived in Kanesville and were preparing to depart for California:

From Iowa:
John Jones
William Jones
Jerome Dutton
Lorenzo D. Dutton
Andrew J. Wilson
Henry Mussetten
Charles H. Haining

John Williams
John Rees /sic/
Melvin Squire
R.S. Dickinson
Martin Sewell
Lorenzo Ellis
Joel Terry

Thomas Edwards and family
James DeLong
A.A. White
John DeLong
Leander G. DeLong

From Illinois:
A.B. Botsford
John Hart
George W. McCulloch
M. Fletcher

Jacob Smith
Ira P. Hale
Clark Haverhill
Valney Wood and Company

John Robertson
Clark Camp
Louis Yearing

From Michigan:
Ocar Nye
W.C. Foster
John E. Jessup
Jesse C. Coleman
Milton Coleman
George Voorhis
Moses Voorhis
William Anderson

Henry Pinckney
Joseph Collins
Bazailed Taft (Bazailed Taft?)
John Hanna
C. C. Putnam
J. A. Patrick

E. G. Gould
W. H. Ells /sic/ (Ellis?)
Zebulon T. Wheaton
H. A. Ells /sic/ (Ellis?)
J. B. Howard
F. A. Howard

From England:
Henry Lunt
From Indiana:
Daniel Carlisle
From Wisconsin:
Benjamin Fowler

From Missouri:
William Flanders
W. L. Freeman
John J. Gray
From Pennsylvania:
Elezer W. Colton
Daniel Greenoch

From Ohio:
John Gochenow Jr. (Gechenow?)
T. B. Smith
L. D. Caster
William Hasson (Hassou?)

The Frontier Guardian of May 29, 1850 also reported that the "Prairie Rover Company" had arrived in Kanesville, Iowa. This California emigrant group was reported to consist of the following individuals:

Charles Sherman
B. B. Williams
William Galloway

George Munford /sic/ (Mumford?)
James B. Brownlee

James Mumford /sic/ (Mumford?)
John T. King

C. Moretz	Luther Moretz	James Moorhead /sic/
Jubin Bosworth	Alexander Casteel (?)	T. C. Hopkins
George Baker	(Castrel?)	John Quinn
Obadiah Hallenbake	William B. Haley	A. T. White
(Hollenbake?)	George Ridgeley	William McCoy
John Wm. M. Eiffert(?)	T. J. Packinpaw	Garrett Rezner /sic/
(John William and M.	James Jackway	Solomon Rezner
Eiffert?)	Thomas Rosborough	Patrick Gleason
John Crane	P. M. Gleason	Simon Nowlan /sic/
James Connell	Joseph Towndrow	Ira B. Dillon
George Brimhall	F. M. Brown	Z. Hansen (?) (Hanser?)
John Brimhall	James Hoover	
Noah Brimhall	A. C. Crouch	

The Frontier Guardian of May 29, 1850 published an article which stated that the "Missouri and Iowa Mining Company" had left Kanesville, Iowa on May 24, 1850, to cross the Missouri River on the south side of the Platte. This California emigrant company had organized at Kanesville on May 23, 1850 and the membership consisted of the following individuals:

James Hanshaw, Captain	Thomas Ward	Edward T. Peake /sic/
Alonzo Barton, Wagon	William Brown	James Shannon
Master	Allen Brown	Wilson Shannon
Henderson Hibbets, Sgt of	Levi Brown	George Clay
the Guard	Lorenzo D. Huntsman	Hubbard Smith
Enoch B. Ripper,	Charles R. Huntsman	William Davis
Inspector of Arms	John White	John Strother
Enoch Richards, Secretary	M. Price	Andrew Little
Committee of Three to	John Ford	Samuel Ellison
Settle all Difficulties:	Jephthah Dunn /sic/	William Bushkirk
Washington Hanshaw	E. L. Thomas	Henry Dawson
Samuel H. Colton	Hazon Wilson	Andrew Spencer
Isaac D. Davis)	John Willis	Joseph Woodward
Diar Taylor /sic/	James Laytham /sic/	Charles Billups
Alfred Allen	(Latham?)	William Billups
The Family of	Daniel South	John Stephens
Washington Hanshaw	Abel Ellis	H. Billups
Nicholas Clark	Samuel Swan	George Tomaugh /sic/
James W. Fowler		

AUGUSTA, MAINE (May, 1850) The Kennebec Journal of May 30, 1850 printed an item dated "St. Louis, Missouri, May 23, 1850" in which reference is made to a letter from S. McAdams stating that cholera had broken out among the California emigrants. The disease had broken out specifically in the train of a Dr. ___Clark and an emigrant named C. H. Moore, of Mulford, Illinois, was reported to have died.

KANESVILLE, IOWA (June, 1850) The Frontier Guardian published articles dealing with the arrival and departure of California emigrants at Kanesville, Iowa. On June 12,

1850, the <u>Guardian</u> reported that the following emigrants had arrived in the city:

L. W. Locker, of Illinois	J. P. Newton, of Michigan	Thomas F. Davis, of Wisconsin
W. H. Ham, of Illinois	Horace Hinman, of Michigan	C. Cattermole, of Iowa
Joseph Glines, of Wisconsin	Alexander Bailey, of Illinois	John O'Loughlin /sic/ of Iowa

The forementioned issue of the <u>Guardian</u> stated that the "Iowa and Wisconsin Emigrant Company No. 3" had departed from Kanesville, Iowa for California. This company had been organized in Fremont County, Iowa on May 9, 1850. Supervision of the company was under the management of a committee consisting of E. M. Tanner, Nathan Tolman, and Aaron Collingwood. Members of the company were listed as:

Nathan Tolman	Robert Mitchell Jr.	John Groom
E. M. Tanner	Aaron Collingwood	Digory Hobbs /sic/
M. R. Byrd	Mitburn Pool (Milburn Pool?)	H. Hill
George Allen		James Peters
Francis Peters	Daniel Hunt	William Griffith
John Palmer	John Benjamin	Joseph Bedell /sic/
Enoch Palmer	Emerson Rogers	John Gill
Hermon Dodd /sic/	Juba Rogers (?) (John Rogers?)	Charles Baker
William Parker		Daniel Rockwell
Edward West	Charles Stokes	John McGrinsey /sic/
A. Hendrickson Sr.	James W. Brown	_____ Sanders
John Hendrickson	Charles Drean	John M. Bennett
Robert Allison	Andrew Shiuier (?) (Shinier?)	Alexander Wiley
E. Zevy Allison		Olderson McGirnsey/sic/
William M. Goodsuca /sic/	Richard Seddell /sic/	

<u>AUGUSTA, MAINE (June, 1850)</u> The <u>Kennebec Journal</u> published a letter which had been written from _____ Goodrich, in California, to his father in Bingham, Maine. Goodrich states that he is the only survivor of a party of thirty who left, via Independence, Missouri, a year ago. The others having died of cholera, exposure or were killed by the Indians.

<u>SACRAMENTO, CALIFORNIA (July 8, 1850)</u> The <u>Sacramento (Calif.) Transcript</u> of July 9, 1850 reported that William H. Moore, of Mishawaka, Indiana, had arrived in Sacramento on July 8, 1850. Moore, along with his wife and son, had crossed the plains by wagon, having left St. Joseph, Missouri on April 10, 1850. He took the "Sublette Cut-off" and followed it and its continuation westward. Some thirty miles of his route was over snow twenty-five to thirty feet deep, but frozen so hard that the wagon wheels did not cut much into it. His wagon team consisted of five horses.

<u>NEW ORLEANS, LOUISIANA (July, 1850)</u> The <u>Daily Picayune</u> of New Orleans, Louisiana published an article on July 15, 1850 which it obtained from the <u>San Antonio</u>

(Texas) Ledger of July 4, 1850. The Ledger had reported that a small party left for California on July 3rd. The group was to travel via Mazatlan, Mexico. James A. Glasscock, a newspaperman with the Ledger, was a member of the party.

SACRAMENTO, CALIFORNIA (July, 1850) The Sacramento Transcript of July 20, 1850 reports the arrival of a Mr. ____Illingsworth, late of St. Louis, Missouri. Illingsworth had just crossed the Plains and the Sierra Range. The article contains references to food costs in the Carson Valley area as well as Mormon activity in that area.

WEAVERVILLE, CALIFORNIA (August 1, 1850)- The Sacramento Transcript of August 6, 1850 reported the arrival of J. M. Sheppards (Sheppard?) in California. Details on his trip across the plains were also carried in the issue of the following day. Sheppard(s) had left Council Bluffs, Iowa on May 5, 1850 and arrived in Weaverville on August 1, 1850. His company crossed the Platte River at Fort Laramie. Sheppard(s) kept daily notes from the time of his departure until his arrival in California. From May 27th up to their arrival in California, they were in sight of snow, with the exception of one day. Sheppard(s) left Fort Laramie on May 27 and arrived at the headwaters of the Humboldt River on June 29th. His company started from Iowa with twelve wagons and only two wagons managed to make it through to California, the ten wagons being destroyed by the rigors of the journey. The two Transcript articles did not mention Sheppard(s) traveling companions. This pioneer was reported to be from Keosauqua, Iowa.

ST. JOSEPH, MISSOURI (July, 1850) The St. Joseph Gazette of July 31, 1850, published six letters received from emigrants enroute to California. All the letters were concerned with the death and suffering that was taking place on the roads to California. In each case the letter-writer was not identified, but they did furnish a number of names which had been collected from the markers on trailside graves.

The first letter was written on June 9, 1850, at a point one hundred and ten miles west of Fort Kearny. Within the letter was the following list of those whose names and places of former residence were written upon slips of board placed at the head of the grave viz:

John Coplinger, aged 74 years, d. June 1, 1850 from Cedar County, Missouri

R. W. Hollan (?), (Hellan?), of Missouri, d. June 2, 1850

Adam Beshear, of Pike County, Ill. d. June 7, 1850

William Allen and brother, sons of Col.___Allen, of Benton, Missouri, one d. June 5 and one d. June 7, 1850

James Johnson, of Pike County, Ill., d. June 6, 1850.

C. Saxton, of Ark., d. June 8, 1850

Dr.___Goodman, of Cole County, Ill., d. June 3, 1850

Benjamin F. Clark, of Linn County, Mo., d. June 4, 1850

George Geitgy, of Ohio, d. June 5, 1850

Moses Wolfe, of Ark., d. June 8, 1850

John Baker, of Ray County, Mo., d. June 6, 1850

Mrs. Sarah A. Sneed, of Jackson County, Mo., no death date

William M'Chesney, of Oxford, Ohio, d. June 6, 1850

John Davis, of Ohio, no death date

Lucius C. Mason, of St. Louis, died June 6, 1850

Thomas Higgs, of Ray County, Mo., d. June 6, 1850 and another unidentified grave at his side with no sign, made at same time

Smith Miller, of Oxford, Ohio, d. June 6, 1850

Mathias Jones, of Hamilton County, Ohio, no date

A. J. Williams, of Dallas County, Mo., d. June 7, 1850

H. C. Swain, a child of, d. June 7, 1850

H. Runyan, a child of,/sic/ d. June 8, 1850

N. Woolsey, no residence no date

H. Uttermich, no residence no date

In a second letter printed in the St. Joseph Gazette of July 31, 1850, there appeared an additional list of graves found enroute to California. This letter was written on June 16, 1850, at a point two hundred and forty miles west of Fort Kearney. The writer was unidentified and the graves were reported as follows: (no death dates)

Robert Walker, of Benton, Missouri

William Beshear, of Pike County, Ill.

Mrs. James Morton, of Pike County, Ill.

Henry Rayman, of Platte County, Mo.

A. H. Winfield, of Georgia

Jefferson Hill, of Cape Girardeau, Mo.

J. Cunningham (no other entries)

J. M. Groms /sic/, of Greencastle, Indiana

William Flourney /sic/ (Flournoy?), of Missouri

George Scofield, of Iowa

John W. Mean, of Iowa

H. Harrison, of Polk County, Iowa

Reese Harrison, of Polk County, Mo.

P. Wheeler, of Jackson County, Mo.

I. T. Burnan /sic/, of same as above

P. A. Getting, of Daviess County, Indiana

J. Osborn /sic/, of Benton, Mo., aged 28 years

James Loffliss /sic/, of Henry County, Mo.

J. P. Box, of Polk County, Mo.

George Gearheart /sic/, of Platte County, Mo.

J. Schni /sic/, of Indiana

John Q. Smith, of Gentry County, Mo.

Harry Gibson, of Shultsburg, Wisc.

Jacob Himelman, of St. Charles, Mo.

Newman Grasley, of Missouri

A. Bennett, of Grundy County, Mo.

A. Taylor, of Polk County, Mo.

Elizabeth A. Hawkins, of Jackson County, Mo.

W. B. Hays /sic/, of Dade County, Mo.

J. W. Belcher, of Jackson County, Mo.

Mrs. Walker Cheesman /sic/, of same as above

Hugh M'Knight, of Buchanan County, Mo.

Robert Eastin /sic/, of Howard County, Missouri

William C. Reeves, of Cape Girardeau, Mo.

James West, of Pulaski County, Mo.

R. B. Brown, of Benton County, Mo.

Mrs. ____ Venable and daughter, of Daviess County, Mo.

Franklin Van Bebler, of Ray County, Mo.

Levi Armstead, of Pike County, Mo.

Newton Griswold, of Missouri

Owen H. Creesy /sic/, of Iowa

Joseph Cezzens /sic/, of Wapello County, Iowa

J. T. Knapp, of Jackson County, Mo.

M. Wadlkey, of Jackson County, Mo.

Alex. N. Stowell, of same as above

Aaron Powers, of Peoria, Illinois

Jesse Ernst, of Peoria, Illinois
Elijah Reed, of Adams County, Ill.
Mrs. E. Hendrix/sic/, of Claiborn Parish, Louisiana
N. Campbell, of Missouri
P.M. Tipton and C. Clark, of Missouri, both in one grave

The St.Joseph Gazette of July 31, 1850 also carried a letter from an unidentified emigrant which had been written on June 19, 1850, at Robidoux-50 miles from Fort Laramie. The writer reported that he had passed several graves since Sunday, viz:

Calvin Green, of Howard County, Mo.
Garret H. Wynckoop/sic/ no resident site
H.J. Perkins, of Gasconado County, Mo.
Thomas Kimball of, Cooper County, Mo.
F. Mascher(?) (Maseher?), of Andrew County, Mo.
A. Wood, of Indiana

Elizabeth Field, of Decatur County, Iowa
William Finnell, of Howard County, Mo.
P. Kirk, of Dade County, Mo.
J. Goodman, of Saline County, Mo.
M. Knight, of Tippecanoe County, Indiana

C.H. Morrow, of Green County, Mo.
T.J. McDonald, of Dark County, Ohio
Lewis Newton, of Marion County, Mo.
Francis M. Foster, of Cooper County, Mo.
Robert Nichols, of Hold County, Mo.
W. Turpen/sic/, of Missouri

In a letter dated June 20, 1850, from Fort Laramie, there appeared additional reports of emigrant deaths. This letter was printed in the St. Joseph Gazette of July 31, 1850 and it contained the following list of emigrant dead:

M.W. Murray, of Orange County, Indiana
Robert Norcross/sic/. of Shelby County, Ohio
Goodson G. Gabbert, of Buchanan County, Missouri
W.A. Garvin, of Franklin County, Missouri
Thomas Morrel /sic/ (Morrell?), of Kane County, Ill.
C.H. Moore, of Syracuse, N.Y.
Peter Waggoner/sic/ of Cass County, Ill.
R. Pierce, of St. Joseph County, Mich.
John Harbinger, of Ralls County, Mo.

John McCarty, of Cape Girardeau, Missouri
Anna Maria Jordon /sic/ (Jordan?), of Dodge County, Missouri
Charles A. Dearing, of Daviess County, Missouri
Rev. M. Jamison/sic/ of Weston, Missouri
Alex. Martin, of Butler County, Penn.
James Walker, of Rock Island, Ill.
A. Malone, of Platteville, Mo.
Mr. ___ Parsons, of Howard County, Mo.
A. Wood, of Boone County, Ill.

John Smith, of Fort Meigs County, Ohio
Joseph Loyd /sic/ (Lloyd?), of Missouri
Samuel Lewis, of Missouri
Hugh Warren, of Carroll County, Missouri
George Kent, of Missouri
D.C. Johnson, of Jefferson County, Wisconsin
John Anderson, of Henderson County, Illinois
G.W. Jordon /sic/ (Jordan?), of Dubuque County, Iowa
W. Hunt, of Scott County, Mo.
Jonathan Hoover, of Cooper County, Mo.

W. Mitchell, of Cooper County, Mo.
A. Lowdermilk /sic/ of LaGrange, Mo.
___ Harris, no residence site
George Corwin, of Chariton County, Missouri
Kane Hector, of Boone County, Mo.
M.A. Brooks, of Andrew County, Mo.
G. Clark, of Camden County, Mo.
H. Dodds, of Camden County, Mo.
George Stanley, of Pike County, Ill.
W. Johnstone /sic/ of Calhoun County, Michigan
Robert Anderson, no residence site
C.H. Squire, of Eaton County, Michigan
___ Cogswell, no residence site
William Lee, of Pulaski County, Mo.
Erastus Lovel /sic/ (Lovell?), of Montgomery County, Missouri
Ed. Lovel /sic/(Lovell?), of Montgomery County, Missouri
H. Francis, of Cole County, Mo.
Newton Stone, of Kentucky
Charles Stonehall(?) (Stonhall?, Stonewall?) of Adams County, Ill.
John Ward, of Gennesee /sic/, Wisc.
Amos L. Hardin, of Warren County, Ill.
B.G. Smith, of DeKalb County, Mo.
D. Binns, of St. Clair County, Mo.
S. McIntyre, of Clinton County, Indiana
N. Harlow, of Chariton County, Mo.
J.G. Ignite, of Chariton County, Mo.
William Ramsey, of Scott County, Mo.

A letter from a California-bound emigrant, dated June 17, 1850, Fort Laramie, also appeared in the St. Joseph Gazette of July 31, 1850. This letter reported that Jerome & Company's wagon train had passed Fort Laramie on June 15, 1850, and that Alexander & Hall's wagon train from St. Louis, Missouri had passed Fort Laramie on June 17th.

SACRAMENTO, CALIFORNIA (June 28, 1850) The arrival of Anson Shinnaberger and a Mr. ___ Saunders in California is announced in the Sacramento Transcript of June 29, 1850. They were the first overland emigrants to arrive in Sacramento during the 1850 season. The newspaper furnishes an account of their departure from St. Joseph, Missouri on April 13, 1850 and their experiences along the travel route.

CARROLTON, MISSOURI (September, 1850) The St. Joseph Gazette of September 4, 1850 reported that letters had been received at Carrolton, Missouri, conveying the news of the death of Captain Benjamin F. White at Pacific Springs, on the California trail. White died on the night of July 4, 1850, of cholera. A strange story is related in which his wife in Missouri dreamed of his death.

ST. JOSEPH, MISSOURI (September 16, 1850) The following individuals arrived in St. Joseph, direct from California. They had left Weaverville, California on July 1, 1850, arrived at Salt Lake (Utah) on August 3rd, and at St. Joseph on September 16th. Alexander Johnson, one of the group, had left St. Joseph eighteen months previously. The returned emigrants were identified as:

Alexander Johnson
Mr. ___ Moore of Kentucky
Aaron Anglin, of Arkansas

Capt. B.F. Furnish
Henry Swearingen, of
  Nodaway County, Mo.
Mr. __ Moore, of
  Kentucky

Pleasant Wilson, of
  Howard County, Mo.
Dr. Clemens, of Pike
  County, Ill.

Squire Griffith, of
  Nodaway County, Mo.
James Anglin, of
  Arkansas

<u>SALT LAKE (UTAH) (May 27,1850)</u> The following is a list of emigrants from Missouri who arrived at Salt Lake (Utah) on May 27, 1850, enroute to California:

<u>Missouri Residents</u>:

John Moke, of St. Louis
William Garwood, of
  Macon County
D. Stephenson, of Macon
  County
J.W. Levy, of Arrow
  Rock
M.T. Hains /sic/, of
  Osecola
C. Cockrill, of Platte
  City
J.T. Crenshaw, of
  Osecola
James R. Watts, of
  Savannah
Joseph Smith, of Trenton
C.R. Roberts, of
  Lexington
James George, of St.
  Louis
A, Skillman, of Cape
  Girardeau
J. Skillman, of Cape
  Girardeau
A. Warnock, of
  Warrensburgh
A.J. Black, of Doniphan
William Wiley, of Fulton
H. Lebaugh, of St. Louis
William Jordan /sic/ of
  St. Louis
A. Miller, of Weston
W.A.F. Hartman, of
  Baldwin
W.J. Hailes /sic/ of
  Boonville
R.M. Woffenden, of
  Baltimore /sic/

Mathew Kelly, of Macon
  County
Jacob Rambe /sic/. of
  Macon County
L. Chambers, of St.
  Louis
T. Chambers, of
  Cambridge
T.L. Chambers, of
  Cambridge
J.T. Davis, of Andrew
  County
J.W. Davis, of Andrew
  County
Dr. J. Ball and wife, of
  Lexington
J.T. Shaw, of St. Charles
J.J. Landrum, of
  Montgomery County
A. McNelly, of Cape
  Girardeau
J.C. Higgins, of
  Jefferson City
R. Phillips, of Newport
O.P. Nelly, of Jefferson
  City
E. Guttridge /sic/, of St.
  Charles
P. Stone, of St. Louis
S.B. Miles, of Hickory
  County
H. Hayes, of Koarhill
G.W. Hedrick, of
  Kirksville
G.W. Woodcock, of
  Savannah
L. Withers, of Columbia

Harling Butner, of
  Macon County
C.B. Elliott, of Boonville
Henry Katz, of Boonville
T. McAfee, of Shelby
  County
L.J.W. Moore, of Shelby
  County
H.J. White, of Shelby
  County
L. Mitchell, of Shelby
  County
J. Glasscock, of Shelby
  County
G.B. Groomer, of St.
  Jopseph
J.C. Westfall, of
  Randolph
A.C. Shelton, of Cape
  Girardeau
D.W. Clark, of
  Columbia
J.R. Mowlray /sic/, of
  Cape Girardeau
J.P. Springer, of
  Washington County
T. Greggs, of Augusta
T. Gordan /sic/, of St.
  Louis
J.A. Mealers, of Union
C. Wells, of Boonville
T. Aikins /sic/, of Linden
P.R. Smith, of
  Springfield

F. Finley, of Weston	B. Ford, of Missouri	A.J. Kelly, of Oregon
L. Corbitt, of Canton	John Long, of Oregon	/sic/
W. Bunce, of Missouri	/sic/	W. Snyder, of Missouri
C.B. Graliot, of St. Louis		

ST. JOSEPH, MISSOURI (September, 1850) The St. Joseph Gazette of September 25, 1850, announced the arrival in Sacramento, California, of W. Crum, late editor of a newspaper in Iowa City, Iowa. The same issue also announced the arrival in Sacramento of S.H.N. Patterson, late editor of the Oquawka (Ill.) Spectator. Patterson arrived in Sacramento on July 29, 1850. He was a member of a company from Oquawka that had departed from Council Bluffs, Iowa on April 26, 1850. The Gazette article furnished particulars relative to Patterson's journey.

ST. JOSEPH, MISSOURI (October 2, 1850) The St. Joseph Gazette of October 2, 1850 printed a list of persons who had died on the road to California. This list was taken from a letter written at the South Pass, on July 10, 1850. The writer of the letter was not identified.

John H. Smith, of Green County, Mo.	Martin A. Woodson, of Platte County, Mo.	Hamilton Turman, of Van Buren County, Iowa
Carr W. Booth, of Boone County, Mo.	Peter Williams, of Davis County, Ill.	John B. Cook, of Ray County, Mo.
M. Thompson, of Arkansas	Matilda Prewett, of Henry County, Mo.	J.P. Wickliffe, of Benton County, Mo.
L.R. Martin, of Benton County, Mo.	David Prewett, of Henry County, Mo.	William Reynolds, of Benton County, Mo.
Dr. __ Wilks /sic/, of Benton County, Mo.	Jonathan Been, aged 22 years no residence listed	P.Q. Bates, of Texas County, Mo.
Dr. __ Wood, of Lexington, Mo.	C.P. Wyatt, of Gasconade County, Missouri	George Murray, of Andrew County, Mo.
O.M. Rowe, of Davis County, Ill.	Sol. Dill, of St. Joseph, Mo.	Markwood Merritt, no residence listed
Mrs. Nancy Wickliffe, of Benton County, Mo.	John M. Colton, of Pike County, Ill.	C. White, of Taney County, Mo.
O.P. Howard, of Saline County, Mo.	Horace Conger, of Iowa	Sarah A. Bowen, of Polk County, Mo.
Jesse Smith, of St. Charles, Mo.	D.W. Townsend, of Erie County, Pa.	C. Sharp, of Knox County, Mo.
Daniel Capps, of Pike County, Ill.	Marion Turley, of Cooper County, Mo.	Thomas Bishop, of Lewis County, Mo.
J. Reed, of St. Joseph County, Michigan	J. Schwenn /sic/, of Burlington, Iowa	Adam Brahm, of Johnson County, Mo.
S. Chandler, of Washington County, Missouri	Phillip Martin, of Washington County, Missouri	Miss Martha Paul, of Washington County, Mo.
John Furguson, of Calloway County, Missouri	James Estell, of Lawrence County, Mo.	William Harshaw, of St. Louis, Mo.

E.W. Cook, of Wisconsin
N.A. Ryan, of Atchison
County, Missouri

A.B. McLaughlin, of
Missouri
William M. Reed, of
Cooper County, Mo.

J. Burns, of Atchison
County, Mo.

ST. JOSEPH, MISSOURI (April 23, 1851) The "Mohican Gold Company" from Delaware and Ashland Counties Ohio, crossed the Missouri River at St. Joseph on April 23, 1851. Members of this California emigrant group consisted of the following individuals:

Joseph Smith, Captain
O.P. Smith
R.B. Han
G. Crull
W.R. Galfin
Thomas Sanford
John Engle (?) (Eagle?)
C.H. Robinson
M. Kimerer
J.S. Paullin /sic/
William Steel
E. Jacobus
T. Wells /sic/

S.C. Snyder
J. Anderson
William Newman
Baltzer Koontz
Jacob Wertsbaugher
James Gammill
William A. Gammill
E. Backley
R.V. Armstrong
S. Bartoe /sic/
C. Davis
J. Kimerer
J.H. Foreman

S.J. Seibert
A. Seibert
F. Foltz
S.H. Young
J.L. Sanburn
Henry Snyder
A.R. Sigler
S.D. Smith
Alexander H. McAfee
G. Joliff
L.W. Condit
A.J. Houser
George Patrick
D. Raugh

ST. JOSEPH, MISSOURI (April 28, 1851) The St. Joseph Gazette of April 30, 1851 published reports of departure from St. Joseph of the "Albion Rangers" and the "Platteville Company". Names of the members of the Ranger group were not listed in the source. Individuals comprising the "Platteville Company", from Wisconsin, were as follows:

Phillip McGaughren
Patrick McGhee

John Bowls /sic/
Mr. __ McMaherr /sic/

Patrick Ring

KANESVILLE, IOWA (May 2, 1851) On May 2, 1851 the Frontier Guardian published a list of the California emigrants who had arrived in Kanesville, enroute across the plains. The list appeared as below:

From Michigan :
Orin Gray
Ira T. Wight /sic/(Wright?)
L.F. Williams
   From Wisconsin :
Alfred Thurston
Jesse T. Pease
John A. Risdon

Charles Chester
A.R. Wisner
G.A. Orton
   From Iowa :
G.A. Cone
   From Indiana :
James K. Hurd
W. Augustus Fairfield

Edwin R. Button
Gustavus Gunney and
wife
   From Illinois :
Charles H. Calmes
   From Pennsylvania :
Alonzo Howard

ST. JOSEPH, MISSOURI (May 1851) On May 7, 1851 the St. Joseph Gazette published a list of members of the "Rhode Island Company" of emigrants who had departed from St. Joseph on May 3, 1851 for California. Members of the group were listed as follows:

C.C. Harrington and lady*

Isaac Gill, of Newport,
R.I.

Thomas Brocken, of
Chicago, Illinois

(*) Residents of Pawtucket, Rhode Island.

William F. Waterman, of Pawtucket, R.I.	Mrs. Fidelia Brockway, of Chicago, Ill.	Alex. E. Harrington, of Wickford, R.I.
Knight Johnson, of Wickford, R.I.	*James J. Harrington, of Providence, Ill.	Nicholas Weaver, of same as above
Clark Johnson, of Wickford, R.I.	*John Harrington, of same as above	Henry Briggs, of Newport, R.I.
Richard Johnson, of Wickford, R.I.	Jonathan Patterson, of Newport, R.I.	Riley Briggs, of same as above
John Grinnell, of Providence, R.I.	Perry Vennum/sic/, of Providence, R.I.	William Brown, of Portsmouth, R.I.
Daniel Allen, of Portsmouth, R.I.	Robert P.S. Allen, of Portsmouth, R.I.	Elisha C. Pechman (Peckman?), of Portsmouth, R.I.

The St.Joseph Gazette of May 7,1851 also reported that Mr. N.V. Sheffer's wagon train, from Warren County, Iowa, passed through St.Joseph, Missouri on May 5,1851. Besides one horse and one ox team, Sheffer was also taking along a drove of thirty head of cows. The names of five men accompanying Sheffer were not reported in the article.

The same issue of the Gazette also reported the May 5,1851 departure, from St.Joseph, Missouri, of the following persons from Wisconsin and Illinois:

William Macky/sic/ (Mackey?)	Hannibal Bray	Charles Harris
Thomas Tamblyn	William Bray	A. Brown
Michael Farnette	John Duvela (?) (Duvels?)	Henry Wilson
	Edward Hays/sic/	

In addition to the foregoing emigrant departures the Gazette of May 7,1851 also reported that the following persons had departed from St. Joseph, for California, during the first week in May, 1851:

From Monroe County, Iowa:	From Decatur, Iowa:	From LaSalle, Ill.:
Joseph Sanders and wife	David D. Gray, wife & four chldrn	George Davis
J.R. Sanders	From Des Moine County, Iowa:	From DesMoine County, Iowa:
George Billings and wife	Robert Ogle, wife & one child	Amelia Millard, son & daughter
P. Patterson		John Allen
Levi Burch and wife		John McCollough/sic/ (McCullough?)

ST. JOSEPH, MISSOURI (May 9,1851) The St. Joseph Gazette of May 14,1851 reported that the "Lafayette Company" had departed from St. Joseph on May 9,1851 for California. The below individuals comprised the company:

J.M. Day and lady	E. Bundran	S. Collins
William R. Clough	J.C. Gear	G.W. Knox
D. Hollinsworth/sic/	L. Berry	M. Clay
William T. Gear	R.B. Chisholm	

KANESVILLE, IOWA (May 7,1851) The Frontier Guardian of May 16, 1851, reported

(*) Author believes residence should read "Providence, R.I.".

the arrival in Kanesville of a number of California bound emigrants from Wayne County, Michigan. They had arrived in Kanesville on May 7, 1851 and intended to cross the Missouri River on May 12th. This group consisted of the following persons:

Dr. B.L. King	Foster Smith and wife	Henry Cramer, lady and
Nelson Clump	James Lovely	child
James Palmer	Isaac McClarry/sic/	Truman Ludd
Mathew Clark/sic/	William Bucklin	Ira Pate
Peter Seper	C. Able	J.K. Preston
J.W. Craff		

PLACERVILLE, CALIFORNIA (August, 1851) On August 18, 1851, the Sacramento Union published a list of emigrants who had just arrived in Placerville, California. The list had originally appeared in the ElDorado News with a publishing date sometime during the first two weeks of August, 1851. The arriving emigrants were members of the "Hillsdale Mutual Company", which was commanded by Captain L.B. Comstock of Galena, Illinois*. Members of this company consisted of the following:

From Galena, Ill.:	From Marshall, Mich.:	From Hillsdale County, Michigan:
L.B. Comstock	N.M. Gilbert	James McConnell
James Comstock	Patrick Cody	Lorenzo Webster
John Martin	Thomas Clark	Stephen Webster
Alex. Downey	Charles Clark	John Warner
From Calhoun County, Michigan:	John Boyden	Henry Shoemaker
John Quingly/sic/	William Boyden	William H. Philbrick
From Coldwater, Michigan:	From St. Louis, Mo.:	Michael Sellers
Dr. F.H. Parish	John Boon	F. Fanning
From Philadelphia, Penn.:	J.D. Adams	C.B. Smith
Charles Mason	From Illinois:	B.E. Brown
From Ovid, N.Y.:	Robert Shooks	S.D. Clark
George Kinney and lady	Chapman Conows/sic/	William Potter Jr.
From Ohio:	From Andover, Ill.:	G.S. Baker
Isaac Anderson and family	William A. Thompson and lady	E.L. Hastings
Jno. Camron/sic/ (Cameron?)	From Kanesville, Iowa:	G.D. Howell
From Hillsdale County, Mich.:	Charles Beebe	Sylvester Whating (?) (Whaling?)
Frank Keefer	From Illinois:	John Wilsey
	Andrew Burr	Edwin Ford
		George Keefer
		Samuel Keefer

KANESVILLE, IOWA (April 29, 1852) The Frontier Guardian of April 29, 1852 published a list of California bound emigrants who had arrived in Kanesville. Some of the emigrants were composed into companies while others were traveling individually or in small groups. The following data appeared in the cited issue:

Arrived in Kanesville during period April 22-29, 1852:

From Indiana:

John Blood	E.E. Wheeler	Lyman Pomeroy

(*) The source at one point states the company leader was Captain I.B. Comstock.

From Indiana:
J.M. Bombarger /sic/ (Bambarger?)
J. Pearsons
Mary Pearsons
Jacob Kiefer
From Ohio:
Orange E. Page
From Michigan:
John Gafner (?) (Gufner)

Charles Doolittle
Jefferson Harper
John Hazelton
Martin Smith
B.F. McCartney
From Wisconsin:
M. McCormick
J.C. Berry

Elijah Carrich /sic/
R.H. Vanbuskirk
John Wood
Thomas Wheeler
Nathaniel McCartney
From Michigan:
C.F. Bradbury
Alexander Stevenson
John Armstrong

Arrived in Kanesville on April 20, 1852:
From Michigan:
George M. Beswick
Pulaski Roberts
From Indiana:
Nathaniel Ayres

Henry Dieffenbucher
Edgar Roberts

John Ryne /sic/ (Ryan?)
Joseph Jaques /sic/

The *Frontier Guardian* issue of April 29, 1852 also reported the departure from Kanesville, Iowa of Messrs. Brooks & Company, of Henderson County, Illinois. The identity of members of this group was not listed in the source. The departure from Kanesville was on April 28, 1852. The same issue also announced the departure of Mr. __ Hume and Mr. __ Blandin from Kanesville. Hume and Blandin were from McDonough County, Illinois and they also departed on April 28, 1852.

On May 4, 1852, a Mr. __ Broughton and Mr. __ Moffat were scheduled to depart from Kanesville for California. They were intending to pack through with a cavalcade of four horses and two mules.

The *Guardian* announced that the "Badger Company" of California emigrants would depart from Kanesville on May 3, 1852. The group was composed of the following residents of Wisconsin:

Albert Greenleaf, of Kingston
Charles E. Phelps, of Kingston
C.A. Whatiley (?) (Whattley?, Whatley?), of Berlin
H.W. Brown, of Granville
William S. Brentwood (Bustwood?), of Madison
Henry Brown, of Weelaunce
Thomas H. Everts, of Milwaukee

Charles Walde, of Kingston
J.Y. Engleton (?) (Eagleton?), of Coresco(?), Fond du Lac County
Aaron G___, of Berlin
John Sy___, of Granville
James Hughes, of Madison
James H. Grout, of Lowell
John O. Everts, of Milwaukee
T.C. Granger, of Milwaukee
C.D. Holbrook, of Kingston

Henry Martin, of Fond Du Lac County
P.H. Phelps, of Berlin
Benjamin Brown, of Berlin
Y.D. Wallace, of Marcellon
Albert France (?), of Lowell
J. Wademan (?), of Eureka
Chester M. Everts, of Milwaukee
F.A. Custis (?) (Curtis?), of Milwaukee

KANESVILLE, IOWA (May, 1852) The <u>Frontier Guardian</u> of May 6, 1852 announced that Lamar Chandle and Raphael Chandle, both of Marion, Iowa, would depart for California on May 7, 1852. Both emigrants stated they would travel with the "Dubuque Company".

The same issue of the <u>Guardian</u> reported that John Pettygrove, of Highland, Wisconsin, would leave for California on May 10, 1852. In addition to the two foregoing announcements, the newspaper also carried a list of emigrants who had arrived in Kanesville during the period of April 30-May 6, 1852. The cited list appears below (former residence locations are noted):

<u>Emigrants Bound for California</u>:

<u>From Michigan</u>:
Sumner Rawson	George Perry	Dr. E.B. Southwick
James R____ (Rawson?)	Thomas Engle	John Dunlap
N. Creen (?) (Cross?)	Stephen Davis	George W. Halstead and
Robert Moore	Nicholas Bunyan	family
C. Thompson	Thomas English	Simeon Dunn
Ames Gold	J.H. Kim(?) (Kiss, Kien?)	Jeremiah Reynolds
Sanford Murphy	G.O,. Kim (Kiss, Kien?)	D.W. Platt
David Bysick (?)	Benjamin Fredenburgh	George Murphy

<u>From Wisconsin</u>:
Chauncy Baird	Robert Gillies/sic/	Robert G__ive (Grieve?)
G. Waller (?)	John Cr__	J.E. Greely/sic/
John M. Drover	R.C. Flanders	John Gillespie
V.E. Huganin (?)	J.A. Norris	David Russell
(Hugunin?)	Andrew C____ (Andrew G__?)	James Sullivan

<u>From Iowa</u>:
A. Alloway	Enos Adamson	Josiah Reever (?)
Martin Baker	George H. Gross	(Reeves?)

<u>From Indiana</u>:
S.P. Matton	John Perry	Doctor White (?) (Decter
James Roop	John Roop	White?)
Benjamin Roop	Joshua Roop	

<u>From Illinois</u>:
Samuel Connell	S. Thomas	J. Montgomery
Benjamin Montgomery	Michael Rairick	

A group of emigrants also arrived in Kanesville, Iowa on May 4, 1852, from Middlesex, Canada West. The <u>Guardian</u> of May 6, 1852 contains a list of these emigrants and it is reproduced below. There was no mention of their destination, but it would appear they were bound for either California or Salt Lake.

William W. Putnam	David A. Peck	Hyram Odell
Patrick Me__	William Higgle (?)	Seth Putnam
Levi Meyrick	(Higgie?)	Isaac Putnam
M.H. Rowley	Henry Meyrick	Thomas Wood____
George Odell	L.E. Rowley	(Woodbuck?, Woodbeck?)

On May 13, 1852 the Frontier Guardian published a list of California bound emigrants who had arrived in Kanesville, Iowa during the period of May 6-13, 1852. The list is reproduced as follows:

From Wisconsin:
- H. Brunt
- Lyttle Hannon
- A.S. Bennet
- Henry Bradley
- Seth Parker
- Thomas Waller(?) (Weller?)
- George Shaw
- Robert Elliot
- F.R. Stryker
- Patrick Archibald
- Samuel Downes

From Iowa:
- Henry Ehrman
- J.M. Williams
- Tunis S. Beaver
- Samuel Marks
- Hugh P. Cox
- James Brawner
- S.J. McAninch/sic/

From Illinois:
- N.W. Randall
- C.W. Brewster
- E.D. Thomson
- Rufus K. McGreery
- Samuel K. McGreery
- William Dunlap
- H. Bellnap
- J.M. Jones
- Edward Fairhurst
- Henry Spaulding
- Frederick Parker
- William Wright
- Richard Sanford
- John Winn
- Jacob Goff
- William Stoddard
- W.C. Stoddard
- P.O. Tool/sic/
- James Low
- A.T. Maltbey
- E.L. Maltbey

From Virginia:
- L.M. Myers

From Pennsylvania:
- William D. Nesmith

- Oscar Judd
- Robert Sigsby
- Ephrian Sigsby
- A.J. Mays
- John C. Richardson
- Stephen T. Church
- Isaac F. Mann
- William Page
- Thomas Box
- James Colton
- Rev. K. Owen

- Joseph Montgomery
- Daniel Morier
- William J. Mikesell
- John W. Mikesell
- Hannah Mikesell
- A.M. Finch
- Stuart Richey

- Jared Preston
- J.S. Mack
- Thomas C. Brewer
- Jacob Linzee/sic/
- William Vanatta
- James Vanatta
- E.N. Linzee (?) (S.N. Linzee?, B.N. Linzee?, L.N. Linzee?)
- Edward Loomis
- Seth Kinman
- William Brophy (?) (Bruphy?)
- W. Horsley
- Lafayette Mackay
- J. Strafford
- M.E. Everts (?) (Evarts?)
- Napoleon Hammon
- Martin Blunt
- A.H. Simons
- E.W. Simons
- John Cain/sic/

From California:
- Livingston Jones

From Pennsylvania:
- John Weinmer

- Merrick Sawyer
- Joseph Foster
- A.P. Vanvleck/sic/
- Nelson Cole
- John Boundey
- George W. Kent
- L.A. Snow
- Lemuel Page
- Charles Knight
- Thomas Basson
- Edward Platte/sic/

- Jacob Ripley
- Homer Aldrich
- Dedridge Alley
- James Wilson
- Lemuel Marmon
- Isaac P. Ellyson
- R.G. McIntire

- Mary Mack
- William Mittenbuger (Miltenbuger?)
- D.C. Blair
- Calvin Witherell (?) (Witharell?)
- Daniel B. Edwards
- Byron Stevens
- George M. Lease(?)(Leese?)
- B.F. Gum
- S.A.V.Y. Ralston /sic/ (S.A. Ralston? V.Y. Ralston?)
- M.T. Crowell
- B. Parmer
- C. Crowell
- F.A. Davis
- Christopher Webb
- William Webb
- William Fagher (?) (Fugher?)
- Mahlon Eastlick

From Prince Edward's Island, Gulf of St. Lawrence:
- Ambrose J.T. Peake

From Michigan:
A.D. Long
Francis McCormick
Henry Bascom
William Brunridge
G.W. Gaskins
Hiram Gaskins
Benjamin A. Cummings /sic/
William J. Henderson/sic/
Isaac Austin

From Ohio:
Jonathan P. Morton
George T. Terry
W.A. Barnes
J.M. Keating
C. Lee
Aaron Flanders

From Indiana:
Moses Church
O. Vanderlip
E.W. Bisley
Mrs. E.W. Bisley
Sam Funk
Thomas Laugh

William Bagley
Betsey A. Gardner
Jared Pond Jr.
Michael Slaven
Benjamin Cummins/sic/
James Budman
John Budman
Alfred Marmon
Alex. Baldwin
James Fowl
Hiram Strang/sic/

H. Brown
Josiah Dibble
David Lawton
Miss E. Harbaugh
Isaac Jackson
S. Temple

John Irvine
Hiram Kennedy
T.H. Chambers
V.A. Simson
Simon Rhoads
Amos Compton

Marion C. Miller
Amelia H. Pevey
Charles Pevey
B.F. Moore
William Bell
William Henderson/sic/
Almond Colton
O.J. Lundy
Benjamin J. Bradley
Samuel Klady
William E. Klady

S.V. Hurlburt
Vincent Payne
Elisha Coone/sic/
S.P. Read
Kendall Jackson

Aley Puterbaugh
George W. Surgui/sic/
F. Harbaugh
J.W. Walker
Mrs. H.A. Walker

The <u>Frontier Guardian</u> of May 13, 1852 reported that the "James Russell Company", of Plymouth, Marshall County, Indiana, had arrived in Kanesville, Iowa on April 26, 1852, and that the company departed for California on May 7, 1852. Members of this company were listed as follows:

James Russell of Plymouth, Ind.
Cyrus Russell, of Valparaiso, Ind.
N. Cadwallader, of Plymouth, Ind.
F.D. Taylor, of Warsaw, Ind.

William Dunbar, of Paris, Ohio
Alfred Jordan, of Blountsville, Ind.
R.T. Weech, of Onandigua, Ind.
Farmon Young, of same as above
Moses Gunn, of same as above

William Cooper, of Rome, Ohio
Cyrus Bliven, of Plymouth, Ind.
W.L. Blakely, of same as above
F. Baker, of same as above
R.A. Scarbrough, of Newark, Ohio

A list of California bound emigrants that arrived in Kanesville, Iowa on May 7, 1852 also appeared in the <u>Frontier Guardian</u> of the forementioned date. The May 7th arrivals were reported as follows:

James Nicholson, of Mount Pleasant, Iowa
L.M. Davis, of Salem, Iowa
Nelson Rogers, of Salem, Iowa

Joel Cook, of Salem, Iowa
Jonathan Cook, of Salem, Iowa
L. Coppick, of Salem, Iowa

E. Morse, of Salem, Iowa
H.C. Arnold, of Salem, Iowa

James Fagan, of St. Louis, Mo.	Robert Coles, of Guernsey, Ohio	Robert Hornson (?) (Hernson?), of Salem, Iowa
T. Baldwin, of Salem, Iowa	John Buffington, of Salem, Iowa	J. Lott Collins and Company, of Saluba County, Iowa
John S. Coe, of Saluba County, Iowa	James Coe, of Saluba County, Iowa	

In addition to the foregoing emigrant listings, the Frontier Guardian of May 13, 1852 also reported the arrival and departure of the following California-bound emigrants:

Arrived at Kanesville, Iowa on May 9, 1852, the "Eagle Prairie Company", composed of:

George Partridge Jr, Company Pilot	George Partridge	John Sprague
Henry Audiss (?) (Andiss?)	Elias Rose	Peter Sprague
William Partridge	Joseph Buckley	Elias D. Marshall

Arrived at Kanesville, Iowa, on May 4, 1852 and departed on May 8, 1852, the "Red Bird Company, No.1 and No.2", composed of:

William Vannatta	E.D. Thomson	Martin Carse (?)
James Vannatta	Wilber Baker	Richard Glasgow
Andrew Weiss	Phillip Kinnan (?) (Kinnen, Kennen?)	Samuel Swift Jr.

Arrived at Kanesville, Iowa from McComb County, Michigan, and left for California on May 7, 1852 (no arrival date):

Zadock T. Burgess	Reuben A. Burgess	Charles O. Burgess
Alexander Stevens		

Arrived at Kanesville, Iowa from Michigan and Wisconsin, and left for California on May 7, 1852 (no arrival date):

Hugh Towining/sic/ (Towning?, Twining?)	E. Green	N.T. Cross
G.W. Holstead/sic/	Robert Moore	J. Williams
	N. Michael	Thomas English

Arrived at Kanesville, Iowa, from Dyersville, Iowa, on May 4, 1852, with a six mule team, and departed for California on May 8, 1852:

Thomas Rigg/sic/	William Woodward	Timothy Walsh
Robert Bell (?) (Ball?)		

The By-Laws and Resolutions of the "Cassville and Beetown Emigrating Company" will be found in the Frontier Guardian of May 13, 1852. The by-laws of the California-bound company were adopted at a meeting held in camp at Council Bluffs, Iowa on May 10, 1852. Membership was reported as follows:

James M. Scott, Captain	*John Rule	*Dr.E.D. Everhart
William Johnston	Samuel Scott	William S. Anderson
R.M. Briggs	C.A. LaGrave	Samuel Cook
William Polkinghorse	Simon Glazier	James Weeks
H.F. Smith	W.S. Coombs/sic/	Thomas Prater
Olando Button/sic/	George H. Pond	P. Tucker
William Thomas	H.M. Branstutter	William McCartny/sic/ (McCartney?)
	P. Mullen/sic/	

(*) At one point the source lists "John Rule" as "John Buel" and "Dr.E.D. Everhart" as "Dr.F.D. Everhart".

O.B. McCartny/sic/ (McCartney?)
Erastus Gates
J.W. Jones
John Garro
Peter Garro

D.F. Brown
B.F. Lenard/sic/ (Leonard?)
Eli Detor/sic/
William McCurdy

E.B. Grandin
William H. Vanhook
D.W. Stark
William Cooly /sic/ (Cooley?)

The Frontier Guardian of May 13, 1852 reported that the "Wisconsin Company" would leave for California on, or about, May 13, 1852. The Captain of this company, John Healy, was reportedly making his second trip to the West. Membership was listed as follows:

John Healy, Captain
John Crawley/sic/
T. Mahoney
Miss. C. Williams
P. Kearney
J. Chamberlain
L. Fox, wife and child
Jared Fox
J. Woolver
Adison Moore/sic/
C. Maxfield
John Crosson

James Cashing and wife (Cushing?)
J. Hammondson
James Kelly
E. Davis
William Angriaves
J. Francis, wife and children
Baxter Thompson
J. Farrer
E.W. Kingman
Alexander Vail

S. Holland
A.W. Phelps
James McGinn
Miss L.S. Howland
F. French
J. Turnick
H.T. Blanchard
T. Dale
Charles Devol/sic/
John Hollenback
L. Woodworth

KANESVILLE, IOWA (May, 1852) The Frontier Guardian and Iowa Sentinel of May 20, 1852, reported on a number of California emigrant arrivals and departures. The newspaper carried the following announcements:

Arrived in Kanesville, Iowa, from Mishawaka, Indiana, and departed for California on May 12, 1852:

O. Hurd and wife
Mr.__ Sumpstine

William Finch
Aaron Usher

Samuel Numan/sic/
Enos Eutsler(?) (Eutaler?)

Departed from Kanesville, Iowa, on May 14, 1852, for California:
Captain S.E. Jones, late Editor of the Telegraph, from Bellefonte, Kentucky, with a party of eighteen (all-unidentified).

Departed from Kanesville, Iowa, on May 15, 1852, for California, the following members of the "Waukesha and Rock County Company":

J.G. Burgess, of Janesville, Wisc., Company Captain
L.W. Gitchell/sic/, of Janesville, Wisc.
Thomas Basson, of same as above
Dr.H. Van Vleck/sic/, of Brookfield, Wisc.
A.P. Van Vleck and family, of same as above

H. Hyd /sic/ (Hyde?), of Janesville, Wisc.
James Culton /sic/ (Colton), of same as above
Thomas Carlton, of Brookfield, Wisc.
Adam J. Fisher, of same as above
David Mitchell/sic/, of Platteville, Wisconsin

Charles Copp, of Janesville, Wisc.
H. Vanwort/sic/, of same as above
D. Vanwort/sic/, of same as above
James Aitkin, of Brookfield, Wisc.
William S. Clock, of same as above
Newton Neely/sic/, of Platteville, Wisconsin

E.O. Clemens, of Platteville, Wisc.
George Maxim, of Rosendale, Wisc.
John H. Deamon, of Bloomfield, Mich.
William Deamon, of same as above
G.W. Eves, of Neenah, Wisc.

Calvin Austin, of Rosendale, Wisc.
J.T. Williams, of Milwaukee, Wisc.
D.B. Phelps, of Bloomfield, Mich.
R.M. Reed, of same as above
Jesse M. Eves, of Neenah, Wisc.

Fredrick Winegar, of Rosendale, Wisc.
Daniel Marshall, of Milwaukee, Wisc.
A.J. Potter, of Waukesha, Wisc.
D.P. Carter, of Johnstown, Wisc.
James Wood, of Neenah, Wisc.

Following California emigrants arrived in Kanesville, Iowa during the period of May 13-20, 1852 and were preparing to depart for the West:

From Canada West:
A. Askin
A. McKee
M. Dwnell/sic/ (Downell?)
From Iowa:
Richey D. Hoover (?) (__ Richey and D. Hoover?)
J. Pickler
__ Brown
D. Calhoun
D. Jameson
J. Day
From Wisconsin:
Alonzo P. Turner
T. Dean
S.W. Beall
James McClure
James Stewart
James Cowden
J.T. Miles
James S. Miles
W.L. Dewitt/sic/
William C. Jennings

From Michigan:
Francis Brown
Anson Benjamin
J.O. Steam
From Indiana:
James Chesnut/sic/ (Chestnut?)
O. Third and wife/sic/
Mrs. __ Finch
S. Numan/sic/
Enos Eutsin (?) (Eutsia?, Eutsla?)
From Missouri:
J. McNeil
M. Come/sic/
J. Dedman and family
J. Green
I. Ripper
L. Dedman
M. Dedman
H. Dedman
J. Phillips
From Wisconsin:
Peter Miller

From Illinois:
John H. Vandemark
Eli Gum
R.S. Burnhill/sic/
A.B. Reed
E.R. Abbees (?) (Abboes?, Abbotts?)
D. Goodwin
A.A. Gillman/sic/
L. Booth
O. Milthon (?) (Miltbon?)
J.G. Sheridan
J.F. Pierce
J. Preston
G. Cleveland
Benjamin Mikesel/sic/ (Mikesell?)
From Ohio:
Isaac C. Patten (?) (Patton?)
Leven Fowler
From Connecticut:
James A. Connor

Following California emigrants in Kanesville, Iowa on May 20, 1852 and expecting to depart for the West on same day:

Reuben Martin, of Iowa
Charles McAmeron, of Iowa

E. Manning & Company
L. Pittman, of Iowa
George Baldwin, of Iowa

Walter Knight, of Iowa
Robert Daugherty/sic/ of Iowa

Following California emigrants arrived in Kanesville, Iowa during the period of May 21-28, 1852 and were preparing to depart for California:

C.R. Visey, of Ohio
P. Ryan, of Mass.

P. Striker of Wisconsin
David C. Hale, of Ill.

C.G. Taylor, of Wisconsin
H. Stockdale, of Indiana

John S. Wilson, of Indiana	Z.S. Bryant, of Indiana	L. Bryant, of Indiana
John M. Howe, of Indiana	Orville Root, of Indiana	Miss Luba Spicer, of New York

<u>Departed from Kanesville, Iowa, on May 20,1852 for California, the following members of the "Tipton Company" of Iowa</u>:

W. Johnson	John Snyder	Mr. ___ Lariper
Mr. ___ Haywood	Mr. ___ Willis	Mr. ___ Harmon
A.W. Morton	___ Beattle	William Butts and family
J.L. Wright and lady	Samuel Beattle	Robert Long
Dr.S.S. Tibens/sic/ (Tibbons?)	W.A. Bebbs	Dr. Ames Wibber/sic/ (Webber?)
Dr.J.E.R. Cutler	M.E. Bebbs	John ___
Peter Buck and Family	Spicer Wells	
	E.W. ___	

KANESVILLE, IOWA (June, 1852) The <u>Frontier Guardian and Iowa Sentinel</u> of June 4, 1852 reported a number of California emigrant arrivals and departures. The following notices appeared in this issue:

<u>Arrived in Kanesville on May 29,1852, from Wayne County, Michigan with departure for California set as June 1,1852</u>:

A. Clark   J. Ford & Company

<u>Arrived in Kanesville on May 6,1852 and departed for California on May 22,1852</u>:
Peter Dubadie and Company

<u>Arrived in Kanesville on May 31,1852 and departed for California on same day</u>:
Horace Deming and three unidentified sons

<u>Following California emigrants from Fairfield, Illinois departed for California, from Kanesville, on May 25,1852</u>:

Capt. R.S. Barnhill	Mathew Crews/sic/	Alexander Eick/sic/
*George L. Alocumb	C. FanFhouser (?)	A.F. Smith
J.T. Day, lady and child	(FonFhouser?)	J.M. Brown, of Potosi
A.F. Barnhill	J.M. Covington	County, Missouri

The <u>Frontier Guardian and Iowa Sentinel</u> of June 11,1852 reported that Colonel H.P. Russell's Company had departed from Kanesville, Iowa on June 1,1852, bound for California, with an unidentified company of twenty individuals. The same issue also reported the departure of the following California emigrants:

William S. Terry, of Ohio	Horace Taber, of Michigan	A. Wilcox, of Illinois

SACRAMENTO, CALIFORNIA (July, 1852) The <u>Sacramento Daily Union</u> reports the arrival in Sacramento of William Mount, his wife, four children, and a Mr.___ Hoover. All of the forementioned emigrants had crossed the plains from St. Joseph's County, Indiana. They arrived in Sacramento on July 2nd, having left Great Salt Lake City (Utah) on April 2,1852. The news announcement also refers to Hoover's brother, Levi Hoover, another emigrant.

(*) Consider alternative of "George L. Alcoumb".

On July 5, 1852 the <u>Sacramento Daily Union</u> announced the arrival of the first overland immigration company. This company had made the trip from St. Joseph, Missouri to Sacramento, California in seventy-two days, arriving in the city on July 3rd. The group was made up of former residents of the Ohio counties of Miami, Clark and Montgomery. The company guide, Captain J. Clark, had crossed the plains previously. The party left Ohio on March 18, 1852 and St. Joseph (Mo.) on April 20th.

A man named James Harwood, was found by the company a short distance beyond Rock Point. He had strayed from a Salt Lake train, while attempting to ferry across the Humboldt River. The Indians had shot him in the hip with an arrow, and when picked up he was nearly dead with loss of blood. Harwood managed to recover. Members of Captain Clark's company consisted of:

Captain J. Clark	W.J. Cutter	J.H. Chaffee
L. Clark	S. Smith	P. Shellebarger
Thomas Corman	S.M.B. Simpson	John Oakes
George Morris	J. Winslit /sic/	D. Oakes
M. Morris	A. Coffman	M. McCoy
J. Morris	S. Crowell	H. Snyder
F. Stein	L. Ramsay	R. Ramsay
W. Stein	J. Dunn	J. Dye
J. Stein	Mr. ___ Peck	

PLACERVILLE, CALIFORNIA (July 17, 1852) The <u>Sacramento Daily Union</u> of July 19, 1852 reported that William Maiden (Malden?) and George Cross arrived in Placerville, California on July 17, 1852. Both of these emigrants had journeyed across the plains from Radford, Michigan.

PLACERVILLE, CALIFORNIA (July 12-17, 1852) The <u>El Dorado (Calif.) News</u> of July 17, 1852 reported a number of overland arrivals in Placerville, California during the period of July 12-17, 1852. The arrivals were re-printed by the <u>Sacramento Daily Union</u> of July 19, 1852 as follows:

From Michigan:	From Ohio:	From New York:
D. Gridley and family	T.B. Croft	J. Smith
J. Gridley	E. Westlake	O. Hambleton
L. Derbing /sic/	J.W. Davis	L.C. Dodge
A.A. Saunders	G.W. Lowery	From Wisconsin:
A. McNiel	Z. Davis	D. Doul
L. Bingham	D. McGulpin	J. Simmon /sic/
A. Dunham	G.G. Walter /sic/	W. Simmon /sic/
J.L.H. Well /sic/	D. Newman	From Indiana:
H.N. Blakeman	J.K. Malker /sic/ (Walker?,	E.H. Walker
E.A. Blakeman	Walter?)	W. Hart
C.J. Saunders	From Missouri:	H. Hall
Dr. J. Allen	W.S. Clearer	W.H. Scudder
G. Squeer /sic/ and wife	J.H. Menefee /sic/	From Illinois:
(Squire?)	S. Reed	J. Hancock
W. Campbell	J.A. Shieford /sic/	J.W. Parks
		D.M. Stuart

From Missouri:
J.H. Shieford/sic/
T. Stewart
E. Kinchloes and family
S.E. Lay
   From Ohio:
W. Dodd
P. Crosby
G.W. Terrier
W.R. Strobles
F.R. Fish
C. Habry
Collier Robbins
G.A. Wilson
D.E. Wilson
A.H. Bills
J. Moneyheffer
E. Eagle
C. Wilton/sic/
   From Pennsylvania:
E.B. Hotsoff
A.S. Waugaman/sic/

From Michigan:
F. Downey
M.R. Lewis
G.W. Coster
   From Kentucky:
G. Sanson/sic/
T. Middleton
O. Howard
   From Wisconsin:
J.H. Watson
F. Bucklain
W.P. Fleming
P. McGraw
   From Michigan:
R. Foules
M.A.G. Chapman
T. Tunigan
S.M. Shaffee/sic/
C. Henry
   From Iowa:
J.O. Laughlin
   From New York:
H. Newland

From Illinois:
J. Doudell/sic/ (Dondell?)
J. Grady
T. Sarrimore
   From Virginia:
M. Strong
   From Pennsylvania:
J. Frear/sic/
E. Whielock/sic/
   (Wheelock?)
J. Chapman
J.B. Shiffer
   From Indiana:
H.C. Hall
P.R. Brown
Robert Mason
H. Mason
   From Illinois:
M.J. Hough
J.L. Pope
Samuel Pope

SACRAMENTO, CALIFORNIA (July 21, 1852) The Sacramento Daily Union of the forementioned date reports the arrival in the city of a party of eight men from the overland route. This party left St. Joseph, Missouri on April 25, 1852, with one wagon, fourteen oxen and two horses. They made the trip in eighty-five days, the shortest time yet made by ox teams. The group consisted of the following men:

Alfred Bowlby, of
   Hamilton County, Ohio
A.B. Medlor/sic/

David Rudicil/sic/
Hugh Miller
James Johnson

D. White
W. Seaman
W. Medlor/sic/

SACRAMENTO, CALIFORNIA (July 23, 1852) The Sacramento Daily Union of the forementioned date reports the return to Sacramento of Robert Forsythe from a visit to Ohio. Forsythe made the journey through Mexico, from Matamoras via Durango to Mazatlan. He previously tried the route across the plains, the route across the Isthmus, and through Mexico, the last was the cheapest and reportedly the most pleasant.

VOLCANO, CALIFORNIA (July, 1852) The Sacramento Daily Union of July 23, 1852 published a report from a correspondent in Volcano, California that an overland train consisting of eleven wagons from Pennsylvania had arrived in Volcano, over a new road to Carson. In compliment to the train, it was christened the "Pennsylvania Cut-off Road". Four of the newly arrived emigrants endorsed the cut-off with signatures, names as follows:

H.J. Grenet, of
   Manchester, Pa.

G.W. Gardner, of Butler
   County, Pa.

J. Boyle, of Pennsylvania

H. Plannett, of
Manchester, Pa.

SACRAMENTO, CALIFORNIA (July, 1852) The Sacramento Daily Union of July 26, 1852 reported the arrival in Sacramento of Mr.__ Alexander and wife, Mr. __ Norton, wife and two sisters and Mr. James Starr. They had come from Edwardsville, Illinois by way of the plains and Carson Valley, arriving in Sacramento on July 24, 1852.

The same newspaper also announced that at 5:00PM, on July 25, 1852, Benjamin Carpenter and family, and David H. Neale and family had passed William Daylor's Ranch enroute from Great Salt Lake. They had been residents there since the winter of 1850.

PLACERVILLE, CALIFORNIA (July, 1852) The Sacramento Daily Union of July 26, 1852 reported that the following emigrants had arrived in Placerville during the period of July 17-24, 1852:

From Indiana:
J. Buckley
J.S. Tart
C.M. Ogden
C.P. Henry
J. McMurry /sic/
J. McGrew
R. Murry /sic/ (Murray?)
G. Ake
D. Farmer
P. Cassidy
F. Cassidy
M. Bassett
P. Patten /sic/
S.B. Linton
E.M. Miller
L.R. Meeker
W. Roberts
C.E. Links
J. Grinnell
M.M. Woody
L. King
C.W. Anderson
J. Grant
W.W. Coburn /sic/
L.A. Smith
H. Clendenen /sic/
S. Hanson
H.D. Jackson
C. Mason
J. McLane
G. Watters /sic/ (Waters?)
A.G. Banganan
R. Mason

From Pennsylvania:
F. Wyrick
W.H. Shields
J.S. Riddle
J. Vaneman
A. Patten /sic/
J.B. Hays /sic/
R. Jameson /sic/
W. Campbell
J. Johnson /sic/
J. McFarland
T. Farrar
D. Marquis
S. Roberts
B. Lemmon
T. Aiken
J. Barratt /sic/
D. House
J. Roberts
J. Peterman
John Peterman
J. Horton
W. Gregory
E. Harkins
J. Inder
W. Brown /sic/
G. Custer
A. Hannegan
J. Johnson /sic/
J. Ceward /sic/ (Seward?)
E.D. Hartman /sic/
W. Brown /sic/
D.J. Lewis
A. Cook
R. Cook

From Ohio:
J.W. Bateman
H. Bateman
A.P. Parker
E.S. Wells /sic/
G. Allen
O. Meredite /sic/
S. Waugh
D.S. Miller
A. Stephens
W.W. Rose
A.J. Carter
S. Myers
W.K. Williamson
W. Borden
D. Hennessy
P. McCarthy
A. Ingalls
J. Bateman
H. Clendenen /sic/
From Illinois:
T. Millsapo /sic/
H.G. Bristow
C. Caston
C.A. Coffman
R.P. Castle
C.F. Lill /sic/ (C.F. Hill?)
C.W. Davenport
T. Davenport
R. Voorhies /sic/
E. Holdrige /sic/ (Holdridge?)
Dr. W.J. Jones
M. Cahoon /sic/
T.R. Welch

From Indiana:	From Pennsylvania:	From Illinois:
T. Mason	J. Roeberry	J. Welch
H. Mason	W.F. White	T.S. Davenport
C. Sutton	L. McBride	J. Burcham (?)
J.C. Perry	H. Eaton	(Bureham?, Burnham?)
J.W. Ewing	R. Jenkins	From Wisconsin:
W.P. Wheeler	J. Spence	P. McGraw
R. White	R.S. Farrar	P. Brown
G. Nevitt	J.B. Matoon	W. Henry
F. Nevitt	R.J. Nichol	J.C. Ritchie
A. Fuller	J. Myers	___ Fugler
H. Dunant	J. Boyles /sic/	From Iowa:
T. Hawley	G.W. Lardner /sic/	W. Jones
T.P. Hawley	H.J. Grennett /sic/	A. Flannegan /sic/
T.C. Keller	H. Plant /sic/	L. Zibler
H. Berdine	T. Hamilton	From Virginia:
From Michigan:	E.D. Armitage	John Tarland
A. McKenzie	J.P. Dykens	H. Connell
E.D. Hartman /sic/	From New York:	From Michigan:
S.M. Platt	W.W. Coburn /sic/	T.F. Moulton
T. Reed /sic/	G.A. Smith	I.K. Read /sic/
E. Sandborn	J. Ellis	D. Stone
T. Sandborn	W. Farmer	

KANESVILLE, IOWA (July 14, 1852) The Frontier Guardian of July 23, 1852 notes the arrival in Kanesville of the following named persons who were enroute to California. This group intended to winter in the Salt Lake area and move on to Califonia in the spring. They were taking along 1,750 sheep, 87 head of cattle, five horses and ten wagons. The company consisted of:

Thomas Sebring, of Freedom, Illinois	J. More /sic/ (Moore?) of Wisconsin	P. Kenepley /sic/, of Jersey Shore, Penn.
L. Durham, of Freedom, Illinois	V. Beckworth, of Freedom, Illinois	D. Beckworth, of Freedom, Illinois
H. Shoup, of Jersey Shore, Penn.	J.W. Hays, of Winesport, Penn.	J.H. Allen, of Winesport, Penn.
C. Thomas, of Jersey Shore, Penn.	S. Milligan, of Jersey Shore, Penn.	William Thomas, of Jersey Shore, Penn.
J. Sebring, of Liberty, Penn.	J. Crist, of Liberty, Penn.	W. Crist, of Liberty, Penn.
	H. Hopkins, of New York	J.A. Todman, of Elmira, New York

DOWNIEVILLE, CALIFORNIA (August 7, 1852) On the forementioned date the Downieville Mountain Echo reported the first overland arrivals for the 1852 season. The article indicated that the immigrants were from Michigan and Illinois and noted that the journey had taken two and a half months. The arrivals were reported as follows:

John Hall and wife*	John Wilson	L. Buttes
	Mr. ___ Beckwith	Lewis Buttes

(*) Mrs. John Hall was reported as "the first lady overland to arrive in Downieville".

H. Stafford   J. McKnight Jr.   Mr. __ Woods
Mr. __ Edgar

DOWNIEVILLE, CALIFORNIA (August 14,1852) The <u>Mountain Echo</u> of the forementioned date referred to the arrival in Downieville of ten men who had left the Missouri River on May 15,1852. The group had utilized horses in crossing the plains and reported little trouble enroute. Members of the group were listed as follows:

M.N. Mason, of Wisconsin	George Forster/sic/, of Pennsylvania	W.B. Johnson, of Wisconsin
Thomas L. Lewellin, of Illinois	Selphatius Schroter, of Wisconsin	Harvey Johnson, of Wisconsin
M. Neal, of Illinois	J.J. Linn, of Illinois	William Starks, of Illinois
	C.H. Linn of Illinois	

COLOMA, CALIFORNIA (July, 1852) On August 3,1852 the <u>Sacramento Union</u> published a list containing the names of emigrants who had arrived in Coloma, California during the period of July 24-31,1852. The <u>Union</u> had obtained the list of emigrants from the <u>El Dorado (Coloma) News</u> of July 31,1852. Names of the overland emigrants appeared as follows:*

Peter Kallenback	S.S. Jeaning/sic/ (Jenning?)	B.T.C. Brandon
R.A. Keene	Edw. St. John	A.B. Jacobs
J.C. Hammond	O.H.P. Baily/sic/ and family (Bailey?)	C.H. Atherton
George Dake		Noble Fish
B.H. Hankey	Thomas Hamilton	E.D. Hartman/sic/
M. Law	W. Troop	G.M. Enners
David Means	M. Street	T. Hayden/sic/
H.T. Tennet	John M. Anderson	John Haydon/sic/
J. Murray	Moses Bates	J.M. Hubbard
S.M. Chaffie	L. Cunningham	George Graham
S.A. Reed	Mr. __ Weatherby	W.H. Edgeston
J. Rardeer /sic/	Fleming Spangier	A.P. Hayward
J.F. Fox	Solomon Freeid/sic/ (Fried?)	David Murssly/sic/
W.W. Birkolet		E. Ryan
Paul Sharpley	A.A. Huse	S. Jonas/sic/
James Finn	Dan C. Smith	A.A. Hall
John Lawkin	Ed Flanegin	D.B. Adney
S.H. Foote	John Green	Francis Johnson
John Thomas	Joseph Pronty/sic/	Thomas Ball
D. McNahl	John Thornton	James M. Lan/sic/ (Lander?)
H. McNahl	Jeremiah Berry	
Eli K. Ludwig	James Duffy	August Lander/sic/
Anias Marcasy /sic/	John Peters	Pat Lynch
C. Dempsey	N. Skarg	John S. Connus/sic/
Michael Carberry	Michael Egan	Marcus Webster
William Seveny/sic/	Jesse H. Ellis	W.R. Welch
William T. Colister/sic/	Lewis Sarrson/sic/	John Delal/sic/
Cyms Colister/sic/	Calvin Wiley	Edward A. Vincent

(*) Author believes emigrants arrived in Placerville, California rather than Coloma, California.

Anthony Rogers
C.W. Case
F.M. Edger/sic/
John S. Street
A. Banyat
G.A.R. Oston
John O. Everts
J. Allen
J.C. Saript/sic/
J. Miller
John Farsing
Charles Anderson
Stephen W. Werither
Sam W. Thomas
John Webb
R.E. Barnes
John Ryne/sic/
James P. Dye
Henry G. Blanshard
 (Blanchard?)
Edw. Blain
E.W. Lemis
Martin L. Smith
J.A. Stephenson
John Gleen
T. Froods/sic/
John Range
P.M. Browning
Pulaski Roberts
John Bidblee/sic/
Dexter Carlton/sic/
John P. Rreen/sic/
 (Breen?)
Daniel Woore/sic/
 (Moore?)

J.B. Herbert
J.S. Shafer
P. Thomas
Thomas Downing
John Harper
J.W. Krengel
Henry W. Brown
H.C. Blanchard/sic/
Amos C. Matteson
R. Piarson/sic/ (Pearson?)
Henry Lambert
Jesse Hall
W. Sweeny/sic/
 (Sweeney?)
J.C. Wendon
John A. Young
Joseph S. Wineford
Levand Orain/sic/
George Reed
James W. Robertson
C. Weed
R.H. Buskisk
R.C. Barnett
Richard Wasden
John Tipto/sic/ (Tipton)
Thomas Boyce
F.C. Good
Thomas Warshal
John G. Weste/sic/
L.D. Murdock
C.A. Pardis
John White

J.M. Bombarger/sic/
John A. Fowler
G. Leihest/sic/
M.S. Thompson
W.A. Thompson
M.C. Belmier
C. Ellis
William Price
John H. Riplinger
Jacob Prickett
B. Simpson
W.E.W. Kee
Charles S. Stnyher/sic/
 (Steiner?)
Volney Wood
J.T. Janson
J.A. Barrelton
John Lambert
Spencer Knapp
W.D. Robertson
Lewis S. Hoffman
Eli Lome
J. Kiefer/sic/
B.F. Denton
James W. Lure/sic/
J.S. Beming
W. Burnett
T.F. Blackburn
J.C. Blackburn
William Sweeny/sic/
 (Sweeney?)
John Bissel
George C. White

PLACERVILLE, CALIFORNIA (August, 1852) On August 9, 1852 the Sacramento Union published a list of overland emigrants who had arrived in Placerville during the period of August 1-8, 1852. The list had originally appeared in the El Dorado (Coloma) News. The overland arrivals were carried as follows:

S. Beardsley
J. White
B.F. Donalson/sic/
 (Donaldson?)
W. Sweeney
Sno Hall/sic/ (John Hall?)
P. Davis
S. Taylor
C.T. Gibson
P.T. Simms/sic/

H.M. Harris
I. Rumgan/sic/ (Rungan?)
J.S. Roe
M.J. Barney/sic/
B.Y. Rungan/sic/
 (Rumgan?)
W.C. Hardlan
E. Trayon
J.R. Mitchell
P.H. Phelps

J.G. Groff
D. Smith
T.F. Engell /sic/ (Engel?)
H.C. Green
E. Ingrove
D.D. Jehus
H. Brown
W. Charlton/sic/
W.B. Aaron
C.E. Phelps

William Charlton/sic/
M. Francess/sic/
   (Frances?)
H. Cornell
John Getter
L.P. Cosperte
F. Hefright
N.B. Buckham
J.H. Parmelee
G.C. Barry
M. Herman
G. Graham
S. Smith
J.C.P. Smith
Charles Smith
W. Webster
W.H. Daniel
P. Lee/sic/
A.J. Campbell
J. Barbin
T. Nelson
C.M. Stillwell/sic/
J. Turnock
N. Hough
J.W. Hough
E. Morgan
P. Lee/sic/
S. Barlow/sic/
Dr. F.D. Ward
J. Luster
J.F. Carter
J.C. Huck
W.M. Fillbright/sic/
E. Decamp/sic/
J.D. Moley and family
J. Muk/sic/
G.W. Wentz
E. Rowe
J.B. Colten/sic/
L. Dunning
J.J. Benden
Dr. J.F. Morse
C. Ferguson
J.H. McDonald
A. Gregory
J.M. Davis/sic/
J.M. Davis/sic/
A. Berden
W.S. Miller
J.M. Moore
C. Marshall

M. Carr
D.H. Fugua
G.N. Mott
L. McIntyre
J. Spinning
M. Francis
J. Pedvin
A.S. Buchanan
J.P. Lewis
L.G. Atwood
A. Wyers
E. Walker
B.L. Howes
J.T. Lewis
D. Townsend
W.W. Eppes
William E. Carder
N. Hammond
J.H. Minter
J. Biddinger
J.P. Holmes
Thomas Dale
W.M. Williams
L. Hiles
M.M. Hilliard
W.F. Waters
J. Laramer
W. Laramer
J. Smith
J.F. Clifford
D.F. Clifford
D. Wise
R. Lee
J. Lee
M. McCormick
A.B. Perfect
E.C. Crane
W. Thompson
P. McMahon
G.R. Suley/sic/
Jason Sowle/sic/
W.H. Kinan/sic/
J. Thompson
R. Richardson
R. Martin
W.A. Gentry
W.E. Doolittle
M.W. Goode/sic/
F.M. James
G.W. Crosby
A.J. Young
J.O. Boon/sic/

Sno Eagle/sic/ (John
   Eagle?)
L.H. Hopkins
L. Howe
T. Brown
S.P. Boles
J.P. Hope
A.S. Lohanan
W. Plemery
G.T. Barron
A. Campbell
J.F. Campbell
A.C. Tilsmiman
T.A. Falconer
E.G. Bradford
W. Desbrough
James Loving
W. Howard/sic/
A. Cline
J. Mulbarger
J. Sheppard
H.J. Blanchard
D. Watts
P. Wolcott/sic/
C. Northway
S.H. Shearer
J. Powell
C. Fisher
J.M. Grable
G.R. Lamper
H. Grable
B.F. Lamper
B. Snider
F. James
V. Currer/sic/
W.M. Carey and family
M. Suttle
W. Howard/sic/
J. Kirk
J. Henderson
B. Estis/sic/
James Williamson
R. Williamson
R. Hill
W. Dogan/sic/
H. Miller
A. Reed
W.D. Drane/sic/
G.P. Morgan
E.D. Reed
W.T. Boon/sic/

N.B. Lemno/sic/ (Lemon?)	J.A. Hays/sic/	S.M. Brown
L.G. Hammond	J. Bordvelle	J.B. Brown
A. Fox	S. Phelps	L.H. Putnam
W. Prophy/sic/	D. Hall	D. Stove
Benjamin C. Donellan	K.C. Hughs/sic/ (Hughes?)	E. Meeks
A. Bowers	E. Silter	W. Tate
P.J. Nolan	B.T. Hunt	L. Emerson
D.W. Cheek/sic/	I. Allen	I. Muncey
S. Barlow/sic/	N.D. Squibb	M. Andrews
J. Mellon	M. Francis	E. Rummel
		Y.M. Gallsep

SHASTA, CALIFORNIA (August 4, 1852) On the foregoing date a party of immigrants arrived in Shasta after having crossed the Sierra Nevada mountains by Noble's new Shasta route. The party came under the pilotage of A.P. Shuel, one of the first surveyors of the route. They had traveled with wagons as far as the Humboldt River, and from that point onward with pack mules. No wagons traveled this road because of the need for improvement. The Sacramento Union of August 11, 1852 published the list of the new arrivals from data obtained in the Shasta (California) Courier of August 4, 1852.

From Stevenson County, Illinois:	From McHenry County, Illinois:	From Boone County Illinois:
L.D. Snyder	Alfred Thomas	Thomas McClure
Uriah Borden	Martin Wescott	___ Bullard
James Stewart	Fleetus Brush	D. Harvey
Mahlon Snyder	From Indiana:	John Powers
Alfred Rowe	William Worden	Francis Bullard
Adam Ecker	___ Pierce	From Illinois:
Thomas Seely/sic/	From Wisconsin:	Duke W. Kendrick
G.S. Freeman	James Taylor	Levi B. Kendrick
Henry Epley	John Yost	From Wisconsin:
John Epley	Peter Reese	Erasmus Olison/sic/

PLACERVILLE, CALIFORNIA (August, 1852) On August 16, 1852 the Sacramento Union published a list of overland immigrants who had arrived in Placerville during the period of August 9-14, 1852. The list had originally appeared in the El Dorado (Coloma) News. The arrivals were listed as follows:

S.S. Workman	J. Rice	G. Alcock
J. Van Amen (?) (Van Aman?)	J. Emerson	A.A. Bloss/sic/
	A. Smith	E.V. Rice
C.J. Blackman	W. Biggers	W. Boling
J.J. Lillard	J.C. Henton	J.D. Kelley
J.W. Ellis	W. Erwin	A. Campth/sic/
D.C. Wilcox	A.N. Read	W.B. Stone
J. Brown	William Venton	J. McWorgan
L.A. Norton	A.C. Raimey (?) (Rainey?)	T.M. Norton
C.H. Atherton		C.D. Johnson
B.R. Coon/sic/	M.F. Lamrester	J.F. Finch
	J.A. Dory	J.R. Grace

J.R. Grace
T.A. Bosler
J.W. Beacham
J. Little
J. Scott
M. Emmens
R.B. Hubbard
J.C. Berry
A.A. Palmer
E.G. Woodburn
B. Franklin
S.H. Fellows
J.D. Garner
D.S. Kirby
H.C. Tickner
C.H. Scott
William P. Laforce
J.D. Ingalls
T. Ingalls
J. Sherburne/sic/
J.C. Nagel/sic/
J.T. Pearson
J.G. Sprague and family
C.J. Allen
K.G. Fraser
C. Allon/sic/ (Allen?)
J. Hollenbeck
William Laforce/sic/
J. Eagle
B.R. Coon/sic/
C. Campbell
O.S. Pierce/sic/
S.H. Little
Dr. J.W. Layton
William Heart
J.C. Carpenter
William T. Purcell
A.E. Kidd
W.H. Hook
J. Kane
L. Kane
R.W. Nayoo
S. Boger
L.M. Neale
F.S. Glass
S. Isham
A. Richardson
J. Frerret
M. Ryan/sic/

R.J. Elliott
E.T. Todd
T.C. Wilson
G. Steny (?) (Steuy?)
Dr. A.A. Allen
N. Milleson
B.T.C. Brandon
M. McCormick
William Wirick (Wyrick?)
  and brother
J.W. Tamoy (?)(Tumoy?)
L. Ingalls
J.X. Scott
H. Buft
S. Jetmore
C. Brando/sic/ (Brandon?)
E.G. Woodbury
J.P. Kates
M.L. Fairservice
J. Kimball
J.L. Dory
G. Cone
W.F. O'Neale
G. Blake
William Tresslor
E.P. Dunne
C.C. Dunne
S. Lyons
W.S. Eaton
John Burlison and two
  daughters
H.N. Chase
C.M. Vrain
G.C. Conner
W. Howard
J. Stone
H.A. Perimo
William de Kay
A. Wood
J. Buyatte
E. Buyatte
F.W.M. Phelps
E.H. Gosnell (?) (Goshell?)
G.W. Kneedler
C.D. Kneedler
T.A. Kimball
H.M. Blodget
Mathew Ryan/sic/
C.T. Gibson

J.W. Snook
H. Starr
M. Kelly
L. Sonder
F. Drish (?) (E. Drish?)
M. Drish
J. Edwards
Ira Analinda (Amalinda?)
  and wife
W.C. Goldsmith
D.A. Rowland/sic/
H. Lewis
D.A. Rowland/sic/
A. Palmer
C. Lewis
L. Baldwin
William McCrarey
W.C. Wallace
G.L. Cole
J.D. Reed
G.M. Thomas
A. Moore
J.A. Clark
A. Smith
W.C. Glassan(?) (Glessan?)
J.S. Brown
L.D.C. Wilcox
B.D. Marston
T. Commary, wife and
  two children
Dr. B.M. Beckhand
J.M. Breneman
M. Francis
S. McCreeny
R. Burgess
A. Corinth
C.W. Howland
G. Raugh
C.A. Burgess
R. Ashlock
P. Giles
A.D. McCoy
W.H.H. Hopkins
J.H. Goodhue
H. Williams
T.J. Guthrie
J.P. McHenry
J. Hale

H. Creelman	C.E. Nash	O.S. Pierce/sic/
W.B. Knowlton	S.D. Nash	I. Calwell/sic/
J. Knowlton	H.O. Morrell	John Rien/sic/
J. Beraus	F. Parker	A. Judd
F. Hammond	A. Currier	F. Chaff
J.M. Finney	O. Sailady	J.C. Rendall/sic/
J.F. Wicker	F. Dunpree	Amos T. Osby
O.H. Downs	H.M. Sinclair	Dr. E.D. Walker
J. Kelly	William Brice	Dr. W. Church
N. Geesly	J. McCarthy	Dr. S.F. Marques
J.D. McCarthy (?) (J.O. McCarthy?)	A. Chine	S. Vanpatter
	Robert Allison	A. Hartford
R. Glass	J. McDonald	M. Dunlap
G.W. Fitzsimmons	C. Tupper	G.W. Hanck(?) (Hauck?)
C.J. Blackard	S. Hanck(?) (Hauck?)	

SHASTA, CALIFORNIA (August 11, 1852) The Sacramento Union of August 17, 1852 reported that the following immigrants arrived at Shasta, via Noble's route, on August 11, 1852. The Union based its report on an item appearing in the Shasta Courier of August 14, 1852.

John Redshaw, of Warren County, Indiana	Andrew J. Sloan, of Mahaska County, Iowa	John Bird, of Wisconsin George Branch, of Wisconsin
William Pierce, of same as above	James Sullivan, of Watertown, Wisc.	Mr. __ Long, of Hazlegreen, Wisc.
John Sprouse, of same as above	William M. McConnell, of Warren County, Indiana	

YANKEE JIM'S, CALIFORNIA (August, 1852) The Sacramento Union of August 21, 1852 printed the following list of emigrants and indicated they had arrived at Yankee Jim's, via "Scott's Route", the week ending August 18, 1852. Yankee Jim's was situated on the "divide" of the Middle and North Fork of the American River.

Isaac McClarry and lady	Charles Coon	Charles Lewis
Frederick Marker	Mathew Jackson	Hiram Coon
Andrew Laland/sic/ (Leland?)	Henry Vaper	Martin Lorr
	Major __ Ward (Major Ward?)	Charles Lorr
John Houck		Marvin Wheeler
Enos Houck	George Bruce and lady	Dennis Sackett
John Laland/sic/ (Leland?)	William Armstrong	Alonzo Sackett
M. Steele	John Igram/sic/ (Ingram?)	A. Johnson
C. Burns	N. Stirrer	Mr. __ Burbank, of Wayne County, Michigan
John Straut	John Voightly	
W. Witsel	C. Sahly	
John Swap	David Domarn	F. Burns
Frederick Brighthoup	Frank Fisher	G. Faas
C. Miller	C. Swartz	John Hani/sic/ (Haney?)
Louis Smether	M. Younger	G. Wagoner
		Jacob Colber

Anthony Gaugher, of
  Pennsylvania

The same issue of the <u>Sacramento Union</u> also reported that the following emigrants from Michigan died of diarrhea on the Humboldt River:

David McClarry	D. H. Ravlin	E. Wheeler
Uriah Coots	Albert Dunning	

SACRAMENTO, CALIFORNIA (August, 1852) The <u>Sacramento Union</u> of August 24, 1852 published an item announcing that Christian Myers, an old resident of Calaveras County, California, had just returned by way of the plains. Myers had left Farmington, Iowa, with an ox team and made the trip in ninety days. The <u>Union</u> based its report on an article which appeared in the <u>Calaveras Chronicle</u> of August 21, 1852.

The <u>Union</u> of August 24th also printed another emigrant item which it had obtained from the <u>Sonora (Calif.) Herald</u> of August 21, 1852. The <u>Herald</u> had stated that a party, numbering seventy-five emigrants, from across the plains were within a few miles of Columbia, California. This train was under the direction of Mr. ____Clarke and Mr. ____ Skidmore. An advance party from the train had reached Columbia and this group consisted of:

J. L. Frost, of Hamilton County, Ohio	James C. Hays /sic/, of Hamilton County, Ohio	Isaac Sherman, of Hamilton County, Ohio
John G. Rabe (?) (Rahe?), of same as above	Nathaniel Clark, (Clarke?), of same as above	John Hughes, of Pittsburgh, Penn.

A final emigrant article appearing in the <u>Union</u> of August 24, 1852 concerned a list of overland emigrants who had arrived at Placerville, California during the period of August 16-19, 1852. The <u>Union</u> secured the list from the <u>El Dorado News</u> and it appeared as follows:

F. Copland /sic/ (Copeland?)	J. Budd	W. B. Reeve /sic/ (Reeves?)
A. C. Allen	G. W. Botts	William Wilkinson
F. J. Birkey	J. P. Cutterson	G. Anderson
B. P. Flinn	W. W. Johnson	S. F. Wood (?)
J. Waggoner	William Farmer	(S. P. Wood?)
H. Carmack /sic/	H. C. Follijamb	P. C. Adams
J. L. Alexander	J. F. Conant	W. Coppers
M. Tradwick (?) (Trailwick?)	A. Miller	W. Fox
Dr. F. D. Ward	M. Boone	J. M. Rankin /sic/
G. W. Johnson	F. Boone	H. Syhox (?) (Synox?)
W. Biggs	M. J. Barney /sic/	J. Patmor /sic/ (Patmore?)
G. Nixon	E. Ingersoll	J. C. Garner
G. W. Stout	A. Ingersoll	A. Moore
J. Cantrey	S. H. Fellows	
	William Halbert	
	J. Woods	

A. L. Morris
J. Blair
P. McGill
A. G. Spaulding
J. Watters /sic/
J. Steller
G. W. Watson /sic/
S. A. Lee
D. A. Blankenship
William Sweeden
J. Frantises /sic/
____ Cooper
N. Syne /sic/
N. Phillips
A. Baker
William Miller
G. W. Watson /sic/
S. T. Davis
A. Burroughs
S. A. Hulbert /sic/
A. F. Cowell
L. Ares /sic/
C. A. Terrill
A. D. Palmer
J. Williams
Ripley Stogden
R. Williams
C. Williams
J. Slattey
R. McMahan
M. Hill
M. Francis
T. Barnes
T. M. Claugry /sic/
J. S. Edgos /sic/
A. Freeman
P. M. Bedgalow /sic/
S. Young
*J. Patmore /sic/
S. Downey
V. W. Philips
J. A. Phelps
____ Myers
W. Pane /sic/
G. W. Coddington
W. McSpencer /sic/
  (Spencer?)
D. Spencer /sic/
  (McSpencer?)
M. W. Spencer /sic/
  (McSpencer?)
G. C. Greenold /sic/

James Woodward
John Woodward
J. H. Constant
A. Martin
W. M. Johnson
W. Lumpion
H. Smith
C. W. Rust
O. Rower
J. H. Fisher
James Burer /sic/
W. N. Snowden
J. Biddeliger
H. Richardson
S. B. Merril /sic/
  (Merrill?)
N. Smith
I. Swift
J. Greeny /sic/ (Greeney?)
M. Jackson
S. E. Anderson
P. Dickerson
R. Wagdloff /sic/
S. B. C. Mombur
Henry Drake
S. Scott
R. Scott
A. Eals
M. Knox
M. Mosely /sic/
C. C. Blevin
J. Sudlum
C. M. Bross
S. N. Carbin
S. Hooke
C. V. Dodge
T. Scott
W. C. T. Gibson
W. T. Gibson
S. Woodworth
D. J. Lake
S. Ogden
W. B. Stephens
D. G. Myers
E. W. Burough /sic/
J. Parks
B. T. Addison
J. P. Carpenter
J. A. Crutchfield
A. T. Beatty
J. S. Howee /sic/
B. Willie /sic/

J. G. Glidden
J. L. Riddle
P. W. Fishburn
J. S. L. Edgar /sic/
G. Spaugle (?) (Spangle?)
W. F. P. Norris
J. M. Stewart
S. Willimer /sic/
E. Hoffman
A. H. Kennedy
C. Jewett
J. White
J. Platt /sic/
K. B. Hudson
G. Trimble
W. R. Kincannon
H. J. Dyer
C. E. Linck /sic/
A. Malory /sic/
R. M. Boutrall
J. B. Boutrall
____ Marshall
J. Yandywine /sic/
J. Pebles sic/
  (Peebles?)
J. Doty
W. Smith
J. Putt (?)
C. O. Burgef
S. Hurbbirt /sic/
  (Hurlbirt?)
J. M. Serland
G. M. Chandler
O. G. Tooker /sic/
N. McGohan
M. Warren
J. H. Wright
H. M. Malvin /sic/
W. Smullio /sic/
  (Smullin?)
R. B. Brown
H. Frasier
W. Frasier
J. Stephenson
H. Staley
E. J. Palmer
A. Cloff
B. M. Sampson
A. H. Warrey /sic/
  (Warren?)

(*) Note entry page 152 for J. Patmor /sic/.

W. B. Hossler	W. Spoon	L. Pilcher and family
D. Greednfield and wife /sic/ (Greedenfield?)	J. R. Cox	G. A. Fuller and wife? (C. A. Fuller and wife?)
	W. Patton	
D. R. Howell	S. Camell /sic/	S. M. Scott
T. L. Beal	M. Blair	F. Baker
J. Miller	T. M. Smith	N. T. Potter
C. Whitney /sic/	J. Matters and son	G. W. Hoblitzee
J. Jeffry /sic/ (Jeffrey?)	I. Ross	S. Fuller /sic/
I. S. Harly /sic/ (Harley?)	J. Parks	S. Huller /sic/ (Fuller?)
William Vermillion	W. M. Smith	R. Huller /sic/ (Fuller?)
W. Wilson	D. W. Parker	J. T. Armstrong
H.O. Naering /sic/	H. Beckney	S. M. Greenville
J. Song	C. Whitney /sic/	C. P. Caoly /sic/
W. Steel	S. W. Reed /sic/	J. McLaughlin
F. Hammond	A. C. Stillman	W. N. Breedlove
G. S. Worman	H. Stillman	W. McMillion /sic/ (McMillian?)
H. Newell	L. W. Wible /sic/	
O. E. Rice	J. Stow	H. Ahalt /sic/
A. Collins	B. Scribners /sic/ (Scribner?)	U. Hatcher
H. Goodfoster and family		H. Hull and family
_____ Barrett	J. Taylor and family	J. Paul and family

DOWNIEVILLE, CALIFORNIA (August, 1852) On August 21, 1852 the Mountain Echo of Downieville published a news story that Mr. S. E. Jones, a printer from Kentucky, had conducted the first overland wagons through to Galloway's Ranch, on the new road to Downieville. Mr. Joseph Driver and family, and Mr. _____ Jones, of Wisconsin, accompanied S. E. Jones. The below individuals were also in the wagon train:

Talten Bramell	Leonard Periner	D. W. Wells
Benjamin Brown	John Steen	I. Bramell
William J. Rogers	F. Schweerkotting	H. Koppelman
Alfred Campbell	M. Williams	Peter Steen
A. Elerandse /sic/	Harrison White	Joseph E. Fitzgerald
R. Weigand	Donald White	Ruben Fenstermaker
Charles Ashton	A. Brownlea /sic/	

The Downieville Mountain Echo of August 28, 1852 contains a list of overland emigrants who arrived in Downieville from the Humboldt Sink. The list is reproduced as follows:

From Jefferson County, Wisconsin:	From Cole County, Missouri:	From St. Louis County, Missouri:
C. H. Wilcox, lady and child	James Caffett	Adam Frick
	Nicholas Ahart /sic/	George Frick
William Allis	Peter Ahart	George Kline
C. Marble	Michael Ahart	John Cribner
A. McEntire /sic/ (McIntire?)	William Rosinbury /sic/	John Stoten, lady and boy
	George Misten	John Cainor /sic/
Daniel Masters		Samuel Hanelett

From Jefferson County, Wisconsin:
William Masters
Lytle Hannen
Jacob Fellows
Chauncey Haskell

From Jefferson County, Wisconsin:
Merrick Sawyer
William Fleming
Benjamin Bludgett

From Jefferson County, Wisconsin:
David B. Pattison
Alonzo McEntire /sic/ (McIntire?)

SHASTA, CALIFORNIA (August 22, 1852) On August 26, 1852 the Sacramento Union published a list of immigrants who had arrived at Shasta, California on August 22, 1852 as following Noble's route. According to the newspaper, this was the first party to follow the route to the town of Shasta. The group had left the old immigrant trail at Black Rock and turned their course into Shasta, a route entirely unknown to them. No wagons had ever preceded them, and having no guide, some of the party became alarmed, left the train and started on the trail for Shasta. The majority, however, remained and dispatched a man to Shasta for assistance. A relief party from Shasta brought in the following immigrants:

Travelling with horses:

David Mitchell, wife and two children
Michael Engless
William Engless
Peter Engless
A. Engless
Mrs. Angelina Wilson

W. F. Miller
S. J. Adams and son
E. O. Clemens
P. Elfbrink
R. A. Pierce, wife and one child
Thomas Egan, wife and son

George Mason
Lewis Thompson
Charles Baker
William Wheeler
Newton Neely
E. J. Comstock
James Decker
R. J. Evans

Travelling with ox teams: (Eight wagons)

William Jackson
William Montgomery, wife and two children
Samuel O. Robinson
James Sals /sic/
John Denver
Thomas Montgomery
John Denny
William Copenhaven /sic/ (Copenhagen?)

John Young, wife and two children
Isaac Cox
Xavier Brisbeau
James Baugh
Thomas Baugh
Woodson Wilkinson
Raphael Wilkinson
Jack Wilkinson
James Denny
Mr. _____ Hurst /sic/

Charles Cook, wife and child
David B. Warren
William C. Payne
Hamilton Frazier
Samuel Sconce
William Cammon /sic/ (Cannon?)
Hadrick Fry
Amos Montgomery

SACRAMENTO, CALIFORNIA (August 25, 1852) The Sacramento Union of August 26, 1852 reported that a party of thirty-five Kentuckians, residents of Madison and Clark Counties, had arrived in Sacramento on August 25, 1852. The group made the overland trip in seven wagons drawn by thirty mules. Only a portion of the train member names appeared in the Union. A daughter of Dr. _____ Cooper, who was one of the party, had died during the trip and was buried at Fort Kearny. Members of the train were reported as follows;

From Madison County:
Edward Tiley
O. F. McIntosh and family

From Clark County:
Mrs. A. H. Cooper and family
Dr. _____ Cooper

From Missouri:
Mrs. _____ Fugett
From Clark County:
J. W. McIntosh

From Madison County:
Harrison Helfenstein and family

From Madison County:
J.P. Helfenstein and family

From Madison County:
J.W. Payden and family

COLUMBIA, CALIFORNIA (August, 1852) The Sacramento Union of August 27, 1852 published a news story stating that a train, under the guidance of General H. Morehead (sic), had reached Columbia, California, by a new route from Carson Valley. This wagon train was a portion of a train known as the "Elizabethtown, Ohio Emigrating Company," which was being guided by W.C. Clark, an old Californian. The Morehead train came along the Carson River Road, about forty miles past the sink of Carson River, and then struck off in a south south-west direction, striking Walker's River in about twenty-five miles-then up the same river to its head, and thence on the same course south of the Stanislaus River. The Morehead segment consisted of:

W.C. Clark	Gen. H. Morehead	Isaac Sherman, of Ohio
John G. Rake, of Ohio	John Hughes, of Penn.	Jacob Frost, of Ohio

COLOMA, CALIFORNIA (August, 1852) On August 30, 1852 the Sacramento Union published an item announcing that Mr. __ Haines, an old Coloma resident, had returned from Thousand Spring Valley, where he had gone for the purpose of meeting his family, who had crossed the plains. Haines had returned to Coloma with his family on August 23, 1852. Members of the Haines family were not identified and the Union had based its news story on an item which appeared in the El Dorado News of August 28, 1852.

A second item removed from the News by the Union reported the following persons, from Polk County, Missouri, all belonging to one train, had died while crossing the plains:

W.C. Campbell	Miss M.C. Campbell	J.A. Smithson
Mr. __ Justice	Dr. __ Beal /sic/	

PLACERVILLE, CALIFORNIA (September, 1852) On September 7, 1852 the Sacramento Union published a list of overland emigrants who had arrived in Placerville during the period of August 29-September 4, 1852. The list is reproduced as follows:

W.G. Romans	A. Newsome /sic/	H. Pykes /sic/
S. Jackson	J. Hey /sic/	C. Howk /sic/
D. Eby /sic/	C.W. Newman	A.C. Plummer /sic/
G.W. Gregory	C.H. Schwenker	L. Pimper
J. Wolford	D. People /sic/	J. Vanorinan
John Wolford	A. Manche /sic/	L.H. Weatherby
F.D.C. Shaw	J.J. Jennings	C. Crittenden
J.H. Shelton	W.J. Hill	E.F. Springer
E. Horine /sic/	J. Jones	W.H. Springer
D. Nicely	C. Stremming	J.P. Springer, wife and child
R.K. Lansden (?) (Lunsden?, Lensden?)	J.C. Hall	
	J.M. Coley	Mrs. S.O. Springer and child
J.W. Jones	A. Hull	
A.G. Burleson	J. Cain	H.B. Wilson /sic/

157

M. Tacks (?)
L.D. Allen
J.A. Shepperd
J. Hammond
H. Whitson
J.G. Dougherty
P. Parcels
P.R. Wellot
P. Fitzpatrick
J. Holt (?)
C. Metcalf
W. Henderson
D.H. Williamson
A.J. Pimberman /sic/
H. Gilbert Jr.
J. Kannatte
W. Griffeth /sic/
  (Griffith?)
W.J. Gilson
G.A. Elmer
J. Anderson
W. Eccleston /sic/
J. Lampton /sic/
T. Clancy
G.S. Kendrick
H.H. Hall
J.J. Randelin /sic/
R.G.C. Houston
I. Cox and lady
L. Ballard
J.A. Pearch /sic/
F. McElroy
S. Burket /sic/
J. Criswell
A. Prince
W.S. Alexander /sic/
W. Garrison
A. Garrison
P. Weir /sic/
O.T. Snider
G.P. Randall
T. Edmonds
J.P. Bower
D.P. Edwards and
  brother /sic/
C.E. Phillips
W. Smith
G. Hugill /sic/
J.A. Maglin
R. Smith
D.J. Hains /sic/

J.W. Smith
H.B. Wilson /sic/
W. Hammond
J.F. Long (?) (Lang?)
L. Ang /sic/ (Long?, Lang?)
M. Echtery /sic/
J. Sharper
H.B. Doolittle
J.A. Powell
J.P. Bower /sic/
L.D. Jones
M. Adams and lady
S. Fulser
H. Aicks /sic/
E. Mack
W.L. McCranor /sic/
R. Powel /sic/ (Powell?)
W. Marwood
J.B. Munson
W. Retter /sic/ (Ritter?)
D. Boyle
E. Gilbert
H.A. Sweet
C.M. Mathias
J.S.C. Cosley
O. Conde /sic/ (Conte?)
W. Inshee
M.F. Furguson /sic/
W.W. Womeldorf
R. Turner
R.J. Womeldorf
W.F. Miller
M.C. Miller
W.A. Smith
H.O. Nearing
A. Flanegan
G. Lucas
W. Parks
S.W. Reed /sic/
B. Moore
M. Kelly
A.C.S. Jamwer /sic/
J.P. Anderson Sr.
J.P. Anderson Jr.
C.W. Durgin
H.M. Hamilton /sic/
T. Cary
C. Cawetes
W.A. Haston /sic/
R. Lunceford

T. Land
L. Gates
W. Bond Jr.
W. Bond
P. Sniter
C.A.C. Bidwell
W. Westfield
J.W. Johnson
W.H. Hand /sic/
H. Harrington
N. Lane and lady
S.M. Hoover
G.W. Morris
B. Treloar /sic/
__ Edwards and brother
  /sic/
L. Wahl
W. Waterford
J. Heely /sic/
W.W. Book
G. Everlort /sic/
F.A. Brainard /sic/
S.W. Bensline
D.L. German
J. Gardener /sic/
H.C. Hall
S. Barton /sic/
J.A. Elston
R. Palding /sic/
O. Brown
R. Ewingo /sic/
C. Smidt /sic/
J.M. Wiant /sic/ (Wyant?)
A. Fisher
J. Lea /sic/ (Lay?)
E.M. Eddy
S. Hamilton
J.T. Walker
H. Sawyer
R. Parker
J. Wilkinson
J.H. Hallett
H. Bengson
W.G. Booth
J.F. Perkins
H. Wickwise
F.H. Hilburn /sic/
G.A. Halllkins /sic/
  (Halkins, Hallkins?)
P. Wood

D.C. Phillips
A. Dunnigan
H. Chase
J.M. Stuart /sic/
R. Uhlrich
J.H. Mapfield
M. Coleman
A. Ward
E.S. Reed
J.M. Short
A.C. Plummer /sic/
P.J. Lay /sic/
J. Thompson
J. Blackburn
J.N. Hodge
S. Warnley
S. Laird /sic/
S. Cooper
J.W. Wilson
B.A. Johnston
G.A. Cross
H.J. Ormsby
J. Vanhorn
V.S. Holderbuck(?) (Holdenbuck?)
W.W. Boak /sic/
S.E. Wriston
R.G. McKee
D.C. Mettison
R. Rogers
A. Stephenson
B.H. Winship
F.B. Winship
C. Warner
D.H. Williams
E.C. McIntire
S. Barton /sic/
J.J. McCall /sic/
W. Miller
T.J. Bennett
W. King
E. Quigly /sic/ (Quigley?)
J.L. Steele
P. Dicson /sic/ (Dickson?)
Dr. E. Buckwell
K.E. Norton
W.W. Waterbury
B. Brown
A.J. Balmey /sic/
W. Blakeley

M. Sprague
C. Dale
E. Fairbrother
J.C. Donaldson
S.P. Russell
F.P. Hall
A. Swan
C. Mitcheltree /sic/
B.S. Craft
J.W. Drake
C.E. Linch /sic/ (Lynch?)
E. Angle /sic/
R.S. Adams
J. Blackinton /sic/ (Blackington?)
L. Milkland
W.E. Rottenhouse
W.W. McCoy
J.P. Bower /sic/
R. King
N.L. Robinson
J. Wallace
L. Laport /sic/
E.W. Kenton
J. Ross
S. Brookford
M. Phelps
E.S. Veach
W. Green
A. Bell
L. McMackin
F.M. Hilberson
D. Dills
E. Dale
A.L. Weston
W.S. Bennett
H.M. Hamilton /sic/
H. Crammer
E.P. Stuart
E. Boree /sic/
C. Holley /sic/
J.S. Jennings
J.D. Wilcox
J.H. Parmer
J.W. Brush
M. Burke
J.B. Hixson /sic/
C.P. Baker
J.N. Lemen /sic/ (Lemmon?, Lemon?)

R.J. Wicks
J. Marton /sic/
D.W. Madden
A.C. Collins
J.P. Witesell /sic/ (Whitesell?)
M.O. Johnson
L. Bishop
D.A. Endicott
F.M. Hilburn /sic/
A.W. Morton
J. Dacke /sic/
J. Rice
C.P. Kley /sic/ (Clay?)
J. Cunningham
B.F. Rogers
J. Morgan
D. Barnay and lady /sic/
J. Wilcox
L.E. Brooche
H.G. Haskell /sic/
N.J. Hammond
B. Griggsby /sic/ (Grigsby?)
J.B. Nash
C. Nash
J. Nash
L. Swartout
S. Hodley
F. Charles
J. Stewart
M.G. Stearns /sic/
J. Carpenter
J.E. Drake
J.E. Shaw
J.W. Vorhees /sic/
O. Wilson
A. Pierce
Z. Pierce
J. Strang /sic/
A. Garnett
J. Carrens
J.M. Sparks
T. Gardiner /sic/
J.E.S. Veach
J. Molter
G.M. Cotton
C. Howk /sic/ (Hawck? Hawk?)
H.H. Ferguson
B. Morton
J.H. Dills

J. Foxell /sic/ (Foxwell?)	L.T. Earthan /sic/	A.E. Wells
E. Sergeant	V.L. Acorn /sic/ (Acord?)	J.H. Fletcher
J. Holmes	J.J. McCall /sic/	J. Tryon /sic/
G. Wilson	R.B. Hall /sic/	Rev. A. Acord /sic/
J.P. Anderson	J.A. Gwinn	(Acorn?)
W.C. Greenleaf	J.H. Hardy	F.B. Badilla /sic/
W. Grace	J.L. Cox	F. Dittema /sic/
W. Allendaffer	B.F. Connelly	L. Teitts /sic/
J.J. Hopkins	W. Burnes /sic/	J.L. Sackett
T.B. Van Winkle and brother	S.S. Beeker (?) (Becker?)	F.M. Schell /sic/
	W.V. Barch	T.M. Slaughter
J.J. McCall /sic/	W.M. Hanloy /sic/ (Hanley?)	A.T. Gillespie
R.H. McIlroy /sic/		J.R. Moulton
G.R. Berford	S. Worduson /sic/	W.H. Benedict
J. Smith	C.W. Saunders	P. Flaerty /sic/ (Flaherty?)
J.W. Vorhees /sic/	H. Sweet	W.S. Alexander /sic/
D.C. Snider	Colonel __ Johnson	J. Kearney /sic/
J. Porter	G. Worick	S. Burket /sic/ (Burkett?)

YREKA, CALIFORNIA (September, 1852) On September 7, 1852 the Sacramento Union published a list of overland emigrants who had arrived in Yreka during the period of August 29-September 4, 1852. The below list was originally published in the El Dorado News and it is reproduced as follows:

From Illinois:	From Wisconsin:	From Michigan:
Capt. Isaac Mead	F.R. Striker	Albert Matthewson
Alford Mead	J. Bonndy /sic/ (Bondy?)	G. Chapman
G.H. Blankinship	Charles Stiles	From Missouri:
Frank Gibbs	Ira Ferris	P.H. Poindexter
J.J. Westbrook	Charles Rice	E.C. Shearer
Four un-identified Germans	Francis Kugeht /sic/	From Iowa:
	Oscar Judd	J.Q. Adams
From Wisconsin:	C. Barrett	From Ohio:
Anson Turner	T. Box	John Henry Parker
J.G. Moss	L.M. Brown	From Wisonsin:
Charles B. Moss		Ford Myers

SHASTA, CALIFORNIA (September, 1852) On September 7, 1852 the Sacramento Union published a list of overland emigrants who had arrived in Shasta during the period of August 29-September 4, 1852. These emigrants followed Noble's Route to Shasta.

From Wisonsin:	From Indiana:	From Illinois:
Nathan Parish and wife	C.E. Edwards	I.P. Miller
Daniel Parish and wife	William Edwards	J.K. Hoyt
Caleb Parish and wife	H. Stockton	W. Strong
H.F. Wood	John Judson	James Eden
D. Dunn	A. Joy, wife and three children	From Ohio:
		Daniel Snyder
	H. Crable /sic/	J. Warren
	William Crable /sic	J.D. Randall

From Wisconsin:
P.K. Kearny /sic/
Mr. __ Madison
Edmund Purdy(?)
  (Burdy?)
Mr. __ Parley
Mr. __ _oble (Noble?)
John Kelly
George McComber, wife
  & child
From Missouri:
A. Price and wife
D. Branch
M. Branch

From Indiana:
Mr. __ Crawford
D. Tripp
Mr. __ Merritt
Mr. __ McIntyre, wife and
  child
Mr. __ Tinkham and wife
From New York:
J. Hibbard /sic/
Joseph Hibbard /sic/
P. Combs /sic/
S. Combs /sic/

From Ohio:
George Rice
William T. Beatty
Edward Chaney
J. Clark
M. Simpkins
William A. Dudley
J.I. Brown
T. McGuire
J. McGinnes /sic/
J. Love
J. Patterson
G. Miles
J. Sandlin
J. McNulty
J. Paskell

DOWNIEVILLE, CALIFORNIA (September, 1852) The Sacramento Union of September 8, 1852 published a list of overland emigrants who had arrived in Downieville a few days prior to September 4, 1852. The list had previously appeared in the Downieville Echo of September 4th. The arrivals were reported as follows:

*Benjamin Hammer, of
  Lee County, Iowa
*William Hammer, of
  same as above
Richard Benson, of same
  as above

W.J. Miksell /sic/, of
  Marion County, Iowa
John Miksell /sic/, of same
  as above

Doddrige Alley, of Marion
  County, Iowa
Phillip Carpenter, of
  Columbia County,
  Wisconsin

On September 11, 1852, the Echo printed another list of recent overland emigrants who had arrived in Downieville and it is reproduced as follows:

S. Crim
William Thompson
Samuel Thompson
L.P. Faust
H.H. Hauselin /sic/
S. Smithers
S. Brennamon /sic/
George Cass
D. Brown
C.W. Atwood
D. Kaufman
Mr. __ Corrells
Thomas Cobb, of Franklin
  County, Iowa
W.E. Davis, of
  same as above
J. Jones, of same as above

Thomas Sturgeon
A. Brown
Thomas A. Black
D. Alexander
James Dallas
S. Ghastez /sic/
A.R. Gingber
J. Stukey
Dr. R. Kibbe and family
E.H. Rogers
Mr. __ Frick
P.D. Howard, of Kingston,
  Wisconsin
H. Blachley /sic/, of same
  as above
H.H. Suddath, of Franklin
  County, Iowa

W.H. Quams /sic/
H. Westlake
H.C. Menhoster
John Boyer
John Miller
R. Miller
William Jacobs
S. Streets
Samuel Wilson
A. Smith
Mr. __ Hyatt, family and
  nephew
Truman Evans, of Illinois
R.V. Engliss /sic/, of
  Walworth County,
  Wisconsin

(*) The Downieville Echo listed the surname of Benjamin and William Hammer as "Hammar".

On September 18,1852, the Downieville Mountain Echo reported that the below emigrants arrived in Downieville on September 16th, after following the Henness Route:

Thomas Freeman and lady, of Rushville, Illinois
Benjamin W. Gray, of same as above
M.C. Ireland, of same as above
James Harrington, of same as above
George Maxwell, of Illinois
James Booth, of Illinois

Mr. __ Kirkpatrick and lady, of Illinois
James Biddel, of same as above
Mr. __ Mann, of same as above
John Legget, of same as above
James Legget, of same as above

P.D. Hayward, of Wisconsin
Benjamin Booth, of same as above
Mr. __ Reed, of same as above
Mrs. __ Haskins, of same as above
M. Shoemaker, son and daughter, of Indiana

The Mountain Echo of September 25,1852 reported the arrival in Downieville of Mr. M. O'Sullivan, late Postmaster of Sullivan (sic), Iowa. Sullivan had just finished an overland trip on the plains, having left his family some forty miles back on the trail. He intended to return for his family after determining trail conditions.

SACRAMENTO, CALIFORNIA (September, 1852) The Sacramento Union of September 14,1852 published a list of persons who had died during the 1852 season on the emigrant trail on the north side of the Platte River. The list had originally appeared in the El Dorado (Coloma) News of September 11,1852. The News had been informed that at Ash Hollow, on the south side of the Platte, the mortality was much greater than on the north-diseases principally cholera and diarrhea. The mortality list is reproduced below:

Margaret Craig, aged 31 years
Rochell Fleener, no age or nativity listed
Charles Stull, deaf and dumb of Pennsylvania, found in a dying condition, June 5,1852 by Willard's Company.
Emily S. Gillard, of Missouri
Harvey Barker, age 54 years, of Missouri
Samuel Dunn, of Hill County, Michigan, age 38 years
Ann E. Hunt, of Illinois

Mrs. __ Rothwick, of Missouri
D. Taggart, of Peru, Iowa
Elias Barker, age 22 years, of Missouri
Louisa A. Emerit /sic/ age 8 years
Ziba Davenport, age 21 years
Sarah A. Bryant, age 12 years
Conrad Turner, of Ohio
A. Maria Kohl, age 9 years, of Missouri
Caleb Brown, age 25 years

Hiram Smith, age 42 years
Edward Smith, of Tennessee, age 50 years
James Skeggs /sic/, of Missouri
Harvery Vrdman (?) (Vorman?) age 26 years
Eleven unknown emigrants
Newell Lothrop /sic/ age 35 years
M.A. Cadwell /sic/ age 11 years
Jacob Edinger, of Missouri

161

Robert Bell, age 6 years
I. Fallen, age 26 years
John Tourman, age 10 years
Charles Truxler, age 23 years died June 25, 1852
W. Starkweather, age 2 years, 9 months
Thomas E. Dart, of Missouri
John Wicklefft /sic/, age 2 years
A. Ferell /sic/ of Illinois
D.I. Hogsett /sic/, age 32 years
C. Langwell, no age or nativity listed
Huldah McHuffe, no age or nativity listed
Mrs. Mary Bush, of Iowa
Mrs. Joseph Cristoe (?) (Criston?) age 22 years
Henry Franklin, age 2 years
W.E. Mott, age 3 years
Zach. L. Johnson, age 27 years
William Watkins, age 45 years
John Fletcher, of Missouri
Dr. James Fargerson /sic/ (Fergerson?) of Ohio, age 42 years
George Crane, age 35 years
Mrs. Mary E. Bailey, of Missouri, age 26 years
A.T. Hrouty /sic/ (Prouty?) age 63 years
Francis Kays /sic/ no age or nativity listed
Martha A. Duncan, no age or nativity listed
Martha Langston /sic/, of Missouri, age 12 years
Charles R. Matton, age 14 months
Richard Hodge, of Illinois
Ab. Newingham, of Illinois
Eliza Cotter, age 50 years
Milly Howard, of Ohio, age 22 years
S.D. Goodman, of Illinois, age 36 years
Edward Pyburn, age 45 years
Rerella Vance, age 19 years, of Illinois
D. Shelley, no age or nativity listed
Louis Helderbrant, of Missouri
R.C. Thompson, of Missouri, age 23 years
M.I. Picken /sic/, age 6 years
Margaret Davis, of Missouri
Sarah Ann Kean /sic/, of Iowa
B.F. Smith, of Michigan
Sarah Stone, age 6 years
Ellen Barlow, of Iowa, age 1 year
Edward Kirby, no age or nativity listed
E.C. Busch /sic/, of Virginia
Susan M. Williams, no age or nativity listed
James Lee, of Ohio, age 49 years
S. Sander Hice /sic/ (Rice?, S. Sander?) no age or nativity listed

PLACERVILLE, CALIFORNIA (September, 1852) On September 14, 1852 the Sacramento Union published a list of overland emigrants who had arrived in Placerville during the first week of September, 1852. The list is reproduced as follows:

G.W. White
E.S. Batse /sic/
J. Lippencott /sic/
J. Conrud /sic/ (Conrad?)
I. Still
T.W. Irymire /sic/
H.C. Crow
J.S. Sanderson /sic/
George Hightower
W.B. Fudge /sic/
C.W. Sanders /sic/
G.W. Morris
T.C.B. Strent /sic/
L.T. Bource
A.E. Mullins
D.A. Basher
W. McClintick /sic/
W. Buckley
W.O. Hughes
N. Stephenson
T. Augent
C.G. Bears
D.C. Littlefield

J.A. Reed
H. Jackson
T.L. Bartholes /sic/
  (Bartholomew?)
W. Trimble
P. Sutter
C. Fierce /sic/ (Pierce?)
A.T. Johnson
J.J. Moore and lady
W.B. Wilcox
S. Cranes (?) (Granes?)
E. Hop /sic/
M.D. Carlos
J.J. McKain /sic/
J. Emmens
J.R. Moulton
J.W. Field
W.F. Miller
W.C. McLain /sic/
J. McLain /sic/
T.P. Hollister
N. Hammell
W. Wales
J.T. Thompson
C.E. Link
J.M. Stuart /sic/
S. Rumfelt /sic/
P. Huss
S. Greeg /sic/ (Gregg?)
J.S. Collins
H. Cold /sic/
W. Caldwell
J.G. Moore
D. Black
C.W. Welch
C.W. Reed
H.B. Doolittle
W.W. Doolittle /sic/
R.J. Hewit /sic/ (Hewitt?)
J. Laston
A. Calhoun
S.W. Shepperd
G. Neagley /sic/
S.F. Hutchinson
J. Beats /sic/
A.B.O. Reading
E. Goodapod(?)
  (Goodspod?,
  Goodspeed?)
James Manor
A.T. Burleson

Ira Fainsworth /sic/
  (Fairmsworth?)
G. Campbell
W. Doolittle /sic/
A. Mullins
R.L. Womeldorff
J. Margo
J.R. Winterson
J.H. Gillett
Miss Sarah Whetstone
C. Jullett (?) (Juilett?)
J.R. Whaloy /sic/
  (Whaley?)
J. Diffen
E.D. Marshall
John Smith
J. Jones
H.B.J. Cranmer /sic/
  (Crammer?)
D.W. Check /sic/
J. Phaler /sic/
O.G. Tooker /sic/
S.D. Hendricks
C.C. Freeman /sic/
J. Keyes
J.T. Tood /sic/ (Todd?)
A.J. Cornwell
W.L. Booth
H.G. Farker /sic/ (Barker?)
A. Greeslier
S. Ramsey
G. Cofr /sic/
J.M. Winship
F.B. Winship
E. Niles
J.M. Massey
W. Rase
E.H. Hhiley /sic/ (Hiley?,
  Whiley?)
M. Frasier
R.K. McFarland
J. Tait
W. Tait
T.S. Bradford
W.G. Crockett
J. Noona /sic/
J. Rees /sic/
A.G. Barnett /sic/
P. Beckquett /sic/
  (Beckwith?)
F. Myers

A. Lee
E.M. Rentway
F.A. Brainard /sic/
S.J. Carper
J. Cancy /sic/
C. Blockman (?)
  (Blackman?)
W.B. McAboy
A.F. Kennedy
W.E. Tisdale
J.J. Smith
Dr. W. Callis
F.M. Heilburn /sic/
T. Keegan
G.W. Ford
I.F. Cox
J.M. Davis
J.P. Frisbee
J. Fitzgerald
I. Davis
S.B. Davis
A. Fisher
A. Hull
J.S. Fisher
A.G. Rergendale /sic/
J.T. Stone
B.F. Balep /sic/
J.C. Wood
P. Waterman
B.J. James
G.H. Leathers
C.T. Givens
D.H. Aale /sic/ (Ale?,
  Able?)
O. Burlingame
N. Cole
J.S. Richardson
J.H. Milton /sic/
D. Sires
J. Tyron /sic/
S. Davis
C.C. Freeman /sic/
B. Salts
A. Wilcox
M. Salts
J. Paulus /sic/
R. Brewer
S. Wickard

W. Balard /sic/ (Ballard?)	T. Hollister	J. Fisher
H. Jeffen	H.G. Haskell /sic/	B. Taylor
A.T. Copelain /sic/	A.R. Fearn	A. Potter
J. Wilson	K.M. White	S.S. Kingory /sic/
W.C. Jennings	G.M. Weaton (Wheaton?)	J.J. Cunton /sic/
J. Shaven	M. Adams	W.H. Ault
H. Anst /sic/	J.D. Van Eaten /sic/ (Van Eaton?)	A. Getham
D. Hollister /sic/		T. Matthews
H.W. Gillett	__ Barlow	R.C. Crockett
J.P. Lynch	J.H. Adams	J.A. Maglin
W. Hardy	H.M. Paul	L. Southard
J. Clark	J. Preston	M. Sparks
J. Evans	J.A. Williamson	G. Sparks
A. Reed	G.D. Stone	W. Sparks
M.L. Campbell	J. Smith	H. Glendenen /sic/
R. Clagearn /sic/	J. Warich	H. Cob /sic/ (Cobb?)
J.M. Rankin /sic/	A.B. Byrd	A.G. Barnett /sic/
W.H. Hoffman	J.F. Meredith	R. Williams
J.R. Myers	A.S. Fagg	C.K. Drum /sic/
R. Long	W. Simpson	R. Nichols
P.J. Mayer /sic/	M. Knox and wife	D. Robertson
A. Jones	P. Knox	M.E. Hartenck /sic/
F. Fulton	J. Knox	J. Jackson
J.M. Parker	J. Miller	D.M. Head
J. Parker	R.K. Harmalf /sic/	J. Hoover
E. Dall	C. Wilson	H.L. Lighter
A. Eettit /sic/	W.J. Henderson /sic/	J. Hemmingway /sic/ (Hemingway?)
E. Gates	J. Henderson	
J. Peterson	E.A. Detor	D. Whaley
J. Eagle	J. Barnard	J. Mitchell
A.T. Warren	T.M. Luca	J.A. McKnight
		D.C. Dickenson /sic/

SACRAMENTO, CALIFORNIA (September 16,1852) The Sacramento Union of September 17, 1852 reported the arrival in the city of a drove of two hundred and fifty cows from Missouri. They were the property of the late Michael Smith, of Missouri, who, however, died on the Platte River. The cows were then taken in charge by another unidentified member of the train who was to deliver them to relatives of the deceased residing on a ranch in the Napa Valley. Smith and his cows had left the Missouri River on May 1, 1852. During the overland journey twenty of the cows had died or strayed.

YREKA, CALIFORNIA (September, 1852) On September 20, 1852 the Sacramento Union published a news story which had been written by a correspondent of the Shasta Courier under date of September 6th. The correspondent, writing from Yreka, California, reported that a train of ten wagons and sixty-nine emigrants had arrived in Yreka on September 3, 1852. One of the emigrants, a Mrs. __ Kimball, from Illinois, had died shortly after arrival. Only a portion of the train emigrants were reported as follows:

George T. Terry	W.A. Barnes /sic/	John Hathaway

John McConanghy	E. Tolf /sic/	J.M. Keating
W. McConanghy	David Lawton	E. Crockett
J.C. Church	S.P. Mead	C. Lee
J. Boofman /sic/	P. Ragan /sic/	W. Walters
A. Smith	E. Ragan /sic/	B. Freels /sic/
J. Wilson	W. Briar /sic/	G. Albert
W. Oliver	S. Southerland /sic/	J. Woodward
J. Davenport	T. Southerland /sic/	

The Courier correspondent also reported that the following overland emigrants arrived in Yreka, California on September 5, 1852. They were under the guidance of Messrs. Coates, Long and Owensby.

D.M. Morrison	W. W. Hanway	George Cook
Capt. W. Donnellan and family	L. D. Cook	W. McKay
	Asa Shinn	George Shenk
W.W. Anson	John M. Shulthies	S. Willard
W.R. Marshall	Thomas McMillan	J. Stow
William Kimball	R. McMillan	George Flock
M.H. Crib	George Cogswell	C. Hartsock /sic/
Conrad Schelley /sic/	Henry Synis /sic/	Henry Croft
Peter Stimant and boy	Mat Marcehoffer	
Benjamin A. Samuels	James Thompson	

PLACERVILLE, CALIFORNIA (September, 1852) The Sacramento Union of September 21, 1852 published a list of overland emigrants who had arrived in Placerville, California during the second week of September, 1852. The list is reproduced as follows:

G. W. Gaskins, lady and ten passengers	H. P. Briscoe	A.D. Blodgett and Company
	A. L. Thayer	
W. J. Henderson /sic/	E. McLaughlin	J. Finehens /sic/
J. Kean	James Cate	S. C. Switzer
J. W. Handsky /sic/	A. W. Wolf	H. A. Clark
J. J. McCall /sic/	J. L. Morton	J. W. Helmer
D. Russell	B. Leonard	G. W. Helmer
C. McGarry	A. W. Davenport /sic/	D. Gilman
J. O. Mullin	F. M. Freeman	G. M. Condor
Sarah M. Cornel /sic/ (Cornell?)	F. A. Wickee /sic/	W. B. Fudge /sic/
	S. P. Condee /sic/	Dr. H. Van Vleck
F. A. Davis	M. B. Evans	C. Crowel /sic/ (Crowell?)
J. Stratford	B. Palmer	
E. R. Davis	W. Hewitt	D. Vanhalie /sic/
B. F. Durlin	R. Hastwell	M. Hardy
F. M. Helburn /sic/	C. Lasolett	C. Cremmons
A. McConnel /sic/ (McConnell?)	P. E. Barloy	G. Salliary
	W. Moore	P. C. A. Saw /sic/
S. Venter	T. R. Dale	I. M. Butler
H. Lofolett	I. M. Swinford /sic/	G. Dillard
J. Jefferson	J. B. Smith /sic/	J. North
J. M. Jefferson	D. B. Edwards	A. T. Mattley
B. F. Jefferson	W. Webb	E. L. Mattley

A. H. Simons
E. Simons
C. Gardnes /sic/ (Gardens? Gardner?)
L. N. Haskins /sic/
O. Ames
J. S. Jones
L.C. Jones
B. F. Mury /sic/ (Murray?)
J. H. Kingsbury
S. Witson /sic/
D. Witson /sic/
S. Fratzy /sic/
C. K. Drumm /sic/
E. Davis
G. Coy
T. Hilton
H. A. Pine
L. Bishop
W. Panton (?) (Pantor? Pantos?)
J. Vanderford
T. Winte
C. H. Bailey
J. M. Robinson
G. Robinson
A. G. McCoy
W. Justice
E. B. Harvy (Harvey?)
N. B. Barfes /sic/
A. W. Davenport /sic/
P. Garrett
B. Satterthwright /sic/
K. G. Welker /sic/
D. Hollister /sic/
W. Amsberry
J. H. Weaver
M. Miller
A. S. Warren
G. W. Sayles
J. Valentine
T. Seary /sic/
H. G. Duncan
W. R. Depus
G. Thrush
J. S. Crain
A. T. Abbey
H. L. Vadder and brother
J. W. Ashley

J. Lowe
W. W. White
S. Rumfelt /sic/
N. Turner
B. C. McFarland
T. S. Burlage
J. Wade
D. Allen /sic/
E. Walker
J. J. Carleton
H. Moon
J. Perkins
M. D. Sharp
L. Hoffiner /sic/ (Hoffner?)
D. Lock
J. Henning
E. Goodspeed /sic/
J. M. Kennedy
G. W. Seaton
T. M.McCauley
J. B. Smith /sic/
J. McNair
S. Asnifiy (?) (Asniffy?)
J. Cossins /sic/
J. Cosar
P. Parcels
J. Wason
J. U. Garwood
O. F. Hagans
W. B. Hagans
J. Rains /sic/
R. B. Hall /sic/
A. J. Blakesley
G. W. Chaffin
P. Anson
R. H. Oxley
N. B. Hubbell
C. Ballon
H. S. Anable
G. Hamilton
D. Allen /sic/
T. Paxton
E. E. Jones
R. C. Lauz /sic/
G. Buden
C. Benson
E. Preston
R. P. Locke, lady and child

O. C. Laws /sic/
W. Faher
N. Newburg
W. Newburg
G. Goodlad /sic/ (Goodland?)
J. Cassins
M. Bush
R. Pollock
J. B. Kung
J. A. Grims /sic/
W. H. Benedict
W. J. McCoy
P. Shaver
W. DeWitt
A. C. Salt
Q. Lice /sic/
G. McNutt
T. F. Henninger
H. M. McCoy
A. Jeffery
R. S. Coleman
W. H. Fall
J. P. Knider
L. H. Jobling
G. Fry
T. Yotes /sic/ (Yates?)
W. J. Still
A. Justice /sic/
W. Parker
R. C. Coleman
W. S. Meacham
W. Dvng /sic/ (Dung?)
A. F. Wing
M. Durr
T. Z. Armstrong
R. P. Wilkes /sic/
T. Hastings
H. Hudson
A. S. Brown
L. Timmons
J. Woods
L. Young
W. Young
A. Wiley
A. Still
E. Luce /sic/
J. W. Garit /sic/ (Garritt?)
W. Blacklock
H. Altenburg

J. Murdoch /sic/
O. Kelsle /sic/ (Kelsley?)
F. McBride
J. Brinkley
A. J. Piper
H. P. Marquam
S. Beck
J. Smith
A. R. Wood
M. Galabert
S. M. Orbison
W. A. Barnes /sic/
J. P. Williams /sic/
W. McCoy
S. Yates /sic/
F. Dunrich
P. Moses

T. Knott
B. Graham
C. D. Benson
L. Hubbard
N.L. Griffin
M. McClenaham
L. Rawlings
W. S. Black
F. Rache /sic/
H. B. Warren
C. C. Bennett
S. Laird /sic/
S. Wamsley
F. M. Schell /sic/
R. Morgan
J. M. Richardson
J. Wright

J. Swift
R. Doncaster Jr. (?)
   (Doucaster?)
S. Doncaster (?)
   (Doucaster?)
Mr. _____ Haydin /sic/ and
   family
A. Wilcox
P. Rosasabaugh /sic/
   (Rosabaugh?)
J. Rosabaugh /sic/
   (Rosasabaugh ?)
T. G. Shaw
J. Garrison
A. McFee
J. Buttles /sic/ (Bottles ?)

PLACERVILLE, CALIFORNIA (September, 1852) The *Sacramento Union* of September 27, 1852 published a list of overland emigrants who had arrived in Placerville during the third week of September, 1852. The list is reproduced as follows:

T. Simmons
A. G. Bergendahl
H. W. Rytson /sic/
J. Bryan Jr.
S. Bingham
J. D. McKnight
W. H. Wyman
R. L. Sharp
C. Bishoff
Capt. _____ Zimmerman
C. D. Genson
D. Click
C. M. Smith
A. Stephenson
P. S. Seaburg
W. Magee
E. Harryman /sic/
   (Harriman?)
W. Harryman /sic/
   (Harriman?)
R. Cleghorn
H. Ahpil /sic/
E. C. Cook
D. Burrows
Mrs. _____ McCormick
J. F. Watson
A. Justice /sic/
D. McRisan

S. Hillis
D. W. Levan /sic/
T. Winter
A. Walton
A. Hewett /sic/
J. M. Scott and family
S. Beatty
E. R. Pliley /sic/ (Philey?
   Plilbey?, Pilbey?
   Philbey?)
W. Wilcox
G. W. Blackstone
A. McBride
W. McDaniel
A. D. McAfee /sic/
W. H. Miller
J. Hager
J. Jones
H. F. Kallum (?)
   (Kellum?)
C. Smith
W. Kelley
W. Cannon
W. S. Clayton
S. B. Martin
J. Martin
A. Bamburth /sic/
S. Mayer

J. M. Burrel /sic/
L. N. Haskin /sic/
J. Paul /sic/
J. R. Smith
G. W. Kenney
A. Rowley
A. Dunlap
T. Sulliban /sic/
E. W. Cooper
C. H. Holmes
J. J. Crittenden
J. A. Songer /sic/ (Singer?)
J. Binkley
R. M. Ware
W. Ward
J. F. McDowell
J. Bostwick
W. Ellis
W. Desserl /sic/
T. Smith and company
T. D. March
T. J. Guthrice (?)
   (Guthriee?, Guthrie?)
H. Cutler
S. A. Cutler /sic/
C. G. Morford /sic/
D. J. C. Hall

PLACERVILLE, CALIFORNIA (September, 1852) The Sacramento Union of October 5, 1852 published a list of overland emigrants who had arrived in Placerville during the last week of September, 1852. The list is reproduced as follows:

J. S. Wilkins	J. A. Taylor	L. Ray
G. W. Wilkins	W. McKnott (?)	W. L. Sanders
W. Fargo	(McKnotts?)	R. M. Hood
G. W. Fox	J. C. Veach	W. F. Trego
J. Boals /sic/	J. Croy	A. Justice /sic/
W.A.H. Hand /sic/	W. A. Gibson	T. Haseled /sic/
Dr. L. A. Brewer	J. M. Gates	J. Lusk
J. Nance	C. Bukes	J. B. Messick
H. R. Hughes	B. Mikesell	R. H. Miller
D. A. Staton /sic/	W. Blakewell	C. Smart
J. Pope	R. D. Seaward	J. H. McHenry
W. D. White	E. Lea /sic/	W. Cusick
T. M. Hopkins	J. S. Caldwell	R. P. Wilkes /sic/
H. B. Smith	A. Y. Luthes	J. Chickester
I. N. Thompson	J. Lampton /sic/	A. R. Gould
F. H. Adams	J. M. Deamky /sic/	B. F. Gum
A. J. Quillin (?) (Quilhin?)	R. R. Ferguson	J. G. W. Smith
S. Hinman	S. F. Walker	W. D. Whitead /sic/
W. E. Davis	N. Stevenson	(Whitehead?)
H. Hawkins	G. P. Mong /sic/	W. _wort (Swort?)
S. W. Drake	D. Dunlap	D. Copeland
A. J. Dallas	J. W. Stout	F. A. Brainard /sic/
W. C. Read	J. Gilmore	H. Francis
J. B. Bussick	J. Paulus /sic/	J. B. Hixson /sic/
J. S. Wilks /sic/ (Wilkes?)	E. Lamarr	D. Strueler /sic/
J. Arown /sic/ (J. A.	T. M. Calvin	T. A. Watson
Brown?, J. Brown?)	J. Penman	R. Jophehe (?) (Jophebe?)
D. Crawford	P. C. Gabbett	J. Forrest
J. S. Carner	H. Terrett	J. Moore /sic/
H. Simmons	H. W. Scott	J. Moore /sic/
D. White	J. Spark	L. J. Dana
R. Mayers and family	E. Knocke /sic/	O. J. Gibbs
A. F. Arterbrook	J. Cole	R. B. Hall /sic/
M. A. Hahm /sic/	R. G. Thrasher	G. W. Coar /sic/ (Carr?)
(Hamm?)	J. B. Racine	B. L. Brown
B. W. Kammerer /sic/	C. L. Crackburn	H. G. Dunham
J. Webb	T. Finch	W. White
T. Sherdon /sic/	M. D. &yres /sic/	
	(Sayres)	

EMIGRANT DEATHS (1852 Season) The Sacramento Union of October 9, 1852 published a list of some of the emigrants who died on the plains during the period of May-June, 1852. The deaths took place between Independence, Missouri and Fort Laramie, a distance of six hundred and fifty miles. The list was compiled by John H. Hays (sic), who had "lately come over the plains." The compilation is reproduced below:

J. Miller, of Ohio, died May 24, 1852

J. Cutler, of Missouri, died May 24, 1852

William F. Staunton, died May 25, 1852

F. Wainger, died June 4, 1852

M. Bays /sic/, of Virginia, died June 3, 1852, age 26 years

Joseph Elviedge /sic/ (Eldridge?), of Illinois, died June 4, 1852, age 25 years

Mary North, died May 26, 1852

Amanda E. Brown, died May 30, 1852

P. A. McWilliams, died May 28, 1852, age 47 years

Mrs. Emiline Barns /sic/
Amanda Bobbins
Mahala Bobbins,
Three sisters in one grave, all of Indiana, no death date

William O. Frost, of Davis County, Missouri, died May 31, 1852, age 22 years

E. S. Markis, died May 25, 1852, age 55 years

T. Martin
D. Wood
Both above in one grave, of Princeton, Kentucky, died May 27, 1852

R. R. Wilkins, died June 5, 1852

W. W. Wilson, of Adams County, Illinois, died May 21, 1852, age 22

Mr. _____ Atwater, of Ohio, died May 24, 1852

J. S. Skidmore, died May 16, 1852

Mary A. Daniel, of Butler County, Penn., died May 27, 1852, age 28 years

Francis D. Kemp, of Pettis County, Missouri, died June 14, 1852, age 5 years

John McCever /sic/, of Illinois, died June 4, 1852

Joseph Crankelton, of Delaware County, Ohio, died May 29, 1852

Leo Weightman /sic/, Penelton County, Virginia, died May 10, 1852

Maberry Splawn, died May 22, 1852

Francis Robinson, of Dane County, Wisc., died May 31, 1852, age 29 years

Joseph Moon, of Jackson County, Missouri, died May 30, 1852, age 59 years

D. A. Hill, of Illinois, died May 29, 1852, age 27 years

Mrs. Nancy Starks, of Collaway County, Missouri, died May 31, 1852

Rosaniah Conlisk, died May 23, 1852, age 26 years

P. Neel /sic/, died June 1, 1852

Fines Bloyed /sic/, of Arkansas, died May 24, 1852

George Ball, of Portsmouth, Ohio, died May 17, 1852, age 20 years

Edward Brown, of Gentry County, Missouri, died May 19, 1852, age 9 years

George Winslow, died May 30, 1852

W. E. Stevens, of Missouri, age 24 years

John Brown, of Clark County, Illinois, died May 28, 1852

Malin Moore, died May 28, 1852

William Brown, of Clark County, Illinois, died May 29, 1852

Mary E. Fenter, died May 31, 1852

S. Trumble, of Batavia, Illinois, died May 30, 1852, age 56 years

G. H. Tandy, of Princeton, Kentucky, died May 30, 1852, age 24 years

Conrad Teneyck, died May 30, 1852, age 27 years

Mrs. Caroline Miner, of Laporte County, Iowa, died on May 31, 1852

J. Carron, of Wayne County, Illinois, died May 24, 1852

Nancy Skean, died June 4, 1852

Dr. _____ Traftan /sic/, died June 3, 1852, age 57 years

Elizabeth Turnbough, of Arkansas, died May 30, 1852

Abigal Springer, of Morgan County, Ohio, died June 5, 1852

Alex. Janes, of Dallas County, Mo., died June 6, 1852, age 21 years

Mrs. Mary Janes, of Johnson County, Mo., died June 5, 1852, age 72 years

Mrs. C. McCubbins, died June 1, 1852, age 42 years

S. Colby, died May 25, 1852, age 53 years

Sarah Crabtree, of Jackson County, Mo., died May 25, 1852, age 23 years /sic/

William Clark, of Casse County, Ill., died June 1, 1852

Sarah Myrtle, of Jackson County, Mo., died June 8, 1852

Hon,. S. F. Myrtle, of Jackson County, Mo., died June 8, 1852, age 22 years

P. Hann, died June 5, 1852

Joel F. Show /sic/, died June 9, 1852

H. D. Dorand, died June 8, 1852

J. A. White, of Andrew County, Mo., died June 4, 1852, age 42 years

B. Liteut (?) (Liedt?), of Wellsburgh, Va., died June 3, 1852

Margaret Burch, of Canon County, Missouri, died May 29, 1852

William Cooper, died June 4, 1852

C. A. Narsen, died May 31, 1852

William F. Rooil /sic/ of Columbus, Ohio, died in May, 1852

J. M. Daugherty, of Ohio, died May 30, 1852

Greater Crane /sic/, died in June, 1852

Wesley Lusk, of Green County, Mo., died June 1, 1852

George W. Benkley, of Henry County, Mo., died June 6, 1852, age 28 years

Jacob France, of Marion County, Iowa, died June 8, 1852. age 4 years

P. Y. Murphy, of Farmington, Mo., died June 5, 1852

Thomas Thomas /sic/, of Ohio, died June 3, 1852, age 19 years

John Strange, of Cedar County, Iowa, died June 7, 1852

J. W. Bell, of Illinois, died June 8, 1852

Lewis Cooper, died June 8, 1852

Thomas Williams Miller of Johnson County, Mo., died June 10, 1852, age 25 years

Martin M. Connet /sic/, of Putman County, Ohio, died May 21, 1852

Enoch Ligget, died June 4, 1852

S. C. Haile /sic/ of Missouri, died June 2, 1852

John D. Swift, died June 1, 1852, age 47 years

James Connor, died May 28, 1852

E. F. Wilson, of Pennsylvania, died May 30, 1852, age 47 years

S. C. Rooker, of Howard County, Mo., died June 2, 1852, age 19 years

Robert Miller, of St. Genevieve County, Mo., died May 28, 1852

R. H. Nelson, of Monroe, Michigan, died June 6, 1852

Permella Nichols, died June 1, 1852

Miller Swan, of Platte County, Mo., died May 28, 1852, age 28 years

Ezekiel White, of Litchfield, Mich., died June 8, 1852, age 44 years

Robert P. Hardcastle, of Cooper County, Mo., died June 2, 1852, age 26 years

J. C. Deavers, died June 4, 1852, age 60 years

David Phenix /sic/, died June 8, 1852, age 23 years

Mrs. R. Dodson, of Franklin County, Mo., died June 4, 1852, age 18 years

David Fewis /sic/ (Lewis?), died May 29, 1852, age 24 years

Milow Wooding, of Connecticut, died June 3, 1852

T. F. Watkin /sic/ (Watkins?), of Pennsylvania, died June 2, 1852, age 26 years

Joseph Eade, of Joe Daviess County, Illinois, died June 4, 1852, age 47 years

Robert Russel /sic/ (Russell?), of Simpsonville, Ky., died June 10, 1852

William J. Robinson, of Maddison County, Illinois, died June 3, 1852

Harvey Emerson, of Saline County, Mo., died June 8, 1852

James W. Music, of Franklin County, Mo., died June 6, 1852

William T. Underwood, of Franklin County, Mo., died June 17, 1852, age 21 years

D. B. Miller, of Ohio, died June 11, 1852, age 36 years

Charles G. Burdett, of Ohio, died June 14, 1852, age 22 years

Eliza B. Matthews, died June 5, 1852, age 38 years

John Hollman, of Missouri, died June 5, 1852

Mrs. ____ Reeves /sic/, died June 9, 1852, age 49 years

William Taylor, of Perry County, Mo., died June 3, 1852

John Strouss (?) (Strouse?), of Cedar County, Iowa, died June 7, 1852

Susan C. Reynolds, of Bates County, no State listed, died June 8, 1852, aged 16 years

John Wirtner, of Platte County, Mo., died June 21, 1852, age 40 years

Henry Sager, of Atchison County, Mo., died June 8, 1852

S. Edbington /sic/, (Eddington?) died June 5, 1852

C. S. Carner, of Akron Ohio, died June 3, 1852, age 34 years

George Ceanard /sic/, of St. Charles County, Mo., died June 11, 1852, age 39 years

Mason Hall, of Wisconsin, died in June 1852, age 23 years

S. Robinson, died June 2, 1852

C. J. Shoffner, of Pittsburgh, Pa., died June 3, 1852

James McDonald, of Franklin County, no State listed, died in June, 1852, age 42 years

Isaac Crig /sic/ (Craig?) of Clark County, Ill., died June 16, 1852, age 45 years

Henry Hill, of Missouri, died June 8, 1852, age 59 years

SACRAMENTO, CALIFORNIA (October 11, 1852) The Sacramento Union of October 12, 1852 reported the arrival in Sacramento of two emigrant trains by the "Beckwith Route". The trains had departed from the Missouri River on May 1, 1852 and had entered Sacramento on October 11, 1852. One of the trains consisted of James Laughlin and Mr. ____ Gillham (sic), together with their families, from Illinois. The second train, made up of five wagons, was from Jackson, Missouri. The latter train belonged to Mr. ____ Hardy and Mr. ____ Rodgers, who also brought their families with them.

DEATHS ON THE PLAINS DURING THE 1852 SEASON The Sacramento Union of November 2, 1852 published a partial list of emigrant deaths on the plains during the 1852 season of travel. The list is reproduced as follows:

Amanda Jennings, no death data

Thomas Bedford, no death data

John McAllister, no death data

Thomas H. Foster, of Cumberland, Md., died May 18, 1852, age 25 years

Joseir Veiger, of Illinois, died June 4, 1852, age 25 years

Henry A. Bedford, of Michigan, died June 1, 1852, age 22 years

Miller A. Madison, of Pike County, Mo., died May 18, 1852, age 22 years

John Barnett, of St. Francois County, Missouri, died May 30, 1852, age 26 years

John Dennison, died June 6, 1852, age 40 years

Mary Macey /sic/ (Macy?), of Michigan, died June 5, 1852, age 19 years

Mrs. Julia A. Berrington, of Ohio, died June 5, 1852, age 22 years

J. Long, age 61 years

____Hubbard, no death data

Preston Muir, of Kentucky

H. Hoggard, of Illinois, died June 1, 1852, age 35 years

D. C. B. /sic/, died June 8, 1852

Mary A. May, died June 1, 1852, age 20 years

A. J. Maddox, of Missouri, died June 18, 1852, age 21 years

R. H. Nelson, of Monroe, Michigan, died May 26, 1852, age 25 years

Sarah A. Sleigh, of St. Louis, Mo., died June 5, 1852, age 22 years

Elizabeth Vaughn, died June 28, 1852

Sarah Crabtree, of Jackson County, Mo., died May 25, 1852, age 23 years

David Lewis /sic/, died May 26, 1852, age 29 years

John Dickson /sic/, of Illinois, died May 25, 1852, age 22 years

Rachael Andrews, no death data

Charles C. McFarlane of Missouri, died June 18, 1852, age 17 years

H. Hickson, no death data

John Hotton /sic/, died May 1, 1852, age 29 years

John D. R. D. /sic/ died May 4, 1852

John Cow, died June 3, 1852

Susan J. Riley, of Rarrington, Ohio /sic/, died June 8, 1852 age 20 years

Samuel N. Brigham, died June 6, 1852

A. Crider, of Missouri, died June 7, 1852, age 47 years

A. C. Pressor, died June 18, 1852, age 26 years

Mary E. Misscard, died June 12, 1852

Levi Lee, of Illinois, died June 1, 1852, age 25 years

George Eddy, of Ohio, died June 1, 1852, age 25 years

W. E. Sterns, of Missouri, died June 4, 1852, age 24 years

John Crawford, died May 18, 1852, age 28 years

Martin M. Conant /sic/, no death data

John Musser, of Richelieu, Ohio, died June 4, 1852, age 24 years

John Holeman /sic/ (Holman?), died June 5, 1852, age 19 years

Joseph Langley /sic/, age 47 years

T. F. Watkins, died June 5, 1852, age 26 years

C. S. Carner /sic/, died June 5, 1852

J. J. Jedson, no death data

N. Campbell, of Chicago, Illinois, died June 10, 1852, age 22 years

Amasa Moore, of Ohio, died June 18, 1852, age 52 years

Eliza Beming /sic/, died June 15, 1852, age 19 years

Perry Runnels, of Harvard, Indiana, died June 3, 1852, age 31 years

Ann A. Cartrell, died June 6, 1852, age 2 years

S. Allen, died June 18, 1852

173

D. Ganger, of Fairfield (no State listed), died June 11, 1852, age 36 years

Samuel R. Patterson, died June 16, 1852, age 26 years

Ira E. McMannus /sic/ of South Bend, Ind., died August 18, 1852

W. O. Smith, of Union City, Mich., died August 2, 1852

Charles B. Greeley, died August 18, 1852, age 22 years

C. Stanley, died August 21, 1852, age 21 years

Sarah May, died August 4, 1852, age 14 years

Frederick Hemily /sic/, died June 20, 1852, age 31 years

H. A. Webb, died June 21, 1852, age 25 years

Mary E. Fitzgerald, of Missouri, died June 20, 1852, age 18 years

James Boyd, of Illinois, died June 30, 1852, age 25 years

J. B. Nicholas, died July 1, 1852, age 34 years

Mrs. E. Mitchell, of Missouri, died July 6, 1852, age 32 years

Mary E. Lamb, of Michigan, died July 4, 1852, age 18 years

Marillo Moon, of Pan Pan, Michigan, died July 22, 1852, age 23 years

D. B. Miller, of Ohio, died June 11, 1852, age 36 years

W. M. Morehead, died June 21, 1852, age 17 years

T. Miller, died June 15, 1852, age 26 years, murdered by R. Tate

Hes Whitney /sic/, of Illinois, died August 9, 1852

Mary A. Hay, died August 8, 1852, age 20 years

M. Young, of Ohio, died August 2, age 31 years

James C. Lamb, no death data

John Brown of Michigan, died June 14, 1852, age 21 years

William Barnes, died June 25, 1852, age 22 years

G. C. Baxton, of Ohio City, Ohio, died June 24, 1852, age 22 years

N. Thairmont, died June 14, 1852 age 41 years

Henry Moss, died July 15, 1852, age 17 years

Julia Ella S. Farmington, of Cleveland, Ohio, died July 2, 1852, age 17 years

Samuel Houk /sic/ (Hook?), died June 7, 1852, age 24 years

Dr. _____ Beatty, of Mt. Morris, Ill., died July 18, 1852, age 55 years

H. R. Allison, died June 4, 1852, age 29 years

W. S. Greeley, died June 4, 1852, age 29 years

W. Meredith, of Mount Pleasant (no State listed), died June 17, 1852

Clement McWair, of Illinois, died on August 15, 1852, age 27 years

Richard King, died August 20, 1852, age 22 years

Olonzo Kane, died August 15, 1852, age 27 years

Mareto C. Ballard, died August 6, 1852, age 27 years

Charles Whitney, died July 1, 1852, age 32 years

Sorellia Haun /sic/ (Hahn?, Hann?) of Missouri, died June 28, 1852, age 8 years, 6 months, 14 days

Jane Coward, of Missouri, died June 30, 1852, age one year

W. H. Bedford, died July 4, 1852, age 28 years

C. Harrison, died July 18, 1852, age 24 years

J. J. Morris, died July 4, 1852, age 25 years

Mary E. Martin, of Cleveland, Ohio, died July 2, 1852, age 17 years

Henry A. Martin, died July 4, 1852, age 20 years (no State)

H.D. Marvin, died June 30,1852, age 25 years

William McCune, of Mt. Morris, Ill., died June 28,1852, age 41 years

Cornelius D'Mont, of Buffalo, N.Y., died July 4,1852, age 22 years

R. Children, of Lancaster, Wisc., died July 18,1852, age 26 years

E.B. Drier /sic/, of Montgomery County, Ill., died July 28,1852, age 20 years

William Hall, of Detroit, Mich., died July 22,1852, age 40 years

W.M. Johnston, died July 12,1852, age 20 years

William J. Moore, of Cook County, Ill., died July 4,1852, age 22 years

G.B. Allcott /sic/, of Michigan, died July 22,1852, age 25 years

J.N. Stanley, died July 21,1852, age 22 years

G.S. Burton, of Ohio City, Ohio, died July 22,1852, age 25 years

Sarah J. Davis, of Michigan, died on August 1,1852, age 23 years

Nancy J. Cook, of Missouri, died August 1,1852, age 13 years

Henry Fair, died May 28,1852, age 38 years

___ Pitzel, of Mt. Morris, Ill., no other data listed

Mary E. Hammond, of Euclid, Ohio, died July 15,1852, age 21 years

Hymelius Pugh, of Peru, Ill., died June 25,1852

William Logan, of Allegany County, Penn., died July 24,1852

Charles Moon, of Michigan, died June 21,1852, age 32 years

Samuel Hough, died July 20,1852, age 30 years

Mrs. Margaret Perkins, died in June 1852

H. Galbraith, of Tiffin, Ohio, died July 19,1852, age 22 years

William Fairley, of Michigan, died July 2,1852, age 39 years

J.B. Wilson, of Indiana, died July 21,1852, age 21 years

L.L. Sutliff, of Michigan, died July 21,1852, age 23 years

M.D. Moran, of Wayne County, Mich., died August 2,1852, age 22 years

Uriah Munson, died June 12,1852 (no other data listed)

John Sperry, of Freeport, Ill., died May 30,1852, age 30 years

D.B. Salver, of Mt. Morris, Ill., died July 30,1852, age 25 years

Eliza D. Bayley /sic/, of Painesville, Ohio, died May 19,1852, age 20 years

Demetrius Munger, of Peoria, Ill., died July 4,1852, age 25 years

J. Blake, of Livingston County, no state listed, died June 25,1852 age 21 years

G.W. Moore, died August 6,1852, age 30 years

G.W. Lancaster, of Illinois, died July 4,1852, age 20 years

D.S. Allen, of Cleveland, Ohio, died July 22,1852, age 23 years

Lawrence Ridgely, of Baltimore, Md., died July 21,1852, age 22 years

Rachael Persons, of Frankfort, Ind., died July 29,1852, age 29 years

J.R. Fisher, died on August 4,1852, (no other data listed)

Eliza M. Parker, of Jackson County, Mo., died August 5,1852, age 23 years

S. Green, died June 8,1852, age 41 years

Thomas Sprague, died July 27,1852, age 22 years

Maria Joneday /sic/, died July 22, 1852, age 32 years

David Henderson, died April 21, 1852, age 40 years

George Smith, died June 8, 1852, age 21 years

J.W. Snodgrass, died June 18, 1852, age 23 years

Martha Langston /sic/, died June 18, 1852, age 2 years

Mrs. Salvina Means, died August 13, 1852, age 32 years

Col. __ Lankeord /sic/ (Lankcord?, Langcord?), died August 8, 1852, age 20 years

Lafayette Tate, hung June 15, 1852 for murder of T. Miller /sic/

Elizabeth Stewart, wife of E. Stewart, died June 13, 1852, age 35 years

Mary J. Kirby, died June 16, 1852, age 14 years, daughter of J.B. Kirby

A. Swan, died June 3, 1852, age 37 years

M.J. Henderson, of Wisconsin, died June 15, 1852, age 1 year, 2 months, 15 days

Nelly Osborne, of Missouri, wife of Willis Osborne, died June 17, 1852

John Edwards, of Ohio, died May 26, 1852, age 32 years

S. Reed (no other data listed)

Henry Barker, of Holt County, Mo., died June 9, 1852, age 55 years

Elias Barker, of Holt County, Mo., died June 2, 1852, age 22 years

Eliza A. Barker, of Johnston County, Missouri, died August 5, 1852 age 22 years

Mary C. Barker, died June 22, 1852, age 2 years (no state listed)

W.C. Hardcastle, died August 16, 1852, age 23 years

R.P. Hardcastle, died June 23, 1852, age 26 years

Mrs. D.A. Hardcastle, died June 6, 1852, age 26 years

J.M. Hardcastle, died June 7, 1852, age 6 years

Mrs. D.J. Hardcastle, died June 16, 1852, age 25 years

Mary C.S. Crobe /sic/, died June 12, 1852

__ Rose, died June __, 1852

George Brooks, of Ohio, died June 4, 1852, age 22 years

J.H. Swansey, of Pike County, Mo., died June 11, 1852, no age listed

Charles Sharp, of Michigan, died June 22, 1852, age 52 years

Mary Pete /sic/ (Peter?), died June 23, 1852

Josephine Gilmore, died June 26, 1852, age 14 years

__ Battsford /sic/, died July 26, 1852, shot by his captain

Mrs. Mary E, Murray, died July 16, 1852, age 23 years

Mrs. M.A. Campbell, died June 2, 1852, age 22 years

Mrs. Mille Irwin /sic/ died June 10, 1852, age 55 years

Cemeal Means /sic/, died August 13, 1852 age 21 years

Thomas H. Cooper, died August 8, 1852, age 21 years

John Lolas /sic/, died August 8, 1852, age 27 years

M.J. Bracket, died August 2, 1852, age 24 years

R. Chambers, died June 9, 1852, age 46 years

S. Rees, of Illinois, died July 2, 1852, age 37 years

P.L. Coleman, of New York, died June 18, 1852, age 24 years

Charles A. Mount, died June 2, 1852, age 24 years

William Jackson, died June 20, 1852, (no other data listed)

A.J.R. Obnetting, of Illinois, died June 2, 1852, age 25 years

William Wilson, of Illinois, died May 21, 1852, age 22 years

Joseph Curtis, of Miami, Ohio, died June 14,1852, age 23 years

A.T. Prouty, died June 19,1852, age 53 years

George Willis, of Lexington, Ky., died May 20,1852, age 26 years

O. Cooper, died May 13,1852 (no other data listed)

F. Frances Kays, died June 16,1852, age 6 years

Martha Duncan, of Missouri, died June 22,1852

John A. Place, died June 27,1852, age 25 years

B.F. Smith, (no other data listed)

G.B. Mandfield /sic/ (Mansfield?) of Indiana, died June 3,1852

G.W. Batty /sic/, died June 16,1852, age 23 years

D.J. Hogsett /sic/, died June 26,1852, age 23 years

John Gusk, died June 23,1852 (no other data listed)

Mrs. Mary E. Bagley, of Missouri, died June 25,1852, age 20 years

James Mount, died June 14,1852, age 50 years

D.D. McCall, died June 27,1852, age 25 years

Joseph Lynn, died June 6,1852, age 3 years

D. Taggart, died June 4,1852, age 49 years

M. Brennan, of Chicago, Ill., died May 20,1852

Daniel Carpenter, of Michigan, died May 13,1852, age 74 years

J.C. Strong, died June 12,1852, age 19 years

Lawrence Cotrell, of Ohio, died June 15,1852, age 36 years

Sarah Anne Kean /sic/ of Missouri, died June 22,1852

Mrs. Margaret Craig, of Indiana, died June 2,1852, age 27 years

Sally Stone, died June 23,1852, age 6 years

A. Straus /sic/, of English Prairie, Ind., died June 12,1852, age 21 years

Daniel Gilleney /sic/ (no other data listed)

William Harshard, of St. Louis, Mo., died June 23,1852, age 39 years

A. Allen, died June 16, 1852, age 13 years

S. Cant /sic/, died June 17,1852, age 23 years

A.C. Thompson, died June 24,1852 (no other data listed)

J.R. Nelsonhy (?) (Nelsonby?), died June 20,1852, age 31 years

John Bush, died May 30,1852, age 40 years

John Fletcher, of Palmyra, Missouri, died June 13,1852, age 26 years

Mary E. Doone, died May 11,1852, age 25 years

James Mann, died June 14,1852, age 32 years

M.J. Pickens, died June 22,1852 (no other data listed)

Margaret Davis, of Missouri, died June 19,1852, age 22, wife of I.Davis

R.B. Oscar, of Boone County, Missouri (no other data listed)

John T. Kindar /sic/, died June 25,1852, age 14 years, son of William and Lydia Kindar

Peter Petty, died May 27,1852, age 22 years

Daniel Miller, of Sweetville, Mo., (no other data listed)

Daniel Wilson, died June 23,1852, age 22 years

W. Wolseman (?) (Toiseman?), died June 23,1852, (no other data listed)

Edward Kirby, died June 22,1852, age 23 years

Eleanor G. Gordon, of Chicago, Ill., died July 27,1852, age 22 years

Russel Jones /sic/, age 23 years (no other data listed)

Mrs. Sarah A. Fitzgerald, of Illinois, died August 7, 1852, age 15 years /sic/

C. Steel, of Illinois, died August 20, 1852, age 21 years

G.W. Gonger (?) (Gouger?), of St. Louis, Missouri, died July 31, 1852, age 44 years

Emma L. Butts, of Pennsylvania, died June 5, 1852, age 27 years, 6 months

Samantha Thornton, died June 8, 1852, age one year

Albert Dunning (no other data listed)

Lizzy Wheeler, of Jackson, Michigan, died July 22, 1852, age 37 years

James B. Personger /sic/, of Boone County, Missouri, (no other data listed)

Andrew J. Ballen, of Sheboygan, Wisc., died June 24, 1852, age 33 years

C.W. Wilson, died August 11, 1852, (no other data listed)

Mary Couise Frey /sic/ (Mary Louise Frey?), of Perry County, Indiana, died August 1, 1852, age 27 years

S.P. Reed (no other data listed)

William Forbes, of Dexter, Michigan, died August 13, 1852, age 32 years

J. Cunningham, died August 1, 1852, age 26 years

Jesse Brown, of Sheboygan, Wisc., died June 21, 1852, age 34 years

Sarah Talbort /sic/ (Talbert?), of Cooper County, Mo., died June 22, 1852

RELIEF TO EMIGRANT TRAINS AT TRUCKEE STATION/ORMSBY'S STATION (July to October, 1852) Provisions were distributed to destitute overland emigrants by John Bodley, agent for the California Relief Post, at Truckee Station and Major L.P. Ormsby's Station, at the "sink of the Humboldt". The period of distribution ran from July 10, 1852 to October 10, 1852. Bodley's distribution record will be found on file in the California State Archives (Governor's Papers GP1:142). Items furnished were recorded as flour, dried apples, potatoes, onions, tea, ground coffee, saleratus, brandy, sugar, ham, cheese, pork, pint bottles of lime juice, pickles, barley, and corn meal.

The original documents were difficult to decipher, hence a number or the names appear with appropriate question marks. Relief provisions were issued as follows:

Emigrants and
Distribution Date:

J.H. Wood and Company, from Iowa, July 10, 1852

William Greggs and Company, from Michigan, July 25, 1852

John Hutzel and family, from Wisconsin, August 3, 1852

D. Hale and Company, from Michigan, July 20, 1852

Thomas Higgins and Company, from Michigan, July 25, 1852

William Ewing, from Illinois, August 8, 1852

David Wilson, from Michigan, July 25, 1852

D. Levi and Company, from Michigan, July 25, 1852

John Helchpin (?) (Helchfin?) and family, from Wisconsin, August 3, 1852

<u>Emigrants and Distribution Date</u>:

David Gephart /sic/ from Indiana, August 8, 1852

Joseph Dennis and family, from Illinois, August 13, 1852

George Myers and family, from Wisconsin, August 15, 1852

Michael Mish, from Missouri, August 17, 1852

J. Dags (Dazo?) and A. Arnold, from Missouri, August 19, 1852

Philip Vaughen /sic/ and Company (Vaughn?), from Missouri, August 20, 1852

E.Z.R. Brown (?) (E.Z.B. Brown?) and H. Cook, from Illinois, August 21, 1852

Philip Morrison, from Wisconsin, August 21, 1852

Jacob P. Miller, from Wisconsin, August 21, 1852

Lewis J. Stinson (ill on arrival, issued one bottle brandy), from Indiana, August 21, 1852

Benjamin Roberts, from Missouri, August 21, 1852

Michael Messman (?) (Mepsman?), from Missouri, August 21, 1852

James Willis, wife and children, from Michigan, August 23, 1852

G.H. Hudson (?) and family (J.H. Hudson?, I.H. Hudson?) from Illinois, August 10, 1852

D. Lindle and Company, from Illinois, August 15, 1852

George Gephart /sic/ and family, August 16, 1852

John Flood and Company, from New York, August 17, 1852

William D. Kelly and brother, from Missouri, August 19, 1852

Robert Owen and two sons, from Wisconsin, August 21, 1852

Mr. __ Willis (eight days sick) from Illinois, August 21, 1852

Israel D. Layman (sick six days), from Bates County, Missouri

E.H. Brown and family, from Missouri, August 21, 1852

S. Cooper and son, from Ohio, August 21, 1852

George Kephart /sic/ (Gephart?) and family, from Indiana, August 21, 1852

Frank Hebble, from Pennsylvania, August 23, 1852

Anthony Bishel (?) (Rishel?, Zishel?), from Wisconsin, August 11, 1852

James Goldweather (sick on arrival), from Illinois, August 11, 1852

William Ketchum and family, from Wisconsin, August 16, 1852

A.J. Carson, from Missouri, August 18, 1852

Michael Hewets /sic/, from Missouri, August 18, 1852

Francis O'Neal, from Wisconsin, August 20, 1852

Patrick __ and L. Nickel, from Pennsylvania and Iowa, August 21, 1852

Patrick Cason, from Illinois, August 21, 1852

Thomas Gibble, from Henry County, Ill., August 21, 1852

W.A. Jones and W.R. Harris, from Ohio, August 21, 1852

Thomas Daniels, from Missouri, August 21, 1852

William Ketchum and family, from Wisconsin, August 21, 1852

Henry Lewis, from Mississippi, August 23, 1852

P. Little (no state or country listed) August 23, 1852

Emigrants and
Distribution Date:

E. Miller and three sons, from Michigan, August 23, 1852

William Fowler, wife and eleven children, from Missouri, August 23, 1852

T.R. Williams and R. Mar__ (Marguis?, Marquis?) (both sick), from Arkansas, August 23, 1852

Malinda Lathrop and eight children, from Missouri, August 25, 1852

William Chase and wife, from Missouri, September 1, 1852

R.Z.W. Guard (?) (Guaro?, Green?), from Illnois, September 1, 1852

John Cassaday /sic/ and family, from Missouri, September 2, 1852

R. Milland and E. Bisham(?) (Risham?), from Wisconsin, September 6, 1852

Israel Irts (?) (Arts?) and family, from Missouri, September 7, 1852

William Simmons (?) (Timmons?), N. Tredwine (?) (W. Tredwine?), Henry Wolf, M. Simmons (?) (W. Simmons?, M. Timmons?, W. Timmons?), I. Simmons(?) (I. Timmons?), S. Green and John Morris, from Pennsylvania, September 10, 1852

E. Lacy and two partners (no names listed), from Michigan, August 23, 1852

Joseph Heat /sic/ (Hart?), ill on arrival, from Missouri, August 23, 1852

R. Holmes and E. Holmes, from Arkansas, August 25, 1852

Mars Shockley, from Missouri, August 25, 1852

Sarah Wright and family, from Indiana, August 25, 1852

Caroline Robinson, three children and driver, from Missouri September 1, 1852

E. Rein (?) (Reis?, Reir?) and J. Brown, from Wisconsin, September 6, 1852

Peter Gish (?) (Gist?) and family, from Wisconsin, September 7, 1852

M. Wilson and Mrs. __ Ganety (?) (Gangtry?, Gansety?, Ganztey?, Ganzetry?) and family, from Missouri, September 10, 1852

Nehemiah Blake, from Iowa, September 10, 1852

A. Hill and family, from Iowa, September 13, 1852

Henry Foley and William Noble, from Michigan, August 23, 1852

John Hartman, wife and two children (team broken down) from Wabash County, Indiana, August 23, 1852

H. Tree and W.M. Brown, from Arkansas, August 25, 1852

Joel Clas (?) (Claz?, Claus?, Clay?), ill on arrival from St. Joseph, Missouri, August 25, 1852

D. Bates (lame and ill on arrival), from Missouri, September 1, 1852

T. McGlochlan, from Missouri, September 2, 1852

Sarah Bennett and family, from Wisconsin, September 6, 1852

Daniel Rants and family (children sick), from Illinois, September 7, 1852

Mrs. __ Davis and family, from Iowa, September 10, 1852

R.V. Sutherland, from Ohio, September 10, 1852

W. McClure and J. Lot, from Ohio, September 10, 1852

Porter Johnson and family, from Iowa, September 10, 1852

William R. Smith and J.W. Wright, from Iowa, September 13, 1852

Emigrants and
Distribution Date:

James Payne (sick on arrival), from Missouri, September 13, 1852
John H. Bradford and family, from Virginia, September 15, 1852
Philip Sumalt (?) (Gumalt?), from Missouri, with family, September 15, 1852
H. Bigler and family, from Illinois, September 17, 1852
John A. Putnam and family, from Wisconsin, September 20, 1852
Mrs. __ Cox and family, from Missouri, September 22, 1852

Philip King and family, from Missouri, September 13, 1852
John Kelly /sic/ (Kelley?) and M. Kelley /sic/ (Kelly?), from Missouri, September 15, 1852
B.H. Jaques (?) (Jagues?), from Illinois, September 16, 1852
R. Atkinson, wife and three children, from Indiana, September 20, 1852
Reese Shrouder /sic/ (Shrorder?, Schrorder?), died at the Station. Departure point not listed, September 22, 1852

Mrs. __ Hopkins, from Illinois, September 13, 1852
William Hunter and family, from Wisconsin, September 15, 1852
John Tryman (eight days sick), from Missouri, September 15, 1852
G. Busson (?) (S. Busson?, G. Russon?, S. Russon?), from Illinois, September 17, 1852
James Baker (ill on arrival), from Illinois, September 20, 1952

The following emigrants received relief provisions at Truckee Station from September 25, 1852 to October 20, 1852. Ledger record did not indicate point of departure.

September 25, 1852:
Michael Mulrover (?)
Joseph Honceladen (?)
William T. Gilkey, wife and three children
October 2, 1852:
Mrs. E.G. Durham (?) (Dunham?) and family
Mrs. __ Johnson and family of six children
October 7, 1852:
E.G. Durham (?) (Dunham?) and family of five children
Mrs. __ Beverly and ten children

September 27, 1852:
Dr. E.W. Pierson, and David Tuttle and familes (eighteen in all)
October 4, 1852:
David Beamer, wife and eight children
October 5, 1852:
David Flea (?) (Tlea?, David T. Lea?) and two others
Ansel Hubbard and five others
October 7, 1852:
George Durham (?) (Dunham?)
John Hargreaves, wife and five children

September 28, 1852:
John McDonald, wife and six children
Louis Wien /sic/ (Wein?) and six in family
Samuel Stetmay (?) and Company
October 6, 1852:
A.H. Brown, wife and five children
Augustus Cork (?) (Cook?)
Benjamin Tannahill
H.C. Russell, wife and seven children
I.H. Moore
John Chandler
Delos Luce

NOTES

Data contained in this section has been incorporated into the index of this book. Primarily, the following citations deal with variations in the spelling of passenger surnames and given names or expansions on the identity of passengers. Readers may find this a curious and interesting part of the work.

Page 3 - (J.H. Levering, President of Cincinnati, Ohio wagon train):- This group of Ohio residents left Cincinnati, Ohio for St. Louis, Missouri in the middle of March 1849. Known as the "California Mining and Trading Company of Cincinnati"; they intended to travel to Independence, Missouri by steamboat. The company's bookkeeper was identified in a contemporary source as A.H. Colter. Three men served on the company's board of finance, Joseph Talbert, Dr. ___ Rogers and G. Letter. These three foregoing individuals will be found on page 3 as "Mr. J. Tabbert", "Mr. L.M. Rogers" and "Mr. G.W. Letter". Variations in spelling arose in listing in second contemporary sources.

Page 4 - (Dr. ___ Woodworth, of St. Joseph, Missouri; F.P. Ward, Dwight Herbert and Jacob Stetzel, of New Carlisle, Ohio):- The foregoing members were camped at Independence, Missouri on April 6, 1849. On April 25, 1849 three members of this group were placed at a camp near St. Joseph, Missouri. However, there was no reference to Dr. ___ Woodworth being in the St. Joseph camp. In addition, variations appeared in spelling of the names at the St. Joseph camp. Dwight Herbert is listed as D. Hubbard, and Jacob Stetzel appears as Jacob Stitzel (see page 37). F.P. Ward is the only entry which agrees with the page 4 entry. All three individuals are listed as residents of New Carlisle, Ohio.

Page 4 - (Lieut. G.W. Paul, of St. Louis, Missouri):- Lieutenant Paul had purchased mules in St. Louis for $70 per head and was offered $100 a head when he arrived at Independence. Paul's company apparently was well-provisioned, for a visitor partaking an evening meal at his campsite indicated that the dinner Paul served "was equal to that set at any St. Louis hotel"- (April 14/49 Republican).

Page 4 - (Lieut. G.W. Paul, of St. Louis, Missouri):- The New York Daily Tribune of May 15, 1849 printed an item which stated that G.W. Paul's company had lost thirty mules while enroute.

Page 4 - (A.A. Ackley, passenger aboard the steamer "Mary Blane"):- The Missouri Republican of April 23, 1849 mentions that a company from Indianapolis, Indiana was organized into four messes, each mess being provided with a wagon, tent, and necessary equipment and provisions. Members of this company were listed as:

A.A. Ackley	J. Hoover	G.W. Larimore (sic)
M. Alford	A.W. Harrison	Samuel Dunlop (sic)
George Baker	T.P. Harrison	W.B. Greer
John Culley	R.C. Grogdon	William L. Morris
W. Bradon (sic)	B.F. Ringland	H.H. Ohr (sic)
Jacob Hoover Sr.	E.R. Myers	J. Latimore

182

Readers should note the listings of J. Latimore and G.W. Larimore and consider alternative of "J. Larimore" and "G.W. Latimore". (Note that A.A. Ackley is on page 4, and that J. Hoover Sr. and J. Hoover were identified out of another source as Jacob Hoover Sr. & Jr.)

Page 4 - (James McElrath, W.C. Hayes, S.K. Dundass, Oliver C. Gray, S.E. Barr):- All names listed as found in source. Note entries on Page 30, for members of Steubenville, Ohio wagon train encamped at Independence, Missouri on April 19, 1849. The below comparison entries are believed to refer to the same individuals:

Page 4 Entry	Page 30 Entry
James McElrath	J. McElrath
W.C. Hayes	William C. Hayes
S.K. Dundass	S.D. Dundall(?) (Dandell?) (Dandall?)
Oliver C. Gray	O.C. Gray
S.E. Barr	S.R. Barr

Page 7 - (Washington California Mining and Trading Association, of Washington County, New York):- This train was still encamped at St. Joseph on April 14, 1849. On page 24 will be found a letter reference to this company in which there appears variations in certain names as listed below:

Entry Page 7	Entry Page 24
Samuel McDoual	Samuel McDoul
J.H. Tilford	John H. Tilford
J. Cowan	John Cowan
J. Robertson	John Robertson
R. Gourlay	Robert Gourley
A. McNaughton	A. McNorton
D.T. Harshaw	B.F. Harshaw
William Harrison	W. Harrison
Andrew Telford	A. Tilford

Page 7 - (Dr. Thomas B. Small, of Schaghticoke, New York, member of the "Schaghticoke Califorina Mining Company"):- The Rome (New York) Sentinel of July 4, 1849 carried a letter written by John M. Muscott dated May 20-21, 1849. Muscott, a member of an emigrant train traveling to California, headed his letter Pawnee Territory, Little Blue River, 224 miles from St. Joseph, Missouri.

In Muscott's letter he mentions coming across two graves of emigrants who died on their route after leaving St. Joseph, both buried near the roadside. The graves contained two physicians, one a Dr.___ Small, of Washington County, New York; the other Con Ferdinand Sims, a Spaniard of St. Louis, Missouri.

Page 10- (Newark Overland Company of Newark, New Jersey):- The proceedings of the New Jersey Historical Society, July 1923, listed this company and a second contemporary source contained variations in spelling of names of company members and residence sites.

Variations are as follows:

Listing Page 10	Second Contemporary Source
Andrew J. Grey	Andrew J. Gray
Charles Grey of New York City	Charles Gray of Newark, N.J.
A. Jerohnen, of Newark, N.J.	Abraham Joralemon, of Belleville, N.J.
C.B. Gillespie	Charles Gillespie
George Sayre	George D. Sayre
Col. J.R. Crockett	Col. John R. Crockett
Moses Camfield	Moses Canfield
James Lewis, of Newark, N.J.	James Lewis Jr. of Hanover, N.J.
H. Johnson	Henry L. Johnson
A. Jobes	Ashfield Jobes
L.B. Baldwin	Lewis B. Baldwin
J.A. Pennington & svt	James A. Pennington
G.W. Martin	George W. Martin
Joseph Denman, of Newark, N.J.	Job Denham of Springfield, N.J.
B. Easterline	Benjamin Casterline
C.D. Bogleston	Caleb Boughton
I. Overton of Elizabethtown, N.J.	Isaac Overton, of Newark, N.J.

Page 10 - (Captain Edward Bryant, or Edwin Bryant of Louisville, Kentucky):- In a letter written to the Rome Sentinel, a New York newspaper, John M. Muscott mentions Bryant's group passing his own wagon train. In Muscott's letter which was dated May 20-21 and written from ____, refers to Bryant traveling with a Louisville company of pack mules.

Page 14 - (Robert Pollock and G.W. Pocock, of Michigan):- Surnames listed as found in source. Consider alternatives of Robert Pocock and G.W. Pollock.

Page 14 - (Wagon Trains from Michigan in St. Joseph, Missouri on April 10, 1849):- On
& 15 April 24, 1849, a wagon train calling itself the "Michigan Company No. 1" departed St. Joseph, Missouri for California. This train was made up of Berrien County & Cass County residents. In reviewing a second contemporary source enumeration (St. Joseph Gazette, April 27, 1849) with the enumeration appearing on pages 14-15 there were found to be variations in names of company members. The listings on pages 14-15 were compiled on April 10, 1849, whereas the enumeration printed on April 27, 1849 was made on April 24, 1849. Variations appeared as noted below:

Second Contemporary Source (April 24, 1849)	Listings on Pages 14-15 (April 10, 1849)
Hobby & Company	same 15
Samuel Hastings	" 15
Lyman Hastings	" 15
Lyman Hastings Jr.	" 15
J.C. Hale	John Hale 15

Second Contemporary Source (April 24, 1849) Continued	Listings on Pages 14-15 (April 10, 1849) Continued
Erastus Ford	E. Ford 15
Cornelius Compton	William H. Compton 14
Martin Cronkhite	J. Cronkhite 15
not listed	David Hobby 15
Joint Stock Company Passengers	
Henry Hass	not listed
Henry C. Shattuk (sic) (Shattuck)	" "
H. Kimberly	L. Kimble 15
S. Hass	not listed
William Welch	" "
V. Washey	" "
George W. Benton	" "
Ezekiel Benton	" "
Seward Benton	" "
Charles W. Shattuck (sic)	" "
Joseph Beadie(?) (Beadle?)	" "
Mathew Balland (sic)	" "
Benjamin W. Veary	Benjamin Veszey 15
Ely Paxson	Eli Paxon 15
N. Hudson	same 15
John Winchester	" 15
J.S. Freese	George S. Freese 14
J.H. Smith	J.C. Smith 14
Asa Dow	same 14
R. Maronville	R. Maranville 15
Ely Eck	Eli Eck 15
Lenard Crane (sic)	Leonard Crane 15
Isaac Thompson Jr.	J.P. Thompson 15
James Wily (sic)	James Wiley 15
F.W. Early	F.W. Earl 15
Charles Kane	same 15
John M. Heisy	John Heisz(?) Heinz(?) 15
James Hull	James Hull(?) Hall(?) 15
Henry Kingsley	H. Kingsley 15
Cicero Towner	C. Towner 15
Samuel Saulpaugh	S. Saulpan 15
Elijah McDougle (sic)	E. McDougall 15
J.E. Pike	G. Pike 15
Fred Vanhorn (sic)	F. VanHorn 15
J. Hartsel (sic) (Hartzel)	J. Hartsall 15
James H. McCord	not listed
Brookfield Gard	B. Guard 14
Ezra Gard	Ezra Guard 15
Henry Myers	same 14
Henry Rudd	H. Rudd 15
James Rudd	J. Rudd 15

185

Second Contemporary Source (April 24, 1849) Continued	Listings on Pages 14-15 (April 10, 1849) Continued
G.W. Jones	same 15
Robert Wilson	Robert W. Wilson 14
Isaac Babcock	same 14
Hamilton Smith	H. Smith 15
George Fay	same 15
Thomas Beady	Thomas Brady 15
James Tuly	James Tooly 15
Not listed	C. Martin 15
" "	H. Schenefelt 15
" "	George Eancs(?)(Evans?) 15
" "	H. Smith 15
" "	J.O. Nickel 15
" "	I. Steinbaugh 15
" "	F. Barker 15
" "	William B. Howard 15
" "	A. Smith 15
" "	William Hood 15
" "	___ Bleauster 15

Page 16 - (Wagon train from Ashtabula County, Ohio):- One contemporary source (St. Joseph Gazette, April 20, 1849) stated this group was from Kingsville, Ashtabula County, Ohio and reported that they were still camped out of St. Joseph on April 20, 1849. The second contemporary newspaper source contained variations in names of the emigrants as follows:

Entry on Page 16	Second Source Listing
C. Tinker	Chauncey Tinker
H. Tinker	Horace Tinker
Lyman Luce	Lyman Lun
L. Beckwith	Samuel Beckwith
A.N. Kenk	A.N. Rent
G. Perkins	John A. Perkins
G. Kendall	James Kendall
G. Hayner	not listed

Pages 17-19 - (Pittsburgh & California Enterprise Company):- This wagon train was still encamped at St. Joseph, Missouri on April 20, 1849, with a departure time set for the following week. Some records of the period refer to this train as "The California Enterprise Company" and a number of variations appear in contemporary sources in respect to names of the members. In some instances duty assignments do not agree. These variations are set forth in paragraphs which follow.

Before leaving Pittsburgh, Pennsylvania for St. Joseph, Missouri the members of the company were subjected to a lengthy address by Colonel S.W.

Black. Colonel Black called on the train's members to act as "one" promising that a perfect unity of interest and affection "will make you prosperous and invincible". Unfortunately, a number of the company failed to follow Colonel Black's advice and the train suffered considerably on the trail and there was discontent among its members after its departure from St. Joseph. Reports told of the company being short of provisions, once without meat for six weeks. Fighting and quarrelling erupted frequently and bowie knives were freely employed in settling quarrels. Before comparing variations in three contemporary sources of the period, some particular questionable listings should be noted. The name "M. Kane Jr." is listed twice on page 17, once denoting a duty assignment as president of the company. Both entries list a residence of Pittsburgh, Penn. The dual entries are listed as found in the primary source.

The entries J.A. McGee, R. McKee and James McKee appearing on page 17 are listed as found in source. All three listings reflect a residency of Pittsburgh, Penn. Readers should consider alternatives of J.A. McKee, R. McGee and James McGee. It would appear that McKee is the correct surname based upon three comparisons which appear in the following source review. On page 17 will be found two Pittsburgh, Penn. residents entries with surnames which appear similar: J. Arnderson and F. Anberson. The alternative spellings of J. Anderson and F. Amberson are worthy of consideration. In a similar vein there are three suspicious variations of Pittsburgh, Pennsylvania residents. They appear as found on page 18: F.J. Beal, A. Beal and Samuel Deal. The alternatives for the foregoing entries would be F.J. Deal, A. Deal and Samuel Beal.

On page 18 will be found an entry for B. Fiffer of Alleghany County, Pennsylvania. The surname is listed as found in source- note entry on page 19 relative to F. Phipper, of Butler County, Pennsylvania. Alternatives of B. Phipper and F. Fiffer would appear reasonable. An entry for J. Shotts, of Westmoreland County, Pennsylvania appears on page 18. Note entry on page 26 for J. Shutt, of Westmoreland County, Penn. Author believes both entries refer to the same individual. An obvious original source error also appears on page 18 for J. Estepp, a resident of Pittsburgh, Pennsylvania. Note entries on same page for "W. Estep", of Pittsburgh, Pennsylvania and "D. Estep of New Brighton, Pennsylvania". Alternatives of "J. Estep", "W. Estepp" and "D. Estepp" must be alternative listings. A further comparison of this surname is noted in the three sources which follow the entry on page 19 for William F. Alderman, of Mohoning County, Ohio is listed as found in source. Note entries on same page of H. Halderman and P. Halderman, of Lancaster County, Pennsylvania. The following three-source comparison also reflects comparisons on the two surnames. However, readers should consider alternatives of "William F. Halderman", "H. Alderman" and "P. Alderman".

W.H. Call is noted on page 17 without a duty capacity. In one contemporary source Call was carried as a Second Lieutenant of the wagon train. Thomas Thornburgh (page 18) was listed as the First Lieutenant of the train, S.H. Sarler is listed as Vice President in place of Charles Coleman (page 17). W.M. Murray was listed as Secretary in place of Charles T. Officer (page 17) and L.G. Berger was carried as Treasurer.

The following variations in the names of the members of the "Pittsburgh & California Enterprise Company" appeared in newspaper period sources:

187

Page Entry Name	Secondary Source	Third Source
T. Dunn (17)	same as 17	Thomas Dunn
J.B. Chamberlain (17)	J.B. Chamberlain	William J. Chamberlain
S.H. Sarler (18)	not listed	S.H. Sarber
S.B.F. Clark(?) (S.Clark and B.F. Clark) (18)	" "	C.B.F. Clark
W.H. Walker (17)	W.H. Taylor	G.S. Walker
J.S. Willock (17)	J.B. Willock	no entry
not listed	not listed	R. Silcox
" "	" "	W.H. Taylor
Dr. ___Orendorf (17)	Dr. Grandorf (no first name)	Dr. ___Orendorf
Jacob Cupps (17)	same as 17	same as 17
J. Knowland (17)	" " 17	L. Knowland
B.C. Quigley (17)	" " 17	B.C. Quigly
James McKee (17) and J.A. McKee	" " 17	J.S. McKee
J.S. Tallanalle (17)	J.B. Tallanalio	J.S. Follanslie
J. Nesmitte (17)	same as 17	J. Nesmith
A.W. Gug (17)	" " 17	A.W. Ing
E.C. Gug (17)	" " 17	E.C. Ing
B. Messersmith (17)	" " 17	B. Mesmith
W.C. Beck (17)	" " 17	William C. Beck
R.P. Glass (17)	" " 17	R.P. Glase
Thomas Suce (17)	" " 17	Thomas Snee
J. Leckey (17)	" " 17	J. Lecky
J. McClaskey (17)	" " 17	J. McCloskey
not listed	not listed	S. Frisbie
R. Phillips (17)	H. Phillips	R. Phillips
J. Aiken (17)	same as 17	J. Aikin
J. McCowan (17)	" " 17	J. McCowen
not listed	not listed	Samuel Jaynes
Samuel Ward (17)	same as 17	Samuel Wand
C.O. Flynn (17)	" " 17	C. O'Flynn
T. Reynolds (18)	same as 18	Thomas Reynolds
G. Winebiddle (18)	not listed	G. Minebiddle
N. McIlwine (17)	N. Mellwine	N. McIlwaine
not listed	not listed	L. Cupps
R.K. Polrouski (17)	same as 17	R.K. Peitrouski
J. Ludwick (17)	" " 17	J. Ludwick
George E. McCrady (17)	" " 17	G.E. McCrady
J. Hunker (17)	" " 17	J. Hunnker
C. Rabun (17)	" " 17	C. Rahm
J. McGreggor (17)	J. McGregor	J. McGreggor
W.C. Reed (18)	same as 18	W.C. Reid

Page Entry Name Continued	Secondary Source Continued	Third Source Continued
J. Kearnes (18)	same as 18	J. Kearns
T. Maxwell (17)	same as 17	Thomas Maxwell
M. Mechling (18)	same as 18	M. Meckling
W.J. Stewart (18)	" " 18	W.J. Stewert
E. Alsip (17)	same as 17	F. Alsip
J. Moore (17)	" " 17	J. Morre
E. Holifant (17)	" " 17	E. Hilifant
William Cadde (18)	same as 18	W. Caddoo
J. Estepp (18)	" " 18	J. Estep
W. Wychoff (18)	" " 18	W. Wychoff (clarified)
W. Angenbraigh (17)	William Angenbraigh	W. Aughenbaugh
T. Galbraith (18)	same as 18	Thomas Galbraith
G. Steiner (18)	" " 18	J. Steiner
W.G. Bender (18)	" " 18	W.J. Bender
John Heiss (18) (Heise?)	John Heiss	John Heise
W. McIlbeny (18)	same as 18	W. McIlheney
G. Sythe (18)	" " 18	J. Sythe
W.M.O. Shelton (19)	same as 19	W.M. O'Shelton
F.C. McClure (19)	" " 19	F.C. M'Clure
J.P. Harbach (18)	same as 18	J.B. Harbaugh
J. Matthews (18)	" " 18	J. Mathews
J. Walls (18)	" " 18	J. Wall
Thomas Perkins (18)	" " 18	Thomas Perkins Jr.
H. Gotsman (18)	" " 18	H. Gottzman
B. Fiffer (18)	" " 18	B. Phiffer
S. Sugder (18)	" " 18	S. Snyder
F.A. McMillan (18)	" " 18	F.A. McMillen
G. Mitchell (19)	same as 19	J. Mitchell
S.M. Stowe (19)	" " 19	S. Stowe
George C. Taylor (19)	" " 19	George W. Taylor
G. Lemon (19)	" " 19	J. Lemmon
H. Halderman (19)	" " 19	H. Halderman (confirming)
P. Halderman (19)	" " 19	P. Halderman (confirming)
F. Phipper (19)	" " 19	F. Phiffer (sic)
P. Bergen (19)	" " 19	P. Bergan
B. Brown (18)	same as 18	R. Brown
D. Houck (19)	same as 19	D. Hough
William F. Alderman (19)	" " 19	W.F. Alderman
*S. Trisbie (17)	S. Triable	not listed
C. Lent (17)	C. Leut	C. Lent
James M. Aitkin (17)	James A. Aitkin	James Aitkin
L. Crepps (17)	L. Crappa	not listed

*Reader should consider alternative of S. Frisbie

Page 19 - (The "Illinois Sucker Company", listed is in some contemporary sources as
& 20 "The Sucker Company"):- was still camped at St. Joseph, Missouri on April 27, 1849. This Alton, Illinois wagon train had apparently made extensive rendezvous plans for as early as February 16, 1849. The St. Joseph press had indicated it was expected that the train would rendezvous in St. Joseph on April 1, 1849. (St. Joseph Gazette, February 16, 1849). Besides the equipment and teams listed on page 19 the train also had an India rubber boat, and all the necessary tools, arms and ammunition. David Adams, the guide, was an old and experienced mountaineer.

Most of the train's forty teams comprised four yokes of oxen, carrying 2,200 to 2,800 pounds each. Two newspaper sources of the period varied emigrant name spellings and are indicated in the following comparison.

The column on the left represents a compilation appearing in the St. Joseph Gazette of April 27, 1849. The column on the right was taken from another Missouri newspaper of the same period.

Contemporary Secondary Source	Primary Source Listing Pages 19-20
H. Buffum	same (19)
A. Stevens and two chldrn	A. Stevens and family (19)
D. Boos	D. Booz (19)
J.G. Beiler	J. Beeler (19)
S. Truitt	Samuel Truitt (19)
W. Mitchell	William Mitchell (19)
___Vannatta	___Vanntee (19)
A. Snitowski	A. Schenitoski (19)
M.T. Smith	same (19)
A.K. Grichline	R.F. Grisihline (19)
W.R. Latham	same (19)
J. Flannegan	J. Flanagan (19)
E. Randall	same (20)
J. Woods	T. Woods (20)
A. Currie	A. Curree (20)
I. Spruance	J. Spruance (20)
G. Settlemire	G. Sittibruive (20)
___Croghan	same (20)
___Anderson	Mr. ___Anderson and family (20)
R. Whyers	same (20)
I. Chapman and wife	not listed
S. Chapman and wife	" "
J. M. Taylor	" " (see ___Taylor page 19)
C.R. Post	L. Post (20) and Rollin Post (19)
J.N. Dow	same (19)
S. McPhail	Samuel McPhaill (19)
J.W. Boothsinger	W. Boothsinger (19)
F. Werrdt (sic)	F. West (19)
J. Goodwin	John Godwin (19)
C.A. Walker	same (20)

Contemporary Secondary Source Continued	Primary Source Listing Pages 19-20 Continued
D. Settlemire	D. Settlemyer (20)
J. Lehman	J. Layman (20)
W. Benson	William Benson (20)
J. Pardee	not listed
C.F. Mitchell	C. Mitchell (20)
D. Gwinn	not listed
W.W. Warren	" "
J. Holtzwart	J. Haltzwert (20)
J. Salee	John Sales (19)
A.R. Ferguson	A. Ferguson (19)
D. Hatton	B. Hutton (19)
W. Powers	William Bowers (19)
A. Taylor	___Taylor (19)
T. Lock	Thomas Lock (19)
G.M. Bride (sic)	George McBride (19)
J. Brooks	John Brooks (19)
J. Jablonski	___Joblauski (19)
M. Brattegan	M. Bratagan (19)
W.B. Moody	W.V. Moody (19)
D.W. Aldrich, wife & two chldrn	D.W. Aldrich and family (19)
J. Patrick	same (20)
___Oakes	T. Oakes (20)
H. Rice	same (20)
P. Lathian (sic)	Peter Lottim (20)
E. Guild	___Guild (20)
R. Waggoner	not listed
James Rowe	J. Rowe (20)
T. Carr	not listed
C. Lewis	" "
T. Primrose	" "
R.S. Greene	Robert S. Green (19)
G.M. Boyd (sic)	George M. Boxer (19)
G.W. Carr	same (19)
C. Vaughn	" "
J. Bills	John Bills (?) (Bells?) (19)
J. Ristin (sic)	John Rislin and son (19)
J. Vedder	same (19)
C.J. Palmer	" " (20)
J.D. Powers	" " (20)
C. Cheney	Charles Chaney (20)
J.F. Burton	same (20)
J. Longwell	" " (20)
J. Hughs	John Hogus (20)
J.A. Pettingale	not listed
W.P. Hendrickson	" "
C. Misendoffer	C. Mizendorfer (20)

Contemporary Secondary Source Continued	Primary Source Listing Pages 19-20 Continued
not listed	John Douglas (19)
" "	F. Starr (19)
" "	John Post (19)
" "	___Brooks (19)
J.C. Post	John Post (20)
J.R. Godfrey	J. Godfrey (19)
M. (Lewis?)	M. Louis (19)
J. Gifford	same (19)
C. Recard	C. Record (19)
T.S. Ramdy (sic) (Randy?)	Thomas T. Rainey (19)
F. Wardzynski	___Wardzinuski (19)
H.S. Latham	H.A. Latham (19)
R.W. Canfield	R.W. Camfield (19)
J. Hughes	John Hughes (19)
N.M. Dorsey	same (19)
A. Starr	" " (19)
B. Pursley	___Purseley (20)
R. Kirkwood	same (20)
E. Case and wife	E. Case and family (20)
C. Barker	not listed
Mr. & Mrs. ___Thomas	" "
L. Clarke & wife	" "
I. Milne	" "
H.J. Moreland	" "
F.H. Curtis	same (19)
J.W. Buffum and wife	J.W. Buffum (no wife listed) (19)
E. Elwell	Ellis Elwell (19)
E. Pomroy	E. Pomeroy (19)
William Pankey	not listed
C. Sinclair	Charles Sinclair (20)
S. Keller	___Keller (20)
J. Dunlap	not listed
B. Lucken	B. Luken (20)
W. White	William White (20)
S. Haynes	not listed
H. Martini (sic)	H. Martin (20)
H.F. Johnson	not listed (see C. Johnson & brother) (20)
A. Grotfend (sic)	A. Groetfield (20)
G.S. Hamly (sic)	G.S. Hanly (20)
Z. Root	not listed
G. Johnson	C. Johnson and brother (20)
H. Johnson	not listed (see C. Johnson and brother) (20)
S. Stuart	not listed
J. Johnson	same (20)
A. Lelleur (?) Leileur (?)	not listed

Page 22 - (Adrian, Michigan Wagon Train):- A second contemporary source refers to this group as "California Squad, No. 2" and noted that it would depart from St. Joseph, Missouri a few days after April 27, 1849. The secondary source listed members of the group as:

Names listed on Page 22	Secondary Source
H. French	Henry French
Same	John Densmore
Edward Lapham	Edmund Lapham
Ephraim Lapham	Dr. E. Lapham
H. Crandall	Not listed

Page 22 & 23 - (Columbia County (Ohio) Wagon Train):- The New York Daily Tribune of May 1, 1849 printed an article relative to this company which contained variations in the emigrant names but also supplied additional data regarding residence sites. Some ommissions were noted in the Tribune list as set forth below:

Tribune List	Page 22-23 Entry
Frederick Eaholtz, of New Lisbon, Ohio	F. Esholtz
Col. Hugh Lee of New Alexander, Ohio	Hugh Lee
Alexander Anderson of West Township	A. Anderson
George Grice, of North Georgetown, Ohio	same name
A.V. Kinnear, of Hanover, Ohio	same name
Hugh Jordan, of Hanover, Ohio	H. Jordan
Z. Downer, of Hanover, Ohio	same name
Joseph O. Evans, of New Garden, Ohio	J.W. Evans
John Lindsay, of New Garden, Ohio	J. Lindsay
F. Hastings, son of Hon. John Hastings	E.O.F. Hastings
Not listed	A. McMillan
Not listed	A.J. Hagan
Not listed	S.M. Holland
Not listed	N.B. Wean
Not listed	J.S. Smith
Not listed	Daniel Willard
Not listed	A. Schindler

Page 23 - (John B. Louck and J. Loach (?) both members of "The Cincinnati and California Joint Stock Company" of Ohio):- Entry reading as "John B. Louck" listed as found in source. Entry reading as "J. Loach" as difficult to decipher and could instead be "J. Leach" or "J. Louck".

Page 26 - (Dr. J.S. Ormsby, of Peru, Illinois):- On July 15, 1850, the Sacramento Transcripts published a notice seeking information on a Dr. ___Ormsby, who left St. Louis, Missouri for California, the previous season. The missing Ormsby was travelling in "Water's Train" and those possessing information were to contact Mr. N.M. Guild, of San Francisco, or the editor of the Pacific News.

Page 26 - (Racine County, Wisconsin Wagon Train):- A number of individuals listed as members of a wagon train from Racine County, Wisconsin were camped at St. Joseph on April 14, 1849. Many of the members of this train associated themselves with a Michigan train which left St. Joseph on April 24, 1849. Spelling variations appeared in the two source lists as cited below:

Listing on Page 26	Listing on Page 41
J.B. Howe	James B. How (sic)
E. Stebbins	A.C. Stebbins
E. Lowry (sic)	Elisha Lowery
___Simonds	Silas Simonds
L. Dutton	D.L. Dulton
A.H. Blake	A.K. Blake
W. Spofford	W.P. Spaford
H. Blake	No listing
E. Gordon	E.E. Gordon
W. Dodge	W.E. Dodge
E. Pearce	Ebenezer Pierce
___Kimball	Sheridan Kimball

Page 33 - (Painsville Mining Company, of Lake County, Ohio):- The name of the company is listed as found in source. Author believes correct name should be "Painesville Mining Company." The New York Daily Tribune of May 3, 1849 also printed an article relative to this company but there were variations in spelling as follows:

Entry Page 33	Tribune Entry
L. Thatcher, President	Leland S. Thatcher, President
S. Mathews (sic), Director	Dr. Samuel Mathews (sic) Treasurer
H.C. Ely	same name
Major ___Downing (sic)	A.D. Downing
C. Turner, Director	C. Turner, Vice President
H.K. Fobes (sic)	H.K. Forhee (sic)
A. Trowbridge	A.B. Trowbridge
E. Bligh (sic)	E.E. Bligh (sic)
H.P. Cady	same name
B.F. Adams, Director	R.F. Adams, Secretary
M. Fox	M.N. Fox
J.W. Amy	same name
E. Manley	Eli. Manley
M.J. Turney	same name
J. Green	Isaac Green

Page 36 - (Joint Stock Company from Cincinnati, Ohio identified as the "Cincinnati Company"):- Additional data on this small group was contained in the New York Daily Tribune of May 1, 1849 where the group was. Variations in the spelling of members appeared in the Tribune article as noted below:

Tribune List	Page 36 Entry
Joseph H. Moore	J.H. Moore
Mr. ___Sperry, of the Cincinnati Globe	W.J. Sperry
George W. Harrington	G.W. Harrington
G.W. Grippon	A.W. Griffin
James Gale Hubbell	J.G. Hubbell
Berry Jones	Barry Jones

Page 36 - (J.C. Crane, J.A. Drake, William Glover, William Mullowy, all members of train from Cincinnati, Ohio):- The New York Daily Tribune of May 3, 1849 printed an article relative to the foregoing emigrants but varied the spelling on J.C. Crane as "H. Crane" and William Mullowy as "William Molony". The Tribune also added the name C.L. Ingalabee.

Page 37 & 38 - (Wagon company from Columbus, Ohio):- The New York Daily Tribune of May 1, 1849 printed an article relative to this company and it contained variations in the emigrant names as noted below:

Tribune Entry	Page 37-38 Entry
H.L. Morgan	same name
L. Green	L.E. Green
B. Johns	B. John
S.F. Hoyt	S.Y. Hoyt
H.C. Riordan	H.C. Rareden
J. Cowen	J. Cowan
B. Carpenter	same name

Page 41 - (S. Hough, of the "Dixon Company", of Dixon Lee County, Illinois):- The New York Herald of July 1, 1849 reported the death of a Silas Hough, of Baltimore, Maryland, seventy miles from Independence, Missouri enroute to California. Silas Hough was accompanied by two young sons (unnamed) and a man named ___Boyd from Philadelphia.

Page 41 & 42 - (Charleston, Virginia Mining Company):- This group was also known as the "Charlestown Company" or the "Charlestown, Virginia Mining Company". The Spirit of Jefferson (Virginia) issue of February 13, 1849 published the names of the company members and its list varied in spelling of the emigrant names with the Missouri newspaper account as follows:

Entry Pages 41-42 (Missouri Newspapers)	Jefferson List
B.F. Washington of Jefferson, Virginia (41)	Benjamin F. Washington

Entry Pages 41-42 (Missouri Newspapers) Continued	Jefferson List Continued
Robert H. Kelland of Richmond, Virginia (41)	Robert H. Keeling
Smith Crany, of Jefferson Cty, Virginia (41)	Smith Crane
J.E.N. Lewis, of Jefferson Cty, Virginia (42)	Joseph E.N. Lewis
Wake Bryarly (42)	Dr. Wakeman Bryarly
E.M. Aisquith (42)	Edward M. Aisquith
J.T. Boley (42)	John T. Boley
J.W. Bowers (42)	John William Bowers
T.C. Brapley (42)	Thornton C. Bradley
W.J. Burwell (42)	Walter J. Burwell
Asa Dlevinger (42)	Asa Clevinger
H. Conway (42)	Hugh Conway
J.C. Davis (42)	Joseph C. Davis
J.H. Engle (42)	Jacob H. Engle
D. Fagan (42)	Daniel Fagan
M. Ferrill (42)	Milton Ferrill
J.W. Gallaher (sic) (42)	John W. Gallaher
J.H. Garnhart (42)	John H. Garnhart
V.E. Geiger (42)	Vincent E. Geiger
F.A. Riely (42)	Edwin A. Riely
C.F. Slagle (42)	Charles F. Slagle
J.C. Walpert (42)	John C. Walpert
H.H. Moore (42)	Henry H. Moore
J.T. Poland (42)	John T. Roland
C.A. Hayden (42)	Charles A. Hayden
E. Hooper (42)	Edward Hooper
J.M. Lupton (42)	John M. Lupton
H.C. Harrison (42)	Hamilton C. Harrison
E. Rohter (42)	Elisha Rohrer
N. Tavener (42)	Newton Tavener (died later at Johnson Ranch)
T.C. Moore (42)	Thomas C. Moore
E. Lock (42)	Elisha Lock
C.C. Thomas (42)	Charles G. Thomas
T. Milton (42)	Taliaferro Milton
J.C. Young (42)	Joseph C. Young (died May 23, near Big Sandy)
R.H. Keeling (42)	not listed
F.R. Simpson (42)	Francis R. Simpson
J.H. Murphy (42)	John H. Murphy
J.T. Humphreys (42)	J. Thomas Humphries
J.A. Strider (42)	Jesse A. Strider
J.S. Showers (42)	John S. Showers
I.K. Strider (42)	Isaac Keys Strider

Entry Pages 41-42 (Missouri Newspapers) Continued	Jefferson List Continued
A.R. Miller (42)	Andrew R. Miller
B.F. Steevers (42)	Benjamin F. Seevers
W.H. Mackaran (42)	William H. Mackaran
P.W. Ripler (42)	not listed
not listed	Richard Barley
" "	James S. Cribs
" "	Charles F. Gittings
" "	T.P. Hardesty
" "	Noble T. Herbert
" "	Dr. Joseph D. Humphreys (note: see page 42 for listing on a J.T. Humphreys)
" "	Edward McIlhany
" "	Frank Smith (Guide for trip)
" "	George Marshall
" "	William Rissler
" "	James B. Small
" "	Lawrence Washington
" "	Thomas F. Washington

The "Camp Bryarly" referred to on Page 42 was undoubtedly named after the Company's Surgeon, Dr. Wakeman Bryarly (Wake Bryarly)

Page 42 - (California Mining & Trading Company, of Dayton, Ohio):- This company was
& 43   still camped at St. Joseph, Missouri on May 4, 1849, and on that date a second tabulation of the company was printed in the St. Joseph Gazette-. In comparing the May 4th list with the enumeration appearing on pages 42-43 (source St. Joseph Gazette, April 27, 1849) there will be noted variations in the names. Variations are listed as follows:

Page 42 Entry- (April 27, 1849)	Second Source-(St. Joseph Gazette of May 4, 1849)
James Odell	James Odell Jr., Secretary
not listed	E. Ealy, Surgeon
John Edmonson	John Edmondson, Treasurer
J.D. Possenoe	Judson Popenoe
H. Marat	H. Marrott
B.F. Kinsely	B.F. Knisely
not listed	William Rosseau
John S. Lewis	S. Lewis
I. Stouder	J. Stouder
D.D. Gilman	B.D. Gilman
J. Haage	J. Hague
S. Hoke	S. Hake
D. Fundiburgh	D. Fundiburg
R. Shadrick	R. Chaddie

Page 42 Entry- (April 27, 1849) Continued	Second Source (St. Joseph Gazette of May 4, 1849) Continued
not listed	H.B. Christ
" "	William Speulda
" "	E.A. King
" "	W.H. Smith
William M. Smith	William Smith
not listed	S.M. Keifer (sic)
" "	W.H. Bickford
" "	J.W. McCorkle
" "	J.H.T. Morris
" "	Thomas Clegg Sr.
" "	J. Hisey
" "	James Pease
" "	Thomas Clegg Jr.
" "	D. Stibbins (sic)
" "	W. Coles
" "	J. Kreiner
" "	D. Engles
" "	J.C. Foster
" "	Webster Clegg

The secondary source also noted that the following individuals were traveling in company with the "California Mining and Trading Company":

C. Arisman	William Smith
J. Favorite	J. Clark
G. Lowery	J. Grauf
A. Warner	H.C. Trebein
William Brogden	H.F. Trebein
A. Clark	

With the exception of William Smith, none of the immediate above individuals were noted as train members on April 19, 1849, which indicates they associated themselves with the company sometime between April 19 - May 4, 1849.

Page 43 - (Cincinnati Mercantile Association of Ohio):- A secondary contemporary source (St. Joseph Gazette, May 4, 1849) noted that this company left their St. Joseph encampment for California on April 30, 1849. The secondary source also varied in identifying company members as follows:

Entry page 43	Secondary Source
R.S. Drummond	same
William M. Stoder	William Stoddart
David Horton	D.C. Horton
S. Merrill	same
Timothy Worthington	Z. (Zee) Worthington

Entry page 43 Continued	Secondary Source Continued
John Henderson	J. Henderson
W. Name	William M. Vance
John R. Patten	J.R. Patton
John Bukham	John Bickham
Dr. W.F. Ames	Dr. F.W. Ames
Dr. John McKenzy	Dr. J.M. Mackenzie
Joseph H. Merrill	not listed

(Rev. Isaac Owens): Another member of the cloth who departed for California from St. Joseph in the spring of 1849 was Rev. James Wright, of Boone County, Missouri. The St. Joseph Gazette of January 11, 1850 contained an interview with Wright who returned to Missouri after going overland to California. Wright preached a "California sermon" to the residents of Columbia, Missouri and during the course of it observed that he found "that the population of California was the most honest, moral and intelligent with which he ever associated". Wright's observations are carried to some length in the article, and it closed with this remark "My serious and honest opinion is that people who are making a living, and all men of families, should remain at home and not go to California".

Page 46 - (Dr. J. Hendricks, E.S. Reynolds, M.B. Miller, G. Pierson, Dr. D.W.C. Willoughby, W. Miller, C. Johnson, W. Snavely, W. Woodward and W. Maslin all of South Bend, Indiana and members of the "Dowdle Family"):-
The New York Daily Tribune of May 3, 1849 also printed an item relative to the foregoing individuals, and indicated they had departed from South Bend on March 24, 1849. However, the Tribune reference did not make any reference to those in the "Dowdle Family" who were listed with residence listings in St Joseph, Missouri, Iowa, and Chicago, Illinois. The Tribune article added the name of John Linderman and varied the spelling of the members as follows:

William Miller, Secty & Treasurer	Cyrenius Johnson George Pierson
M.B. Miller	D.W.C. Willoughby
William Maslin	W.L. Woodward
Dr. J.A. Hendricks	W.J. Snavely
E.S. Reynolds	John Linderman

Page 46 - (Wagon trains in St. Joseph, Missouri, May 4, 1849):- The "Green and Jersey County Company" Wagon Train was also meeting in St. Joseph, Missouri on May 4, 1849. The complete Constitution and By-Laws of the Company, signed by Elon Eldred and A.R. Knapp, will be found in the St. Joseph Gazette, of May 4, 1849.

Page 49 - (Wagon train from Canton, Ohio):- Further data on this wagon train appeared in the New York Daily Tribune of May 1, 1849. Some variations and omissions occur between the Tribune list and the list contained on page 49. The Tribune article stated that this company left Steubenville, Ohio about April 1, 1849. All were residents of Canton, Ohio except as noted:

Tribune list	Page 49 entry
O.P. Stidger (?)	not listed
Robert Gillespie	" "
George Evans	" "
Joe Vosbey (?)	" "
George Hampson	" "
James Anderson	same name
Mr. ___Platt	George B. Platt
Alison Dunbar	same name
George S. Dunbar	" "
Darwin Estep	" "
D. Raffensperger	Daniel Raffensperger
J. Wagoner	John W. Wagner
William Haas	same name
Amos Piersong (?)	Amos Pierrong (sic)
Mr. ___Martin	not listed
___Reed, of Massillon, Ohio	" "
___Searl, of Massillon, Ohio	" "
Benjamin Page, of Jackson, Ohio	" "

The Tribune article also noted that N.M. Harris, John Mobley, William Hicks and John Fitzsimmons, of Fulton, Ohio had left Steubenville, Ohio for California a few days prior to the departure of the above company.

Page 49 - (The "Illinois and California Mutual Insurance Company, No. 1):- The Constitution of the "Illinois and California Mutual Insurance Company, No. 2" will be found fully detailed in the St. Joseph Gazette, (Missouri) of May 4, 1849. Members of Company No. 2 consisted of:

P.W. Webber (sic)	James Parkerson
Henry Shepherd	Lewis Campbell
James Shepherd	Joseph Crane
Thomas Moffat (sic)	A. Eastman

Page 49 - (Wheelersburg, Sciota County, Ohio Wagon Train):- The New York Daily Tribune of May 1, 1849 claimed this company was from Portsmouth, Ohio, whereas, a Missouri newspaper source reported it as being from Whellersburg, Ohio (sp?). Emigrant name variations between the two sources appear below:

Tribune List	Entry page 49
T.S. Enslow	same name
W. Reddick	William Raddock
Uri Nurse	same name
W. Enslow	" "
G. Duke	" "
Thomas Burke	T.J. Burke
Finton Kendall	A.F Kendall
T.S. Moxley	Dr. T.S. Moxly (sic)
Robert McConnel (sic)	Robert McConnell
M. Narse	Morrison Nurse

Tribune List Continued	Entry page 49 Continued
W. Crichton	William Crichton
W.J. Finton	same name
W. McKinney	William McKinney
John B. Miller	John Miller

Page 64 - (Members of "Knox County, Illinois Company," from Knox County, Illinois):-
& 65   The New York Daily Tribune of May 1, 1849 printed an article relative to some members of this company, though not specifically identifying them as members of the unit. The Tribune article supplied pinpoint resident data, but varied in spelling some of the emigrant names. The comparison is as follows:

Tribune Listing-	Entry on Page 64 or 65
Nelson D. Moore, of Henderson, Ill.	N.D. Morse, of Knox County
Orris Clark, of Henderson, Ill.	Oren Clark, of Knox County
James E. Hale, of Henderson, Ill.	J.E. Hale, of Knox County
Alex. Ewing, of Knoxville, Ill.	Alex Ewing, of Knox County
John Ewing, of Knoxville Ill.	John H. Ewing, of Knox County
L. Dow Montgomery, of Knoxville, Ill.	L.D. Montgomery, of Knox County
Edward McGowan, of Knoxville, Ill.	E. McGowan, of Knox County
Josephus Arms, of Knoxville, Ill.	Lt. Cephas Arms, of Knox County (listed in two places)
E. Taylor, of Knoxville, Ill.	E.N. Taylor, of Knox County
J.L. West, of Knoxville, Ill.	John L. West, of Knox County
J.W. Plummer, of Knoxville, Ill.	J.W. Plummer, of Knox County
A. Haynes, of Knoxville, Ill.	Asa Haynes, of Knox County
Thomas McGrew, of Knoxville, Ill.	Thomas McGrew, of Knox County
George Allen, of Knoxville, Ill.	George Allen, of Knox County
Robert Kimball, of Knoxville, Ill.	Robert Kimble, of Knox County
D.C. Norton, of Knoxville, Ill.	D.C. Norton, of Knox County (above name on p. 65)
Nathaniel Hulbert of Knoxville, Ill.	Nath. Hurlbut, of Knox County
Wilson Temple, of Knoxville, Ill.	J.W. Semple, of Knox County
Leander Woolsey, of Knoxville, Ill.	J.L. Woolsey, of Knox County
Alex Palmer, of Knoxville, Ill.	Alex. Palmer, of Knox County
Aaron Larkin, of Knoxville, Ill.	Aaron Larkin, of Knox County
Thomas Shannon, of Knoxville, Ill.	Thomas Shannon, of Knox County

Page 74 - (Frederick Rohrer, of Andrew County, Missouri):- The St. Joseph Gazette of April 12, 1850 printed a letter written by Fred Roher (sic) and datelined "Near Hangtown, Dry Diggins, California, January 31, 1850". It will be noted the spelling of the surname in this instance was "Roher" as opposed to "Rohrer".

    The same issue of the Gazette contained extracts from a letter written by R.B. Fulkerson at Deer Creek Village, California bearing the date January 16, 1850. Fulkerson stated he had a pleasant trip across the plains and arrived in the mines on August 17, 1849.

A third article in the Gazette issue concerned an interview held with Captain ___Griggsby (sic Gribsby?) by the St. Louis Union. Grigsby had recently returned to Missouri from California to purchase milk cows which he intended to take back to the west in May, 1850. He was identified as a former resident of Missouri who had emigrated from the south-western portion in 1845, and arrived in California at a time when few white men were to be found there. He raised and commanded a company which served throughout the struggle of Independence of California.

Page 78 - (Oxford, Ohio, Ezra Bourne):- Research source for this entry is taken from
& 79 carbon typescript of the Journal of Ezra Bourne. Typescript is in the Bancroft Library, University of California, Berkeley. Bourne reached Fort Laramie on June 12, 1849, the Humboldt Sink on July 26, 1849 and crossed the Sierra Nevada by Carson Pass. He reached Weaverville, California on August 5, 1849.

Page 79 - (New York Daily Tribune):- The Tribune printed a number of articles dealing with the departure of individuals to California by the land or the land-sea-land route. The following references to departures and progressions appeared on indicated dates:

1849

April 18:- Report of the departure to California of Edwin Robinson, late publisher of the Vermont Gazette and the actor C.R. Thorne, accompanied by two sons. The same issue carried a reference to a company of eighty-five in camp near Van Buren, Arkansas under the command of Dr. W.B. Smith, of Alabama. A passing mention was made of a horse tamer named Professor ___Offutt.

April 19:- Report of the landing at St. Josephs Island (sic) of the "Essex Mining and Trading Company" under command of William C. Waters. The schooner which carried this company, the "John W. Herbert", sank after leaving them in its departure for Galveston, Texas. This company had left Corpus Christi, Texas on March 31, 1849.

On June 6, 1849 the New York Daily Tribune printed an article which it had copied from the Salem Massachusetts Register. The Register had received a letter from George W. Copeland of the Essex Mining & Trading Company. Copeland wrote that he was left at Laredo on the Rio Grande with another member of the company, Mr. Warren Prince. The article also noted that William E. Cox, of Lynnfield, Massachusetts, John C. Walton, of Salem and Stephen Jones, of Boston, had died of cholera. The remainder of the company had proceeded on its route.

On June 12, 1849 the Tribune printed a letter from a Robert McCloy (no attachment company given) in which there was a reference to the death of a C.F. Boyden of Beverly, Massachusetts and D.E. Parker of Lynn, Massachusetts. Mention was also made that Stephen Jones died of cholera on April 18, 1849.

April 20:- Letter signed by the initials "H.C.W.", datelined Mexico City, Mexico, concerning the Manhattan Company, Enterprise division of thirty men.

April 21:- Mr. ___Coote (sic) of Massachusetts, accidently wounded by a shotgun on the Rio Grande while enroute to California. Passing mention of a Mr. ___Peoples and reference to the "Carson Association" leaving for Houston, Texas. The "Persifer F. Smith Association" reported taking passage to Port Lavaca, Texas, and movement thence to San Antonio, Texas.

April 25:- Letter printed from Michael McClellan, of Jackson County, Missouri announcing his safe arrival in California after an overland trip taken in 1848. McClellan's family accompanied him on the journey.

April 27:- The "Massachusetts & California Company" formed at Northampton, Massachusetts. William H. Hayden, a Yale graduate, was to act as the company's assayer. (This group had a capital of $50,000 and its purpose was to establish a private mint.) Josiah Hayden of Haydenville, Massachusetts, father of the companies assayer, was the President S.S. Wells and Miles G. Moles, also of Haydenville were the directors. Rev. F.P. Tracy was to act as the agent.

April 28:- Report of the departure to California of the "Memphis, Tennessee Company". This group going overland, via Fort Smith, Arkansas, consisted of: E. Wilkins, John Willis, Mr. Ledgerwood, P.W. Kirkpatrick, E. Mallory, R.S. Param, J.P. Param, G. Davis, Capt. Larke, Lagrange; John Gary, Lamar; W. Macon, Shelby County; R.B. Macon, Hardeman; E. Williamson, Fayette; E. Morris, H. Hart, P.W. Fulingee, Simon Fant, Mr. Morrison, Mississippi; M.D. Floyd, Salem, Massachusetts; R. Steele, B. Doxy, Mr. Foster, Mr. Neley, Spring Hill; Jas Ballord, Sommerville.

The Tribune of the same date also carried lists of the "Peoria Pioneers" and the "Peoria Californians" overland companies both from Peoria. The location of Peoria is not listed but it could refer to New York State or Illinois. The following are the members of the "Peoria Pioneers":

Thomas Phillips, Captain	J. Angel	Thos. Carlyle
John S. Bowers, Lieutenant	B.H. Banvard	John R. Crandall
	Dan'l. Banvard	Jacob Culver
	Benk. Booker	John Collin
James Armstrong	A.H. Brown	Edmund Durst
Howel Armstrong	Benj. O'Brien	Elisha Douglass
Long'th Armstrong	Jesse O'Brien	Flemming Dunn
Wm. Armstrong	C.W. Boyden	George Dullen
C.L. Armstrong	Henry Bowman	Samuel S. Durmand
Jacob Adams	J. Crable	Ellis Dunn
M. Angel	Wm. Carman	Andrew Drury

203

Stephen W. Eastman	Horace Tarble	Myron Lisk
John R. Forsyth	Wm. Tappin	H.G. Miller
M. Fritchery	Ira Ward	L.M. Miller
James Rankin	George Wells	Joab Moffat
E. Snow	W. Frury	Hugh Moffat
Peter Shroff	George Ford	James Mitchell
Henry Stevens	G.H. Farron	John Monroe
Leonard Somers	Wm. Giles	Thos. J. McGrew
John Shull (sic, Sholl?)	Nathaniel Giles	Warren Nash
	Nelson Giles	J. Nicholson
Rees Stevens	M. Greenman	Obadiah Oakley
Valentine Shutts	E. Greenman	Allison Philley
W.H. Simmerman	A. Hughs	Wm. Pearce
James Simpson	C.M. Hinman	Wm. E. Post
A.L. Seward	Robert W. Haynes	Robert Pack
Adam Sholl (sic, Shull?)	Nathan Hull	C.W. Reese
	Samuel R. Hicks	John Rankin
Wm. Sterling	W.H. Holland	John Winter
Joshua Thurwell	Paul Keim	Stephen Winter
John Tucker	Orrin Kingsley	M. Watson
Samuel Tart	Isaac Lockman	R. Watson
		Josephus Wood

The following are the members of the Peoria Californians:

Benj. White	James Swan	Abijah Hunt
Joseph Ellis	Wm. Howes	Reuben Crowell
George F. Pledge	George Oakley	Jerome Stevers
Mr. Tripp	James Murgins	Andrew Johnson
Orrin Oakley	Seth Sturgess	Joseph Hunt
George Lawrens (Lawrence?)	Henry Hahn	Wm. G. Tryall
	James Maxwell	D. M. McConnell
Wm. Spurk	Wm. Stillwell	James S. Cleveland

Page 79 - (Captain Blanton McAlpin and the "Mobile Company" from Alabama):- The New York Daily Tribune of April 18, 1849 stated that McAlpin left Mobile on April 6, 1849. The Picayune of New Orleans reported that the company left Vera Cruz, Mexico on April 13, 1849 for California. The Kennebec Journal (Augusta, Maine) of April 26, 1849 stated that three other California-bound companies left Vera Cruz the same week that McAlpin departed. The Journal did not identify the other companies by name nor did they print a list of members.
    The same issue of the Augusta newspaper printed an article reporting that Charles Dunham, from the vicinity of Hartford, Connecticut, was killed in a dispute with Mexican soldiers at Irapauto, Mexico, supposedly over nine pence owed for breakfast.

Page 86 - ("Boston & Newton Joint Stock Association"):- The New York Daily Tribune of May 3, 1849 did not print a full list of the members of this association and names contained in the Tribune list varied in spelling with Staples/Gould diary account contained in the Bancroft Library in Berkeley, California. This association left Boston on April 16, 1849 and arrived in California in September, 1849. There follows a comparison of the Tribune list of members and Bancroft source records list:

Page 86 Entry	Bancroft Source List
Brachet Lord	Brackett Lord
Jesse Winslow	Jesse Winslow
A.C. Sweetser	Albion C. Sweetzer
Thomas H. McGrath	Thomas H. McGrath
Walton C. Felch	Walton C. Felch
D.J. Staples	*David J. Staples
H.W. Dickinson	Harvey Dickinson
S.D. Osborne	S.D. Osborn
A.J. Hough	James A. Hough
Ben. C. Evans	Benjamin C. Evans
Not listed	Milo J. Ayer
" "	Robert Coffey
" "	Daniel E. Easterbrook
" "	Harry Noyes
" "	John White
" "	James St. Clair Wilson
" "	Benjamin Burt Jr.
" "	*Charles Gould
" "	Dean Jewett Locke, physician to Company
" "	Nathaniel B. Loring
" "	William H. Nichols
" "	John Frederick Staples
" "	George Thomason
" "	Lewis K. Whittier
" "	# George Winslow
" "	Edward Jackson, of Newton, Massachusetts. (joined association from another small emigrant group)

(*) Copies of diary in Bancroft Library
(#) Died on June 8, 1849 and buried 30 miles west of Big Blue River. Grave marked in 1912 with permanent monument.

GEOGRAPHICAL NOTES

AMERICAN FORK RIVER - about half a mile below Sutter's Mill, 74

ASH HOLLOW - South side of the Platte, 161

BEAR RIVER - 80 miles from Salt Lake, 74

CARSON RIVER ROAD - about 40 miles past the Sink of Carson River, 156

FORT CHILDS - A Fort Kearny was established in 1846 on the Missouri River where Nebraska City is located today. One year later the army decided that the Fort was not close enough to the Oregon Trail, so it was moved to a location on the Platte River, just west of where the Oregon trail reached the Platte River, and south of present-day Kearney, Nebraska. At this time it was renamed Fort Childs. Approximately one year later the Fort was renamed again as Fort Kearney. The new fort was in operation from 1848 to 1871.

Travellers recorded that the fort was 208 miles from Kanesville, Iowa; 270 miles from St. Joseph, Missouri; 340 miles from Fort Laramie; 50 miles from the Little Blue River and 275 miles north of Scotts Bluff. 69, 72

FORT HALL - is on the banks of the Lewis River, the southern main branch of the Columbia. 74, 75

GALLOWAY'S RANCH - on the road to Downieville. 154

GREEN HORN VILLAGE - at the base of the Rocky Mountains. 95

HANGTOWN - 60 miles from Sacramento, California, in the Dry Diggings. 75, 77

HOCK FARM - about 8 miles below Yuba City, as you ascend the Feather River, (site of residence of Captain Sutter). It is situated on a high plain and in 1850 consisted of about 600 acres.

KANESVILLE, IOWA - The name from 1848 to 1853 of the present-day city of Council Bluffs. In approximately 1846, Col. T.L. Kane came to the town that was then called Trader's Point to register Mormons for the Mexican War. The Mormons were fleeing persecution in Missouri and Illinois. They were in need of help, and Col. Kane gave them aid. They then renamed their town to Kanesville in his honor.

LITTLE BLUE RIVER - 224 miles from St. Joseph, Missouri, and 55 miles from Fort Childs on Platte River. 182

LOUP FORK or (Loop Fork) - is 75 miles form North Platte, Nebraska.

MARY'S RIVER - called this by the Mormon's. Fremont called it the Humbolt River. 74

NEBRASKA TERRITORY - when that territory was created in ____ (some 5 years after 1849), it was divided as Kansas and Nebraska.

NINIHAM RIVER - native term for Nemaha River in Nebraska, about 80 miles from St. Joseph, Missouri.

SALT CREEK - about 60 miles from Missouri River, 69.

SCOTT'S BLUFF - is near the North Fork of the Platte River, about 75 miles below Fort Laramie and some 275 miles above Fort Childs, Nebraska. 95

SPRING CREEK - 345 miles form Kanesville, Iowa. 72

SUBLETT'S CUTOFF - in Oregon Territory.

WEAVERS CREEK - 45 miles north of Sacramento, California. 75

WEAVERTOWN DRY DIGGINS (DIGGINGS?) - 50 miles east of Sacramento, California, 2 miles north of Weavertown and 1 1/2 miles southeast of Hangtown California. 74

WOLF CREEK - 18 miles from St. Joseph, Missouri. 53

Surname Index

(x)- Denotes more than one entry for name on cited page. See "Key to Abbreviations and Symbols" for the definition of symbols, abbreviations and figures. Index for passengers with surnames that have missing letters will be found either at the beginning of the index, or, if the first letter of the last name is known, within the index.

____, Albert, 93
____, C., 108
____COCK, Peter, 40
____, E. W., 141
____, "Henry," 104
____, J. W., 113
____, John, 141
____, Nathaniel, 121
____OBLE, ____ (Mr.), 160
____, Patrick, 178
____, William, 93
____WORT, W., 168

-A-

AALE, D.H. (sic), 163
AARON, W.B., 147
ABBEES, E.R., 140
ABBEY, A.T., 166
  R., 3
  William, 44
ABBITT, William L. (sic), 117
ABBOES, E.R., 140
ABBOT, G. wife & 3 chldrn (sic), 22
  G.E., 113
  John, wife & child (sic), 22
ABBOTT,____(grave of), 93
  George E., 113
  John, 14
  M.D., 118
  William, 67
  William L. (sic), 117
ABBOTTS, E.R., 140
ABER, D., 28
ABLE, C., 133
  D.H., 163

ABRAHAM,____, 119
ABRENT,____, 35
ACKER, P.P., 65
  Peter P., 59
ACKERS, Austin, 57
  W., 57
ACKLEY, A.A., 4, 181(x), 182
ACORD, A. Rev (sic), 159
  V.L., 159
ACORN, A. Rev, 159
  V.L., 159
ADAMS,____ (Dr.), 69
  ____ (Mr.), 55
  B.F. (death of), 33, 94, 193
  C.A., 48
  Daniel, 107, 119
  David, 19, 189
  F.H., 168
  George, 91
  J., 68
  J.D., 133
  J.H., 164
  J.O., 20
  J.Q., 159
  Jacob, 106, 202
  John, 69
  M., 164
  M. & lady, 157
  P.G., 152
  R.F., 193
  R.S., 158
  S.J. & son, 155
  Sebastin, 98
  W., 69
ADAMSON, Enos, 135
ADDISON, B.T., 153
ADKINS, C.C., 90
ADNEY, D.B., 146

AGNEW, Abraham, 116, 118
  J.A., 25
AHALT, H. (sic), 154
AHART, Michael, 154
  Nicholas, 154
  Peter, 154
AHPIL, H., 167
AHRENT,____, 35
AICKS, H. (sic), 157
AIGEN, James, 114
AIKEN, J., 17, 187
  T., 144
AIKIN, J., 187
AIKINS, T., 129
AINSWORTH, John M., 116
AISQUITH, E.M., 42, 195
  Edward M., 195
AITKIN, James, 139, 188
  James A., 188
  James M., 17, 188
AKE, G., 144
AKIN, William, 86
AL____, R. M., 116
ALBERT, G., 165
  John (death of), 94
ALBRE, William H., 7
ALBRO, William A., 7
ALCOCK, G., 149
ALDERMAN, H, 186
  P. 186
  W.F., 188
  William F., 19, 186, 188
ALDRICH, D.W. & fam, 19, 190
  D.W., wife and 2 chldrn, 190
  Garner, 103
  Homer, 136
  L.D., 85
  William, 48

ALDRIDGE,____, 87
  Isaac, 97
  J., 39
  W.W., 108
ALE, D.H., 163
ALEXANDER,____
  (Mr.) & wife, 144
  A.C., 55
  C.G., 47
  D., 160
  J.L., 152
  J.W., 81
  James & fam, 9
  R.B. (Major), 86
  R.N., 111
  W.S., 157, 159
ALFORD,____ (Dr.), 84
  M., 181
ALGEO, J.L., 4
  John M., 4
ALGER, Abner, 110
  James B., 110
ALLAN, Ethan, 91
ALLANDER, Edward, 45
  William, 45
ALLARDT, A., 23
ALLCOCK, Isaac, 117
ALLCOTT, G.B., 174
ALLEN,____, 115
  ____ (Colonel), 125
  A., 176
  A.A. (Dr.), 150
  Abin, 13
  A.C., 152
  Alfred, 123
  C., 150
  C.J., 150
  D., 63, 166 (x)
  D.S., 174
  Daniel, 132
  Edwin, 99
  Edwin W., 106
  G., 144
  George, 64, 119, 124, 200
  George M., 34
  Grovinor, 40
  H., 33
  I., 149
  I. J., 83
  Ira M., 82
  J., 100, 147
  J. (Dr.), 142
  James, 61
  Jeremiah, 114
  John, 42, 100, 132
  L.D., 157
  L.J., 83
  Lafayette, 40
  Levi, 99
  R.L., 82
  Robert P.S., 132
  S., 172
  T.S., 82
  Thomas, 70
  William & brother, 125
ALLENBACH, Jacob, 116
ALLENDAFFER, W., 159
ALLENWORTH, C., 29
ALLESWORTH, C., 29
ALLEY, Dedridge, 136
  Doddrige, 160
ALLIN, G.P., 46
ALLINGHAM, W., 98
ALLIS, F., 113
  P., 113
  William, 154
ALLISON, E. Zevy, 124
  H.R., 173
  James, 88
  John R., 112
  Robert, 124, 151
ALLON, C. (sic), 150
ALLOWAY, A., 135
ALLWORTH, N.B., 6
ALOCUMB, George L., 141
ALSEN, S.F. (sic), 52
ALSIP, E., 17, 188
  F., 188
ALSOP, Thomas, 71
ALSTAD, Joseph, 101
ALTENBURG, H., 166
ALVERSON, L.M., 86
ALVIRUS,____ (Mr.), 60, 61
AMALINDA, Ira & wife, 150
AMBERSON, F., 186
  J., 17, 186
AMEL, Louis, 20
AMES, F.W. (Dr.), 198
  J.W., 59
  O., 166
  O.N.J., 59
  W.F. (Dr.), 43, 198
AMMON, Jackson, 91
AMOS, Henry, 54
AMSBERRY, W., 166
AMY, J.W., 33, 193
ANABLE, H.S., 166
ANALINDA, Ira & wife, 150
ANDERFORM, C., 35
ANDERSON,____, 115, 189
  ____ (General), 92
  ____ (Mr.) & fam, 20, 189
  A., 23, 192
  A.B., 31
  Alexander, 192
  C., 35
  C.A., 29
  C.W., 144
  Charles, 147
  D., 30
  David, wife & 2 chldrn, 26
  F., 17, 186
  G., 152
  G.S., 15
  G.W., 56
  George, 107
  George Alexander, 92
  Isaac & fam, 133
  J., 55, 131, 157, 186
  J.B., 65
  J.C., 17
  J.L., 38, 107
  J.P., 159
  J.P. Sr., 157
  J.P. Jr., 157
  J.W. (Mr.), 3
  James, 49, 199

John, 127
John M., 146
John S., 83
Onestis, 107
Robert, 90, 128
S.E., 153
William, 38, 108, 122
William S., 121, 138
William W., 107
ANDERSTON,____
  (Mr.), 95
ANDISS, Henry, 138
ANDREW, M.O., 52
  W.H., 67
ANDREWS,____, 71
  A.B., 110
  G., 100
  G.H., 85
  James, 46
  Lewis, 102, 111
  M., 149
  Rachael, 172
  V.S., 119
ANG, L. (sic), 157
ANGEL, J., 202
  M., 202
ANGENBRAIGH, W.,
  18, 188
  William, 188
ANGEVINE, W.H., 45
ANGLE, E., 158
ANGLIN, Aaron, 128
  James, 129
ANGRIAVES, William,
  139
ANKNEY, J.F. (Dr.), 23
ANKRIM, William J., 17
ANSETT, W.H., 70
ANSON, P., 166
  W.W., 165
ANST, H. (sic), 164
ANTECS,____ (Dr.), 28
ANTEES,____ (Dr.), 28
ANTHONY, Alex (Dr.),
  86
  William, 86
ARCHIBALD, Patrick,
  136
ARES, L., 152

ARISMAN, C., 197
ARMITAGE, E.D., 145
  Thomas, 84 (x)
ARMS, Cephas, 64 (x)
  Cephas (Lt.), 200
  Josephus, 200
ARMSTEAD, G.W., 70
  Levi, 126
ARMSTRONG,____, 50
  C.L., 202
  Elijah, 55
  Howel, 202
  J., 13
  J.A., 23
  J.S., 83
  J.T., 154
  James, 202
  John, 134
  Long'th, 202
  M., 48
  R.V., 131
  T.Z., 166
  William, 151, 202
ARNOLD, A., 178
  Green, 107
  H.C., 137
  J.C., 37
  P.R., 24
ARNWELL, Lyman, 67
AROWN, J. (sic), 168
ARRICK, Jacob, 90
ARROWSMITH,____,
  91
ARTERBROOK, A.F.,
  168
ARTHUR, E.F., 1
  G., 25
ARTS, Israel & fam, 179
ASBURRY, George M.,
  107
  Isaac, 107
ASBURY, George M.,
  107
  Isaac, 107
ASGOLM, T., 35
ASHBURY, George M.,
  107
  Isaac, 107
ASHBY, J.T., 61

ASHLEY, D.R., 5
  J.W., 166
  Z.W., 22
ASHLOCK, R., 150
ASHTON, Charles, 154
ASHWORTH, James, 118
ASKIN, A., 140
ASNER, Lewis, 99
ASNIFFY, S., 166
ASNIFIY, S. (sic), 166
ASPER, M., 100
ATHERTON, A.J., 37
  C.H., 146, 149
  E.B., 33
ATKINSON, H., 166
  Isom, 117
  John, 29
  R., wife & 3 chldrn, 180
ATKISON, Isom (sic),
  117
ATWATER,____ (Mr.),
  169
  J.R., 68
ATWOOD,____, 89
  C.W., 160
  John, 24
  L.G., 148
AUCHUST, Philip, 53
AUDISS, Henry, 138
AUGENT, T., 162
AUGER, Lorin, 111
AUGHENBAUGH, W.,
  188
AULICH, B., 34
  K., 34
AULT, W.H., 164
AUSCHUST, Philip, 53
AUSTIN, Calvin, 140
  Charles, 78
  D.H., 14
  Henry, 47
  Isaac, 137
  L.B., 90
  Lucius, 90
AVERELL, D.L., 112
AVERILL, Charles, 110
AVIRI, Charles, 110
AVIRL, Charles, 110
AX, Joseph, 88

AYER, Milo J., 204
AYLIFF, C., 99
AYLIFFE, George, 3
AYRE, Edward, 38
  George W., 38
AYRES, G., 55
  Nathaniel, 134
  O.H.P., 99
  Samuel, 23, 27

-B-

B____NET, Augustus, 118
BA____GETT, Ruben, 69
BABB, Henry, 92
  William, 92
BABBITT,____ (Mr.), 72
  Horace F., 102, 106
BABCOCK, Isaac, 14, 185
  Peter, 40
BACHANANER, W., 34
BACHELDER,____ (Dr.), 40
BACKENBAUGH, Peter, 38
BACKLEY, E., 131
BACON, J.M., 52
BADDLE, John, 100
BADGER, J., 64
BADGETT, Ruben, 69
BADILLA, F.B., 159
BAER, 42
BAGLEY, Mary E. (Mrs.), 176
  William, 137
BAHDEN, J., 61
BAILEY,____ (Mr.), 44, 54
  A.S., 86
  A.W., 112
  Alexander, 124
  C.H., 166
  David (Colonel), 47
  H., 54
  Henry, A., 47
  Joel, 105, 110
  Mary E. (Mrs.), 162
  O.H.P. & fam, 146
BAILY, O.H.P. & fam, 146
BAINE,____ (Mr.), 74
BAIRD, Chauncy, 135
  Jefferson, 119
BAKE, Henry, 99
BAKER, A., 153
  A.J., 58, 65
  B.C., 117
  C., 53
  C.P., 158
  Charles, 124, 155
  D.J., 86
  E.B., 41
  F., 137, 154
  G.S., 133
  George, 123, 181
  George A., 78
  J.M., 105
  James, 180
  James E., 82
  John, 126
  John B., 117
  Martin, 135
  R.N., 60
  Samuel T., 121
  Timothy, 38
  Wilber, 138
  William, 57, 63
  William H., 121
BALARD, W., 164
BALDWIN,____, 89 (x)
  A.C., 37
  Alex, 137
  Alexander H., 28
  Dosson, 67
  George, 140
  H., 100
  L., 150
  L.B., 10, 183
  Lewis B., 183
  N., 100
  R., 65
  T., 138
BALEP, B.F., 163
BALES, Charles, 59
  Eleanor, 64
  G., 99
  Jasper, 64
  O., 59
BALL, C., 63
  F., 18
  George, 169
  H.M., 69
  J. (Dr.) & wife, 129
  Noah, 91
  Richard, 91
  Robert, 138
  Thomas, 146
BALLAND, Mathew, (sic), 184
BALLANTINE, D., 63
BALLARD, G., 80
  L., 157
  Mareto C., 173
  W., 164
BALLEN, Andrew J., 177
BALLEW, Leonard, 71
BALLON, C., 166
BALLOON, Leavitt, 106
BALLORD, Jas., 202
BALLOW, Samuel, 9
BALM, A., 34
BALMEY, A.J., 158
BALTGELL, J., 30
BALTZELL, J., 30
BAMAY, D. & lady, 158
BAMBURTH, A., 167
BANCROFT, William, 27
BANDEN, J., 61
BANDY, H., 108
  John, 105
  Thomas, 105
BANEHAST, P.A., 48
BANGANAN, A.G., 144
BANGS, A., 15
BANKS, Charles C., 57
  W., 57
BANNON, Patrick, 87
BANTA, Isaac, 2
BANVARD, B.H., 202
  Daniel, 202
BANYAT, A., 147
BARBER, M.R., 54
  R. 22

BARBIN, J., 148
BARBY, William C., 112
BARCH, W.V. (sic), 159
BARCLAY, C.C., 40
BARCUS, E. Jr., 88
BARD, George W., 9
BARDIN, C.P., 80
BARDSALL, D.S., 10
BARDSHAR, Solomon, 12
BARFES, N.B., 166
BARKDELL, J.D., 113
BARKDULL, Enos E., 116
  J.D., 116
  J.D. (Capt), 115
BARKER, C., 191
  E.W., 50
  Elias, 161, 175
  Eliza A., 175
  F., 15, 185
  H.G., 163
  Harvey, 161
  Henry, 175
  James H., 47
  John 103, 111, 118
  Joseph, 48
  Mary C., 175
  Reuben, 103, 111
  Thomas, 17
  William, 64
  William F., 115
  William N., 47
BARLEY,_____ (Mr.), 54
  Richard, 196
BARLOW,_____ 164
  Ellen, 162
  Joseph, 102
  S., 148, 149
BARLOY, P.E., 165
BARNARD,_____ (Mr.), 103
  J., 164
BARNES, Barnet, 119
  David, 103, 111
  Franklin L., 107
  George, 109
  Hiram, 118 (x)
  James, 101

Joel S., 106
John, 63
H., 57
Hamilton, 66
R.B., 55
R.E., 147
Reason, 119
T., 153
W.A., 137, 164, 167
William, 173
William C., 117
William H., 84
BARNET,_____ (Mr.), 47
  Augustus, 118
  J.W. (sic), 55
BARNETT,_____ (Mr.), 47
  A.G., 163, 164
  John, 172
  R.C., 147
BARNEY, C., 14
  H.B., 12
  M.J., 147, 152
BARNHART,_____, 29
  Henry Jr., 97
BARNHILL, A.F., 141
  R.S. (Capt), 141
BARNS, Barnet, 119
  Emiline (Mrs.), 169
  Hiram (sic), 118 (x)
  Joel S. (sic), 106
  Reason, 119
BARR, S.E., 4, 182
  S.R., 30, 182
  Stephen, 120
BARRACHMAN, J., 19
BARRATT, J., 144
BARRELTON, J.A., 147
BARRET, Samuel (sic), 36
BARRETT,_____, 154
  C., 159
  R., 28
  W.G., 15
  William G., 105
BARREY, Richard, 121
BARRON, G.T., 148
BARROW, D., 101
BARRY, Dow C., 117

G.C., 148
BARTHOLES, T.L., 163
BARTHOLOMEW, E.F., 65
  L., 65
  T.L., 163
BARTLETT, E.D., 9
  E.M. (Dr.), 111
  H., 108
  J., 113
  John, 26
  Joseph, 96
  William, 5
  William H., 112
BARTMESS, James R., 112
BARTOE, S., 131
BARTON,_____ (Mr.), 54
  A., 65
  Alonzo, 123
  J.H., 90
  M., 121
  S., 157, 158
BARUH, Harman, 84
BASCOM,_____ (Mr.), 76
  Henry, 137
BASHER, D.A., 162
BASS, John L. (Capt), 83
  Nathan, 105
BASSET, William, 104
BASSETT, Elisha, 2
  M., 144
  W.D., 60
BASSON, Thomas, 136, 139
BATEMAN, H., 144
  J., 144
  J.W., 144
BATES, D., 179
  Edward B., 106
  John, 47
  Moses, 146
  P.Q., 130
  R.S., 57, 63
BATSE, E.S., 162
BATTSFORD,_____, 175
BATTY, G.W., 176
BAUDEN, J., 61

BAUDY, John, 105
    Thomas, 105
BAUGH, James, 155
    Thomas, 155
BAXTER, Henry, 58, 65
    J.H., 80, 107
BAXTON, G.C., 173
BAYLES, C., 63
    O., 63
BAYLEY, Eliza D., 174
    Peter & fam, 21, 87
    William, 31
BAYS, M., 169
BEACH, E., 100
    Julius, 68
    Julius C., 68
    W., 29
BEACHAM, J.W., 150
BEADIE, Joseph, 184
BEADLES, R.M., 52
BEADY, C., 47
    Thomas, 185
BEAHAM, Thomas, 88
BEAL,_____ (Dr.), 156
    A., 18, 186
    F.J., 18, 186
    Samuel, 186
    T.L., 154
    William, 66
BEALE, P., 100
    Richard, 87
BEALES, Hiram, 44
BEALL, John, 88
    R., 39
    S.W., 140
BEALS, William, 60
BEAM, Jacob L., 89
BEAMER, David,
    wife & 8 chldrn, 180
BEAN, E., 38
    J.F., 56
    J.T., 55
    William & fam, 40
BEARD,_____ (Mr.), 47
    C., 28
    Charles, 106
    O.T., 85
BEARDSLEY, S., 147
BEARS, C.G., 162

BEATS, J., 163
BEATTLE,_____, 141
    Samuel, 141
BEATTY,_____, 115
    _____ (Dr.), 173
    A.T., 153
    J.W., 30
    S., 167
    W.J., 18
    William, 2
    William T., 160
    Zaccheus, 88
BEAVER, Tunis S., 136
BEBBS, M.E., 141
    W.A., 141
BECK, Robert, 79
    S., 167
    W.C., 17, 187
    William C., 187
BECKER, J.A., 24
    S.S., 159
BECKET, F.O., 90
BECKHAND, B.M. (Dr.), 150
BECKLEY, George, 29
BECKNEY, H., 154
BECKQUETT, P., 163
BECKWITH,_____
    (Mr.), 145
    L., 16, 185
    P., 163
    Samuel, 185
    William, 59, 63
BECKWORTH, V., 145
BEDDISON, J.A., 25
BEDELL, Joseph, 124
BEDFORD, Francis, 67
    Henry A., 172
    Thomas, 171
    W.H., 173
BEDGALOW, P.M., 153
BEEBE, Charles, 133
BEECH,_____, 12
BEEKER, S.S., 159
BEELER, J., 189
    J.G., 19
BEEN, Jonathan (sic), 130
BEGGS, William H., 114

BEILER, J.G., 189
BEIRCE, J. (Dr.), 107
BELANGEE, Enoch, 13
BELCHER, J.W., 126
BELKNAP, Clarinda, 64
    J., 63
    Jonas, 59
    Polly, 64
    S., 64
    Silas, 59
BELL,_____ (Capt), 62
    A., 158
    C.H., 37
    Charles, 63
    Christopher, 3
    G.W., 98, 108 (x)
    H.M., 69
    J.W., 170
    John, 3
    Robert, 138, 162
    William, 66, 137
BELLNAP, H., 136
BELLOWS, Eph, 99
BELLS, John, 19, 190
BELMIER, M.C., 147
BEMING, Eliza, 172
    J.S., 147
BENDEN, J.J., 148
BENDER, Jacob, 42
    W.G., 18, 188
    W.J., 188
BENDETT, C. (sic), 83
BENEDICT, D.K., 14
    J.D. (Mr.), 3
    Julius, 2
    W.H., 159, 166
BENEY, Andre J., 67
BENGSON, H., 157
BENHAM, C., 11
BENINGER, Caroline
    Josephine, 64
    Jacob, 63
    Lewis, 63
BENJAMIN, Anson, 140
    John, 124
BENKLEY, George W., 170
BENN, Henry, 111
BENNER, I., 60

BENNESON, William H., 91
BENNET, A.S., 136
  Daniel (sic), 67
  Henry, 121
  Simon (sic), 117
BENNETT, A., 126
  Augustus, 118
  C., 83
  C.C., 167
  Christopher, 121
  D.C., 86
  E., 68
  Edgar, 103
  G., 83
  Isahel, 67
  J. (Mr.), 74
  J.N., 54
  Jacob, 29
  John M., 124
  L.F., 115
  Robert, 121
  Sarah & fam, 179
  Simpson, 86
  T.J., 158
  Valentine, 98
  W.S., 158
  William, 119
  William M., 84, 85
BENRONGLES, E.B., 70
BENSHAW, D.W.C., 79
BENSLINE, S.W., 157
BENSON, A., 68
  B., 63
  C., 166
  C.D., 167
  Ezra T., 72
  H.A., 113
  Richard, 160
  W., 190
  William, 20, 190
BENTON, Charles, 107
  Ezekiel, 22, 184
  George, 22
  George W., 184
  Leonard, 22
  Nathaniel, 90
  Seward, 184
BENTS, F.G., 85

BENWELL, William, 67
BERAUS, J., 151
BERDEN, A., 148
BERDINE, H., 145
BERGAN, P., 188
BERGE, E.D., 66
BERGEN, P., 19, 188
BERGENDAHL, A.G., 167
BERGER, L.G., 17, 186
BERKSHIRE, Otho, 65
BERLING, ____ Sr., 35
  ____ Jr., 35
BERRINGTON, Julia A. (Mrs.), 172
BERRY, Andrew, 41
  H. Jr., 41
  J.C., 134, 150
  Jeremiah, 146
  L., 132
  Thomas, 9
BERTHOLF, James, 109, 110
  Peter, 109, 110
BESBY, Horace, 5
BESHEAR, Adam, 125
  William, 126
BEST, George, 100
BESWICK, George M., 134
BETNER, ____ (Dr.), 81
BEVARD, C.M., 119
BEVENS, J.I., 61
BEVERLY, ____ (Mrs.) & 10 chldrn, 180
  J. R., 49
BEVINS, William, 20
BICKFORD, J., 119
  W.H., 42
  William, 197
BICKHAM, John, 198
BICKNELL, G.W. (Dr.), 50
  J.W. (Colonel), 60
BIDBLEE, John, 147
BIDDEL, James, 161
BIDDELIGER, J., 153
BIDDINGER, J., 148
BIDDLE, B.R., 49
BIDWELL, C.A.C., 157

C.W., 37
  Eli Jr., 39
BIFFLE, William D., 83
BIGELOW, O.O., 66
  Oaks, 60
BIGGE, Mathew (sic), 104
BIGGERS, W., 149
BIGGS, W., 152
BIGLER, H. & fam, 180
BIGLOW, George, 117
BILLING, J.G., 85
BILLINGS, C., 31
  George & wife, 132
  William, 120
BILLS, A.H., 143
  J., 190
  John, 19, 190
  Sherman, 103
BILLSON, T., 49
BILLUPS, Charles, 123
  H., 123
  R.M., 59
  William, 123
BINGHAM, L., 142
  S., 167
  W.H., 54
BININGER, A., 64
  Charles, H., 64
  E. Manuel, 64
  Elizabeth, 64
  Margaret, 64
BINKLEY, J., 167
BINNEL, Thomas, 40
BINNEY, Andrew J., 67
BINNS, D., 128
BIRD, H.L., 6
  J. (Mr.), 3
  John, 151
  P.M., 120
  William, 61
BIRKEY, F.J., 152
BIRKOLET, W.W., 146
BISHAM, E., 179
BISHEL, Anthony, 178
BISHOFF, C., 167
BISHOP, A.D., 106
  Charles, 47, 95
  L., 158, 166

M., 100
T.A. (Mr.), 3
Thomas, 130
W., 18
BISLEY, E.W. & (Mrs.), 137
BISSEL, John, 147
BIVEN, R., 81
BIVINS, Walker, 56
BL____, Phineas U., 82
BLACHLEY, H. (sic), 160
BLACK, A.J., 129
  D., 163
  J., 63
  James M., 114
  S.W. (Colonel), 186
  Thomas A., 160
  W.S., 167
BLACKARD, C.J., 151
BLACKBURN, Ames, 105
  Amos, 103
  J., 158
  J.C., 147
  R.S., 44
  T.F., 147
BLACKINGTON, J., 158
BLACKINTON, J. (sic), 158
BLACKLOCK, W., 166
BLACKMAN, A.J., 43
  A.M., 67
  C., 163
  C.J., 149
  Hiram, 117
  John W., 102, 111
BLACKSTONE, G.W., 167
BLACKWELL, William, 91
BLAIN, Edw, 147
BLAIR, A.W., 44
  Alex, 108
  C.C., 17
  D., 17
  D.C., 136
  Harvey, 90
  J., 153
  M., 154

Milton, 90
BLAKE, A.H., 26, 193
  A.K., 41, 193
  G., 150
  H., 26, 193
  Henry, 99
  J., 174
  James, 98, 108
  John, 78
  Joseph (death of), 94
  Nehemiah, 179
  Robert Jr., 85
  Samuel Sr., 78
  William M., 88
BLAKELEE, V., 120
BLAKELEY, W., 158
BLAKELY, Daniel, 104
  Joseph, 95
  W., 17
  W.L., 137
BLAKEMAN, E.A., 142
  H.N., 142
BLAKEMORE, R.M., 42
BLAKESLEE, V., 120
BLAKESLY, A.J., 166
BLAKEWELL, W., 168
BLANCHARD, G.G., 119
  H.C., 147
  H.J., 148
  H.T., 139
  Henry G., 147
  J.M., 103
  L., 102
BLAND, T., 11
BLANDIN,____ (Mr.), 134
  J.C., 102
BLANKENSHIP, D.A., 153
BLANKINSHIP, G.H., 159
BLANSETT, Joseph L., 106
BLANSHARD, Henry G. (sic), 147
BLEAUSTER,____, 15, 185
BLEIGHTNER, George, 101

BLEVIN, C.C., 153
BLIGH, E., 33, 193
  E.E. (sic), 193
  J., 41
BLISS, A.F., 7, 24
BLIVEN, Cyrus, 137
BLOCKMAN, C., 163
BLODGETT, A., 58
  A.D. & co., 165
  H.M., 150
  V., 45
BLOOD, John, 133
  Henry S., 106
BLOOMER, John A., 59
BLOOMFIELD, John, 87
BLOSS, A.A., 149
BLOTE, J., 63
BLOXHAM, William, 117
BLOYED, Fines (sic), 169
BLUDGETT, Benjamin, 155
BLUE, William, 114
BLUMY, Alex, 110
BLUNT, Martin, 136
BLY, P., 108
BLYTHE, A.F., 17
BOAK, W.W., 158
BOALS, J. (sic), 168
BOARDMAN, J.H., 83
BOBBINS, Amanda, 169
  Mahala, 169
BOCKNELL, James B., 105
BODEN, Charles, 42
  E., 56
BODKIN, Joseph, 16
BODLEY, John, 177
BOEKNELL, James B., 105
BOENGESSER, A., 50
BOGARD, Perry, 100
BOGER, S., 150
BOGERT, John H., 82
BOGGS, William A., 27
BOGLESTON, C.D., 10, 183
BOISMENNE, John, 20
BOISMENUE, N., 20

BOLDMAN, P., 29
BOLEMENE, Nicholas
  (death of), 94
BOLES, John, 20
  S.P., 148
BOLEY, Henry, 40
  J.T., 42, 195
  John T., 195
BOLING, W., 149
BOLLINGER, E.C., 83
BOMAN, Nathaniel, 69
BOMBARGER, J.M.,
  134, 147
BOMLER, Henry, 46
BOND, ____, 90
  Hermann, 16
  Levy, 68
  Robert, 10
  W., 157
  W. Jr., 157
BONDY, J., 159
BONE, Fed (sic), 80
  Fred, 80
BONHAM, B.N., 67
BONINE, E.J., 5
BONNDY, J. (sic), 159
BONNELL, A.C., 51
BONNET, J., 108
BOOFMAN, J., 165
BOOK, W.W., 157
BOOKER, Benj., 202
BOOMER, Almon, 7
BOON, J.O. (sic), 148
  John, 133
  W.T., 148
BOONE, Daniel, 79
  F., 152
  M., 152
BOORSMAN, C., 27
BOOS, D., 189
BOOTH, A., 98
  Benjamin, 161
  Carr W., 130
  Hamilton, 56
  James, 161
  Joseph, 11
  L., 140
  W.G., 157
  W.L., 163

BOOTHSINGER, J.W.,
  189
  W., 19, 189
BOOZ, D., 189
  David, 19
  E.D., 51
BORDEN, Uriah, 149
  W., 144
BORDVELLE, J., 149
BOREE, E., 158
BORLEAND, J., 19
  M., 18
BOREN, L.E., 1
BOSLER, T.A., 150
BOSTWICK, C.R., 79
  E., 62, 63
  J., 167
  O., 79
BOSWORTH, Jubin, 123
BOTS, Campbell D. (sic),
  88
BOTSFORD, A.B., 122
BOTTLES, J., 167
BOTTS, Campbell D., 88
  D., 38
  G.W., 152
BOUDELEAR, D., 38
BOUDRAY, Charles, 84
BOUGHMAN, George,
  38
BOUGHTON, Caleb, 183
BOUNDEY, John, 136
BOURCE, L.T., 162
BOURNE, Ezra, 79, 201
BOUTRALL, J.B., 153
  R.M., 153
BOUZ, E.D., 51
BOW, Erastus, 104
BOWDEN, H.B., 83
BOWEN, D.L., 107
  Daniel L. (Lt.), 107
  Sarah A., 130
BOWER, J.P., 157, 158
  T., 157
BOWERS, A., 149
  Benjamin D., 7
  G.W., 89
  Harbut, 7
  J.W., 42, 195

  John S. (Lieut.), 202
  John T., 7
  John William, 195
  William, 19, 190
BOWLBY, Alfred, 143
BOWLIN, J.A., 90
BOWLS, John (sic), 131
BOWMAN, D.D., 80
  Henry, 202
BOX, J.P., 126
  T., 159
  Thomas, 136
BOXER, George M., 19,
  190
BOYCE, Thomas, 147
BOYD, ____, 194
  G.M., (sic), 190
  H., 98
  J.H., 26
  J.P., 18
  James, 173
  John, 88
  John H., 29
  M.W., 101
  T., 15
BOYDEN, C.F., 201
  C.W., 202
  John, 133
  William, 133
BOYER, John, 160
BOYLE, C.E., 88
  D., 157
  J., 143
  Joseph, 85
  W.C., 9
BOYLES, J., 145
BOYNTON, G.H., 109
  S.W., 117
BOZER, George M., 19
BRACKET, M.J., 175
BRACKETT, J.W. (Dr.),
  55
BRADBURY, A., 106
  C.F., 134
BRADEN (see also
  BRADON)
  James M., 17
BRADFORD, ____
  (Mr.), 47

E.G., 148
I., 119
John H. & fam, 180
T.S., 163
William, 111
BRADLEY,____, 112
A.B., 99
Benjamin J., 137
Henry, 136
J.S., 22
L., 100
Thornton C., 195
W.C., 86
William, 99
BRADNER, Ezra, 58
BRADON (see also BRADEN)
W., 181
BRADSHAW, John D. (Death of), 94
BRADY, J., 89
Thomas, 15, 185
William, 108
BRAHM, 130
BRAINARD, Charles, 98
F.A., 157, 163, 168
BRALEY, L.H., 36
BRAMELL, I., 154
Talten, 154
BRAMLETT, D.B., 8
BRANCH, D., 160
George, 151
M., 160
BRANDERS,____ (Dr.), 80
BRANDO, C., 150
BRANDON, B.T.C., 146, 150
C., 150
G.W., 14
BRANEN, James (sic), 106
BRANNEN, James, 106
BRANNON, Thomas, 114
BRANSTUTTER, H.M., 138
BRANT, J.C., 90
BRANTLACH, F., 35
BRANTLEY, Jonas, 12

BRAPLEY, T.C., 42, 195
BRASHER, Robert, 103
Thomas R., 103
BRATAGAN, M., 19, 190
BRATTEGAN, M., 190
BRATTON, S., 39
BRAUSHEED, William, 81
BRAWNER, James, 136
BRAY, Hannibal, 132
William, 132
BRAYTON, A.S., 24
BRAZDON, A., 64
BRAZIL, Wiley, 54
BRECKER, Isaac, 5
BREDIN, J., 101
BREEDLOVE, Balling, 79
W.N., 154
BREEM, M., 100
BREEN, John P., 147
BREESE, James H., 98
BREEZE, A.N., 63
BREMMER, H., 63
BRENEMAN, J.M., 150
BRENNAMON, S., 160
BRENNAN, M., 176
BRENTWOOD, William S., 134
BRESSETT, L., 13
BREVARD, William, 86
BREWER, D.H. (Dr.), 109
Jacob J., 118
John, 45
L.A. (Dr.), 168
R., 163
Thomas C., 136
BREWSTER, C.W., 136
J.A., 51
BREYFOGLE, C., 88
BREZEL, Francis, 7
BRIAR W., 165
BRICE, William, 151
William H & wife, 5
BRIDE, G.M. (sic), 190
BRIDGE, C.P., 111
Galusha, 58
BRIDWELL, James W. (sic), 114

BRIGGS, B.B., 23
Henry, 132
J.G., 23
James, 43
Milton, 100
BRIGGS, R.M., 138
Riley, 132
W., 61
BRIGHAM, Samuel N., 172
BRIGHTHOUP, Frederick, 151
BRIMHALL, George, 123
George W., 106
John, 123
Noah, 123
BRINKERHOFF, J. Jr., 85
BRINKLEY, J., 167
BRINKRHOFF, J. Jr. (sic), 85
BRISBEAU, Xavier, 155
BRISCOE, H.P., 165
BRISKELL, William, 30
BRISON, F., 11
BRISTO, T.J., 83
BRISTOL, S., 63
BRISTOW, H.G., 144
BRITTEN, Henry, 63
BRITTON, Henry, 63
S., 6
BROADERS, R., 55
BROADMEADOW, James, 82
BROADUS, R.H., 38
BROADWELL, S., 42
William B., 49
BROCK, J.A., 102
BROCKAWAY, A.W., 5
BROCKEN, Thomas, 131
BROCKWAY, Fidelia (Mrs.), 132
BROGDEN, William, 197
BROGDIN, R.W., 52
BROKAW, W., 80
BROLASKI, H.L., 81
BRONER, William, 11
BROOCHE, L.E., 158
BROOK,____ (Mr.), 97

C., 55
BROOKE, W., 61
BROOKFORD, S., 158
BROOKS,____, 19, 191
  B., 70
  E.W., 23
  Edwin, 102
  F.W., 90
  Francis, 69
  George, 175
  Gideon, 47
  H.W., 70
  J., 58, 190
  J.C., 102
  John, 19, 190
  Lafayette, 90
  M.A., 128
  P.F.W., 90
  V., 70
BROPHY, William, 136
BROSS, C.M., 153
BROTHERS, Henry, 112
  Thomas, 112
BROTHERTON, J.R.
  (Dr.), 25
BROUGHTON,____
  (Mr.), 134
BROWER, Jacob J., 118
BROWN,____, 115, 140
  ____(Mr.), 50, 54, 91
  A., 97, 132, 160
  A.H., 202
  A.H., wife & 5 chldrn, 180
  A.S., 166
  Aaron, 5
  Allen, 123
  Amanda E., 169
  B., 18, 158, 188
  B.E., 133
  B.F., 14
  B.L., 168
  Bartlett, 62
  Benjamin, 134, 154
  C.W., 59
  Caleb, 161
  Cyrus E., 102 (x)
  D., 160
  D.F., 139

  D.P., 42
  Daniel, 117
  E., 30
  E.H. & fam, 178
  E.Z.B., 178
  E.Z.R., 178
  Ebenezer, 56
  Edmund, 6
  Edward, 169
  F.M., 123
  Francis, 140
  G.H., 15
  H., 32, 137, 147
  H.W., 134
  Harrison, 57, 121
  Henry, 27, 134
  Henry W., 147
  J., 60, 149, 168, 179
  J.A., 168
  J.B., 149
  J.I., 160
  J.M., 141
  J.S., 150
  J.W., 104
  James, 26, 82
  James W., 124
  Jesse, 177
  John, 46, 85, 169, 173
  Jonathan, 57
  L.M., 159
  Levi, 123
  M., 80
  Miner (sic), 107
  N., 113
  O., 157
  P., 145
  P.R., 143
  R., 188
  R.B., 126, 153
  R.C., 66
  R.C.S. (Judge), 104-105
  S.D., 5
  S.M., 149
  Sandy, 11
  Simon, 45
  T., 148
  Thomas J., 2
  V., 25
  W., 144 (x)

  W.M., 179
  William, 47, 59, 81, 123, 132, 169
  William L., 112
BROWNING, George, 121
  M.A., 56
  P.M., 147
  Rich S. (sic), 33
BROWNLEA, A. (sic), 154
BROWLEE, James B., 122
BROWNSON, Reuben, 102
BRUBAKER, Francis, 46, 75
  Frank, 75
BRUBANKS,____
  (Mr.), 71
BRUCE,____ (Mr.), 54
  George & lady, 151
  Hezakiah, 117
BRUDLON, E.B., 70
BRUEN, Josiah H., 82
BRUFF, J. Goldsborough, 47
BRUMBARRY, J.M., 27
BRUN, J., 55
BRUNER, Alexander, 90
  J., 55
BRUNOT, H.J., 18
BRUNRIDGE, William, 137
BRUNSON, W.B., 52
BRUNT, H., 136
BRUPHY, William, 136
BRUSH, Fleetus, 149
  J.W., 158
  Jessee (sic), 82
BRYAN,____ (Mrs.), 96
  Charles W., 105
  J. Jr., 167
  S.E., 59
BRYANT, A., 15
  Edward (Capt), 10, 11 (x), 183
  Edwin (Capt), 11, 183
  Harrison, 114

Jackson, 114
L., 141
Samuel, 112
Z.S., 141
BRYARLY, Wake, 42, 195, 196
　Wakeman (Dr.), 195, 196
BRYD, M.R., 124
BRYDEN, D., 88
BRYNE, E.D. (Dr.), 79
BUCHANAN,____, 39
　A.S., 148
　D.C., 83
　Henry H., 7
BUCHANANER, W., 34
BUCK, Costellow D., 67
　E., 80
　George H., 68
　George W., 65, 103
　Norman, 106
　Peter, 65
　Peter & fam, 141
　Samuel, 106
　William, 4
BUCKHAM, N.B., 148
BUCKHOLDER, W., 25
BUCKINGHAM, John, 101
BUCKLAIN, F., 143
BUCKLEY, J., 144
　Joseph, 138
　L.P., 3
　R.P., 25
　W., 162
BUCKLIN, William, 133
BUCKNAM, Caleb, 105
　W.J., 105
BUCKNELL, James B., 105
BUCKWELL, E. (Dr.), 158
BUDD, J., 152
　J.A., 24
BUDEN, G., 166
BUDMAN, James, 137
　John, 137
BUEL, John, 138
BUELL, Wallis S., 106

BUFFINGTON, John, 138
BUFFUM, H., 19, 189
　J.W., 19, 191
　J.W. & wife, 191
BUFORD, Jer (sic), 90
　Jerome (sic), 90
BUFT, H., 150
BUKES, C., 168
　F., 81
BUKHAM, John, 198
　John (sic), 43
BULKLEY, H., 5
BULLARD,____, 149
　Frances, 149
BULLOCK, A., 83
　Isaac, 105
　N.B., 106
　S.S., 106
　Samuel, 70
BUMHISER,____ (Mr.), 55
BUNALL, Edward (sic), 46
BUNCE, W., 130
BUNDRAN, E., 132
BUNDY, H., 108
　Harlow E., 106
BUNN, F., 95
　Nathan, 105
BUNYAN, Nicholas, 135
BURBANK, Bradford, 60
　F., 151
BURCH, Levi & wife, 132
　Margaret, 170
BURCHAM, J., 145
BURDETT, Charles G., 171
BURDSALL, J., 11
BURDY, Edmund, 160
BUREHAM, J., 145
BURER, James (sic), 153
BURGEF, C.O. (sic), 153
BURGEON, P., 12
BURGESS, C.A., 150
　Charles O., 138
　Henry S., 97
　J., 86, 109
　J.G., 139
　P., 12

R., 150
Reuben A., 138
S.P., 97
William H., 85
Zadock T., 138
BURGETT, D., 30
BURGY, John, 25
BURHITT, Ashbel, 58
BURIP, Stephen, 54
BURISH, Charles, 110
BURKE, M., 158
　T.J., 49, 199
　Thomas, 199
BURKER, Thomas, 92
BURKET, S. (sic), 157, 159
BURKETT, S., 159
BURKHOLDER, John, 90
BURKSLOW, William, 91
BURLAGE, T.S., 166
BURLESON, A.G., 156
　A.T., 163
　R., 2
　R.B., 2
BURLINGAME, Hiram, 66
　Jacob, 66
　O., 163
　Orson, 103
BURLISON, John & 2 dau, 150
BURNAN, I.T. (sic), 126
BURNE, Phillip, 24
BURNEL, R.W., 112
BURNES, W. (sic), 159
BURNETT, A., 81
　Henry, 115
　M.W., 7
　Thomas S., 37
　W., 147
BURNHAM, J., 145
　O.S., (Capt), 86
BURNHILL, R.S., 140
BURNS, C., 151
　J., 131
　James O., 36
　L.M., 1
　Philip, 8

W.J., 52
BOROUGH, E.W. (sic), 153
BURR, Andrew, 133
  E., 23
  George W., 67
  James P., 82
  Marshal B., 106
  Stephen, 120
BURREL, J.M., 167
BURRILL, L.I., 23
BURRIS,____ (Dr.), 40
  John, 67
BURROUGHS, A., 153
  Asa G., 97
  D. (Capt), 97 (x)
  F.H., 41
BURROWS,____ (Mr.)
  (Death of), 92
  D., 167
  John, 58
BURSHE, B.F., 47
BURT, Benjamin Jr., 204
BURTON, G.S., 174
  J.F., 20, 190
  Joshua, 95
  M.J., 102
  V.B., 83
BURWEIL, W.J., 42
BURWELL, W.J., 195
  Walter J., 195
BURZELL, Francis, 7
BUSCH, E.C., 162
BUSH, John, 176
  M., 166
  M.S., 113, 115
  Mary (Mrs.), 162
BUSKIRK, William, 123
BUSKISK, R.H., 147
BUSS, Nathan, 105
BUSSELL, E., 64
  William, 64
BUSSICK, J.B., 168
BUSSON, G., 180
  S., 180
BUSTWOOD, William S., 134
BUTLER, E.D., 117
  I.M., 165

J.O., 20
James, 40
John, 102, 106
John H., 20
R.B., 18
Thomas, 102, 108
BUTNER, Harling, 129
BUTT, Abel, 119
BUTTERFIELD, Henry, 97
  N., 29
BUTTES, L., 145
  Lewis, 145
BUTTLES, J., 167
  James, 90
BUTTON, Alexander, 7
  Edwin R., 131
  Orlando, 138
BUTTS, Emma L., 177
  William & fam, 141
BUYATTE, E., 150
  J., 150
BYERS,____ (Dr.), 115
  Henry, 80
  James L., 82
BYINGTON, George, 47
BYNAM, Sashel, 69
BYRAM, Bruen, 64
BYRD, A.B., 164
BYRGE, James, 110
BYRNES, Isaac, 86
BYRNS, Isaac (sic), 86
BYSICK, David, 135
BYWATER, William, 67

-C-

C____, Andrew of Wisc., 135
CABINIS, E.T., 49
CABLE, Hezekiah G., 45
CADDA, William, 18
CADDE, William, 18, 188
CADDOO, W., 188
CADWALLADER, N., 137
CADWELL, M.A., 161

CADY, H.P., 33, 193
  William, 29
CAFFETT, James, 154
CAHOON, M. (sic), 144
CAIN, G., 63
  J., 156
  J.T.J., 32
  John, 136
  Thomas, 7
  W., 88
CAINOR, John, 154
CALBOUGH, R., 55
CALDERWOOD,
  Thomas, 119
CALDWELL, A.J., 110
  A.S., 90
  Anthony W., 110
  C., 13
  H.H., 1
  J., 18, 113
  J.J., 119
  J.S., 168
  John, 92
  M. (Dr.), 56
  W., 163
CALHOUN, A., 163
  D., 140
CALL, Elias, 67
  W.H., 17, 186
CALLAHAN, William, 117
CALLANDER, A.D., 14
CALLEN, G.W.S., 91
CALLENDINE, Edward, 30
CALLIS, W. (Dr.), 163
CALLOWAY, A.R., 8
  H.N., 8 (x)
  S.G., 8
CALMES, Charles H., 131
CALTENDER, John, 110
CALVIN, T.M., 168
CALWELL, I., 151
  John, 115
  Rufus, 80
  S., 80
CAMDEE, S., 51
CAMELL, S., 154

CAMER, Charles, 99
CAMERON, James (Dr.), 98
  Jon, 133
  John, 47
  T.B., 67
CAMFIELD, Moses, 10, 183
  R.W., 19, 191
CAMMON, William, 155
CAMP, Clark, 122
  Elijah, 106, 121
  Oliver, 121
  William, 121
CAMPBELL, A., 60, 61, 148
  A.J., 148
  A.W., 102
  Alfred, 69, 70, 154
  Andrew, 109
  Annis, 78
  C., 150
  Charles A., 27
  D. & 3 svts, 60, 61
  D.J., 31
  Deland, 119
  Enos, 53
  F., 81
  G., 55, 163
  H.M., 79
  Hector, 27
  Hector B., 27
  Hugh, 56
  J., 60, 61
  J.D., 65
  J.F., 148
  J.N., 53
  J.W., 60
  James, 107
  James H., 115
  John, 95
  Lewis, 53, 199
  M.A. (Mrs.), 175
  M.C. (Miss), 156
  M.L., 164
  N., 127, 172
  P., 12
  R., 60
  Samuel, 72

Samuel (Death of), 94
Samuel L., 27
W., 142, 144
W.C., 156
William B., 27
CAMPTH, A. (sic), 149
CAMRON, Jno (sic), 133
  Michael, 46
CAN____ELD, William, 82
CAN, P., 55
CANCY, J. (sic), 163
CANDEE, Joel G., 82
CANFELD, William, 82
CANFIELD, E.E., 88
  Moses, 183
  R.W., 191
CANNON, Charles, 26
  John (Death of), 94
  N.C., 26
  T.S., 105
  W., 167
  William, 155
CANT, S., 176
CANTREY, J., 152
CAPPS, Daniel, 130
CAPRON, Augustus S., 47
CARBERRY, Michael, 146
CARBIN, S.N., 153
CARD, Orson, 108
CARDER, William E., 148
CAREY, B., 10
  George (Dr.), 113
  W.M. & fam, 148
CARGILL, N.E. (Dr.), 16
CARL, M., 34
CARLETON, J.J., 166
CARLISLE, Daniel, 122
CARLOS, M.D., 163
CARLTON, Dexter, 147
  G., 40
  R., 98
  Thomas, 139
CARLYLE, Thos., 202
CARMACK, H., 152
CARMAN, Wm., 202

CARNER, C.S., 171, 172
  J.S., 168
CARNES, Abraham, 104
  Robert, 20
CARPENTER, A.J., 63
  B., 38, 194
  Benjamin & fam, 144
  Daniel, 176
  E.G., 13
  J., 158
  J.G., 150
  J.P., 153
  John, 105
  Phillip, 160
  S. (Colonel), 68
CARPER, S.J., 163
CARR, Arthur, 27
  F.W., 8
  G., 3
  G.W., 19, 168, 190
  H.E., 39
  Houston, 87
  J.H., 39, 87
  J.P., 8
  M., 148
  Michael, 44
  T., 190
CARRENS, J., 158
CARRICH, Elijah, 134
CARRON, J., 169
CARRSON, Phillip, 121
CARSE, Martin, 138
CARSON,____, 116
  A., 48
  A.J., 178
  D., 83
  Elisha J., 111
  Mark, 120
  Phillip, 121
CARTER, A.J., 144
  C., 61
  D.P., 140
  George, 31
  J.E., 30
  J.F., 148
  J.M., 70
  John, 63
  John B., 8
  R., 27

221

Zenes, 119
CARTNER, ____ (Mr.), 87
CARTON, R., 98
CARTRELL, Ann A., 172
CARTWRIGHT,
   Alexander J. Jr., 10
CARY, P., 107
   Pat, 119
   T., 157
CASE, C.W., 147
   E. & fam, 20, 191
   E. & wife, 191
   George, 23, 91
   George S., 37
   William, 14
CASEY, Charles, 27
   James, 27
   William P., 111
CASHING, James & wife, 139
CASON, Patrick, 178
CASS, George, 160
CASSADAY, John & fam, 179
CASSIDY, F., 144
   James, 110
   P., 144
CASSIM, F., 28
CASSIN, Stephen J., 47
CASSINS, J., 166
CASSON, William, 63
CASTEEL, Alexander (sic), 123
CASTER, L.D., 122
CASTERLINE, Benjamin, 183
CASTLE, R.P., 144
CASTON, C., 144
CASTREL, Alexander, 123
CATE, James, 165
CATHERWOOD, F.S.P., 120
   R., 41
CATLETT, C.C., 68
CATTERMOLE, C., 124
CAUDEL, James, 90
CAWETES, C., 157

CAYTON, Alex S., 59
   William, 59
CEANARD, George, 171
CELLARS, Nathan, 120
   Samuel, 121
CEWARD, J., 144
CEZZENS, Joseph, 126
CHABOT, Tousaint, 52
CHACE, J.H. (sic), 80
CHADDIE, R., 196
CHADDOCK, William, 121 (x)
CHADWICK, G., 88
CHAFER, Benjamin, 41
CHAFEY, G., 5
CHAFF, F., 151
CHAFFEE, J.H., 142
CHAFFIE, S.M., 146
CHAFFIN, G.W., 166
CHAMBERLAIN., J.B., 17, 187
   S., 105
CHAMBERLAND, ____, 67
CHAMBERLIN, J., 139
   Wiliam J., 187
CHAMBERS, L., 129
   P., 23
   R., 175
   T., 129
   T.H., 137
   T.L., 129
CHANDLE, Lamar, 135
   Raphael, 135
CHANDLER, G. M. 153
   H., 23
   James, 99
   John, 20, 180
   K., 23
   P., 23
   S., 99, 120
   T., 38, 55
CHANEY, Charles, 20, 190
   Edward, 160
   S. W., 61
CHAPIN, S., 64
CHAPMAN, A., 100
   B.D., 52

C.J., 25
E., 121
G., 159
G. J., 23
I. and wife, 189
J., 143
J.C., 117
Joel, 98
John C., 102
M.A.G., 143
S. and wife, 189
William (death of), 94
CHAPPEL, E. T., 16
CHARLES, F., 158
   J. E. (Dr.), 56
CHARLTON, W., 147
   William, 148
CHASE, ____, 115
   E. B., 51
   H., 158
   H. N., 150
   Henry W., 57
   J., 83
   Levi, 63
   S.C., 61
   William & wife, 179
CHATBOURN, Moses 119
CHATBURN, Moses, 107
CHATFIELD, Silas P., 62
CHATTERTON, John, 65
CHECK, D. W., 163
CHEEK, D. W., 149
CHEESEMAN, Zebedee 68
CHEESMAN, Walker (Mrs.) (sic), 126
CHENEY, C., 190
CHENY, Peter, 89
CHESEBROUGH, E., 113
CHESHIRE, P., 108
CHESHOLM, Samuel, 84
CHESNUT, James, 59, 140
   James A., (sic) 59
CHESSHIRE, P., (sic) 108
CHESTER, Charles, 131
CHESTNUT, James, 59, 140

James A., 59
CHEVER, W. H., 25
CHICHESTER, William, 90
CHICKESTER, J., 168
CHILDERS, Lewis, 30
CHILDERS, M. B. 63
   Mosby 59
   W.H., 31
CHILDREN, R., 174
CHILDS, Charles W., 40
   Clark W., 109
   John W., 111
CHINE, A., 151
CHINN, M. A., 11
CHISHOLM, R. B., 132
CHITHAM, G., 38
CHITTENDEN, Zophar, 34
CHOATE, G. C., 33
CHREVISTON, William (sic) 118
CHRISMON, F. H., 67
CHRIST, H.B., 197
CHRISTIAN, William, 107
CHRISTY, J., 100
   John, 20
CHURBELLO, H. Marie, 53
CHURCH, A.M., 46
   Amos, 27
   Austin, 58
   J.C., 165
   Moses, 137
   Stephen T., 136
   W. (Dr.), 151
CHURCHILL, Charles, 82
   George, 82 (X)
   George W., 82
CIRKWOOD, James (sic), 46
CISSON, _____, (Mr.), 54
CLAGEARN, R. 164
CLAMPET, J.J.F., 53
   Moses (Rev.), 53
CLANCY, T., 157
CLAPP, P., 83
CLARK, _____, (Dr.), 123

A., 141, 197
Asa (Dr.), 39
B. F., 18, 187
Benjamin F., 125
C. (death of), 127
C.B.F., 187
Charles 133
D. W., 129
Daniel B., 114
E. F., 59
Ezekiel, 59
Francis C., (Major), 47
G., 128
G. W., 80
H. A., 165
J., 160, 164, 197
J. (Capt.), 142 (x)
J. A., 150
J. M., 59
J. T., 24
James, 81
Jesse, Jr., 96
John, 109
John L., 68
John M., 88
L., 68, 142
Mason, 109
Matthew (sic), 133
Nathaniel, 72, 152
Nicholas, 123
Oliver, 87
Oren, 64, 200
Orris, 200
Philip, 53
R. B. (Capt.), 109
Reuben, 105
Rufus B., 109
S., 18, 187
S. B. F., 18, 55, 187
S. D., 133
Thomas, 133
Thomas M., 105
W. C., 156
W. M., 2
William, 170
William, Jr., 106
Y. E., 99
CLARKE, _____ (Mr.), 152

A., 53
John, 43, 70
L. & wife, 191
CLARY, N., 29
CLAS, Joel, 179
CLAUDET, C., 83
CLAUDOT, C., 83
CLAUGRY, T,. M. (sic), 153
CLAUS, Joel, 179
CLAY, A.C., 64
   Francis. 58
   George, 123
   Joel, 179
   M., 132
CLAYTON, W. S., 167
CLAZ, Joel, 179
CLEARER, W. S., 142
CLEARY, D. C., 103
CLEAVER, Henry, 81
   Thomas, 81
   William, 81
CLEGG, J., 30
   J. M., 79
   John, 105
   Thomas, Sr., 42, 197
   Thomas, Jr., 42, 197
   Webster, 43, 197
CLEGHORN, R., 167
   William, 87
CLEMENS, _____ (Dr.), 129
   E. O., 140, 155
CLEMENT, Thomas, 87
CLEMENTS, A. B., 2
   F. H. 79
CLENDENEN, H., 144 (x)
CLEVELAND, A. S., 6
   G., 140
   James S., 203
   M., 6
CLEVINGER, Asa, 195
CLICK, D., 167
CLIFFORD, D. F., 148
   J. F., 148
CLINE, A., 148
   G., 63
   James, 22
   Philip, 63

CLINGAMAN, Stephen, 23
CLINGMAN, C., 110
CLOCK, William S., 139
CLOFF, A., 153
CLOSE, C., 1
CLOUGH, J.P. Jr., 42
　James P., 83
　Pike, 83
　William R., 132
CLOUSER, Nelson, 114
CLUFF, Hamilton, 16
CLUMP, Nelson, 133
COACH, J.S., 80
COAD, John, 67
COAKLEY, Andrew, 111
　John, 57
COAKLY, Andrew, 111
COAR, G. W. (sic), 168
COATES, ____, (Mr.), 165
COATS, B. M., 63
COB, H. (sic), 164
COBB, C. L., 59, 65
　H., 164
　Thomas, 160
COBESTY, Enoch, 63
COBINSON, Leonard (sic), 120
COBURN, John, 62
　W. W., 144, 145
COCHRAN, G., 51
　Horace, 62
　J. S., 68
　James, 90
　John L., 91
　Robert, 99
　Samuel T., 83
COCKERELL, James, 114
COCKILL, C. S., 6
COCKRELL, Daniel, 42
COCKRILL, C., 129
　C. S., 6
COCKS, N. P., 63
CODDINGTON, G. W., 153
CODE, J., 67
CODY, ____, 52,

Clark, 33
Patrick, 133
COE, Archibald, 50
　James, 138
　John S., 138
COFFEE, Benjamin, 116
COFFEEN, Joseph B., 67
COFFENBERRY, Andrew, 115
COFFEY, Joseph B., 67
　Robert, 204
COFFIN, Benjamin, 116
　J. W., 110
　Jerome W., 105
　Thomas, 27
COFFMAN, A., 142
　C. A., 144
COFR, B. (sic), 163
COGSWELL, ____, 128
　George, 165
COKE, A., 99
COLBER, Jacob, 151
COLBURN, F. M. (Mr.), 74
　Luke, 52, 90
COLBY, A. H., 58
　S., 170
COLD, H., 163
COLE, C. H., 85
　E. A., 83
　G. E., 116
　G. L., 150
　J., 168
　J. H., 70
　J. M., 113
　J. W., 31
　James, 83
　John, 63
　John T., 2
　L. L., 103, 109
　Lewis L., 105
　N., 163
　Nelson, 136
　R. C., 64
COLEMAN, ____, (Mr.), 87
　A., 33
　C., 52
　Charles, 17, 186

H., 31
Jesse C., 122
M., 158
Milton, 122
P. L., 175
R. C., 166
R. S., 166
Robert, 138
Stephen O., 81
U. P., 81
W. D., 85
COLERICK, Charles F., 9
COLES, J., 14
　W., 42, 197
COLEY, J. M., 156
COLISTER, CYMS (sic), 146
　William T., 146
COLLEY, J. B., 113
　James H., 71
　S. G., 113
COLLIN, J. W., 110
　John, 202
COLLINGWOOD, Aaron, 124 (x)
COLLINS, A., 154
　A. C., 158
　J. Lott & Company 138
　J. R., 30
　J. S., 163
　Jesse, 56
　John, 104
　Joseph, 122
　S., 132
COLLY, W. K., 95
　William, 71
COLT, Benjamin, 107
　George, 106
　N., 107
COLTEN, J. B. (sic), 148
COLTER, A. H., 3, 181
COLTON, Almond, 137
　C. P., 83
　D. D., 98
　Elezer W., 122
　J. B., 64
　James, 136, 139
　John M., 130
　Samuel H., 123

223

William, 120
COLVIN, Alfred, 103, 109
COLWELL, Rufus, 80
 S., 80
COMBS, P., 160
 S., 160
COME, M., 140
COMEGYS, George W. (sic), 42
COMMARY, T. wife & 2 children, 150
COMPTON, Amos, 137
 Cornelius, 182
 David, 75
 G. D., 59, 63
 Henry S., 57
 Thomas 114
 William H., 14, 184
COMSTOCK, E. J., 155
 James, 133
 L. B. (Capt), 133
 L. M., 100
CONANT, J. F., 152
 Martin M., 172
CONDE, Ara, 55
 O., 157
CONDEE, S. P., 59, 165
CONDIT, L. W., 131
CONDOR, G. M., 165
CONE, G., 150
 G. A., 131
 G. C., 21, 68
CONEY, _____, 35
CONGAR, O. N., 109
CONGDON, E. S., 57
CONGER, Gary, 103
 Horace, 103, 130
 John, 85
 O. H., 103
 W. K., 118
CONGLETON, Adin (sic), 58
CONIG, John, 110
CONKLIN, H., 2
 H. S., 86
CONLISK, Rosaniah, 169
CONNELL, lex, 41
 H., 145

James, 123
 Samuel, 135
CONNELLY, B. F., 159
 James, 91
CONNER, E. W., 89
 G. C., 150
 George, 75
CONNET, Martin M, 170
CONNOR, _____, 21
 D., 30
 J., 17
 James, 87, 170
 James A., 140
 Monroe, 68
CONNOVER, M., 21
CONNUS, John S., 146
CONORER, Monroe, 68
CONOVER, M., 95
CONOWAY, Thomas, 33
CONOWS, Chapman (sic), 133
CONRAD, Adam, 88
 J., 162
 John, 41
CONROY, H., 11
CONRUD, J. (sic), 162
CONSTABLE, Charles, 91
CONSTANT, J. H., 153
CONWAY, A., 35
 H., 42, 195
 Hugh, 195
 W. H., 55
 William C., 23
CONWELL, JOHN, 29
COOK, _____, (Mr.), 53
 A., 144
 Alfred, 88
 Augustus, 180
 C. P., 30
 Charles, wife & child, 155
 E., 100
 E. C., 167
 E. W., 131
 Edward J., 9
 G., 55, 97
 George, 165
 H., 80, 178
 Henry, 87

J., 18, 55
Joel, 137
John, 99
John B., 130
John P., 80
Jonathan, 137
L. D., 165
Milton, 80
N. S., 1
Nancy J., 174,
Peter, 109
R., 96, 144
R. W. (Mr.), 3
Robert, 108
S. H., 1
Samuel, 138
W. C., 38
Wallace, 10
COOKE, A., 99
 William S. & svt., 79
COOLEY, G. C., 65
 Gustavus C., 58
 James H., 82
 O., 109
 William, 139
COOLIDGE, J. P., 81
COOLY, Benjamin, 102
 William (sic), 139
COOMBS, W. S., 138
COON, B. R., 149, 150
 Charles, 151
 Hiram, 151
COONE, Elisha, 137
COONS, James, 91
 W., 61
COOPER, _____, 89, 153
 _____, (Dr.), 155
 _____, (Dr) 7 dau, 155
 A. H. (Mrs.) & fam, 155
 E. W., 167
 Isaac, 45
 J., 51
 J. H., 65
 J. M., 107
 Lewis, 170
 O., 176
 S., 158
 S. & son, 178
 Thomas H., 175

William, 17, 25, 64,
    137, 170
COOTE, ___ (Mr.), 202
COOTS, Uriah, 152
COOVER, C. S., 36
COPELAIN, A. T., 164
COPELAND, D., 168
    F., 152
    George W., 201
    J. S., 86
COPENHAGEN,
    William, 155
COPENHAVEN, William
    (sic), 155
COPLAND, F. (sic), 152
COPLINGER, John, 125
COPP, Charles, 139
COPPERS, W., 152
COPPERSMITH, J., 19
COPPERWAITHE,
    Thomas, 81
COPPICK, L., 137
COPUR, W. (sic), 58
CORBIN, E., 98
CORBITT, L., 130
CORD, Orson, 108
CORDING, J. B., 90
COREY, Manning, 16
CORINTH, A., 150
CORK, Augustus, 180
CORMAN, Thomas, 142
CORMANY, P., 38
CORNAGLE, Henry, 106
CORNEL, Sarah M. (sic),
    165
CORNELIUS, Richard H.,
    112
CORNELL, G. C., 68
    H., 148
    Sarah M., 165
CORNOIER, N. C., 20
CORNWELL, A. J., 163
    Cornelius, 82
CORRELLS, ___,
    (Mr.), 160
CORRIELL, W. W., 86
CORSAUL, David, 57
CORSAUT, David, 57
CORSEGNER, F. W., 85

CORWELL, G. H., 94
CORWIN, George, 128
    Harmon, 67
CORWINE, James (Rev.),
    71
CORYELL, George, 109
COSAR, J., 166
COSIG, John, 110
COSLEY, J. S. C., 157
COSPERTE, L. P., 148
COSSINS, J., 166
COSTER, G. W., 143
COTHRIN, W., 108
    W. S., 102
COTRELL, Lawence, 176
COTTER, Eliza, 162
COTTEREL, E., 115
    W., 115
COTTERELL,
    William, 59
COTTLE, Oliver, 90
COTTON, ___, (Dr.),
    53
    G. M., 158
COTTRELL, G. W., 52
    J. C. P., 52
COUGHRAN, James, 41
COULTER, John, 88
COUMBE, John T., 47
COURTRIGHT, M., 18
COUTS, ___, (Mr.), 54
COVENEY, Joseph, 45
COVENTRY, Charles,
    104
COVINGTON, Edward,
    112
    J. M., 141
COW, J., 53
    John, 172
COWAN, D. S., 63
    J., 7, 182, 194
    J. W., 38
    John, 24, 182
    Thomas, 105
COWARD, Jane, 173
COWDEN, James, 140
    S. D., 43
COWDREY, B., 32
COWELL, A. F., 153

COWEN, J., 194
COWLES, ___, (Mr.),
    87
    Alfred, 87 (x)
COWMAN, Thomas, P.,
    59
COX, ___, (Mrs) &
    Fam, 180
    Henry, 86
    Hugh P., 136
    I. & lady, 157
    I. F., 163
    Isaac, 155
    J. L., 159
    J. R., 154
    M. W., 39
    N. W., 87
    R., 86
    S., 86
    W. B., 52
    William E., 201
COY, G., 166
COYLE, Patrick, 110
COZARD, J. M., 38
CR___, John of
    Wisconsin, 135
CRABLE, H. L, 159
    J., 202
    William, 159
CRABTREE, B., 58
    L. A., 58
    Sarah, 170, 172
CRACKBURN, C. L., 168
CRAFF, J. W., 133
CRAFT, B. S., 158
CRAIG, Isaac, 171
    J. B., 68
    Margaret, 161
    Margaret (Mrs.), 176
CRAIL, J. R., 31
CRAIN, J. S., 166
CRAMB, H., 16
CRAMER, Henry, lady &
    child, 133
CRAMMER, H., 158
    H. B. J., 163
CRANDALL, H., 22, 39,
    192
    H. S., 7, 24

225

John R., 202
Royal, 91
CRANE, Azra, 51
E. C., 148
E. O., 82
George, 162
Greater (sic), 170
H., 194
J. C., 36, 194
John, 123
Joseph, 199
Lenard (sic), 184
Leonard, 15, 184
O. A., 57
Smith, 195
Thomas, 59
CRANES, S., 163
CRANKELTON, Joseph, 169
CRANMER, H. B. J. (sic), 163
CRANMORE, ___, (Mr.), 49
CRANSON, C. C., 51
CRANY, Smith, 41, 195
CRAPPA, L., 188
CRAWFORD, ___, (Mr.), 160,
A. J., 39, 87
D., 168
F., 11
J., 63
John. 172
Joseph, 45
William, 1, 8
William D., 64
CRAWLEY, Daniel, 79
John, 139
CRAYTON, Peter, 102
CREAMER, Charles M., 88
CREANER, Charles M., 88
CREARY, H. G., 116
CREEL, E. (Major), 110
CREELE, E., 103
CREELMAN, H., 151
CREEN, N., 135
CREERY, N. G., 116

CREESY, Owen H. (sic), 126
CREIGHTON,F. B., 42
CREMMONS, C., 165
CRENSHAW, J. T., 129
James, 86
R. W., 2
CREOLE, F., 103
CREPPS, L., 17, 188
CRERRAN, Hiram, A., 7
CREVIER, J., 59
CREWES, George, 4
CREWS, Mathew, 141
CRIB, M. H., 165
CRIBLIN, C., 31
CRIBS, James S., 196
CRICHTON, W., 200
William, 49, 200
CRIDER, A., 172
CRIG, Isaac (sic), 171
CRIGER, G., 109
George, 105
CRIM, John (Dr.), 98
S., 160
CRIPPEN, Charles, 105
Hiram, 66
James, 116
CRIST, A. B., 88
J., 145
CRISTOE, Joseph (Mrs.), 162
CRISTON, Joseph (Mrs.), 162
CRISWELL, J., 157
CRITES, Lucy P., 105
CRITTENDEN, C., 156
J. J., 167
L., 98
S. G., 5
CROALON, James, 31
CROATHWAIT, S. M., 31
CROBE, Mary C. S. (sic), 175
CROCKER, Charles, 106
J. D. Charles, 106
CROCKETT, E., 165
J. R. (Col.), 10, 183
John R. (Col), 183

R. C., 164
W. G., 163
William T., 56
CROFT, ___, (Mr.), 47
Henry, 165
T. B., 142
CROGHAM, ___, 20
CROGHAN, ___, 20, 189
CROGHIN, R. S., 95
CROMBIE, Elizabeth P. (Mrs.) widow, 40
CRON, Nelson V. A., 105
CRONEMILLER, David, 107
CRONKHITE, J., 15, 184
Martin, 184
CROOKS, N., 108
CROSBY, ___, (Mr.), 4
G. W., 148
P., 143
R., 19
CROSLIN, James, 31
CROSS, A. C., 59
D.,115
G. A., 158
G. W., (Dr.), 43
George, 142
J. H., 59
Jesse, 46
N., 135
N. T., 138
Samuel E., 68
Thomas, 120
CROSSMAN, O., 83
CROSSON, John, 139
CROSTHWAIT, S. M., 31
CROUCH, James, 83
CROW, H. C., 162
James, 42
CROWEL, C. (sic), 165
CROWELL, C., 136, 165
D. A., 30
M. T., 136
Reuben, 203
S., 142
CROY, J., 168
CRUICKSHANK, William, 81

CRULL, G., 131
CRUM, S., 92
  W., 130
CRUMPACKER, L., 43
CRUTCHFIELD, J. A., 153
CULBERTSON, J. S., 119
  Rosetta, 119
CULL, C. H., 112
CULLEY, John, 181
CULTON, James (sic), 139
CULVER, A. C., 101
  H. A., 101
  Henry, 98
  Jacob, 202
  Samuel H., 50
CULVERSON, A., 37
CULVERWELL, Richard, 47
  Stephen, 47
CUMBERFORD, H. S., 70
CUMINGS, C. J. & Company, 104
CUMMINGS, Benjamin, 137
  C. J. & Company, 104
CUMMINS, ____, 115
  Benjamin, 137
  C., 56
  E., 98
  R. K., 44
CUNDIFF, Milton, 71
CUNIG, John, 110
CUNNING, Franklin, 79
CUNNINGHAM, ____
  (Capt.), 93
  Charles, 42
  George, 42
  J., 126, 158, 177
  J. G., 8
  J. H., 52
  J. Q. A., 68
  J. T., 8
  James, 42
  L. 146
  N. C. (Capt.), 50
  R., 65

T. A., 111
Theodore A., 102
William, 63
William M., 8
CUNTON, J. J., 164
CUPPS, Jacob, 17, 187
  L., 187
CURFES, A., 23
CURL, Robert, 106
CURLEY, Amos, 25
  John, 25
CURRAN, H. A., 7
CURREE, A., 20, 189
CURRELL, S., 32
CURRER, V., 148
CURREY, G., 25
CURRIE, A., 189
  A. S., 24
CURRIER, A., 151
  Cyrus, 10,
CURTIS, ____, 98
  F. A., 134
  F. H., 19, 191
  G. D., 25
  G. W., 18
  Joseph, 176
  Marshall, 118
  S. T., 28
CURTISS, C. T., 50
CURTY, Henderson, 113
CUSHING, James & wife, 139
CUSICK, W., 168
CUSTER, G., 144
CUSTIS, F. A., 134
CUTHBERT, E., 79
CUTLER, Edmund S., 102
  H., 167
  Henry, 14
  J., 169
  J. E. R., (Dr.), 141
  John, 14
  L. H. (Dr.), 102
  L. K., 121
  Otis M., 77
  S. A., 167
  T. L., 35
CUTTER, A. F., 55

Charles, 25
W. J., 142
CUTTERSON, J. P. 152
CUTTING, J. H. (Col) 73

-D-

D____, M____, 121
DACKE, J., 158
DAFT, T., 18
  Thomas, 18
DAGGETT, William, 68
DAGS, J., 178
DAIL, S., 54
DAKE, George, 146
DALAMATTER, ____(Mr.), 49
DALE, C., 158
  E., 158
  H. (Mess of), 114
  Henry (see also H. DALE), 114
  James, 83
  Joseph, 83
  T., 139
  T. R., 165
  Thomas, 148
DALL, E., 164
DALLAM, Richard B. Jr., 81
DALLAS, A. J., 168
  James, 160
DAMON, ____, 68
DANA, H., 59
  L., 59
  L. J., 168
  Lester F., 106
  Loren, 66
DANDALL, S. D., 30, 182
DANDELL, S. D., 30, 182
DANIEL, Alex B., 59
  (death of), 94
  Mary A., 169
  W. H., 148
DANIELS, F., 90
  J. M., 113
  Johns A., 107

227

T. J., 70
Thomas, 178
William, 30
DANSBEE, Thomas, 11
DANY, L. D., 110
   S. F., 110
DARCY. John S.
   (General)
   & svts 10 (x)
DARLING, C. T., 90
DARNELL, Benjamin, 97
DARNIELL, T. R., 31
DARNING, Thomas, 60
DARR, David, 33
DARRAGH, D., 18
   J. 18
DART, Thomas E., 162
DAUGHERTY, J. M., 170
   Robert, 140
DAUGHTERY, Enos, 42
DAVENPORT, A. W.,
   165, 166
   C. W., 144
   J., 165
   J. L., 79
   T., 144
   T. S., 145
   Ziba, 161
DAVID, J. S., 90
DAVIDSON, J. M., 51
   James, 15, 42
   K., 44
   Robert, 44
   Samuel, 15, 42
DAVIES, _____, (Mr.) 53
   Daniel, J. C., 67
DAVIS, _____, 99
   _____, (Mrs) & fam,
   179
   Alfred, 116
   Andrew, 102
   Benjamin, 83
   C., 131
   C. C., 56
   Charles D., 105
   E. , 139, 166
   E. R., 165
   F. A., 165
   G., 202

G. W., 105
George, 132
I., 163, 176
Isaac D., 123
J., 109
J. B., 55
J. C., 25 (x), 42, 54, 195
J. D., 18
J. F., 31
J. H., 56
J. M., 148 (x), 163
J. T., 129
J. W., 129, 142
James 32
James E., 11
James V., 88
John, 40, 103, 126
John H., 44
John W., 88
Joseph C., 195
L., 100
L. M., 137
Margaret, 162, 176
P., 147
R. S., 44
Russell, 108
S., 163
S. B., 163
S. T., 153
Samuel, 11
Sarah J., 174
Stephen, 135
T., 88
Thomas, 114
Thomas F., 124
W., 41
W. E., 160, 168
W. F., 103
William, 123
William C., 83
William F., 106, 117
William V., 3
Z., 142
Z. P., 15
DAVISON, John, 17
   Ubin P., 64
DAWSON, A. H., 106
   Henry, 123
DAY, G. B., 45

G. B. (Rev.), 103
J., 18, 140
J. M. & Lady, 132
J. T., Lady & child, 141
James T. & wife, 91
John, 13
John G., 83
O. J., 102
William, 117
DAYE, John & lady, 27
DAYKON, William, 109
DAYLOR, William (sic),
   144
DAYTON, William, 109
DAZO, J., 178
D. C. B., (sic), 172
D. R. D., John (sic), 172
DEACONS, Gilbert, 81
DEAL, A. 186
   F.J., 186
   Samuel, 18, 186
DEALS, Thomas, 47
DEAMKY, J. M., 168
DEAMON, John H., 140
   William 140
DEAN, D., 55
   F. S., 49
   S., 2
   T., 140
   W., 55
DEARING, Charles A.,
   127
DEAVER, H., 44
DeBOIS, James, 7
DEBOW, Lafayette H., 86
De BUTTS, Arch., 37
DECAMP, E., 148
DeCAMP, William, 68
DECKER, _____, 75
   _____ (Mr.), 76
   James, 155
   John, 3
DEDMAN, H., 140
   J. & fam., 140
   L., 140
   M., 140
DEFFEMBACH M., 97
De FOE, A., 27
DEFRASE, W. R., 119

De FREES, Wilkinson, 102
DeGRACIE, E. H., 2
DeGRAFF, G. S., 13
DEGRAFF, J. C., 16
DEGUIRE, John (death of), 94
DeHART, S., 10
DEHAVEN, A., 99
   Jacob, 76
DEITZ, William H., 47
de KAY, William, 150
de LAFAYETTE, Sylvanus (see Sylvanus de Lafayette Fox)
DELAL, John, 146
DELANO, Cyrus, 118
DELANY, John, 37
DELEEP, J. S., 91
DELLAM, J. W., 38
DELLMARSH, R., 32
DeLONG, James, 122
   John, 122
   Leander G., 122
deLORIMIER, George G. G., 102
   V., 105
DELORINE, B., 20
DELUDE, B., 20
DEMARES, James, 91
   John, 91
DEMAREST, S., 15
DEMGAN, J. S., 88
DEMING, A., 79
   Horace & 3 sons, 141
   John, 80
DEMMING, Alfred, 111
DEMPSEY, C., 146
DENBAR., Patrick, 110
DENHAM, Job, 183
DENIG, L. A., 88
DENION, S. W., 118
DENLON, S. W., 118
DENMAN, Joseph, 10, 183
DENMARK, C., 90
DENNIS, Joseph & fam., 178

DENNISON, John, 172
DENNISTON, William, 97
DENNY, James, 155
   John, 155
   William J., 106
DeNOVILLE, P., 20
DENSMORE, John, 22, 192
DENTON, B. F., 147
   J. A., 8
DENVER, John, 155
DENZ, G., 35
DEPUS, W. R., 166
DERBING, L., 142
DERBYSHIRE, P. S., 119
de RO, Charles, 67
De ROUSSE, M., 20
De ROUSUE, M., 20
DERRICK, George, 82, 83
DESBROUGH, W., 148
DeSENE, T., 59
DESPAIN, Benjamin, 98
   Benjamin Jr., 98
DESS, Charles, 109
DESSERL, W. (sic), 167
DESSIEUX, J. C., 52
DETOR, E. A., 164
   Eli, 139
DETTER, M. L., 26
DEUION, S. W., 118
DEULON, S. W., 118
DEUTSCH, John, 57
DEUZ, G., 35
DEVILBIAN, Andrew, 121
   John, 121
DEVILLION, Andrew, 121
   John, 121
DEVIN, John (sic), 99
DEVINE, John, 99
DEVOL, Charles, 139
DEWEL, A., 121
DEWEY, C. C., 100
   L., 29
   Ulysis S. (sic), 101
DEWITT, ____ (Mr.), 114

   C., 88
   James R., 25
   W., 166
   W. L., 140
DeWOLF, J. B., 108
DEXTER, A. A., 102
DIBBLE, A. M., 65
   Ambrose M., 58
   Josiah, 137
DICHOLSON, Isaac, 67
DICK, David, 85
   L. D., 101
DICKENSON, D. C. (sic), 164
DICKERMAN, B. F. & wife, 99
   Marie (Miss), 99
DICKERSON, P., 153
DICKEY, Samuel, 104
DICKINSON, B. H., 119
   H. W., 86, 204
   Harvey, 204
   Hawley, 107
   R. S., 122
   Seth J., 88
DICKSON, Hugh, 55
   John, 172
   Joseph, 55
   P., 158
   W., 8
DIEFEL, F., 35
DIEFFENBUCHER, Henry, 134
DIFFEN, J., 163
DIFFENDAFFER, Samuel, 39
DIFFENDOFFER, Samuel, 39
DILL, Sol., 130
DILLARD, G., 165
   J. J. (Capt.), 81
DILLAY, D. J., 68
DILLION, Daniel, 103 (see also Daniel Dillon)
   Ira, B., 123
   Moses, 102, 108
   R., 68
DILLS, D., 158

J. H., 158
DIMICK, DeLivan, 101
　L. R., 101
DIMMICK, O., 55
　Ziba, 106
DINGMAN, J. W., 116
DINNEY, Joseph, 37
DINNIN, J. R., 19
DISMY, George (sic), 107
DISNOPH, William, 108
DITTEMA, F., 159
DIVER, W. B. (Mr.), 3
DIXON, ____, (Capt.), 89
　Ellis, 114
　H., 17
　J., 18
　J. H. (Dr.), 9
　Kelly, 114
DLEVINGER, Asa, 42, 195
D'MONT, Cornelius, 174
DOAN, R., 102
DOBBINS, ____, 91
DODD, Herman (sic), 124
　W., 143
　Ziba, 60
DODDS, H., 128
DODGE, B., 121
　C. V., 153
　F. H., 121
　Francis, 103
　H. S., 7
　J., 54
　L. C., 142
　M. R., 103
　Miles B., 121
　S. F., 111
　W., 26, 193
　W. E., 41, 193
DODSON, B. E. (Dr.) & lady, 113
　Buton, 45
　C. B., 51
　Joseph, 45
　N. B., 113
　R. (Mrs.), 170
DOGAN, W., 148
DOING, Robert, 54

DOLE, E. J., 113
　W., 113
DOLIVER, John, 21
DOLLIVER, Ira, 57
　John, 21
DOLLVER, John, 21
DOMARN, David, 151
DOMO, Mayo, 53
DONAHOE, A., 63
　John, 120
DONALD, Jonathan, 90
DONALDSON, B. F., 147
　J. C., 158
DONALSON, B. F. (sic), 147
DONCASTER, R., Jr., 167
　S., 167
DONDELL, J., 143
DONEL, A. B. (death of), 94
DONELLAN, Benjamin C., 149
DONN, John Y., 48
DONNELL, S. F., 59
DONNELLAN, W. (Capt.) & fam., 165
DONNEVAN, P. J., 54
DONOHOE, Francis, 13
DOOLITTLE, Charles, 134
　H. B., 157, 163
　Lyman, 87
　W., 163
　W. E., 148
　W. W., 163
DOONE, Mary E., 176
DORAND, H. D., 170
DORAR, HENRY (sic), 49
DOREY, Thomas S., 107
DORMAN, William B., 16
DORRINGTON, J., 17
DORSEY, A. A., 106
　H. C., 48
　N. M., 19, 191
　P. M., 8 (x)
DORY, J. A., 149

J. L., 150
DOSS, Charles, 109
DOTY, Edward, 64 (x)
　J., 153
　Joseph T., 10
DOUCASTER, R., Jr., 167
　S., 167
DOUD, Philemon, 6
DOUDELL, J., 143
DOUGALL, William, 106
DOUGHERTY, J. G., 157
　William H., 79
DOUGLAS, John, 191
DOUGLASS, B. (sic), 44
　Elisha, 202
　G. L., 108
　John, 20
　John H., 15
DOUL, D., 142
DOUZ, G., 35
DOW, Asa, 14, 184
　J. N., 19, 189
　James, 2
　L. C., 121
　Thomas, 110
DOWNELL, M., 140
DOWNER, D. C., 44
　E. H., 97
　J. S., 44
　Z., 22, 192
DOWNES, Samuel, 136
DOWNEY, Alex., 133
　F., 143
　S., 153
DOWNING, ____, (Major), 33, 193
　Major (sic), 33, 193
　A. D., 193
　Thomas, 147
DOWNS, E. M., 105, 119 (x)
　Henry, 83
　O. H., 151
DOWS, W. B. (DR.), 91
DOXSEE, A. A., 106
DOXY, B., 202
DOYLE, H., 70
DRAKE, ____, 100

Andrew Jackson, 109
Dennis, 55
Henry, 153
J. A., 36, 194
J. D., 85
J. E., 158
J. W., 158
S. W., 168
DRAN, R. (sic), 63
DRANE, W. D., 148
DRAPER, Josiah, 6
DREAN, Charles, 124
DREHER, E., 43
DREIBELBIS, Martin, 67
DRENNON, W., 96
   William, 25
DRERER, David, 105
DRESSER, ___, 41
DREVER, David, 105
DREYER, David, 105
DRIER, E. B., 174
DRISH, E., 150
   F., 150
DRIVER, Joseph & fam,
   154
DROUILLARD, Simon,
   59
DROVER, John M., 135
DRUM, C. K., 164
   John, 24, 54
DRUMM, C. K., 166
DRUMMOND,
   Archibald, 54
   R. A., 38
   R.S. 43, 197
DRURY, Andrew, 202
DUBADIE, Peter &
   company, 141
DUBB, J., 63
DUBOIS, A., 55
   Jonathan, 6
DUDLEY, ___, (Mr.),
   78
   B. F., 39
   J. P. (Dr.), 85
   William A., 160
DUELL, John, 110
DUFFY, Francis Jr., 86
   James, 146

Patrick, 121
Peter, 110
Thomas, 86
DUFRIEND, Lewis, 120
DUGAL, E., 98
DUHRING, A., 51
DUKE, F. W., 42
   G., 199
DULIN, Samuel, 100
DULLEN, George, 202
DULLY, Patrick, 111
DULSEY, E. F., 11
DULTON, D. L., 41, 193
DUMBLE, John, 89
DUMONT, J., 12
DUNANT, H., 145
DUNBAR, Alison, 49,
   199
   George S., 49, 199
   Patrick, 110
   William, 137
DUNCAN, Daniel, 71 (x)
   H. G., 166
   James, 107, 108
   James M., 79
   Joseph, 62
   Martha, 176
   Martha A., 162
   R., 70
   Robert, 114
   T. P., 87
   William, 71
DUNDALL, S. D., 30,
   182
DUNDASS, S. K., 4, 182
DUNE, T., 17
DUNG, W., 166
DUNHAM, A., 142
   Charles, 203
   E. G. & fam of 5 chldrn,
   180
   E. G. (Mrs.) & fam, 180
   George, 180
   H. G., 168
   J. H., 14
   S., 68
DUNKAM, C., 15
DUNKS, O., 47
DUNKUM, C., 15

DUNLAP (see also
   DUNLOP)
___, (Mr.), 93
A., 167
D., 168
J., 191
John, 135
M., 151
Presley, 90
R., 52
William, 136
DUNLOP (see also
   Dunlap)
Samuel, 181
DUNN, Ambrose, 59
D., 159
Ellis, 202
Flemming, 202
J., 142
James, 65, 87
Jephthah (sic), 123
John, S, 8
John Y., 48
Justus, 80
L. N., 12
S., 109
Samuel, 161
Simeon, 135
T., 17, 187
Thomas, 187
Thomas B., 18
W. D., 41
DUNNE, C. C., 150
E. P., 150
DUNNIGAN, A., 158
DUNNING, Albert, 152,
   177
H., 52
L., 148
Warren, 106
DUNPREE, F., 151
DUNRICH, F., 167
DUNTON, Stephen, 12
DUPE, G. F., 49
DuPUI, James, 67
DURBAN, Charles L.,
   118
DURBEN, Eli, 108
DURBIN, Eli, 108

Joseph L., 120
DUREE, J. C. & son, 14
DURGIN, C. W., 157
DURHAM, C., 2
  C. H., 63
  D. T., 63
  E. G. & fam of 5 chldrn, 180
  E. G. (Mrs.) & fam, 180
  George, 180
  L., 145
  T., 63
DURLIN, B. F., 165
DURMAND, Samuel S., 202
DURNING, Thomas, 60
DURR, M., 166
DURST, Edmund, 202
DUSTAN, J. G., 108
  William, 108
DUTCHER, Joseph, 85
DUTRICH, ____, 35
DUTTON, Enos, 107
  Isaac, 48
  Jerome, 116, 122
  Joseph. 63
  L., 26, 193
  L. D., 116
  Lorenzo D., 122
DUVELA, John, 132
DUVELS, John, 132
DUYER, John E., 101
DVNG, W. (sic), 166
DWELLY, Horace, 106
DWINAL, Harrison (sic), 89
DWNELL, M. (sic), 140
DWYER, John, 98
DYCHMAN, Smith, 102
DYE, E., 51
  J., 142
  James P., 147
DYER, H. J., 153
  John, 50
  M., 44
  Morgan, 7
  Robert, 84
DYKENS, J. P., 145
DYKES, G. P., 40

-E-

EADE, Joseph, 171
EADS, Granville O., 81
EAGLE, E., 143
  J., 150, 164
  John, 131, 148
  Sno (sic), 148
EAGLETON, J. Y., 134
EAHOLTZ, Frederick, 192
EALS, A. (sic), 153
EALY, E., 196
EANCS, George, 15, 185
EARL, F. W., 15, 184
  J., 41
EARLE, G. M., 31
EARLY, F.W., 184
EARTHAN, L. T., 159
EASLEY, W., 121
  William, 2
EASTERBROOK, Daniel E., 204
EASTERLINE, B., 183
EASTIN, Robert, 126
EASTLICK, Mahlon, 136
EASTMAN, A., 199
  C. H., 62
  J.J., 51
  Stephen W., 203
EASTON, W.M.C., 57
  William C., 63
EATHEY, John (death of), 94
EATON, H., 145
  J., 83
  Jeremiah, 58
  Robert T., 103
  W., S., 150
EBBETTS, John A. N. (Capt.), 82
EBERLE, Charles, 3
EBY, D., 156
  Peter, 108
ECCLESTON, W., 157
ECHTERY, M. (sic), 157

ECK, Eli, 15, 184
  Ely, 184
ECKER, Adam, 149
ECKHOFF, L., 18
ECKLEY, Dow, 107
  John, 107
  Levi, 107 (x)
ECLESTON, Ranson, 66
EDBINGTON, S. (sic), 171
EDDINGTON, S., 171
EDDY, E. M., 157
  George, 172
  Henry & fam, 87
  James E., 44
EDEN, James, 159
EDGAR, ____ (Mr.), 146
  George, 47
  J. S. L., 153
  William, 115
  William F., 71
EDGERTON, M. P., 64
  S. P., 65
EDGESTON, W. H., 146
EDGOS, J. S., 153
EDINGER, Jacob, 161
EDISON, Snow, 33
EDMONDS, B. F.., 31
  T., 157
EDMONDSON, J. H., 8
  John, 196
EDMONSON, Benjamin B., 47
  John (sic), 42, 196
EDSON, J. H., 83
EDWARDS, ____, & bro., 157
  ____, (Mr.), 60
  C. E., 159
  D. B., 165
  D. P. & bro., 157
  Daniel B., 136
  F. D., 79
  J., 150
  J. A., 83
  John, 21, 89, 175
  John F., 89
  T. D., 70

233

Thomas & fam., 122
William, 67, 159
EELBACK, Thomas, (sic), 105
EELS, A. J., 58
Franklin, 58
EENBOOM, H. (sic), 89
EETTIT, A. (sic), 164
EFNER, Goerge B., 7
EGAN, H. (Mr.), 69
Michael, 146
Thomas, wife & son, 155
William, 120
EGGLESTON, J. W., 18
Morris, 105
EHRENSTROEN, E. W., 85
EHRMAN, Henry, 136
EICK, Alexander, 141
EIFFERT, M., 123
John Wm. M., 123
EIKENBURY, Samuel, 90
EINER, George B., 7
EISTNER, J. (Mr.), 3
ELDEN, B., 52
R., 52
ELDER, William H., 21
ELDRED,
Elon, 198
Oliver, 102
ELDRIDGE, Albert G., 7
D. T., 35
Joseph, 169
Norman, 97
ELERANDSE, A. (sic), 154
ELERGOFF, P., 34
ELFBRINK, P., 155
ELLANWOOD, Benjamin, 40
ELLCESSOR, J., 18
ELLENSWORTH, Benjamin, 61
Thomas, 61
ELLENWOOD, Benjamin, 40
ELLETT, B. D. (sic), 46

ELLIOT, William (sic), 12
ELLIOTT, C. B., 129
C. C., 43
J., 52
Jacob, 90
John, 56
Joseph, 56
R. J., 150
Robert, 136
William H., 68
ELLIS, A., 86
Abel, 123
C., 147
D. C., 38
George, 31
H. A., 122
J., 145
J. W., 119, 149
James H., 65
Jesse H., 146
John M., 84
Joseph, 203
Lorenzo, 122
Nathan, 117
Nathan B., 118
R. B., 111
R. B. (Dr.), 111
R. W., 112
W., 167
W. H., 122
William, 31
ELLISON, J., 51
J. R., 53
John, 28
Samuel, 123
ELLS, H. A., 122
W. H. (sic), 122
ELLSWORTH, ____, (Mr.), 79
Chandler W., 116
William, 105
ELLYSON, Isaac P., 136
ELMER, ____, (Mr.), 87
G. A., 157
ELROD, Thomas, 32
ELVIEDGE, Joseph, 169
ELWELL, E., 191
Ellis, 19, 191
ELY, H. C., 33, 193

EMERIT, Louisa A., 161
EMERSON, Harvey, 171
J., 149
L., 149
EMERY, David, 10
Joel, 120 (x)
T. S., 120
Walter, 120
William, 10
EMILY, S. C., 79
EMMENS, J., 163
M., 150
EMMET, Simon, 117
EMMONS, H., 118
EMORY, G. H., 15
Joel, 120 (x)
T. S., 120
Walter, 120
ENDICOTT, D. A., 158
W., 23
ENGEL, T. F., 147
ENGELL, T. F., 147
ENGLE, George, 14
J. H., 42, 195
Jacob H., 195
John, 131
Jonathan, 118
Joseph, 42
Thomas, 135
William, 107, 118
ENGLES, D., 43, 197
ENGLESS, A., 155
Michael, 155
Peter, 155
William, 155
ENGLETON, J. Y., 134
ENGLISH,. Thomas, 135, 138
ENGLISS, R. V. (sic), 160
ENNERS, G. M., 146
ENNIS, Gregory, 48
James A., 48
John V., 48
ENOOR, Thomas, 54
ENSEY, E. A., 115
ENSLEY, W., 121
ENSLOW, T. S., 49, 199
W., 49, 199
EPLEY, Henry, 149

John, 149
EPPERLY, George, 54
EPPES, W. W., 148
ERICKSON, Charles H., 69
ERMAN, A. B., 67
ERMON, A. B., 67
ERNST, Jesse, 127
ERSKINE, H. W., 102
ERWIN, W., 149
ESHOLTZ, F., 22, 192
ESRY, Thomas, 71
ESTELL, James, 96, 130
ESTEP, Darwin, 49, 199
  D., 18, 186
  J., 186, 188
  W., 18, 186
ESTEPP, D., 186
  J., 18, 186, 188
  W., 186
ESTIS, B., 148
ESTLOW, B. S., 107
ETDERTON, Robert, 45
EUSEY, E. A., 113
EUTALER, Enos, 139
EUTSIA, Enos, 140
EUTSIN, Enos, 140
EUTSLA, Enos, 140
EUTSLER, Enos, 139
EVANS, A. M., 101
  Ben C., 86, 204
  Benjamin C., 204
  D., 27, 55
  Daniel, 91
  Edwards, 91
  George, 15, 110, 185, 199
  Hezekiah, 91
  Isaac, 32, 54
  J., 164
  J. W., 6, 23, 192
  James, 91, 120 (x)
  James E., 91
  James H., 91, 114
  John, 23, 65
  Joseph O., 192
  M. B., 165
  R. J., 155
  Truman, 160

  Watson, 54
EVARTS, M. E., 136
EVERETT, B. R., 56
  D., 100
  Milton, 56
  W. J., 56
  William, 56
EVERHART, E. D. (Dr.), 138 (x)
  F. D. (Dr.), 138
  William, 16
EVERLORT, G., 157
EVERSON, _____, 20
EVERTS, Chester M., 134
  F. B., 14
  John O., 134, 147
  M. E., 136
  Thomas H., 134
EVES, G. W., 140
  Jesse M., 140
EVEY, David, 20
  John, 20
  Joseph, 20
EVINGER, A. 49
  W. 49
EWING, ALEX, 64, 200
  J. W., 145
  John, 83, 200
  John H., 64, 200(x)
  Samuel, 98
  W., 42
  William, 177
EWINGO, R., 157

-F-

FAAS, G., 151
FAGAN, D., 42, 195
  Daniel, 195
  James, 138
FAGG, A. S., 164
FAGHER, William, 136
FAHER, W., 166
FAINSWORTH, M Ira, 163
FAIR, _____, 90
  Henry, 174

FAIRBANKS, Augustus, 45
  Hiram, 90
  James J., 121
FAIRBROTHER, E., 158
FAIRCHILD, Luther, 87
FAIRCHILDS, John, 33
FAIRFIELD, W. Augustus, 131
FAIRHURST, Edward, 136
FAIRLEY, William, 174
FAIRMSWORTH, Ira, 163
FAIRSERVICE, M. L., 150
FAIRVILLE, E., 55
  R., 55
FAKE, David, 87
  George S. (Col.), 87
FALCONER, T. A., 148
FALL, W. H., 166
FALLEN, I., 162
FALM, J., 100
FanFHOUSER, C. (sic), 141
FANNING, F., 133
  George W., 111
  James, 59
FANT, S., 83
  Simon, 202
  William B., 83
FARGERSON, James (Dr.) (sic), 162
FARGO, W., 168
FARKER, H. G. (sic), 163
FARMBARGE, Joseph, 101
FARMER, C., 32
  D., 144
  John, 90
  W., 145
  William, 152
FARMINGTON, Julia Ella S., 173
FARNETTE, Michael, 132
FARNHAM, L. G., 119
FARNSWORTH, M. S., 63

William, 47, 63
FARR, ____, (Mr.), 59
FARRAR, John M., 47
　R. S., 145
　T., 144
FARRER, J., 139
FARRINGTON, Joseph
　A., 62
FARRIS, John, 120
FARRON, G.H., 203
FARSING, John, 147
FARWELL, L. G., 38
　S. B., 106
FASH, A. H., 30
　J., 30
FASSETT, C. S., 13
　Richard, 100
FAUCHER, Nelson, 102
FAULDS, ____, 11
FAULKNER, C. D., 52
　Robert, 6
FAUSETT, Thomas, 46
FAUST, L. P., 160
FAVORITE, J., 197
FAWCITT, William (sic), 85
FAY, ____, (Col.) (death of), 93
　Edward & son, 106
　George, 15, 185
FEARN, A. R., 164
FEATHERSTONE, R. J., 83
FEHAN, Thomas, 54
FEIFFER, G. F., 52
FELAND, G. W., 31
FELCH, Walton C., 86, 204
FELLOWS, Francis L., 87
　Jacob, 155
　S. H., 150, 152
FELT, Edward, 91
FELTON, Lewis, 98
FELTS, J., 100
FENDERICH, Charles, 48
FENN, ____, 99
　A., 99
　Fowler, 85
　Theo, 100

FENNESY, Willaim, 87
FENSTERMAKER,
　Ruben, 154
FENTER, Mary E., 169
FERBER, A., 35
FERELL, A. (sic), 162
FERGERSON, James
　(Dr.), 162
FERGUSON, A., 19, 52, 190
　A.R., 190
　Alex B., 119
　Alexander B., 107
　C., 148
　George, 107
　George (Capt.) 119
　H. H., 158
　Jacob, 88
　R. R., 168
　W. S., 95
　W. W., 67
FERN, John, 116
FERRALL, Elijah, 55
FERREE, A., 42
FERRILL, M., 42, 195
　Milton, 195
FERRINGTON, Joseph
　A., 62
FERRIS, David 109 (x)
　Ira, 159
　J. W. G., 98
　John, 120
　L., 109
FERRISS, Reed, 109
FERRY, James, 110
FESTER, O. F., 69
FEWIS, David (sic), 170
FICK, H ., 63
　P., 63
FICKAS, John L., 33
　Samuel R., 33
FICKETT, James H., 78
FIDDICK, James, 54
FIDLER, D. L., 65
FIELD, E. (Dr.), 48
　Elizabeth, 127
　J. W., 163
FIELDS, ____, 91
FIERCE, C., (sic), 163

FIFFER, B., 18, 186, 188
　F., 186
FIGGIN, W., 83
FIKE, A. Y., 54
　Ausby, 54
　Moses, 54
FILE, Conrad, 47
FILLBRIGHT, W. M., 148
FINCH, A. M., 136
　C. F., 58
　J. F., 150
　O. D., 42
　Robert, 58
　T., 168
　William, 100, 139
FINDLEY, C. W., 32
　D. Boyd, 92
　George B., 39
　J., 2
　J. L., 32
　John Jr., 97
　L., 14
　William, 121
　William H., 8
FINEHENS, J., 165
FINK, William, 58
FINLAY, James, B., 102
　Thomas, 102
　William, 102
FINLEY, F., 130
　Oscar, 44, 58
FINLOCK, P., 33
FINN, James, 146
FINNELL, William, 127
FINNEY, J. M., 151
FINNIN, B. & lady, 27
FINTON, W. J., 49, 200
FISH, F. R., 143
　John, 109
　Noble, 146
FISHBURN, P. W., 153
FISHELOR, J., 21
FISHER, A., 157, 163
　Adam J., 139
　C., 148
　Frank, 151
　J., 164
　J. H., 154

J. R., 174
J. S., 163
John, 24
M., 18
P., 3
William, 30
FISK, C. M., 88
John, 14
L. C., 51
FITCH, George C., 47
Henry S., 47
W. W., 22
FITE, Eli, 120
FITTS, James R., 1
FITZGERALD, G. K., 23
J., 163
Joseph E., 154
Mary E., 173
N. D., 57
Sarah A. (Mrs.), 177
FITZHUE, William (sic), 56
FITZHUGH, ____, (Mr.), 61
William, 56
FITZPATRICK, B., 36
P., 157
FITZSIMMONS, G. W., 151
John, 199
FLACK, John A., 91
FLAERTY, P. (sic), 159
FLAHERTY, P., 159
FLANAGAN (see also FLANNEGAN)
J., 19, 189
M., 52
FLANDERS, Aaron, 137
F., 117
R. C., 135
William, 122
FLANEGAN, A., 157
FLANEGIN, Ed., 146
FLANNEGAN (see also FLANAGAN)
A., 145
J., 189
FLATT, M., 41
FLEA, David & 2 others, 180
FLECK, John, 9
FLEENER, Rochell, 161
FLEMING, W. P., 143
William, 155
FLEMMING, Anthony, 116
Jesse, 58
N., 58
William, 58
FLETCHER, Andrew, 102, 110
J. H., 159
John, 162, 176
M., 122
FLINN, B. P., 152
R., 56
C. D., 42
Thomas, 24
FLOCK, George, 165
FLOOD, John, 18
John & company, 178
FLOURNEY, William, 126
FLOURNOY, William, 126
FLOYD, A. B., 52
M.D., 202
FLYNN, A., 51
C. O., 17, 187
John, 82
M. J., 80
P., 51
FOBES, H. K., (sic) 33, 193
FOIBLE, David, 48
FOLEY, Henry, 179
FOLLANSLIE., J.S., 187
FOLLETT, A. D., 117
FOLLIJAMB, H. C., 152
FOLTZ, F., 131
FonFHOUSER, C., 141
FONT, J., 1
FOOTE, G. W., 58
Mark, 91
S. H., 146
FORBES, A., 23
William, 177
FORBUSH, Charles L., 47
FORCUM, Joseph D., 41
Moses, 41
FORD, A. G., 13
B., 105, 130
Charles N., 2
E., 15, 184
Edwin, 133
Erastus, 184
G. W., 163
George, 203
J. & company, 141
John, 123
William F., 82
FORDICE, Asa, 44
FOREMAN, J. F. (Mr.), 71
J. H., 131
Thomas C., 110
FORHEE, H.K. (sic), 193
FORMAN, S., 48
FORMEVAUL, J. A., 8
FORNIER, Asa, 44
FORREST, J., 168
FORSINGER, D. L., 30
FORSTER, George, 146
FORSYTH, C. A., 105
John R., 203
FORSYTHE, Robert, 143
FORWARD, Joseph R., 102
FORYE, J. B., 25
FOSDICK, G. W. (Mr.), 3
FOSTER, ____(Mr.), 202
E., 92
Francis M., 127
George, 102
Isaac, 63
J., 51
J. A., 18
J. C., 43, 197
J. G., 63
Joseph, 136
Thomas H., 172
Vincent, 63
W. C., 122
FOTHINGHAM, John & fam., 40
FOULES, R., 143
FOULKES, John Jr., 112
FOUTCH, W. J., 56

FOUTS, Lemon, 90
FOWL, James, 137
FOWLER, Almon, 106
　Benjamin, 122
　George D., 106
　Gilbert, 84
　J., 64
　James W., 123
　John A., 147
　Leonard D., 59
　Leven, 140
　Thomas, 10
　William, wife & 11
　　chldrn, 179
FOX, A., 149
　Amos, 107
　B., 2
　Charles, 38
　G., 55
　G. W., 168
　Henry, 80
　J. F., 146
　Jacob, 80
　Jacob B., 80
　Jared, 139
　L. wife & child, 139
　Lauren F., 102
　M., 33, 193
　M.N., 193
　Sylvanus de Lafayette, 105
　W., 152
FOXELL, J., 159
FOXWELL, J., 159
FOY, James, 47
FRAGGINS, Daniel, 114
　Presley, 114
FRAME, Andrew, 45
FRANCE, ____, 31
　Albert, 134
　D., 31
　Jacob, 170
　M., 148
FRANCESS, M. (sic), 148
FRANCIS, H., 128, 168
　J., wife & chldrn, 139
　M., 148, 149, 150, 153
　Morrison, 57
　Thomas, 105

William, 101
FRANCISCUS, Louis, 79
FRNKELERGER, J. C., 79
FRANKLIN, B., 150
　D., 61
　Henry, 162
　S. W., 41
　William, 48
FRANKS, Isaac, 67
　John, 67
FRANS, H. B. (sic), 64
FRANTISES, J., 153
FRANTZ, Nicholas, 116
FRANZ, Seler, 34
FRASER, K. G., 150
FRASIER, H. (sic), 153
　M., 163
　W., 153
FRATZY, S. (sic), 166
FRAUNBERGER, A., 21
FRAUNBORGER, A., 21
FRAZIER, Griffin, 109
　Hamilton, 155
　Jacob, 108
　John, 87
FREAR, J., 143
FREDENBERG, L., 95
FREDENBURGH, Benjamin, 135
FREDERICK, John, 45
　William, 5
FREEID, Solomon (sic), 146
FREEL, Jer (sic), 90
　Jerome, 90
FREELAND, Orlando, 118
FREELS, B., 165
FREEMAN, A., 58, 106, 153
　C. C., 163 (x)
　F. M., 165
　G. S., 149
　J. P., 31
　John, 83
　S., 10
　Thomas & lady, 161
　W. L., 122

William, 35
William H., 53
FREESE, George S., 14, 184
　J.S., 184
FREMONT, John (Col.), 25
FRENCH, A., 52
　F., 139
　H., 22, 192
　Henry, 192
　Jacob, 45
　Robert, 45
FRERRET, J., 150
FREY, Mary Couise (sic), 177
　Mary Louise, 177
FRICK, ____ (Mr.), 160
　Adam, 154
　George, 154
FRIED, Solomon, 146
FRIEND, C. W., 12
　John, 12
FRIGGS, James, 108
FRISBEE, ____, 23
　J. C., 118
　J. P., 163
FRISBIE, S., 187
FRITCH, J. M., 4
FRITCHERY, M., 203
FRITZLAND, J., 31
FRIZZLE, ____ (Capt.), 55
FROODS, T., (sic), 147
FROST, J. L., 152
　Jacob, 156
　L., 100
　William O., 169
FROTIER, H., 20
　Joseph, 20
FRURY, W., 202
FRY, E., 100
　G., 166
　Hadrick, 155
FUDGE, D., 32
　W. B., 162, 165
FUGETT, ____ (Mrs.), 155
FUGHER, William 136

FUGITT, J., 30
FUGLER, ____, 145
FUGUA, D. H., 148
FUHRUP, H., 23
FULGHMER, F., 32
FULINGEE, P.W., 202
FULKERSON, P. (Dr.), 1
    R.B., 201
FULLER, A., 145
    Amos, 44
    C. A. & wife, 154
    E., 49
    G. A. & wife, 154
    Nelson, 108
    R., 154
    R. M., 49
    Randall, 21
    Richard, 67
    S., 154
FULLIGAN, P. W., 83
FULLMAN, D., 23
FULMER, Daniel, 66
FULSER, S., 157
FULTON, Alexander, 11
    F., 164
    J., 18
    J. B., 17
FUNCK, E., 63
FUNDIBURG, D., 196
FUNDIBURGH, D., 42, 196
FUNK, D. R., 68
    Sam, 137
FUNNELLS, ____, 80
FURGESON, Elihue, 97
FURGUSON, John, 130
    M. F., 157
FURNISH, B. F. (Capt.), 129

-G-

G____, Aaron (of Berlin, Wisc.) 134
G____, Andrew (of Wisc.), 135
G__IVE, Robert (of Wisc.), 135
GABBERT, Goodson, G., 127
GABBETT, P. C., 168
GADDEN, Henry, 110
GAFF, E., 63
GAFFIELD, E., 57
GAFNER, John, 134
GAGE, J. B., 40
    J. D., 40
    S. W., 40
GAINES, Richard, 121
GALABERT, M., 167
GALBRAITH, H., 174
    T., 18, 188
    Thomas, 188
GALBREATH, Joseph, 101
GALE, A. C., 51
    Abner, 106 (x)
    G. A., 65
    G. H., 59
    G. W., 98
    J. V., 61
    Joseph W., 119
GALFIN, W. R., 131
GALLAGHER, Grovesnor, 1
    J. G., 18
    James, 87
GALLAHER, J. W. (sic), 42, 195
    John W., 195
GALLAWAY, James E., 25
GALLING, Francis, 120
GALLOWAY, William, 122
GALLSEP, Y. M., 149
GALLUP, P., 55
GALORD, Joseph, 39
    S. (sic), 39
    W. (sic), 39
GAMBLE, G. W., 59
    Philip, 79
    S. J., 116
    William G., 116
GAMLIN, A., 20
GAMMILL, James, 131
    William A., 131
GANETY, ____, (Mrs.) & fam., 179
GANGER, D., 173
GANGTRY, ____ (Mrs.) & fam., 179
GANNON, Joseph, 117
GANSETY, ____(Mrs.) & fam., 179
GANSON, Joseph, 117
GANTHER, Leroy, 119
GANTT, H. C. (sic), 31
GANZETRY, ____(Mrs.) & fam., 179
GANZTEY, ____, (Mrs.) & fam., 179
GARD, Brookfield, 184
    Ezra, 184
GARDENER, A. B., 10
    J., 157
GARDENS, C., 166
GARDINER, ____, 115
    J., 99
    T., 158
    T. B., 12
GARDNER, Betsy A., 137
    C., 166
    D., 54
    G. W., 143
    Joseph, 8
    Joshua, 55
    Melvin S., 82
GARDNES, C. (sic), 166
GARFIELD, H., 23
GARIT, J. W. (sic), 166
GARNER, Conrad, 59
    J., 59
    J. C., 152
    J. D., 150
    Jefferson, 105
GARNETT, A., 158
GARNHART, J. H., 42, 195
    John H., 195
GARR, S., 70
GARRATT, Thomas, 108
GARRETT, A. O., 52
    Alexander, 47

Emily, 99
Henry, 99
Hiram, 99
J. O., 3
J. O. & wife, 99
J. O. Jr., 99
James, 38
Joseph, 38
P., 166
Sarah, 99
T., 96
William H., 100
GARRISON, A., 157
  E. F., 9
  J., 167
  W., 157
GARRO, John, 139
  Peter, 139
GARSEY, Hans, 107
GARTHER, Faulkner, 119
  Leroy, 119 (x)
GARTON, Morrison, 117
GARVER, John (Dr.), 78
GARVEY, Patrick, 82
GARVIN, James, 24
  W. A., 127
GARWICK, P., 23
GARWOOD, J. U., 166
  William, 129
GARY, John, 202
GASAWAY, N., 24
GASKINS, G. W., 137
  G. W., lady & 10
    passengers, 165
  Hiram, 137
GASSNER, V., 79
GASTON, C. B., 63
  Morrison, 117
GATES, E., 164
  Erastus, 139
  J., 61, 100
  J. M., 168
  L., 157
  Reuben, 59
  Seth, 106
GAUGHER, Anthony, 152
GAVETT, Jonathan, 78
GAY, William, 38

GAYNE, S., 17
GEAR, J. C., 132
  N., 99
  William T., 132
GEARHEART, George (sic), 126
GECHENOW, John Jr., 122
GEE, D., 14
GEESLY, N., 151
GEIGER, V. E., 42, 195
  Vincent E., 195
GEITGY, George, 125
GENSON, C. D., 167
GENTRY, W. A., 148
  Z. B. (Dr.), 32
GEORGE, E. R., 87
  James, 129
  T., 96
GEPHART, David, 178
  George, 178
GEPHEART, John, 38
GERARD, A. C., 44
GERMAN, D. L., 157
GEROLD, T., 80
GETHAM, A., 164
GETTER, John, 148
GETTING, P. A., 126
GETZENDINER, J., 81
GETZLER, A., 87
  Charles, 87
GHASTEZ, S. (sic), 160
GIBBLE, Thomas, 178
GIBBONS, A., 10
  J. B., 100
GIBBS, Frank, 159
  H. B., 91
  J. C., 59
  O. J., 168
  William A., 118
GIBSON, C. T., 147, 150
  Harry, 126
  Nathan, 87
  S., 99
  W. A., 168
  W. C. T., 153
  W. T., 153
  William, 70, 81
GIDDINGS, Isaac D., 118

GIESE, J., 67
GIESS, J., 67
GIFFARD, Freeman, 97,
GIFFORD, J., 19, 191
GILBERT, _____, 115
  D. T., 101
  E., 157
  F. D. (Mr.), 4
  H. Jr., 157
  J. L., 3
  Jonathan R., 3
  N. M., 133
GILCHRESE, Ira, wife & 3 chldrn, 22
GILCHRIST, R. C., 19
GILER, John, 121
GILES, Charles, 55
  Cyrus, 55
  Nathaniel, 203
  Nelson, 203
  P., 150
  S. L., 45
  William, 203
GILFORD, E., 27
GILHAM, Samuel, 117
GILKERSON, E. S., 14
GILKEY, C. M., 59
  William T., wife & 3 chldrn, 180
GILKINSON, W., 51
GILL, Cornelius, 98, 104
  I. B., 83
  Isaac, 131
  John, 124
  Joseph, 37
  L. B., 83
  M., 53
GILLAM, Samuel, 117
GILLARD, Emily S., 161
  Thomas (Dr), 2
GILLENEY, Daniel, 176
GILLESPIE, A. T., 159
  C. B., 10, 183
  Charles, 183
  John, 135
  Joseph, 54
  Robert, 199
GILLETT, C., 99
  H. W., 164

J. H., 163
M., 48
GILLHAM, ____, (Mr.)
   & fam., 171
   James H., 67
GILLIES, Robert, 135
GILLILAND, J. F.; 58
   John, 117
GILLIS, George F., 89
   James S., 50
GILLMAN, A. A., 140
   W. S. (sic), 86
   William, 116
GILLMEN, William, 116
GILLMON, William, 116
GILLMORE, Robert, 37
GILLUM, ____, (Mr.), 103
GILMAN, B.D., 196
   C. D., 52
   Charles S., 95
   D., 165
   D. D., 42, 196
GILMORE, J., 168
   Josephine, 175
   Lyman, 103
GILPIN, L. S., 89
   William, 71
GILSON, J. J., 106
   W. J., 157
GIRARD, J., 63
GISH, D. E., 13
   John, 116
   Peter & fam., 179
GIST, Peter & fam., 179
   Samuel J., 13
GITCHELL, L. W., 139
GITTINGS, Charles F., 196
GIVENS, C. T., 163
GLASE, R.P., 187
GLASGOW, Richard, 138
GLASS, F. S., 150
   James, 92
   John & fam., 92
   R., 151
   R. P., 17, 187
   Robert, 92
   Thomas W., 107

GLASSAN, W. C., 150
GLASSCOCK, J., 129
   James A., 125
   Z. P., 121
GLAZEBROOK, ____, 75
GLAZIER, Simon, 138
GLEASON, C. Willard, 78
   P. M., 123
   Patrick, 123
GLEEN, John, 147
GLEESON, E. F., 5
GLEICH, Michael, 116
GLENAT, N., 96
   V., 59
GLENDENEN, H., 164
GLENN, J., 18
   John, 114
GLESSAN, W. C., 150
GLIDDEN, J. G., 153
GLINES, Joseph, 124
GLITNER, Ira, 121
GLOVER, William, 36, 194
   William M., 102
GLYM, John (sic), 67
GOBLE, Josephus, 89
GOCHENOW, John Jr., 122
GODDARD, A., 59
   E., 113
GODFREY, J., 19, 191
   J.R., 191
GODLAD, G., 166
GODWIN, John (sic), 19, 189
   William (sic), 67
GOFF, Jacob, 136
GOGERTY, E., 11
GOLD, Ames, 135
GOLDEN, William, 84
GOLDER, ____, 91
GOLDSMITH, W. C., 150
GOLDWEATHER, James, 178
GOMAN, Samuel N., 37
GONGER, G. W., 177
GOOCH, Mary Ann

(Mrs.)
   & child, 40
GOOD, F. C., 147
   John, 99
   William, 7
GOODAPOD, E., 163
GOODE, B. A., & svt, 25
   M.W., 148
GOODFELLOW, M., 18
GOODFOSTER, H. & fam., 154
GOODHUE, George, 38
   J. H., 150
GOODING, J. A., 73
GOODLAND, G., 166
GOODMAN, ____ (Dr.), 125
   J., 127
   S. D., 162
GOODNOUGH, Charles (sic), 45
GOODRICH, ____, 124
   C. G., 104
   Charles, 33
   H., 58
   Ira, 118
   J., 21
   James E., 107
   L. B., 8
   Philip, 58
GOODSON, Joseph, 83
GOODSPEED, E., 163, 166
GOODSPOD, E., 163
GOODSUCA, William M. (sic), 124
GOODWIN, A. S., 18
   D., 140
   J., 18, 189
   William, 67
GOODWYN, T. W. (sic), 120
   T. W., Jr., (sic), 120
GOODYEAR, Andrew, 40
   H., 108
   Henry A., 106
   Miles M. (Capt.), 40
GOOKIN, T. M. S., 81, 82

GOOLE, F. A., 27
GORDAN, T., 129
GORDEN, Marion W. (sic), 111
GORDON, A. W., 90
  E., 26, 193
  E. E., 41, 193
  Eleanor G., 176
  J., 113
  J. O., 27
  John & son, 27
  Marion W., 111
  Milton B., 105
  Thomas, 62, 65
GORE, A., 83
  Isaac B., 78
GORMAN, Edward, 119
  John, 105
  Robert, 83
GOSHELL, E. H., 150
GOSNELL, E. H., 150
GOTSMAN, H., 18, 188
GOTTZMAN, H., 188
GOTZMAN, H., 18
GOUGER, G. W., 177
GOUGH, John, 44
GOULD, A. R., 168
  Charles, 204
  E. G., 122
GOULDING, William R., 82
GOURLAY, R., 7, 182
GOURLEY, Robert, 24, 182
GOVE, A.F, (Mr.), 3
GOWDY, George, 64
GOWLEY, George, 57
GRABLE, H., 148
  J. M., 148
GRACE, J. R., 150
  W., 159
GRADY, J., 143
GRAF, Abraham, 80
  Ferdinand, 80
GRAFF, P., 57
GRAHAM, ___, (Dr.), 68
  A. M., 32
  B., 167

C. C., 47
Charles, 117
Francis, 57
G., 148
George, 146
H. J., 55
J. (Mr.), 3
Jared, 40
Stephen, 119
Theodore, 117
W. D., 18
GRALIOT, C. B., 130
GRANDIN, E. B., 139
GRANDORF, ___ (Dr.), 187
GRANES, S., 163
GRANGER, T. C., 134
GRANT, D., 68
  David, 111
  J., 144
  N., 40, 73
  Thomas W., 58
  W. B., 85
GRAPE, B., 19
GRASLEY, Newman, 126
GRASSMAN, James, 101
  Robert, 101
GRATIOT, C. H. (Col.), 85
GRAUF, J., 197
GRAULECH, Casper, 81
GRAVES, E. S., 77
  N. (Mr.), 3
GRAY, ___, 93 (x)
  Andrew J., 183
  Benjamin W., 161
  C., 61
  Charles, 183
  David D., wife & 4 chldrn, 132
  J. C. (Dr.), 53
  Jacob, 88
  John J., 122
  John W., 29
  Joshua & fam., 40
  Nelly, 105
  O. C., 30, 182
  Oliver C., 4, 182
  Orin, 121, 131

Pleasant (Capt.), 95
Samuel, 67
W. H., 50
W. W., 31
William, 54
GREATRAKE, George, 7
GREEDENFIELD, D. & wife, 154
GREEDNFIELD D. & wife, 154
GREEG, S. (sic), 163
GREELEY, Charles B., 173
  W. S., 173
GREELY, J. E., 135
GREEN, A., 66
  Bazle, 100
  Calvin, 127
  E., 138
  H. C., 147
  Hiram, 82
  Isaac, 100, 193
  J., 34, 140, 193
  John, 146
  L., 194
  L. E., 38, 194
  Nicholas, 100
  R. Z. W., 179
  Robert C., 52
  Robert S., 19, 190
  S., 174, 179
  W., 158
  William, 53
GREENE, B. B., 99
  George, 112
  J. D., 99
  Moses, 116
  R.S., 190
GREENEY, J., 153
GREENLEAF, Albert, 134
  L., 109
  L. K., 105
  W. C., 159
GREENMAN, E., 203
  M., 203
GREENOCH, Daniel, 122
GREENOLD, G. C., 153
GREENVILLE, S. M., 154

242

GREENWOOD, B., 117
  Henry, 59
  N., 52
GREENY, J., 153
GREER, John, 20
  O., 16
  W.B., 181
GREESLIER, A., 163
GREGG, S., 163
  Thomas, 19
GREGGS, T., 129
  William & co., 177
GREGORY, A., 148
  David, 120
  G. W., 156
  Henry, 59, 65
  J., 33
  Thomas, 117
  W., 144
GRENET, H. J., 143
GRENNETT, H. J., 145
GRESSARD, C., 3
GREW, S. L. (Dr.), 117
GREY, Andrew J., 10, 183
  Charles, 10, 183
  Daniel D., 48
  George, 11
  Nelson, 48
GRICE, George, 23, 192
GRICHLINE, A.K., 189
GRIDLEY, D. & fam., 142
  J., 142
  Thomas M., 78
GRIER, Thomas P., 47
GRIEVE, Edwin, 121
GRIFFERMAN, P., 99
GRIFFETH, W. (sic), 157
GRIFFIN, A. W., 36, 194
  G., 95
  H., 108
  John, 106
  M., 11
  N. L., 167
  S. H ., 45
GRIFFITH, Jacob, 118
  James, 91
  John, 43

  Squire, 129
  W., 157
  William, 124
GRIFFITHS, Samuel, 82
  Thomas J., 48
GRIGGSBY, ____, (Capt.) (sic), 201
  B., 158
GRIGSBY, ____, 201
  B., 158
GRIMM, Jacob, 65
GRIMS, J. A., 166
GRINDELL, John, 119
GRINNEL, J., 144
  John, 132
GRIPPON, G.W., 194
GRISIHLINE, R. F., 19, 189
GRISWOLD, Harrison, 109
  Newton, 126
GRITZNER, F., 87
GROETFIELD, A., 20, 191
GROFF, J. G., 147
GROGDON, R.C., 181
GROMS, J. M. (sic), 126
GROOM, J. S., 8
  John, 124
  R., 8
  V. C., 8
GROOMER, G. B., 129
GROOMS, Ormsby, 54
GROOT, James H. (death of), 94
GROSS, E. S., 51
  F., 35
  George H., 135
  W. T. A. H. (sic), 38
GROSSCUP, J., 64
GROTFEND, A., 191
GROUT, James H., 134
GROVE, C., 48
GROVER, Mannassah, 62
GROVES, J., 18
GROW, S. L. (Dr.), 117
GRUBB, S., 5
  Thomas R., 114
GUARD, B., 14, 184

  Ezra, 15, 184
  R. Z. W., 179
GUARO, R. Z. W., 179
GUDLEY, George, 110
  John, 110
GUERNSEY, O. (Col.), 115
GUFFITH, H., 60, 61
GUFFEY, A. H., 66
GUFNER, John, 134
GUG, A. W., 17, 187
  E. C., 17, 187
GUGER, John, 104
GUILD, ____, 20, 190
  E., 190
  John E., 102
  N.M. (Mr.), 193
GUILTNER, Ira, 102
GUINN, J. T., 108
GUISLER, Peter, 81
GUITERIA, Francisco, 53
GUITERIO, Francisco, 53
GUITERIS, Francisco, 53
GULLFORD, G. J. (Mr.), 3
GULLING, Francis, 120
GULLY, Samuel, 73
GUM, B. F., 136, 168
  Eli, 140
  William, 54
GUMALT, Philip, 180
GUNDER, W., 99
GUNETT, William E. (sic), 30
GUNLEY, George, 110
  John, 110
GUNN, Moses, 137
GUNNEY, Gustavus & wife, 131
GURTHER, Faulkner, 119
  Leroy, 119
GURTHRIE, Faulkner, 119
  Leroy, 119
GUSK, John, 176
GUTH, Horace, 51
GUTHRICE, T. J., 167
GUTHRIE, Elisha, 12
  Faulkner, 119

Harvey, 116
Leroy, 119
T. J., 150, 167
GUTHRIEE, T. J., 167
GUTTRIDGE, E., 129
GUY, W. R., 17
GUYER, Joseph F. 103, 111
GWALTNEY, William H., 16
GWINN, D., 190
  J. A. (sic), 159
GYER, Cowden, 98
  John, 98

-H-

H____,. Joshua M., 108
HAAGE, J., 42, 196
HAAS (see also HASS) William 49, 199
HABER, C., 35
HABERMANN, ____, 35
HABRY, C., 143
HACKETT, E. W., 50
  F. H., 50
  John B., 82
  Simon, 12
  Susan, 12
HADLEIGH, John, 78
HADLEY, Mark, 110
HAGAN, A. F., 27
  A. J., 22, 192
HAGANS, O. F., 166
  W. B., 166
HAGEN, Jonathan, 4
  S. 22
HAGER, J., 42, 167
HAGGARD, Dennison, 91
  Edward, 72
HAGUE, ____, 83
  J., 196
HAHM, M. A., 168
HAHN, Henry, 203
  Sorellia, 173
HAIGHT, Henry, 120
HAILE, S. C., 170

HAILES, W. J., 129
HAINES, ____, (Mr.), & fam., 156
  C. W., 30
  G. W., 13
  Guy, 19
HAINING, Charles H., 122
HAINS, D. J. (sic), 157
  M. T. (sic), 129
HAISLEP, J. B., 61
HAKE, ____, 89
  S., 196
HALBERT, William, 152
HALDERMAN, H., 19, 186, 188
  P., 19, 186, 188
  William F., 186
HALE, D. & Co., 177
  David C., 140
  Ira P., 122
  J., 150
  J.C., 183
  J. E., 64, 200
  James E., 200
  John, 15, 183
  Moses, 68
  R., 1
HALEY, William B., 123
HALL, ____, 110
  A. A., 146
  A. S., 9
  C., 99
  Charles, 25
  D., 149
  D. J. C., 167
  D. M., 7, 24
  F. P., 158
  George H., 106, 121
  H., 142
  H. C., 143, 157
  H. H., 157
  Henry, 47
  Ira, 109
  Isaac C., 102
  J., 110
  J. C., 156
  J. H., 8
  J. R., 16

J. W., 23
James, 15, 184
Jesse, 147
John, 147
John & wife, 145
L., 108, 109
L. B., 111
Mason, 171
R. B., 159, 166, 168
Samuel, 106
Sno (sic), 147
Sylvester, 109
T. B., 111
William, 174
HALLENBAKE, Obadiah, 123
HALLETT, J. H., 157
HALLLKINS, G. A. (sic), 157
HALSTEAD, George W. & fam., 135
  J., 108
  Jerome, 106
HALSTED, G. W., 65
HALTZWERT, J., 20, 190
HAM, W. H., 124
HAMBLETON, O., 142
HAMILTON, ____, (Col.), 87
  ____, (Mr.), 103
  Alexander, 45
  D., 38
  E. E., 25
  E. G., 116
  G., 166
  G. B., 105
  H. M., 157, 158
  Hiram, 118
  Jacob, 91
  O., 83
  R., 87
  S., 157
  T., 145
  Thomas, 146
HAMLIN, C. P., 63
  Charles, P., 57
  F. (Mr.), 3
  John, 100
  Seth, 100

HAMLINS, Charles P., 57
HAMLY, G.S., 191
HAMM, M. A., 168
HAMMAN, J., 2
HAMMAR, Benjamin,
    160 (x)
    William, 160 (x)
HAMMELL, N., 163
HAMMER, Benjamin,
    160 (x)
    William, 160(x)
HAMMIN, James, 26
HAMMITT, M. F., 104
HAMMON, Napoleon,
    136
HAMMOND, ____,
    (Mr.), 54
    Andrew, 91
    Charles D., 70
    E. D. (Dr.), 79
    F., 151, 154
    J., 157
    J. C., 146
    L. A., 5
    L. G., 149
    Mary E., 174
    Minor, 106
    N., 148
    N. J., 158
    W., 157
HAMMONDS, T. L., 91
HAMMONDSON, J., 139
HAMPSON, George, 199
HAMPTON, Christopher,
    33
HAMTON, O., 57
HAN, R. B., 131
HANAN, James, 63
    John D., 63
    Thomas, 62, 63
HANCE B. M., 33
    George, 30
HANCK, G. W., 151
    S., 151
HANCOCK, ____, (Dr.),
    86
    J., 142
    John, 61
    John M., 101

R., 119
HAND, E., 67
    E. O., 67
    N. B., 67
    O., 67
    W. A. H., 168
    W. H., 157
HANDLER, Isaac, 92
HANDSKY, J. W., 165
HANDY, David, 58
    J. B., 70
    J. W., 70
HANELETT, Samuel, 154
HANEY, John, 151
    Valentine, 45
HANGER, A. E., 103
HANI, John, 151
HANKEY, B. H., 146
HANLEY (see also
    HANLY)
    W. M., 159
HANLOY, W. M., 159
HANLY (see also
    HANLEY)
    G. S., 20, 191
HANN, P., 170
    Sorellia, 173
HANNA, A. J., 8
    Andrew, 88
    Green, 92
    James P., 118
    John, 92, 122
    Sam Jr., 92
    William Jr., 92
HANNAH, A. M., 112
    Henry, R., 87
HANNAN, James, 67
    Wesley, 67
HANNEGAN, A., 144
HANNEN, Lytle, 155
HANNON, Lyttle, 136
HANSCOM, D., 98
HANSEN, Z., 123
HANSER, Z., 123
HANSHAW, James
    (Capt.), 123
    Washington, 123
    Washington fam of, 123
HANSON, Ole, 90

S., 144
HANVET, A. W., 63
HANWAY, W. W., 165
HARAZTHY, A., 87
HARBACH, J. P., 18, 188
HARBAUGH, E. (Miss),
    137
    F., 137
    J.B., 188
HARBINGER, John, 127
HARCKNESS, ____,
    (Dr.) (sic), 5
HARD, B., (Dr.), 15
    Edward, 29
    Lafayette, 66
HARDCASTLE, D. A.
    (Mrs.), 175
    D. J. (Mrs.), 175
    J. M., 175
    R. P., 175
    Robert P., 170
    W. C., 175
HARDESTRY, James,
    107
HARDESTY, James, 107
    T.P., 196
HARDIN, Amos L., 128
    M., 8
    Mark, 8
HARDINBOOK, William,
    63
HARDING, E. D., 18
HARDLAN, W. C., 147
HARDY, ____, (Mr.), 91
    ____ (Mr.) & fam.,
    171
    J. H., 159
    J. J., 118
    J. J. (death of), 94
    J. J. (grave of), 93
    M., 165
    W., 164
HARE, M. D., 31
HARFACLIFT, Henry, 47
HARGER, A. E., 103
    Andrew, 111
HARGREAVES, John,
    wife
    & 5 chldrn., 180

HARKDULL, Enos E., 116
HARKER, George M., 89
HARKINS, E., 144
HARKNESS, ____, (Dr.), 55
  David, 40
HARLAN, Joshua, 106
  William, 6
HARLEY, B., 113
  I. S., 154
  J. P. (Mr.), 3
HARLOW, N., 128
HARLY, I. S. (sic), 154
HARMALF, R. K., 164
HARMON, ____, (Mr.), 141
HARNESS, Seaton L., 118
HAROLD, J. M., 102
HARPER, A. T., 9
  Henry, 109
  J. W., 4
  Jefferson, 134
  John, 147
  Robert, 8
HARREL, Abel, 91
HARRELL, Robert, 107
HARRIMAN, E., 167
  W., 167
HARRINGTON, Alex. E., 132
  C., 70
  C. C. & lady, 131
  G. W., 36, 68, 194
  George W., 194
  H., 157
  James, 161
  James J., 132
  John, 132
  W. P., 23
HARRIS, ____, 38, 128
  ____, Mr. 55, 69
  ____, (Mr.) (death of), 92
  A., 18
  B. C., 16
  C. R., 8
  Charles, 109, 132
  Felix M.. (see Phelix M. Harris)
  H., 80
  H. M., 147
  J. B., 1
  James, 93, 104
  John, 2
  Joseph, 54
  Matthew, 80
  N. M., 28, 199
  Phelix M. (sic), 106
  R. C., 16
  Samuel, 13
  W. R., 178
HARRISON, A. C., 9
  A. W., 181
  C., 173
  H. C., 42, 195
  Hamilton C., 195
  O. H., 61
  R. E. (Dr.), 58
  Reese, 126
  Rufus K., 16
  T.P., 181
  W., 24, 182
  William, 7, 182
  Willaim F., 16
HARRYMAN, E., 167
  W., 167
HARSHARD, William, 176
HARSHAW, B. F., 24, 182
  D. T., 7, 182
  William, 130
HARSHBARGER, Daniel, 116
HARSMAN, William, 20
HART, A., 98
  H., 202
  H. M., 32
  Henry, 83
  J. T., 15
  John, 117, 122
  John B., 29
  Joseph, 179
  Joseph P., 111
  Morgan, 116
  Thomas, 26
  Thomas S., 5
  W., 142
  William, 27
  William W., 107
HARTENCK, M. E. (sic), 164
HARTFORD, A., 151
HARTLEY, J. B., 19
HARTMAN, Andrew, 58, 65
  E. D., 144, 145, 146
  John, wife & 2 chldrn, 179
  P., 35
  W. A. F., 129
HARTNELL, J., 110
HARTNETT, J., 110
HARTON, Benjamin T.
  D. L., 103
HARTSALL, J., 15, 184
HARTSEL, J. (sic), 184
HARTSOCK, C., 165
HARTWELL, James, 45
HARTZEL, ____, 116
HARVEY, C., 12
  D., 149
  E. B., 166
  James, 84
  Thomas C., 84
HARVY, E. B. (sic), 166
HARWOOD, James, 142
HASALD, Nathaniel N., 63
HASBROOK, J., 65
HASELED, T., 168
HASELTON, ____, 115
HASEY, A., 109
  S., 109
HASKELL, Chauncey, 155
  George W., 50
  H. G., 158, 164
HASKIN, L. N., 167
HASKINS, ____, (Mrs.), 161
  C., 100
  L. N., 166
HASLEP, J. B., 61
HASLETT, James H., 37

HASLIP, J. B., 61
HASS (see also HAAS)
  Esquire, 22
  Henry, 22, 184
  S., 184
HASSETTON, ____, 115
HASSON, William 122
HASSOU, William, 122
HASTINGS, E. L., 133
  E. O. F., 23, 192
  F., 192
  John (Hon.), 192
  Lymnan, 183
  Lyman & son, 15
  Lyman Jr., 15, 183
  Samuel, 15, 183
  T., 166
  William, 111
HASTON, W. A., 157
HASTWELL, R., 165
HASWELL, D. R., 24
HATCH, Ezra, 109
  George F., 109
  Henry, B., 109
  S., 41
HATCHER, J., 31
  U., 154
HATE, John, 107
HATFIELD, Isaac, 111
HATHAWAY, John, 164
HATTON, D., 190
HAUCK, G. W., 151
  S., 151
HAUGH, J. A., 112
HAUN, Sorellia, 173
HAUSCHUTE, R., 51
  W., 51
HAUSELIN, H. H., 160
HAVDEN, N., 87
HAVEN, P. A., 87
HAVERHILL, Clark, 122
HAWCK, C., 158
HAWK, C., 158
  W. M., 54
HAWKINS, A., 12
  B. M., 61
  Elizabeth A., 126
  H., 168

Henry, 74
J.F., 61
J. H., 61
Samuel Jr., 74, 81
HAWLEY, Lucius E., 89
  Sherman, 59
  T., 145
  T. P., 145
  Thomas T., 67
HAWTHORN, William A., 105
HAY, George, 109
  J. M., 96
  John, 118
  Mary A. 173,
  Walter, 62, 68
  William, 112
HAYDEN C. A., 42, 195
  Charles A., 195
  Josiah, 202
  M., 18
  N., 87
  N. (Capt.), 39
  T., 146
  William H., 202
HAYDIN, ____, (Mr.) & fam. (sic), 167
HAYDON, John 146
HAYES, E. W., 31
  H., 129
  H. O., (death of) (sic), 93
  John, 91
  John F., 79
  W. C., 4, 182
  William C., 30, 182
HAYNARD, J. P., 85
HAYNER, G., 16, 185
HAYNES, A., 200
  A. (Dr.), 40
  Asa, 64 (x), 117, 200
  H., 80
  J. (Dr.), 2
  Jacob, 106
  Jonathan, 40
  Robert W., 203
  S., 191
HAYS, Amhal Jr., 117
  David, 84

E., 100
Edward, 132
H. O. (death of) (sic), 93
J., 104
J. A., 149
J. B., 144
J. W., 145
James C., 152
John H., 168
Thomas, 108
W. B. (sic), 126
William, 104
HAYSEY, A., 109
  S., 109
HAYWARD, A. P., 146
  P. D., 161
HAYWOOD, ____ (Mr.), 141
HAZARD, A. W., 109
  J., 79
HAZELTON, John, 134
HEAD, D. M., 164
  G., 55
  George W., 38
  J. 63
  W. Y., 47
HEADINGTON, David, 114
HEADLEY, James, 91
HEADLY, Thomas (sic), 67
HEAGER, John, 27
HEALY, John (Capt.), 139 (x)
HEARD, Edward, 109
HEARN, Charles, 110
  John, 111
HEART, Joseph P., 103
  William, 150
HEAT, Joseph, 179
HEATH, M. M. (Capt.), 80
  S. & son, 51
  Solimon & son (sic), 78
  Solomon & son (sic), 78
  Solyman & son (sic), 78
HEAZLITT, R. A., 82
HEBBLE, Frank, 178

HECTOR, Kane, 128
HEDRICK, G. W., 129
HEELY, J., 157
HEFRIGHT, F., 148
HEIGHT, Henry, 120
HEILBURN, F. M., 163
HEINZ, John, 15, 184
HEISE (see also HEISS)
  John, 18, 188
HEISKELL, H. B., 60
  T. D., 60
HEISS (see also HEISE)
  John, 18, 188
HEISY, John M., 184,
HEISZ, John, 15, 184
HELBURN, F. M. (sic),
  165
HELCHFIN, John & fam.,
  177
HELCHPIN, John & fam.,
  177
HELDERBRANT, Louis,
  162
HELFENSTEIN, Harrison
  & fam., 156
  J. P. & fam., 156
HELLAN, R. W., 125
HELLIS, George, 105
HELM, H. (Mr.), 3
HELMER, G. W., 165
  J. W., 165
HELMS, James, 82
HEMILY, Frederick, 173
HEMINGWAY, J., 164
HEMMINGWAY, J. (sic),
  164
HEMPREED, John, 82
HENCHBACK, N., 101
HENDERSON, A., 116
  A. J., 105
  A. J. (Dr.), 107
  Adam, 107
  David, 175
  J., 148, 164, 198
  J. B., 18
  James A., 111
  John, 43, 198
  M. J., 175
  Robert, 68

W., 157
W. J., 164, 165
William, 137
William, J. 137
William P., 32
HENDRICKS, H., 6
  J. (Dr.), 46, 198
  J.A. (Dr.), 198
  John M., 82
  S. D., 163
  Samuel E., 112
  William, 6
HENDRICKSON, A. Sr.,
  124
  John, 124
  Robert M., 114
  W.P., 190
HENDRIN, William, 90
HENDRIX, E., (Mrs.) 127
HENDRON, John, 100
HENLEY, Columbus, 117
  John, 7, 113
HENNESSEY, M., 99
HENNESSY, D., 144
HENNESY, M., 99
HENNING, J., 166
HENNINGER, T. F., 166
HENRY, B. E., 51
  C., 143
  C. P., 144
  W., 105, 145
HENTON, J. C., 149
HERALD, John, 65
  Richard, 47
HERBERT, Dwight, 4,
  181
  J. B., 147
  Noble T., 196
HERBST, John E., 16
HERD, E. H. (Capt.), 31
  Lafayette, 66
HERMAN, M., 148
HERMANE, Marshall,
  103
HERMON, John, 99
HERNANDEZ, R. S., 9
HERREL, Royal, 91
HERRICK, Hiram, 111
  M. S., 108

Morris S., 106
HERRIN, Harvey, 111
HERRING, Job, 91
HERROLD, J. & lady, 54
HERRON, A. M., 15
  John (sic), 108
HERRYFORD, S. H., 117
HERSEY, Joshua, 6
HERWOOD, John W.,
  119
HESELP, J., 95
HESLER, Chancy (sic),
  120
HESLEY, Columbus, 106,
  117
HESLIP, A. J., 81
HESS, G. W., 68
HESSLER, George, 118
HESTON, William, 11
HETSLER, H., 100
HEUSTIS, A. J., 64
HEWETS, Michael (sic),
  178
HEWETT, A., 167
  Thomas, 63
HEWIT, R. J. (sic), 163
HEWITT, R. J., 163
  W., 165
HEYS, C. J., 99
HEYWOOD, D. W., 85
  Jonathan, 106
HHILEY, E. H. (sic), 163
HIBBARD, J., 160
  Joseph, 160
HIBBETS, Henderson,
  123
HICE S. Sander (sic), 162
HICKCOX, T. B., 6
HICKEL, H., 90
HICKEN, Edward, 46
  George, 46
HICKERSON, S., 85
HICKNELL, G. W. (Dr.),
  50
HICKOCK,P., 99
HICKOX, Alfred, 109
  Charles D., 121
  Mark, 109
  R. D., 109

HICKS, Charles, 10
    Edward D,, 103
    George D., 101
    J. B., 120
    Samuel R., 203
    T. C., 41
    William, 199
HICKSON, H., 172
HICOCK, Peter, 40
HIDDON, C., 36
HIDE, William, 70
HIDY, William (sic), 114
HIERS, Henry, 107
HIGBEE, Oscar B., 118
HIGGIE, William, 135
HIGGINGS, Benjamin, 103
HIGGINS, E. H., 60
    J. C., 129
    Thomas & Co., 177
HIGGLE, William, 135
HIGGS, Thomas, 126
HIGHTOWER, George, 162
HIGLEY, O. N., 105
HILBERSON, F. M., 158
HILBURN, F. H., 157
    F. M., 158
HILDRETH, Thomas, 74
HILES, L., 148
HILEY, E. H., 163
HILIFANT, E., 188
HILL, A., 34
    A. & fam., 179
    C. F., 144
    D. A., 169
    E. G., 57
    E. P., 8
    H. 113, 124
    Henry, 171
    Isaac, 102, 111
    J. B., 6
    J. O., 31
    J. P., 64
    James, 7, 24
    Jefferson, 126
    John, 71, 99
    Joseph, 116
    L. H., 83

    Leander, 21
    M., 153
    R., 148
    Samuel, 32
    W. J., 156
    Werner, 35
HILLERY, W., 48
HILLIARD, M. M., 148
HILLIS, S., 167
HILLMAN, James, 39, 117
HILLS, Josiah B., 48
HILLYER, Edwin, 44
HILT, ____, (Mr.), 39
HILTON, Hiram, 108
    John H., 47
    T., 166
HILYER, W. D., (sic), 50
    W. D. (Capt.), 113
HIMEBAUCH, Enos, 107
HIMEBAUCK, Henry, 105
HIMEBOUCH, Enos, 107
HIMELMAN, Jacob, 126
HIMROD, David, 98
HINDMAN, David, 47
HINEMAN, William, 45
HINES, Haven, 87
HINKLEY, R., 15
HINMAN, C.M., 203
    Horace, 124
    S., 168
HINSON, ____, (Mr.), 45
HIPES, David, 96
HIRES, H. P., 119
HISEY, J., 42, 197
HITCHCOCK, T. A., 108
HITCHING, J., 30
HITE, David, 6
HITT, W. Y., 75
HIXSON, J. B., 158, 168
HOBBE, George, 25
HOBBIE, William M., 62
HOBBS, Carles (sic), 121
    Charles 121
    Digory (sic), 124
    George 25
    Thomas, 53

HOBBY, David, 15, 184
HOBLITZEE, G. W., 154
HODGDEN, C. (sic), 40
HODGE, H. C., 49
    J. N., 158
    John S., 116
    Justin, 79
    Richard, 49, 162
HODGES, E., 32
HODGINS, George W., 98
HODGKINS, ____, (Mr,), 49
HODLEY, S., 158
HOES, Schuyler, 82
HOFFINER, L, 166
HOFFMAN, A., 81
    Benjamin, 42
    C., 81
    E., 153
    F. H., 84
    Lewis S., 147
    Peter, 27
    W., 42
    W. H., 164
HOFFNER, L., 166
HOGE, John, 30
HOGGARD, H., 172
HOGLE, George, 59
HOGSETT, D. I., 162
    D. J., 176
HOGUS, John, 20, 190
HOHNER, J., 98
HOICE, Timothy, 113
HOKE, S., 42, 196
HOLBROOK, C. D., 134
HOLCOMB, D. H., 57
    O. M., 66
    Oscar N., 66
HOLCOMBE, P. E., 35
HOLDEN, C.,
HOLDENBUCK, V. S., 158
HOLDERBUCK, V. S., 158
HOLDRIDGE, E., 144
HOLDRIGE, E. (sic), 144
HOLEMAN, John, 172
HOLESBERG, G., 90

HOLFEMANY, C., 99
HOLIBAUGH, G. A., 89
HOLIDAY, B. R., 54
   John J., 81
   Samuel N., 81
HOLIFANT, E., 17, 188
HOLLADAY, Jesse, 75
HOLLAN, R. W., 125
HOLLAND, John, 16
   Joshua, 90
   S., 139
   S. M., 23, 192
   W.H., 203
HOLLAWAY, W. A., 116
HOLLENBACK, John, 139
HOLLENBAKE, Obadiah, 123
HOLLENBEC, William W. (sic), 116
HOLLENBECK, J., 118, 150
HOLLEY, C., 158
HOLLINSWORTH, D. (sic), 132
HOLLISTER, D., 164, 166
   T., 164
   T. P., 163
HOLLMAN, John, 171
HOLLY, C. F. (Judge), 74
HOLM, H., 2
HOLMAN, John, 172
HOLMES, C. H., 167
   E., 179
   J., 98, 159
   J. P., 148
   R., 179
HOLOCHAR, B., 89
HOLSTEAD, G. W., 138
   J., 108
   Jerome, 106
HOLSTED, G. W. (sic), 58
HOLT, Calvin, 100
   J., 157
HOLTON, Oscar M., 57
HOLTZWART, J., 190
HOLZMAN, M., 18

HOMER, J., 120
   Norman, 64
HONCELADEN, Joseph, 180
HONNELL, Eli B., 116
   M., 116
HOOD, R. M., 168
   William, 15, 185
HOOK, G. W., 20
   Samuel, 173
   W. H., 150
HOOKE, S., 153
HOOKER, Alvah, 98
HOOPER, E., 42, 195
   Edward, 195
   F., 23
HOOVER, ____,(Mr.), 141
   D., 140
   J., 164, 181, 182
   Jacob Sr., 181, 182
   James, 123
   James A., 23
   John, 95
   Jonathan, 127
   Joshua B., 23
   L. (Dr.) wife & 5 chldrn, 22
   Levi, 141
   Richey D., 140
   S. M., 157
HOP, E. (sic), 163
HOPE, J. P., 148
HOPKINS, ____, (Mrs.), 180
   H., 145
   J. J., 42, 159
   L. H., 148
   R. S., 25
   T. C., 123
   T. M., 168
   W. A., 83
   W. H. H., 150
HOPPS, Henry, 114
HORINE, E., 156
HORN, H. B. & Co., 105
HORNE, George, 19
HORNSON, Robert, 138
HORRISON, James, 109

HORSLEY, W., 136
HORTON, Benjamin T.D.L., 103
   D.C., 197
   David, 43, 197
   J., 144
   J. B., 67
   James, 42
   William, 106
HOSKINS, T. Henry,. 78
HOSLEY, Columbus, 106
HOSSLER, George, 118
   W. B., 154
HOTSOFF, E. B., 143
HOTSPILLER, Jacob, 109
HOTTON, John, 172
HOTUS, Jeremiah, 20
HOUCK, D., 19, 188
   Enos, 151
   John, 151
HOUGH, A. J., 86, 204
   Clark A., 67
   D., 188
   J. F., 82
   J. W., 148
   James A., 204
   M. J., 143
   N., 148
   P. Y., 2
   R., 54
   S., 41, 194
   Samuel, 174
   Silas, 194
   Warren, 110
HOUGHTON, ____, 91
   Howard, 117
HOUK, Samuel, 173
HOUSE, D., 144
   I. G., 80
HOUSER, A. J., 131
HOUSTON, G. W. (Mr.), 40
   Lemuel, 121
   R. G. C., 157
   Robert, 3
   Samuel (Dr.), 121
HOW, James B. (sic), 41, 193
HOWARD, ____, 53

A. S., 64
Alonzo, 131
Austin, S., 59
C., 60
Clarinda, 64
F. A., 122
H. E., 113
Homer, 64
J. B., 122
J. H., 63
J. W., 66 (x)
James, 59
Joseph, 37, 38
Milly, 162
Nancy, 64
O., 143
O. P., 130
P. D., 160
Rachel, 64
Samuel, 117
W., 148 (x), 150
William B., 15, 185
HOWE, J. B., 26, 193
  John M., 141
  L., 148
  Philenus, 44
  William, 118
HOWEE, J. C. (sic), 153
HOWEL, J. H. (sic), 54
  William M., 54
HOWELL, D. R., 154
  E. P. (Mr.), 70 (x)
  G. D., 133
  H., 61
  J. H., 54
  J. J., 70
  John, 21, 57
  William M., 54
HOWES, B. L., 148
  William, 203
HOWK, C., 156, 158
HOWLAND, A., 150
  C. W., 150
  L. S., (Miss), 139
HOXIE, ____, (Dr.), 121
HOY, A. B. (Dr.), 52
  J., 31
HOYT, E. R. (Dr.) &
  fam., 21

F. A., 85
J. K., 159
J. P., 40
John P., 82, 83
S. F., 194
S. Y., 38, 194
W., 59
HROUTY, A. T., 162
HUBBARD, ____, 172
  Allen, 35
  Ansel & 5 others, 180
  D., 37, 181
  G. W., 71
  J. M., 146
  Jedidiah, 117
  L., 167
  R. B., 150
  William T., 102
  Winslow, 84
HUBBELL, ____, 115
  J. G., 36, 194
  James Gale, 194
  N. B., 166
HUBER, C., 35
HUBERMANN, ____,
  35
HUCK, J. C., 148
HUDSON, G. H. & fam.,
  178
  H., 166
  I. H. & fam., 178
  J. H. & fam., 178
  James M., 112
  John, 41
  K. B., 153
  N., 15, 184
HUEY, Catharine, 119
HUFF, James, 107
  L. B., 46
  S., 46
  W. P., 121
HUFFIN, Andrew, 105
HUFFMAN, Augustus,
  109
  Chauncey, 110
HUGANIN, V. E., 135
HUGHES, Charleston, 90
  E., 112
  F. H., 119

George, 70
H. R., 168
J., 17, 191
J. L., 116
J. L. (Mr.), 115
James, 134
John, 19, 40, 152, 156,
  191
K. C., 149
R. T., 116
Thomas, 39, 89
W., 18
W. O., 162
William, 89
HUGHEY, D., 18
HUGHS, A., 203
  F. H., 119
  J., 190
  John, 54
  K. C., 149
HUGHSON, E. L., 82
HUGILL, G., 157
HUGUNIN, V. E., 135
HULBERT, Nathaniel, 200
  S. A., 153
HULE, ____, (Dr.) &
  lady, 80
  J. B., 80
HULL, A., 156, 163
  E., 99
  H. & fam., 154
  John, 119
  James, 15, 184
  Nathan, 203
  Philip, 57
HULLER, R. (sic), 154
HULSE, S. B., 102
HULTZ, James, 102
HUME, ____, (Mr.), 134
  Andrew, 14
HUMMELL, Jacob, 43
HUMMER, J. J., 119
  John, 6
  Levi, 6
HUMPHREY, James M.,
  106 (x)
HUMPHREYS, A. A., 60
  J. M., 32
  J. T., 42, 195, 196

Joseph D. (Dr.), 196
L. H., 83
HUMPHRIES, J. Thomas, 195
HUNADEN, J. H., 111
HUNKER, J., 17, 187
HUNNKER, J., 187
HUNSDEN, J. H., 111
HUNT, Abijah, 203
  Ann E., 161
  B. T., 149
  C. A., 2
  Daniel, 124
  J. C., 52
  John, 38, 120
  Joseph, 203
  W., 127
HUNTER, Benjamin F. & fam., 20
  Edward E., 81
  J., 17
  John A., 82
  Jonah, 81
  Joseph, 88
  Joseph (death of) 94
  L. & fam., 180
  Samuel, 12
  William & fam., 180
HUNTINGTON, John, 68
  William, 23
HUNTSMAN, Charles R., 123
  Lorenzo D., 123
HUPP, S., 51
HURBBIRT, S. (sic) 153
HURBURT, H. M., 9
HURD, Edward, 29
  J. B., 81
  James K., 131
  O. & wife, 139
HURFF, D., 52
HURLBIRT, S., 153
HURLBURT, A. W., 115
  J. W., 6
  S. V., 137
HURLBUT, Egbert R., 105
  Nath., 64, 200
HURLEY, A. D., 120

C., 63
E. D., 63
J., 7
John, 115
HURRELL, William, 91
HURST, _____, (Mr.), 155
  Joseph, 83
  S., 83
  S. W., 83
HURVEY, Thomas C., 84
HUSE, D., 146
HUSS, P., 163
HUSTIN, H., 107
HUSTON, Lemuel, 121
  Samuel (Dr.), 121
  William, 11
HUTCHERSON, G., 51
HUTCHINGS, James M., 82
HUTCHINSON. G., 51
  G. W., 117
  R., 1
  S. F., 163
  Thomas, 90
  W. H., 80
HUTCHISON, G. W., 117
  John, 88
HUTTON, B., 19, 190
  C. C., 52
  William, 105
HUTZEL, John & fam., 177
HUYETT, J., 17
HYATT, _____, (Mr.), fam., & nephew, 160
HYD, H., 139
HYDE, H., 139
  Stephen, 82
  W. W., 37
HYERS, Henry, 107
HYMER, E., 107
  J. B., 107
HYNARD, J. P. (sic), 85

-I-

IARDELLA, L. A., 48

IBERTSON, George, 106
IGNITE, J. G., 128
IGRAM, John, 151
ILLINGSWORTH, _____, (Mr.), 125
ILLINSKI, A. X. (Dr.), 20
INDER, J., 144
ING, A.W., 187
  E.C., 187
INGALABEE., C.L., 194
INGALLS, A., 144
  J. D., 150
  L., 150
  T., 150
INGERSOL, James (sic), 50
  Theodore (sic), 65
INGERSOLL, A., 152
  C., 21
  E., 152
  E. P., 56
INGHAM, F., 98
INGRAM, A., 17
  C., 61
  J. H., 31
  John, 151
  W. J., 17
INGROVE, E., 147
INMAN, Anthony, 6
  H. H., 67
  Israel, 67
  L., 108
  P. H., 67
INNMAN, Andrew, 91
  Daniel, 91
  John, 91
INMANN, P. H., 67
INSHEE, W., 157
IRELAND, _____, 91
  A. S., 111
  M. C., 161
IRTS, Israel & fam., 179
IRVINE, B., 55
IRWIN, J. P., 18
  James, 30, 117
  James A., 18
  John, 116
  Richard, 56
  Mille (Mrs.) (sic), 175

Willaim, 102
IRVINE, John, 137
IRYMIRE, T. W., 162
ISGNIGG, W. L., 29
ISHAM, G. S., 22
  Joseph, 91
  S., 150
  Susan, 22
ISNIGG, W. L., 29
ISRAEL, S. G., 36
IVES, N. M., 90
  William, 99

J-

JABLONSKI, J., 190
JACK, A., 70
  A. J., 18
  J., 18
  L. C., 70
JACKS, W. S., 57
JACKSON, Andrew, 26
  Benjamin, 109
  Edward, 204
  G., 30
  H., 163
  H. D., 144
  Isaac, 137
  J., 60, 164
  James, 47
  John, 82
  Kendall, 137
  M., 153,
  Mathew (sic), 151
  Peter, 90
  Robert, 4
  S., 156
  Samuel, 84
  W., P., 9
  W. T., 74
  William, 59, 155, 175
JACKWAY, James, 123
JACOBS, A., 83
  A. B., 146
  Charles, 27
  George W., 27
  Hiram, 45
  John D., 48

Owen W., 97
R., 18
William, 160
JACOBSON, ____, 37
JACOBUS, E., 131
JAGGER, Daniel, 89
JAGUES, B. H ., 180
JAMES, B. J., 163
  F., 148
  F. M., 148
  H., 70
  J., 51
  James Jr. (sic), 105
JAMESON, D., 140
  R., 144
  Robert, 64
JAMISON, W. (Rev.), 127
  Robert, 57
JAMWER, A. C. S., 157
JANES, ALEX, 170
  Mary (Mrs.), 170
JANSON, J. T., 147
JANUARY, Ephr. (Sen.), 71
  Ephraim P., 71
JAQUES, B. H., 180
  Joseph, 134
JARROT, Vital, 20
JARVIS, C. B., 108
JAY, Alonzo, 108
JAYNES, Samuel, 187
JEANING, S. S., 146
JEDSON, J. J., 172
JEFFEN, H., 164
JEFFERSON, B. F., 165
  D., 12
  J., 165
  J. M., 165
JEFFERY, A., 166
JEFFREY, J., 154
JEFFREYS, W. P., 28, 51
JEFFRIES, Andrew J., 114
  James W., 111
JEFFRY, J. (sic), 154
JEHUS, D. D., 147
JENKINS, ____, 6
  R., 145

JENKS, C. F., 13
  G. D., 118
  O. A., 102
JENNETT, Moses C., 84
  Robert, S., 10
JENNING, S. S., 146
JENNINGS, Amanda, 171
  H. M., 12
  J. H., 105
  J. J., 156
  J. S., 158
  O., 9
  R. F., 84
  Samuel, 14
  W. C., 164
  William, 33
  William C., 140
JEPTHA, ____, 110
JEPTHS, ____, 110
JEROHNEN, A., 10, 183
JEROME, ____, (Mr.), 97
JESSUP, John E., 122
JETMORE, S., 150
JEWELL, W. Jr., 48
JEWETT, C., 153
  G. E., 63
  George E., 59
  Henry, 100
  James R., 100
  M., 99
JEWITT, Charles, 117
JINKIN, Matthew J., 103
JINKINS, ____, (Mr.) & (Mrs.) (sic), 76
JOBES, A., 10, 183
  Ashfield, 183
JOBLAUSKI, ____, 19, 190
JOBLING, L. H., 166
JOHN, B., 38, 194
  Jones (sic), 99
  Robert, 6
JOHNS, B., 194
  E., 54
JOHNSON, ____, (Col.), 159
  ____ (Mr.), 24, 71
  ____ (Mrs.) & fam of

6 chldrn, 180
A., 41, 151
A. (Mr.), 3
A. T., 163
Alexander, 128 (x)
Andrew, 203
Asbury, 29
C., 46, 198
C. & brother, 20, 191(x)
C. D., 149
C.M., 119
C.M. (Colonel), 40
Charles, 59, 85
Clark, 132
Cyrenius, 198
D.C., 127
E.A., 121
Edward, 30
Edward L., 105
Francis, 146
G., 191
G. W., 152
H., 10, 183, 191
H.F., 191
H. T. (death of), 94
Harvey, 146
Henry, 29, 106
Henry L., 183
Isaac, 85
J., 20, 144 (x), 191
J. (Mr.), 3
J. A., 1
J. L. F., 18
J. N., 47
J. R., 18, 36,
J. W., 157
James, 54, 85, 125, 143
John, 12, 27, 29, 100
Knight, 132
Lemuel, 44
Lewis, 49
M. O., 158
P. N., 13
P. P., 31
Peter, 110
Philip, 44, 45
Porter & fam., 179
R., 41
Richard, 132

S., 11
S. T., 32
Sam, 46, 75, 76 (x)
Samuel, 88
Simeon H., 112
Thomas, 107
Timothy, 86
W., 18, 141
W. B., 146
W. M., 153
W.W. 152
Walter & Co., 117
William J. W., 110
Zach. L., 162
JOHNSTON, B. A., 158
  Epaminondas, 86
  F. G., 120
  J., 60, 61
  M. B., 80
  S. J., 60, 61
  W. G., 6
  W. M., 174
  William, 121, 138
JOHNSTONE, W. (sic), 128
JOLIFF, G., 131
JOLLY, David, 121
  William, 121
JONAS, S., 146
JONEDAY, Maria, 175
JONES, ____ (Mr.), 154
  ____, (Mr.) & Co. 97
  A., 9, 164
  A. S., 15, 56
  Augustus, 105, 110
  Augustus Jr., 98
  Barry, 36, 194
  Berry, 194
  Dan. (Capt.), 62
  David, 105
  E. E., 166
  E. H., 51
  Elizabeth (Miss), 58
  F., 84
  F. A., 31
  G. H., 29
  G. W., 15, 185
  George, 117
  Gustavus, 120

  Heath, 81
  J., 156, 160, 163, 167
  J. A. Z., 36
  J. E. S., 51
  J. F., 84
  J. M., 83, 136
  J. S., 166
  J. W., 46, 139, 156
  Jackson, 81
  James, 18, 102, 111
  James P., 121
  John, 81, 99, 122
  John Jr., 82
  L. C., 166
  L. D., 157
  Livingston, 136
  Mathias, 126
  Orville, 65
  Russel (sic), 177
  S., 9
  S. E. (Capt.), 139
  S. E. (Mr.), 154
  S. T., 3
  Stephen, 81, 201, 202
  T., 17
  Taylor, 81
  Theodore, 117
  Thomas, 54
  Thompson, 102, 111
  W., 145
  W. A., 178
  W. F., 59
  W. J. (Dr.), 144
  William, 60, 67, 99, 106, 122
  William Jr., 102, 111
  William A., 48
  William E., 103
  Z., 99
JOPHEBE, R., 168
JOPHEHE, R., 168
JORALEMON, Abraham, 183
JORDAN, Alfred, 137
  Ann Maria, 127
  Charles H., 90
  G. W., 127
  H., 22, 192
  Hugh, 192

J. L., 104
James, 92
Moses, 90
R. G., 104
William, 129
JORDON, Ann Maria, 127
G. W., 127
JOURNEY, Peter, 91
JOY, A., wife & 3 chldrn, 159
Alonzo, 108
JOYCE, J., 17
William W., 84
JUCE, H., 110
J. S., 110
Luther, 110
JUDD, A., 151
Oscar, 136, 159
William B., 99
JUDSON, John, 159
JUDY, Jacob (Maj.) & bro., 122
JUILETT, C., 163
JULIAN, H., 63
John S., 68
JULLET, C., 163
JUSTICE, ____, (Mr.), 156
JUSTICE, A., 166, 167, 168
F. M., 102
W., 166
JUSTIRE, John, 91

-K-

K'HLER, Peter, 90
KAEMIES, Gottlieb, 92
KAHE, Owen, 116
KAHO, Owen, 116
KALLENBACK, Peter, 146
KALLER, F., 35
KALLUM, H. F., 167
KAMMERER, B. W., 168
KAMP, B., wife & 8 chldrn, 26

KANE, Charles, 15, 184
D., 109
J., 150
James, 17
L., 150
M., Jr., 17 (x), 186
Olonzo, 173
P., 17
KANNATTE, J., 157
KANOUSE, J. Alfred, 82
KARNEY, Stephen H., 101
KARR, J., 115
KASER, William, 119
KATES, J. P., 150
KATZ, Henry, 129
KATZLER, Fred, 65
KAUFMAN, D., 160
KAY, J. M., 56
KAYE, F. A., Jr., 11
John, 11
KAYS, F. Frances, 176
Francis, 162
KEALY, Thomas, 69
KEAN, E., 2
J., 2, 165
Sarah Ann, 162
Sarah Anne, 176
KEARNER, JACOB, 101
KEARNES, J., 18, 188
KEARNEY, J., 159
James, 102
P., 139
KEARNS, J., 188
John, 11
KEARNY, P. K., 160
KEATH, Samuel, 43
KEATING, J. M., 137, 165
KEE, W. E. W., 147
KEEFER, Frank, 133
Geroge, 133
J. L., 6
Samuel, 133
KEEGAN, T., 163
KEELING, Eldridge, 56
R. H., 42, 195
Robert H., 195
KEENAN, ____, 95

KEENE, R. A., 146
KEENER, George, 97
Henry, 92
KEFNER, Henry, 121
KEIFER, S. M., 42
S.N., 197
KEIFFER, James, 110
KEIM, Paul, 203
KEINER, Henry, 121
KEITH, Elisha, 106
J., 52
Joseph, 106
Peter, 106
KELL, James, 30
KELLAND, Robert H., 41, 195
KELLER, ____, 20, 191
Anton, 68
D. P., 30
Edward, 45
F., 35
John, wife & 5 chldrn, 22
S., 191
KELLEY, J. D., 149
Jacob, 107
John, 180
M., 180
P., 83
W., 167
KELLOG, A., 3
KELLOGG, A., 72
Edw., 65
F. S., 64, 65
Hiram, 59
O. E., 60
William, 65
KELLUM, H. F., 167
KELLY, A. J., 130
G. W., 103
J., 35, 151
J. Harrison, 42
James, 139
James K., 79
John, 160, 180
M., 150, 157, 180
Mathew, 129
Samuel, 82, 101
T., 49

William A. (Dr.), 79
William D. & bro., 178
KELLYHAN, Nicholas, 100
KELS, John, 112
KELSEY, A., 32
C. M., 51
E., 59
Erastus, 66
G. W., 51
KELSLE, O., 167
KELSLEY, O., 167
KEMP, C. L., 96
D., 42
Francis D., 169
J. B., 97
KENDALL, David, 119
A. F., 49, 199
Finton, 199
G., 16, 185
James, 185
Lorenzo, 2
Theodore, 109
Y. L., 59
KENDRICK, G. S., 157
Duke W., 149
Levi B., 149
KENEPLEY, P., 145
KENK, A. N., 16, 185
KENLY, Thomas, 69
KENNARD, M., 91
Stephen, 91
KENNEDY, A. F., 163
A. H., 153
Hiram, 137
J., 49
J. M., 166
John, 104
Joseph C., 5
Samuel S., 111
T. B., 5
KENNEN, Phillip, 138
KENNEY, G. W., 167
KENT, A., 99
G. E., 99
George, 127
George W., 136
Horace A., 110
R. D., 90

S., 32
KENTON, E. W., 158
KEPHART, George & fam., 178
KERCHEVAL, A. F., 30
KERME, Francis M., 41
KERN, M., 63
KERR, Henry, 97
J., 18
J. M., 36
John F., 112
W. (Mr.), 3
KESER, William, 119
KESSLER, Frederick, 109
Peter, 92, 93
KETCHUM, William & fam., 178 (x)
KETNER, Henry, 121
KETZLER, Fred, 65
KEYES, J., 163
L., 109
Leander, 105
KEYS, William N., 68
KIBBE, R. (Dr.), & fam., 160
KIDD, A. E., 150
KIDDER, John, 99
Joseph, 99
L. L., 99
KIDWELL, M. A., 13
KIEFER, J., 147
Jacob, 134
KIEN, G. O., 135
J. H., 135
KIERNAN, James, 9
KILBOIN, ____, (Mr.), 54
KILBOURNE, Lewis, 99
KILLBORNE, R. & Co., 104
KILLEN, John, 56
KILLER, T. A., 67
KILLINGSWORTH, J., 84
KILPATRICK, David, 91
KIM, G. O., 135
J. H., 135
KIMBALL, ____, 26, 193

____, (Mrs.), 164
Erastus, 45
J., 150
James, 54
Marvin, 103, 107
Oliver, 91
Robert, 200
Sheridan, 41, 193
T. A., 150
Thomas, 127
William, 165
William F., 50
KIMBELL, James (sic), 54
KIMBERLY, ____, (Dr.), 87
E., 87
H., 184
N. C., 101
KIMBLE, A., 99
Charles, 100
L., 15, 184
R. C., 98
Robert (sic), 64, 200
Thomas V., 41
KIMDERLIN, John, 112
KIMERER, J., 131
M., 131
KIMMER, Henry, 22
KINAN, W. H. (sic), 148
KINCAID, C., 6
KINCAIDE, Oliver, 101
KINCANNON, W. R., 153
KINCHLOES, E. & fam., 143
KINDAR, John T., 176
Lydia, 176
William, 176
KINESBURY, T. P., 48
KING, ____, 20, 41, 93
B. F., 57
B. G. (Dr.), 81
B. L., 65, 66 (x)
B. L. (Dr.), 60, 133
C., 39
E., 79
E. A., 42, 197
E. H., 98

E. W., 103
G. B., 67
G.W. 98
Henry, 32
Isaac J., 112
J., 52
J. (Mr.), 3
J. F., 99
James A., 117, 120
John, A., 102
John D., 38
John T., 122
Joseph (death of), 93
L., 144
L. Jr., 106, 108
Leicester Jr., 102
Philip & fam., 180
R., 158
Richard, 173
Samuel B., 106
Thomas T., 9
W., 158
KINGMAN, E. W., 139
KINGORY, S. S., 164
KINGSBURY, J., 117
J. H., 166
S., 51
William, 117
KINGSLEY, H., 15, 184
Henry, 184
Orrin, 203
KINMAN, Seth, 136
KINNAN, Phillip, 138
KINNEAR, A. V., 22, 192
KINNEN, Phillip, 138
KINNEY, F., 27
George & lady, 133
Patrick, 27
William D., 10
KINNINGSWORTH, J., 84
KINSELY, B. F., 42, 196
KINSEY, A. G. (Mr.), 3
C., 52
David, 3
P. W., 13
KINZELL, Z., 90
KINZENBACH, G., 5
KIRBY, B., 99

D., 99
D. S., 150
Edward, 162, 176
J. B., 175
KIRK, J., 148
M. J., 9
Mary J., 175
P., 127
Robert J., 106
KIRKLAND, C. T., 19
KIRKPATRICK, _____,
(Mr.) & lady, 161
J. S., 67
James, 88
P.W., 202
T. A., 54
KIRKWOOD, _____,
(Mr.), 73
James, 46
R. 20, 191
KIRLAND, George, 5
KIRTLAND, Samuel, 118
KISER, J., 19
KISNER, A., 101
KISS, G. O., 135
J. H., 135
KITTREDGE, Edward L., 78
KIZER, George, 115
KLADY, Samuel, 137
William E., 137
KLANBERY, Daniel, 66
KLAUBERY, Daniel, 66
KLEECHER, F. B., 119
KLEECKER, F. B., 105
KLEIN, J ., 50
KLEY, C. P., 158
KLINE, George, 154
KLING, D., 61
E., 61
KLOPPENBURGH, D., 36
KLUMP, _____, 35
KNAPP, A.R., 198
Albert & lady, 113
Cornelius, 106
J. T., 126
Spencer, 147
W. W., 28, 53

KNEAR, William, 119
KNEEDLER, C. D., 150
G. W., 150
KNIDER, J. P., 166
KNIGHT, Charles, 136
George, 120
James F., 106
John, 106
Joseph, 35
Josiah M., 62, 63, 127
N., 58
Seymore, 58,
Walter, 140
KNISELY, B.F., 196
KNOCKE, E., 168
KNODE, À. B., 3
KNOTT, John M., 119
T., 167
KNOUER, C., 35
KNOWER, Eli, 21
Elk, 21
KNOWLAND, J., 17, 187
L., 187
KNOWLTON, J., 151
Levi, 109
W. B., 151
KNOX, G. W., 132
J., 164
James J., 11
M., 153
M. & wife, 164
P., 164
Shannon, 90
William F., 47
KOHL, A. Maria, 161
KOONTZ, Baltzer, 131
KOPF, V., 35
KOPPELMAN, H., 154
KRAMER, F., 35
KRAUSZ, George, 36
KREINER, J., 43, 197
KRENGEL, J. W., 147
KREPPS, B. G., 56
KRIDER, Levi, 99
KROBE, Frederick, 47
KROHE, Frederick 47
KRUMM, J., 88
KRYTZER, John, 100

KUGEHT, Francis, 159
KUNG, J. B., 166
KUNTZ, J. W., 51
KURTZ, Charles, 38
KYLE, H. T., 79
   R. G., 84
   Thomas, 26
KYLES, Andrew, 108
KYNION, H., 99

-L-

LACEY, G. O., 100
   H. C., 100
   R. J., 103
LACK, B., 83
LACKEY, C. D., 68
   John, 100
LACKORE, T. W., 106
LACY, E. & 2 partners, 179
LADEW, James, 27
LAFORCE, William, 150
   William P., 150
LaFOUNTAIN, Lewis, 60
LaFOUNTAIN, Lewis, 66 (x)
LAGRANGE, C. C., 2
LAGRAVE, C. A., 138
LAIDSY, J. (sic), 63
LAIRD, Michael, 45
   S., 158, 167
LAKE, D. C., 82
   D. J., 153
   J., 82
   John, 65
LAKUE, J. W. & Co., 117
LALAND, Andrew, 151
   John, 151
LALLY, Edward, 102
LAMARR, E., 168
LAMB, Charles, 9
   F. A., 8
   James C., 173
   Joseph, 106
   Mary E., 173
   W. H., 110
   William, 100

LAMBDIN, W. McK. 25
LAMBERT, Henry, 147
   J. S., 32
   John, 147
LAMFEAR, George W., 106
LAMFORD, H. L., 83
LAMM, F. J., 60
LAMPER, B. F., 148
   G. R.. 148
LAMPHERE, Judson, 102
LAMPTON, J., 157, 168
LAMRESTER, M. F., 149
LAN, James M., 146
LANCASTER, ____, (Mr.), 56
   G. W., 174
   J. P., 91
   Jerry, 76
LAND, J. (death of), 94
   T., 157
LANDER, August, 146
   James M., 146
LANDON, G. H., 111
LANDROW, L. W., 31
LANDRUM, J. J., 129
LANDSDALE, ____, (Dr.), 44
LANE, A. F., 14
   N. & lady, 157
   P., 91
   R., 51
LANG, J. F., 157
   L., 157
LANGCORD, ____, (Col.), 175
LANGDON, William, 63
LANGE, Joseph, 1
   N., 35
LANGEMAN, J., 12
LANGFORD, L. F., 65
LANGLEY, Henry C., 85
   Joseph, 172
LANGSTON, Martha, 162, 175
LANGTON, J. A., 59
LANGWELL, C., 162
LANIER, R., 84
LANKCORD, ____,

(Col.), 175
LANKEORD, ____, (Col.), 175
LANSDALE, ____, (Mr.), 46
LANSDEN, R. K., 156
LANSFORD, T. A. (Mr.), 60
LANSFORERD, T. A. (Mr.), 60
LANWEISTER, F. W., 80
LAPHAM, E. (Dr.), 192
   Edmund, 192
   Edward, 22, 192
   Ephraim, 22, 192
LAPORT, L., 158
LARABEE, George W., 29
   Henry, 29
LARAMER, J. (sic), 148
   W., 148
LARDNER, G. W., 145
LAREBEE, George W., 29
   Henry, 29
LARIMORE, G.W. (sic), 181, 182
   J., 182
LARIPER, ____, (Mr.), 141
LARISON, William, 82
LARK, John, 83
LARKE, ____, (Capt), 202
LARKIN, Aaron, 64, 200
LARROWAY, Jonas, 87
LASAK, E. F., 85
LASOLETT, C., 165
LASSELLE, S. (Capt.), 83
LASTLEY, J., 61
LASTON, J., 163
LATHAM, Charles C., 115
   H. A., 19, 191
   H.S., 191
   Ira, 58, 65
   James, 123
   W. R., 19, 189
LATHIAN, P. (sic), 190

LATHROP, Levi L., 110
  Malinda & 8 chldrn, 179
  William B., 110
LATIMER, ____, 109
LATIMORE, G.W. (SIC), 182
  J., 181, 182
LATSHAW, B. T., 17
  J. Jr., 18
LAUGH, Thomas, 137
LAUGHLIN, J. O., 143
  James & fam., 171
  L., 1
LAURY, William, 5
LAUZ, R C., 166
LAVIDGE, R., 31
LAW, M., 146
LAWKIN, John, 146
LAWRENCE, Charles A., 107
  George, (sic), 203
  Jasper H., 91
  John, 65
  S. K., 91
  William, 27
  Willaim D. 37
  William L., 107
LAWRENS, George, 203
LAWS, O. C., 166
LAWSON, Benjamin, 58
  Thomas, 107
  William, 86
LAWTON, David, 137, 165
  Robert T., 119
LAY, P. J., 158
  S. E., 143
LAYMAN, Israel D., 178
  J., 20, 190
LAYTHAM, James (sic), 123
LAYTON, J. W. (Dr.), 150
LEA, David T. & 2 others, 180
  E., 168
  J., 157
LEACH, J., 23, 192

M., 91
LEAHE, J. J., 84
LEARIGHT, Alex, 83
  William, 83
LEASE, George M., 136
  John (Dr.), 117
  T. T., 95
LEATHERS, G H., 163
LEAVITT, J. H., 99
  James, 66
LEBAUGH, H., 129
LECKEY, J., 17, 187
LECKY, J., 187
LECOMPTE, M., 20
LEDGERWOOD, ____(Mr.), 202
LEE, A., 163
  C., 137, 165
  G. H., 67
  H. G., 89
  Hugh, 23, 104, 192
  Hugh (Colonel), 192
  J., 148
  J. M., 89
  James, 162
  James C., 11
  Joseph & lady, 54
  Lemuel, 95
  Levi, 172
  P., 148 (x)
  R., 148
  Robert, 46, 71
  S. A., 153
  W. G., 72
  William, 128
LEECH, ____ (Mr.), 97
LEEDS, Ellis, N., 81
LEEK, S. J., 104
LEELAND, Charles (sic), 121
LEER, W., 61
LEESE, George M., 136
  John (Dr.), 117
LEFFLER, Hugh M., 107
  Jacob, 90
  Richard, 107
  W., 43
LeFOLLETT, D. D., 108
LEGG, Lewis, 81

LEGGET, James, 161
  John, 161
LEHMAN, J., 190
LEIB, Daniel, 114
LEIHEST, G., 147
LEILEUR, A., 191
LELAND, Andrew, 151
  C. M., 8
  Charles, 121
  George, 109
  John, 151
LELLEUR, A., 191
LEMEN, J. N., 158
LEMMON, B., 144
  J., 188
  J. N., 158
LEMMONS, Aaron, 107
LEMNO, N. B., 149
LEMOIN, Reuben E., 98
LEMOINE, R. E., 106
LEMON, Adams W., 114
  G., 19, 188
  George, 105
  J. B., 13
  J. N., 158
  James, 13
  N. B., 149
LENARD, B. F. (sic), 139
LENNEN, John P., 112
LENSDEN, R. K., 156
LENT, C., 17, 188
  John, 97
LEONARD, B., 165
  B. F., 139
  Charles, 110
  Charles Jr., 106
LEONARDSON, J. C., 50
LEPPER, Phillip, 106
LERNIS, E. W., 147
LESTER, Lewis, 29
LETS, Jeremiah, 87
LETTER, G., 181
  G.W. (Mr.), 181
LETTS, Jeremiah, 87
LEUT, C., 188
LEVAN, D. W., 167
LEVERIDGE, Alfred C., 116
LEVERING, J. H., 3, 181

LEVI, D. & Co., 177
LEVY, Harrison, 79
  J. W., 129
LEWELLIN, Thomas L., 146
LEWIS, ____, (Mr.), 71
  A., 22
  C., 150, 190
  C. W., 13
  Charles, 151
  D. J., 144
  David, 170, 172
  David C., 117
  Evan, 40
  F., 109
  F. B., 110
  H., 150
  H. H., 63
  H. J., 109, 110
  Henry, 178
  Homer, 117
  J. E. N., 42, 195
  J. P., 40, 148
  J. S., 65
  James, 10, 183
  James, Jr., 183
  John, 25, 46
  John S., 42, 58, 196
  Joseph E.N., 195
  Lewis (sic), 34
  M., 63, 191
  M. R., 143
  P. D., 105
  P. T., 52
  Philip, 114
  S., 63, 108, 196
  S. D., 48
  Samuel, 127
  William, 99
LICE, Q., 166
LIDDELL, ____, 83
LIDDY, ____, (Mr.), 55
LIEDT, B., 170
LIESER, ____, (Mr.), 87
LIGGET, Enoch, 170
LIGGETT, A. J., 28
LIGHT, George W., 45
LIGHTER, H. L., 164
LIGHTFOOT, Robert, 54

LIGHTNER, C. W., 81
LILES, R., 8
LILL, C. F., 144
LILLARD, J. J., 149
LILLARS, James, 55
LILLIE, George, 99
LIM, Daniel, 92
LINCBECK, Peter (sic), 110
LINCH, C. E., 158
LINCK, C. E. (sic), 153
LINDBECK, Peter, 110
LINDERMAN, John, 198
LINDLE, D. & Co., 178
LINDSAY, Charles R., 110
  J., 23, 192
  John, 192
  L., 92
  R. S., 111
  William, 111
LINDSEY, T., 13
LINDSTRAM, Paul, 105
LINDSTROM, Paul, 105
LINK, C. E., 163
LINKS, C. E., 144
LINN, C. H., 146
  Daniel, 92
  J. J., 146
LINSLEY, Charles, 59
LINTON, S. B., 144
LINZEE, B. N., 136
  E. N., 136
  Jacob (sic), 136
  L. N., 136
LIONBERGER, D., 52
LIONS, John, 91
LIPPENCOTT, J., 162
LISCOM, Charles, 78
LISK, Myron, 203
LITEUT, B., 170
LITMAN, A. M., 17
LITTER, G. W. (Mr.), 3
LITTICK, I., 55
LITTLE, Andrew, 123
  Herman, 121
  J., 150
  P., 178
  S. H., 150

LITTLEFIELD, D. C., 162
LIVERMORE, James, 97
  T. A., wife & fam., 54
LLOYD, W. W., 48
LOACH, J., 23, 192
LOCK, D., 166
  E., 42, 195
  Elisha, 195
  J., 61, 81
  T., 190
  Thomas, 19, 190
LOCKE, Dean Jewett, 204
  E. T., 90
  R. P., lady & child, 166
LOCKER, L. W., 124
LOCKHART, James, 82
LOCKHEART, James (sic), 82
LOCKMAN, Isaac, 203
LOCKWOOD, B., 100
LODEWICK, Peter, 82
LOEHR, Thomas H., 109
LOFF, Thomas, 30
LOFFLISS, James, 126
LOFLAND, William 88
LOFOLETT, H., 165
LOGAN, Robert, 105
  William, 55, 174
LOHANAN, A. S., 148
LOLAS, John (sic), 175
LOME, Eli, 147
LONE, J. S. (Major), 12
LONG, ____, (Mr.), 151, 165
  A. D., 137
  C. (Mr.), 3
  Ferman, 113
  H. S., 3
  J., 61, 172
  J. F., 157
  John (sic), 41
  John, 130
  L., 157
  R., 164
  R. W., 67
  Robert, 141
  W. B., 61
LONGENECKER, John

(Dr.), 42
LONGMIRE, John, 63
LONGWELL, J., 20, 190
LONGWORTH, George, 106
LOOFBOURROW, David, 115
LOOMIS, A. J., 56, 116
  Abner, 119
  Andrew, 118
  Edward, 136
  Leander V., 116
  T. L., 43
LORD, Bracket, 86, 204
  Brackett, 204
  Edwin Harvey, 117
LOREE, Samuel (sic), 38
LORING, J. M., 53
  Nathaniel B., 204
  Philip, 53
  W. A., 48
LORR, Charles, 151
  Martin, 151
LOSHMET, A., 107
  Elias, 107
LOT, J., 179
LOTHROP, J., 104
  Newell, 161
LOTT, J. J., 85
LOTTIM, Peter, 20, 190
LOUCK, J., 192
  John B., 23, 192
LOUDERBACK, Daniel, 106
LOUGE, Joseph, 1
LOUIS, M., 19, 191
LOUSE John (Dr.), 117
LOVE, _____ (Mr.), 71
  J., 160
  Samuel, 67, 75
  Samuel E., 77
LOVEL, Ed (sic), 128
  Erastus (sic), 128
LOVELAND, H., 41
  Henry, 1
LOVELL, Ed., 128
  Erastus, 128
LOVELY, James, 133
LOVING, James, 148

LOW, James, 136
LOWDERMILK, A., 128
LOWE, Byron N., 103, 108
  J., 166
LOWERY, Elisha, 41, 193
  G., 197
  G. W., 142
LOWRY, Amelia, 119
  D. H., 119
  D. H. (see also David Lowry)
  David (sic) 118
  (see also D. H. LOWRY)
  E. (sic), 26, 193
LOYD, Joseph, 127
LUCA, T. M., 164
LUCAS, B. D., 71
  G., 157
  S., 63
  Samuel, 59
LUCE, Delos, 180
  E., 166
  Lyman, 16, 185
LUCK, Frank, 117
  G. W. D., 31
LUCKEN, B., 191
LUDD, R., 81
  Truman, 133
LUDWICK, C. P., 14
  J., 17, 187
LUDWIG, Eli K., 146
  L. W., 11
LUFF, Thomas, 30
LUGER, Barney, 6
LUKEN, B., 20, 191
LUKENS. George, 4
LULL, Adam, 69
LUM, Samuel Y., 82
LUMPION, W., 153
LUN, Lyman, 185
LUNCEFORD, R., 157
LUNDREY, S., 49
LUNDY, O. J., 137
LUNN, J. C., 88
LUNNICE, J. L., 9
LUNSDEN, R. K., 156
LUNT, Henry, 122

LUPTON, J., 55
  J. M., 42, 195
  James, 38
  John M., 195
LURE, James W., 147
LUSK, J., 168
  Wesley, 170
LUSTER, J., 148
  T., 55
  Thomas (Dr.), 38
LUTHER, I. M., 60
LUTHES, A. Y., 168
LUTMAN, Anthony, 70
LYE, H., 100
LYKES, N. N., 48
LYLY, James (sic), 114
LYMAN, E., 21
  H., 68
LYNCH, C. E., 158
  Henry C., 81
  J. P., 164
  Pat, 146
  William, 112
LYNN, Joseph, 176
LYON, Ames, 117
  H., 60
  J., 40
  J. P., 67
LYONS, S., 150
LYTLE, James, 44
LYTTLE, John, 16

-M-

MAR_____, R., 179
MABIE, Jeremiah, 117
MACDONALD, J. H., 85
MACE, Charles, 63
MACEY, Mary, 172
MACK, E., 157
  J. S., 136
  Mary, 136
MACKARAN, W. H., 42, 196
  William H., 196
MACKAY, Lafayette, 136
MacKENZIE, J.M., (Dr.), 198

MACKEY, J., 64
  William, 54, 132
  William A., 112
MACKLIN, S., 108
MACKY, William (sic), 132
MacNALLY, James, 82
MACOMBER, J., 14
MACON, R.B., 202
  W., 202
MACY, Mary, 172
MADDEN, D. W., 158
MADDIN, Charles, 40
MADDOX, A. J., 172
  J. W., 121
  William B., 39
MADDUX, William R., 87
MADISON, ___, (Mr.), 160
  J. W., 20
  Miller A., 172
  R., 20
MAGAW, I., 84
MAGEE, W., 167
MAGLIN, J. A., 157, 164
MAGOFFIN, John M., 97
MAGRUDER, F. M., 48
  Lloyd, 89
MAGURY, W., 117
MAHAN, M., 23
  W. K., 114
MAHONEY, David, 31
  John, 31
  T., 139
MAHONY, Stephan (sic), 118
MAIDEN, William, 142
MAINEY, William M., 56
MAJOR, John, 45
MAJORS, Thomas, 112
MALAY, Asbury (sic), 37
MALCOM, Ferguson, 114
MALCOMB, J. G., 89
MALEN, William, 142
MALKER, J. K. (sic), 142
MALLERSON, Moses, 52
MALLORY, E., 202
  W. T., 84

MALONE, A., 127
  F. J ., 32
  John W., 39
MALONEY (see also MOLONY)
MALONY, A. P. (sic), 56
MALORY, A. (sic), 153
MALTBEY, A. T., 136
  E. L., 136
  J. R., 84
MALVIN, H. M., 153
MANCHE, A., 156
MANDELL, E. W., 109
MANDFIELD, G. B. (sic), 176
MANGUM, Emeline & child, 40
MANIFOLD, B., 4
MANLEY, E., 193
  Eli, 193
MANLOVE, John H., 26
  John N., 26
  M. D., 26
MANN, ___, (Mr.), 161
  C. B., 116
  Christopher, 113
  H. C.(Dr.), 48
  Isaac F., 136
  J., 31
  James, 176
  Joseph, 29
  Zenos, 103, 105
MANNING, E. & Co., 140
  James H., 47
  W., 108
MANOR, James, 163
MANSFIELD, E., 61
  Eber L., 105
  G. B., 176
MAPFIELD, J. H ., 158
MARA, H., 113
MARANVILLE. R. 15, 184
MARAT, H., 42, 196
MARBLE, C., 154
MARBLEY, John, 28
MARCASY, Anias, 146
MARCEHOFFER, Mat, 165

MARCH, T. D., 167
MARDEN, John M., 48
MARGAN, O., 84
MARGO, J., 163
MARGUIS, R., 179
MARIAN, T. C., 51
MARKER, Frederick, 151
MARKHAM, Lorin, 58
MARKIS, E. S., 169
MARKLE, J. A., 18
MARKS, Samuel, 136
MARLETT, T. J., 32
MARMADUKE, A. J., 42
MARMON, Alfred, 137
  Lemuel, 136
MARONVILLE, R., 184
MARPLE, J. M., 88
MARQUAM, H. P., 167
MARQUES, S. F. (Dr.), 151
MARQUIS, D., 144
  E., 18
  R., 179
MARRILL, J. E. (sic), 61
MARROTT, H., 196
MARRS, Henry (sic), 116
MARS, H., 113
MARSH, ___, 41, 115
  Charles. 50
  J., 58
  Josh S., 84
MARSHAL, Green (sic), 93
MARSHALL, ___, 153
  ___, (Dr.), 99
  Alexander, 45
  C., 148
  Columbus S., 117
  Daniel, 140
  E. D., 163
  Elias D., 138
  George, 196
  Green (death of), 93
  H., 11
  J. H., 11
  James M., 11
  James W., 112
  John (Dr.), 30

M., 80
Simon, 63
W. R., 165
MARSTON, B. D., 150
MART, Robert S. 5
MARTHENS W. F., 17
MARTIN, ____, (Dr.), 80
____, Mr., 199
A., 104, 153
Alex, 127
Andrew, 99
C., 14, 185
C. L., 83
D., 104
D. D., 11
G. W., 10, 183
George, 3, 9
George W., 183
H., 20, 191
H. (Mr.), 4
H. D., 11
Henry, 116, 134
Henry A., 173
Hugh, 81
J., 18, 167
James, 102
James H., 86
John, 133
John J., 63
John W., 112
L. R., 130
M., 55
M. J., 29
Mary E., 173
Mike, 38
Morris, 105
Nelson, 102
Phillip, 130
R., 148
R.H., 57
Reuben, 140
S. B., 167
Samuel, 119
T., 169
MARTINDALE, John, 16
MARTINI, H. (sic), 191
MARTLING, J. W., 108
MARTON, J., 158

MARVEL, H. C., 120
MARVIN, George, 109
H. D., 174
W. R., 40
MARWOOD, W., 157
MASCHER, F., 127
MASEHER, F., 127
MASLIN, W., 46, 198
William, 198
MASON, A. J., 5
C., 144
Charles, 133
Charles E., 48
George, 155
H., 143, 145
Isaac H., 117
L., 63
Lucius, C., 126
M. N., 146
R., 144
Robert, 143
T., 145
V., 41
MASSEY, George, 81
J. M., 163
MASSICK, J. B., 105
MASTER, F., 99
MASTERS, Daniel, 154
William 120 (x), 155
MASTIN, John B., 96
MATHER, Elisha, 79
MATHEWS, J., 188
S., 33, 193
Samuel (Dr.), 193
MATHIAS, C. M., 157
MATLOCK, John, 30
MATOON, A., 119
J. B., 145
MATSLER, George, 43
MATSON, James, 117
MATTAX, Silas T., 45
MATTERS, J. & son 154
MATTESHEIMER, ____, 35
MATTESON, Amos C., 147
Oscar, 109
MATTHEWS, C. F., 90
Eliza B., 171

J., 18, 188
O., 59, 63
S. B., 63
T., 164
MATTHEWSON, Albert, 159
MATTHIS, John S., 90
MATTICKS, ____ (Mr.), 54
MATTLEY, A. T., 165
E. L., 165
MATTON, Charles R., 162
S. P., 135
MATTOON, George (sic), 81
MAULE, C., 32
MAURY, Reuben F., 89 (x)
MAVEY, Jonathan, wife & 6 chldrn, 26
MAXFIELD, C., 139
H. H., 30
MAXIM, George, 140
MAXSON, O. T. (Dr.), 113
MAXWELL, George, 161
George M., 32
James, 203
T., 17, 188
Thomas, 188
W., 52
MAY, Henry, 120
Mary A., 172
N., 99
Sarah, 173
MAYER. P. J., 164
S., 167
MAYERS, R. & fam., 168
MAYES, A., 116
MAYHALL, W. D., 80
MAYNARD, M. E., 87
MAYS, A. J., 136
G. M., 48
Mc____, W. P. of Tippecanoe County, Indiana, 26
M'CHESNEY, William, 126

M'CLARY, Henry &
    wife, 71
M'CLURE, F.C., 188
M'CREA, Charles, 46
M'GEE, R. K., 70
M'KINNEY, Wilson, 71
M'KNIGHT, Hugh, 126
McABOY, W. B., 163
McADAMS, S., 123
McADOW, S. (Dr.), 122
McAFEE, A. D., 167
    Alexander H., 131
    T., 129
McALLISTER, James
    (death of), 94
    John, 171
    Lewis, 110
    William, 110
McALPIN, Blanton
    (Capt.), 79 (x), 203
McAMERON, Charles,
    140
McANINCH, S. J., 136
McBETH, ____, (Dr.),
    (death of), 93
McBRAYER, John M., 2
McBRIDE, A., 167
    D., 19
    F., 167
    George, 19, 190
    L., 145
    W. B., 6
McBRIDGE, James C.,
    106
McCADDIN, William, 53
McCAIN, J. L., 79
McCALL, D. D., 176
    J. J., 158, 159 (x), 165
    W. W. P., 84
McCALLISTER, Jesse, 33
McCAMRON, John (sic),
    67
McCAN, ____, (sic) 121
McCANDLESS, J., 17
    J.W., 18
McCANN, ____, 121
    James. 24
    John, 120
McCARTER, James, 17

McCARTHY, J., 151
    J. D., 151
    J. O., 151
    P., 144
McCARTNEY, B. F., 134
    D. T., 63
    Nathaniel, 134
    O. B., 139
    William, 138
McCARTNY. O. B., 139
    William (sic), 138
McCARTY, John, 127
    John F., 41
    M., 70
McCASLIN, M., 90
McCAULEY, T. M., 166
McCEVER, John (sic),
    169
McCHESNEY, J., 63
    William, 126
McCLAIN, W. H., 84
McCLANAHAM, W., 2
McCLARE, H. C., 61
McCLARRY, David, 152
    Isaac (sic), 133
    Isaac & lady, 151
McCLASKEY, J., 17, 187
McCLASKY, Francis, 44
McCLEARY, James, 54
    Joseph, 11
McCLELAND, William
    (sic), 82
McCLELLAN, Edward, 7
    Michael, 202
McCLELLAND, E., 7
    John, 63
    William, 63, 82
McCLENAHAM, M., 167
McCLENTHEN, J. H., 98
McCLINTICK, W., 162
McCLORY, A., 17
    W., 17
McCLOSKEY, J., 17, 187
McCLOY, Robert, 201
McCLURE, F. C., 19, 188
    J ., 42
    J. S., 90
    James, 140
    N. (Mr.), 77

Roan, 101
S., 51
S. J., 33
Thomas, 149
Thomas J., 112
W., 179
W. D., 100
McCOLLOUGH, John,
    132
McCOMBER, George,
    wife &
    child, 160
McCOMMENS, David,
    105
McCOMMON, P., 88
McCONANGHY, John,
    165
    W., 165
McCONNEL, A. (sic),
    165
    Robert (sic), 199
McCONNELL, ____, 53
    ____ (Judge), 53
    A., 165
    D.M., 203
    J. A., 12
    James, 133
    John S., 91
    O., 19
    P., 118
    Robert, 49, 199
    William .M., 151
McCONNELLY, H., 30,
    37
McCORD, James H., 185
McCORKLE, J. H. T., 42
    J.W., 197
McCORMACK, F. A., 88
McCORMICK,
    ____(Mrs.), 167
    B., 29
    D., 68
    Francis, 137
    L., 6
    M., 134, 148, 150
McCOWAN, J., 17, 187
    James, 31
McCOWEN, J., 187
McCOY, A. D., 150

A. G., 166
Alexander W., 28
D., 142
H. M., 166
J., 112
John, 100
L., 55
M. M., 13
T. J., 104
W., 167
W. J., 166
W. W., 158
William, 100, 123
McCRACKEN, M., 11
  Robert, 20
McCRADY, G.E., 187
  George E., 17, 187
McCRANOR, W. L., 157
McCRAREY, William, 150
McCREENY, S., 150
McCUBBINS, C., (Mrs.), 170
McCULLOCH, George W., 122
  J., 25
McCULLOGH, W. S., 13
McCULLOUGH, John, 115, 132
McCULLUM, D. F., 51
McCUMMINGS, L. M., 13
  Perry, 13
McCUNE, W. B., 99
  William, 174
McCURDY, James, 42
  William, 139
McDALE, B., 108
McDANIEL, A., 99
  C., 63
  W., 167
McDERMITT, ____ (Dr.), 96
McDERMOTT, Patrick, 120
McDOLE, B., 108
McDONALD, ____, 68
  ____ (Dr.), 52
  A., 30

A. D.,, 46, 61, 77
Alexander, 85
C. R., 16
D., 51
E. J., 79
F. A., 81
J., 17, 51
J. D., 16
J. H., 148
James, 171
John, 16
John, wife & 6 chldrn, 180
R. B., 113
T. J., 127
McDONNELL, D. A., 30
McDOUAL, Samuel (sic), 7, 182
McDOUGALL (see also McDOUGLE)
  E., 15, 184
McDOUGLE (see also McDOUGALL)
  Elijah (sic), 184
McDOUL, Samuel, 24, 182
McDOWELL, ____ (death of), 93
  Alex, 103
  J. (Mr.), 72
  J. F., 167
  John, 96
  John F., 46
  William, 26
McDUFFY, B., 81
McELRATH, J., 30, 182
  James, 4, 182
McELROY, F., 154
  Jackson, 105
McELWAIN, E. F., 53
McELWAIT, ____, 92 (x)
McENTIRE, A., 154
  Alonzo, 155
McEWAN, Johnson A., 105
McEWEN, William, 8
McFARLAND, B. C., 166
  J., 144
  J. W., 91

James, 39
John, 61
R. K., 163
W., 11
McFARLANE, Charles C., 172
  George, 63
McFEE, A., 167
McGAHEM, Archibald, 115
McGARREN, Robert, 118
McGARRON, Robert, 118
McGARRY, C., 165
McGAUGHEY, J. F., 19
McGAUGHREN, Philip, 131
McGAVRON, Robert, 118
McGEE, Daniel, 30
  H., 69
  J. A., 17, 186
  James, 186
  Oscar, 58
  R., 186
McGENNES, William (sic), 87
McGEORGE, L.H., 12
McGHEE, Patrick (sic), 131
McGILL, D., 19
  P., 153
McGINN, James, 139
McGINNES, J. (sic), 160
McGINNIS, Robert, 91
  William, 54, 87
McGINNY, Edward, 67
McGIRNSEY, Olderson, 124
McGLOCHLAN, T., 179
McGLOVERN, William H., 115
McGOHAN, N., 153
McGOWAN, E., 200
  Edward, 64, 200
  R. L. (Mr.), 3
McGOWEN, R., 54
McGRATH, James, 108
  John, 67

Joseph H., 109
Thomas H., 86, 204
McGRAW, J., 17
   P., 143, 145
McGREERY, Rufus K., 136
   Samuel K., 136
McGREGGOR, J., 17, 187
McGREGOR, J., 187
McGREW, J., 144
   Thomas, 64, 200
   Thomas J., 203
McGRINSEY, John, 124
McGUIRE, T., 160
McGULPIN, D., 142
McHENRY, ____ (Mr.), 45
   J. H., 168
   J. P., 150
McHUFFE, Huldah, 162
McILBENY, W., 18, 188
McILHANY, Edward, 196
McILHENEY, W., 188
McILROY, R. H., 159
McILWAINE, H., 187
McILWINE, N., 17, 187
McINTIRE, A., 154
   Alonzo, 155
   E. C., 158
   R. G., 136
   William, 67
McINTOSH, J. C., 60
   J. W., 155
   John, 7
   M., 7
   O. F. & fam., 155
   Peter, 87
   Tally A., 87
McINTYRE, ____ (Mr.), wife & child, 160
   John, 67
   L., 148
   S., 128
McJILTON, Ely, 52
McKAIN, J. J., 163
McKAINEY, R. C., 31

McKARSHER, J. G., 51
McKAY, Thomas, 4
   W., 165
McKEE, ____, 91
   ____ (Mr.), 54, 103
   A., 140
   J.A., 186, 187
   J.S., 187
   James, 17, 186, 187
   R., 17, 186
   R. G., 158
McKELVEY, J., 99
   John, 88
McKENNEY, D. C., 41
   H., 41
   John A., 111
   Leslie H., 41
   P., 41
   R., 41
McKENZIE, A., 145
McKENZY, John (Dr.), 43, 198
McKEY, George, 100
McKIBBEN, J., 98
   J. C., 5
McKIBBON, J. C., 5
McKILE, Charles, 68
McKINLEY, George, 93
McKINLY, George (sic), 93
McKINNEY, John A., 102
   W., 200
   William, 49, 200
McKINSTRY, Bryon W., 117
McK.LAMDIN, W., 25
McKNIGHT, G. S., 80
M'KNIGHT, Hugh, 126
   J. Jr., 146
   J. A., 164
   J. D., 167
McKNOTT, W., 168
McKNOTTS, W., 168
McKUNE, J., 12
McLAIN, A., 26
   J., 163
   W. C., 163
McLANE, Allin (sic), 56
   J., 144

J. D., 63
McLAUGHIN, James, 67
McLAUGHLIN, ____ (Mr.), 54
   A. B., 131
   E., 165
   E. R., 102
   J., 154
   James, 67
   Patrick, 24
McLEAN, Chambers, 47
   D. (company of), 114
   William, 119
McLEOD, C. C., 47
McMACKIN, L., 158
McMAHAN, R., 153
McMAHERR, ____ (Mr.) (sic), 131
McMAHON, P., 148
McMANNUS, Ira (sic), 173
McMANUS, J., 26
McMASTER, S. W., 67
McMATH, William, 39
McMICHAEL, T., 66
McMILLAN, A., 22, 32, 192
   F. A., 18, 188
   H. M., 62
   H. W., 59
   R., 165
   Sloan (death of), 94
   Thomas, 165
McMILLEN, F.A., 188
   H. W. (sic), 63
   S. (sic), 80
   Thomas, 104
McMILLIAN, W. (sic), 154
McMILLION, W. (sic), 154
McMORROW, J., 79
McMULLEN, Samuel, 117
McMULLIN, J., 102
McMURRAY, A., 17
   F., 54
   James, 72
McMURRY, J. (sic), 144

McNAHL, D., 146
  H., 146
McNAIR, J., 166
  R., 19
  Thomas, 19
McNAMARA, Charles P., 98
McNAUGHTON, A., 7, 182
McNEAL, Marshall, 44
  S. D., 99
McNEIL, Hugh, 108
McNELLY, A., 129
McNIEL, A., 142
  J., 140
McNORTON, A., 24, 182
McNULTY, A. J., 17
  J., 160
McNUTT, G., 166
  J., 63
McPHAIL, S., 189
McPHAILL, Samuel, 19, 189
McPHERRIN, George, 111
McPHERSON, _____ (Mr.), 55
  W. A., 121
  William, 118
McPIKE, James, 113
  John, 113
McQUAT, R. S., 112
McRISAN, D., 167
McSPENCER, D., 153
  M. W., 153
  W., 153
McTARNAHAN, _____, 116
  Francis, 116
  Isaac, 116
  M. C. (Miss), 116
  R. (Mrs.), 116
McWAIR, Clement, 173
McWILLIAMS, P. A., 169
  Robert, 56
  Samuel, 117
McWORGAN, J., 149
ME____, Patrick, 135

MEACHAM, W. S., 166
MEAD, Alford, 159
  Isaac (Capt.), 159
  John, 15
  Luther, 90
  M. B., 102
  S. P., 165
MEALERS, J. A., 129
MEAN, John W., 126
MEANS, Alfred & 2 svts, 32
  Cemeal (sic), 175
  David, 146
  H. H., 32
  J., 18
  Salvina (Mrs.), 175
MEASE, William, 99
MECHAM, _____, (Mr.), 39
  Alfred B, 105
  H. J., 105
MECKLIN, S., 108
MECKLING, M., 18, 188
MECUM, C. B., 64
  Charles B., 64
MEDLOR, A. B., 143
  W., 143
MEEKER, L. R., 144
  S. H., 10
  T. G., 115
MEEKS, E., 149
MEGGISON, George, 92
MEHAN, W., 17
MEHANY, _____, 115
MELEE, Thomas, 35
MELLBURN, Joseph (sic), 39
MELLON, J., 149
MELLWINE, N., 187
MELONY, _____ (Mr.), 54
MELVILLE, James, 17
MENDENHALL, Amos, 117
  Hiram, 117
MENEFEE, J. H., 142
MENEFER, W. H., 112
MENHOSTER, H. C., 160
MEPSMAN, Michael, 178

MERABIN, J., 17
MEREDITE, O. 144
MEREDITH, _____, 91
  J. F., 164
  J. M., 17
  W., 173
  William C., 17
MERICK, J., 63
  S. F., 63
MERRICK, T. A., 83
MERRIFIELD, James, 65
MERRIL, S. B. (sic), 153
MERRILL, J. E., 61
  Joseph H., 43, 198
  S., 43, 197
  S. B., 153
MERRITT, _____ (Mr.), 160
  F. W., 68
  Markwood, 130
MERRYFIELD, _____, 108
  J. C., 102
MERRYFORD, S. H., 117
MERRYMAN, Henry, 11
MERS, C. L. (Mrs.), 118
MESMITH, B., 187
MESSERSMITH, B., 17, 187
MESSICK, J. B., 168
MESSMAN, Michael, 178
MESSRELL, John M., 117
MESSROLL, John M., 117
METCALF, _____, 76
  Almonson, 106
  C., 157
  John, 76
  Robert, 83
METTISON, D. C., 158
METTS, John, 121
MEYER, Louis, 90
MEYRICK, Henry, 135
  Levi, 135
MICHAEL, George, 114
  N. 138
MICHLER, M., 99
MICHOLSON, John, 67

MICKELWAIT, James, 45
  John, 44
  Whitcomb, 44
  Willerby, 45
MIDDLEHAM, Robert, 101
MIDDLETON, T., 143
MIKESEL, Benjamin, 140
  Hannah, 136
  John W., 136
  William J., 136
MIKESELL, B. 168
  Benjamin, 91, 140
MIKSELL, John (sic), 160
  W. J. (sic), 160
MILARHY, Timothy, 121
MILES, E. E., 85
  G., 160
  J., 41
  J. T., 140
  James S., 140
  R. W. (Capt.), 110
  S. B., 129
MILKLAND, L., 158
MILLAN, William, 29
MILLAND, R., 179
MILLARD, Amelia, son & dau., 132
  William H., 118
MILLEN, W., 52
MILLENCHOP, J. H., 51
MILLER, A., 90, 129, 152
  A. G., 113, 116
  A. J., 2
  A. R., 42, 196
  Abraham, 43
  Alexander, 78
  Andrew R., 196
  B. (Dr.), 80
  C., 151
  C. W., 65
  Charles, 90
  D., 27
  D. B., 171, 173
  D. C., 38
  D. S., 144
  Daniel, 176
  David, 78, 118
  E. & 3 sons, 179
  E. M., 144
  F. M., 2
  G., 5
  George, 5, 100
  H., 148
  H. B., 102, 111
  H.G., 203
  H. M., 39
  Henry, 3, 16, 120
  Hugh, 143
  I. P., 159
  J., 147, 154, 164, 169
  J. A., 13
  J. C., 49
  J. H. B. & 2 unidentified accompanists, 80
  Jacob P., 178
  James B., 2
  Jason, 53
  John, 5, 49, 160, 200
  John B., 200
  Joseph, 107
  L.M., 203
  M., 18, 166
  M. B., 46, 198
  M. C., 157
  Marion C., 137
  Morgan, 42
  N., 99
  O. F., 91
  Peter, 140
  R., 160
  R. H., 168
  Robert, 40, 170
  Samuel, 16
  Sinclair K., 76
  Smith, 126
  T., 173, 175
  Thomas Williams, 170
  W., 46, 158, 198
  W. F., 155, 157, 163
  W. H., 167
  W. S., 148
  William, 16, 25, 153, 198
MILLESON, N., 150
MILLET, Martin, 121
MILLIGAN, James B., 120
  S., 145
MILLIHAN, Baldwin, 114
  Samuel, 115
MILLIKIN, John, 37
MILLIMAN, Schuyler, 66
MILLNER, J. H., 84
MILLS, Abraham, 68
  John, 1
  Peter, 57
MILLSAPO, T., 144
MILNE, I., 191
MILNER, E. J. C., 70
  John T., 70
MILTBON, O., 140
MILTENBUGER, William, 136
MILTHON, O., 140
MILTON, J. H., 163
  T., 42, 195
  Taliaferro, 195
MINARD, Abel & fam., 21
MINCHELL, G. R., 102
MINEBIDDLE, G.187
MINEHART, Samuel, 56
MINER, Caroline (Mrs.), 169
  J., 90
  J. M., 107
  John D., 99
MINGFIELD, A. H., 70
MINIS, W., 18
MINSHALL, G. K., 111
MINSTER, Willim H., 56
MINTER, J.H. 148
MINTON, B., 91
MISCHART, L., 31
MISENDOFGER, C., 190
MISER, J., 55
MISH, Michael, 178
MISSCARD, Mary E., 172
MISTEN, George, 154
MITCHELL, C., 20, 190
  C.F., 190
  David, 139

267

David, wife & 2 chldrn, 155
E. (Mrs.), 173
G., 19, 188
G. R., 102
George, 44
H. S., 32
J., 164, 188
J. A., 49
J. J. 84
J. R., 147
J. W., 84
James, 67, 203
James B., 5
John, 108
L., 129
Robert Jr., 124
S., 49
W., 128, 189
W. (Rev.), 48
W. H. C., 23
William, 19, 189
MITCHELTREE, C., 158
MITLEN, W., 52
MITTENBUGER, William, 136
MITTENBURGER, William, 136
MIZENDORFER, C., 20, 190
MOATS, J., 26
MOBLE, Jeremiah, 117
MOBLEY, John, 199
MOFFAT, ____ (Mr.), 134
Hugh, 203
Joab, 203
Thomas (sic), 199
MOFFETT, Joseph, 90
Levi, 90
MOHR, C. (Mr.), 3
MOKE, John, 129
MOLES, Miles B., 202
MOLEY, J. C. & fam., 148
MOLONY (see also MALONEY)
William, 194
MOLTER, J., 158

MOMBUR, S. B. C., 153
MONEYHEFFER, J., 143
MONFORT, David, 66
MONG, G. P. (sic), 168
MONICHE, C., 79
MONROE, Edwin, 102
John, 203
MONTAGUE, George, 57
MONTGOMERY, Amos, 155
Benjamin, 135
G. B., 63
J., 135
Joseph, 136
L. D., 64, 200
L. Dow, 200
Timothy, 4
Thomas, 155
William, wife & 2 chldrn, 155
MONTILLIUS, Edward, 5
MONTRASS, A. B., 14
MOODY, A., 81
Joseph L., 6
P. H., 6
R., 68
W.B., 190
W. V., 19, 190
MOON, Charles, 174
H., 166
Joseph, 169
Marillo, 173
MOONEY, S., 68
MOONY, S., 68
MOOR, R. (sic), 41
MOORE, ____ (Mr.), 128
A., 150, 152
Adison, 139
Alex., 58
Alexander, 38
Amasa, 172
B., 157
B. F., 137
C. A., 92
C. H., 123, 127
C. H. (death of), 122
D. S., 97
Dan, 57

Daniel, 147
Edward, 40
Ephraim, 90
F., 35
G. G., 11
G. W., 174
H. H., 42, 195
Henry, 111
Henry H., 195
Hubbard, 50
I. H., 180
J., 17, 145, 168(x), 188
J. D., 44
J. G., 163
J. G. (Dr.), 88
J. H., 36, 108, 194
J. J. & lady, 163
J. M., 148
J. T., 81
J. W., 111
James H., 42
Jesse (Dr.), 50
John, 111
John Jr., 42, 57
John T., 11
Jonathan, 5
Joseph H., 194
L. J. W., 129
Malin, 169
Nelson D., 200
R., 41
R. G. R., 101
R. W., 11
Robert, 135, 138
Rufus, 106, 111
S., 113
S. W., 95
T. C., 42, 195
Thomas C., 195
W., 165
W. M., 54
W. S., 97
William, 29, 82, 96
William C., 112
William H., 96
William H., wife & son, 124
William J., 174
William O., 117

MOORES, H. (sic), 88
MOORHEAD, James, 123
MORALEW, Mathew, 109
MORAN, M. D., 174
MORE, J. (sic) 145
  John Jr., (sic), 57
MOREHEAD, A. Jr., 30
  C., 6
  H. (Gen.), 156
  John H., (sic), 70
  T. G., 30
  W. M., 173
MORELAND, F. (Mr.), 3
  H.J., 191
MORELL, David, 67
MORETZ, C. (sic), 123
  Luther, 123
MORFORD C. G., 167
MORGAN, C. C., 11
  David, 84
  E., 148
  G. P., 148
  H. L., 38, 194
  J., 17, 99, 158
  John, 18
  O., 84
  R., 167
  Robert, 84
  William, 67
MORIER, Daniel, 136
MORLEY, J. C., 118
MORRAN, W. W. (sic), 67
MORRE J., 188
MORREL, Thomas, 127
MORRELL, H. O., 151
  Thaddeus, 108
  Thomas, 127
MORRIE, R., 52
MORRILL, F., 61
MORRIS, A. L., 153
  D. C., 29
  E., 202
  G. W., 157, 162
  George, 142
  H., 49
  J., 142
  J.H.T., 197
  J. J., 173
  Jacob, 40
  John, 32, 179
  M., 142
  W. L., 4
  William, 49
  William L, 181
MORRISON, ____, (Mr.), 202
  D. M., 165
  Elam, 83
  J., 17, 30
  James, 97, 109
  John, 65, 103
  M., 20
  Philip, 178
  R. T., 25
  Robert, 107
MORROW, A., 8
  C. H., 127
  James, 38
  L., 8
  T., 23
  Thomas (Rev.), 112
MORS, C. L. (Capt.), 118
MORSE, E., 52, 95, 137
  Henry, 114
  J. F. (Dr.), 148
  N. D., 64, 200
  Stewart, 51
  Warren, 109
  William, 70
MORSLEW, Mathew, 109
MORTLAND, Alex, 104
MORTON, A. W., 141, 158
  B., 158
  E., 99
  J. L., 165
  J. M., 46
  James (Mrs.), 126
  Jonathan P., 137
MORY, Alfred (Capt.), 111
  John E., 64
MOSELEY, Benjamin, 11
  C. G., 48
MOSELY, M. (sic), 153

MOSES, P., 167
MOSFORD, William, 64
MOSS, ____ (Mr.), 71
  Albert, 26
  Charles B., 159
  Charles L., 105
  D. H., 46, 73
  D. H. T., 96
  D. H. T. & fam., 54
  David, 77
  David H., 76
  Henry, 173
  J. G., 159
  M. F., 46
  Mason F., 75, 76
  Mildred (Mrs.), 96
MOTT, G. N., 148
  W. E., 162
MOTTS, Thomas B., 38
MOUFORT, David, 66
MOULTON, J. R., 159, 163
  T. F., 145
MOUNT, Charles A., 175
  James, 176
  William, wife & 4 chldrn, 141
MOWER, George, 36
MOWLRAY, J. R., 129
MOXLEY, Francis, 117
  T.S., 199
MOXLY, T. S. (Dr.), 49, 199
MUER, F., 65
MUFFIT, Christian, 106
MUIR, Preston, 95, 172
MUK, J. (sic), 148
MULBARGER, J., 148
MULBY, John, 43
MULFORD, C. W., 51
  Charles, 44
MULKINS, A., 61
MULL, G. W., 56
MULLEN, John, 81
  P. (sic), 138
MULLENS, B. B., 31
  R. (Mr.), 31
MULLIN, J. O., 165
MULLINS, A., 163

A. E., 162
MULLONS, B. B., 31
  R. (Mr.), 31
MULLOWY, William, 36, 194
MULLREY, S., 80
MULROVER, Michael, 180
MULVILLE, N. B., 70
MUMFORD, George, 122
  James, 122
MUMMS, D., 109
  David, 106
MUNCEY, I., 149
MUNFORD, George, 122
  James, 122
MUNGER, Devetrius, 174
MUNN, Joseph, 29
MUNSON, J. B., 157
  Pennell, 119
  Uriah, 174
MURDOCH, J. (sic), 167
MURDOCK, L. D., 147
MURGINS, James, 203
MURPHY, Andrew, 24, 54
  George, 135
  J., 39
  J. H., 42, 195
  John, 82, 117
  John & son, 106
  John C., 67
  John H., 195
  Joseph, 48
  Mathew (sic), 24
  P. Y., 170
  Philip, 101
  Sandford, 135
  Thomas, 24
MURRAY, Alfred, 54
  B. F., 166
  George, 130
  J., 146
  John, 114
  John & fam., 40
  M. W., 127
  Mary E. (Mrs.), 175
  O. T., 11
  R., 144

Thomas, 68
  W. M., 17, 186
MURRY, John & fam. (sic), 40
  R., 144
MURSSLY, David, 146
MURY, B. F. (sic), 166
MUSCOTT, John M., 182
MUSE, Jos. (sic), 83
  Joseph, 83
MUSIC, James W., 171
MUSSELMAN, Andrew, 11
MUSSER, John, 172
MUSSETTEN, Henry, 122
MYERS, ____, 153
  Absolam, 67
  Christian, 152
  D. G., 153
  E.R., 181
  Enoch, 4
  F., 163
  Ford, 159
  George & fam., 178
  H. W., 5
  Henry, 14, 184
  J., 145
  J. J., 99
  J. R., 164
  John, 48
  John, Q., 105
  Jos., 90
  L. M., 136
  Peter, 23
  S., 144
  W. C., 53
  W. D., 100
  William, 91
MYRES, Jos. (sic), 90
MYRTLE, S. F., 170
  Sarah, 170

-N-

NAERING, H. O., 154
NAGEL, J. C., 150
NAHAN, U. M., 83

NAME, W., 43, 198
NANCE, J., 168
NARSE, M., 199
NARSEN, C. A., 170
NASH, C., 158
  C. E., 151
  F. A., 6
  J., 158
  J. B., 41, 158
  M., 27
  S. D., 151
  Warren, 203
  William, 27
NAYLOR, J., 38, 55
NAYOO, R. W., 150
NEAGLEY, G., 163
NEAL, C., 64
  D., 63
  George W., 116
  J. O., 98
  M., 146
  O., 98
NEALE, David H. & fam., 144
  L. M., 150
NEARING, H. O., 157
NEBLITT, E., 11
NEEL, P., 169
NEELEY, W. C., 84
NEELY, A. J. (death of), 92
  Newton, 139, 155
NEESE, George, 4
NEGLEY, F. C., 19
NEIHMERT, A., 35
NEITESKY, Joseph, 38
NELEY, ____ (Mr.), 202
NELLIS, Henry, 119
NELLY, O. P., 129
NELSON, J. R., 96
  J. T., 117
  R. H., 170, 172
  T., 148
  W., 100
NELSONBY, J. R., 176
NELSONHY, J. R. (sic), 176
NESBIT, William, 67
  William N., 8

NESMITH, J., 187
  William D., 136
NESMITTE, J., 17, 187
NESS, Richard, 66
NETHERLAND, J. H., 111
NETWARE, C. N., 98
NEVINS, Robert W., 82
NEVITT, F., 145
  G., 145
NEVLAND, Joseph (death of), 93
NEWBRACH, Jack, 116
NEWBURG, N., 166
  W., 166
NEWCOMER, C., 61
  V. S., 45
NEWELL, B., 61
  H., 154
  J., 98
NEWING, James, 100
NEWINGHAM, Ab., 162
NEWLAND, H., 143
  Joseph (death of), 93
  Thomas J., 112
NEWLIN, Calvin, 100
  Enoch, 100
  Frederick, 100
  Jonathan, 100
  Kelly, 100
NEWMAN, D., 142
  Thomas, 84
  William, 131
  William K., 83
NEWRY, John, 93
NEWSOME, A., 156
NEWTON, Hollis, Jr., 117
  J. P., 124
  J. W., 30
  James H., 7, 24
  Job, 25
  John, 116
  Lewis, 127
  P. H., 118
  S., 6
NEY, Joseph, 67
NEYES, J. W., 66
NIBLACK, Alonzo L., 118

NIBLOCK, Alonzo L., 118
NICELY, D., 156
NICHOL, R. J., 145
NICHOLAS, J. B., 173
  J. J., 87
NICHOLIS, John (sic), 89
NICHOLS, A. K., 110
  E. L., 4
  J. J., 39
  James, F., 70
  Permella, 170
  R., 164
  Robert, 127
  T. B., 54
  William H., 204
NICHOLSON, D. W., 92
  J., 86, 203
  James, 137
  John, 57
  M., 67
NICKEL, J. O., 15, 185
  L., 178
NICKSON, B., 73
  B. D., 70
NIGH, Adam S., 114
NILES, E., 163
  W. S., 63
NILSON, J. O., 18
NITTERHOUSE, Franklin L., 114
NIVER, George J., 102, 121
NIXON, A. B. (Mr.), 3
  G., 152
  Robert, 120
NOBLE, _____, (Mr.), 160
  Charles, 106
  O. F., 119
  William, 179
NOBLES, J., 102
NOBLITT, E., 11
NOE, B. L., 85
NOLAN, P. J., 149
NOONA, J. (sic), 163
NORCROSS, Robert, 127
NORCROST, Robert, 116

NORDYKE, Hiram, 68
  Jacob, 686
NORFOLK, N., 49
NORMAN, W. B., 3
NORRIS, H., 108
  J. A., 135
  J. W., 87
  W. F. P., 153
NORTH, Almer, 98, 101
  J., 165
  Mary, 169
NORTHROP, L. (Dr.), 100
  S., 67
NORTHRUP, T. J., 56
NORTHWAY, C., 148
NORTON, _____ (Mr.), wife & 2 sisters, 144
  C. N., 105
  D. C., 65, 200
  Ed, 55
  Edward, 85
  John, 33
  K. E., 158
  L. A., 149
  Noah, 68
  O. T., 30
  P., 59
  T. M., 149
  William, 13
NOTCROST, Robert, 116
NOWLAN, Charles & fam., 40
NOYES, Harry, 204
  J. W., 59, 66
  James, 106
  Loren A., 106
NUMAN, S., 140
  Samuel, 139
NUNN, Alexander, 9
NURSE, Morrison, 49, 199
  Uri, 49, 199
NUSSBARNER, L., 35
NUTTING, Alden B., 40
NYE, James, 70
  Newton, 117
  Oscar, 122

NYS, Newton, 117

-O-

OAKES, ___, 190
  D., 142
  John, 142
  Stephen, 13
  T., 20, 190
OAKLEY, George, 203
  Obadiah, 203
  Oliver B., 82
  Orrin, 203
OATMAN, J. E. (Dr.), 39
OBNETTING, A. J. R., 175
O'BRIAN, J. J., 51
O'BRIEN, Benjamin, 202
  J. J., 51
  Jesse, 202
O'CALLAHAN, J., 27
OCLAND, John (death of), 94
O'CONNOR, M. P., 24
ODELL, George, 135
  Hyram, 135
  James, 42, 196
  James Jr., 196
  R., 44
ODENHEIMER, William, 49
OFFICER, Charles T., 17, 186
OFFUTT, ___, (Professor), 201
O'FLEWEL, Thomas, 69
O'FLOWEL, Thomas, 69
O'FLYNN, C., 187
OGDEN, Benjamin, 45
  C. M., 144
  Hiram, 53
  S., 153
  William, 20
OGLE, Alfred M., 114
  Franklin, 78
  Hiram, 78
  Jesse, 16
  M., 37

Robert, wife & 1 child, 132
Theodore, 37
OGLESBY, R. G., 43
O'HANA, E., 50
OHLSON, Amond, 67
O'HOWELL, ___, 70
OHR, H.H., 181
OLAND, Anson, 21
OLDHAM, J. C., 70
  Samuel, 70
OLIN, William A., 68
OLISON, Erasmus (sic), 149
OLIVER, J., 17
  John, 117
  Mersay, 11
  W., 165
OLLIOD, J., 84
OLMSTEAD, J. D., 52
OLNEY, A. B., 25
O'LOUGHLIN, John, 124
ONDERDONK, Jonathan, T. (Dr.), 58
O'NEAL, Francis, 178
O'NEALE, W. F., 150
O'NEIL, James, 97
OPT, Henry, 67
ORAIN, Levand, 147
ORBISON, David, 15
  S. M., 167
ORENDORF, ___, (Dr.), 17, 187
ORMSBY, ___ (Dr.), 193
  Erastas N., 106
  H. J., 158
  J. S. (Dr.), 26, 193
  L. P., 26
  L. P. (Maj.), 177
  William (Maj.), 26
ORR, J., 64
  J. W., 113
  James G., 120 (x)
  Joseph, 57
  S., 57, 64
  William, 1, 57, 64, 91
ORSBORNE, T. C. (sic), 102
ORTON, G. A., 131

ORVIN, Charles, 118
ORVIS, A. M., 66
  Charles, 118
OSBORN, A. H., 85
  C. E., 85
  J. (sic), 126
  J. W., 85
  Philander (sic), 58
  S.D., 204
OSBORNE, A. H., 85
  A. P., 12
  C. E., 85
  J. W., 85
  John, 67
  John L., 12
  Nelly, 175
  S. D., 86, 204
  T. C., 102
  W. T., 8
  Willis, 175
OSBY, Amos T., 151
OSCAR, R. B., 176
O'SHELTON, W.M., 188
OSTERBURY, D., 67
OSTON, G. A. R., 147
OSTRANDER, A., 21
  R., 119
OSTROM, William, A., 6
O'SULLIVAN, M, (Mr.), 161
OTIS, John C., 80
OTWAY, W. B., 28
OVERALL, J. W., 46
OVERTON, I., 10, 183
  Isaac, 183
OWAN, Thomas E., 70
OWEN, ___, (Capt.), 73
  Isaac (Rev.) & fam., 71
  Isaac E., 48
  James, 87
  Jesse, 80
  John, 67
  K. (Rev.), 136
  Martin P., 103
  Robert & 2 sons, 178
  Stephen, 67
  Thomas H. (Judge), 69
  William, 7, 24

273

OWENS, Edward, 28
  Isaac (Rev.), 43, 198
  J., 70
  James H., 70
  M. A., 70
  N., 70
  Thomas E., 70
  William H., 32
OWENSBY, _____ (Mr.), 165
OWSLEY, G., 48
OXLEY, R. H., 166

-P-

PACEY, John, 30
PACK, Robert, 203
PACKARD, _____, 89
  A. Jr., 99
  John, 16
PACKINPAW, T. J., 123
PADDOCK, D. W., 35
  John H., 106(x)
PAGE, _____, 115
  Benjamin, 199
  Ether (sic), 91
  Lemuel, 136
  Orange E., 134
  William, 136
PAGGETT, J., 63
PAGITT, Joseph, 57
PAIGE, Harry, 33
PAINE, Hy, 92
  M. R., 99
  Seth, 55
PALCHEN, Volney, 45
PALDING, R., (sic), 157
PALL, H. M., 69
PALMER, A., 150
  A. A., 150
  A. D., 153
  Alex., 64, 200
  B., 165
  C. J., 20, 190
  E. J., 153
  E. M., 108
  Enoch, 124
  George A., 105

  James, 133
  John, 124
  Lorenzo, 105
  N., 6
  Robert, 66
  W. C., 12
  William, 42, 50
PANDEGAN, Joseph, 66
PANE, W., (sic), 153
PANKEY, William, 191
PANNELL, Eli, 105
PANTLAN, William P., 49
PANTON, W., 166
PANTOR, W., 166
PANTOS, W., 166
PAPY, J. G., 9
PAQUIN, James, 109
PARAM, J.P., 202
  R.S., 202
PARCELS, P., 157, 166
PARDEE, J., 190
PARDIS, C. A., 147
PARDY, Joseph, 60
PARIS, J. H., 31
PARISH, A. H., 47
  Caleb & wife (sic), 159
  Daniel & wife (sic), 159
  F. H. (Dr.), 133
  Nathan & wife (sic), 159
  W. E., 30
PARK, E. F., 70
  F., 79
  J. A. (grave of), 93
  Starke, 79
PARKE, F. A., 5
  Robert (sic), 33
PARKER, _____, 115
  A. F., 110
  A. P., 144
  A. V., 51, 78
  D., 44
  D.E., 202
  D. W., 154
  Daniel, 70
  E., 49
  Eliza M., 174
  F., 67, 151

  F. J., 67, 68
  Frederick, 136
  H. A., 48
  J., 49, 118, 164
  J. M., 164
  J. R., 64, 65
  James A., 91
  John Henry, 159
  Lewis F., 106
  M., 44
  Moses, 107
  R., 157
  Samuel, 121
  Samuel J., 103
  Seth, 136
  W., 166
  W. E., 106
  William, 100, 124
  Z. D., 11
  Zacchus, 102
PARKERSON, James, 199
PARKHURST, Lewis, 67
PARKS, Charles, 81
  E. H., 70
  J., 153, 154
  J. A., 8
  J. W., 142
  John, 112
  W., 157
  William, 30
PARLEY, _____ (Mr.), 160
  John, 45
PARMELEE, J. H., 148
PARMER, B., 136
  J. H., 158
PARR, Ell., 45
PARROTT, J., 30
PARRY, George, 23
  Isaac, 23
  Thomas C., 67
PARSHALL, Simon (sic), 63
PARSONS, _____ (Mr.), 127
  Jerry, 105
  L. D., 32
  Theron, 110

Thomas, 85
PARTRIDGE, George, 138
  George Jr., 138
  William, 138
PASKELL, J., 160
PATCHIN, F. B., 103
  L. W., 103
PATE, Ira, 133
PATERSON, F. (sic), 53
PATMOR, J. (sic), 152
  J., 153
PATMORE, J., 152, 153
PATRICK, Francis A.,
  114
  George, 131
  J., 20, 190
  J. A., 122
PATRIN, George, 79
PATTEN, A., 144
  Isaac C., 140
  John R. (sic), 43, 198
  P., 144
  Robert (Capt.), 69 (x)
  William, 108
PATTERSON, A., 81
  A. D., 18
  Aaron, 88
  Andrew, 6
  Augustus, 92
  C., 92
  C. H., 59
  C. R., 14
  E. H. M., 102
  F. C., 109
  G. K., 85
  J., 98, 160
  J. B., 51
  John, 106
  Jonathan, 132
  Joseph C., 102, 111
  M. R., 106
  M. R. (Mr.), 102
  P., 132
  S. H. N., 130
  Samuel R., 173
  W., 17
  William, 27, 48, 60
PATTISON, David B.,
  155

Rachel E., 95
PATTON, C., 7
  Isaac C., 140
  J.R., 198
  John Q., 104
  W., 154
  Warren H., 104
  William, 93
PAUL, Edward A. (Capt.),
  78
  G. W., (Lt.), 4, 5, 181
  H. M., 164
  J., 167
  J. & fam., 154
  Martha (Miss), 130
  W., 81
  William, 4
PAULLIN J. S. (sic), 131
PAULUS, J., 163, 168
PAXON, Eli, 15, 184
PAXSON, Charles, 7
  Ely, 184
PAXTON, J. R., 84
  Robert, 16
  T., 166
PAYDEN, J. W. & fam.,
  156
PAYNE, C. H., 63
  J. H., 8
  James, 180
  Vincent, 137
  William C., 155
PAYNTER, L. R., 63
PEABODY, N., 89
  Sylvanus, 67
PEACE, O. W., 103
PEAK, John G., 107
PEAKE, A., 54
  Ambrose J. T., 136
  Edward T., 123
  Luke, 54
PEARCE, E., 26, 193
  William, 203
PEARCH, J. A., 157
PEARKS, Fred (sic), 52
PEARL, William M., 58
PEARONS, ____(Dr.),
  52
PEARSALL, W. R., 68

PEARSON, George, 90
  J. (Mr.), 3
  J. T., 150
  R., 147
PEARSONS, J., 134
PEASE, James, 42, 197
  Jesse T., 131
PEATROSS, W. W., 2
PEBLES, J. (sic), 153
PECHMAN, Elisha C.
  (sic), 132
PECK, ____, 30
  ____, (Mr.), 142
  B. F., 112
  David A., 135
  S. S., 100
PECKETT, James, 97
PECKHAM, Frederick
  119
  Elisha C., 132
PEDVIN, J., 148
PEEBLES, J., 153
  John C., 106
PEIRCE, J. (Dr.), 107
PEIRRONG, Amos, 49
PEITROUSKI, R.K., 187
PELHAM, James E., 89
PELL, H. M., 69
PELROUSKI, R. K., 17
PENCE, O.W., 103
PENCHAL, Albert, 120
PENDICORD, N. W., 43
PENDLETON, J., 100
PENDRY, R. S., 112
PENIX, Jeremiah, 112
PENMAN, J., 168
PENN, J. B., 104
PENNELL, Eli, 105
  J. P., 70
PENNINGTON, J. A. &
  svt., 10, 183
  James A., 183
PENTLAND, Edward, 34
PEOPLE, D., 156
PEOPLES, ____(Mr.),
  202
PEPPER, D. L., 67
  Daniel, 62
  Thomas, 62

PERCIVAL, W., 80
PERCY, ____, 115
PERFECT, A. B., 148
PERIMO, H. A., 150
PERINE, J. N., 56
PERINER, Leonard, 154
PERKINS, Douglass, 68
  G., 16, 185
  H. J., 127
  J., 166
  J. F., 157
  John A., 185
  L. S., 113
  Margaret (Mrs.), 174
  Thomas, 18, 188
  Thomas Jr., 188
PERON, P., 20
PERRINE, Samuell, 119
PERRY, A. T. (Mr.), 3
  Charles S., 24
  George, 27,. 135
  J. C., 145
  John, 9, 135
  Samuel, 116
PERRYMAN, James, 20
PERSELL, William, 68
PERSONGER, James B., 177
PERSONS, Rachael, 174
PESEN, New (sic), 68
PESTROSS, W. W., 2
PETE, Mary (sic), 175
PETER, Mary, 175
PETERMAN, J., 144
  John, 144
PETERS, A. N., 24
  C., 19
  Francis, 124
  J. L., 51
  James, 124
  John, 146
PETERSON, B. A., 44
  J., 164
PETRE, William, 65
PETRICAN, John, 41
PETTIBONE, A., 38
  W. C., 12
PETTINGALE, J.A., 190
PETTIT, ____ (Mr.), 25

George W., 91
PETTY, Peter, 176
  R. C. (Capt.), 121
PETTYGROVE, John, 135
PEVEY, Amelia H., 137
  Charles, 137
PEYTON, McGonigle, 78
PFLAGRATU, G., 35
PHALEN, John, 117
PHALER, J., 163
PHELPS, A. W., 139
  C. E., 147
  Charles E., 134
  D. B., 140
  F. W. M., 150
  J. A., 153
  M., 158
  O. R., 109
  P. H., 134, 147
  S., 149
PHENIX, David, 170
PHETTERPLACE, E. H., 65, 66 (x)
PHIFFER, B., 186, 188
  F. (sic), 188
PHILBEY, E. R., 167
PHILBRICK, William H., 133
PHILEY, E. R., 167
PHILIPS, V. W., 153
PHILLEY, Allison, 203
PHILLIPS, B., 84
  C. E., 157
  D. C., 158
  George, 89
  H., 187
  J., 140
  John G., 9
  Lewis, 67
  N., 153
  N. T., 95
  R., 17, 129, 187
  S., 67
  Thomas (Capt.), 202
  William, 29, 67
PHIPPER, B., 186
  F., 19, 188
PIAFF, Mathias, 5

PIARSON, R. (sic), 147
PIATT, Richard, 43
PICKEN, M. I., 162
PICKENS, M. J., 176
  S. D., 98, 101
PICKERING, Albert, 121
  Charles, 41
PICKETTS, Thomas, 29
PICKLE, F., 41
PICKLER, J., 140
PICKREL, Daniel, 106
PICO, Manuel, 53
PIERCE, ____, 149
  ____, (Mr.), 27
  A., 158
  C., 163
  Clark, 111
  Ebenezer, 41, 193
  Ezek, 110
  George, 67
  H. E., 51
  Hiram E., 78
  J. C., 52
  J. F., 140
  O. S., 150, 151
  R., 127
  R. A., wife & 1 child, 155
  Robert, 98
  Samuel, 110
  William, 151
  William A. J., 117
  Stephen, 67
  Z., 158
PIERCY, W., 39
PIERRONG, Amos (sic), 199
PIERSON, E. W. (Dr.) & fam., 180
  Frank, 38
  G., 46, 198
  George, 198
  Gustavus, 87
PIERSONG, Amos, 199
PIGUE, James A., 104
PIKE, Alfred, 113
  Anderson, 116
  Barnabas, 82
  Daniel, 117

275

G., 15, 184
J.E., 184
PILBEY, E.R., 167
PILCHER, L. & fam., 154
PIMBERMAN, A.J., 157
PIMPER, L., 156
PINCKNEY, Henry, 122
PINE, H.A., 166
PINKHAM, D.C., 50
  E., 41
  S., 117
PINNEY, A.P., 46
  Austin, 40
PINO, Manuel, 53
PIPER, A.J., 167
PISER, Oliver, 104
PITCHER, George C., 96
PITTMAN, L., 140
PITTS, F. (Dr.), 51
PITZEL,____, 174
PIXBY,____ (Mr.), 95
PIXLEY, William, 13
PLACE, John A., 176
PLACKETT, William L., 119
PLAGRUTER, G., 35
PLANNETT, H., 144
PLANT, H., 145
PLASKETT, William, 119
PLATT,____, Mr., 199
  D.W., 135
  George B., 49, 199
  H.W., 65
  J., 153
  S.M., 145
PLATTE, Edward, 136
  Hiram (sic), 58
PLEASANTS, C.E., 81
PLEDGE, George F., 203
PLEMERY, W., 148
PLILBEY, E.R., 167
PLILEY, E.R., 167
PLUCKETT, William L., 119
PLUM, Joseph, 106
PLUMBNER, James, 102
PLUMEY, E., 63
PLUMMER, A. C., 156, 158

Benjamin, 88
Frederick, 118
J. W., 64, 200
James, 102, 108
S. C. (Dr.,), 102
Samuel C., 108
Wesley D., 102, 111
PLUSKETT, William L., 119
POCOCK, G. W., 14, 183
  Robert, 183
POGUE, A. E., 1
  J. G., 1
POINDEXTER, C. W., 31
  P. H., 159
POINTS, Charles, 39
POLAND, J. T., 42, 195
  John T., 195
POLHEMUS, C. B., 109
POLING, J., 53
POLK, W., 59
  Wesley, 66
POLKHAMUS, C. B., 109
POLKINGHORSE, William, 138
POLLARD,____, (Mrs.), 113
POLLOCK, G.W., 183
  R., 166
  Robert, 14, 183
POLROUSKI, R. K., 17, 187
POMEROY, E., 19, 191
  Lyman, 133
POMROY, E., 191
POND, Alfred, 91
  George H., 138
  Jared Jr., 137
PONNER, Stephen, 87
POOL, Milburn, 124
  Mitburn, 124
  William, 114
POOR,____, 89
  William, 23
POPE, J., 168
  J. L., 143
  Joe, 91
  Robert, 11

Samuel, 143
Wallace, 11
William, 48
POPENOE, Judson, 196
PORLEY, John, 45
PORTER, Benjamin F., 110
  D. J., 116
  George W., 97
  Henry, 107
  Henry F., 119
  J., 41, 159
  J. B., 110
  M., 99
  W. T., 51
  William S., 4
POSEY, O., 39
POSSENOE, J. D., 42, 196
POST, B. F., 24
  C.R., 189
  J.C., 191
  John, 19, 191(x)
  L., 20, 189
  O. A., 7
  Rollin, 19, 189
  Stephen, 103, 108
  Wiliam, E., 203
POSTELTHWAITE, P. H., 106
POTTER, A., 164
  A. J., 140
  Eric, 119
  N. T., 154
  William Jr., 133
POWEL, R. (sic), 157
POWELL, D. A., 29
  J., 29, 148
  J. A., 157
POWERS, Aaron, 126
  J. D., 20, 190
  John, 149
  S., 87
  W., 190
  William, 66
POWLES, Daniel, 100
PRATER, Thomas, 138
PRATHER, Henry, 43
  J. S., 80

PRATT, Gideon, 14
  Henry, 57
  Leva, 109
  Levi, 109
  Thomas, 6
PRENELL, Silas, 37
PRENESS, F., 35
PRENTISS, Joseph, 119
  Stanton, 106
  William (Dr.), 104
PRESSON, ____,(Rev.), 107
  Butler, 107
  Harrison, 98, 107
  Reuben, 107
PRESSOR, A. C., 172
PRESTON, E., 166
  J., 140, 164
  J. K., 133
  Jared, 136
PRETZMAN, Ezra, 115
PREWETT, David, 130
  Matilda, 130
PRICE, ____, 115
  A., 12
  A. & wife, 160
  C., 61
  John, 82
  M., 123
  R. C., 64
  R. H., 81
  S. J., 88
  T., 14
  William, 147
PRIMROSE, T., 190
PRITCHETT, G. W., 55
PRICKETT, Jacob, 147
PRIEST, J., 111
  John W., 111, 112
PRINCE, A., 157
  Warren (Mr.), 201
PRITCHARD, John (Dr.), 87
PRIZER, Thomas, 114
PROBASCO, H. (Mr.), 3
PROBST, ____, 115
PROCTOR, William, 108
PRONTY, Joseph, 146
PROPHY, W., 149

PROSE, Daniel, 30
  Daniel H., 30
  Jacob H., 30
PROSSER, W. F., 103, 109
PROTHERS, David, 55
PROUTY, A. T., 162, 176
PROVEST, Thadeus (sic), 48
PRUDE, J. W., 8
PRULL, George, 108
PUCKET, David, 114
PUGH, Hymelius, 174
PULLAM, H. W., 83
PUNCHES, Samuel, 106
PURCELL, D., 90
  John, 42
  William T., 150
PURCY, S., 51
PURDY, Edmund, 160
PURSEL, Isiah W. (sic), 101
PURSELEY, ____, 20, 191
PURSLEY, B., 191
PURVIANCE, C. E., 101
PURVIS, Henry, 117
PUTERBAUGH, Aley, 137
PUTNAM, Alden, 58
  C. C., 122
  Isaac, 135
  John A. & fam., 180
  L. H., 149
  Seth, 135
  William W., 135
PUTNEY, C. M., 105
PUTT, J., 153
PYATT, John, 47
PYBURN, Edward, 162
PYE, Edward R. & son, 4
  William, 4
PYKES, H., 156

-Q-

QUAMS, W. H., 160

QUEAR, Lewis, 108
QUEEN, J. H., 48
  Lewis, 108
  O. B., 48
QUEER, Lewis, 108
QUENCH, Louis, 54
QUICK, John, 60
  William, 66
QUIGLEY, B. C., 17, 187
  E., 158
  John P., 105
  William, 9
QUIGLY, B.C., 187
  E. (sic), 158
  R. (sic), 89
QUILHIN, A. J., 168
QUILLIN, A. J., 168
QUINGLY, John, 133
QUINN, John 123
  Richard, 121
QUINTON, James, 2
QUIRK, William, 60
QUIRY, Virgil, 120
QUISENBERRY, J. H., 84

-R-

R____, James,135
RABE, John G., 152
RABUN, C., 17, 187
RACHE, F., 167
RACINE, J. B., 168
RADDOCK, William, 49, 199
RADENBOUGH, A., 118, 119
RADER, John, 70
RAE, James, M., 109 (x)
RAEDELL, William, 87
RAFFENSPERGER, D., 199
  Daniel, 49, 199
RAGAN, E., 165
  P., 165
RAHE, John G., 152
RAHM, C., 187
RAHN, John, 117

RAHU, John, 117
RAIMEY, A. C., 149
RAINEY, A. C., 149
   John, 4, 30
   Thomas T., 19, 191
RAINKING, Conrad, 45
RAINS, J., 166
RAIRICK, Michael, 135
RAKE, John G., 156
RALPH, C. R., 65
   Calvin R., 58
   William, 91
RALSTON, S. A., 136
   S. A. V. Y., 136
   V. Y., 136
RAMBE, Jacob (sic), 129
RAMDY, T.S. (sic), 191
RAMSAY, David P., 103, 109
   L., 142
   R., 142
   S., 163
RAMSBEY, Robinson, 106
RAMSDALL, S. L., 33
RAMSDELL, Joseph, 106
RAMSELL, John, 30
RAMSEY, J., 41
   R., 113
   William, 128
RANCKER, Gerard, 82
RANDALL, Calvin, 98
   E., 20, 99, 189
   G. P., 157
   J. D., 159
   N. W., 136
RANDELIN, J. J., 157
RANDOLPH, J. F., 85
RANDY, T.S., 191
RANGE, John, 147
RANKIN, _____, 90
   A., 80
   J. M., 152, 164
   James, 203
   Thomas M., 114
   Thomas M., 96
   William, 17
   William H., 20
RANNEY, H. (sic), 88

RANSOM, John (death of), 93
RANTS, Daniel & fam., 179
RAPHAEL, S., 80
RARDEER, J., 146
RAREDEN, H. C., 38, 194
RARISON, A. P., 23
RASE, W., 163
RATAN, _____, 119
   Abraham, 119
RATCLIFF, Robert B., 102
RATHBURN, James, 55
RATTLE, Samuel, 99
   William, 99
RAUGH, D., 131
   G., 150
RAUSE, George, 54
   James, 54
   William, 54
RAVLIN, D. H., 152
RAWLINGS, L., 167
RAWSON, James, 135
   Sumner, 135
RAY, _____ (Mr.), 75
   Edwin, 117
   James, 120
   L., 168
   Moses, 25
   Reson, 56
   Shorty, 4
RAYBUM., J. P., 61 (x)
RAYBURN, W. A., 8
RAYMAN, Henry, 126
RAYMOND, A., 2
RAYNER, Daniel O., 109
RAYWALT, E., 56
REA, Evan, 117
   James M., 103
   William (sic), 43
READ, A. N., 149
   Charles F. (Lt.), 78
   I. K., 145
   John L., 78
   S. P., 137
   W. C., 168
READER, S. P., 80

READING, A. B. O., 163
REAM, S. A., 30
REAMS, A. J., 83
RECARD, C., 191
RECORD, C., 19, 191
RECTOR, W., 96
REDD, R. H., 80
REDDICK, W., 199
REDDING, D., 90
REDENBOUGH, A., 119
REDENOR, P., 16
REDICK, J., 99
REDINGTON, E. S., 103
REDSHAW, John, 151
REE, James M., 103
REED, _____, 199
   _____ (Mr.), 161
   A., 148, 164
   A. B., 140
   Alexander H., 82
   C. W., 163
   Casper, 107
   Charles, 48
   E. D., 148
   E. S., 158
   Elijah, 127
   George, 101, 147
   H. J., 52
   J., 130
   J. A., 163
   J. B., 60
   J. D., 150
   James, 44
   John, 54
   John B., 66
   Jonas, 66
   L. P., 90
   R. M., 140
   S., 142, 175
   S. A., 146
   S. P., 177
   S. W., 154, 157
   T., 145
   W. C., 18, 187
   William, 42, 54
   William M., 131
   William T., 108
REEDER, _____ (Mr.), 54

REES, George, 11
    J. (sic), 163
    John, 2, 122
    S., 175
    William C., 105
REESE, C.W., 203
    Peter, 149
REEVE, W. B., 152
REEVER, Josiah, 135
REEVES, ____ (Dr.) &
    fam., 20
    ____(Mrs.), 171
    B. D., 49
    Edward & fam., 40
    G. W., 55
    John, 89
    Josiah, 135
    W. B., 152
    William C., 126
REID, B. J., 51
    W.C., 187
REILEY, N. N.(sic), 66
REILLY J. N., 57
REILY, Joseph C. (sic), 48
REIN, E., 179
REINHART, P., 118
REIR, E., 179
REIS, E., 179
RELLER, William, 38
REMINGTON, C., 83
    J., 99
REN, James M., 103
RENDALE, J. R., 84
RENDALL, J. C., 151
RENDEL, R. Y., 105
RENNY, Moses, 41
RENOIS, B. C., 20
RENT, A.N., 185
RENTWAY, E. M., 163
RENYON, A. S., 48
RERGENDALE, A. G., 163
RES, James M., 103
RESLEY, J. W., 95
RESS, George, 11
RESSETER, Nathan, R., 117
RETTER, W., 157

REVFRO, W., 53
REXFORD, Lyman 43
REYNOLDS, ____, 99
    ____(Mr.) & bro., 44
    A., 8, 63
    Alonzo, 59
    Benjamin W., 117
    E., 33
    E. S., 46, 198
    J., 18
    James L., 118
    Jeremiah, 135
    L. B., 63
    Levi, 105
    Lucian B., 59
    N. Nazro, 101
    O., 63
    R., 58
    Russell S., 103
    S. D., 52
    Samuel, 110
    Susan C., 172
    T., 18, 187
    Thomas, 187
    W., 58
REZNER, Garrett, 123
    Solomon, 123
RHINIE, J., 100
RHOADS, Simon, 137
RHODES, G. W., 6
    J., 63
    J. A., 59
    L., 108
    Samuel, 107
    William, 80
RICE, Abel H., 53
    Charles, 159
    E. V., 149
    George, 29, 54, 116, 160
    H., 20, 190
    J., 149, 158
    James F., 106
    Joel, 53
    Josiah, 103
    Mathias, 20
    O. E., 154
    Robert, 92
    S. Sander, 162

    William, 54
RICHARD, M. A., 2
RICHARDS, A. M., 92
    Charles, W., 30
    Enoch, 123
    H. J., 23
    J. W. & fam., 103
    John C., 10
RICHARDSON, A., 83, 150
    A. J., 80
    Francis, 45
    H., 153
    J. M., 167
    J. S., 163
    James H., 54
    John, 57
    John C., 136
    N. W., 105
    R., 148
    Samuel, 59
    W. P., 11
RICHEY, ____, 140
    George, 99
    Stuart, 136
RICHMOND, D., 100
    John, 112
    S., 39
    Thomas G., 98
RICHTER, C., 35
RICKCORD, A., 109
RIDDLE, A. J., 12
    Hugh, 73
    J., 104
    J. L., 153
    J. R., 17
    J. S., 144
    James Jr., 98
    Lewis, 86
    S., 104
    William, 11
RIDER, J., 64
RIDGELEY, George, 123
RIDGELY, Lawrence, 174
RIDGEWAY, J., 26
RIEBER, J. C., 5
RIELY, Edwin A., 195
    F. A. (sic), 42, 195

RIEN, John, 151
RIGBY, George, 25
RIGG, Thomas (sic), 138
   William, 57
RIGGS, D., 67
   Frank, 58
   J., 115
   J. R. (Dr.), 68
   P., 115
   William R., 67
   Z. F., 54
RILEY, J., 84
   J. N., 66
   Susan J., 172
RINENEY, R. G., 64
RING, Patrick, 131
RINGLAND, B.F., 181
RIORDAN, H.C., 194
RIPLER, P. W., 42, 196
RIPLEY, Jacob, 136
RIPLINGER, John H., 147
RIPPER, Enoch B., 123
   I., 140
RISDON, John A., 131
RISHAM, E., 179
RISHEL, Anthony, 178
RISINGTON, E. S., 109
RISK, William, 103, 108
   William (Capt.), 107
RISLIN, John & son, 19, 190
RISSLER, William, 196
RISTLIN, J. (sic), 190
RITCHEY, Josiah, 104
   William, 90
RITCHIE, J. C., 145
RITHEY, Josiah (sic), 104
RITTER, W., 157
RITYET, Conrad, 101
ROACH, James, 24
ROBBINS, C., 38
   Collier, 143
   Edwin D., 117
   Lorain, 5
   William H., 37
ROBERSON, L. H. (sic), 55
ROBERT, Darnas (sic), 102

ROBERTS, _____ (Dr.), 95
   Benjamin, 178
   C. R., 129
   Edgar, 134
   J., 113, 144
   J. G., 82
   J. P., 63
   J. W., 49
   John, 68, 108
   John & fam., 44
   L. W., 31
   Pulaski, 134, 147
   Robert (sic), 68
   S., 144
   Samuel M., 88
   W., 144
   William, 68
   William H., 112
ROBERTSON,
   _____(Mr.), 47
   D., 164
   Henry, 67
   Henry J. R., 67
   J., 7, 182
   J. M., 32
   James (Capt.), 108 (x)
   James W., 147
   John, 24, 122, 182
   John J., 67
   W. D., 147
ROBINS, C. (sic), 38
ROBINSON, _____,
   (Mr.), 47
   A., 20
   A. G., 13
   B. R., 53
   C. H., 131
   Caroline, 3 chldrn & driver, 179
   Charles, 23
   D. C., 53
   Edwin, 201
   Elijah, 47
   F. P., 18
   Francis, 169
   G., 166
   H. H., 48
   Henry & lady, 55

   J. D., 18
   J. F. (Dr.), 23
   J. M., 166
   J. O., 91
   James, 27, 64
   James W., 121
   John, 114
   John H., 114
   L. H., 38
   Lemuel, 43
   Leonard, 120
   M. W., 98
   Moses, 102
   N. L., 158
   R. G., 18
   Richard, 121
   S., 48, 107, 171
   Samuel O., 155
   W., 90
   William J., 171
ROBSON, Joseph, 66
ROBY, James, 95
ROCKAFELLAR,
   William H., 117
ROCKE, Edward, 121
ROCKEFELLER,
   William H., 117
ROCKENBAUGH, F., 5
ROCKS, Edward, 121
ROCKWELL, Alfred H., 102
   Daniel, 124
   James B., 102
   William, 92
RODENBOUGH, A., 118, 119
RODGERS, _____ (Mr.) & fam., 171
   A., 16
   James M., 106
   Morris, 102
   T. W., 18
   William, 116
RODHAM, John, 49
   S. F., 41
ROE, _____ (Mr.), 71
   J. S., 147
   S. M., 56
   Silas, 102

ROEBERRY, J., 145
ROGER, David, 32
  J. D., 51
ROGERS, ___(Dr.), 181
  A., 29
  A. W., 12
  Anthony, 147
  B. F., 158
  B. F. (death of), 94
  E. H., 160
  Elizabeth, 58
  Emerson, 124
  George, 63
  Jedediah & sons, 60
  John, 91, 124
  Juba, 124
  L. M. (Mr.), 3, 181
  Nelson, 137
  R., 158
  W., 52
  William J., 154
ROHER, Fred (sic), 200
ROHRER, Elisha, 195
  Frederick, 74, 200
ROHTER, E., 42, 195
ROLLINS, David M., 110
ROM, N. (sic), 80
ROMANS, W. G., 156
ROMINO, Frank, 53
ROOD, H. W., 45
  Obadiah, 59
ROODS, L., 108
  Samuel, 107
ROOIL, William F., 170
ROOKENBAUGH, F., 5
ROOKER, S. C., 170
ROOP, Benjamin, 135
  James, 135
  John, 135
  Joshua, 135
ROOT, Henry, 21
  James, 99
  Orville, 141
  Z., 191
ROPER, William, 42
RORER, Daniel, 90
ROSABAUGH, J., 167
  P., 167
ROSASABAUGH, J., 167

  P., 167
ROSBOROUGH,
  Thomas, 123
ROSE, ___(death of), 175
  Benjamin, 112
  C. B., 110
  Daniel, 30
  Daniel H., 30
  Elias, 138
  Ezekiel, 45
  Francis, 14
  H., 110
  Ira, 3
  Jacob, 121
  Jacob H., 30
  John, 117
  W. W., 144
  William, 104, 107
ROSENBERGER, W., 47
ROSENKRANS, H. (Dr.), 61
ROSINBURY, William, 154
ROSS, ___ (Mr.), 55
  Benjamin, 84
  C. P., 38
  Charles T., 117
  D. S., 23
  H. C., 98
  I., 154
  J., 158
  W., 41
  William S., 82
ROSSE, Daniel, 67
ROSSEAU, William, 196
ROTH, G., 35
  John A., 65
  L., 35
ROTHWICK, ___(Mrs.), 161
ROTTENHOUSE, W. E., 158
ROUNTREES, ___ (Maj.) & company, 90
ROUSE, Collin, 98
ROWAN, Hugh, 87
  Patrick, 87

ROWAND, W. D., 84
ROWE, Alfred, 149
  Cyrus, 78
  E., 149
  J., 20, 190
  James, 114, 190
  Morris, 114
  O. M., 130
  T. K., 84
ROWER, O., 153
ROWLAND, D. A., 150 (x)
ROWLEY, A., 167
  Aldrich M., 109
  Calvin, 27
  L. E., 135
  M. H., 135
ROWSON, Asa, 54
ROY, James, 120
  W. S. Sr., 112
  W. S. Jr., 112
ROYSTON, John H., 70
RREEN, John P. (sic), 147
RUBLE, Owen, 121
RUCKER, Thomas, 53
RUCKLE, Matthew, 37
RUDD, H., 15, 184
  Henry, 184
  J., 15, 184
  James, 184
RUDDY, M. S., 30
RUDE, W. B., 64
RUDICIL, David, 143
RUDOLPH, A., 5
RUFFNER, H. (Mr.), 3
RUGER, A. P., 90
RUGG, D., 88
  T., 88
RULAND, Lindley, H., 47
RULE, John, 138 (x)
RUMFELT, S., 163, 166
RUMGAN, B. Y., 147
  I., 147
RUMMEL, E., 149
RUMRILL, F., 99
RUMSEY, W. H., 52
RUNDEL, R. Y., 105
RUNGAN, B. Y., 147
  I., 147
RUNNELS, Perry, 172

R., 32
William, 32
RUNYAN, A., 31
  A. N., 31
  H., 126
  O. R., 31
  S., 31
RUPLE, John, 45
RUSCHE, W., 35
RUSE, Jacob, 121
RUSK, Benjamin, 13
RUSSEL, Robert, 171
RUSSELL, ____(Mrs.), 113
  Boggs, 60
  C., 81
  Cyrus, 137
  D., 165
  David, 90, 135
  E., 64
  Ellis, 95
  G. P., 58
  H. B. (Dr.), 1
  H. C. wife & 7 chldrn, 180
  H. P. (Col.) & company, 141
  James, 137
  P. S., 1
  Robert, 171
  S. P., 158
  Samuel, 108
  T. A., 63
  W., 101
  W. H. (Col.), 2, 9, 12 (x)
  William, 64
  William G., 63
RUSSON, G., 180
  S., 180
RUSSUM, T. B., 81
RUST, C. W., 153
RUTHERFORD, H., 31
  J. R., 53
  R., 31
RYAN, ____(Dr.) (death of), 94
  ____(Mr.), 71
  E., 146

Joel, 46, 73, 76
John, 67
M., 150
Mathew (sic), 150
N. A., 131
P., 140
William, 97
RYMER, P. J., 80
RYNE, John (sic), 134, (sic) 147
RYNNEARSON, A. C., 78
RYON, William (sic), 97
RYTSON, H. W. (sic), 167

-S-

SABINE, David, 43
SACKEIDER, S., 117
SACKET, J., 52
SACKETT, Alonzo, 151
  Dennis, 151
SADDLER, O. R., 32
SADORUS, Henry, 43
SAERS, Edward, 91
SAGE, J., 24
  Jonathan, 119
  Redmond, 24
SAGER, Henry, 171
SAHLY, C., 151
SAHUMBRIE, H. J., 4
SAID, William, 48
SAILADY, O., 151
SAILSBERRY, Dennis, 97
SAINT CLAIR, W. M., 53
SAINT JOHN, A. C., 67
  Edward, 146
  John, 6
  John & 2 svts., 31
  M. G., 109
  Thomas, 6
SALE, J. K., 31
SALEE, J., 190
SALES, Caleb, 108
  John, 19, 46, 190
SALLIARY, G., 165
SALS, James (sic), 155

SALSBURY, D. C., 79
SALSWORTH (see also SAULSWORTH)
SALT, A. C., 166
SALTS, B., 163
  M., 163
SALVER, D. B., 174
SALTZER, Herr, 96
SAMPLE, A. L., 17
SAMPSKE, W. W., 72
SAMPSON, ____(Lt.), 54
  B. M., 153
  Samuel, 112
SAMUELS, B. Y., 31
  Benjamin A., 165
  John, 79
SANBORN, Abram, 1
  H., 113
  Jeremiah, 118
  L. W., 109
SANBURN, J. L., 131
SANDBORN, E., 145
  T., 145
SANDER, S., 162
SANDERS, ____, 124
  ____(Mr.), 54
  C. W., 162
  J. R., 132
  Joseph & wife, 132
  W. L., 168
SANDERSON, J. S., 162
SANDFORD, B. F., 119
  F. H., 79
  R. F., 119
SANDILAN, Alex, 65
SANDLIN, J., 160
SANFORD, F. H., 70
  George A., 27
  Richard, 136
  Thomas, 131
SANGER, D. F., 9
SANKEY, Samuel, 5
SANSON, G., 143
SANTON, D., 99
SARBER, S.H., 187
SARGEANT, ____(Mr.), 24
  Alonzo, 90

283

J. B., 29
Nahum, 90
SARGENT, Alonzo, 90
Nahum, 90
William S., 106
SARIPT, J. C. (sic), 147
SARLER, S. H., 18, 186, 187
SARLES, Simeon B., 103
SARRIMORE, T., 143
SARRSON, Lewis, 146
SARVER, J. H., 86
SATER, Thomas, 90
SATERTY, Albert, 49
SATTERFIELD, J. F., 98
SATTHERTHWRIGHT, B. (sic), 166
SAUDILAN, Alex, 65
SAULPAN, S., 15, 184
SAULPAUGH, Samuel, 184
SAULSWORTH (see also SALSWORTH)
SAUNDERS,_____ (Mr.), 128
  A. A., 142
  C. J., 142
  C. W., 159
  Henry, 118
  Ira J., 102
  J. N., 105
  Robert T., 79
  William J., 105
SAVAGE, Margon, 48
  Morgan, 48
SAW. P. C. A., 165
SAWIN, John, 60
SAWTELL, D., 98
SAWYER, H., 157
  J., 11, 23
  L., 113
  Merrick, 136, 155
  Thomas S., 28
SAXTON, C., 125
SAYLES, G. W., 166
SAYRE, George, 10, 183
  George D., 183
SAYRES, M. D., 168

SAYWARD, William T., 77
SCARBOROUGH, A., 80
SCARBROUGH, R. A., 137
SCHAEFFER, David, 37
SCHAFFER,_____ (Mr.) & 4 young men, 22
SCHAIBROCK, G., 35
SCHARMAN, B., 35
  T., 35
SCHAUB, T., 35
SCHEIBROCK, G., 35
SCHEID, F. S., 35
SCHELL, F. M., 159, 167
SCHELLEY, Conrad (sic), 165
SCHELLING, John, 120
SCHENCK, C. S., 84, 85
  Jackson, 102, 111
SCHENEFELT, H., 15, 185
SCHENITOSKI, A., 19, 189
SCHEUTEN, N. N., 85
SCHILLING, John, 120
SCHILLINGER, Benjamin, 109
SCHINDLER, A., 23, 192
SCHLAGIDER, F., 35
SCHMIDT, T., 35
SCHNAEIDER, D., 35
SCHNAIDER,_____, 35
SCHNEIDER,_____, 35
  D., 35
  G., 34
SCHNI, J. (sic), 126
SCHOTIN, W., 89
SCHRADER, Frederick, 107
SCHRAFFT,_____(sic), 35
SCHRORDER, Reese, 180
SCHROTER, Selphatius, 146
SCHWALKA, A. E., 54
SCHWEERKOTTING, F., 154

SCHWENKER, C. H., 156
SCHWENN, J., 130
SCIMMERS, M., 34
SCOFFIELD,_____ (Dr.), 45
SCOFIELD, George, 126
SCONCE, Samuel, 155
SCOTT,_____(Mr.), 2, 92
  Andrew, 73
  C. H., 150
  D. B., 5
  David, 3
  George, 30, 67
  H. C., 30
  H. W., 168
  Hiram, 100
  J., 150
  J. D., 63
  J. M. & fam., 167
  J. X., 150
  James M. (Capt.), 138
  John, 73
  John (Sr.), 73
  John A., 88
  John B., 105
  N., 107
  P. M., 67
  R., 153
  R. B. F., 63
  S., 153
  S. M., 154
  Samuel, 138
  Smith, 39
  T., 153
  Thomas, 45
  Thomas B., 48
  W., 63
  William, 79, 110
  William W., 90
SCOVILL, William, 121 (x)
SCRIBER, C., 98
SCRIBNER, B., 154
  S., 107
SCRIBNERS, B. (sic), 154
SCRIVENER, Alexander, 86

SCROFORD, J., 2
SCRUGGINS, John, 20
SCUDDER, W. H., 142
SCULLY, W. O. H., 6
SCUTTER, J. G., 6
SEABAUGH, John, 89
SEABURG, P. S., 167
SEABURY, Edgar, 82
SEAMAN, J. W., 81, 82
  W., 41, 143
  William, 45
SEARCY, William B., 89
SEARL, ___, 199
SEARLES, Daniel, 45
  Jesse, 45
SEARSEY, Albert, 86
SEARY, T., 166
SEATON, G. W., 166
SEAWARD, R. D., 168
SEAWGOOS, H. (sic), 52
SEBRING, J., 145
  Thomas, 145
SECKET, Samuel, 53
SEDDELL, Richard, 124
SEEBORN, Alpha Jr., 91
  Eli, 91
  Elisha, 91
SEED, Ellis, 105, 111
SEEHORN, Alpha Jr., 91
  Eli, 91
  Elisha, 91
SEELEY, T. W., 10
SEELY, Thomas, 149
SEERE, J. B. (sic), 59
SEEVERS, Benjamin F., 196
  Nathaniel, 42
SEGVENS, S. F., 90
SEIBERT, A., 131
  Jacob L., 90
  R. W., 90
  S. J., 131
SELANDEK, S., 48
SELICK, F., 66
SELLERS, J. H., 80
  Michael, 133
SELLS, D. S., 32
SELSER, A., 81
  J. W., 81

William, 81
SEMPLE, J. W., 64, 200
SEPER, Peter, 133
SERGEANT, E., 159
SERLAND, J. M., 153
SETTLEMIRE, D., 190
  G., 189
SETTLEMYER, D., 20, 190
SEVENY, William, 146
SEVIER, Joseph, 86
  V. (Maj.), 86
SEWARD, A.L., 203
  J., 144
  J. M., 39
SEWELL, Martin, 122
  S. S., 108
SEWIN, John, 60
SEXTON, M., 39
  N., 20
SEYMOUR, H., 112
  H. J. B., 98
SGEVENS, S. F., 90
SHACKELFORD, James, 71
  John, 71
SHADRICK, R., 42, 196
SHAFER, Henry, 108
  J. S., 147
SHAFF, J. W., 10
SHAFFEE, S. M., 143
SHAFFENR, C. S. (sic), 103
SHAFFER, A., 108
  Chris S., 109
  G. J., 108
  H., 108
  Henry, 102
  J., 63
  John W., 102
  W., 17
SHAFFNER, C. S., 103
SHALLOWHOUSE, E., 58
SHANELY, J., 44
SHANKS, ___(Dr.), 57
SHANLY, Christian, 115
SHANNON, Andrew, 44
  F. B., 65

Francis, 114
  James, 123
  Thomas, 64 (x)
  Wilson, 123
SHAPPER, John W., 121
SHARE, H. J., 82
SHARP, C., 130
  Charles, 175
  Isaac, 1
  James, 4
  M. D., 166
  P. T., 2
  Peter G., 2
  R. L., 167
  W. B., 5
  William, 2
SHARPE, Joseph (death of), 94
SHARPER, J., 157
SHARPLEY, Paul, 146
SHATLOCK, Charles, 22
  Henry, 22
SHATSWELL, Richard, 68
SHATTUCK (see also SHATTUK)
  Charles W., (sic), 184
  Henry C., 184
  William H., 119
SHATTUK (see also SHATTUCK)
  Henry C. (sic) (Shattuck?), 184
SHAVEN, J., 164
SHAVER, P., 166
SHAW, Barlett, 106
  Bart, 111
  F. D. C., 156
  George, 136
  J. E., 112, 158
  J. T., 129
  J. W., 37
  P. F., 29
  S., 108
  T. G., 167
  Willaim, 98
SHAEFFER, F. W., 11
SHEARER, Arthur, wife & 5 chldrn, 78

E. C., 159
S. H., 148
SHEARMAN, Phineas, 117
SHEDDEL, Bernard, 80
SHEEK, M. L., 121
SHEFFER, N. V. (Mr.), 132
SHEFFIELD, James E., 119
SHEHAN, Thomas (sic), 89
SHEILDS, Benjamin (sic), 71
SHELDON, G., 63
SHELHAMMER, S., 65
SHELL, J. C., 81
SHELLEBARGER, P., 142
SHELLEY, D., 162
SHELLHAMMER, Aaron, 108
John, 108
SHELTON, A. C., 129
J. H., 156
Peter, 106
W. M. O., 19, 188
William C., 47
SHENABARGER, Miller, 102
SHENK, George, 165
SHEPARD, Benjamin W., 103
James, 31
SHEPPARD, G. D., 28
H., 19
J., 148
SHEPHERD, Edmund, 105
Henry, 199
James, 53, 199
SHEPPARDS, J. M., 125
SHEPPERD, J. A., 157
J. M., 125
Miles, 106
S. W., 163
SHERBURNE, J., 150
SHERDON, T. (sic), 168
SHERIDAN, J. G., 140

SHERLAND, G. A., 9
SHERMAN, B. & fam., 35
Charles, 122
Isaac, 152, 156
L. H., 88
SHERRILL, L. J., 31
M., 31
SHERVIN, P., 59
SHERWOOD, J., 98
John, 107
SHETTENKIRK, D. G., 117
SHEURMAN, Phineas, 117
SHEWER, G. L., 57
SHIEFORD, J. A., 142
J. H., 143
SHIELDS, ____, 92
Benjamin, 71
W. H., 144
SHIFFER, J. B., 143
SHIMBERGER, M., 108
SHIN, Thomas, 64
SHINEBERGER, M., 108
SHINER, John, 37
SHINIER, Andrew, 124
SHINN, Asa, 165
SHINNABERGER, Anson, 128
SHIPMAN, G. M., 61
W. B., 115
SHIRLEY, E. A., 117
SHIUIER, Andrew, 124
SHIVELY, Henry, 88
James, 30
SHOBERT, F., 41
SHOCKLEY, Mars, 179
SHOEMAKER, Henry, 133
M., son & dau., 161
W., 53
Woodford, 56
SHOFFNER, C. J., 171
SHOLL, Adam (sic), 203
John, 203
SHOMAKER, Woodford (sic), 56
SHOOK, Martin L., 102

SHOOKS, Robert, 133
SHORE, James, 104
Thomas, 104
Thomas P., 104
SHORT, J. A., 21
J. M., 158
John, 65
Thomas, 20
SHOTSWELL, Richard, 68
SHOTTENKIRK, D. G., 117
SHOTTS, J., 18, 186
SHOUP, H., 145
SHOW, Joel F., 170
SHOWERS, J. S., 42, 195
John S., 195
SHOWMAN, P. B., 42
SHRADE, J., 72
SHROFF, Peter, 203
SHRORDER, Reese, 180
SHROUDER, Reese, 180
SHUAR, A. (sic), 55
SHUBAR, A., 54
SHUEL, A. P., 149
SHUGERT, Jacob, 101
SHUHAN, William, 119
SHULL, Adam, 203
John, 203
SHULTHIES, John M., 165
SHUMAN, Andrew, J., 68
SHUMWAY, S. B., 98
SHUN, ____ (Mrs.), niece & nephew, 97
SHUPE, David, 58
SHUTT, J., 26, 186
SHUTTS, Valentine, 203
SIBECK, Frederick, 109
SIDELL, ____ (Mr.) & wife, 90
SIGLER, A. R., 131
SIGSBY, Ephrian, 136
Robert, 136
SILCOX, R., 187
SILLHEIMER, P. B., 113
SILLSBRIDGE, J. S., 13
SILMON, T., 29
SILSBY, H. A. (Dr.), 105

SILTER, E., 149
SIMAN, ____(Mr.), 61
SIMMERMAN, W.H., 203
SIMMERS, ____, 87
SIMMON, J., 142
  W., 142
SIMMONS, H., 168
  Joseph M., 118
  M., 179
  T., 167
  William, 179
SIMMS, P. T., 147
SIMONDS, ____, 26, 193
  Silas, 41, 193
SIMONS, A. H., 136, 166
  E., 166
  E. W., 136
SIMPKINS, M., 160
SIMPSON, B., 147
  D., 100
  F. R., 42, 195
  Francis R., 195
  James, 104, 203
  S. M. B., 142
  W., 164
SIMS, ____(Mr.), 73
  Con Ferdinand, 182
  H., 53
SIMSON, ____, 115
  D., 100
  V. A., 137
SINCLAIR, C., 191
  C. M., 51
  Charles, 20, 191
  H. M., 151
  J. N., 18
SINEX, Samuel, 32
SING, Jacob, 116
SINGER, J. A., 167
SIRES, D., 163
SISSON, Ed., 112
  George E., 112
SITES, George, 114
  Horris (sic), 114
SITTIBRUIVE, G., 20, 189
SKAGG, Eli, 75
SKAGGS, Eli, 75

SKARG, N., 146
SKARZYNSKI, A., 84
SKEAN, Nancy, 169
SKEGGS, James, 161
SKELLY, W. P., 17
SKIDMORE, ____(Mr.), 152
  J., 49
  J. S., 169
SKILES, W. H., 31
SKILLMAN, A., 129
  J., 129
SKINNER, B. R., 116
  Charles, D., 118
  E. D., 118 (x)
  Elisha, 41
  James, 39
  John D., 79
  M., 68
  W. B., 98
  William, 83
SLADE, W. H., 52
SLAGLE, C. F., 42, 195
  Charles F., 195
  James M., 103
  Levi, 96
SLATER, L., 63
SLATOR, L., 63
SLATTEY, J. (sic), 153
SLAUGHTER, R. P. (Dr.), 11
  T. M., 159
  William, 111
SLAVEN, Michael, 137
SLEIGH, Sarah A., 172
SLIFER, Tilghman, 111
SLIGHT, Robert, 48
SLOAN, Andrew J., 151
  John, 105, 119
  Samuel, 119
  William, 37
SLOCUMB, Stillman, 106
SLOSS, L., 52
  L. L., 31
SLUMAN, Andrew J., 68
SLYE, ____(Dr.) & fam., 21
  Edwin D., 48
SMAGG, William, 99

SMALL, ____(Dr.), 182
  James B., 196
  Thomas, 6
  Thomas B. (Dr.), 7, 182
  Thomas W., 58
SMALLEY, T. C., 63
SMART, C., 168
  J. B., 36
SMETHER, Louis, 151
SMIDT, C., 157
SMITH, ____, (Capt.), 60
  ____(Mr,), 45, 87. 103
  A., 15, 66, 149, 150 160, 165, 185
  A. F., 141
  A. J., 113
  Alfred, 114
  Alino F., 101
  Andrew, 82, 83
  B. F., 7, 176
  B. G., 128
  C., 2, 99, 167
  C. B., 133
  C. D., 4
  C. G., 18
  C. M., 167
  Charles, 148
  Charles L., 81
  D., 121, 147
  Dan C., 146
  Darius, 107
  E. J., 79
  E. P., 55
  Edward, 110, 161
  Eli, 5
  F. W., 112
  Francis A., 98
  Frank, 196
  Foster & wife, 133
  G. A., 145
  G. C., 63
  G. J. & fam., 35
  G. W., 100
  George, 70, 175
  George A., 72
  George C., 92
  George E., 9
  H., 15, 153, 185

287

H. B., 168
H. D., 60
H. F., 138
Hamilton, 185
Henry, 105
Henry (Gov.), 121
Hiram, 161
Hubbard, 123
Isaac, 78, 115
J., 18, 79, 115, 142, 148, 164, 167
J. A., 58
J. B., 165, 166
J. C., 14, 25, 116, 184
J. C. P., 148
J. G., 79
J. G. W., 168
J.H., 184
J. J., 163
J. R., 61, 167
J. S., 23, 192
J. T., 80
J. W., 2, 157
Jacob, 122
James, 107, 114
James W., 97
Jesse, 130
Joe, 45
John, 42, 70, 89(x), 127, 163
John B., 81
John H., 130
John L., 98
John M., 1
John Q., 126
Joseph 5, 129, 131
King, 99
L., 11
L. A., 144
Laertes S., 102
Leo. Jr., 75
Levi, 95
Levi (death of), 94
M., 2, 33
M. D., 59
M. T., 19, 189
Martin, 134
Martin L., 147
Michael, 164

N., 153
Nelson, 87
O. P., 131
P. R., 129
Patrick, 54
R., 52, 157
R. B., 47
R. D., 82
R. P., 99
Robert, 33
S., 52, 142, 148
S. D., 131
Samuel R., 6
Silas, 23
T., 100
T. & Co., 167
T. B., 122
T. M., 154
Thomas, 41, 47
W., 57, 153, 157
W. A., 157
W.B. (Dr.), 201
W. E., 63
W. H., 42, 197
W. M., 154
W. O., 173
W. P., 49
William, 24, 69, 197(x)
William M., 42, 197
William R., 179
William T., 102
Willis & Co., 57
SMITHERS, S., 160
SMITHSON, J. A., 156
SMOKER, P., 19
SMOOT, E. L., 112
SMULLIN, W., 153
SMULLIO, W., 153
SNAVELY, W., 46, 198
   W.J., 198
SNEADE, Samuel, 27
SNEE, Thomas, 187
SNEED, Sarah A. (Mrs.), 125
SNESSBY, Henry, 110
SNEVELEY, William, 115
SNIDER, B., 148
   D. C., 159
   H., 61

O., 61
O. T., 157
SNIFFIN, G. F., 85
SNITER, P., 157
SNITOWSKI, A., 189
SNODGRASS, J. W., 175
SNOOK, J. W., 150
SNOW, E., 203
   L. A., 136
   Noah J., 105
   S., 100
SNOWDEN, W. N., 153
SNYDER, C. K., 31
   Daniel, 159
   H., 142
   Henry, 131
   John, 141
   L. D., 149
   Mahlon, 149
   S., 188
   S. C., 131
   W., 130
SOFLEY, E., 32
SOLOMON, W., 30
SOMERFIELD, James, 46, 75
   John 46, 75
SOMERS, Leonard, 203
SON, Jacob, 37
   Reuben, 8
SONDER, L., 150
SONG, J., 154
SONGER, J. A., 167
SOO, Reuben, 8
SOO____, Reuben, 8
SORGENFRY, W. H., 53
SOULE, B. M., 118
   Joseph Sr., 89
SOUTH, Daniel, 123
SOUTHARD, L., 164
SOUTHER, William, 68
SOUTHERLAND, Roderick, 67
   S., 165
   T., 165
SOUTHWICK,____(Mrs.), 107
   E. B. (Dr.), 135
   G. W. (Dr.), 48 (x)

M. J., 119
SOWLE, Jason, 148
SPAFORD, W. P., 41, 193
SPANGIER, Fleming, 146
SPANGLE, G., 153
SPARK, J., 168
SPARKS, G., 164
  J. M., 158
  L., 44
  M., 164
  P., 44
  S. W., 70
  W., 164
SPARS, Joseph (death of), 93
SPARROW, William (Dr.), 10
SPARROWHAWN, S., 99
SPAUGLE, G., 153
SPAULDING, A. G., 153
  E. C., 77
  Henry, 136
SPEAR, A., 17
SPEARS, H. T. M., 51
  J., 64, 111
  John, 113
SPEEKMAN, Jonas, 119
SPEELMAN, Jonas, 119
SPEER, Moray T., 118
SPEES, John, 65
  Joseph C., 118, 119
SPENCE. J., 145
SPENCER, Andrew, 123
  D., 153
  E., 49
  E. F. (death of), 94
  James, 30, 82
  M. W., 153
  O., 73
  R., 17
  W., 153
  W. B., 104
  W. H., 119
  William, 63
SPERRY, ___ (Mr.), 194
  Jacob, 114
  John, 174
  M. S., 119

W. J., 36, 194
SPEULDA, William, 197
SPICER, Ezekiel, 117
  J., 99
  Luba (Miss), 141
SPIKER, Joseph, 100
SPINGER, James B. (sic), 104
  S. W., 104
SPINNING, J., 148
SPLAWN, Maberry (sic), 169
SPOFFORD, A. J., 80
  W., 26, 193
SPOON, W., 154
SPOONER, E. A., 33
SPRAGUE, J. C. & fam., 150
  John, 138
  M., 158
  Peter, 138
  R. T., 12
  Thomas, 174
SPRECHER, Frederick, 114
SPRING, C. A., 55
  John, 67
SPRINGER, Abigal, 170
  Charles, 75
  E. F., 156
  J. P., 129
  J. P. wife & child., 156
  James B., 104
  Robert, 75
  S. O. (Mrs.) & child, 156
  S. W., 104
  S. W. (Mr.), 75
  W. H., 156
SPROUSE, John, 151
SPRUANCE, I., 189
  J., 20, 189
SPURK, William, 203
SQUEER, G. & wife (sic), 142
SQUIBB, N. D., 149
SQUIRE, C. H., 128
  G. & wife, 142
  Melvin, 122

S. H., 18
SQUIRES, E. W., 71
  John, 71
  Ogden, 109
  R. J., 71
  Zacharias, 109
STAFFORD, H., 146
  J. G., 52
STALEY, H., 153
  R., 19
STALL, C. S., 111
STANBUROUGH, Charles, 68
STANDEFORD, M. G. (sic), 107
STANDFORD, M. G., 107
STANFIELD, Robert, 93
  S. H., 63
STANLEY, C., 173
  C. G., 84
  George, 128
  J. N., 174
  S. F., 80
STANTON, Andrew, 13
  B., 99
  F. S., 15
STAPLES, D. J., 86, 204
  David J., 204
  John Frederick, 204
STARK, D. W., 139
STARKEY, John, 93
STARKS, Henry P., 105
  Nancy (Mrs.), 169
  William, 146
STARKWEATHER, W., 162
STARR, A., 19, 30, 191
  F., 19, 191
  H., 150
  James, 144
STATES, William, 25
STATIS, J. J., 20
STATON, D. A., 168
STAUNTON, A., 26
  James, 91
  William F., 169
STAUTS, Joseph P., 103
ST. CLAIR, W. M., 53

STEAM, J. O., 140
STEAN, J. W., 70
STEARNS, A. C., 78
   M. G., 158
STEBBINS, A. C., 41, 193
   E., 26, 193
   Rufus, 110
   William P., 81
STECK, Amos, 90
STEDMAN, William L., 55
STEEL, A. H. (Dr.), 51
   C., 177
   J. S., 19
   W., 154
   William, 131
   Z. D., 84
STEELE, Henry, 24
   J. L., 158
   M., 151
   R., 202
   Samuel C., 75
STEEN, John, 154
   Peter, 154
STEES, F., 100
STEEVERS, B. F., 42, 196
STEFFEY, C. H., 103
STEIN, F., 142
   J., 142
   W., 142
STEINBACKER, E., 3
STEINBAUGH, I., 15, 185
STEINBECKER, E., 3
STEINBUCHER, John, 99
STEINBURG, H., 34
STEINER, Charles S., 147
   G., 18, 188
   J., 188
STELLER, J., 153
STENTELL, Samuel E., 84
STENY, G., 150
STEP, Elijah, 38
STEPHENS, ____, 84
   A., 144

   B. R., 41
   G. D., 55
   John, 123
   John W., 33
   Joshua W., 33
   Luke, 16
   Robert, 16
   Samuel, 120
   W. B., 153
STEPHENSON, A., 158, 167
   D., 129
   J., 153
   J. A., 147
   John, 106, 118
   John S., 116
   N., 162
   R., 105
   W. C., 81
STERLING, Andrew, 87
   E., 41
   William, 203
STERN, L., 31
STERNS, W. E., 172
STETMAY, Samuel & Co., 180
STETZEL, Jacob, 4, 181
STEUY, G., 150
STEVENS, A. & 2 chlrn., 189
   A. & fam., 19, 189
   Alexander, 138
   Byron, 136
   Henry, 203
   J., 68
   James, 90
   Rees, 203
   W. E., 169
STEVENSON, Alexander 134
   J. W., 1
   N., 168
STEVERS, Jerome, 203
STEWART, A., 62
   A. Jr., 102
   Alexander, 85, 111
   B. F., 89
   Daniel, 97
   E. (Mr.), 175

   Elizabeth, 175
   George, 38
   J., 158
   J. M., 84, 103, 109, 153
   J. Q. A., 90
   J. T., 90
   James, 4, 81, 140, 149
   James J., 11, 115
   James V. S., 85
   John W., 85
   Joseph, 20
   L. D., 20
   O., 81
   Robert. 38, 67, 114
   T., 143
   Thomas P., 97
   W. G., 11
   W. H., 53
   W. J., 18, 188
   William, 43
   William L., 117
   William W., 13
STEWERT, W.J., 188
STIBBINS, D. (sic), 42, 197
STIDDINS, J., 32
   P., 32
STIDGER, O.P., 199
STILES, Charles, 159
   W. C., 88
STILL, A., 166
   I., 162
   W. J., 166
STILLMAN, A., 87
   A. C., 154
   H., 154
STILLWAGON, William W. (Dr.), 98
STILLWELL, C. M., 148
   James P., 67
   Paine, 98
   William, 203
STIMANT, Peter & boy, 165
STIMPSON, Stephen, 90
STIMSON, Faucher, 109
STINE, John, 100
STINSON, Lewis J., 178
STIRRER, N., 151
STITH, F., 84

Willis, 63
Willis & Co., 57
STITLES, Joseph, 117
STITZEL, Jacob, 37, 181
STIVERS, A., 115
  C. G., 115
  G., 115
  J., 115
  R. Jr., 115
  R. Sr., 115
ST., JOHN, A. C., 67
  Edward, 146
  John, 6
  John & 2 svts., 31
  M. G., 109
  Thomas, 6
STNYHER, Charles S., 147
STOCKDALE, H., 140
STOCKING, E., 113
STOCKTON, E., 36
  H., 159
STODDARD, Asa A.,
  (Lt.), 22
  John, 120
  W. C., 136
  William, 136
STODDART, William,
  197
STODDERT, T. E., 49
STODER, William M.,
  43, 197
STODGER, O. P., 4
STOGDEN, Ripley, 153
STOKES, B. F., 30
  Charles, 124
  E. A. (Mr.), 3
  H., 30
  Isaac, 37
  William H., 30
STOKESBERRY, John,
  114
STONE, D., 145
  D. C., 80
  G. D., 164
  George, 14, 39, 87
  H. B., 16
  J., 150
  J. P., 88
  J. T., 163

James, 111
John, 89
Joseph, 118
Newton, 128
P., 57, 63, 129
Sally, 176
Sarah, 162
W. B., 149
William B., 100
STONEBRAKER, G. C.,
  42
STONEHALL, Charles
  128
STONEWALL, Charles,
  128
STONHALL, Charles
  (sic), 128
STOOPS, W. J., 48
STOPP, M. H., 79
STORM, Frank, 115
STOTEN, John, lady &
  boy, 154
STOTT, Hiram, 100
STOTTS, Joseph P., 111
STOUDER, I., 42, 196
  J., 196
STOUFER, Samuel, 26
STOUGHTON, Clouden,
  105
  S. P., 109
STOUT, B., 80
  Benjamin, 6
  G. W., 152
  J. W., 168
  Peter, 6
STOVE, D., 149
STOW, J., 154, 165
STOWE, S., 188
  S. M., 19, 188
STOWELL, Alex N., 126
STOYELL, R. S., 51
STRAFFORD, J., 136
STRAHAN, J. M., 111
STRANG, Hiram, 137
  J., 158
STRANGE, John, 170
STRATFORD, J., 165
STRAUB, P., 31
STRAUS, A. (sic), 176

STRAUT, John, 151
STRAWBRIDGE,
  William, 54
STREET, J. H., 63
  John S., 147
  M., 146
STREETER, L., 118
STREETS, S., 160
STREMMING, C., 156
STRENT, T. C. B., 162
STRICKLAND, Nelson,
  120
STRICKLER, Joseph R.,
  117
STRIDER, I. K., 42, 195
  Isaac Keys, 195
  J. A., 42, 195
  Jesse A., 195
STRIKER, F. R., 159
  P., 140
STROBLES, W. R., 143
STRONG, J. C., 176
  Leander, 14
  M., 143
  S., 104
  W., 159
STROTHER, B. C., 112
  E. J., 113
  John, 123
STROUD, A. A., 54
STROUSE, John, 171
STROUSS, John, 171
STRUELER, D. 168
STRYKER, F. R., 136
STUART, D. M., 142
  David, 67
  E. P., 158
  J. M., 158, 163
  James W., 40
  John, 67
  S., 191
  Thomas, 67
STUBEN, John, 1
STUKEY, J., 160
STULL, Charles, 161
STUM, Thomas J. & 2
  sons, 2
STURGEON, Thomas,
  160

Thomas L., 11
STURGES, H. M. (sic), 82
T. C. (sic), 82
STURGESS, H. M., 82
Seth, 203
T. C., 82
STURGIS, Andrew, 90
David, 103
SUCE, Thomas, 17, 187
SUDDATH, H. H., 160
SUDLUM, J., 153
SUFFRINS, Isaac, 87
SUGDER, S., 18, 188
SULEY, G. R., 148
SULLERS, John, 20
SULLIVAN, Arthur, 90
James, 135, 151
SULLIBAN, T., 167
SUMALT, Philip, 180
SUMMERS, John, C., 53
W. F., 31
SUMNER, Edward, 106
F., 99
G., 99
I., 6
W. E., 106
SUMPSTINE, ____(Mr.), 139
SUNDERLAND, T. W., 87
SUNDERLY, L. D., 37
SURGUI, George W., 137
SURMEIER, H., 65
J. B., 65
SUTHERLAND, Brush, 103
L., 83
Mason, 121
R. V., 179
Sidney, 121
Silas, 121
T., 83
SUTLIFF, L. L., 174
SUTTER, P., 163
SUTTLE, Campbell, 90
Josiah, 90
M., 148
SUTTON, C., 145

James, 54
Joseph, 54
SUUSFRANK, Absalom, 88
SUYDAM, C. B., 25
John, 25
SUYDON, David S., 88
SWZO____, J. B., 5
SWAIN, H. C., 126
Joseph, 92
Joses, 56
SWAN, A., 158, 175
C., 68
James, 203
Miller, 170
N. P., 66
Samuel, 123
SWANSEY, J. H., 175
SWAP, John, 151
SWARTOUT, L., 158
SWARTWOUT, C. F. (sic), 58
T. (sic), 58
SWARTZ. C., 151
SWASEY, Samuel, 62
SWAYER, J. (sic), 11
SWEARAGEN John, 47
SWEARINGEN, Henry, 129
SWEEDE. William, 153
SWEENEY, Charles, 30
W., 147 (x)
William, 147
SWEENY, M., 5
W. (sic), 147
William (sic), 147
SWEET, H., 159
H. A., 157
SWEETSER, A. C., 86, 204
SWEETZER, Albion C., 204
SWIFT, D. C. H., 51
I., 153
J., 167
Jesse, 6
John D., 170
Samuel, 98
Samuel Jr., 138

SWIND, ____, 31
SWINERTON, Henry, 57, 64
J., 64
SWINFORD, I. M., 165
SWINGLEY, Michael, 45
SWINGLY, G., 61
SWITZER, J., 91
S. C., 165
SWORT, W., 168
SWZORT, J. B., 5
SY____, John (of Granville, Wisc.), 134
SYHOX, H., 152
SYLVESTER, ____, 115
SYNE, N., 153
SYNIS, Henry (sic), 165
SYNOX, H., 152
SYTHE, G., 18, 188
J., 188

-T-

TABER, Horace, 141
TACKABORRY, J., 2
TACKS, M., 157
TAFT, Bazailed, 122
Bazalled, 122
TAGGART. D. 161. 176
John, 98
John H., 101
William, 30
TAINTER, A., 63
TAIT, J., 163
W., 163
TAKER, E. (Dr.), 24
TALBERT, ____, 12
J. (Mr.), 3, 181
James, 32
Joseph, 181
Sarah, 177
TALBORT, Sarah, 177
TALEY, Theodore, 117
TALLANALE, J. S., 17
TALLANALIO, J.B., 187
TALLANALLE, J.S., 187
TALLEY, J. N., 103

TAMBLYN, Thomas, 132
TAMOY, J. W., 150
TANDY, G. H., 169
TANNAHILL, Benjamin, 180
TANNENWOOD, L., 105
TANNENWOULD, L., 105
TANNER, E. M., 124 (x)
   William, 97
TANSEY, J., 63
TAPLIN, ____ (Mr.), 60, 61
TAPPEN, C. B., 85
   David, 98
TAPPIN, David, 101
   William, 203
TARBLE, Horace, 203
TARLAND, John, 145
TART, J. S., 144
   Samuel, 203
TATE, Lafayette, 175
   R., 173
   W., 149
TAVENER, N., 42, 195
   Newton, 195
TAYLOR, ____, 19, 190
   A., 15, 126, 190
   Andrew J., 89
   B., 164
   Benjamin, 49
   C., 41
   C. G., 140
   Diar (sic), 123
   E., 15, 18, 200
   E. N., 64 (x), 200
   Egbert, 45
   F. D., 137
   George, 1, 41
   George C., 19, 188
   George W., 188
   H., 2, 99
   Henry, 48
   Hugh B., 117
   J. & fam., 154
   J. A., 168
   J. D. P., 101
   J. L., 111
   J.M., 189

Jacob, 48
James, 4, 90, 149
James H., 27
John, 4, 44, 48, 109
John L. (Dr.), 111
John N., 63
L. C., 118
Matilda (Mrs.), 95
Robert, 30, 65
S., 147
Samuel R., 106
W., 99
W. G., 43
W.H.(x), 187
Walter, 5
William, 171
William H. (Dr.), 91
TEATS, W. P. (Dr.), 117
TEETAHORN, Marcellus, 103
TEITTS, L., 159
TELBERT, James, 32
TELEY, Theodore, 117
TELFORD, Andrew, 7, 182
TELLER, W., 85
TELVER, Henry, 109
TEMPLE, James, 107
   John, 70
   S., 137
   Wilson, 200
TEMPLETON, C., 18
   J., 18
TENEYCK, Conrad, 169
TENNET, H. T., 146
TENTS, W. P. (Dr.), 117
TEPRELL, M. M., 48
TERMAN, M. 28
   N., 28
TERRELL, H. E., 116
   M. C., 116
TERRETT, H., 168
TERRIER, G. W., 143
TERRILL, C. A., 153
   H., 69
   H. C., 105
TERRY, George T., 137, 164
   Joel, 122

William S., 141
TERUTER, Augustus, 57
TERWILLIGER, Lorenzo P., 106
   William, 106
TESTE, W. P.L (Dr.), 117
THAIRMONT, N., 173
THATCHER, A. T., 106
   John P., 1
   L., 20, 33, 193
   Leland S., 193
   William, 32
THAW, Joseph, 48
THAYER, A. L., 165
THEURING, Fohann Frederick, 103
THIRD, O. & wife, 140
THOM, Robert (sic), 40
THOMAS, ____(Mr. & Mrs.), 191
   Albert, 117
   Alfred, 149
   Burroughs, 101
   C., 145
   C. C., 42, 195
   Charles G., 195
   E., 25
   E. L., 123
   F., 25, 34
   G. M., 150
   J. D., 27
   Jesse, 91
   John, 146
   L. K., 11
   Leonard, 106
   P., 25, 147
   S., 135
   Sam W., 147
   Stephen, 91
   Thomas (sic), 170
   W. H. R., 120
   William, 138
   William (Capt.), 50
THOMASON, George, 204
THOMASSON, John, 8
THOMPSON, ____, (Lt.) of U.S.N., 80
   A., 81

A. C., 176
Amos & 2 sons, 57
Andrew, 71
Baxter, 139
C., 135
C. P., 110
Charles, 25
E., 111
Elias, 111
Ellus, 111
George, 69, 70
Henry, 78
I. D., 80
I. N., 168
I. S. (Dr.), 102
Isaac Jr., 184
J., 148, 158
J. (Dr.), 29
J. B., 106
J. B. (Gen.), 70
J. P., 15, 106, 184
J. T., 163
J. W., 85
James, 78, 165
James P., 109
John, 104
John B., 47
John D., 64
L. F., 118
L. M., 118
Leonard, 119
Lewis, 155
M., 29, 130
M. S., 147
Michael, 57
Otis C., 119
R., 29
R. C., 162
S. V., 109
Samuel, 160
Thos. C., 109
V., 76
W., 148
W. A., 147
W. C., 32
W. W., 121
William, 71, 160
William A. & lady, 133
William H., 111

Wm. P., 38
THOMSON, ____, 115
  E. D., 136, 138
  James P., 109
  L. S., 110
  L. Sims, 111
  Thos. C., 109
  William W., 106
THORN, J., 49
  J. (sic), 63
  Reuben T. & fam. (sic), 79
THORNBURGH, John, 18
  Thomas, 18, 186
THORNDIKE, K., 77
THORNE, C.R., 201
THORNTON, John, 146
  Samantha, 177
THORP, Edward (sic), 111
THORPE, Allen, 27
  D. W., 31
  Edward, 111
  S. 25 (x)
THRASHER, R. G., 168
THRUSH, G., 166
THURBER, Erastus, 103
THURSTON, Alfred, 131
THURWELL, Joshua, 203
THUSTIN, L. D., 60
TIBBATTS, William, 83
TIBBETTS, A. P., 117
  James A., 103
  William, 83
TIBBONS, S. S.(Dr.), 141
TIBBS, Wesley, 91
TIBENS, S. S. (Dr.), 141
TICER, John, 99
TICKNER, H. C., 150
TICKNOR, Almon, 106
TIDBALL, A. P., 90
TIFFANY, Calvin, 106
  P. D., 50
  Sylvester, 106
TIFIELD, Gilvin S., 40
TILEY, Edward, 155
TILFORD, A., 24, 182
  F., 11

J. H., 7, 182
John H., 24, 182
TILSMIMAN, A. C., 148
TIMERMAN, John, 97
TIMMONS, I., 179
  L., 166
  M., 179
  W., 179
  Williams, 179
TINGLE, A. J., 5
TINGLEY, G. R., 87
  Ira, 42
TINKER, C., 16, 185
  Charles (Lt.), 16
  Chauncey, 185
  H., 185
  Horace, 185
TINKHAM, ____ (Mr.) & wife, 160
TINNY, W. (sic), 55
TIPTO, John (sic), 147
TIPTON, John, 147
  P. M. (grave of), 127
TISDALE, W. E., 163
TITLOO, T. G., 32
TITSNER, W., 48
TLEA, David & 2 others (sic), 180
TOAY, James, 105
TOBIN, David M., 56
  E., 22
TODD, C. (Capt.), 93
  E. T., 150
  George, 30
  J. T., 163
  John, 11
  Samuel, 52
  William (Dr.), 56
TOISEMAN, W., 176
TOLAN, John, 54
TOLBERT, James, 32
TOLEN, John, 54
TOLEY, Theodore, 117
TOLF, E., 165
TOLMAN, Nathan, 124 (x)
  Samuel W., 44
TOLSEMAN, W., 176
TOMAUGH, George, 123
TOOD, J. T. (sic), 163

TOOKER, O. G., 153, 163
TOOL, P. O. (sic), 136
TOOLY, James, 15, 185
TOPF, George (sic), 35
TORIAN, D., 31
TOURMAN, John, 162
TOURTCLETT, William D., 105
TOWER, J. M., 113
TOWINING, Hugh (sic), 138
TOWNDROW, Joseph, 123
TOWNE, P. A., 8
TOWNER, C., 15, 184
  Cicero, 184
TOWNING, Hugh, 138
TOWNSEND, D., 148
  D. W., 130
  J., 54
  L., 55
  M. Q., 112
TRACE, ___ (Mr.), 91
TRACY, F.P. (Rev.), 202
  John M., 75, 76 (x)
TRADWICK, M., 152
TRAFTAN, ___ (Dr.), 170
TRAILWICK, M., 152
TRAINER, J., 13
TRAITKILL, ___ (Mr.), 44
TRALL, Francis, 117
TRAPP, Nicholas, 116
TRAVERS, Nathan, 60, 66
TRAVEY, J. B., 16
TRAVIS, W. H., 70
TRAYON, E., 147
TREADWAY, A. D., 55
  S. V., 30
TREADWELL, C., 51
  Charles, 78
TREBEIN, H.C., 197
  H.F., 197
TREDWINE, N., 179
  W., 179
TREE, H., 179
TREGO, W. F., 168

TRELOAR, B., 157
TREMBLE, Nancy, 96
TRENELL, Jacob, 117
TRESSLOR, William, 150
TRIABLE, S., 188
TRIER, John, 90
TRIGGS, James, 105
TRIMBLE, G., 153
  W., 163
TRIPP, ___ (Mr.), 203
  D., 160
  Truman B., 116
TRISA, Charles, 4
TRISBIE, S., 17, 188
TRISBIN, S., 17
TROOP, W., 146
TROTH, Joseph, 56
TROTT, T. P., 86
TROTTER, Robert, 112
  Thomas, 30
TROWBRIDGE, A., 33, 193
  A.B., 193
  O., 52
TRUAX, W. D., 117
TRUE, A. B., 103
  Thomas J., 40
TRUESDALE, C., 19
TRUITT, S., 189
  Samuel, 19, 189
TRULL, Francis, 117
TRUMAN, William H., 48
TRUMBLE, S., 169
TRUMBULL, J. K., 26
TRUSSELL, A., 63
TRUXLER, Charles, 162
TRYALL, William G., 203
TRYMAN, John, 180
TRYON, J, 159, 163
TUBBS, ___, 115
  L. W., 14
TUCKER, George, 91
  John, 203
  P., 138
  Robert, 67
  Thomas, 91
TUFFI, John, 104

TUFLI, John, 104
TULEY, Theodore, 117
TULLER, N., 96
TULY, James, 185
TUMOY, J. W., 150
TUNIGAN, T., 143
TUPPER, C., 151
  H., 35
TURCOT, N., 20
TURLEY, Marion, 130
TURMAN, Hamilton, 130
TURNBOUGH, Elizabeth, 170
TURNER, Alonzo P., 140
  Anson, 159
  C., 8, 33, 193
  Conrad, 161
  E., 55
  G. N., 16
  G. W., 83
  J. W., 35
  James, 102
  Joseph P., 102
  N., 166
  R., 157
  Robert, 67 (x)
  S. G., 8
  S. K., 28
  S. R., 52
  William, 105
TURNEY, M. J., 34, 193
TURNICK, J., 139
TURNOCK, J., 148
TURPEN, W., 127
TURR, John, 20
TURVILL, S. N., 2
TUTIL, Smith (sic), 111
TUTT, C. M., 13
TUTTLE, C. C., 50
  David & fam., 180
  John, 29
  Joseph, 25
  Joseph B., 117
  M., 58
  M. H., 57
  Smith, 111
TWINING, G. W., 138
TWOMLEY, B., 81
TYLER, E. R., 57

George, 106
H., 91
S. C., 66
TYREL, Miles, 121
TYRIE, George, 106

-U-

UBER, Peter, 104
UHLER, Jacob, 49
UHLRICH, R., 158
ULSIE,B. L., 112
UMBERFIELD, Robert, 1
UMSTAD, William J., 97(x),
UNDERDONK, J. F. (Dr.), 65
UNDERDOUK, J. F. (Dr.), 65
UNDERWOOD, T. M., 117
Thomas C., 67
William T., 171
UPCHURCH, A., 32
UPDEGRAFF, J. H., 38
UPDERGRAFF, H., 55
UPDERGRUFF, H ., 55
UPDIKE, R. J., 52
UPTON, S. J., 51
URNER, H. (Mr.), 3
P. K. (Mr.), 3
URY, Jackson, 43
USHER, Aaron, 139
R., 51
UTE, E. B., 33
UTT, David D., 67
G. D., 67
Henry, 67
UTTERMICH, H., 126

-V-

VADDER, H. L. & bro., 166
VAGEBY, E., 101
John, 101
VAIL, Alexander, 139

W. D., 43
VALENTINE, J., 166
Job, 120
William, 90
Van ALLEN, J. D. & son, 39
John, 62
Van AMAN, J., 149
Van AMEN, J., 149
VANATTA, James, 136
William, 136
Van BEBLER, Franklin, 126
VANBORN, _____, 29
Van BUREN, _____, 81
VANBUSKIRK, R. H., 134
VANCE, James, 118
Joseph, 37
Rerella, 162
William M., 198
VANDECAR, C. F., 85
William, 85
VANDEMARK, John H., 140
VANDERCOOK, Roberts, 85
VANDERFORD, J., 166
VANDERHOOF, Henry, 62, 73
VANDERLIP, O., 137
VANDEVER, H., 85
VANDIMACK, George, 110
VANDLING, Abraham, 79
Van DOREN, Joseph, 82
VAN DUREN, Joseph, 82
Van EATEN, J. D., (sic) 164
Van EATON J. D., 164
VANEMAN, J., 144
Van GARDINER, C., 21
Van GELDER, Abram A., 82
VANHALIE, D. (sic), 165
VANHOOK, William H., 139
Van HORN, F., 15, 184
VANHORN, J., 158

Fred (sic), 184
Van HOUTEN, H., 89
VANKIRK, J. K., 18
VANNATTA, _____, 189
James, 138
William, 138
VanNESS, Thomas, 78
VANNTEE, _____, 19, 189
VANORINAN, J., 156
VANPATTER, S., 151
VANPELT, A. S., 81
VANSANT, A., 59
J., 29
VANSCOIT, James, 70
John, 70
Van SCOYOC, Jackson, 78
Jonathan, 78
Van SCOYSE, W., 12
VANSICKLE, James H., 60
Van TASSER, N., 14
S., 14
Van TASSON, N., 14
S., 14
Van TRACE, D., 29
Van VAULKENBURGH, John, 44
VANVECTHEN, Tunis, 57
VanVLECK, A. P., 136
A. P. & fam., 139
H. (Dr.), 105, 139, 165
VANVOLKENBURGH, Noah, 104
Van WINKLE, P. W., 28
T. B. & bro., 159
VANWORT, D., 139
Van WYCK, C. H., 85
VAPER, Henry, 151
VARNER, Henry, 100
VAUGH, C., 19
VAUGHAN, _____ (Dr.), 103
A., 99
H. P. (sic), 33
VAUGHEN, Philip & Co., 178

295

VAUGHN, A., 105
  C., 190
  Elizabeth, 172
  Philip & Co., 178
  T. H., 8
  W. H., 14
  William, 64, 91
VAUNXEN, A., 32
VEACH, E. S., 158
  J. C., 168
  J. E. S., 158
VEARY, Benjamin W., 184
VEBLER, ____, 83
VEDDER, George F., 108
  J., 19, 190
VEIGER, Joseir (sic), 172
VENABLE, ____(Mrs.)
  & dau., 126
VENNUM, Perry, 132
VENTER, S., 165
VENTON, William, 149
VERMILLION, Henry, 48
  William, 154
VERNON, J. S., 40
VERTREES, A., 59
VESZEY, Benjamin, 15, 184
VICKORY, S. J., 24
VIGIEL, John, 53
VILLINGER, George & fam., 21
VINCENT, Dow, 106
  Edward A., 146
  George, 106
  J., 67
  William., 105
VINEYARD, William B., 90
VIRDEN, James, 104
  L. P. H., 51
  M., 51
VISEY,C. R., 140
VOIGHTLY, John, 151
VOORHIES, R. (sic), 144
VOORHIS, George (sic), 122
  Moses, 122
VORHEES, A. J. (Mr.), 3

J. W., 158
  John, 81
VORMAN, Harvery, 161
VOSBEY, Joe, 199
VOSE, William, 81
VRAIN, C. M., 150
VREDENBURGH, J. S., 37
  J. V., 37
VRDMAN, Harvery (sic), 161
VROMAN, D., 41

-W-

W____, Charles D., 121
WACKMAN, Harrison, 103
WADDIE, John W., 80
WADE, David, 38
  Harry & fam., 87
  J., 166
  J. E., 25
  Lemuel, 87
WADEMAN, J., 134
WADLKEY, M. (sic), 126
WADSWORTH, F., 104
  Francis, 98
  J. V., 80
WAGDLOFF, R. (sic), 153
WAGGONER, J., 152
  Peter, 127
  R., 190
WAGNER, Abraham, 84
  Andrew, 42
  John W., 49, 199
  P., 42
WAGONER, G., 151
  J., 199
WAHL, L., 157
WAINGER, F., 169
WAIT, F. W., 6
WAITE, J. S. & fam. of 5 chldrn, 87
  James S. & Fam., 21
WAKEFIELD, J. R. (Dr.) & wife, 22

WAKEMAN W. B., 11
WALBERT, S. T. (death of), 94
WALBRIDGE, G., 14
  S., 14
WALDE, Charles, 134
WALDING, A. G., 56
  E., 56
WALDRON, Henry, 90
WALES, W., 163
WALKER, C. A., 20, 189
  C. F., 44
  E., 148, 166
  E. D. (Dr.), 151
  E. H., 142
  G.S., 187
  H. A. (Mrs), 137
  H. D., 65
  J. K., 142
  J. P., 44
  J. T., 157
  J. W., 137
  James, 32, 108, 127
  Joseph, 97
  L. A., 48
  M., (Dr.), 91
  Robert, 126
  Robert J., 109
  S. F., 168
  W. H., 17, 187
  William H., 111
WALL, D. R., 48
  J., 188
WALLACE, F. (Dr.), 35(x)
  H., 17, 110
  H. W., 71
  J., 158
  J. B. V., 65
  T., 84
  W. C., 150
  Y. D., 134
WALLACK, Green, 9
WALLARD, Samuel, 45
WALLER, G., 135
  Thomas, 136
WALLIE, C., 56
WALLING, William, 104
WALLS, J., 18, 188

WALONG, Albert G., 90
WALPERT, J. C., 42, 195
   John C., 195
WALSATH, Jacob, 115
WALSH, Timothy, 138
WALTER, G. G., 142
   H. A., 8
   J. K., 142
WALTERS, ____(Mr.), 28
   W., 165
   W. T., 51
WALTON, A., 167
   G., 88
   John C., 201
   John W., 29
WALWORTH, J. D., 116
WAMSLEY, S., 167
WAND, Samuel, 187
WANNELL, Thomas K., 81
WARD, ____ & son, 91
   ____(Maj.), 151
   A., 158
   D. C., 2
   E. L., 53
   Eli & son, 89
   F. D. (Dr.), 148, 152
   F.P., 181
   F. P. (Mr.), 4, 37
   H. J., 64
   Ira, 203
   J. M., 70
   John, 16, 128
   L. B., 51
   Major, 151
   P., 17
   R. L., 111, 112
   Robert (death of), 93
   Samuel, 17, 187
   T. C., 21
   Thomas, 123
   W., 167
   William, 53
WARDELL, James, 48
WARDZINUSKI, ____, 19, 191
WARDZYNSKI, F., 191
WARE, R. M., 167

Robert, 91
   W., 51
WARFIELD, John, 46
WARICH, J., 164
WARMBAKER, John, 113
WARNER, A., 197
   C., 158
   H. L., 113
   John, 133
   T. F., 46
   W. A., 58
WARNEY, William A., 57
WARNLEY, S., 158
WARNOCK, A., 129
WARNSTAFF, James, 120
WARREN, A. H., 153
   A. S., 166
   A. T., 164
   David B., 155
   H. B., 167
   Hugh, 127
   J., 18, 159
   M., 153
   M. J., 90
   T. D., 35
   W.W., 190
WARREY, A. H. (sic), 153
WARSHAL, Thomas, 147
WASBELY, G., 70
WASDEN, Richard, 147
WASHBURN, L., 98
   Lorinda (Miss), 99
WASHEY, V., 184
WASHINGTON, B. F. 41, 194
   Benjamin F., 194
   Crawford, 6
   Lawrence, 196
   Richard, 48
   Thomas F., 196
WASON, J., 166
WASSON, George M., 5
WATERBURY, W. H., 158
WATERFFORD, W., 157

WATERHOUSE, ____(Mr.), 54
WATERMAN, Lewis, 97
   P., 163
   William F., 132
WATERS, G., 144
   George M., 102
   R. M., 32
   W. F., 148
   William C., 201
WATERWORTH, John, 67
WATKIN, T. F., 171
WATKINS, Solomon, 101
   T. F., 171, 172
   William, 162
WATSON, B. A., 49
   C., 38
   G. K., 48
   G. W., 153(x)
   George C., 50
   J. B., 49
   J. F., 167
   J. H., 143
   M., 203
   R., 203
   S., 67
   T. A., 168
   W., 92
WATTERS, G., 144
   J., 153
   W. T. (sic), 51
WATTS, D., 148
   James R., 129
WATTY, Joseph, 120
WAUGAMAN, A. S., 143
WAUGH, S., 144
   Sandy, 89
WAY, H. M., 16
   J. W., 36
WAYBUREN, Samuel, 14
WAYMAN, William & son, 27
WEAMS, F. M., 11
WEAN, N. B., 23, 192
WEATHERBY, L. H., 156
WEATON, G. M., 164

WEAVER, Harris, 107
  J. H., 166
  Jacob, 4
  James A., 32
  Nicholas, 132
WEBB, Christopher, 136
  H. A., 173
  J., 168
  John, 147
  John, S., 4
  W., 165
  William, 136
WEBBER, Ames (Dr.), 141
  P.W. (sic), 199
  R. A., 2
WEBER, F., 35
  George A., 29
  J. B., 49
WEBLEY, John Wesley, 108
WEBSTER,____(Mr.), 78
  A. S., 85
  A. W., 16
  G. P., 32
  H., 32. 63
  Henry, 63
  James, 81
  James P., 121
  Joseph P., 121
  Kimball, 40
  Lorenzo, 133
  Marcus, 146
  Royal, 6
  Stephen, 133
  W., 148
WEECH, R. T., 137
WEED, C., 147
  O. F., 103, 109
  Samuel M., 98
  William, 109
WEEKS, James, 138
WEES, Charles, 16
WEEVER, Charles (sic), 54
WEIGAND, R., 154
WEIGHTMAN, Leo, 169
WEIL, Mayer, 99

Meyer, 99
WEIN, Louis & 6 in fam., 180
WEINMER, John, 136
WEIR, P., 157
WEISS, Andrew, 138
WELCH, A. S., 58, 65
  C. W., 163
  J., 145
  Nicholas, 97
  T. R., 144
  W. R., 146
  William, 184
WELDEN, Levi, 105
WELK, William, 111
WELKEL, John, 12
WELKER, K. G., 166
  O., 45
WELL, J. L. H., 142
WELLER, S. B., 36
  Thomas, 136
WELLOT, P. R., 157
WELLS,____(son of A. WELLS), 76
  A., 76
  A. E., 159
  Aaron & Co., 104
  Alex, 65
  C., 129
  D. W., 154
  E. S. (sic), 144
  G., 100
  George, 203
  Giles, 44
  Ira, 65
  J. M., 107, 118
  Jacob, 9
  James B., 112
  John S., 81 (x)
  Luke, 65
  S.S, 202
  Spicer, 141
  T., 131
  W., 4
  William (death of), 94
  William P., 116
WELS, Aaron & Co. (sic), 104
WELSH, William, 22

WENDEL, Ham, 115
WENDON, J. C., 147
WENT, F., 19
WENTZ, G. W., 148
WENTZE John M., 42
WERITHER, Stephen W., 147
WERNER, F., 21
WERRDT, F., 189
WERTSBAUGHER, Jacob, 131
WESCOTT, Martin, 149
WESHE, ____, 22
  Fred, 22
WESSON, C. H., 51
  J., 51
WEST, A., 58
  A. J., 101
  E. B., (Dr.), 21
  Edward, 124
  F., 19, 189
  George, 58
  J. L., 64, 200(x)
  James, 126
  John L., 64, 200
  M. (Mr.), 3
  R., 119
  William, 21
WESTBROOK, J. J., 159
  S., 48
WESTE, John G. (sic), 147
WESTFALL, ____(Dr.), 115
  J. C., 129
  J. G., 24
WESTFIELD, W., 157
WESTLAKE, E., 142
  H., 160
WESTON, A. L., 158
WETHERALL, J. E., 8
  S. W., 8
WETHERELL, J. E., 8
  S. W., 8
WETHINGTON, George, 5
WHALEN, Andrew, 50
WHALEY, D., 164
  J. A., 85

J. R., 163
William, 65
WHALING. Sylvester. 133
WHALOY. J. R., 163
WHATILEY, C. A., 134
WHATING, Sylvester, 133
WHATLEY, C. A., 134
  H., 84
  W., 84
WHATTLEY, C. A., 134
WHEATLEY, David, 90
WHEATON, G. M., 164
  Zebulon T., 122
WHEELER, ____, 68
  C. B., 4
  E., 152
  E. E., 133
  J. R., 27
  John F., 81
  Levi, 106
  Lizzy, 177
  M. A., 98
  Marvin, 151
  P., 126
  Simeon, 56
  Theodore O., 84
  Thomas, 87. 134
  W. P., 145
  William, 155
WHEELLOCK, Marvel, 120
WHEELOCK, E., 143
  Marvel, 120
WHETSTONE, Sarah (Miss), 163
WHIELOCK, E., 143
WHILEY, E. H., 163
WHIPPLE, S. G., 12
WHITAKER, A. S., 117
  Joseph, 9
WHITBRIDGE, M. D., 38
WHITE, ____(Dr.), 135
  ____(Mr.), 68
  A. A., 122
  A. H. & Co., 109
  A. T., 123
  Benjamin, 203

  Benjamin F. (Capt.), 128
  C., 130
  D., 143, 168
  D. C., 32
  David, 110
  Decter, 135
  Doctor (sic), 135
  Donald, 154
  Ezekiel, 170
  G. W., 162
  George C., 147
  H. J., 129
  Harrison, 154
  Henry, 27
  Hiram, 87
  Isaac N., 18
  J., 147, 153
  J. A., 170
  James, 59, 63
  John, 112, 114, 123, 147, 204
  Jonathan, 86
  Joseph, 59, 63
  K. M., 164
  N., 98
  O. P. (Dr.), 60
  R., 145
  R. L., 60
  Robert M., 101
  Robertson, 110
  T. W., 79
  Thomas K., 121
  W., 168, 191
  W. D., 168
  W. F., 145
  W. W., 166
  William, 20, 99, 121, 191
WHITEAD, W. D. (sic), 168
WHITEHEAD, S. (Mr.), 3
  W. D., 168
WHITEHILL, D. M., 5
WHITEHURST, Thomas, 49
WHITEMAN, R., 51
WHITEMORE, ____, 115

  D., 21
  Levi, 100
  S., 21
WHITESEAS, W. B. & lady, 54
WHITESELL, J. P., 158
WHITESIDES, A. R., 59
  E. M., 59
  Samuel, 104
  William H., 104
WHITFORD, F. H., 70
WHITHAM, William, 54
WHITING, L. L., 17
WHITLOCK, William B., 16
WHITMAN, Jarvis, 67
  L. O., 118
  W. B., 13
  W. G., 13
  W. O., 13
WHITMORE, D. (Dr.), 87
  Hill, 109
  Samuel, 87
WHITNEY, C., 154 (x)
  Charles, 173
  Hes, 173
  J. D., 99
  J. J., 117, 120
  Nelson, 57, 90
WHITSON, H., 157
WHITTIER, Lewis K., 204
WHITTINGTON, E., 30
WHITTLEREY, S., 44
WHITTOCK, James, 104
WHOLLY, H. L., 107
WHYERS, R., 20, 189
WIANT, J. M., (sic), 157
WIBBER, Ames (Dr.)(sic), 141
WIBLE, L. W., 154
WICHROWSKY, A., 35
WICHTERMAN, G. J., 89
  Joseph, 89
WICKARD, S., 163
WICKEE, F. A., (sic), 165
WICKER, J. F., 151
WICKHAM, M. T., 14
  Samuel, 33

William, 119
WICKLEFT, John, 162
WICKLIFFE, J. P., 130
   Nancy (Mrs.), 130
WICKS, Coleman, 68
   R. J., 158
WICKWISE, H., 157
WIDENER, James, 117
   R., 44
WIDNER, C. N., 109
WIDO, J. (sic), 99
WIEN, Louis & 6 in fam., 180
   Michael, 120
WIGHT, Ira T., (sic), 131
WIGHTMAN, Robert, 5
WILBARGER, Harry, 112
WILBER, James, 84
WILBRIGHT, E., 11
WILCOX, A., 141, 163, 167
   C. H., lady & child, 154
   D. C., 149
   H., 52
   J., 158
   J. D., 158
   L. D. C., 150
   W., 167
   W. B., 163
WILDER, Joshua, 108
   O. C., 67
WILDRIDGE, James, 39
WILE, H., Jr., 90
   N. W., 90
WILEY, A., 166
   Alexander, 124
   Benjamin F., 114
   Calvin, 146
   Egbert A., 105
   J., 55
   James, 15, 184
   James R., 27
   John, 38
   M. W., 27
   R., 49
   William, 129
WILHINUS, F., 70
WILKES, Coleman, 62

J. S., 168
R. P., 166, 168
WILKIN, Stephen Jr., 115
WILKINS, E., 202
   G. W., 168
   J. S., 168
   R. R., 169
WILKINSON, George, 109
   George M., 103
   J., 49, 157
   Jack, 155
   Raphael, 155
   William, 152
   Woodson, 155
WILKS, ____ (Dr.)(sic), 130
   Coleman (sic), 62
   J. S. (sic), 168
WILLARD, ____ (Mrs.), 99
   Daniel, 192
   H., 99
   H. O., 99
   Harrison P., 105
   R., 119
   S., 165
   Samuel, 45
   Theo., 99
WILLCOX, John, 38
WILLEY, Morris, 109
WILLIAM, John (sic), 123
WILLIAMS, ____ (Mr.), 25
   A. C., 63
   A. J., 126
   Alfred, 40
   B. B., 122
   C., 153
   C. (Miss), 139
   Connell, 68
   D. H., 158
   David, 59
   E., 63
   Edward T., 66
   Elias, 59
   F., 56
   G. W., 67

George W., 57
H., 150
H. S., 99
J., 138, 153
J. C., 109
J. H., 121
J. M., 136
J. P., 167 (x)
J. T., 140
James, 98
James L., 114
James S., 101
John, 45, 122
John M., 87
L. F., 131
M., 23, 154
Peter, 130
R., 153, 164
R. & 2 svts., 8
R. L., 20
Richard, 58, 103, 109
S. S., 67
Septius (Capt.), 89
Susan M., 162
T. R., 179
Thomas, 3, 48
W., 4
W. J., 112
W. M., 148
Washington, 116
William G., 84
William H., 70
William Isaac, 7
WILLIAMSON, ____, 35
   D. H., 157
   E., 202
   J. A., 164
   James, 148
   R., 148
   R. M., 32
   W., 104
   W. K., 144
WILLIARD, Daniel, 23
WILLIE, B. (sic), 153
WILLIMER, S., 153
WILLIS, ____, (Mr.) 141, 178
   C. E., 112

301

C. J., 9
E. E., 68
George, 176
J. C., 48
James, 112
James, wife &chldrn, 178
John, 123, 202
Thomas, 76
WILLOCK, J.B., 187
  J. S., 17, 187
WILLONGBY, A., 56
WILLOUGHBY, A., 56
  D. W. C. (Dr.), 46, 198
WILLSON, J. S. 50
  Samuel (sic), 46
WILMANS, C., 61
  D., 75
  D. I., 61
  D. I. & bro., 46
WILSEY, John, 133
WILSON, ____,(Mr.), 71, 87
  A., 18, 155
  Andrew J., 122
  Angelina (Mrs.), 155
  C., 164
  C. W., 177
  D., 115
  D. E., 143
  D. W. & 2 sons, 17
  Daniel, 176
  David, 177
  E. (death of), 94
  E. F., 170
  E. R., 69
  G., 159
  G.A., 143
  H., 18
  H. B., 156, 157
  Hazon, 123
  Henry, 132
  J., 115, 164, 165
  J. B., 174
  J. C. F., 60
  J. S., 17
  J. W., 23, 158
  James, 103, 136
  James St. Clair, 204

  John, 91, 111, 145
  John (Gen.) & wife, 77
  John S., 141
  M., 179
  O., 158
  O. B. W., 87
  P. C., 82 (x)
  Pleasant, 129
  R., 17, 19
  Robert, 185
  Robert W., 14, 185
  S., 57, 64
  Samuel, 61, 73, 91, 114, 160
  Samuel S., 41
  T., 61
  T. C., 150
  Truvius, 43
  W., 154
  W. (Mr.), 3
  W. W., 169
  William, 5, 175
  William L., 55
WILTON, ____, 91
  C., 143
WILY, James (sic), 184
WIMBELY, G., 70
WIMBLEY, G., 70
WINCHELL, G. R., 102
WINCHESTER, John, 15, 184
  M. C., 41
WINDERS, J. W., 109
  John W., 105
WINDSOR, F. R., 48
WINEBIDDLE, G., 18, 187
WINEFORD, Joseph S., 147
WINEGAR, Fredrick, 140
WINER, Isam, 61
WINFIELD, A. H., 126
WING, A. F., 166
WINGATE, J. C., 37
  R. A., 11
WINGHAM, R. S., 5
WINN, C. C., 9
  John, 136
  Tristran, 7

WINNER, E. B., 119
WINSHIP, B. H., 158
  F. B., 158,163
  J. M., 163
WINSLIT, J, 142
WINSLOW, E. D., 51
  George, 169, 204
  George (death of), 94
  H., 23
  Jesse, 86, 204
WINSOR, Alonzo, 43
WINSTOCK, J. W., 61
WINTE, T., 166
WINTER, John, 203
  Stephen, 203
  T., 167
  W. C., 70
WINTERS, H., 42
  J. D., wife & 2 dau., 54
  Theodore & lady, 54
WINTERSON, J. R., 163
WIRICK, William & bro., 150
WIRTNER, John, 171
WISE, B., 61
  D., 63, 148
  G., 61
  George, 61
  John, 63, 116
  S., 65
WISEHOFF, C., 34
WISNER, A. R., 131
WISTENDORF, L., 3
WITESELL, J. P., 158
WITHARELL, Calvin, 136
WITHERELL, Calvin, 136
WITHERS, L., 129
WITHINGTON, S. (Mr.), 3
WITMER, W. D., 7
WITSEL, W., 151
WITSON, D., 166
  S., 166
WITT, J. B., 59, 65, 66 (x)
WITTENMYER, L. C., 57
WITTER, E., 59
WITTERMYER, L. C., 46

WITTY, James, 17
WITWER, William D., 7
WOOD____,Thomas, 135
WOFFENDEN, R. M., 129
WOHMEN, J., 99
WOLCOTT, P., 148
WOLF, ____, 87
____(Mr.), 55
A. W., 165
Henry, 179
J. F., 63
Joshua, 39
WOLFE, Moses, 125
P., 51
WOLFORD, J., 156
John, 156
WOLVERTON, N. L., 88
WOMELDORF, R. J., 157
W. W., 157
WOMELDORFF, R. L., 163
WOOD, ____, 89
____(Dr.), 130
A., 99, 127 (x), 150
A. R., 167
Amesworth, 101
C. D., 88
Clement, 118,. 119
D., 169
D. F., 12
H. F., 159
J. C., 163
J. H. & Co., 177
James, 140
John, 114, 134
Josephus, 203
Mills, 54
O. F., 103
P., 157
S. D., 30
S. F., 152
S. P., 152
Solomon, 81
Thomas, 114
Valney & Co., 122
Volney, 147
W. H., 54

WOODBECK, Thomas, 135
WOODBUCK, Thomas, 135
WOODBURN, E. G., 150
J. B., 43
WOODBURY, D. A., 5
E. G., 150
Erastus, 40
WOODCOCK, G. W., 129
WOODFON, W. (sic), 26
WOODFORD,
____(Dr.), 59
A., 59
Daniel, 110
WOODHOUSE, John, 105, 110
Levison, 103, 110
WOODING, Milow, 171
WOODMAN, S. P., 98, 111
WOODROE, Edward, 70
WOODRUFF, T., 10
WOODS, ____, 91
____(Mr.), 146
Charles R., 110
Daniel T., 87
David B., 87
J., 152, 166, 189
J. G., 18
L., 41
Lewis, 97
R. B., 25
T., 20, 189
William, 85
William B., 97
WOODSIDE, John, 96
WOODSON, H., 1
John, 1
Martin A., 130
T. J., 1
W., 26
WOODWARD, George, 21
J., 165
J. E., 13
James, 153
John, 153

Joseph, 123
Luther, 106
W., 46, 198
W.L., 198
William, 138
WOODWORTH,
____(Dr.), 4, 181
G. W., 68
H. P., 62
Joseph, 98
L., 139
L. H., 62
S., 153
WOODY, M. M., 144
WOOLDRIDGE, John R., 121
WOOLEY, L. A., 51
WOOLFOLK, Shapburgh R., 47
WOOLSEY, B. F., 10
J. L., 64, 200
Leander, 200
N., 126
WOOLVER, J., 139
WOORE, Daniel, 147
WOOTLY, John, 104
WORCESTER, G. W., 66
J. M., 66 (see also John M.)
J. W., 66
John M. (see also J. M.)
WORDEN, G., 68
William, 149
WORDUSON, S. 159
WORICK, G., 159
WORKMAN, S. S., 149
WORMAN, G. S., 154
WORRELL, George, 90
Reuben, 90
William, 32
WORSLEY, John, 40
Sarah & 6 chldrn, 40
WORTHINGTON, O. A., 30
Timothy, 43, 197
Z., 197
WRAY, Caleb P., 118
WRIGHT, Amos, 70
D., 99 (x)

David, 114
Edward, 101
F. M. (Capt.), 47
G. B., 12
George, 108
George W., 47
Henry, 48
Ira T., 131
J., 167
J. H., 153
J. L. & lady, 141
J. P., 95
J. W., 179
Jacob, 102
James, 84
James (Rev.), 198
Lucian, 60
O., 99
Samuel, 23
Sarah & fam., 179
T. S., 24
Thomas, 114
W. C., 8
William, 92, 136
WRISLEY, Robert A., 105
WRISTON, S. E., 158
WUSTENFELD,____(Mr.), 80
WYANT, J. M., 157
WYATT, C. P., 130
  F., 104
  James, 104
  Mathew (sic), 91
  Matthew (sic), 91
  T., 103
  William, 104
WYCHOFF, W., 18, 188
WYCKOFF, H., 12
  W., 18
  William W., 82
WYERS, A., 148
WYMAN, W. H., 167
WYNCKOOP, Garret H. (sic), 127
WYNKOP, John H., 102
WYNNE, H. S., 17
WYRICK, F., 144

Peter, 44

-Y-

YAGER, George W., 117
YAN, Peen, 84
YANDYWINE, J. (sic), 153
YARNELL, Green, 116
YATES, John P., 102
  S., 167
  T., 166
YAW, Henry, 106
YEARING, Louis, 122
YEOMAN, Eli, 114
YETTER, E., 18
YOCMM, G., (sic), 49
YOCUM, G., 48
  Joseph M., 100
YORCK, George, 100
YORK, William, 91
YOST, John, 149
  Michael, 38
YOSTER, G., 81
YOTES, T. (sic), 166
YOTTEY, A. G., 2
YOUNG,____, 115
  A., 19
  A. J., 148
  B., 112
  David, 62
  F. E., 60
  Farmon, 137
  G., 2, 31
  George A., 48
  I. Y., 98
  J. C., 42, 195
  John, 101
  John, wife & 2 chldrn, 155
  John A., 147
  Joseph C., 195
  L., 166
  Limon, 101
  M., 173
  M. M., 12
  S., 153
  S. H., 131

Samuel, 81
Sheldon, 87
Thomas, 10
Uriel, 58
W., 166
W. W., 84
William, 84, 87
YOUNGER, M., 151
YOUNGS, C., 4

-Z-

ZABRISKIE. William, 4
ZANDER, Tacitus P., 101
ZEAGER, C., 21
  G., 21
ZIBLER, L., 145
ZIMMERMAN,____(Capt.), 167
ZISHEL, Anthony, 178
ZUMALT, Joseph & fam. of 9 chldrn., 21
ZUNWALT, J. & fam., of 8 chldrn., 87

304

GEOGRAPHICAL INDEX

See also Geographical Notes. Additional area information will also be found in the Subject Index. An "(x)" refers to more than one entry for site on listed page.

NO STATE LISTED:
Ash Hollow, 161
Bates County, 171
Big Sandy, 96, 195
Black Rock, 155
Chimney Rock, 71, 95
Durango, 143
Fairfield, 173
Fayette, 202
Franklin County, 171
Galena, 96
Humboldt Sink, 154, 201
Lagrange, 202
Lamar, 202
Livingston County, 174
Loup Fork (or Loop Fork), 72
Magadore, 99
Mecklenburg County, 47
Mount Pleasant, 95, 173
Nemaha Sub Agency, 72
Ormsby's Station, 177
Pacific Sandy, 96
Pacific Spring (Pacific Springs), 96, 128
Pawnee Territory, 182
Peoria, 202
Platte Crossing, 96
Pymatuning (sic), 97
Robidoux, 127
Rock Point, 142
Shelby County, 202
Sommerville, 202
Spring Creek, 72
Spring Hill, 202
South Pass, 130
Sulphur Springs, 88
Thousand Spring Valley, 156
Truckee Station, 177, 180
Washington City, 95
West Township, 192

ALABAMA:
State of, 40, 79, 83(x), 201, 203
Butler County, 9
Courtland, 51
Demopolis, 79(x)
Florence, 60(x), 61, 94
Gravilly Spring, 60
Greenville, 79
Hormer, 60(x)
Lowndes County, 9(x)
Madison County, 52
Mobile, 72, 79(x), 94
Turnball, 51

ARKANSAS:
State of, 40, 80(x), 104, 125(x), 128, 129, 130, 169, 170, 179(x)
Batesville, 89
Fort Smith, 80, 81, 82(x), 83(x), 84(x), 85(x), 88, 202
Fort Smith Herald, 81, 82(x), 83(x), 84(x), 85
Helena, 81
Little Rock, 77, 82
Van Buren Newspaper, 105, 201
Washington County, 94

BEAR RIVER, 74

BIG PLATTE, 70, 71, 73, 93, 123, 125, 161, 164

CALIFORNIA:
State of, 1(x), 3(x), 4(x), 6, 7(x), 8(x), 10(x), 11, 12(x), 13, 14, 16(x), 17, 20, 21, 22(x), 24(x), 25(x), 26, 27(x), 28(x), 29, 31(x), 32(x), 33(x), 34, 35(x), 36(x), 37(x), 38(x), 39(x), 40(x), 41(x), 42, 43(x), 44(x), 46(x), 47(x), 48(x), 49(x), 50, 53(x), 54, 55(x), 56(x), 57, 59(x), 60(x), 61(x), 62(x), 65, 66, 67, 68(x), 69(x), 71(x), 72(x), 73(x), 74(x), 75(x), 76(x), 77(x), 78(x), 79(x), 80(x), 81(x), 82, 83(x), 84(x), 85(x), 86(x), 87(x), 88(x), 89(x), 90(x), 91(x), 92(x), 93(x), 96, 97(x), 98(x), 100, 101(x), 102(x), 103, 104(x), 105(x), 108, 109, 110, 111, 113(x), 114, 115, 116(x), 118, 119, 120(x), 121, 122(x), 123(x), 124(x), 125(x), 126, 128(x), 129, 130, 131(x), 132(x), 133(x), 134(x), 135(x),

136(x), 137(x), 138(x), 139(x), 140(x), 141(x), 145, 182, 183, 193, 194, 197, 198(x), 199, 201(x), 202(x), 203(x), 204
American Fork River, 74
Berkeley, 204
Calaveras County, 152
Coloma, 75, 146, 156(x)
Columbia, 152, 156(x)
Deer Creek Village, 201
Downieville, 145, 146(x), 154(x), 160(x), 161(x)
Downieville - Henness Route, 161
Downieville, new road, 154
Dry Diggings, 75(x)
Feather River, 74, 75
Galloways Ranch, 154
Gold, 76, 77
Gold Mining, 74(x)
Hangtown, 74, 75, 76(x), 77(x)
Hangtown, Dry Diggins, 200
Indians, 76, 77
Kelso Diggings, 75(x), 76(x)
Mining, 75 (See Subject Index: California)
Napa Valley, 164
Placerville, 133(x), 142(x), 144(x), 146, 147(x), 149(x), 152, 156(x), 162(x), 165(x), 167(x), 168(x)
Sacramento City, 73(x)
Sacramento, 74, 75(x), 77, 124(x), 125, 128, 130(x), 141(x), 142, 143(x), 144(x), 152, 155(x), 161, 164, 171(x)

Sacramento, large drove of cows arrive, 164
Sacramento, First Emigrants to arrive during 1850 season, 128
Sacramento Valley, 75
San Francisco, 77(x), 193
Shasta, 149, 151, 155(x), 159(x)
Sierra Nevada, 56, 74, 75, 149
Stanislaus River, 156
Sutter's Fort, 19
Sutter's Mill, 74
Volcano, 143
Volcano, new road, 143
Weaver Town, 74
Weaver Town Dry Diggins, 74
Weaver's Creek, 74, 75
Weaverville, 125(x), 128, 201
Yankee Jim's, 151
Yreka, 159, 164(x), 165
Yuba River, 74
Yuba River Diggins, 74
BEAR RIVER, 74
BIG BLUE RIVER, 204
CANADA:
  Montreal, 52
  Prince Edward Island, 136
CANADA WEST: 52(x), 62(x), 140
  Middlesex, 135
  London, 52
  Tousaint Chabot, 52
CAPE HORN: 3
COLORADO RIVER: 95
CONNECTICUT: 4, 140, 171
  Hartford, 79(x), 203
  New Haven, 22
DELAWARE:
  State of, 97
DISTRICT OF COLUMBIA:

Washington, 79
(See also No State Listed, Washingon City)
DURANGO, 143
ENGLAND: 62, 122
FEATHER RIVER, 74, 75
FLORIDA:
  St. Johns, 9(x)
FORT:
  Fort Childs, (See Nebraska), 69, 72
  Fort DesMoines, (See Iowa), 45(x)
  Fort Hall, (See Idaho), 74
  Fort Hall Road, 74, 75
  Fort Kearny (Fort Kearney), (See Nebraska), 39, 69(x), 70(x), 71, 78, 92, 93, 96, 113, 114, 125, 126, 155
  Fort Laramie, (See Wyoming Territory), 71(x), 72, 93(x), 94(x), 96, 125(x), 127(x), 128(x), 168, 201
  Fort Madison, (See Iowa) 51(x)
  Fort Smith, (See Arkansas), 80, 81, 82(x), 83(x), 84(x), 85(x), 88, 202
  Fort Washington, (See Wisconsin), 68(x)
  Fort Wayne, (See Indiana), 9
  Sutter's Fort, (See California), 19
GEORGIA:
  State of, 79, 126 (See Subject Index: Wagon Trains-By Name: Missouri & Georgia California Mining Co's.)
  Atlanta, 79

Chattanooga County, 9
Cobb County, 9
Elberton, 51(x)
Floyd County, 9(x)
Milledgeville, 79(x)
Paulding County, 9(x)
GERMANY, 80(x)
GILA RIVER, 93
GRAND ISLAND: (See
   Nebraska)
GREAT BRITAIN:
   Great Britain, 40
GREEN HORN
   VILLAGE, 95
GREEN RIVER, 96
GULF OF ST.
   LAWRENCE, 136
HOLLAND:
   Country of, 27
IDAHO:
   Fort Hall, 74, 75
ILLINOIS:
   State of, 2, 27, 28,
      30(x), 32(x), 40, 41,
      43, 44, 52, 55, 80, 92,
      94, 95, 101, 106,
      124(x), 131, 132,
      133(x), 135, 140,
      141, 142, 143(x),
      144, 145(x), 146(x),
      159(x), 160, 161(x),
      162(x), 164, 169(x),
      170, 172(x), 173(x),
      174, 175(x), 177(x),
      178(x), 179(x),
      180(x)
   Adams, 65
   Adams County, 57(x),
      62, 96, 112, 127, 128,
      169
   Alton, 189
   Andover, 133
   Aurora, 33
   Batavia, 169
   Beardstown, 47
   Belleville, 52(x)
   Belvedere, 80
   Bond County, 54
   Boone County, 127, 149

Brown, 53
Bureau County, 2
Carlyle, 52(x)
Cass County, 46, 47(x),
   127
Casse County, 170
Centre Grove, 92
Champaigne County, 43
Chemung, 66
Chicago, 13, 20, 39(x),
   46, 52(x), 57, 58(x),
   66, 87, 97, 131, 132,
   172, 176(x), 198
Chicago, "Chicago
   Directory", 87
Clark County, 48, 54,
   169(x), 171
Clinton County, 32
Cole County, 125
Coles County, 27(x). 48
Collinsville. 52
Cook County, 66(x),
   174
Danville, 52
Davis County, 101,
   130(x)
De Witt County, 43
Dixon Lee County, 40,
   194
Edgar County, 48, 112
Edwardsville, 55, 122,
   144
Elgin, Kane County, 61
Ewington, 52
Fairfield, 141
Freedom, 145(x)
Freeport, 174
Fremont, 52
Fulton, 65
Fulton County, 46,
   57(x)
Galena, 27, 38(x), 54,
   133(x)
Galesburgh, 65
Gross Point, 57(x)
Grundy County, 27(x),
   28(x)
Gundy County, 113
Hampshire Township,

Hane County, 101
Hancock County, 38,
   46, 94
Henderson, 200(x)
Henderson County, 127,
   134
Henry County, 57(x),
   96, 178 (See also
   McHenry County)
Jacksonville, 91
Jefferson County, 53
Joe Daviess County, 46,
   171
Jo Daviess County,
   57(x)
Kane County, 27, 32,
   127
Kendall County, 54, 97
Knox County, 64(x),
   65(x), 200(x) (See
   Subject Index:
   Wagon Train - By
   Name, Knox County,
   Illinois Company)
Knoxville, 57, 92(x),
   200(x)
Lake County, 52
Land Office-Register
   (Registrar), 87
La Salle County, 27(x),
   102(x), 132
Lewistown, 52(x)
Linden, Whitesides
   County, 62(x)
Little Fort, Lake
   County, 58(x)
Macon County, 43(x)
Macoupin County, 19,
   43
Maddison County, 171
Madison Coutny, 46, 96
McDonough County,
   38, 134
McHenry County, 60,
   62, 149 (See also
   Henry County)
Menard, 53
Menard County, 95
Mercer County, 62, 65

Millcreek, 91
Moline, 66
Montgomery County, 174
Morgan County, 19, 46, 53
Mt. Morris, 173, 174(x)
Milford, 122
Mulford, 123
Naples, 71
Nauvoo, 57
Newspaper: Joliet Signal, 87
Ogle County, 45, 57(x), 58(x), 61, 62, 111
Oquawka, 92(x), 130
Ottawa, 52(x), 57, 58, 87
Palestine, 100
Payson, Adams County, 52
Peoria, 30, 52(x), 65, 126, 127, 174
Peru, 26(x), 62, 174, 193
Piatt County, 43(x)
Pike County, 48, 112(x), 113(x), 125(x), 126(x), 128, 129, 130(x)
Praire Du Rocher, 52
Providence (sic), 132(x)
Quincy, 91, 112
Randolph County, 24
Rock Island, 25, 55, 57(x), 65, 66(x), 101, 127
Rock Island County, 65(x)
Rock River, Ogle County, 57
Rushville, 161(x)
St. Clair County, 19, 54
Sangamon County, 53
Schuyler County 39(x), 44(x), 101(x)
Scott County, 54
Shelby County, 20, 27(x)

Southern (area), 41
Stephenson County, 60 (See also Stevenson County)
Sterling, 62(x)
Stevenson County, 149 (See also Stephenson County)
Tazewell County, 2
Vandalia, 95
Warren, 64
Warren County, 128
Waukegan, 107, 119
Wayne County, 169
Weston, 122
White County, 53
Will County, 21, 27(x), 30
Winchester, 91, 93, 94
Winnebago County, 15(x)
Woodstock, 58
INDIANA,
State of, 26(x), 32(x), 51(x), 69, 96, 106, 112, 126, 127, 131, 133, 134, 135, 137, 140, 141(x), 142, 143, 144, 145, 159, 160, 161, 169, 174, 176, 178(x), 179, 180
Bloomington, 71
Blountsville, 137
Bluffton, 52
Centerville, 87
Cleveland, Elkhart County, 45(x)
Clinton County, 32(x), 128
Daviess County, 126
Economy, 87
Elkhart County, 15(x)
English Prairie, 176
Evansville, 33
Fort Wayne, 9
Frankfort, 174
Grant County, 6
Greencastle, 126
Harvard, 172

Henry County, 1
Indianapolis, 51, 112, 181(x)
Jefferson County, 43
Kane County, 32
Lafayette, 52(x)
Lafayette County, 32
La Porte, 13(x), 14(x), 15, 16, 43
Mesheehakee, 96
Michigan City, 13
Middlebury, 14
Milford, 14
Mishawaka, 45, 124, 139
Montgomery County, 52
New Albany, 22, 26, 94
Onandigua, 137(x)
Orange County, 127
Oswego, 96
Perry County, 177
Plymouth, 13(x), 137(x)
Plymouth, Marshall County, 137
Richmond, 23, 87
Rushville, 39, 87
St. Joseph's County, 141
South Bend, 13, 46(x), 101, 173, 198(x)
Tippecanoe County, 26(x), 127
Valparaiso, 137
Wabash, 62
Wabash County, 66(x), 179
Warren County 151(x)
Warsaw, 137
Wayne County, 3, 32
White County, 1
Wilmington, 94
IOWA:
State of, 50, 119, 124(x), 126, 131, 135, 136, 140(x), 145, 159, 162(x), 177, 179(x), 198
Askaloosa, 72

Augusta, Lee County, 45(x)
Bonaparte, 44(x)
Bonaparte, Van Buren County, 112
Burlington, 66(x), 90, 130
Cedar County, 170, 171
Council Bluff, First to leave in 1850, 107
Council Bluffs, 35, 66, 70, 125, 130, 138
Davenport, 25
Decatur, 132
Decatur County, 127
Des Moine County, 132(x)
Des Moines (see also Iowa/Fort Des Moines)
Dodgeville, 66
Dubuque, 59, 86, 96
Dubuque County, 127
Dyersville, 138
Fairfield, 96, 103, 109
Farmington, 56, 152
Fort Des Moines, 45(x)
Fort Madison, 51(x)
Franklin County, 160(x)
Fremont County, 124
Henry County, 44, 45, 58
Indianapolis (sic) (Indianola?), 112(x)
Iowa City, newspaper editor, 130
Iowa City, 130
Iowa Mission, 55
Jackson County, 15
Kanesville, 44, 46, 57, 58(x), 59(x), 60(x), 62(x), 63, 64(x), 65, 66(x), 67, 68, 72(x), 73, 98, 102, 105, 107, 108(x), 109, 110(x), 111, 116(x), 118(x), 119, 120(x), 122(x), 123(x), 124(x), 131, 132, 133(x), 134(x), 135(x), 136, 137(x), 138(x), 139(x), 140(x), 141(x), 145(x)
Kanesville, "Frontier Guardian Newspaper", 63, 98, 102, 105, 107, 109, 110, 111, 116, 118, 120, 121, 122(x), 123(x), 124(x), 131, 132, 133, 134(x), 135(x), 136, 137(x), 138(x), 139(x), 141(x), 145
Keokuk, 47(x), 57(x)
Keosauqua, 125
Laporte County, 169
Lee County, 44(x), 112, 160(x)
Linn County, 44(x), 58(x)
Louisa County, 45(x), 120(x)
Mahaska County, 151
Marion, 135
Marion County, 59, 160, 170
Monroe County, 132
Mount Pleasant, 95, 137
N. Albany, 111
Peru, 161
Polk County, 44(x), 126
Portland, 57(x)
Red Rock, 94
St.Joseph, Berrien County, 46
Salem, 137(x), 138(x)
Saluba County, 138(x)
Scott County, 111, 112(x)
Sullivan, Postmaster of, 161
Van Buren County, 44(x), 45(x), 130
Wapello County, 126
Warren County, 132
Washington, 66(x), 112(x)
Washington County 57(x), 65
IRELAND:
Country of, 26, 27(x), 80, 112
Roscommon County, 52
Prince Edward, 136
ISLE OF MAN: 107
ISTHMUS, 143
KANSAS: (area), Salt Creek, 69
KENTUCKY:
State of, 10, 26(x), 31(x), 128, 129, 143, 154, 172
Anderson County, 2, 11
Bellefonte, 139
Breckenridge County, 80, 81
Campbell County, 31
Clark County, 155(x)
Cynthiana, 101
Grant County, 31
Greene County, 62, 95
Hancock County, 80(x)
Henderson, 11
Jackson County, 31
Kenton County, 31
Knox County, 1
Lebanon, 52
Lexington, 11(x), 80(x), 176
Louisville, 10, 11, 52(x), 60, 80(x), 89, 183
Madison County, 11, 155(x), 156(x)
Madisonville, 52
Midway, 95
Newspaper "Telegraph", 139
Owensborough, 11
Paducah, 94
Paris, 11(x)
Pendleton County, 31(x)
Princeton, 169(x)
Scott County, 111(x)
Shelbyville, 11

Simpsonville, 171
Steuben County, 6
Westport, 112
Woodford County, 31
LOUISIANA:
State of, 53, 83(x)
Claiborn Parish, 127
Hinds County, 53
Logansport, 83
New Orleans, 51(x), 104, 121, 122, 124
Picayune Newspaper, 104, 105, 121, 122(x), 124, 203
MAINE:
State of, 40(x), 80, 84(x)
Augusta, 77(x), 78(x), 123, 124, 203
Augusta, "Kennebec Journal", 78(x), 123, 124, 203
Bath, 84(x)
Belfast, 50(x), 51(x), 78
Bingham, 124
Charleston, 78
Gardiner, 78
Holton, 93
Limerick, 77
Lime Rock, 77
Limestone, 77
Newcastle, 51(x)
Newspaper, "Republican Journal", 78
Portland, 78
Roxbury, 78(x)
South Thomaston, 77
Waldo, 51(x), 78
MARYLAND:
State of, 51
Baltimore, 73, 78, 174, 194
Cumberland, 172
MARY'S RIVER, 74
MASSACHUSETTS:
State of, 140, 202
Beverly, 201

Boston, 4, 51, 52, 77, 78(x), 86, 201, 204(x)
Hampden County, 27
Haydenville, 202
Lowell, 77, 78
Lynn, 202
Lynnfield, 201
Newton, 94, 204
Northampton, 202
Salem, 201, 202
Sturbridge, 51
MEXICO:
Country of, 143
Irapauto, 203
Matamoras, 77, 143
Mazatlan, 125, 143
Mexico City, 77, 202
Monterey, 77
Saltillo, 77
Tampico, 78
Vera Cruz, 77, 79, 203(x)
MICHIGAN:
State of, 4, 14(x), 22, 40(x), 41, 44(x), 55, 56, 58, 60, 94, 97, 119, 124(x), 131, 134(x), 135, 137, 138, 140, 141, 142, 143(x), 145(x), 152, 159, 162, 172(x), 173(x), 174(x), 175, 176, 177(x), 178, 179(x), 183, 193
Central Area, 60
Adrian, 22, 33, 35(x), 39, 68(x), 192
Adrian County, 5
Albion, 57
Albion, 58 (See Subject Index: Wagon Trains - By Name, Albion Company)
Ann Arbor, 44, 51(x), 66
Berrien, 15, 45, 58, 62(x)
Berrien County, 58, 62(x), 183

Bloomfield, 140(x)
Buchanan, 8, 58(x)
Calhoun County, 44, 45(x), 57, 128, 133
Cass County, 5, 14, 15, 22, 44(x), 97(x), 183
Centreville, 97(x)
Coldwater, 133
Dearborn, 66(x)
Detroit, 66(x), 95, 174
Dexter, 177
Eaton County, 128
Edwardsburg, 45
Grand Rapids, 112
Hill County, 161
Hillsdale County, 133(x)
Ionia County, 22
Jackson, 177
Jonesville, 58, 65
Joseph County, 127 (Note there is also a St. Joseph County)
Kalamazoo, 22, 59, 65(x)
Litchfield, 170
Livonia, 66
Mackinac County, 8
Macomb County, 66(x) (See also McComb County)
Marshall, 133
McComb County, 138, (See also Macomb County)
Monroe, 170, 172
Monroe City, 5
Monroe County (sic) (Munroe County?), 51
New Buffalo, 13
Niles, 45(x), 57(x), 58
Oakland, 66
Pan Pan, 173
Paw Paw, 15
Prairie, St. Joseph County, 45
Radford, 142
St. Joseph, 15

St. Joseph County, 58(x), 130
St. Joseph, Berrien County, 46(x)
St. Louis, 57(x)
Schoolcraft, 101
Sturgis Prairie, St. Joseph County, 45(x)
Union City, 173
Utica, 66
Wayne County, 60, 66(x), 133, 141, 151, 174
MISSISSIPPI:
State of, 32 (x), 80, 83(x), 92, 178, 202
Coffeville, 8
Hillsorough, 85
Jackson, 85(x)
Lafayette County, 32
Madison County, 32
Pontatoc, 96
Pontotoc, 8, 93
Rankin County, 9
Wilkerson County, 8(x)
MISSOURI:
State of, 17, 56, 69, 86, 93, 96, 112, 122, 126(x), 127(x), 128(x), 129, 131, 140, 143, 159, 160, 161(x), 162(x), 164(x), 169(x), 170, 171(x), 172(x), 173(x), 174, 175, 176(x), 178(x), 179(x), 180(x), 201(x) (See Subject Index: Wagon Trains-By Name, Missouri & Georgia California Mining Companies)
Andrew County, 52, 74, 127(x), 128, 129(x), 130, 170, 200
Arrow Rock, 129
Ashley P. C., 112
Atchison County, 69, 131(x), 171

Augusta, 129
Baldwin, 129
Baltimore, (sic) 52, 129
Bates County, 178
Benton, 125, 126(x)
Benton County, 130(x)
Boone County, 75, 95, 128, 130, 176, 177, 198
Boonville, 129(x)
Buchanan County, 126, 127
Calloway County, 130 (See also Collaway County)
Cambridge, 129(x)
Camden County, 128(x)
Camp Bryarly, 41
Canon County, 170
Canton, 130
Cape Girardeau, 126(x), 127, 129(x)
Carroll County 70, 127
Carrolton (sic), 128
Cedar County, 52, 125
Chariton County, 69(x), 128(x)
Clair County, 128
Clark County, 112(x), 120
Clarksville, 111, 112(x)
Cole County, 128, 154
Collaway County, 169 (See also Calloway County)
Columbia, 129(x), 198
Cooper County, 127(x), 128, 130, 131, 170, 177
Dade County, 126, 127
Dallas County, 126, 170
Daviess County, 126, 127 (See also Davis County)
Davis County, 169 (See also Daviess County)
DeKalb County, 128
Dodge County, 127
Doniphan, 129

Farmington, 170
Fayette, 95
Frankfort P. C., 112
Franklin County, 127, 170, 171(x)
Fulton, 129
Gasconade County, 130
Gasconado County, 127
Genevieve County, 170
Gentry County, 69(x), 70(x), 126, 169
Glasgow, 77
Green County, 127, 130, 170
Grundy County, 126
Hannibal, 112
Hannibal, Postmaster, 78
Henry County, 126, 130(x), 170
Hickory County, 129
Hold County, 127 (See also Holt County)
Holt County, 175(x) (See also Hold County)
Howard County, 69(x), 126, 127(x), 129, 170
Independence, 1, 2, 3, 4(x), 5(x), 6(x), 8(x), 9(x), 10(x), 11(x), 12(x), 13, 28(x), 29(x), 30(x), 31(x), 32(x), 33(x), 34(x), 35(x), 36, 53(x), 78(x), 80, 86(x), 92, 93, 121, 124, 168, 181(x), 182, 194
Independence, Prices of stock in, 34
Jackson, 171
Jackson County, 126(x), 169, 170(x), 172, 174, 202
Jefferson City, 72, 129(x)
Jefferson County, 72
Johnson County, 94, 130, 170(x)(See also

311

Johnston County)
Johnston County, 175
(See also Johnson County)
Kirksville, 129
Knox County, 130
Koarhill, 129
LaGrange, 128
Lawrence County, 95, 96, 130
Lewis County, 52, 120, 130
Lexington, 52(x), 96, 129(x), 130
Lexington Express Newspaper, 96
Linden, 129
Linn County, 125
Louisiana, 111(x), 112(x)
Macon County, 129(x)
Madison County, 29
Marion County, 111(x), 112(x), 127
Montgomery County, 128(x), 129
New Madrid, 11
Newport, 129
Newspaper, 73, 74(x), 77
Newspaper "Lexington", 96
Nodaway County, 69(x), 114, 129(x)
Oak Springs, 89
Oregon, 130(x)
Osage County 52(x)
Osecola, 129(x)
Palmyra, 4, 111, 176
Perry County 171
Pettis County, 169
Pike County, 43, 112(x), 113(x), 129, 172, 175
Platte City, 74 , 129
Platte County, 126, 130, 170, 171
Platteville, 127
Pleasant Hill, 95(x)

Polk County, 126, 130, 156
Potosi County, 141
Pulaski County, 126, 128
Ralls County, 43, 74, 127
Randolph, 129
Randolph County, 53(x), 69
Ray County, 70, 95, 126(x), 130
St. Charles, 52, 126, 129(x), 130
St. Charles County, 171
St. Clair Coutny, 128
St. Francois County, 172
St. Joseph, 4, 7(x), 13(x), 14(x), 15, 16(x), 17(x), 19, 20(x), 21(x), 22(x), 24(x), 25(x), 26(x), 27(x), 33(x), 34(x), 35(x), 36(x), 37(x), 38(x), 39(x), 40(x), 41(x), 42(x), 43(x), 44(x), 46(x), 47(x), 48(x), 49(x), 50(x), 53(x), 54, 55(x), 56(x), 60(x), 61(x), 62, 68(x), 69(x), 70(x), 71(x), 72(x), 73(x), 74(x), 75(x), 76(x), 77(x), 79, 89, 94, 96, 97(x), 100, 101(x), 103(x), 104(x), 111(x), 113(x), 114, 115(x), 119(x), 124, 125, 128(x), 129, 130(x), 131(x), 132(x), 142, 143, 179, 181(x), 182(x), 183(x), 185(x), 186, 189(x), 192, 193(x), 196, 197, 198(x)
St. Joseph, (Cholera in), 62
St. Joseph Gazette, 100,
101(x), 102, 103(x), 104(x), 111, 113(x), 114(x), 115(x), 125, 126, 127(x), 128(x), 130(x), 131(x), 132(x), 183, 185, 189(x), 196, 197, 198(x), 199, 200(x)
St. Joseph, Hotel Edgar House, 36
St. Joseph, Newspaper, 77
St. Louis, 4, 13, 19, 24(x), 39, 40, 52(x), 74, 78, 79(x), 80(x), 81, 85, 86(x), 98, 125, 126, 128, 129(x), 138, 172, 176, 177, 181(x), 182, 193
St. Louis County, 154
St. Louis Hotel, 181
St. Louis, Newspaper, "St. Louis Union", 89, 201
Saline County, 127, 130, 171
Savannah, 103, 129(x)
Scott County, 112, 127, 128
Shelby County, 129(x)
Springfield, 129
Sweetville, 176
Taney County, 130
Texas County, 130
Trenton, 129
Troy (Lincoln County), 47
Union, 129
Van Buren County, 52, 53
Warrensburgh, 129
Washington County, 33, 104, 129, 130(x)
Weston, 127, 129, 130
Willow Springs, 96
Wolf Creek, 53
LITTLE BLUE RIVER, 182

MISSOURI RIVER: 33, 39, 60, 70, 73(x), 97, 119, 120, 121, 123, 131, 133, 146, 164, 171
  Cholera on, 62
MONTANA:
  Big Sandy, 96, 195
  Warm Spring, 96
NEBRASKA:
  Fort Childs, 69, 72
  Fort Kearny (Fort Kearney), 39, 69(x), 70(x), 71, 78, 92, 93, 96, 113, 114, 125, 126, 155
  Fort Kearney, 70(x) (Old Fort Kearny)
  Fort Kearney, Old, 113
  Grand Island, 35, 69
  Nichtenabotna Township, 39
  Praire Creek, 72
  Scott's Bluff, 95(x)
NEVADA:
  Carson, 143
  Carson River, 73, 74, 156
  Carson Pass, 201
  Carson Sink, 74
  Humboldt River, 125, 142, 149, 152
  Humboldt Sink, 154, 177, 201
  Sierra, 149, 201
  Sierra (summit of), 74
NEW HAMPSHIRE:
  State of, 4, 24 (See Subject Index: Wagon Trains-By Name, Granite State & California Mining & Trading Company)
  Greenfield, 58(x)
  Nelson, 78
  Pittsfield, 51
NEW JERSEY:
  State of 4, 24, 68

Belleville, 183
Breeden, 96
Elizabethtown, 10(x), 183
Hanover, 183
Jersey City, 10
Martinville, 85
Newark, 10, 182, 183(x)
Salem, 51
Springfield, 183
NEW MEXICO (Territory):
  Territory, 53
  Sante Fe, 56, 82(x), 93
NEW YORK:
  State of, 2, 4, 7, 24(x), 34, 43, 55, 56(x), 80(x), 82(x), 84(x), 92, 96, 141, 142, 143, 145(x), 160, 175, 178
  Albany, 2, 24
  Albany County, 51
  Baldwinsville, 98, 101(x)
  Brooklyn, 85
  Buffalo, 7, 39, 85(x), 95, 174
  Cambridge, 7
  Cattaraugus County. 24
  Cheektowaga, 86
  Clarence, 86(x)
  Elbridge, 101
  Elmira, 145
  Elmyra, 28
  Geneva, 51
  Jamestown, 19
  Monroe County, 32
  Moravia, 51
  New York, 84, 85
  New York City, 10(x), 51(x), 84, 183
  New York Daily Tribune, 79, 82, 83, 84, 85, 88, 89(x), 92(x), 97, 98(x), 181, 192, 193, 194(x), 198(x), 199(x), 200(x), 201(x), 203(x), 204(x)

Oswego, 32, 51(x)
Ovid, 133
Rochester, 18, 95
Schagticoke (or Schaghticoke), 7, 182
Schoharie, 7
Scottsburgh, 52
Steuben County, 39
Syracuse, 127
Utica, 86
Washington County, 7, 24, 182
White Plains, 7
NORTH CAROLINA:
  State of, 1, 83
  Hyde County, 10
OHIO:
  State of, 11(x), 12(x), 16, 22, 23(x), 29(x), 30, 31(x), 36, 43, 53, 56(x), 94, 95, 96, 125, 126, 134, 137, 140(x), 141, 142, 143, 144, 156(x), 159(x), 160(x), 161, 162(x), 169(x), 170(x), 171(x), 172(x), 173(x), 175(x), 176, 178(x), 179(x)
  Adams, Seneca County, 62(x)
  Akron, 98, 171
  Allen County, 23, 116
  Ashland County, 131
  Ashtabula County, 16, 185
  Athens, 55
  Aurora, 99, 100
  Bainbridge, 100(x)
  Bellaire, 52
  Bellefontaine, 52
  Belmont County, 101
  Brooklyn, 98
  Butler County, 16
  Cambridge, 88
  Canton, 49, 198(x)
  Champaign County, 4(x)

Chillicothe, 51
Cincinnati, 28 (See
  Subject Index:
  Wagon Trains - By
  Name, Western
  Mining Company of
  Cincinnati)
Cincinnati, 43 (See
  Subject Index:
  Wagon Trains - By
  Name, Cincinnati
  Mercantile
  Association)
Cincinnati, 1, 2, 3,
  23(x), 29, 36(x),
  37(x), 53, 94, 181,
  194(x)
Clark County, 142
Cleveland, 23, 29, 44,
  173(x), 174
Columbia County, 27,
  192
Columbiana County, 22,
  27
Columbus, 37, 51, 94,
  170, 194
Cooper County, 94
Copley, 100
Covington, 116
Crawford County, 29
Cuyahuga Falls, 99
Dark County, 127
Dayton, 26, 42, 79, 196
Defiance, 80
Delaware County, 48,
  131, 169
Elizabethtown, 156
Erie County, 2
Euclid, 174
Fayette County, 114
Fort Meigs County, 127
Franklin, 88
Fulton, 199
Gallia, 30
Guernsey, 138
Hamilton, 29
Hamilton County, 11,
  12, 28, 29, 126, 143,
  152(x)

Hanover 192(x)
Harrison County, 27, 29
Huron County, 12
Jackson, 199
Kalida, Putnam County,
  89
Kenton, 23
Kingsville, Ashtabula
  County, 16, 185
Lake County, 33, 193
Lima, 100
Loraine County, 23
Lower Sandusky, 1 (See
  also Sundusky)
Mansfield, 5(x)
Marietta, 68
Marion, 89
Marion County, 29(x)
Massillon, 51, 53,
  199(x)
Medina County, 23
Megadoar, Summit
  County, 101
Meigs County, 115
Miami, 176
Miami County, 116, 142
Miamisburg, 38
Middleburgh, 6
Milan, 33
Mohoning County, 19,
  186
Monroeville, 38
Montgomery County, 142
Morgan, 23
Morgan County, 12,
  170
Morrow County, 29
Neville, 66
New Alexander, 192
Newark, 137
New Carlisle, 4, 37,
  112, 181(x)
New Garden, 192(x)
New Lisbon, 192
North Georgetown, 192
Ohio City, 101, 173,
  174
Oxford, 16, 78, 126(x),
  201

Painesville, 174
Paris, 137
Perrysburg, 80(x)
Poland, 95
Portsmouth, 169, 199
Putnam County, 170
Randolph, 100
Rarrington, 172
Richelieu, 172
Richfield, 100
Richland, 14
Richland County, 12
Richmond County, 11
Ripley, 51(x)
Risdon, Sececa County,
  101
Rome, 137
Sandusky, 1 (See also
  Lower Sandusky)
Sandusky City, 30
Sandusky County, 1, 2
Seneca County, 62, 101
Sharon, 66
Shelby County, 44, 113,
  115, 127
Sidney, Shelby County,
  113
Springfield, 100
Stark County, 100
Steubenville, 29, 182,
  198, 199
Stow, 100(x)
Suffield, 100
Summit County, 3
Tiffin, 52, 174
Trumbull, 37
Trumbull County, 89
Wadsworth, 66
Wayne County, 33
Wheelersburg, Sciota
  County, 49, 199
Whellersburg, 199
Woodford County, 11
Wooster, 5
Zanesville, 51(x), 53
OREGON (Territory):
  69
PANAMA:
  Isthmus, 143

PENNSYLVANIA:
  State of, 4(x), 5, 8, 27,
    35(x), 55, 80, 131,
    136(x), 143(x), 144,
    145, 146, 152, 161,
    170, 171, 177,
    178(x), 179
  Allegany County, (sic)
    174
  Allegheny (sic), 7
  Alleghany County, 18,
    186
  Beaver, 23
  Beaver County, 9
  Birmingham, 19
  Blainsville, 93
  Bond County, 35
  Butler, 18
  Butler County, 19, 101,
    104, 127, 143, 169,
    186
  Centre County, 5
  Chester County, 27(x)
  Clarion, 51
  Columbia County, 41
  Crawford County, 97
  Erie County, 6(x),
    27(x), 65, 130
  Fayette County, 52, 56
  Findley Township, 97
  Hamilton County, 8
  Jersey Shore, 145(x)
  Juniata, 79
  Lancaster County, 19,
    112, 186
  Liberty, 145(x)
  Manchester, 143, 144
  Mercer, 97
  Mercer County, 18
  Montgomery, County,
    51
  New Brighton, 18, 186
  Northampton, 51
  North Liberty, 97(x)
  Philadelphia, 23, 27(x),
    51(x), 78, 81, 133
  Pittsburgh, 5(x), 9, 17,
    18. 51, 152, 171, 185,
    186(x)
  Portsmouth, 199
  Schuylkill County, 6
  Shipensburgh, 51
  Somerset County, 9
  Springfield, 97
  Tioga County, 6
  Washington County,
    51(x)
  Wayne County, 33
  West Greenville, 97
  Westmoreland, 26(x)
  Westmoreland County,
    18, 186(x)
  Winesport, 145(x)
PLATTE RIVER, (or Big
  Platte) 70, 71, 73, 93,
  123, 125, 161, 164
PRINCE EDWARD'S
  ISLAND (Gulf of St.
  Lawrence), 136
RHODE ISLAND:
  State of, 24
  Newport, 131, 132(x)
  Pawtucket Island, 131,
    132
  Portsmouth, 132(x)
  Providence, 132(x)
  Wickford, 132(x)
RIO GRANDE, 201, 202
ROCKY MOUNTAINS:
  95
SAN FELIPE, 121
SANTE FE: 93 (No state
  or country
  mentioned)
ST. JOSEPH ISLAND,
  201
SIERRA NEVADA: 56,
  74, 75, 149, 201 (See
  also Sierra Nevada
  under California)
SOUTH CAROLINA:
  State of, 9, 79(x), 83
  Charleston, 51(x)
SUBLETTE CUT-OFF,
  124
TENNESSEE:
  State of, 26, 32, 83, 90,
    161
  Campbell County, 26,
    27
  Carroll County, 86
  Clarksburg, 80
  Clarksville, 80
  DeKalb County, 32
  Germantown, 112(x)
  Jackson, 86
  Knox County, 12(x),
    60(x)
  Knoxville, 92
  Memphis, 60, 202
  Montgomery County,
    26(x)
  Monroe County, 60(x)
  Nashville, 27(x)
  Natchez, 80, 83(x)
  Summit County, 27(x)
  Sumner County, 86
TEXAS:
  State of, 88
  Corpus Christi, 77, 201
  El Paso, 121
  Galveston, 201
  Houston, 202
  Huntsville, 95
  Laredo, 201
  Nacogdoches, 27
  Port Lavaca, 80, 202
  San Antonio, 125, 202
  San Antonio,
    Newspaper, 125
  Victoria, 88
TRUCKEE RIVER, 74
UTAH: (Territory)
  Deseret, 98
  Great Salt Lake, 75, 144
  Salt Lake, 68, 72, 128,
    129, 135, 145
  Salt Lake City, 74, 141
VERMONT:
  State of, 55, 107
  Brattleboro, 78
  Derby Line, 51(x)
  Essex, 94
VIRGINIA:
  State of, 2, 9(x), 15, 16,
    25, 47, 79, 83, 107,
    136, 143, 145, 162,

169, 180
Appomattock County (sic)(Appomattox), 51
Augusta, 16
Bath, 16(x)
Campbell County, 2, 33
Charleston, 41, 194 (See Subject Index: Wagon Trains - By Name, Charleston Virginia Mining Company)
Chesterfield, 51
Essex, 94
Franklin County, 2(x)
Greenbrier County, 51
Henry County, 2
Hollidays Cove, 47
Jefferson, 41, 194
Jefferson County, 18, 41, 42, 195(x)
Lynchburgh, 2(x), 27
Orange Counrty, 52
Penelton County, 169
Pittsylvania County, 2(x)
Pocohantos County, 15
Powhatan County, 15
Powhattan, 51
Richmond, 41, 195
Roanoke County, 16
Rockbridge, 15(x), 16(x)
Short Creek, 18
Sussex County, 16
Wellsburgh, 170
WALES: 40, 62
WALKER'S RIVER, 156
WASHINGTON, D.C., 79
WEST VIRGINIA:
  West Wheeling, 25
  Wheeling, 11, 25, 51(x)
WISCONSIN:
  State of, 9, 13, 15(x), 21, 26(x), 35(x), 41, 44(x), 45, 71, 73, 77, 106, 113(x), 124(x), 131(x), 132, 134,
135, 136, 138, 140(x), 142, 143, 145, 146(x), 149(x), 151(x), 154, 159(x), 160, 161, 171, 175, 177(x), 178(x), 179(x), 180(x) (See Subject Index: Wagon Trains - By Name, Badger Company)
Beloit, 49, 50(x), 113
Berlin, 134(x)
Brookfield, 139(x)
Columbia County, 160
Dane County, 169
Dodge County, 44
Dodgesville, 55
Eureka, 134
Fond du Lac County, 134(x)
Fort Washington, 68(x)
Gennesee (sic), 128
Grant County, 57
Granville, 134(x)
Hazlegreen, 151
Highland, 135
Iowa County, 58, 101
Jamestown, Grant County, 104
Janesville, 50(x), 115, 139(x)
Jefferson, 50
Jefferson County, 44, 127, 154, 155(x)
Johnstown, 140
Kingston, 134(x), 160
Lafayette County, 58
Lake Maria, Marquette County, 66
Lancaster, 174
Lowell, 134(x)
Madison, 86, 134(x)
Marcellon, 134
Marquette County, 66(x)
Milwaukee, 21, 22, 101, 102, 134(x), 140
Monroe, 59
Neenah, 140
Oak Grove, 52
Platteville, 50, 57(x), 62, 90, 139(x), 140
Potosi, 51(x)
Racine, 41
Racine County, 13(x), 26, 35, 45(x), 58(x), 193
Rochester, 57, 59
Rock County, 13(x), 26
Rosendale, 140(x)
Shallburgh, 101
Sheboygan, 177(x)
Shullsburgh, 57
Shultsburg, 126
Southport, 61
Walworth, 34
Walworth County, 34, 62, 160
Waterford, 101(x)
Waterloo, 57
Watertown, 45, 57, 90, 151
Waukashaw County, 57(x)
Waukesha, 68, 94, 95, 140
Waukesha County, 21, 57(x), 95
Weelaunce, 134
WYOMING: (Territory)
  Fort Laramie, 71(x), 72, 93(x), 94(x), 96, 125(x), 127(x), 128(x), 168, 201
YUBA RIVER: 74
YUBA RIVER DIGGINS, 74

SUBJECT INDEX

ACCIDENTS:
  Broken finger, 97
  Buffalo attack, 95
  Drown, 96
  Reports of, 92
  Shipwreck "Dahcota", 58 (See Ships/Shipwreck)
  Shooting, 28, 35, 73, 76, 93, 95(x) (See also firearms accident)
ACTOR, 201
AMERICAN FORK RIVER (See Rivers)
AMMUNITION, 189
ANIMAL:
  Antelope, 70
  Buffalo, 95
  Cattle, disagreement over selection, 28
  Cattle, prices paid, 34
  Cows, 38, 132
  Cows, large drove arrive, 164
  Feed, 41, 107
  Mules, prices paid, 34
  Oxen, prices paid, 34
  Ox Team (Shortest time to Sacramento), 143
  Sheep, 145
  Stock, prices paid, 34
  Wolves, 72
APPLES, dried, 177
ARMS, 189
ASSAYER, 202
ASSOCIATIONS (WAGON TRAIN) (see Wagon Trains-By Name)
ATTORNEY, 78
AUTHOR, 10, 87
AWAKENING TIME, 111
BACON, 3
BARLEY, 177

BEAR RIVER (See Rivers)
BECHWITH ROUTE, 171
BIG BLUE (See Rivers)
BLEEDING, price of, 77
BOARDING HOUSES, 21, 36
BOAT, RUBBER, INDIA, 10
BOATS, wagons as, 2
BOOK, What I Saw In California, 10
BOWIE KNIFE, 13
BRANDY, 177, 178
BREAD, 3
BUFFALO (See Animal)
BURNING (See Crime, Murder)
BUSINESS CAPITAL FOR, 16
CALAVERAS CHRONICLE (See Newspaper)
CALIFORNIA (For Geographical data see Geographical Index)
  Archives, State, 177
  Business intentions, 16, 28, 29
  Capital for Business, 16
  Cost of Living, 77(x)
  Emigrant, Relief for, 177-181
  Feather River, 74, 75
  First Downieville lady overland, 145
  First Downieville 1852 arrivals, 145
  Gold (see Gold and Mining)
  Guide, 196
  Governor's Papers, 177
  Indians, 76
  Indians, with pack mule train, 40

Miners, pre-experience, 59
Newspapers (See Newspaper)
Newspaper, "Calaveras Chronicle" (See Newspaper)
Newspaper, "Downieville Mountain Echo" (See Newspaper)
Newspaper, "Shasta Courier" (See Newspaper)
Newspaper, "Sonora Herald" (See Newspaper)
Pioneers (Mentioned as), 152, 156
Pioneer of Calaveras County, 152
Pioneer of Coloma, 156
Prices, 77
Prices, high, 28
Relief Post, 177
Relief (See California Emigrant Relief)
Resident from, 136
Roads or Routes to (See Routes, Trails, or Roads)
Road, new to Carson, 143
Road, Pennsylvania Cut-off, 143
Road, new to Volcano, 143
Route or Road, Columbia, new route from Carson Valley, 156
Sacramento, First recorded overland immigration company arrival in 1852, 142

317

Sacramento, shortest recorded time made by ox team, 143
Saw Mill, 28
Sermon, 198
State Archives, 177
Trip return to Calaveras County, 152
CAMP BRYARLY, 41, 196
CAPITAL FOR BUSINESS, 16
CARRIAGES (See also Wagons)
  Light (See also Wagons, Light), 20
  Light, spring, 25
  Mule drawn, 25
CARSON PASS, 201
CARSON RIVER (See Rivers)
CARSON RIVER ROAD (See Road and Route)
CARSON VALLEY (See Route)
CATTLE (see Animal)
CHEESE, 177
CHEST, Medicine, 10
CHICAGO DIRECTORY, (Publication), 87
CHOLERA (see Medical)
CINCINNATI GLOBE (see Newspaper)
COFFEE, Ground, 177
COFFEE, Price in California, 77
COLD (see weather)
COLORADO RIVER (See Rivers)
COLORED, 104
COMMENCEMENT OF DAY, 111
COMMERCIAL EDITOR, 89
COMPANIES, JOINT STOCK COMPANIES (see Joint stock Companies)

COMPANY CLERK, 119
COMPASS, 10
CONSTITUTION (See Wagon train By-Laws)
CORN, 107
CORNMEAL, 177
CORPORATION:
  Treadwell & Marshfield, 78
  Corbin & Shaw, 98
  Turner Allen & Company, 50
COST OF LIVING/ CALIFORNIA, 77(x)
COUNTERFEITING (See Crime)
COWS (See Animal)
CRIME:
  Adultery, 53
  Assault, 28
  Attack by deserters, 96
  Attach by Indians, 142
  Counterfeiting, 53
  Desertion, 96
  Gambling, 110
  Immoral Practices, 110
  Infidelity, 78, 92
  Insubordination, 21
  Killing by Indians, 124
  Murder, 53, 78, 92, 93, 173, 175
  Murder, Burning, 76
  Murder, by Indians, 71, 72, 124
  Rape, 92
  Shooting, 28, 53, 76, 78, 92, 93, 175
  Shooting, Indian, 94
  Theft, Indians, 77
  Villainy, 53
CROSSING BY FOOT, 101
DAILY PICAYUNE, (See Newspaper)
DAYLOR'S RANCH, 144
DEAF & DUMB (See Medical)

DEATHS (see medical & graves):
Abbott, (grave of), 93
Adams, B. F., 33
Blake, Joseph, 94
Bolemene, Nicholas, 94
Daniel, Alex B., 94
Deguire, John, 94
Donel, A. R., 94
Eathey, John, 94
Groot, James H., 94
Hardy, J. J. (grave of), 93
J. J. (death of), 94
Harris, ____ (Mr.), 92
Hays, H. O., 93
Hunter, Joseph, 94
Johnson, H. T., 94
King, Joseph, 93
Land, J., 96
Lists of: 1, 47, 53(x), 61, 62(x), 69(x), 70(x), 71, 72(x), 73(x), 76(x), 78, 82, 92(x), 93(x), 94(x), 95(x), 96(x), 123, 125(x), 126(x), 127(x), 128, 130(x), 155, 156(x), 161(x), 162(x), 164(x), 169(x), 170(x), 171(x), 172(x), 173(x), 174(x), 175(x), 176(x), 177(x), 182(x), 194, 201(x), 204
Marshall, Green, 93
McAllister, James, 94
McBeth, ____, (Dr.), 93
McDowell, ____, 93
McMillan, Sloan, 94
Neely, A. J., 92
Nevland, Joseph, 93
Newland, Joseph, 93
Ocland, John, 94
Park, J. A. (grave of), 93
Ransom, John, 93

Rogers, B. F., 94
Rose, ____, 175
Ryan, ____, (Dr.), 94
Sharpe, Joseph, 94
Smith, Levi, 94
Spars, Joseph, 93
Spencer, E. F., 94
Tipton, P. M., 127
Walbert, S. T., 94
Ward, Robert, 93
Wells, William, 94
Wilson, E., 94
Winslow, George, 94
DIARY, (Staples/Gould), 204
DIFFICULTIES, Committee to Settle all, 123
DIRECTOR, 86(x)
DOCTOR/SURGEONS, 1(x), 2(x), 4, 7, 9, 10, 11, 15, 16, 17, 20(x), 21(x), 22(x), 23(x), 24, 25, 26, 28, 29, 30, 32, 35(x), 38, 39(x), 40(x), 42(x), 43(x), 44, 45(x), 46(x), 47, 48(x), 49, 50(x), 51(x), 52(x), 53(x), 55(x), 56(x), 57, 58(x), 59, 60(x), 61, 65, 68, 69, 71, 78, 79(x), 80(x), 81(x), 84, 85, 86(x), 87(x), 88, 89, 91(x), 93, 94, 95, 96, 98, 99, 100, 102(x), 103, 104, 105(x), 107(x), 108, 109, 110, 111(x), 113(x), 115(x), 117(x), 121(x), 122, 123, 125, 129(x), 130(x), 133(x), 135, 138, 139, 141(x), 142, 144, 148(x), 150(x), 151(x), 152, 155(x), 156, 158, 160, 162, 163, 165, 168, 170, 173, 180,
181(x), 182, 187(x), 192, 193(x), 195, 196(x), 198(x), 199, 201, 204
DOWNIEVILLE MOUNTAIN ECHO (See Newspaper)
DREAM (Nightmare), 128
EDGAR HOUSE (St. Joseph), 36
EDITOR, 87(x)
  Commerical, 89
  Newspaper, 130(x), 139
EL DORADO NEWS (See Newspaper)
EL DORADO (COLOMA) NEWS (See Newspaper)
EMIGRANTS:
  Attitude toward, 36
  Deaths on Plains, (Partial 1852), 171-177 (See also Graves and Medical/Deaths)
  Deceased, unidentified, 161
  In Distress, 39
ENGINEER, 108
EXCELSIOR (Motto), 49
EXECUTION, HANGING, 175
EXPRESS, (Lexington, Missouri) (See Newspaper)
FEATHER RIVER (See Rivers)
FEED, ANIMAL, 41
FERRY, 142 (Reference to on Humboldt River)
FIELD GLASS, 10
FIREARMS: 28, 35
  Careless Handling, 28, 35
FIRM:
  Treadwell & Mansfield, 78
FIRST:
  Emigrants to arrive in Sacramento, California in 1850 season, 128
  Lady overland to arrive in Downieville, California, 145
  Overland wagons to Galloway's Ranch, 154
  Ox team travel time record to Sacramento, 143
  Sacramento, Overland Company, arrives in 1852, 142
  To leave Council Bluff, Iowa in 1850, 107
  To arrive in Downieville, California in 1852, 145
  To Shasta (California) via Noble's Route, 155
  Wagon Train from Ohio for California, 12
FLOUR, 177
FOOD:
  Average poundage per man, 6
  Reference to cost in Carson Valley, 125
FOOT COMPANY, (Mode of travel), 101
FORBODING OF DEATH, 128
FORTS:
  Fort Childs, Nebraska, 69, 72
  Fort DesMoines, Iowa, 45(x)
  Fort Hall, Idaho, 74, 75
  Fort Kearney (Fort Kearny) Nebraska, 39, 69(x), 70(x) 71, 78, 92, 93, 96, 113, 114, 125, 126, 155

Fort Laramie,
  Wyoming, 71, 72,
  93(x), 94(x), 96,
  125(x), 127(x),
  128(x), 168, 201
Fort Madison, Iowa,
  51(x)
Fort Smith, Arkansas,
  80, 81, 82(x), 83(x),
  84(x), 85(x), 88, 202
Fort Wayne, Indiana, 9
Fort Washington,
  Wisconsin, 68(x)
Sutter's Fort, California,
  19
FORT HALL ROAD (See
  Road)
FORT SMITH HERALD
  (See Newspaper)
FRACTURE (see
  Accident, broken)
FRONTIER GUARDIAN
  (See Newspaper)
GALLOWAY'S RANCH,
  154
GAMBLING (See
  Crime)
GERMANS, 20, 25, 31,
  34, 37(x), 159
GERMANS, fear of
  taxation, 25
GILA RIVER (See
  Rivers)
GOLD (See also
  California; and
  Mining, California)
  California, 73, 74, 75,
  76, 77
  Feather River, 75
  Grubstake for, 31
GOVERNOR (of Texas),
  121
GOVERNOR'S
  (California), Papers
  re: relief effort, 177
GRADUATE, YALE, 202
GRAIN, 41
GRAVE(S), 71, 72(x),
  73(x), 125-128

GREEN RIVER (See
  Rivers)
GRUBSTAKE, 31
GUARD, (Sergeant of
  the), 123
GUIDE (See also Wagon
  Train, Guide), 19, 62,
  121, 142, 189, 196
GUNS (see Firearms)
HAM, 177
HANGING (Execution),
  175
HEIRS, 3
HENNESS ROUTE, (See
  Road)
HORSE TAMER, 201
HOSPITAL STORES, 10
HOTEL:
  Edgar House, 36
  Emigrants Lodge in, 21
  In St. Joseph, 21, 36
  St. Louis, 181
  Use of 21, 36
HUMBOLDT RIVER
  (See Rivers)
HUMBOLDT SINK (See
  Rivers)
HUNTING, 75
ICE (See Weather)
IMMORAL PRACTICES
  (See Crime)
INDIA RUBBER BOAT,
  10, 189
INDIAN TERRITORY,
  13, 19
INDIANS: 72, 77
  Apache, 93
  Attack, 142
  Attack Wagon Trains,
  93(x)
  California, 76
  California with pack
  mule train, 40
  Cholera introduced, 94
  Indian shoots emigrant,
  94
  Murder by, 124
  Murder Emigrant, 71,
  72

Sioux, 71
INSPECTOR OF ARMS,
  123
INSPECTOR OF TEAMS
  AND WAGONS,
  120
IOWA SENTINEL (See
  Newspaper)
IRON, SHEET, 2
JOLIET SIGNAL (See
  Newspaper)
JOURNAL (of Ezra
  Bourne), 201
JUDGE, 104
KENNEBEC JOURNAL
  (Maine) (See
  Newspaper)
KNIFE/BOWIE, 13
LADY, First overland to
  Downieville, 145
LAND OFFICE,
  REGISTER
  (Registrar), 87
LANGUAGE, Profane, 110
LEXINGTON
  MISSOURI
  EXPRESS (See
  Newspaper)
LIBRARY, (Bancroft in
  Berkeley, Calif.), 204
LIME JUICE, 177
LIQUOR (See name of
  particular liquor)
LITTLE BLUE RIVER
  (See Rivers)
LOST (In mountains), 77
MACHINISTS, 86
MAINE AUGUSTA (See
  Newspaper)
MAPS, 10
MARQUEE, 2
MARY'S RIVER (See
  Rivers)
MASONIC SYMBOL, 95
MECHANICS, 28, 29
MEDICAL:
  Bleeding, 77
  Cholera, among Indians,
  94

Deaf & Dumb, 161
Deaths, 84 (See also Deaths) Emigrant on plains, partial list 1852, 171-177 (See also Graves)
On plains (during May-June 1852), 168-177
Dream, 128
Gout, 36
Inflamatory sore throat, 122
Lame, 179
MEDICAL DOCTORS (See Doctors/Surgeons)
MEDICAL FRACTURE (See Accident, Broken)
MEDICINE CHEST, 10
MILL, saw, for California, 28
MINING, California, 75
MINING OPERATIONS (Experienced men), 59
MISSOURI NEWSPAPER (See Newspaper)
MISSOURI REPUBLICAN NEWSPAPER (See Newspaper)
MISSOURI RIVER (See Rivers, see also Missouri)
Settlers from Wagon Trains, 17
St. Joseph Hotels, 21
MISTRESS, 53
MORMON (Mention of), 93
MORMON, Religion, 125
MOTTO, ("Excelsior"), 49
MOUNTAIN ECHO (See Newspaper, Downieville Mountain Echo)
MOUNTAINEER:
Miles M. Goodyear, 40

David Adams, 189
MOUNTAINS, Sierra Nevada, 149
MOUNTED RIFLES (See U.S. Army)
MULES (See Animal)
MURDER (See Crime)
NEGRO, 104
NEGRO, Unidentified emigrant, 44
NEW ROAD TO CARSON (See Road)
NEW JERSEY HISTORICAL SOCIETY, 182
NEWSPAPER:
Calaveras Chronicle, 152
Cincinnati Globe, 194
Daily Picayune, 104, 105, 121, 122, 124, 203
Downieville Mountain Echo (see Newspaper, Mountain Echo) 145, 146, 154(x), 160(x), 161(x)
Editor, 87(x), 89, 130(x), 139, 193
El Dorado News, 133, 142, 152, 156(x), 159
El Dorado (Coloma) News, 146, 147, 149, 161
Express (Lexington, Missouri), 96
Fort Smith Herald, 81, 82(x), 83(x), 84(x), 85
Frontier Guardian (Kanesville, Iowa), 63, 98, 102, 105, 107, 109, 110, 111, 116, 118, 120, 121, 122(x), 123(x), 124(x), 131, 132, 133, 134(x), 135(x),
136, 137(x), 138(x), 139(x), 141(x), 145
Iowa Sentinel, 139, 141(x)
Joliet Signal, 87
Kennebec Journal, 78(x), 123, 124, 203
Lexington (Missouri) Express, 96
Maine-Augusta, 77(x)
Missouri, (See also St. Joseph or Missouri Newspaper), 77
Missouri Republican, 181
Mountain Echo, (See Newspaper Downieville Mountain Echo), 145, 146, 154(x), 160(x), 161(x)
New York Daily Tribune, 79, 82, 83, 84, 85, 88, 89(x), 92(x), 97, 98(x), 181, 192, 193, 194(x), 198(x), 199(x), 200(x), 201(x), 203(x), 204(x)
New York Herald, 79, 88(x), 194
New York Sentinel (Rome Newspaper), 182, 183
Oquawka (Illinois Spectator), 130
Pacific News, 193
Picayune (New Orleans) 104, 105, 121, 122(x), 124, 203
Republican Journal (Maine), 78
St. Joseph Gazette, 100, 101(x), 102, 103(x), 104(x), 111, 113(x), 114(x), 115(x), 125, 126, 127(x), 128(x), 130(x), 131(x), 132(x), 183, 185,

189(x), 196, 197, 198(x), 199, 200(x)
St. Louis Union, 89, 201
Sacramento California Transcript, 124, 125(x), 128, 193
Sacramento Union, 133, 141, 142(x), 143(x), 144(x), 146, 147, 149(x), 151(x), 152(x), 155(x), 156(x), 159(x), 160, 161, 162, 164(x), 165, 167, 168(x), 171(x)
Salem Massachusetts Register, 201
San Antonio (Texas) Ledger, 125
Shasta (California) Courier, 149, 151, 164, 165
Sonora (California) Herald, 152
Spirit of Jefferson (Virginia), 194
Telegraph (Bellefonte Kentucky), 139
True Democrat, 87
Van Buren Intelligencer (Arkansas), 105
Vermont Gazette, 201
Whig, 87
NEWSPAPERMAN, 125
NEW YORK DAILY TRIBUNE (See Newspaper)
NIGHTMARE, 128
NOBLE'S SHASTA ROUTE, (See Road)
OHIO (first wagon train to leave for California), 12
ONIONS, 177
OQUAWKA (Illinois) SPECTATOR, (See Newspaper)
OREGON BATTALION, 96

ORGANIZATION
  Masonic (Symbol on grave), 95
  Odd Fellow, 62
ORMSBY'S STATION, 177
ORPHAN, 12
OVERLAND CROSSING BY FOOT, 101
OXEN (See Animals)
PACIFIC NEWS (See Newspaper)
PACIFIC SPRINGS, 128
PACK COMPANY (Type of company), 104
PENNSYLVANIA CUT-OFF ROAD (See Road)
PHYSICIAN (See Also Doctor/Surgeon)
PICAYUNE (New Orleans) (See Newspaper)
PICKLES, 177
PIONEERS, California (Old, reference to), 152, 156
PISTOLS (See Firearms)
PLATTE CROSSING (See Rivers)
PLATTE RIVER (or Big Platte) (See Rivers)
POSTMASTER, 78
POSTMASTER (of Sullivan, Iowa), 161
POTATOES, 177
PRINTER, 154
PROFANE LANGUAGE, 110
PROFESSIONAL MEN, 29
PROFESSOR, 201
PROPRIETOR, 87(x)
PROVISIONS, forwarded by sea, 3, 25
PUBLICATIONS (See Newspapers)
PUBLICATION, "Chicago Directory," 87

RAILROAD, 77
RAIN (see Weather)
RANCH, Galloway's, 154
  Johnson, 195
  William Daylor's, 144
RECORD (See also First)
RECORD:
  First to leave Council Bluffs in 1850, 107
  First in Downieville, California in 1852, 145
  First lady overland to Downieville, California, 145
  First overland wagons to Galloway's Ranch, 152
  First to Shasta (California), via Noble's Route, 155
  First Wagon Train from Ohio, 12
  Shortest travel time by oxteams to Sacramento, 143
REGISTRAR (Register)LAND OFFICE, 87
RELIEF POST CALIFORNIA, 177 (See also Wagon Train, Relief)
RELIGION/MORMON, 125
RELIGION/SABBATH DAY, 110
REPUBLICAN JOURNAL (Maine) (See Newspaper)
REVERENDS, 53, 71(x), 103, 107, 112, 125, 127, 128, 136, 159, 198, 202
RESIDENTS:
  old of Calaveras County, 152
  old of Coloma, 156

RIO GRANDE (See Rivers)
RIVERS:
  American Fork, 74
  American (Middle and North Fork), 151
  Bear, 74
  Big Blue, 204
  Carson, 73, 74, 156
  Carson Sink, 74
  Colorado, 95
  Feather, 74, 75
  Gila, 93
  Green, 96
  Humboldt, 125, 142, 149, 152
  Humboldt, sink of 154, 177, 201
  Little Blue, 182
  Mary's, 74
  Missouri, 33, 39, 60, 70, 73(x), 97, 119, 120, 121, 123, 131, 133, 146, 164, 171
  Platte (Or Big Platte), 70, 71, 73, 93, 123, 125, 161, 164
  Platte Crossing, 96
  Rio Grande, 201, 202
  Stanislaus, 156
  Truckee, 74
  Walker's River, 156
  Yuba River 74
ROAD (See also Trail and Route)
  Carson River Road, 156
  Fort Hall, 74, 75
  Henness Route, 161
  New Road to Carson, 143
  New to Downieville, California, 154
  Noble's Shasta Route, 149, 151, 155, 159
  Pennsylvania Cut-off Road, 143
  Santa Fe, 1, 2, 3, 4(x), 5(x), 6(x), 82(x), 93

Scott's Route, 151
ROUTE: (See also Road and Trail)
  Beckwith Route, 171
  Carson Pass, 201
  Carson River Road, 156
  Carson Valley, new route to Columbia, 156
  Emigrant deaths on trail, North side of Platte River, 161
  Henness Route, 161
  Noble's Shasta Route, 149, 151, 155, 159
  Scott's, 151
  South Pass, 130
  Sublette Cutoff, 124
RUBBER, BOAT, INDIA, 10
SABBATH DAY, Restrictions, 110
ST. JOSEPH GAZETTE (See Newspaper)
ST. LOUIS UNION (See Newspaper)
SACRAMENTO TRANSCRIPT (See Newspaper)
SACRAMENTO UNION (See Newspaper)
SALEM MASSACHUSETTS REGISTER (See Newspaper)
SALERATUS, 177
SAN ANTONIO LEDGER (see Newspaper)
SANTA FE (See Road and Trail)
SAW MILL, for California, 28
SCOTT'S ROUTE (See Road)
SECLUSION OF WOMEN, 12
SERVANT (unidentified), 55

SERVANTS (unidentified), 60, 61
SHASTA (California) COURIER (see Newspaper)
SHASTA ROUTE (Nobles), 149, 151, 155, 159
SHEEP (See Animals)
SHEET IRON (Wagons), 2
SHIPMENT OF SUPPLIES BY SEA, 78
SHIPS:
  British Mail Steamer (Unnamed), 79
  Celia No. 2 (Steamboat), 81
  Cholera in, 62
  Cotton Plant, 85
  Dahcota (Steamer), 39, 40, 58
  Edward Bates (Steamer), 78
  Embassy (Steamer), 42
  John W. Herbert (Schooner), 201
  Mary, 62
  Mary Blane (Steamer), 4, 181
  Meteor (Steamboat), 33
  Mustang, 7
  Princeton (Steamer), 40
  Timour, 60
SHIPWRECK, "Dahcota", 39, 40, 58
SHOOTING (See Crime, shooting and Accident, shooting)
SICK (See Medical)
SIERRA NEVADA MOUNTAINS, 149
SIOUX INDIANS, 71
SNOW (See Weather)
SONORA (California) HERALD, (See Newspaper)
SOUTH PASS (See

Route)
SPANISH COUNTRY, 50
SPIRIT OF JEFFERSON
 (Virginia) (See
 Newspaper)
STANISLAUS RIVER
 (See Rivers)
STEAMBOATS (See
 Ships)
STORES, Hospital, 120
SUBLETTE CUT-OFF
 (see Route)
SUGAR, 177
SUPPLIES, Forwarded by
 sea, 3, 25
SUPPLIES, Shipment by
 sea, 78
SURGEON (See Doctors)
SURVEYOR (Of Noble's
 Shasta Route), 149
SURVIVOR, Sole of
 Wagon Train, 124
TAXATION, Fear of, 25
TEA, 177
TEACHER, 86
TELEGRAPH
 (Bellefonte,
 Kentucky) (See
 Newspaper)
TELESCOPE, 10
TENTS, Marquee (See
 Marquee)
TEXAS, Governor, 121
TOMB (See Graves)
TOOLS, 55, 189
TRAIL (See also Road
 and Route)
 Black Rock, 155
 California, 128
 Emigrant on North side
  of Platte River, 161
 Sante Fe, 83
TRUCKEE RIVER (See
 Rivers)
TRUE DEMOCRAT (See
 Newspaper)
UNIDENTIFIED
 DECEASED
 EMIGRANTS, 161

U. S. ARMY:
 Mounted Riflemen, 71
 Mounted Rifles, 95
 Regular Mounted Rifles
  (Company "G"), 71
 Surgeon (Assistant) of,
  71
U. S. NAVY, member of,
 80
U. S. POSTMASTER (of
 Sullivan, Iowa), 161
VAN BUREN
 INTELLIGENCER
 (See Newspaper)
VERMONT GAZETTE
 (See Newspaper)
WAGON, Boats, 2
WAGON TRAIN:
 Assistant Master, 52
 Awakening Time, 111
 By-Lay and,
  Resolutions, 138
 California Relief Post, 177
 Captain, 78, 79, 80, 81,
  82, 83(x) 84, 151
 Captain or Guide,
  Second time West,
  139, 142
 Clerk, 52
 Commisary, 52
 Company Clerk, 119
 Company Guide, 142
 Company Pilot, 138
 Commencement of day,
  111
 Constitution, 63, 64
 Constitution and By-
  Laws, 3, 64, 65, 66,
  111, 198
 Directors, 86(x)
 Dissension in, 28, 34
 Dissolution cause, 28
 Drivers, 22
 Emigrants leave, 17
 Expulsion from 93
 Guide, 19, 63, 121, 142,
  189, 196
 Germans (seeGermans)
 Indian attacks, 71, 72,

  93, 94, 124, 142,
 Inspector (of teams and
  wagons), 120
 Insubordination in, 21
 Lieutenant, 78
 1st. Lieutenant, 82, 83
 2nd Lieutenant, 82, 83
 3rd Lieutenant, 83
 Light, preference for, 34
  (See also Carriages)
 Master, 118, 120, 123
 Minutes of
  organization, 63
 Pack Company, 104
 Quartermaster, 78
 Secretary, 82, 84, 86
 Selling en route, 60
 Sheet Iron, 2
 Surgeon, 83
 Survivor, sole of, 124
 Teams, prices for, 34
 Require to pull, 34
 Teamsters, 71
 Treasurer, 82, 84, 86
 Vice President, 86
 Women, seclusion of,
  12
WAGON TRAINS - BY
 NAME
 A.D. Blodgett &
  Company, 165
 A. H. White &
  Company, 109
 Aaron Wels (Wells) &
  Company, 104
 Albany Overland
  Association, 24
 Albion Company, 58
 Albion Rangers, 131
 Alexander & Hall's,
  128
 Badger Company (Left
  Kanesville, May 29,
  1849), 67, 68
 Badger Company (Left
  Kanesville, May 3,
  1852), 134
 Badger Gold Hunters
  (of Beloit,

Baltimore & Frederick Mining & Trading Company, 89
Banner Company (See California Banner Company & Waukegan Banner Company of Californians), 73
Barry Union Pioneer Company, 48(x)
Bellevue Mining Company, 1
Berkshire Company, 89
Birmingham Emigrating Company, 118
Boston & Newton Joint Stock Association, 86, 203
Brooks & Company, 134
Brookville California Company, 41(x)
Buchanan Agricultural & Mining Company, 56
Buckeye Rovers, 55
Buffalo Exploring & Mining Company, 7, 48
Buffalo Mining Company, 48
C. J. Cumings & Company (Cummings ?), 104
California Banner Company, 120
California Company (of Hollidays Cove, Virginia), 47
California Company (of Rochester, Wisconsin), 59
California Enterprise Company, 185
California Express Company, 65, 66(x)
California Mining Company (of Franklin, Ohio), 88

California Mining Company (of Washington, D. C.), 79
California Mining & Trading Company (of Cincinnati), 181
California Mining & Trading Company, (From Dayton, Ohio), 42, 196, 197
California Squad, No. 2, 192
Cambridge, Ohio California Company, 88
Capt. _____ Clark's Company, 142
Captain _____ Owen's Company, 73
Captain Dixon's Sacramento Company, 89
Carson Association, 202
Cassville & Beetown Emigrating Company, 138
Central Michigan California Emigrant Company, 49
Charleston (Virginia) Mining Company, 41, 194 (Charlestown Company or Charlestown Virginia Mining Company)
Chautaugee Mining Company, 43
Chicago Excelsior Company, 118
Cincinnati and California Joint Stock Company, 23, 192
Cincinnati Company, 194
Cincinnati Mercantile Association, 43
Cincinnati Mercantile Association of Ohio, 197

Clarksville Company, 80
Clinton County Company, 68
Coldwater Company, 107
Colonel H.P. Russell's Company, 141
Compton's Mess, 114
Congress and California Mutual Protection Association, 78
Cutler Company, 121
D. Hale & Company, 177
D. Levi & Company, 177
D. Lindle & Company, 178
D. McLean's Company (See also Taylor McLean Company), 114
Daniel Boone Company, 58
Defiance Company, 80
Desmoine Company No. 1 (sic), 107
Dewitt's Mess, 114
Diamond K. Company, 5
Dixon Company, 40, 194
Dixon's Mess, 114
Dixon's Sacramento Company, 89
Dowdle Family, 46, 198(x)
Dubuque Company, 135
E. Manning & Company, 140
Eagle Prairie Company, 138
East Tennessee & California Gold Mining Company, 92
Eickenberry's Company, 93
Elizabethtown, Ohio Emigrating Company, 156

Elk Horn California Company, 34
Essex Mining and Trading Company, 201(x)
Excelsior Company No. 1, 108
Experiment Club, 23
Express Company, 66
Extract Company, 107, 119
Faette Rovers (sic), 65
Fayette Rovers, 58, 65
Fort Smith California Emigrating Company, 81(x), 82
Fort Smith Company, 81
Fulton Star Company, 56
G.W. Paul's company, 181
General ____ Anderson's Company, 92
German California Mining Company, 34, 35
Grand Mustang Company No. 1, 111
Granite State & California Mining & Trading Company, 40
Green and Jersey County Company, 198
Green River Mining Company of Kentuck (sic) (Kentucky ?), 31
H. B. Horn & Company, 105
H. C. Hodge Company, 60
H. Dale's Mess, 114
H. P. Russell's Company, 141
Havilah Mining Association, 84
Hawkeye Company, 72(x)

Hendrickson's Mess, 114
Hillsdale Mutual Company, 133
Hobby & Company, 183
Hule's California Company, 80
Illinois & California Mutual Insurance Company No. 1, 49, 199
Illinois & California Mutual Insurance Comapny, No. 2, 199
Illinois Sucker Company, (See also Sucker Company), 19, 189
Illinois Union Band, 53
Independent Company, 43
Iowa Company No. 1 of California Emigrants, 62
Iowa & Wisconsin Emigrant Company No. 3, 124
Iron City Rangers, 5
Ithica Pack Train, 95
J. Ford & Company, 141
J. H. Wood & Company, 177
J. Lott Collins & Company, 138
J. W. Lakue & Company, 117
Jackson County Company, 68
James Russell Company, 137
Janesville Gold Hunters No. 1, 115
Jerome & Company, 128
John Flood & Company, 178
Johnston County Company, 68

Jones & Company, 97
Juniata, Pennsylvania, California Company, 79
Knickerbocker Emigrating Company, 82
Knickerbocker Exploring Company, 82(x), 83
Knox County Illinois Company, 64, 200
Knoxville, Tennessee Company, 92
Lafayette Company, 132
Little Rock Company, 82
Louisville, Kentucky Emigrating Company, 89
Mackinac Mining Company, 7, 48(x)
Madison Company, 43
Maine & New York Company, 84
Manhattan Company, (Enterprise Division), 202
Massachusetts and California Company, 202
McPike & Strother, 111(x)
Mechanicsville & California Mining Company, 33
Memphis, Tennessee Company, 202
Michigan Company, 60
Michigan Company No. 1, 183
Mississippi & Alabama Emigrating Company, 88
Missouri Company, 69
Missouri & Georgia California Mining Company, 69

Missouri & Iowa Mining Company, 123
Mobile Company (Mobile, Alabama), 79, 203
Mohican Gold Company, 131
Mormon (group - attended to), 68
Mormon (mention of), 93
Mound City Association of St. Louis, 25
Mutual Mining Association of Cincinnati, 29
Mutual Protection Company No. 1, 119
N. V. Sheffer's Wagon Train, 132
Newark Overland Company, 10, 182
New Durham Temperance Mess, 43(x)
New Orleans Mining & Trading Association, 84(x)
Nodaway Company, 69(x)
Northern Illinois Union Company, 108
Odd-Fellow Wagon, 62
Olentangy Mining Company, 48
Oregon Battalion, 96
Osborn Company (sic) (Osborne ?), 85
Painesville Mining Company, 33, 193
Painsville Mining Company, 33, 193
Pawpaw Mining Company of Michigan, 15
Penfield Company, 97
Peoria Californians, 202, 203
Peoria Pioneers, 202(x)

Persifer Company, 110(x)
Persifer Division, 110
Persifer F. Smith Association, 202
Peter Dubadie & Company, 141
Philip Vaughen & Company (sic) (Vaughn ?), 178
Pioneer Company of California Emigrants, 109(x)
Pioneer Line, 50-53
Pittsburgh & California Enterprise Company, 17, 185, 186
Pittsburgh Independent California Company, 38
Platteville Company, 131(x)
Pokehagan California Company, 22
Pontotoc & California Exploring Company, 8, 9, 10
Prairie Rover Company, 122
Quincy Company, 120
R. Killborne (sic) & Company, 104
Randolph Company, 70
Red Bird Company No. 1 & No. 2, 138
Red Rock Mining Company, 59
Rhode Island Company, 131
Rock Island Pioneers, 55
Rollin Enterprise California Company, 69(x)
Rountrees, ___ Major & Company, 90
Sacramento Company (Capt. Dixon's), 89

Sacramento Union Company of Wheeling, 25
St. Clair Mining Company, 20
St. Joseph Company, 46, 75, 76
St. Louis Proc (sic) Company, 24
Samuel Stetmay(?) & Company, 180
Schaghticoke California Mining Company, 7, 182
Smith's Mess, 115
Social Band of Liberty, 120
South Bend Joint Stock California Mining & Operating Company, 13
Spartan Band, 60
Spencer Creek Company, 44
Springfield, Illinois Company No. 3, 50
Sucker Company, 189
Summit, Train, 3
T. Smith & Company, 167
Tailor McLean Company (sic), 113
Taylor McLean Company (See also D. McLean's Company), 113
Thomas Higgins & Company, 177
Tipton Company, 141
Troy Mining Company, 47
Turner Allen & Company's "Pioneer Line", 50
Union Company (See also Union Company of Fairfield, Iowa), 109(x)

Union Company of Fairfield Iowa (See also Union Company), 109(x)
Union Packing Company, 119
Valney Wood & Company, 122
Victoria California Company, 88
Victoria Company, 88
Walter Johnson & Company, 117
Washington California Mining & Trading Association, 7, 182
Washington City & California Mining Association, 47
Waterford Mutual Mining Association, 85
Water's, 193
Waukegan Banner Company of Californians, 110
Waukesha & Rock County Company, 139
Wellington Mining Company, 86
Wendel's Mess, 115
Western Mining Company of Cincinnati, 28(x)
Western Rovers, 83
Westfield Mining Company, 40
West Point Company, 110
West Point Division, 110, 111
Willard's Company (mention of), 161
William Greggs & Company, 177
Willis Stith and Company (sic) (Smith), 57
Wisconsin Company, 139
Wisconsin & Iowa Union Company, 66, 67
Wright's Mess, 114
WAGONS, PASSENGER CARRIAGES, 50
WALKER'S RIVER (See Rivers)
WEATHER:
Cold, 17, 21
Ice, 21
Rain, 17
Snow, 124, 125
WHIG NEWSPAPER (See Newspaper)
WIDOW, 40(x)
WILLIAM DAYLOR'S RANCH, 144
WOMEN, Seclusion of, 12
WRITER, 10
YUBA RIVER (See Rivers)

www.ingramcontent.com/pod-product-compliance
Lightning Source LLC
Chambersburg PA
CBHW031705230426
43668CB00006B/112

General Editor's Introduction

Asbury Theological Seminary Series in World Christian Revitalization Movements

This volume is published in collaboration with the Center for the Study of World Christian Revitalization Movements, a cooperative initiative of Asbury Theological Seminary faculty. Building on the work of the previous Wesleyan/Holiness Studies Center at the Seminary, the Center provides a focus for research in the Wesleyan Holiness and other related Christian renewal movements, including Pietism and Pentecostal movements, which have had a world impact. The research seeks to develop analytical models of these movements, including their biblical and theological assessment. Using an interdisciplinary approach, the Center bridges relevant discourses in several areas in order to gain insights for effective Christian mission globally. It recognizes the need for conducting research that combines insights from the history of evangelical renewal and revival movements with anthropological and religious studies literature on revitalization movements. It also networks with similar or related research and study centers around the world, in addition to sponsoring its own research projects.

Harris' insightful study of independent Pentecostal churches is written from the perspective of a participant-observer who brings important analytical insights tools to his work, especially in viewing these communities within their cultural context. He offers a helpful examination of the pathologies and potential of congregations in this growing segment of the Pentecostal movement. For this reason, it demonstrates congruence with the mission of the Center and serves to advance its research objectives of understanding movements of revitalization within world Christianity.

J. Steven O'Malley, Director
Center for the Study of World Christian Revitalization Movements
Asbury Theological Seminary

Sub-Series Foreword

The Pentecostal and Charismatic Sub-Series

Of all the renewal traditions that have engaged the theological landscape, the Pentecostal Movement has undoubtedly made the most significant impact since it emerged at the turn of the twentieth century. Starting as a revival in a small African-American congregation on Azusa Street in Los Angeles, California, the movement soon swept the world, establishing itself in more than forty countries in the first three years. One hundred years later Pentecostalism has grown to an estimated 500 million global adherents or approximately twenty-five percent of all of Christendom. In the same manner that Wesleyanism burst beyond the bounds of Methodism to embrace an interdenominational holiness movement following the American Civil War in the nineteenth century, Pentecostalism transcended denominational lines in the form of the Charismatic Movement during the second half of the twentieth century.

This sub-series is designed to explore the historical, theological and intercultural dimensions of these twin twentieth-century Restorationists traditions from a global perspective. In this volume Antipas Harris brings these dimensions to bear as he focuses on the pastoral theology of two African American Independent pentecostal churches. The first, the Rock of Life Church, was initially affiliated with the United Pentecostal Church, the largest "Oneness" Pentecostal denomination in the United States that has been historically white. The second, a Church of God Pillar of Truth Church, was initially associated with the Church of God in Christ, the largest Pentecostal denomination in the United States that is Trinitarian and historically African-American. In each case, he argues, there is a breakdown in the relationship between their interpretation of scripture, experiences of the Spirit, and culture. Instead of this "trilateral" resulting in a liberating power of the gospel, it has led repressive measures, particularly as applied to women. The problem, he maintains, stems from inadequate critical reflection, often made unilaterally by a single male leader that is "imposed" upon a congregation. Using biblical models of decision-making such as illustrated by Jerusalem Council recorded in Acts 15, Harris is confident that these churches possess the recourses necessary that will enable them to shape and reshape church practices that do not compromise core theological beliefs while at the same time remain open to redefining the church's identity and mission in such a way that is truly liberating.

D. William Faupel
Sub-series Editor